THE INTEGRATING STRUCTURE OF THE BASIC ISSUES APPROACH

Theorists / Pages	Freud	Adler	Jung	Erikson	Fromm	Horney	Allport	Rogers	Maslow	May	Frankl	Skinner	Kelly	Ellis	Bandura
Conscious vs. Unconscious	49	85	119	173	196	229	254	281	321	356	382	411	437	465	510
Determinism vs. Freedom	48	86	136	172	196	230	254	282	318	357	378	408	436	471	517
Heredity vs. Social	34	75	119	163	193	224	251	276	311	354	380	403	435	464	505
Early vs. Continuous Development	43	77	133	164	197	225	256	278	316	358	382	409	440	474	511
Subjective vs. Objective Reality	46	84	125	172	204	230	253	277	315	357	381	412	436	473	521
Uniqueness vs. Universality	53	85	137	174	204	231	253	283	319	360	379	413	437	477	522
Explanation of Learning Process	48	85	136	174	205	230	255	282	319	362	383	407	441	472	508
Role Assigned to Self-Concept	52	87	137	175	205	224	253	278	320	359	383	412	441	470	514
Number & Weight of Motivational Concepts	47	75	135	176	199	228	251	277	311	360	380	410	442	478	519
Centrality of Reinforcement	52	88	139	176	205	232	257	284	322	362	384	404	443	479	518
Role Assigned to Group Determinants	53	80	138	177	199	231	256	284	322	361	385	408	443	478	520

Theories of Personality

Theories of Personality

William A. Wallace
Marshall University
Division of Human Development and Technology

Allyn and Bacon
Boston • London • Toronto • Sydney • Tokyo • Singapore

Editor-in-Chief, Social Sciences: Susan Badger
Senior Editor: Laura Pearson
Editorial Assistant: Marnie Greenhut
Production Editor: Cheryl Ten Eick
Editorial-Production Service: Spectrum Publisher Services
Cover Administrator: Linda Dickinson
Composition Buyer: Linda Cox
Manufacturing Buyer: Louise Richardson

Library of Congress Cataloging-in-Publication Data

Wallace, William A.
   Theories of personality : a basic issues approach / William A.
Wallace.
     p.   cm.
   Includes bibliographic references and index.
   ISBN 0-205-14700-3
   1. Personality—Philosophy. 2. Personality. I. Title.
   BF698.W33 1993
   155.2—dc20   92-28118
                                     CIP

Printed in the United States of America
10 9 8 7 6 5 4 3 2 1   96 95 94 93

To Lois

Contents

Preface xxiii

1   Introduction to Personality Theory and Basic Issues   1
Chapter Overview   1
Human Nature Defined Has Consequences   2
History of Personality Theory   3
Personality Defies Scientific Definition   4
The Ambitions of Personologists   4
A Call For Open and Adventurous Minds   5
The Book's Structure   6
Basic Issues: An Integrative Structure to Personality Theory   7
  Characteristics of Basic Issues   8
Eleven Basic Issues   11
  Conscious versus Unconscious Determinants   11
  Determinism versus Freedom of Choice   12
  Heredity versus Social Determinants   12
  Uniqueness versus Universality   13
  Early versus Continuous Development   13
  Subjective versus Objective Reality   14
  Explanation of the Learning Process   15
  Role Assigned to the Self-Concept   16
  Number and Weight Assigned to Motivational Concepts   17
  Centrality of Reinforcement   17
  Role Assigned to Group Determinants   18
Special Features of the Book   18
  Biographical Sketch of the Theorist   18
  Psychological Health and Psychopathology   20
  Heuristic Influences   21
  Applications to Psychotherapy   22
  Extended Applications   22
  Critique   22
  Annotated Bibliography   23
  Glossary   23
References and Suggested Readings   23

PART 1:   *Pioneers of Personality Theory*   25

2   Freud's Psychoanalytic Theory   27
Chapter Overview   27
Introduction   28

Biographical Sketch of the Theorist   30
    Early Years   30
    Education   30
    Emergence of Psychoanalysis   32
    Accomplishments and Awards   33
Freud's Resolutions of the Eleven Basic Issues   34
    Heredity versus Social Determinants   34
    Early versus Continuous Development   43
    Subjective versus Objective Reality   46
    Number and Weight Assigned to Motivational Concepts   47
    Explanation of the Learning Process   48
    Determinism versus Freedom of Choice   48
    Conscious versus Unconscious Determinants   49
    Role Assigned to the Self-Concept   52
    Centrality of Reinforcement   52
    Uniqueness versus Universality   53
    Importance of Group Determinants   53
Psychological Health and Psychopathology   54
    Psychology and Health   54
    Psychopathology   56
Heuristic Influences: Research Methods and Techniques   57
Applications to Psychotherapy   58
    Therapeutic Goals   58
    Therapeutic Relationship   59
    Initial Procedures and Strategies   60
    Course of Psychoanalysis   60
Extended Applications   64
Critique   65
Annotated Bibliography   66
References and Suggested Readings   67

3   Adler's Theory of Individual Psychology   69
Chapter Overview   69
Introduction   70
Biographical Sketch of the Theorist   71
    Early Years   72
    Education   72
    Emergence of Individual Psychology   73
    Accomplishment and Awards   74
Adler's Resolutions of the Eleven Basic Issues   74
    Heredity versus Social Determinants   75
    Number and Weight Assigned to Motivational Concepts   75
    Early versus Continuous Development   77
    Role Assigned to Group Determinants   80
    Subjective versus Objective Reality   84

Conscious versus Unconscious Determinants   85
Uniqueness versus Universality   85
Explanation of Learning Process   85
Determinism versus Freedom to Choose   86
Role Assigned to Self-Concept   87
Centrality of Reinforcement   88
Psychological Health and Psychopathology   90
Psychological Health   90
Psychopathology   91
Heuristic Influence   94
Consensual Validation   94
Empirical Validation   95
Applications to Psychotherapy   96
Therapeutic Goals   96
Therapeutic Relationship   96
Initial Procedures and Strategies   97
Course of Psychotherapy   99
Additional Methods and Techniques   102
Extended Applications   104
Critique   105
Annotated Bibliography   107
References and Suggested Readings   107

4   Jung's Analytic Theory of Personality   111
Chapter Overview   111
Introduction   112
Biographical Sketch of the Theorist   113
Emergence of Jung's Theory   116
Recognition, Awards, and Tributes   118
Resolutions of Eleven Basic Issues   118
Heredity versus Social Determinants   119
Conscious versus Unconscious Determinants   119
Subjective versus Objective Reality   125
Early versus Continuous Development   133
Number and Weight Assigned to Motivational Concepts   135
Determinism versus Freedom of Choice   136
Explanation of Learning Process   136
Role Assigned to Self-Concept   137
Uniqueness versus Universality   137
Role Assigned to Group Determinants   138
Centrality of Reinforcement   139
Psychological Health and Psychopathology   139
Healthy Personality and the Good Life   139
Psychopathology   141
Heuristic Influences: Research Methods and Techniques   143

Applications to Psychotherapy   145
    Therapeutic Goals   145
    Therapeutic Relationship   146
    Initial Procedures and Strategies   147
Extended Applications   149
    Education   149
    Aging and Human Development   150
    Criminology and Biofeedback Research   150
    Anthropology and Folklore Studies   150
Critique   150
Annotated Bibliography   152
References and Suggested Readings   152

PART 2:   *Analytic and Neoanalytic Theories*   157

5   **Erikson's Theory of Ego Psychology   159**
    Chapter Overview   159
    Introduction   160
    Biographical Sketch of the Theorist   161
        Early Childhood   161
        Education   161
        Emergence of Erikson's Theory   162
        Honors   163
    Resolution of Basic Issues   163
        Heredity versus Social Determinants   163
        Early versus Continuous Development   164
        Subjective versus Objective Reality   172
        Determinism versus Freedom of Choice   172
        Conscious versus Unconscious Determinants   173
        Uniqueness versus Universality   174
        Explanation of Learning Process   174
        Role Assigned to Self-Concept   175
        Number and Weight Assigned to Motivational Concepts   176
        Centrality of Reinforcement   176
        Role Assigned to Group Determinants   177
    Psychological Health and Psychopathology   177
        Psychological Health   177
        Psychopathology   179
    Applications to Psychotherapy   180
        Therapeutic Goals   180
        Therapeutic Relationship   180
        Therapeutic Process and Strategies   181
        Course of Therapy   181

Extended Applications   *181*
    Dreams and Dream Interpretation   181
    Psychohistory   182
    Play Therapy   182
    Art Therapy   183
Critique   *183*
Annotated Bibliography   *184*
References and Suggested Readings   *185*

6   **Fromm's Humanistic Social Analysis**   **188**
Chapter Overview   *188*
Introduction   *189*
Biographical Sketch of the Theorist   *190*
    Early Years   190
    Education   191
    Emergence of Fromm's Theory   192
    Awards   193
Resolutions of the Eleven Basic Issues   *193*
    Heredity versus Social Determinants   193
    Determinism versus Freedom of Choice   196
    Conscious versus Unconscious Determinants   196
    Early versus Continuous Development   197
    Role Assigned to Group Determinants   199
    Number and Weight Assigned to
        Motivational Concepts   199
    Subjective versus Objective Reality   204
    Uniqueness versus Universality 204
    Explanation of Learning Process   205
    Role Assigned to Self-Concept   205
    Centrality of Reinforcement   205
Psychological Health and Psychopathology   *206*
    Healthy Personality and the Good Life   206
    Psychopathology   208
Heuristic Influence   *209*
    Fromm's Single Attempt at Empirical Research   210
Application to Psychotherapy   *211*
    Therapeutic Goals   211
    Therapeutic Relationship   211
    Initial Procedures and Strategies   212
    Course of Therapy   212
Extended Applications   *212*
    Dreams   212
    Society and Culture   213

Critique   214
    Too Cross-Disciplinary?   214
    The Criticism of Psychoanalysts   215
    The Criticisms of Psychologists   215
    A Contributor to Social Psychology   215
    Appeal to Western Youth   216
    Conclusion   216
Annotated Bibliography   216
References and Suggested Readings   217

7   **Horney's Theory of Psychosocial Analysis   219**
Chapter Overview   219
Introduction   220
Biographical Sketch of the Theorist   221
    Early Years   221
    Education   222
    Emergence of Theory   222
    Honors and Awards   223
Resolution of the Basic Issues   223
    Heredity versus Social Determinants 224
    Role Assigned to Self-Concept   224
    Early versus Continuous Development   225
    Number and Weight Assigned to
        Motivational Concepts   228
    Conscious versus Unconscious Determinants   229
    Subjective versus Objective Reality   230
    Determinism versus Freedom of Choice   230
    Explanation of Learning Process   230
    Uniqueness versus Universality   231
    Role Assigned to Group Determinants   231
    Centrality of Reinforcement   232
Psychological Health and Psychopathology   233
    Psychological Health   234
    Psychopathology   234
Application to Psychotherapy   235
    Therapeutic Goals   235
    Therapeutic Relationship   235
    Initial Procedures and Strategies   236
    Course of Psychotherapy   237
Extended Applications   238
    Feminine Psychology 238
    Self-Analysis   239
Critique   240
Annotated Bibliography   241
References and Suggested Readings   241

PART 3: *Organismic Theories*   **245**

8   **Allport's Theory of Personalism**   **247**
Chapter Overview   *247*
Introduction   *248*
Biographical Sketch of the Theorist   *249*
       Early Years   249
       Education   249
       Emergence of Allport's Theory of Personality   250
       Honors and Awards   250
Resolutions of Eleven Basic Issues   *250*
       Heredity versus Social Determinants   251
       Number and Weight Assigned to Motivational Concepts   251
       Uniqueness versus Universality   253
       Subjective versus Objective Reality   253
       Role Assigned to Self-Concept   253
       Determinism versus Freedom of Choice   254
       Conscious versus Unconscious Determinants   254
       Explanation of the Learning Process   255
       Early versus Continuous Development   256
       Role Assigned to Group Determinants   256
       Centrality of Reinforcement   257
Psychological Health and Psychopathology   *258*
       Psychological Health   259
       Psychopathology   260
Applications to Psychotherapy   *261*
       Therapeutic Goals   261
       Therapeutic Process and Strategies   261
Extended Applications   *261*
       Expressive Behaviors   261
       Religion   262
       Prejudice   262
       Personal Documents   263
Critique   *264*
Annotated Bibliography   *264*
References and Suggested Readings   *265*

9   **Rogers' Person-Centered Theory**   **269**
Chapter Overview   *269*
Introduction   *270*
Biographical Sketch of the Theorist   *272*
       Early Years   272
       Education   273
       Awards and Honors   275

Resolutions of the Eleven Basic Issues   276
   Heredity versus Social Determinants   276
   Number and Weight Assigned to Motivational Concepts   277
   Subjective versus Objective Reality   277
   Early versus Continuous Development   278
   Role Assigned to Self-Concept   278
   Conscious versus Unconscious Determinants   281
   Determinism versus Freedom of Choice   282
   Explanation of Learning Process   282
   Uniqueness versus Universality   283
   Role Assigned to Group Determinants   284
   Centrality of Reinforcement   284
Psychological Health and Psychopathology   285
   Psychological Health   285
   Psychopathology   288
Heuristic Influences: Research Methods and Techniques   289
   Rogers' Philosophy of Science   290
   Research Methods and Techniques   291
Applications to Psychotherapy   293
   Therapeutic Goals   293
   Therapeutic Relationship   294
   Initial Procedures and Strategies   296
   Course of Therapy   297
Extended Applications   298
   The Intensive Group Experience   298
   Education   300
   Marriage and Its Alternatives   300
   Recent Efforts to Extend Applications   301
Critique   301
Annotated Bibliography   303
References and Suggested Readings   304

10   Maslow's Metamotivational Theory of Personality   306
Chapter Overview   306
Introduction   307
Biographical Sketch of the Theorist   308
   Childhood   308
   Education   308
   Emergence of a Theory   309
   Awards and Honors   310
Resolutions of the Eleven Basic Issues   311
   Heredity versus Social Determinants   311
   Number and Weight Assigned to Motivational Concepts   311
   Subjective versus Objective Reality   315
   Early versus Continuous Development   316

Determinism versus Freedom of Choice   318
Uniqueness versus Universality   319
Explanation of the Learning Process   319
Role Assigned to Self-Concept   320
Conscious versus Unconscious Determinants   321
Role Assigned to Group Determinants   322
Centrality of Reinforcement   322
Psychological Health and Psychopathology   323
Psychological Health and the Good Life   323
Characteristics of Self-Actualizing People   325
Psychopathology   330
Heuristic Influences: Research Methods and Techniques   333
Maslow's Philosophy of Science   333
Research Methods and Techniques   334
Current Assessment   335
Applications to Psychotherapy   337
Therapeutic Goals   337
The Therapeutic Relationship   338
The Therapeutic Process   338
Group Therapy   339
Extended Applications   339
Work and the Work Environment   339
Management   340
Education   340
Critique   341
Annotated Bibliography   342
References and Suggested Readings   343

PART 4:   *Existential Theories*   347

11   May's Existential Theory of Personality   349
Chapter Overview   349
Introduction   350
Biographical Sketch of the Theorist   351
Early Years   351
Education   352
Emergence of the Existential Approach to Therapy   353
Accomplishments and Awards   353
Resolution of the Eleven Basic Issues   354
Heredity versus Social Determinants   354
Conscious versus Unconscious Determinants   356
Subjective versus Objective Reality   357
Determinism versus Freedom of Choice   357

Early versus Continuous Development   358
Role Assigned to Self-Concept   359
Uniqueness versus Universality   360
Number and Weight Assigned to Motivational Concepts   360
Role Assigned to Group Determinants   361
Explanation of the Learning Process   362
Centrality of Reinforcement   362
Psychological Health and Psychopathology   363
Healthy Personality and the Good Life   363
Psychopathology   364
Heuristic Influences: Research Methods and Techniques   365
Applications to Psychotherapy   366
Therapeutic Goals   366
Therapeutic Relationship   367
Initial Procedures and Strategies   368
Course of Therapy   368
Extended Applications   369
Other Therapeutic Settings   369
Dreams   369
Critique   370
Annotated Bibliography   371
References and Suggested Readings   372

12   Frankl's Theory of Logotherapy   374
Chapter Overview   374
Introduction   375
Biographical Sketch of the Theorist   376
Early Years   376
Education   376
Emergence of the Theory of Logotherapy   376
Honors and Awards   377
Resolution of the Eleven Basic Issues   378
Determinism versus Freedom of Choice   378
Uniqueness versus Universality   379
Heredity versus Social Determinants   380
Number and Weight Assigned to Motivational
    Concepts   380
Subjective versus Objective Reality   381
Conscious versus Unconscious Determinants   382
Early versus Continuous Development   382
Explanation of Learning Process   383
Role Assigned to Self-Concept   383
Centrality of Reinforcement   384
Role Assigned to Group Determinants   385

Psychological Health and Psychopathology   385
    Psychological Health   385
    Psychopathology   387
Applications to Psychotherapy   388
    Therapeutic Goals   388
    Therapeutic Relationship   388
    Therapeutic Process and Strategies   388
    Course of Therapy   389
Extended Applications   390
Critique   390
Annotated Bibliography   391
References and Suggested Readings   392

PART 5:   *Radical Behaviorism*   395

13 Skinner's Operant Reinforcement Theory   397
Chapter Overview   397
Introduction   398
Biographical Sketch of the Theorist   399
    Early Years   400
    Education   401
    Emergence of Operant Conditioning   402
    Accomplishments and Awards   402
Resolutions of the Eleven Basic Issues   403
    Heredity versus Social Determinants   403
    Centrality of Reinforcement   404
    Explanation of Learning Process   407
    Determinism versus Freedom of Choice   408
    Role Assigned to Group Determinants   408
    Early versus Continuous Development   409
    Number and Weight Assigned to Motivational Concepts   410
    Conscious versus Unconscious Determinants   411
    Role Assigned to Self-Concept   412
    Subjective versus Objective Reality   412
    Uniqueness versus Universality   413
Psychological Health and Psychopathology   413
    Healthy Personality and the Good Life   413
    Psychopathology   415
Applications to Psychotherapy   416
    Therapeutic Goals   417
    Therapeutic Relationship   418
    Initial Procedures and Strategies   418

Course of Psychotherapy   422
Extended Applications   422
Critique   423
Annotated Bibliography   424
References and Suggested Readings   425

PART 6:   *Rational-Cognitive Theories   427*

14 Kelly's Theory of Personal Constructs   429
Chapter Overview   429
Introduction   430
Biographical Sketch of the Theorist   432
Early Years   432
Early Education   433
Education   433
Emergence of the Theory of
    Personal Constructs   434
Honors and Recognition   434
Resolution of the Eleven Basic Issues   435
Heredity versus Social Determinants   435
Subjective versus Objective Reality   436
Determinism versus Freedom of Choice   436
Conscious versus Unconscious Determinants   437
Uniqueness versus Universality   437
Early versus Continuous Development   440
Explanation of Learning Process   441
Role Assigned to Self-Concept   441
Number and Weight Assigned to
    Motivational Concepts   442
Centrality of Reinforcement   443
Role Assigned to Group Determinants   443
Psychological Health and Psychopathology   443
Healthy Personality and the Good Life   443
Psychopathology   445
Kelly's Diagnostic Constructs   446
Heuristic Influences: Research Methods and Techniques   447
Use of the Rep Test in Empirical Studies   448
Applications to Psychotherapy   449
Therapeutic Goals   449
Therapeutic Relationship   450
Therapeutic Process and Strategies   450
Cycles of Construction   451

Extended Applications   452
   Institutions   452
   Nations   453
Critique   453
   Strengths   453
   Weaknesses   454
Annotated Bibliography   456
References and Suggested Readings   457

15   Ellis's Rational-Emotive Theory   459
Chapter Overview   459
Introduction   460
Biographical Sketch of the Theorist   461
   Early Years   461
   Education   462
   Emergence of a Theory   462
   Honors and Awards   463
Resolution of the Eleven Basic Issues   464
   Heredity versus Social Determinants   464
   Conscious versus Unconscious Determinants   465
   Role of the Self-Concept   470
   Determinism versus Freedom of Choice   471
   Explanation of Learning Process   472
   Subjective versus Objective Reality   473
   Early versus Continuous Development   474
   Uniqueness versus Universality   477
   Role of Group Determinants   478
   Number and Weight Assigned to Motivational Concepts   478
   Centrality of Reinforcement   479
Psychological Health and Psychopathology   481
   Healthy Personality and the Good Life   481
   Psychopathology   483
Heuristic Influences: Research Methods and Techniques   484
   Comparative Studies of RET with Other
         Therapeutic Approaches   485
   Noncomparative Studies of RET   486
Applications to Psychotherapy   486
   Therapeutic Goals   487
   Therapeutic Relationship   489
   Initial Procedures and Strategies   490
   Course of Psychotherapy   491
Extended Applications   493
Critique   494
Annotated Bibliography   495
References and Suggested Readings   496

PART 7: *Social-Cognitive Theory*   **499**

16 **Bandura's Social-Cognitive Theory**   **501**
Chapter Overview   *501*
Introduction   *502*
Biographical Sketch of the Theorist   *503*
    Early Years   503
    Education   503
    Emergence of Social Learning Theory   504
    Accomplishments and Awards   504
Resolutions of the Eleven Basic Issues   *505*
    Heredity versus Social Determinants   505
    Explanation of Learning Process   508
    Conscious versus Unconscious Determinants   510
    Early versus Continuous Development   511
    Role Assigned to Self-Concept   514
    Determinism versus Freedom to Choose   517
    Centrality of Reinforcement   518
    Number and Weight Assigned to Motivational Concepts   519
    Importance of Group Determinants   520
    Subjective versus Objective Reality   521
    Uniqueness versus Universality   522
Psychological Health and Psychopathology   *522*
    Psychological Health   522
    Psychopathology   524
Heuristic Influences: Research Methods and Techniques   *526*
Application to Psychotherapy   *526*
    Therapeutic Goals   526
    Therapeutic Relationship   527
    Initial Procedures and Strategies   528
    Individual and Group Counseling and Psychotherapy   528
    The Course of Social Learning Therapy   529
Extended Applications   *532*
Critique   *533*
Annotated Bibliography   *534*
References and Suggested Readings   *534*

17 **Conspectus of the Theories**   **537**
Chapter Overview   *537*
Introduction   *537*
A Conspectus of the Eleven Basic Issues   *538*
    Heredity versus Social Determinants   538
    Conscious versus Unconscious Determinants   539
    Determinism versus Freedom to Choose   540

Early versus Continuous Development   542
Subjective versus Objective Reality   544
Uniqueness versus Universality   544
Role of Self-Concept   544
Number and Weight Assigned to Motivational Concepts   546
Explanation of Learning Process   547
Role Assigned to Group Determinants   547
Centrality of Reinforcement   548
Psychological Health   549
When Psychological Health Is Viewed as Utopia   549
When Psychological Health Is Viewed as Normality   550
Psychological Health as Adjustment   550
Final Commentary   551
References and Suggested Readings   551

Glossary   553

Index of Authors   569

Subject Index   575

Preface

Theories of Personality: A Basic Issues Approach is an introductory text to the psychological study of human personality. In addition to presenting a survey of fifteen major, representative, and influential theories of personality, this book focuses on the theorists' resolutions of eleven basic and recurrent issues that serve as a distinctive organizational framework not found in most survey books. Not only is the blending of the basic issues approach with the survey method conceptually challenging, it provides students with a common, relevant, and flexible format that may be used to analyze, compare, contrast, and evaluate present personality theories without insisting on conformity to a rigid model. Further, for those students who want more than just knowledge of existing theories and wish to discover personal meaning in the theories they study, this book offers an approach to personal theory construction.

The basic issues teaching–learning approach is an invitation to openness, a dynamic fusion of personal and objective information. It offers students the opportunity to examine those assumptions inherent in their beliefs and values and to make their implicit beliefs explicit. It warns against clinging to beliefs simply because they are generally accepted and comfortable. It helps remove expectations of authoritatively defined right and wrong answers and of imposed truths and values, and it encourages independence of observation, thought, and action. The basic issues approach also reduces the likelihood of surrendering to individual theorists or groups who zealously advocate the superiority of their particular school or theory. In short, a basic issues teaching–learning approach enables students to direct their attention to questions of substance in the human condition, specifically, to those unresolved basic issues in the field that keep the study of personality alive and vibrant.

While it would be presumptuous to claim that the eleven issues selected for presenting the personality theories in this book are the only, or even the most fundamental, theoretical issues in the field of personality psychology, it can be stated that these eleven issues have survived numerous attempts at resolution by brilliant people over the years and merit the label *basic*. Basic issues have demonstrated their capacity to serve as an organizing and integrating framework, not only for the presentation and evaluation of theories in a diverse and contradictory theoretical discipline, but also for the construction of personal theories. The eleven basic issues used in this book and discussed in some depth in Chapter 1 represent an invitation to become a theorist as well as a personologist or psychotherapist.

Because of the book's structure, it may be used in a variety of ways. With the exception of the introductory and final chapters, each chapter focuses on a single theory. When a survey of the major theories of personality is the course objective, the book may be studied chapter by chapter (in any order), with each reader concentrating on a single theory until fully satisfied with his or her level of understanding. Because the same set of eleven basic issues is used throughout, it is possible, also, to study this book across chapters: (1) to compare one theorist's resolution of a particular issue with that of another theorist, or to the resolutions of all theorists; or (2) to study a single issue across chapters, analyzing the commonalities and differences of the various theories.

Each theory chapter opens with a chapter overview in outline form, a brief introductory statement about the theory, and a biographical sketch of the theorist. Where biographical data are sufficient, attempts are made to demonstrate how various theoretical constructs *might* have been influenced by specific life events and experiences. These sections are followed by the presentation of the theorist's resolutions of the eleven basic issues. The eleven issue resolutions offer comprehensive coverage of the theorist's principal theoretical constructs, appear in hierarchical order, and, as much as possible, are stated in the language and tone of the theorist. Key terms are printed in **boldface** type and defined at the point they appear in the text. Examples of research studies supporting or refuting the theorist's resolutions are cited when relevant. And visual illustrations, created to emphasize, clarify, or simplify the theorist's issue resolutions, are inserted. The next two sections are the theorist's views of psychological health and psychopathology. While most personality books deal with psychopathology, few discuss psychological health. Many of today's health-conscious students are genuinely interested in wellness and the good life. The sections on health and pathology are followed by two sections on the theory's application: (1) applications to psychotherapy, and (2) extended applications to other areas and disciplines. Next, there is a critique of the theory's strengths and weaknesses, voiced in the strong terms of advocates and adversaries. The final two sections of each chapter are an annotated bibliography and the references and suggested readings. Each section is designed to encourage further reading of both primary and secondary sources. A comprehensive glossary is provided for the student's convenience in the back of the book.

Acknowledgments

Although writing is a lonely task, no one I know who has written a textbook has done so without assistance. It is much more a pleasure than a sense of duty to acknowledge the many debts I have accumulated during the three years I worked on this book.

My greatest debt is to my wife, Lois. There would be no book without her sustained encouragement, patience, and support. She was always there to listen when I became blocked or discouraged, or to celebrate a completed chapter or the arrival of a favorable set of reviews. I am deeply grateful.

I am especially indebted to Donald Hall, a colleague, and Toni Hardy, a graduate assistant, who read and criticized nearly every chapter of this book. Their ideas and suggestions were most helpful, and I learned to rely on their honest and constructive criticism. Toni also contributed to the initial editing process. I also wish to express my gratitude to Pat LaMaster, Lynn Cole Fritts, and Kathy Vallance, who at various phases of writing managed to track down elusive research articles and books when they were most needed. Kathy Vallance also read and critiqued two chapters.

I am grateful for the illustrations prepared by Deb Hogshead, Clyde Collins, and Vicki Boatright. Their unique and thoughtful illustrations appear throughout the book.

I owe a special debt to those students who participated in the field testing of the basic issues approach to the study of personality theories. It was largely their effort and response that first convinced me of the merit of this approach and stimulated me to write this book.

Although I assume full responsibility for its content, including all errors and shortcomings, this book would not have been written were it not for the inspiration and challenge of the fifteen theorists whose ideas and theoretical constructs were selected for presentation.

Finally, I would like to thank the editors at Allyn and Bacon: Susan Badger, Editor-in-Chief, Social Sciences; Laura Pearson, Senior Editor; and the following reviewers whose ideas and suggestions had a great influence on the final structure of this book: Joel Aronoff, Michigan State University; Angela Burke, North Texas State University; David Cuevas, El Paso Community College; Angela Curiale, Sacramento Community College; Leon Gorlow, Penn State University; Bruce Haslam, Weber State University; Cooper Holmes, Emporia State University; Ralph Hood, University of Tennessee; and Mischel Nietzel, University of Kentucky.

C h a p t e r **1**

Introduction to Personality Theory and Basic Issues

Chapter Overview

    Human Nature Defined Has Consequences

    History of Personality Theory

    Personality Defies Scientific Definition

    The Ambitions of Personologists

    A Call for Open and Adventurous Minds

    The Book's Structure

    Basic Issues: An Integrative Structure to Personality Theory

    Eleven Basic Issues
        Conscious versus Unconscious
        Determinism versus Freedom of Choice
        Heredity versus Social Determinants
        Uniqueness versus Universality
        Early versus Continuous Development
        Subjective versus Objective Reality
        Explanation of Learning Process
        Role Assigned to Self-Concept
        Number and Weight Assigned to Motivational Concepts
        Centrality of Reinforcement
        Role Assigned to Group Determinants

    Special Features of the Book
        Biographical Sketch of the Theorist
        Psychological Health and Psychopathology

Heuristic Influences
Applications to Psychotherapy
Extended Applications
Critique
Annotated Bibliography
Glossary

References and Suggested Readings

There are few, if any, endeavors more intriguing and compelling or more elusive and frustrating to humans than the study of human personality. Human fascination with the nature of being human appears both natural and irrepressible. In their search for answers, humans have permitted their imaginations to carry them far beyond the immediate. Some look to the heavens or the stars for answers to their destinies, some to past events or anticipated consequences, some to nature or the study of animal behavior, and some explore deeply within themselves. Others attempt to demonstrate the influence of individual perception or cognition. And still others strive to incorporate the impact of situational factors or social and cultural influences. Whatever the path taken, the study of human personality can be a most exciting human adventure.

Even more impressive than the quest for answers to the human condition are the number, range, and diversity of the answers put forward. Humans have described themselves, among other things, as divine creations, products of evolution, members of the animal kingdom, rational beings, unfeeling automatons in a technical world, organic computers, imaginative creators, insensitive killers, ultimate world destroyers, even experimental subjects of superior beings from a distant planet.

Humans viewed by humans have been construed as aspiring, noble, rational, and actualizing. They have been portrayed also as petty, insignificant, aggressive, and savage. Humans have been said to be governed by their unconscious instincts, ruled by their biological needs, conditioned by environmental stimuli, motivated by a sovereign drive to actualize innate potentials, shaped by their past experiences, and directed by their present perceptions and cognition. They have been described as passive, active, proactive, and reactive.

Human Nature Defined Has Consequences

If humans have learned anything about themselves, it is that their ideas of human nature are contradictory. Further, they have learned that the contradictory images that emerge from their descriptions carry very real consequences. Indeed, personality theories have strongly affected the world-view of the human condition.

Matson (1976) expresses a strong belief that history reveals "men's ideas of man" have a compelling force and far-reaching consequences of their own that interact with and powerfully influence other phenomena—most noticeable of all, political movements and political constitutions (pp. 11–12). If Matson (1976) is correct, the images constructed by humans to depict their nature significantly influence all their thinking about human potential, abilities, and responsibilities, their concepts of good and evil, fate and freedom, values and beliefs, even their hopes, dreams, and aspirations.

History of Personality Theory

The roots of personality theories run deep in human history. Although it is impossible to establish a specific time in history when humans were first capable of self-reflection, Eccles and Robinson (1984) remind us that the ultimate concern of self-awareness—death awareness—is manifest in the ceremonial burial customs practiced by the Neanderthal, some 80,000 years ago.

Most **personologists** (individuals dedicated to the study of human personality) are a bit more cautious in their reviews of history. Allport (1955, 1968) and Hall and Lindzey (1978, 1985), for example, trace the roots of personality psychology from Greek antiquity. They point to the early conceptions of human nature forged by the Greek physician Hippocrates (460–377 B.C.) and the Greek philosophers Socrates (470?–399 B.C.), Plato (427–347 B.C.), and Aristotle (384–322 B.C.). Questions raised by these ancient scholars stimulated intellectual discourse on the nature of human personality for nearly twenty-five centuries.

From the intervening centuries, Hall and Lindzey (1978, 1985) look to the works of such philosophers as St. Thomas Aquinas (1225–1274), Niccolo Machiavelli (1496–1527), Thomas Hobbes (1588–1697), John Locke (1636–1704), Jeremy Bentham (1748–1832), Auguste Comte (1798–1857), Soren Kierkegaard (1813–1855), and Friedrich Nietzsche (1844–1900). Many of their contributions to the nature of being human are still detectable in contemporary theoretical formulations.

While the psychology of personality owes much to philosophy, its greatest debt is to medicine and the practical need to understand the troubled or abnormal personality. The clinical observations of Jean Charcot (1825–1893), Pierre Janet (1859–1947), Sigmund Freud (1856–1939, see Chapter 2), Alfred Adler (1870–1937, see Chapter 3), and Carl Jung (1875–1961, see Chapter 4) significantly impacted the study of personality theory. Seeking rational explanations and procedures to guide them in their attempts to cope with the psychological problems presented by their patients, these early practitioners viewed personality theory as functional and valued its practical application.

The ancient quest for answers—to perceive significance and find meaning for human ideas on the nature of being human—persists, and is rightly shared today by specialists and scientists representing many disciplines. In addition to psychologists and counselors, philosophers, theologians, poets, novelists, psychiatrists, neurologists, biologists, anthropologists, and sociologists are invested in the pursuit of a common subject, the study of human personality. The answers devised by so many diverse disciplines to explain the nature of human personality must be expected to differ. Indeed, differences, inconsistencies, and contradictions between and across theoretical orientations and discipline boundaries are presently the norm. Not only are the groups splintered, there is an astonishing lack of agreement. There is yet no consensus regarding the "best" theory of human personality or the "good life." The study of personality is still evolving, however. Despite the lack of agreement, personologists continue to serve as an important integrative force in psychology by gathering, organizing, and integrating the works of many specialists—in itself a most worthy and necessary endeavor.

Personality Defies Scientific Definition

Manifest in interpersonal relations, with social, cultural, and political consequences, human personality exists, visibly, as its own proof. Although personality has been an object of psychological study for many years, it continues to defy scientific definition. Personologists have formulated numerous theories, but human personality, while reflected partially in all the existing theories, proves more subtle, more deeply integrated, and more strangely unified than any present theory of it. The object of personologists' theoretical formulations is elusive. The images they paint of human personality in their theories are, at best, incomplete and imprecise impressions. Like present concepts of truth, justice, and beauty, human personality remains a psychological enigma, a multifaceted subject for which there is no single, universally accepted, all-encompassing theory.

The Ambitions of Personologists

No other area of psychology is as ambitious as the psychology of personality: The object of study is the *total* person over the *entire* life span, and the ultimate goal is the integration of *all* aspects of human behavior into a *single* theoretical framework. Unable to define the object of their study, or to agree how such integration might be realized or where their research efforts should be directed, personologists find that their interests and work not only overlap with other specialty areas in psychology (perception, development, motivation, learning, adjustment, change, and pathology, for example), but also cross the boundaries of neighboring disciplines (medicine, neurophysiology, biology, sociology, anthropology, philosophy, and computer science, to name but a few). While the broad range of interests and approaches and the cross-fertilization of thought in personality theory brings a rich abundance of data, ideas, and issues into the personality arena, it brings, as well, numerous unanswered questions, substantial differences, and strong disagreements. The grand theory of human personality awaits formulation.

There are many psychologists who find the ambitions of personologists absurd. They point to the comparative lack of recent advancement in the field as evidence for their conviction. Considering the current state of development in the area of personality, these same critics not only believe that a fusion of existing theories into a single, comprehensive theory of personality is impossible, they also express serious doubt that personologists will ever be able to formulate a single master theory that can account for all the phenomena in human personality.

Personologists are aware that, when viewed in light of their ultimate goal, present theories of personality are inadequate. They agree with their critics that advancement in recent years has been minimal. Nevertheless, they remain steadfast in their conviction that their goal, human personality *as a system*, is worth pursuing. There is always the possibility that converging lines of inquiry will ultimately lead to a new science of personality. Personologists point to other disciplines, physics in particular, where theories of time and space, long held to be true, were transcended in important ways by a conceptual revolution. However, even if a conceptual revolution should never occur in the psychology of personality, there is urgent need and intrinsic value in the study of human nature and the human condition.

A Call for Open and Adventurous Minds

While it is true that the psychology of personality is not a mature science, it is nonetheless a most fascinating, impressive, and rewarding field when approached with an open and adventurous mind. When minds are sufficiently open, adherents of one theory can, by force of imaginative insight, understand theories of personality that differ from their own, even those that differ significantly. They may find other theories unacceptable, but as long as their minds are open, they can grasp the major assumptions, constructs, and values presented in theories that are incompatible with their own.

This book is best approached by readers as an adventure. An exploration of the many implications inherent in today's personality theories does not require the denial of any presently held values, attitudes, or beliefs, nor does it require the application of such valuative criteria as true–false, right–wrong, good–bad, or useful–futile. No existing theory of personality meets all the criteria of a grand theory, yet all the theories selected for presentation in this book (and many that were not) are provocative and stimulating for the person who manages to maintain an open and adventurous mind. All theories of personality have the potential to encourage thought, to engender feelings (the delight or fear of self-exploration), and to evoke questions and issues, insight and doubt. In short, all the theories presented in this book have something worthwhile to say about the essence of being human to those who are willing to listen and to remain open to new or different ways to construe themselves and others.

Unfortunately, there is also the potential for confusion when members of a single area embrace a large number of diverse and conflicting theoretical viewpoints. Worse, the potential for confusion is compounded when the theorists are an enthusiastic and persuasive lot with large numbers of dedicated and loyal followers—many, regrettably, with a tendency toward theoretical zealousness. Beck (1967), aware of this trend, lists three shared characteristics of the adherents of major theoretical schools: ". . . a conviction of the ultimate truth of their own system, disdain for opposing theories, and a steadfast emphasis on purity of doctrines and techniques" (p. 7). Beck (1967) was writing of the patient's dilemma in choosing a therapist, but the student of human personality also may be intimidated and coerced by zealous adherents of the dominant (most popular) theories.

When theoretical enthusiasm evolves into theoretical zealousness, followers can easily lose sight of the impossibility of theoretical certainty and become disciples. No longer open to new experiences and ideas, zealous theorists and their followers are convinced that their theoretical constructs are truths rather than hypotheses. They begin to criticize other theorists, even to the point of telling them how to theorize. Once convinced of the truthfulness of their theory, they see no need to question, test, or research it. Again, an open and adventurous mind can help the intimidated student separate the zealous from the enthusiastic, the dogmatic from the persuasive, and the cult from the camp.

The Book's Structure

The theorists selected for inclusion in this volume are recognized as major contributors to the literature of personality. Moreover, their theories are considered by many personologists to be relatively comprehensive and representative of the major theoretical schools or divisions of personality and psychotherapy. Some of the theorists presented were pioneers in the psychology of personality (Freud, Jung, and Adler, for example); others (such as Ellis and Bandura) are relative newcomers. Some of the theorists found the data for their theories in the therapeutic setting (Freud, Jung, Adler, Fromm, Horney, Rogers, Frankl, May, and Ellis, for example); others looked for their data in the laboratories of an academic setting (Allport, Bandura, Maslow, and Skinner). Some crossed the boundaries of numerous related disciplines (Fromm, Jung, and May, in particular); others never strayed far from their specialty (Bandura and Skinner). Some concentrated on the experience of self (Rogers, in particular); others on identity (Erikson, for example) and still others on enduring characteristics or traits (Allport). Some stressed motivation (Maslow), others environmental stimuli (Skinner), and still others looked to cognition (Kelly, Ellis, and Bandura). To varying degrees, all have influenced the psychology of human personality.

There will almost certainly be readers who question the absence of such theorists as K. Lewin (1935), W. H. Sheldon (1944), and Harry Stack Sullivan (1947). While there is little doubt that their contributions to the field of personality were significant, interest in their theories today appears to be declining. This assessment, along with the limitations of space and time, led to their omission. Some readers may question, also, the inclusion of Bandura (Chapter 16), Ellis (Chapter 15), and Kelly (Chapter 14). While their theories can, with some justification, be viewed as less than comprehensive theories of personality, their work *is* representative of a strong and growing movement in the field to integrate human cognition, emotion, and behavior. Considering that personologists have been criticized severely for the field's lack of advancement and growth, it would seem that those whose theoretical formulations and research are responsible for revitalizing the psychology of personality by providing new directions and advancement merit attention.

To offer some organization to what initially can be an overwhelming and confusing field of study, personologists have attempted through the years to create a series of divisions, classifications, or models into which they could fit, however loosely, all the existing theories of personality. One of the earliest attempts was that of Allport (1937), who after collecting fifty definitions of personality, divided them into five types: Omnibus, Arrangement, Hierarchical, Adjustment, and Distinctiveness. Thirty years later, Rotter (1967) offered six comparative dimensions, three that deal with the formal characteristics of theories and three that relate to personality differences among humans: Systematic versus Unsystematic, Operational versus Nonoperational, Content versus Process, Experience versus Heredity, Generality versus Specificity, and Internal versus Situational. Hall, Lindzey, Lochin, and Manosevitz (1985) assign twenty-four theories to four general areas of focus: Psychodynamic Forces, the Experiencing Person, Enduring Characteristics, and Learning and the Environment. Ryckman (1985) assigns the sixteen theories he selected for presentation to six perspectives: Psychoanalytic and Neopsychoanalytic, Trait, Cognitive, Social-Behavioristic, Humanistic, and Constitutional. Rychlak (1981) divides the theories he presents into three broad historical traditions or models: Mixed Kantian–Lockean Models in Classical Psychoanalysis, Lockean Models in American Psychiatry and Behaviorism, and Kantian Models in the Phenomenological Outlook.

It should be clear by now that the assignment of any of the existing theories of personality into a particular category, model, or school is strictly arbitrary and an expression of the author's views and need for structure. Certainly, it is not an expression of the theorists who would much prefer students of their theories read their works rather than others' summaries of their theories in a survey text, regardless of how accurate or comprehensive those summaries.

To achieve the purpose stated above, this book is divided into seven parts: Pioneers of Personality Theory, Analytic and Neoanalytic Theories, Organismic Theories, Existential Theories, Radical Behavior Theory, Rational-Cognitive Theories, and Social-Cognitive Theories. Each of the fifteen theories selected for presentation in this book was then assigned to one of the seven major parts of the book.

Basic Issues: An Integrative Structure to Personality Theory

Even the most contemporary theories of personality produce more questions than answers and uncover more issues than resolutions. The unanswerable questions about the nature of being human have given rise to the primary issues of concern to today's theorists. Those fundamental, constant, recurring issues appear to have a number of intrinsic characteristics that make them especially relevant to the personologist in the process of developing a theory or of analyzing and comparing existing theories.

Characteristics of Basic Issues

A basic issue is one that cannot be avoided. Theorists may sidestep a basic issue, but only temporarily. Sooner or later, a basic issue will surface and force the theorist to take a stand. Existing theories of personality are conscious or unconscious attempts by individual theorists to resolve basic issues. Fortunately, potential theorists who choose to employ the basic issues approach in their study have a variety of resolutions of each basic issue readily available to them.

Once identified, basic issues may be employed by the theorist or the student to evaluate existing theories as well as personal theories under development. The comprehensiveness of a theory, for example, may be determined and evaluated by the number of basic issues resolved and the degree of depth of each resolution.

If an issue is basic, it is value laden; leaving it unresolved activates the potential for producing tension. Working toward a personal resolution of a value-laden issue offers the theorist and student some distinct advantages. Because basic issues have specifiable values, work with these issues will be personally relevant and significant. This effort will nearly always lead to an increased understanding of both self and others. Because basic issues are value laden, they may be arranged in hierarchical order of significance; this hierarchical order can then be used as an integrating structure for one's personal theory of personality as well as for understanding or contrasting the theories of others.

Although basic issues are fairly easy to separate and to arrange in hierarchical order, they are composed of interrelated questions. Any attempt to resolve an issue will converge with or overlap the resolution of other basic issues. This overlapping gives the theorist or student the opportunity to check for inconsistencies within the theory and to look for gaps in resolutions of other issues. In addition, issue resolution provides an opportunity to expand the comprehensiveness and clarity of one's theoretical thinking, since overlapping can complement the resolutions of other issues and can provide experimental recall of events supportive of a particular direction of resolution.

Often a basic issue involves **polar opposites** (e.g., unconscious versus conscious determinants of behavior). When polar opposites are involved, either extreme serves to define the other, although neither extreme is simply the absence of the other. For example, life requires death, its polar opposite, to give it meaning. Unlike *either–or* opposites, such as *good* versus *evil*, polar opposites can be viewed as integrative, internal differences within a single structure, system, or organism or different parts of a single process. When good and evil are viewed as polar opposites, good that blocks a greater good can be evil, and evil that motivates good can be good. Good is not entirely good unless there could be nothing better; evil cannot be totally evil until there is nothing worse.

Polar opposites exist together as a dimension of the unified organism, the whole human being. They make up the being's uniqueness. Wertheimer (1972) asserts the advantage of the phenomenon of working with an issue composed of two polar opposites when he writes that these issues "have the intriguing property that if their opposites were combined, a new, higher level and more productive structure emerges" (p. 9). Shostrom, Knapp, and Knapp (1976) refer to this new, higher level of understanding as the *tertium quid*. Every value has an equal opposite or counter-value; neither can be fully understood without the other. In fact, neither could exist without the other (e.g., a concept of freedom would have little meaning without a concept of determinism).

When theorists and students are able to resolve a basic issue in some depth, they discover that their resolution holds clear implications for specific therapeutic goals and equally clear directions (specific therapist behaviors) for achieving those goals. The process of resolving the basic issues, then, helps the student make the leap from theory to application.

The cognitive exercise of issue consideration and resolution encourages theorists and students to work beyond present knowledge. To resolve a basic issue, it is necessary to reach beyond certainty. This effort, and the realization that they are exploring the unknown, teaches students that a resolution of a basic issue is no more than a theoretical construct, justified by need, expediency, and the tentativeness of time. Theorists and students who realize fully that they are going beyond the known are more likely to consider and to value their theoretical constructs through perceptual-cognitive frames open to new experiences. Their theories motivate them to commitment and action rather than to closed thinking and rigid behavior. Further, the critical significance of their thinking will allow for examination, refinement, and revision of theory as new data accumulate. As they experiment with this issue-resolution approach, even those who adhere closely to some existing popular theory of personality are less likely to become mere followers or, worse, disciples who distrust their own experience and force themselves into a mold of another's making. Further, the basic issues approach provides the students with awareness of and insight into current controversies that exist within their profession, thereby stimulating new thoughts, discussion, and creativity among professionals.

Resolving the basic issues requires close self-examination. Personal values must be stated explicitly and arranged carefully in hierarchical order. Once this is accomplished, these personal resolutions to the basic issues give students and therapists personal bases for valuation. Whatever they are most certain about in themselves, they can also be most certain of in others.

In addition to assisting the student's growth toward a personal theory, the basic issues approach offers the student a framework for analyzing and evaluating existing theories. This same framework may be used to view major differences and commonalities between theories or major strengths and weaknesses within a single theory.

A personal theory of personality, constructed from the individual's resolutions of the basic issues, provides a framework or valuational base for positive mental health. It offers criteria for the good life, the facilitative interpersonal relationship, the productive learning process, and the healthy environment.

Perhaps more than any other approach to the teaching and learning of theories of personality, the basic issues approach is less likely to become quickly dated. Basic issues are by definition significant, relevant, and timeless. They have always been with us and seem likely to remain.

Like all other approaches, the basic issues approach has distinct disadvantages. First, basic issues abound with judgmental controversy. If various theorists or therapists were asked to identify the basic issues in personality theory, it is unlikely that any two lists would be identical, and even less probable that these listings would rank the issues in the same hierarchical order. Those who have worked in this area state emphatically that it is necessary to be subjective, arbitrary, and more than a little presumptuous to define a list or set of basic issues (Ford & Urban, 1963; Wertheimer, 1972). Few wish to be tagged with those adjectives; consequently, few books on theories of personality have been written wherein the basic issues approach is employed as the primary structure to analyze each theory presented. Second, as stated earlier, examination of a basic issue introduces value consideration. Since no value classification system has been devised on which the majority of personologists can agree, this too must be included among the disadvantages of the basic issues approach. Third, it often appears that data support both polarities of a given basic issue. Nevertheless, if a theory is to be comprehensive and consistent, each theorist must take a stand, even if that stand is firmly in the middle of the road. Failure to take a stand can result in a theory that is less comprehensive than it might otherwise be.

Given that basic issues in the study of human personality are controversial, arbitrary, idiosyncratic, and elusive, why employ this approach? The unique advantages already cited are reasons enough, but Wertheimer (1972), who uses a basic issues approach in an introduction to general psychology, adds this bit of interesting logic:

> *No one needs to agree with the particular set of issues included, nor with the characteristics of particular ideas, men, or movements on these issues, but the exercise of thinking in terms of these issues or another comparable set of issues may well provide a framework that can help organize the fascinating diversity that is psychology today (p. vii).*

In addition, Wertheimer (1972) notes that this approach can "fit with a wide range of prejudices, a broad diversity of different orientations, and a great variety of special interests" (p. vii). Certainly, a book written with this teaching–learning approach may prove controversial, but there seems at least an equal chance that it might well prove compatible with the many diverse theories of personality available today.

In the basic issues approach, values are not forced on students. Rather, they are encouraged only to confront what they already claim to believe and to value. Excessive concentration on existing theories of personality may diminish the motivation to develop a personal theory. By following a basic issues approach, however, students become aware of the values they serve, and they can examine their values for clarity, consistency, and comprehensiveness. Through the discovery of clear meaning in what they are doing, students can commit themselves to firm professional identities and effectiveness.

Eleven Basic Issues

Eleven basic issues make up the structure of the theories presented in this book. Six contain the characteristics of polar opposites discussed previously; five concern the theorists' positions on more specific issues. While not limited to the examples below, each of the eleven basic issues evokes numerous questions.

Conscious versus Unconscious Determinants

Do we humans possess an unconscious, an inherited, inaccessible entity, outside our sphere of control, or are we conscious beings with the power to choose among alternatives? Are we capable of self-awareness, thinking, and decision making, and therefore responsible for our existence and destiny? Is our behavior genetically predetermined and unconsciously conditioned by our environment, or can we consciously select potentials and aspirations? Are we the unconscious results of our unique combination of personal experiences, circumstance, chance, and life scripts, or do we consciously create ourselves through our choices and the lessons we learn? Is our behavior predictable and controllable because of its mechanistic and unconscious origin in genetics and the environment, or are we unknowable and unpredictable because of our ability to transcend genetic endowment and environmental circumstances? Are we capable of full awareness moment to moment, or must we seek self-knowledge through unconscious recall, dream analysis, defense mechanisms, free associations, projective techniques, and hypnosis? Is consciousness a myth we have created to justify our existence? Do some areas of our minds lie beyond the realm of our knowledge (ESP [extrasensory perception], other dimensions, other worlds)? Are the conscious and unconscious compartments of our personalities part of our total awareness, or are these concepts we have invented to describe the regions of an awareness continuum within us? Does our conscious awareness extend beyond the present, beyond the moment, beyond what seems apparent? Is it justifiable to reject any concept of conscious/unconscious because neither can be observed? Does consciousness imply self-awareness, thereby increasing choice?

One of the oldest issues in philosophy and psychology, the debate over the conscious and unconscious aspects of being human continues. Theorists reconcile their stance on this issue from questions similar to those asked here.

Determinism versus Freedom of Choice

Are we free to choose our behavior in any set of circumstances, or is this freedom a contingency we hold because it has been well reinforced in the past? Are our decisions based on innate needs and antecedent causes, or can we transcend our biological dimensions and past learning to reach a level of personal objectivity? Are we passive victims of fate, circumstance, and conditioning, unable to assert responsibility for our existence and choice of behavior, or do we initiate our own goals, methodologies, and achievements? Do we learn merely to accept and adjust to our environments and/or life circumstances, or do we choose our attitudes toward all we encounter, past, present, and future? Do we differ from other animals only in our degree of complexity, and is this degree of complexity something self-defined or part of a determined environment in which we exist? Is our ability to choose an attitude the ultimate human freedom, giving us the resources to view ourselves and reality from an especially personal and relevant inner locale? Are we enmeshed in the web of reinforced behaviors we experience from the moment of birth? Do we, if victims of fate, relinquish responsibility for our approach to life? Are our behaviors justified because we cannot exercise a freedom of choice? Is personal insight an integral factor in our life changes? Are we reactive beings, simply responsive to stimuli introduced through the environment on a personal level, or proactive beings, able to encounter the environment on a personal level and able to make choices designed to minimize difficulty and maximize effectiveness? Can we reach beyond the conditioning of government, education, and conventionality to make of ourselves what we wish to become, or are we pawns in a macrocosmic chess game?

These are but a few of the many considerations to be confronted in pondering the issue of determinism versus freedom of choice. We must evaluate and critically decide who and/or what governs us. Are we in control or are we moving in a flow that surrounds everyone?

Heredity versus Social Determinants

Will future discoveries and interpretations of DNA-RNA research lead to a belief in genetically prescribed limitations to our endeavors, or will this research lead to an even stronger affirmation of our ability to choose our own destinies from the available alternatives? Is our growth and development a dynamic, ongoing set of processes subject to innumerable experiential and/or environmental factors? Is our love for our children rooted in the fact that our children will reproduce our genes, or do we establish this loving relationship on a higher level of social awareness and innovative emotion? Are our most pressing problems to be resolved by genetic manipulation, cloning, psychosurgery, molecular biology, the manufacture of humanoids/androids, the surgical/biochemical intervention in the embryonic and neonatal life phases? Can therapy, education, and improved interpersonal communications/relationships lead to the answers we are seeking? Are we biologically fixed without fluctuation, or do we have experiential elasticity? Should we focus our investigations of human nature on the interaction of inherited or environmental factors, or should we work toward an understanding of the significance of both elements in our growth and development processes? Are we complex primates to be studied with mammalian biology, or must we also seek out a novel methodology for the study of our subjective experiences? Is human intelligence an attribute or an entity? Does the **selfish-gene theory** (an innate predisposition to protect and preserve the genetic line) explain our powerful emotions regarding abortion, child abuse, divorce, suicide, and euthanasia, or is there a humanistic explanation for these feelings? Are we ultimately pushed, pulled, and driven by impulses, basic needs, and urges that override the influences of environment?

We should consider our personal feelings about this issue. What element has played the greater part in our development? Is it the society of which we are members or those attributes we receive from parents and ancestors? Resolution of this issue has definite implications for helping resolve the other issues. All issues are interrelated, and to provide consistency to our own theory, we must provide consistent resolutions of the individual issues.

Uniqueness versus Universality

What are the specific constituent parts of our uniqueness, and how do these parts interact to form our entirety? What factors, characteristics, and experiences do we share with all other individuals, regardless of race, color, or societal configuration? Does uniqueness, for individuals and nations, lead to an unhealthy egocentrism and ethnocentrism? Are personal feeling and appreciation of our uniqueness beneficial or detrimental to our interactions with others? Can we feel that we are unique without feeling that all other persons are also unique? If we share a human ancestral and hereditary commonality, why do we impose war, famine, and interpersonal hardship on ourselves? Does commonality imply a herd mentality we cannot transcend, or does this commonality imply a social instinct that is beneficial to us and our society? Is uniqueness a biological nuance, or is uniqueness something we can foster and utilize for our personal growth and development? How much do we incorporate from the environment and transform into something we consider unique to ourselves? Is human commonality a part of the *Zeitgeist* (spirit of the present and the legacy of the past), or is it something that reaches deeper into each person throughout the history of humankind? Does a concept like Jung's *collective unconscious* imply that we are all linked by a chain of being that exists in the twilight regions of our understanding and being? Is uniqueness or (universality) the cause or the result of our various behaviors?

This particular issue encourages us to view how we perceive ourselves in a personal and social context. As mentioned before, this issue links with other issues to form a whole conception of self, others, and the world.

Early versus Continuous Development

Are there stages or critical periods we must traverse to develop normally and healthfully? Are there developmental tasks within such stages or periods that we must accomplish so we can grow and approach or acquire self-awareness? Can we transcend early trauma and grow continually in the present, or are we linked with inescapable misery and stagnation because of familial or environmental deprivation we experienced as children? Are early experiences permanently imprinted on us, or is personal development amendable by choice and advancement throughout life? Is the past indispensable in the understanding of development, or if we have full understanding of the present, is there any reason to consider or understand the past? Are convenient life milestones—for example, the ages 18, 30, 40, 65, 100—and the characteristics of these ages something we are taught and encouraged to accept as real and inescapable? What factors contribute to a stagnation of personal growth? Are some regions of our being undeveloped or underdeveloped because we are educated to question and to doubt their existence? Are there more than two seemingly natural developmental events—birth and death? Are theories of early development amendable by the pursuit of self-awareness during adulthood? Is there a natural developmental process that fosters self-realization if uninhibited, or is development the result of chance circumstance and interactions? Does our educational system instruct us to seek self-development and personal growth actively, or does this system encourage us to accept things as they are with little opportunity for change and improvement? Can deprivation in some critical stage of development stifle and possibly destroy our attempts to express and activate our potentials? Is mental health something we acquire at a certain time in life, or is it something we develop, perpetuate, and prosper by throughout our lives?

We should develop questions based on consideration of the ideas and concepts that are personally relevant—thus, meaningful. While others may provide a framework for resolution of this issue, a personal resolution is the result of much self-searching. The developmental issue is especially important because it is a statement of where we believe we are at the moment and an expression of where we will be in the future.

Subjective versus Objective Reality

Do we live in an objective world—a reliable, rational, measurable entity—or do we live in a private world of subjective perception, valuing, and emotion? If objective reality is a fact, if a constant and ordered environment exists, how can we know this reality when we have only our unique experiences in it and our personal perceptions and interpretations of it? Although dreams and visions appear to exist in an inner psychological realm, how are we to know where this inner reality is? If our experiences and perceptions are personally and psychologically unique, how can we ever enter into the world of another person? Is understanding of ourselves and others best approached through analysis or synthesis, or is a dual approach the better choice? Do we exist as objective realities unto ourselves, motivated or pushed by universal natural laws, or are we potentialities moving toward actualization and discovery of realities beyond those we now consider? How far does our inner reality extend to influence what we encounter outside ourselves? If we were robbed of our sense of perception, would awareness and sense of being continue to exist? Does truth exist on a universal level, or are we tied to a prejudiced view of our existence because of our attachment to an inner psychological reality? Can our perceptions and, thus, our understanding of reality ever approach completeness given the fact that our senses are imperfect and subject to deterioration and disease? Are all persons given the same potential for understanding their inner psychological being, or is there an inequity of potential that belies concepts such as survival of the fittest and natural selection? Is consideration of and belief in this psychological being something that has occurred in the societal development of humans in civilization, or is it something that lies innately within us and provides us with identity?

Many of the great thinkers of the world have long pondered the question of reality. Since none has resolved the question, it has become a basic theoretical issue that still confronts the personologist.

Explanation of the Learning Process

What are our biochemical bases of learning? Is our learning a completely biochemical exercise, or is it influenced by factors and considerations we can initiate for ourselves? Is learning a natural, continual process, or is it something we must discipline ourselves to undertake? How do we store and recall the information that is presented to us? Is there a difference between how we learn about ourselves and how we learn about the environment? Does significance or relevance of information affect our ability to remember and associate it? Can we be certain that what we learn is valid, or at least beyond the probability of revision? What is the process that allows us to know this? Is knowledge acquired because we desire to acquire it or because we cannot stop ourselves from acquiring it? Is the learning process purposive, determined, or teleological? How do others affect or influence our learning? When others attempt to influence us, why do some succeed and others fail? Is there a facilitative relationship, or is teaching simply the arrangement of the contingencies of reinforcement? Do we teach others in the same manner we were taught? How do learning processes such as recall and association operate? Can learning occur as a result of personal insight into knowledge? Can the learning process be reduced to naturalistic or mechanistic determinants? How many different types of learning are there? What variables—for example, motivation, maturation, attending power, relevance, and reinforcement—facilitate learning in others, and which of these are particularly significant in the therapeutic setting? Do we learn through personal experiences and validate this learning through interpersonal relationships?

We are learning all the time, but do we understand how our learning occurs? We must look at numerous considerations as we determine how we personally go about collecting, organizing, and utilizing the information we gather. The answer or resolution may have many dimensions, and it is the task of personality theorists to sort through these dimensions and arrive at personal conceptions of the learning process.

Role Assigned to the Self-Concept

What is a self-concept? How do we develop this form of self-perception? Is self-concept established within us, beyond us, or somewhere in between, in a middle zone of interaction between our inner psychological state and what we perceive as reality? Is self-concept simply a personally relevant perception of ourselves, or does it affect the way we work, play, and relate to others? Should self-concept be assigned a central position in our theory development since it may significantly influence our behavior, or should we discard the concept because it is an abstract, unobservable concept that has little meaning beyond our own personal experience?

When we object to or deny those qualities of ourselves which seem valid, are we pathological? Are self-awareness, authentic behavior, and honesty with ourselves prerequisites for personal growth and development? Is self-acceptance purely a matter of choice and readily available to anyone whose definitions are in good order? Under what conditions might significant others influence our self-concepts? Does the modeling process lead us to improvement of our self-concept or to dependence on role models for definition of ourselves? Can significant others come to some point of understanding of how we feel about ourselves? Is there a biological predisposition toward the development of a self-concept? Are self-awareness and self-concept the same thing? Without the existence of self-concept, is there a personal identity above the animal level? Is the self-concept a flexible concept that changes according to our age, life circumstance, and emotional stability, or is it established at an early or critical period in our lives without the possibility of revision or improvement? Do we possess many different constituent selves? Is our conception of self a continuous process? Is it possible to expand and improve our self-concept? What conditions or relationships contribute to the creation of a healthy self-concept? Conversely, what conditions or relationships contribute to formation and maintenance of a negative self-concept? Can our self-concept be communicated to others? Do our behaviors serve as an extension of our self-concept into the world? Is it possible to create and maintain a neutral self-concept? For our concepts of self to be favorable, must our concepts of others be less favorable? Will or must our self-concept influence our conception of others? Can we rate ourselves as competent without rating others as less or more competent? Is there a difference between how we act with others and how we act with ourselves? Is self-acceptance more important to self-actualization than self-concept? Are feelings of personal value and significance related to our self-concept? Does the positivity or negativity of our self-concept tend to attract positive and negative people to us?

As can be seen by the number of questions for consideration, self-concept is an important factor to consider in theory development. The issue of self-concept can put us in touch with our innermost personal feelings and how these feelings help or hinder our personal operation and therapeutic effectiveness.

Number and Weight Assigned to Motivational Concepts

What motivates us to behave as we do? Where and when does motivation begin? How can we best recognize, investigate, and measure our motivation? Are we motivated in the present by the cloudy laws of human nature? Are we motivated in the present by childhood experiences, appetites, hopes, and aspirations? Does our motivation change as our life experiences or circumstances change? Is there an innate motivating power, essence, or principle in human life, and what conditions provide for its discovery and enhancement? Is love a legitimate motivational force? Are there motivational concepts that are common to all of us—for example, will to live, to power, to procreate? Are we motivated by a complex array of habit patterns that were intentionally or inadvertently reinforced in our past? Can we come to awareness and appreciation of new things and add them to our motivational inventory? Are we motivated by the principle of pleasure more than by pain, avoidance, tension reduction, conflict/anxiety elimination, equilibrium, system unity and harmony, or an internal belief or value system? Are our motivations stimulated, conditioned, reinforced, sublimated, or elaborated by innate and unconscious drives? How much do parents and significant others influence our development of motivational patterns? Are we motivated only by objects associated with primary drives and then only to the degree our responses were rewarded or gratified in the past? Why can some of us delay gratification in pursuit of a goal, while others seem unable to exist without constant gratification? Is self-actualization a legitimate motivational goal? Does the value we place on life increase our motivation in a general sense? What nuances of constitution make one individual motivated by spiritual or ethical concerns and another by prurient or material concerns? Does our educational system encourage us to develop our potentials or to compete with others for rewards such as money, fame, and ego gratification? Are we sometimes motivated by fear and insecurity, and is this type of motivation important to movement and personal growth?

Our resolutions of this issue depend on what we hold dearest and what we are willing to work and fight for the hardest. We can gain some insight into our personal motivations through resolution of this issue, and such insight will no doubt help us with resolution of some of the other issues.

Centrality of Reinforcement

Do we operate on a pleasure–pain continuum, or is life innately rewarding to us most of the time? What makes life rewarding to some and not to others? How much of our behavior is guided by rewards/reinforcement? Are we reacting beings directed by socio-cultural reinforcements, or is internal personal reward possible? Do we exist from day to day on the premise that there is some long-term reward to life, or do we go from one transient reward to another just to maintain some degree of comfort? Is it realistic to believe that life is its own reward? If we were to lose everything, what is the one thing we would retain if we could do so? Is all civilization and society based on a reward system, and if so, does this mean that we cannot advance beyond the system? Can cultures be purposefully designed through the shaping of humans? Should concern about reward and reinforcement be central to theory development, or do other considerations account for the rightful place of reward as a constituent part of our existence? How are our alternative values of reward determined?

We are dealing with concepts that perpetuate our growth or stagnation as human beings. The things that motivate and reward us have grown out of our value systems and, as such, provide a window from which to view ourselves.

Role Assigned to Group Determinants

Are we really social animals with an innate and powerful instinct toward social interest? If we are members of a group, regardless of the constituency, do we assume a group identity at the sacrifice of personal identity, or can we discover ourselves as we move toward commitment and concern within the group environment? If we accept a self-as-group-member concept of ourselves, how do we maintain and balance this concept with our self-as-individual concept? Is group affiliation necessary for mental well-being? In opposition to group affiliation, are there any advantages to a life of solitude and retreat? Can we come to valid self-awareness in solitude? Does group affiliation facilitate learning? Does group affiliation provide us with a testing ground for our self-concept and for any changes we may want to make in our lives? Are we attracted to groups that mirror our nuances of character, our weaknesses, our strengths? Are we predisposed toward group affiliation since birth, or does our societal environment inculcate a belief in group affiliation?

We must review our personal history to decide how significant group membership has been for us.

Special Features of the Book

Biographical Sketch of the Theorist

In *Ideology and Utopia*, Karl Mannheim (1949) concluded that all scientists are biased in their research interests by their own personal problems. Further, Mannheim (1949) asserts, the areas of research selected and the meaning assigned to the result of research may, for some scientists, be dictated by life experiences and personal difficulties. Ann Roe's (1953) investigation of eminent psychologists and anthropologists appears to lend some credibility to Mannheim's viewpoint. Roe (1953) was impressed with how frequently the subjects of her study seemed to view their research activities as a way to find answers to problems of deep personal concern. She noted also that many of her subjects experienced lengthy periods of soul searching before choosing scientific research as a vocation. H. F. Ellenberger (1970) expressed the idea that a wide range of influential psychological theories originated in the "creative illnesses" of their founders. Freud (Chapter 2) and Jung (Chapter 4) are only two examples that he cited. Christopher Monte (1987) recommends that personality theories be examined in "light of their creators' personal histories" (p. 9). Even further, he proposes, the history of personality theory should be viewed as an exposure of "human nature reflecting on itself. . . . a psychohistory, illuminated by the human character of its creators and opaqued by the character of their human limits" (Monte, 1987, p. 9).

Whether or not one views the biographical data of personality theorists with the importance attributed to it by Mannheim (1949), Roe (1958), Ellenberger (1970), and Monte (1987), it seems only natural to want to know more about persons whose ideas are stimulating and challenging. Moreover, when those persons are the originators of major theories of personality, it is intriguing to speculate about what impact their life experiences might have on their research and theoretical formulations. Were the emotional disturbances of Freud (see Chapter 2) and Jung (see Chapter 4) creative illnesses? What influence did early childhood feelings of inferiority have on Adler's (see Chapter 3) motivational construct? Did the forced early independence of Kelly (Chapter 14) and Ellis (Chapter 15) have anything to do with the role they assigned to cognition in their theories? What, if any, impact did May's (Chapter 11) near-death experience with tuberculosis and Frankl's (Chapter 12) experiences in the Nazi concentration camps have on their theories?

Serious students of personality theories often enhance and expand their understanding of a particular theory by studying the life of the theorist. Indeed, it appears that the genesis of ideas and development of constructs that make up the theories of certain theorists can, in some instances, be unveiled in the theorists' autobiographies. However, it appears also that the ease with which biographical material can be located is directly related to a theorist's stance on the issue of developmental directions. Those theorists who see little or no relationship between their early years and later accomplishments are less likely to disclose their life histories. Conversely, those who espouse causal theories are more inclined to discuss early childhood events and experiences that they consider to be crucial or significant in their personal and theoretical development. Freud (Chapter 2) and Jung (Chapter 4), for example, have provided autobiographies. Skinner (Chapter 13), a radical determinist, has written a three-volume autobiography: *Particulars of My Life* (1976), *The Shaping of a Behaviorist* (1979), and *A Matter of Consequence* (1983). Although Rogers (Chapter 9) believes in continuous development, he trusts personal experience as his ultimate guide in formulating a theory of personality; more, he willingly shared his experiences with his readers.

All theory chapters in this book present a biographical sketch of the theorist. The length of each sketch reflects *only* the availability of biographical information; it bears *no* relation either to importance or to any attempt on the part of the author to personalize one theorist more than another.

Psychological Health and Psychopathology

"There is a group of persons who are entirely mortal, who have their imperfections, and yet have discovered a way of life that is beyond what most people attempt to create for themselves" (Jourard & Landsman, 1980, p. 3). In this book, the writer examines the works of fifteen major personality theorists for their own unique views of the healthy personality and the good life. Since few personality theories focus explicitly on the normal personality, and even fewer attempt to advance any conceptual clarity of the healthy personality and the good life, the writer has had to rely on inferences from their theories.

Historically, the laboratories for the majority of personality theorists have been hospitals, clinics, or institutions where observations are limited primarily to human personalities in conflict—the anxious and the neurotic, the disturbed and the maladjusted, the diseased and the injured, the criminal and the deviant. For theorists who work exclusively with abnormal personalities, **normality** (behavior that is in accordance with social norms) too often becomes a desired goal. When this is the case, there are no theoretical endeavors to conceptualize ways of being that transcend the normal in actualization.

For Freud (Chapter 2), the healthy personality is an achievement of harmony among id, ego, and superego, an achievement largely due to ego's defensive sublimation of id's animalistic and demonic instincts, and the ability of the individual to love and work. Jung (Chapter 4) believes in an innate, continuous, archetypal will to health that develops gradually and becomes more pronounced during the second half of life. While he listed characteristics of the **individuated** person, he considered individuation an ideal level of health that was impossible to achieve fully. Adler (Chapter 3) equated healthy personality growth with the conscious development of the individual's innate predisposition for **Gemeinschaftsgefuhl** (translated as social interest or social feeling toward fellow human beings). In Adler's view the healthy personality, either directly or indirectly, contributes to the well-being of others and to society through work, love, and friendship. For Ellis (see Chapter 15), personality health is largely a matter of rational sensitivity. And while Ellis is more directly involved with therapy than with a state of ideal health, he too describes some of the characteristics of the rationally sensitive person. Fromm (see Chapter 6) refers to the healthy personality as the personality in the productive frame of orientation. Similar to Allport's mature personality (see Chapter 8) and Rogers's fully-functioning personality (see Chapter 9), Fromm's productive personality is the outcome of the fullest realization of all the individual's inherent intellectual, emotional, and sensory potentials. Bandura (see Chapter 16) equates the healthy personality with self-efficacy.

Unlike the theorists who were primarily concerned with therapy, Maslow (see Chapter 10) intentionally set out to view humans at their "full psychological height." His subjects for study were the healthiest of the healthy, that upper one half of one per cent of the general population that he labeled self-actualized. His descriptions of meta-motivated personalities are both vivid and explicit. Maslow, perhaps more than any single theorist selected for presentation in this volume, was interested in developing a psychology of possibility, and the possibility that fascinated him most was the possibility of the ideal level of psychological health.

What do we *know* about psychological health and psychopathology? What are the affective, cognitive, interpersonal variables that lead to psychologically healthy or psychopathological development in different ages? Are there regional, cohort, and ethnic historical differences in the definitions of psychological health and psychopathology? Are the discrepancies between industrial and preindustrial countries in incidence and prevalence of psychological health and psychopathology a reflection of national policies rather than true incidence? Are the intrinsic values of positive psychological health biologically rooted? Must a full definition of psychological health include intrinsic values? Do sweeping social, ethical, political, and economic changes on intrapsychic development render longitudinal studies impractical? Do early childhood experiences leave significant healthy or pathological marks on adults? Are there invariant sequential life stages common to all humans through which all must progress successfully to develop healthfully? Does holding to a view of development that has an intrinsic order cause us to miss much crucial data? Is the difference between psychological health and psychopathology simply a matter of degree? Do the characteristics of the healthy personality differ at various ages or life stages? In different cultures? Between the sexes? In various social classes? What is normal human behavior? Why, under seemingly similar circumstances, does one person function successfully and another find it impossible to cope? Is there the need to examine concepts of normal development through the life cycle and across cultures before we attempt to understand psychological health and psychopathology? How strong are genetic, hormonal, and psychophysiological factors in determining an individual's healthy or pathogenic responses to the environment? What are the consequences of viewing psychological health as typical? As normal or average? As ideal? What must be done to encourage more empirical studies of normality? Of psychological health and the good life? Of psychopathology? Is there an acceptable scientific approach to the study of the subjective experiences of psychological health? Of psychopathology?

Heuristic Influences

The ultimate value of every theory of personality is determined, at least partially, by its capacity to generate research. Whether by suggesting specific empirical hypotheses or even by arousing disbelief and resistance, a personality theory can stimulate attempts to confirm or reject its theoretical constructions in light of controlled, empirical investigations. Each theory chapter contains some discussion of the theorist's views of psychological research methods and techniques. Further examples of representative research studies are cited in the body of the issue resolutions.

In addition to its generative effect upon significant research, a personality theory should also prove capable of incorporating known empirical data within a logically consistent and reasonably parsimonious framework. In short, it should lead to the systematic expansion of knowledge on the human condition.

Applications to Psychotherapy

While it may be argued that the study of personality theories is justified by its own value, theories of personality must demonstrate practical application if they are to be understood fully and used effectively by practitioners in the field. Indeed, there has been a link between personality theory and practitioners in the mental health fields throughout the history of psychology. Most practitioners who express interest in personality theories are concerned with behavior and personality change. More specifically, they are concerned with changing disturbed behavior and with restructuring maladjusted personalities. These individuals want a theory of personality they can apply in both the assessment and the treatment of their clients and patients. They want to know what practical suggestions a theory offers for human growth and development, for psychological health and the good life, and for psychopathology.

Each theory chapter discusses the application of the theory presented to psychotherapy, for it is only natural that practitioners should focus on the theoretical formulations that can be applied to the assessment and treatment of the emotional disturbances that are stifling, disabling, and even endangering their clients' lives. Resolutions of the eleven basic issues have implications for the therapeutic relationship, the goals of therapy, the methods and techniques of therapy, and therapy assessment.

Extended Applications

As personality theorists gain greater confidence in the validity of their theories, their interests often move beyond their original purpose to a much wider social context. Many of the theorists whose works are presented in this book tested the limits of their theories' applicability. Extended applications can be traced to such areas as: education, at all levels; the military; criminal justice and prison reform; business relations; industrial management; interracial and interactional struggles on community, regional, national, and even world levels. Both theorists and followers of personality theories have applied certain theories to the arts and literature, particularly to biographies, novels, and drama. Although primary emphasis on a theory's applicability is given to the theory's application to psychotherapy, extended applications of each theory are also discussed at the end of each theory chapter.

Critique

At the completion of each theory chapter, readers are provided a critique of the theory's major strengths and weaknesses. Every theory of personality has its advocates and its adversaries. There are no exceptions. The advocates praise the theory's strongest features, and the adversaries point to the theory's most prominent weaknesses. Any presentation of a theory that does not recognize and discuss the more salient arguments of both advocates and adversaries would be incomplete. The problem, of course, is to eliminate as much of the bias as possible. The basic issues approach does just that.

Annotated Bibliography

One purpose of this book is to prepare students for advanced study in the field. Full understanding of personality theories can only be achieved by reading the theorists' own works. It is only in primary sources that students can appreciate the theorists' expression of ideas, the logic they employ, and the nuances of their language. An annotated bibliography is included at the end of each theory chapter. Students who wish to continue their study will find here the author's recommendations of specific primary and secondary sources that, after completing the chapter, they should be prepared to read with greater facility and appreciation.

Glossary

The language of personality theory is often more literary than explicit, more persuasive than empirical, more abstract than concrete, and more descriptive than predictive. Indeed, some personality theorists, particularly those from a clinical tradition, have a tendency to create new terms or, even more confusing, to modify or redefine the meaning of existing terms to describe their theoretical concepts. Not only are these practices confusing to students, they make empirical verification of the theoretical constructs they describe extremely difficult. While vivid descriptions may stimulate interest and enthusiasm, lack of explicit and operational terminology precludes consistency of derivations. That is, students attempting to understand a theory will often arrive at different, even conflicting derivations of the same term.

To aid in student understanding of the theorists' idiosyncratic use of language, technical or special terms are printed in boldface type and defined at the initial point of appearance. Further, a comprehensive glossary is provided at the end of the book for the students' convenience. Definitions of terms that are theory specific or that are assigned different meanings by different theorists are identified by the theorist.

References and Suggested Readings

Allport, G. W. (1955). *Becoming.* New Haven: Yale University Press.

Allport, G. W. (1960). *Personality and social encounter: Selected essays.* Boston: Beacon Press.

Allport, G. W. (1968). *The person in psychology: Selected essays.* Boston: Beacon Press.

Beck, A. T. (1976). *Cognitive therapy and emotional disorders.* New York: International Universities Press.

Berlin, I. (March 17, 1988). On pursuit of the ideal. *The New York Review of Books, XXXV*(4), 11–18.

Chiang, H., & Maslow, A. H. (Eds.). (1960). *The healthy personality* (2nd ed.). New York: D. Van Nostrand.

Eccles, J., & Robinson, D. N. (1984). *The wonder of being human: Our brain and our mind.* New York: The Free Press.

Ellenberger, H. F. (1970). *The discovery of the unconscious.* New York: Basic Books.

Ford, D. H., & Urban, H. R. (1963). *Systems of psychotherapy: A comparative study.* New York: John Wiley & Sons.

Hall, C. S., & Lindzey, G. (1978). *Theories of personality* (3rd ed.). New York: John Wiley & Sons.

Hall, C. S., Lindzey, G., & Contributors. (1985). *Introduction to theories of personality.* New York: John Wiley & Sons.

Horney, K. (1937). *The neurotic personality of our time.* New York: W. W. Norton.

Jourard, S., & Landsman, T. (1980). *Healthy personality* (4th ed.). New York: Macmillan.

Lewin, K. (1935). *A dynamic theory of personality.* New York: McGraw–Hill.

Mannheim, E. (1949). *Ideology and utopia: An introduction to the sociology of knowledge.* London: Routledge & Kegan Paul.

Maslow, A. H. (1968). *Toward a psychology of being* (2nd ed.). New York: Van Nostrand Reinhold.

Matson, F. W. (1976). *The idea of man.* New York: Holt, Rinehart and Winston.

Monte, C. E. (1987). *Beneath the mask: An introduction to theories of personality* (3rd ed.). New York: Holt, Rinehart and Winston.

Roe, A. (1953). A psychological study of eminent psychologists and anthropologists, and a comparison with biological and physical scientists. Psychological Monographs, 67(2).

Rotter, J. B. (1976). Personality theory. In H. Helsen & W. Bevan. (Eds.). *Contemporary approaches to psychology.* New York: Van Nostrand.

Rychlak, J. F. (1981). *Introduction to personality and psychotherapy: A theory construction approach* (2nd ed.). Boston: Houghton Mifflin.

Ryckman, R. M. (1985). *Theories of personality* (3rd ed.). Monterey, CA: Brooks/Cole.

Schultz, D. (1977). *Growth psychology, models of the healthy personality.* New York: D. Van Nostrand.

Sheldon, W. H. (1944). Constitutional factors in personality. In J. McV. Hunt. (Ed.). *Personality and the behavior disorders.* New York: Ronald Press, 526–549.

Shostrom, E. L., with Knapp, L., & Knapp, R. (1976). *Actualizing therapy, foundations for a scientific ethic.* San Diego: Edits.

Skinner, B. F. (1976). *Particulars of my life.* New York: McGraw–Hill.

Skinner, B. F. (1979). *The shaping of a behaviorist.* New York: Alfred A. Knopf.

Skinner, B. F. (1983). *A matter of consequences.* New York: Alfred A. Knopf.

Sullivan, H. S. (1947). *Conceptions of modern psychiatry.* Washington, D.C.: William Alanson White Psychiatric Foundation.

Wertheimer, M. (1972). *Fundamental issues in psychology.* New York: Holt, Rinehart & Winston.

Pioneers of Personality Theory

The theories of Sigmund Freud, Alfred Adler, and Carl Jung, whose conceptions of human nature pioneered the field of personality theories, are presented in chapters 2, 3, and 4. Although Adler and Jung were charter members of Freud's Wednesday Night Discussion Group, and played significant leadership roles in the organization of the Vienna Psycho-Analytic Society, they were later criticized as revisionists and asked to resign their memberships when it became evident that their ideas on the importance of libido and human sexuality were antithetical to Freud's. Both Adler and Jung went on to formulate their own theories of personality.

Contrary to the opinion of his day, Freud presented a causal view of human personality. Instinctual drives of an unconscious and demonic id impel object choice and demand immediate gratification. The single goal of the id is relief of tension. Freud's ego exists only to serve id, placate superego, and protect the personality from destroying itself. Survival depends solely on ego's ability to gratify id's needs and bind surplus energy for secondary processes—thinking, reasoning, planning, and adapting to the outer world of reality.

Freud made us aware that a vast amount of our behavior is determined by unconscious forces, the impact of critical psychosexual stages during the first five years of life on the development of the adult personality, and the amount of psychic energy we spend on unconscious defensive postures and maneuvers.

Attempts of other theorists to expand, revise, or reject Freud's theoretical concepts have led to the development of new theories of personality. While many disagree with parts or all of Freud's psychoanalytic theory, few ignore it. Each of the neoanalytic theorists, for example, attempts either to justify his or her differences or to demonstrate that his or her theoretical constructs are merely modifications or elaborations of constructs in Freud's theory.

Adler's mature theory differed radically from Freud's. We are viewed by Adler as social beings, motivated to strive for completion and perfection. Born dependent on family groups for survival, we naturally develop feelings of inferiority and a need to belong. These needs facilitate an early formulation of a life plan and, by the age of five, a life style. We may be influenced by our ordinal position in the family constellation, and the quality of our relationship with our mothers during the formative years is particularly crucial to the development of our social interest: for Adler, the major criterion for mental health.

Adler was convinced that all behavior is purposive. Instincts, lost in the evolutionary process, have become mere biological tendencies or predispositions. Hopes, plans, and aspirations are motivating factors in our striving for completion. We are future oriented, as well as influenced by our past experiences.

Though not always credited (see Chapter 3), Adler's theoretical concepts continue to echo in the theories of many current personologists, including the organismic and existential theorists whose works are presented in this volume.

Like Freud, Jung also emphasized unconscious forces; however, his perceptions of the personal unconscious (and its complexes) and the collective unconscious (and its archetypes) differ significantly from the unconscious presented by Freud. We are, according to Jung, motivated by the interactions and diverse polar tendencies of our psyches' subsystems, a process that he labels individuation. For Jung, the self, an inherent propensity at birth, is both an archetype and an accumulation of our development. As an archetype, the self represents the ultimate goal of life.

Viewing human personality through the works of these three pioneers can be both exciting and disconcerting. It is, however, well worth the effort. Perhaps more than any of the other theories presented in this book, the theories of these three pioneers have proved especially influential and provocative over the years. They have provided the foundation for the study of theories to come—both those presented later in this text and those that will be formulated in the years ahead.

C h a p t e r 2

Freud's Psychoanalytic Theory

Chapter Overview

Introduction

Biographical Sketch of the Theorist

Freud's Resolutions of the Eleven Basic Issues
    Heredity versus Social Determinants
    Early versus Continuous Development
    Subjective versus Objective Reality
    Number and Weight Assigned to Motivational Concepts
    Explanation of the Learning Process
    Determinism versus Freedom of Choice
    Conscious versus Unconscious Determinants
    Role Assigned to the Self-Concept
    Centrality of Reinforcement
    Uniqueness versus Universality
    Importance of Group Determinants

Psychological Health and Psychopathology

Heuristic Influences: Research Methods and Techniques

Applications to Psychotherapy
    Therapeutic Goals
    Therapeutic Relationship
    Initial Procedures and Strategies

Course of Psychoanalysis
    Free Association
    Interpretation
    Dream Analysis
    Analysis of Resistances
    Analysis of Transference

Extended Applications

Critique

Annotated Bibliography

References and Suggested Readings

Introduction

Sigmund Freud (1856–1939), the founder of the first formal, comprehensive theory of personality and approach to psychotherapy, has had a tremendous and controversial impact on Western civilization's view of what it means to be human. The influence of his theory and the controversy it provokes remain with us today, more than a half century following Freud's death. Addressing Freud's impact on the Western world, Peter Gay (1988) writes:

> *Copernicus had shown that the earth, and hence man, is not the center of the universe; Darwin had linked man to the animal kingdom; and now he, Freud, had demonstrated that reason is not the master of its own house (p. xvii).*

Freud's view of humanity is certainly not the flattering picture painted by the romanticists or the humanists who believe in will, reason, and purpose. Indeed, Freud's picture of human nature and destiny is insistently biological and, hence, rather stark and dismal.

According to Freud, humans are not guided by their reason or intellect; rather, they are driven by innate, primitive, instinctual forces of which they are unaware, which they do not understand, and over which they have little control. Further, Freud claims, self-deceit is a universal characteristic of humans—they continually deceive themselves by distorting or repressing unpleasant or painful truths. Even their learning and loving are little more than **sublimations** (unconscious gratification of feared instinctual urges). Their religion may be their greatest illusion. Their sense of freedom is a myth, for every human thought, feeling, and act is determined and can be traced back to some earlier cause. Perhaps most controversial in his final theory, Freud (1961a, 1961c) proposed that the human tendency to aggression is an innate, independent, instinctual disposition, making life a continual struggle between **Eros** (the instincts of life) and **Thanatos** (the instincts of aggression, destruction, and death).

As the first modern personality theorist, Freud not only filled a void in human understanding, he also supplied the theoretical foundation upon which later theorists could build. Freud became the pacesetter for all future theorists, particularly for those who were critical of his ideas. Indeed, many personality theorists and theorists of counseling and psychotherapy owe Freud a great debt, for they developed their theoretical formulations as they tried to prove Freud wrong. Fritz Perls (1969), the founder of Gestalt Therapy, is a prime example of this. Perls spent most of his professional life arguing with Freud, and three decades after a devastating experience at the 1935 International Psychoanalytic Congress and the humiliating meeting with Freud that followed, Perls (1972) records in his autobiography that he still considered his meeting with Freud as one of the unfinished situations of his life. Perls's lifelong love–hate relationship with Freud became the prime motivating force for much of his theoretical effort.

Regardless of the controversy he created, or perhaps because of it, the impact of Freud's extensive and inclusive theory quickly moved beyond psychology and psychiatry. His theoretical constructs crossed the boundaries of numerous other disciplines, including philosophy, biology, anthropology, sociology, social work, political science, biography, literary criticism, and the arts (painting, poetry, theater, and literature).

Many people throughout Europe and the Americas recognize Freud's name. Some are acquainted with one or more of his books and have read others' works about him. Few, however, possess a thorough understanding of his theory. While there is no escaping Freudian thought, Freud's Theory of Psychoanalysis, along with the goals and methods of his approach to psychotherapy, are poorly understood and cast in half truths by the general public and, unfortunately, by more than a few professionals in the field (Gay, 1988).

Every theorist presented in this book made specific references to Freud's theoretical concepts. Indeed, many began their careers as **psychoanalysts** (those who sought the roots of human behavior in unconscious motivation and conflict—Jung [Chapter 4], Adler [Chapter 3], Fromm [Chapter 6], May [Chapter 11], Ellis [Chapter 15], for example). Motivation for some (particularly Adler, Jung, May, Allport [Chapter 8], Ellis, and to a lesser degree, Rogers [Chapter 9] and Maslow [Chapter 10]) seemed to emerge from their direct opposition to the orthodox psychoanalytic stance on human behavior and Freud's approach to psychotherapy. The theories of others (Erikson [Chapter 5] and Fromm, for example) evolved largely from attempts to modify, expand, or integrate Freud's therapeutic concepts and techniques. Although Freud's impact varies considerably among the theorists whose ideas are presented in this volume, it can be neither ignored nor denied. Freud's work served as a direct or indirect catalyst for the development of many of the current theories of personality and psychotherapy, whether the theorists were building onto his foundation or trying to tear it down.

Biographical Sketch of the Theorist

When studying the life of a theorist, personologists are often tempted to search for specific life experiences or psychological traumas that might explain a particularly original theoretical assumption or construct. Yet even as they search, they realize that while such links or connections might be uncovered (at least in hindsight), seldom are they ever simple and direct.

The life and achievements of few individuals have been investigated more thoroughly, or for that matter more critically, by so many. While Ernest Jones's (1953–1957) three-volume biography is accepted as the major presentation of Freud's history and theory development, numerous authors over the years have attempted to discredit or at least question both the objectivity and the value of Jones's work. Sulloway (1983), Masson (1984), Gay (1988), and Holt (1989) are only four of the more recent authors of such investigative efforts. While the research quality of some of these works is high, legends, once given birth, have a remarkable resilience, as well as the capacity for distorting objective appraisal.

Early Years

Sigmund Freud was born on May 6, 1856, in the village of Freiburg, a province of Moravia, Austria (now part of Czechoslovakia). Freud was the eldest son of his father's second marriage. His mother, Amalia (Nethansohn) Freud, was twenty-one years old at Freud's birth, half her husband's age. During the next ten years Jacob Freud's family grew. In addition to the two sons from his first marriage, who were by this time married with children of their own, Sigmund was followed by five daughters—Anna, Rosa, Marie, Adolfine, and Paula—and two other sons—Julius, who died at eight months, and Alexander. Since Alexander was ten years Freud's junior, Freud's nephew, only a year older, was Freud's closest boyhood companion and major rival.

In 1859, when Freud was four years old, his father, an independent merchant dealing principally in wool, moved the family to Vienna where he thought business opportunities might improve. Initial movement toward industrialization and mass production made competition for small business owners difficult. Vienna was to remain Freud's home for nearly eighty years.

Education

Adored and protected by his mother, who was convinced her precocious firstborn was destined for greatness, Freud held a privileged position in the family. Their apartment was overcrowded, but Freud alone had a room of his own. Moreover, while all other rooms had to be lighted by candles, Freud's room, a combination bedroom and study, was lighted by an oil lamp. When Freud complained that his sister's piano practice interfered with his study, her lessons were stopped and the piano removed.

Encouraged by an indulgent mother and his dreams of becoming a famous Austrian general or minister of state, Freud became a serious young student. Gifted in language, he mastered Hebrew, Latin, Greek, French, and English and taught himself Italian and Spanish. He was especially interested in English and enjoyed reading Shakespeare at the age of eight. At nine years of age, he passed the entrance examination to the Speri Gymnasium where he stood at the head of his class the last six of his eight years at the school. At seventeen, Freud was graduated summa cum laude.

Professional career choices for an impoverished young Jew in Vienna were limited to industry, business law, or medicine, none of which Freud found especially appealing. Attracted to natural science, particularly after reading the theories posited by Darwin, Freud decided to become a medical student shortly before finishing his final year of high school.

Freud entered the University of Vienna to study medicine in 1873. With Ernst Brucke, the famous physiologist and a leader of the Helmholtz School of Medicine, as his model of the disciplined scientist, Freud became involved in research and, in 1876, he was accepted to work under Brucke's supervision in the Institution of Physiology. It was here that Freud, immersed in the study of the histology of nerve cells, was introduced to the standard of scientific method and intellectual honesty that were to be with him for life. It was here, too, that he became acquainted with Joseph Breuer, a Viennese physician who, though forty years Freud's senior, became a close friend and colleague and assisted Freud financially in later years with substantial loans.

Freud's medical education was interrupted when he was called in 1879 for a year's military service in the Austrian Army. He passed his final medical examination in March, 1881. Brucke, who was aware of Freud's poor financial position and knew of his limited prospects for promotion within the institute, urged Freud to leave research and begin private practice as a physician.

Freud resigned his position at Brucke's institute in 1882 to begin his residency at General Hospital. After two months in the department of surgery, Freud applied for and gained the position of aspirant in internal medicine. In 1883, Freud transferred to the Psychiatric Clinic, where he began a specialty in neurology the following year and for five months undertook a course of psychiatric studies.

In 1885, Freud was appointed lecturer in neuropathology. Also that year, Freud visited Jean Charcot (famous French neurologist and hypnotist). Freud was so impressed to see Charcot induce and cure hysterical paralysis by means of direct hypnotic suggestion that he volunteered his services as a German translator for Charcot's lectures. He published *Lessons,* a three-volume set, the following year. In 1886, Freud accepted the post of director for a new neurological department at the Institution for Children's Diseases. In addition to his clinical duties, Freud opened his private practice and gave his first paid consultations. He married Martha Bernays that year, after a four-year engagement. Their marriage, often described as ideal, lasted fifty-three years and produced six children: Mathilde, Jean Martin, Oliver, Ernst, Sophie, and Anna.

Emergence of Psychoanalysis

Finding prevalent methods of psychiatric treatment ineffective, Freud turned to hypnosis, not only to trace the origin of a symptom but also, through hypnotic suggestion, to arrest the symptom. However, while he sometimes appeared miraculously to cure cases of hysteria and some forms of neurosis, he discovered that changes produced through hypnosis seemed to depend on the relationship between the doctor and the patient. The benefits of therapy were often lost on termination of that relationship; that is, the patient apparently overcame his or her symptoms to please the doctor. This phenomenon, and the inability to hypnotize some recalcitrant patients as deeply as he thought necessary to effect a cure, motivated Freud to search for other more effective and lasting therapeutic methods.

In 1889, Freud returned to Breuer's cathartic method. The cathartic method required hypnosis, but Freud discovered that all forms of suggestion, whether by hypnosis, touching the patient's forehead, or asking questions, interrupted or covered client transference and **resistance** (clients' attempts to sabotage the purpose of therapy). He therefore reduced his use of hypnosis and developed the so-called concentration technique. While reclining on a couch with eyes closed, the client is asked to concentrate on the symptom and, without censoring, recall all memories of the symptom. At the sign of initial resistance, Freud urged, pressed his hand on the client's forehead, and questioned, all methods used to assure the client that the memories were there and could be recalled.

When some of his clients complained that his interventions interfered with their efforts to recall early or painful memories, Freud gradually withdrew to the background. **Free association** (reporting whatever comes to mind) as a therapeutic method had evolved. Though his procedure lengthened the therapeutic process considerably, his patients eventually became able to recall the early childhood events responsible for their traumatic hysterias.

From this point, Freud moved rather rapidly toward his theory of psychoanalysis—far too rapidly for his friend Breuer, his colleagues in the medical community, and the lay public, all of whom reacted with incredulity when he presented his ideas. Through his clients' free associations and the wealth of symbolism in their dreams, Freud ascertained the significance of the unconscious and began to map its structure and **topography** (an early conceptual model later replaced with a structural model). More important, he assigned early sexuality and aggressive impulses new and greater importance in the etiology of later emotional disturbances. Thus he intuitively constructed the foundation upon which his theory of psychoanalysis would rest. Since Freud needed data to confirm his ideas, in 1897 he decided to undertake in-depth self-analysis to obtain answers to many of his questions.

Freud's engrossing self-analysis, accompanied at times by serious neurotic disturbances, continued for nearly four years, but he emerged from it a different person (Ellenberger, 1970; Jones, 1955). The turmoil of his life had largely subsided, personal relationships were less intense and upsetting, and his life was more ordered and harmonious. As a result, his thinking seemed clearer and his judgments more critical. He gained greater confidence, in both himself and his discoveries, and he channeled his energy into development, application, and advancement of his ideas. In reference to this period of Freud's life, Ellenberger (1970) presents a convincing argument for **creative illness** ("a polymorphous condition that can take the shape of depression, neurosis, psychosomatic ailments, or even psychosis" [p. 447]). Ellenberger (1970) describes a creative illness as one that "succeeds a period of intense preoccupation with an idea and a search for a certain truth," the termination of which may be spontaneous, rapid, and marked by a permanent transformation in personality along with the conviction of the discovery of a great truth and a feeling of elation (p. 447). Whether neurosis or creative illness, this period of Freud's life was followed by one of high productivity and increasing recognition. He was appointed to the prestigious position of extraordinary professor.

In 1902, the Wednesday Psychological Society (often referred to informally as the Wednesday night discussion group) was formed by a small group of interested friends who met weekly at Freud's home to discuss problems of psychoanalysis. By 1908, this group became the Viennese Psychoanalytic Society. In 1907, after returning to Zurich from a visit with Freud, C. G. Jung (see Chapter 4) and Ludwig Binswagner (an existential analyst) founded a similar group. The first International Congress of Psychoanalysis met in Salzburg in 1908. Freud's psychoanalytic movement had acquired an international character in only a few years.

In 1909, Freud, with Jung and Ferenczi (an analyst in Budapest), was invited to the United States to present lectures on psychoanalysis at Clark University, Worcester, Massachusetts. This event, for Freud, marked the beginning of world recognition and support. During the Second International Congress in Nuremberg, the International Psychoanalytic Association was created and, along with it, a second professional journal. Although tainted by a shaky beginning (for example, Freud's break with Adler in 1908, with Stekel [one of the original members of Freud's discussion group] in 1912, with Jung in 1913, and the interruption of two world wars), the International Psychoanalytic Association continues to serve as the parent organization for psychoanalytic societies and institutes all over the world, as well as the organization behind the World Congress, which meets every two years.

Accomplishments and Awards

Freud's accomplishments and awards are too extensive to be fully documented in this brief biographical sketch. He was, as indicated, the author of the first comprehensive theory of personality development. This achievement alone assures him a place in history. However, in addition to his original and dynamic theoretical constructs, Freud developed a new approach to psychotherapy, a new method of dealing with the unconscious, and a new science. Further, Freud was the founder and prime mover of the worldwide psychoanalytic association with its own publishing house. More than creating a psychotherapeutic theory, method, and organization, Freud created a world movement and lived to see his name become synonymous with it.

Freud's Resolutions of the Eleven Basic Issues

Most presentations of Freud's theory are historical, covering more than four decades of his work. While this approach may be necessary for a full understanding of theoretical development, such a presentation risks the introduction of confusion for the beginning student. By including all early conceptions, many of which Freud later discarded, modified, or supplemented, clearly specified hypotheses are not evident. Further, such a presentation lacks integration or synthesis.

Resolutions of the eleven basic issues are largely based on, though not limited to, Freud's third and final theory, often referred to as the *tripartite model* or the *structural conception* to distinguish it from the earlier topographic formulations. Freud first presented this model in *The Ego and the Id* (1962) and elaborated more fully on it a decade later in the "New Introductions Lectures" (Freud, 1962).

It should be noted here that Freud did not directly address all eleven basic issues (Explanation of Learning Process, for example). Implications for his resolutions to certain issues do appear in other theoretical constructs of his theory, however, and are brought to the attention of the reader by the writer.

Heredity versus Social Determinants

While Freud does not deny the influence of social determinants, he relegates the external world of reality to a secondary role in personality development. Human nature, according to Freud, is *essentially* biological. As with all living creatures, we are viewed as closed, complicated, and dynamic energy systems. Our energy, derived from the food we eat, takes mechanical, thermal, electrical, and chemical forms. Moreover, this energy, when necessary, swiftly converts from one form to another to serve better our various physical and psychic processes, functions, mechanisms, and dynamism. **Physical energy** (the force that powers all psychic activity) may be used for bodily processes, such as circulation, respiration, digestion, and motor activities. **Psychic energy** may be used for mental functions, such as perceiving, thinking, emoting, and remembering.

Psychic energy originates in the **id** (the innate component of our personality) from excitations or tension caused by some tissue or organ of our body that is experiencing a deficit. These excitations create mental representations or wishes. Freud refers to a collection of wishes as **instincts,** the aim of which is to reduce tension. Hence, all instincts have a **source** (the state of excitation within the body), an **aim** (the removal of that excitation), and an **object** (that which can be found in either the body or the environment to satisfy the aim).

Freud (1960, 1962) identified two essential instincts, **Eros** and **Thanatos** (Freud's life and death instincts). Positive and constructive aspects of behavior, such as hunger, sexual desire, and thirst, as well as creative aspects of culture, including art, music, literature, cooperation, and love, represent the life instincts. He refers to the energy behind the life instincts as the **libido.** Thanatos, or the death instinct, is responsible for the negative, aggressive aspects of our nature and accounts for all destructive behavior, violence and cruelty, murder and suicide. The death instinct, the energy of which is not named, is defined simply as the unconscious desire to return to an inanimate or tensionless state that is the ultimate aim of all instincts. Although in conflict, all normal mental activity involves both life and death instincts.

Structure of Personality   The structural formulations of Freud's (1960b) mature theory—**id** (the unorganized part of the psyche that contains everything inherited or repressed), **ego** (the modified part of the id that has been influenced by the external world), and **superego** (the third part of the psyche that evolves from ego and reflects society's rules, norms, values, ethics, and attitudes)—are not representations of empirical data. Rather, they are presented by Freud merely as a theoretical *model* of the personality structure. The function of the model is to assist with the organization of the many empirical findings into a coherent, integrated conceptual system of processes, functions, mechanisms, and dynamism within the total personality.

The Id.   Freud (1960b) named the original system of the structure of human personality the id, the Latin word for "it." The id is the product of human

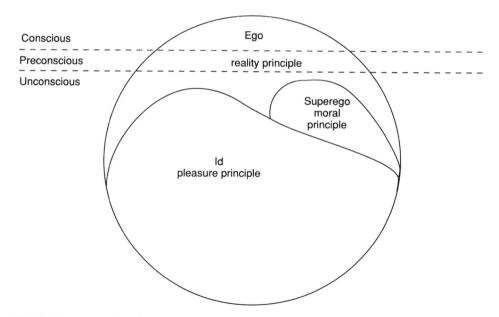

FIGURE 2-1   Tripartite Model of Personality Development

evolution and the psychological representative of biological endowment, including all bodily needs. As such, id is the deepest and most inaccessible unconscious dimension of personality. All the primitive, impulsive, unorganized instincts once shared with the lower animals are present in the id. Further, id serves as a communication link between somatic and mental processes, translating the body's sexual and aggressive needs into mental expression.

Id is a true psychic reality. It is closed to any contact with an **objective reality** (the external world). It does not change with the passage of time (there is no time dimension in the id). And because the id is a closed system, it cannot be modified with either experience or learning. Devoid of any values, morals, ethics, logic, or reason, the id knows no fear and takes no precautions to ensure its own survival.

The energy stored in the id is free, unfettered, and uncontrolled, and the id operates on the homeostasis Nirvana principle and the hedonistic **Pleasure Principle** (to achieve pleasure by gratifying instinctual urges and avoiding pain). The id seeks only the immediate and unconditioned discharge (Pleasure) of the intolerable sensory excitations (Pain) created by instinctual urges. Id has only **reflex action** (blinking, sneezing, coughing, gagging) and **primary process** (wish fulfillment—fantasies, dreams, and hallucinations) at its command to reduce the intolerable tensions produced by instinctual urges or drives. When reflex action and primary process are ineffective in gratifying id's needs, id must yield its psychic energy to the influence of the ego.

The Ego. With the infant's realization that there is a separate world of external reality, **ego** (literally the "I") begins to evolve from the id. Because the ego is formed from the id, both its structure and its function are acquired from this original psychic system. Ego is essentially an acquired representative of reality, but its relationship with the id remains both intimate and complex. Ego evolves either to serve or control id, to test reality, and to seek within both the body and the external world those instinctual **object choices** (whether people or things) that will satisfy, postpone, or repress id's needs. Of the three systems of personality, only ego has contact with extra-organic reality and the capacity to reduce the instinctual excitations and their resultant tension so intolerable to the id.

Ego operates on a **Reality Principle** (finding a safe and socially acceptable object choice for an instinctual urge) and concern for the safety and survival of the organism, a concern ignored by both id and superego. With its **secondary process** (the cognitive capacities to perceive, think, use language, reason, memorize, imagine, decide, and learn), ego is able to distinguish between what is only in the mind and what actually exists in the world. Ego differentiates between the "I" and the "not I," between fact and fantasy. Although the secondary process of the ego is identical to the activities of consciousness and the ego seeks to bring the influence of reality to bear on the irrational id, ego is not entirely conscious. **Censorship** (dream distortion) and **repression** (unconsciously relegating threatening material to the unconscious) are also ego functions; hence, some parts of ego are preconscious and some are unconscious.

Operating on a higher dynamic level than either the id or the superego, ego is able to tolerate moderate amounts of tension and check panic reactions. Considering the consequences of its actions, the ego represses, suppresses, redirects, or discharges gradually the psychic energy of the id within the restrictive bounds set by society and the conscience of the superego. To capture and bind the psychic energy it needs to operate effectively, while at the same time avoiding the pain of guilt, ego must, on a conscious level, meet some of the id's demands and the superego's restrictions. Ego is more than simply a buffer between the blind instincts of id and reality; it is also a mediator of psychic energy and societal dictate.

Ego Defense Mechanisms   In one sense, *all* the mental activity of ego is defensive. By the very nature of the personality system, ego must constantly defend itself from the conflict (and the anxiety that accompanies it) that emanates from three fronts: the extra-organic world of reality, the irrational dictates of superego, and the impulsive, often dangerous, demands of id. All techniques employed by ego to master, control, and discharge the anxiety-arousing forces that may lead to neurosis usually fall under the general designation of **defense mechanisms.**

In quite another sense, Rycroft (1968) points out:

> *Since psychoanalysis holds that anxiety is a spur to DEVELOPMENT, some, perhaps all, of the defenses play a part in normal development and it is assumed that certain defenses belong to specific stages of development, e.g. introjection, projection, denial, and splitting to the ORAL phase; reaction-formation, isolation, and undoing to the ANAL phase (p. 28, emphasis in original).*

With the exception of sublimation, which Freud reserved for normal development, all defense mechanisms of ego are expressions of inner conflict and an intolerable state of anxiety.

Repression.   The most common and most important of the ego defense mechanisms is repression. Freud distinguishes between two kinds of repression, **primal repression** and **repression proper.**

As the name implies, primal repressions are inherited barriers (e.g., incest) that have evolved as a result of repeated painful experience over thousands of years of human evolution and that are responsible for holding certain contents of the id permanently unconscious. Repression proper is ego's barring from consciousness threatening and anxiety-producing impulses, memories, and ideas by pushing the threatening material into the unconscious and then acting as if it did not exist. As long as ego's anticathexis is stronger than a **cathexis of the id** (investment of psychic energy in a mental representation or image of an object or another person), repression is successful and the repressed material does not reach consciousness.

When ego employs repression as a defense mechanism, it pays a price. An **anticathexis** requires psychic energy to establish and maintain, draining ego of the energy it needs to deal with the external world of reality. Moreover, a repressed cathexis may emerge from the unconscious in a displaced or disguised form. It may, for example, emerge in the form of a physical symptom (e.g, a repressed sexual cathexis may emerge as impotence). It may seek symbolic fulfillment in dreams, parapraxes, or hallucinations. It may also appear in one of the other defense mechanisms.

Fixation. Libidinal fixation during the pregenital stages of development is discussed at length elsewhere in this chapter (see "Fixation and Character Typology"). However, fixation can occur any time stress and anxiety threaten ego. Ego's strategy is to remain in the present where it is coping successfully rather than to advance in life where it may be threatened. The college senior who is quite comfortable with his life as a student, but anxiety ridden at the prospect of leaving the college campus and finding a job, may suddenly decide his chosen major is really a serious mistake. By changing his major field of study, which will require another year on campus to complete, he discharges the threat to ego and the anxiety disappears. All this, of course, occurs on an unconscious level. The college senior is genuinely convinced of his error and of the wisdom behind the decision to correct it.

Denial. Denial, as a defense mechanism, involves either a painful experience or some impulse or aspect of the self. All painful experiences must overcome the pleasure principle and wishful thinking. Denying some aspect of the self usually involves the denial of the inner significance of experience (e.g., the manic's denial of reality, brought about by the denial of depressive feelings, or the diabetic's denial of the danger of the disease and consequent ignoring proper diet and insulin injections).

Displacement. Displacement permits ego to find a less threatening way to discharge or satisfy a threatening cathexis that is creating painful feelings of anxiety. A person embarrassed or angered by a supervisor's remarks and afraid to respond in kind for fear of being fired may direct his or her anger onto others who are less threatening. For example, the person serving his or her table at lunch, the cashier at the grocery store, the children at the dinner table, or the newscaster on television may represent convenient targets. The class bully, disciplined by his teacher and afraid to strike back, may pick a fight with a younger and weaker classmate during recess. None of the substitute subjects at whom the displaced anger is directed is in position to cause as much harm as the supervisor or the teacher.

Displacement can also occur in dreams or fantasy. Anger at the authority figure can be repressed and later emerge in symbolic form in dreams; here, where reality is no longer a factor, the source of threat may magically be made to disappear or to suffer for the anxiety incurred by the dreamer.

Sublimation. Sublimation, considered by some a defense mechanism but by Freud a developmental process, is the discharge of instinctual energies (sex and aggression) in non-instinctual forms of behavior. The sublimation process involves the substitution of socially acceptable behavior for unacceptable behavior. Freud used sublimation processes to explain the evolution of higher cultural goals, as, for example, in art, literature, and music. Freud believed that sublimation is responsible for the highest achievements of humankind. All sublimations depend on symbolization. The writer may satisfy instinctual needs for aggression by killing off characters in his or her novel. The attorney may reduce oral tension in arguing a case; the surgeon may discharge aggression by operating on a patient; the scholar may express inquisitiveness by becoming competent in his or her discipline.

Projection. When ego is made to feel anxious by pressure from the id or superego, anxiety can be relieved by attributing its cause to another person or the world. Rather than feeling hate for another person, which would bring the punishment of guilt from superego, the anxious person may convince himself or herself that the other person hates him or her. In short, inner feelings or pressures from instinctual urges or drive are projected outwardly to another person or event. The purpose is to transform a neurotic (inner) anxiety to an objective (outer) anxiety which is not only more acceptable to ego, hence less anxiety arousing, but also makes it easier for ego to cope.

Regression. Threatened by a particular stage of development that creates anxiety, a person may revert to an earlier and less threatening stage of development. This defense is called regression. The seriousness of this defense to ego development is wide-ranging. It may be as simple as an adult running home to mother after an argument with a spouse or a child reverting to baby talk, or as dangerous as withdrawing from reality by living in a private world of fantasies and dreams, alcohol, or drugs. Any unconscious flight from controlled rational thinking constitutes regression.

Reaction Formation. In reaction formation the repressed cathexis emerges disguised as its opposite, for example, love–hate, action–passivity, dominance–submission, life–death. Reactive behavior is exaggerated and showy and, while unconscious to the ego employing it, it is manifestly visible to the outside observer.

A woman, highly successful in her career, faces an unwanted pregnancy that threatens to interfere with her career plans. When the child is born, she suffers from anxiety because she experiences feelings of hatred toward the child. Ego, threatened by superego (to hate one's child is terrible), unconsciously masks the feelings of hatred with an anticathexis—strong feelings of love. All the mother's "loving" behaviors toward the child are exaggerated and affected; indeed, she smothers the child with her love. She never lets the child out of her sight. She does not permit the child to play with other children. She insists that the child remain spotlessly clean. She is constantly (compulsively) touching, holding, and stroking the child. In short, her "loving" behavior is inflexible, and she is interfering with the normal development of the child.

A man with extremely strong sexual urges that result in feelings of anxiety may become a leader in the community to clean up pornography in the theaters, video tape outlets, newsstands, bookstores, and record stores. Now, for the sake of protecting youth in the community from pornography, he can view films and video tapes, read the magazines and books, listen to the records, tapes, and disks to decide which should be labeled pornographic and either not shown or taken from the shelves. He is, of course, discharging a cathected instinctual impulse for a moral (anticathected) reason.

Rationalization.   A defense mechanism used after the fact to justify an act and at the same time conceal its true motivation is rationalization. "Because everybody cheats on examinations in that class, cheating is the only way to compete successfully." This rationalization not only justifies the act of cheating (everybody cheats), but also hides the fact that the person cheating fears he or she may not have the ability to compete successfully with the other class members. The person who has just been served divorce papers decides suddenly that his or her spouse is impossible to please and will never be able to live with anyone. On the third strike in an important game, the player who just struck out glares at the sun— there isnt anything wrong with his batting technique: "No one could see the ball with the sun in his eyes."

Undoing.   Undoing is the defense mechanism used to make some prior thought or action "unhappen"—a kind of negative magic that will undo not only the consequences of the thought or action, but also the thought or action itself (e.g., obsessional rituals). In a less neurotic form, an example of undoing would be the person with whom a friend has shared a very personal experience and swears him to secrecy. When confronted after telling the secret to another, he responds: "I didn't mean to tell your secret; it just slipped out." Undoing, in this instance, resolves the person from responsibility, and he need not own the behavior or suffer any loss of self-esteem. Not walking under ladders, or stepping on cracks in the sidewalk, or crossing the street to avoid crossing the path of a black cat are also lesser forms of undoing, *if* these actions are intended to cancel out another preceding action, thought, or feeling that created anxiety in ego.

Recent Research Studies of Defense Mechanisms   Kline (1972) and Tribich and Messer (1974) conclude that while there appears to be evidence supportive of the oral receptive and the anal retentive character types (see "Fixation and Character Typology," this chapter), the phallic character type is not supported. Here again, however, there are formidable problems in interpreting the findings of the character type studies (Liebert & Spiegler, 1987), for Freud's hypotheses can be stretched to cover conflicting outcomes. For example, if a study of oral character types shows dependency, the hypothesis is supported. However, the hypothesis is also supported if the study of oral character types shows independence, for "independence can be a defense—reaction formation—against independence"

BOX 2-1   Recent Instruments to Measure/Test Freud's Defense Constructs

There have been a number of studies in recent years devised to measure and/or test Freud's defense constructs. Two examples are the studies of Blancha (1981) and Marshall (1983).

Blancha (1981) devised *The Inventory of Defense* (ID), a self-report inventory to measure individual differences in preferences for twelve psychoanalytic defense mechanisms. The ID consists of ten short stories describing situations in which sexual, aggressive, or self-esteem conflicts are aroused. Each story is followed by twelve responses representing the twelve defense mechanisms of avoidance, denial, displacement, isolation, negation, projection, rationalism, reaction formation, regression, intellectualization, turning against self, and repression. These responses are rated by the subjects in terms of how characteristic each would be of them if they found themselves in the situation described. The ID's content validity and test–retest reliability were relatively good. Blancha (1981) concludes that, while there are some methodological problems that warrant consideration, early findings with the ID are encouraging.

Marshall (1983) devised the *Marshall Personality Measure* (MPM), an objective test of defense mechanisms. The MPM was evaluated in light of psychometric analysis, clinical validity findings, and relationships to theoretical model based on the psychoanalytic concept of ego differentiation and Welsh's empirically established Origence/Intelligence personality types. The clinical validity study involved the comparison between patients' scores on the MPM and the therapists' ratings of these mechanisms. The Undoing scale showed an inverse relationship to its rating. Marshall (1983) concludes that these results should be viewed in light of methodological problems inherent in the rating procedure and an unavoidably biased clinical sample. Intercorrelation and a complex pattern of relationship among defense mechanisms were found both on the test and between test and clinical ratings. While defenses appear to fall as predicted into two general categories of "primary" and "secondary processes," the delimitation of secondary defensive variables is unclear.

(Liebert & Spiegler, 1987, p. 147). In short, hypotheses that explain and predict contrasting and conflicting behaviors are impossible either to prove or disprove.

Seegert (1984) reports on a study designed to discern the effects of stress management treatment (SMT) in an academic military setting. Fifty-two students in the Russian department at the Defense Language Institute were divided into three groups: a wait-list control group, a relaxation group, and a cognitive restructuring group. Treatment groups attended six weekly sessions of SMT. Relaxation subjects were taught techniques for inducing physical and psychological relaxation. Subjects in the cognitive restructuring group were taught to identify dysfunctional thinking patterns and to replace them with rational thoughts that facilitate calm and coping. The subjects' grades showed significant correlation with language aptitude scores, but not with the intelligence measures. However, most of the variance in grades was accounted for by Turning Against Self, the defense mechanism that involves self-directed aggression. The data also show that reversal (e.g., denial) is the defense strategy most effective in managing anxiety, or at least in reducing anxiety.

Koller (1982), who looked at the role of depression in reducing anxiety by returning environmental predictability and/or control to a person, found support for the idea of depression as an ego defense mechanism at low levels of anxiety, but no significant correlation at higher levels of anxiety. His subjects were 120 female undergraduates, assigned randomly to one of the twelve experimental conditions. Participation was a partial requirement for the Introductory Psychology class.

Investigating the relationship of gender, self-esteem, and cognitive style to ego defense mechanisms, Narov (1983) found that (1) males show a preference for the use of defenses of Turning Against Object and Projection, while females show a preference for the defenses of Turning Against Self and Reversal; (2) high self-esteem individuals tend to employ more Reversal than low self-esteem individuals, while low self-esteem individuals tend to employ more Turning Against Object and Projection than high self-esteem individuals; and (3) field-independent individuals tend to rely more on the differentiated defense of Turning Against Object and Projection. Field-dependent individuals tend to rely more on the undifferentiated defense of Reversal than field-independent individuals. Narov's investigation found no sex differences in self-esteem. Males were found to be more field independent than females. And no statistically significant correlations were found between verbal intelligence, social class, birth order, and religion to ego defense mechanisms. Some significant correlations were found between factors in parent-child relationships to ego defense mechanisms.

The Superego. The superego, a reflection of society's rules, norms, values, ethics, and attitudes, is the last of the three major personality systems to evolve. Just as ego evolves from id, so superego evolves from ego. More specifically, the superego develops from that part of ego in which self-observation and self-criticism develop and in which parental introjection occurs. Fears of punishment, rejection, and abandonment (first during the anal stage and later during the phallic stage and the Oedipus complex) force the child's ego to introject, identify with, and idealize parental prohibitions and moral values *as the child perceives them.* Superego begins to differentiate right from wrong, good from bad, and moral from immoral, and to develop a **conscience** (introjected standards and values imposed by parents) and an **ego ideal** (an idealized image of the self one believes he or she must be). While initially ego processes, near the end of the phallic stage of development superego begins to evolve from ego as a separate personality system. It is not fully developed, however, until the individual has replaced parental control with self-control. Full development of superego occurs only after the resolution of the Oedipus complex.

Although superego evolves from ego, it is exclusively the product of the social world and, operating on a *Moral Principle,* shares many characteristics of the id. Like the id, superego is unconscious, irrational, and demanding. Like id also, superego is unconcerned with the safety and survival of the organism. Indeed, if superego accumulates enough psychic energy (by joining forces with the id against ego, for example) it could overpower, even destroy, ego. Recognizing its destructive potentialities, Freud (1960b) sometimes referred to the superego in his final theory as the agent of Thanatos, the death instinct.

Early versus Continuous Development

According to psychoanalytic theory, development occurs largely as a consequence of two pervasive inseparable phenomena: (1) maturation or natural growth processes, and (2) learning associated with the avoidance of pain, through the conquest of frustration, the resolution of conflicts, and the reduction of anxiety. For Freud (1949, 1963), early life stages, particularly those in the first five years of life, are both *essential* and *decisive*—that is, *critical* to personality formation. During infancy and early childhood we first encounter conflicts and frustrations that force us to learn numerous and varied forms of adaptation, compromise, defense, displacement, and sublimation, and these conflicts and frustrations can influence our personalities in subsequent years. Moreover, Freud (1949) identified these early critical life stages with the erogenous zones of the body.

According to Freud (1954, 1960b, 1963), whose theoretical stance is insistently and consistently causal, human personality and behavior should be viewed developmentally. That is, adult personality and behavior are the result of and can be understood and explained as an elaboration or evolution of the personality and behavior of early childhood. In like manner, more complex and integrated personality and behavior can be conceptualized as the elaboration of simple, primitive behavioral patterns and drives. Psychological development, like physical development, is a gradual, evolving process. Moreover, Freud (1960b) claimed psychological development progresses through rather well-defined overlapping psychosexual stages, the most important of these being the pregenital stages occurring during the first five or six years of life. The pregenital stages—oral, anal, and phallic—are both essential and decisive to personality formation.

Psychosexual Stages of Development As with human motivation, Freud's theory of the development of personality is tied to the division of mind (**ego development,** the acquisition of ego functions) and body (**libidinal development,** the transformation of pregenital sexual and aggression drives), hence Freud's term, **psychosexual stages of development.**

The Oral Stage. In Freud's theory, in the first stage of both libidinal and ego development (birth to approximately eighteen months), the mouth, lips, and tongue are the primary sources of pleasure and thus the focus of the infant's attention. At birth the human infant is a small and helpless but demanding, narcissistic blob of id, totally dependent on others, particularly the mother, for survival. The child is limited at this stage to reflex action and the **primary process** (wish fulfillment—unconscious fantasies of libidinal urges) and is unable to tolerate the tension created by hunger; the mouth thus becomes the first of the erotogenic zones to produce both irritating excitations and experiences of pleasure. The gentle, tactile oral pleasure resulting from nursing (sucking), whether the nipple of mother's breast or a bottle, becomes associated with nourishment, love, and approval. Conversely, the withholding of this pleasure becomes associated with the pangs of hunger, rejection, and disapproval. The infant's perceptions of others and of the world as good or bad and safe or dangerous are reflections of the infant's perceptions of its mother's responses.

Hall (1954) hypothesizes that the infant's mouth has at least five modes of functioning: "taking in, holding on, biting, spitting out, and closing" (p. 104). Moreover, each mode is a *prototype* for certain personality traits that can, if the infant experiences either overgratification or deprivation of its oral needs, serve as a model for later adaptations. "Taking in through the mouth is the prototype for acquisitiveness, holding on for tenacity and determination, biting for destructiveness, spitting out for rejection and contemptuousness, and closing for refusal and negativism" (Hall, 1954, p. 104). Scheduled feedings, increased time lapses between feedings, and eventual weaning before the infant can learn to tolerate the frustration and tension, for example, may result in a personality trait of dependence and holding on to others and to things. Indeed, through various displacements and sublimations, fixation on any one of the prototype oral modes may result in a constellation of functional and dysfunctional interests, attitudes, and behaviors that become incorporated into the personality.

The Anal Stage. At approximately the age of two, when the child's instinctual needs to defecate and urinate conflict with the external prohibitions imposed by parental toilet training, the child is asked to control the sphincters and voluntarily delay gratification. There is, at this stage, a transition in the erotogenic zones from the mouth to the anus and the urethra.

The anal stage introduces the necessity of learning to tolerate the privation and prohibition imposed by society, and the child, accustomed to immediate gratification, resists. Inordinately harsh or demanding training methods at the anal stage of development can cause distress and frustration in the child. Defiance may manifest itself in intentional soiling or withholding feces or urine, and the immediate response, "No!" to every request made of the child. Retention-and-release "games" may also contribute to a clash of wills between parents and child.

Phallic Stage. The third and possibly the most important of the psychosexual stages of development is the phallic stage, for it is during this stage that object cathexes are directed outwardly toward a parent. Children, as early as three years of age, discover the sensual pleasure of genital stimulation and become conscious of sexual differences. Exhibitionism and voyeurism are often evident during this period. The phallic stage is also the period when children experience an intensification of sexual longing for their parents. The difference in the genitals of male and female led Freud to view this period differently for the two sexes.

With the emergence of the phallic stage, late in the second or third years of life, the male child moves from loving his mother and identifying with his father to incestuous feelings for his mother and feelings of jealousy for his father, along with the fear of forfeiture of his father's love and protection. Borrowing from Greek mythology, Freud (1949, 1963) referred to this as the **Oedipus complex.**

The incestuous desire for exclusive sexual possession of his mother's love and attention places the male child in a dangerous, antagonistic position with his father. He fears physical punishment in the form of castration and suffers a **castration anxiety.** His defense against castration anxiety is the repression of his incestuous feelings for his mother and the hostility he feels toward his father, and he reverts from object choice to identification and introjection with the father's superego standards. This defensive process sets the stage for the development of the child's superego.

As with the male, the female's first cathexis is the mother. Unlike the male, however, she has not identified strongly with the father prior to the Oedipus complex. The discovery that she lacks a penis (castration complex) weakens the cathexis with the mother, whom she partially blames for bringing her into the world without a penis, and strengthens her preference for her father. At this time, her feelings of love for her father are mixed with feelings of envy, because he possesses a penis.

The female Oedipus complex weakens with maturity and the realization that sexually possessing the father is impossible. Identification occurs with one of the parents, depending on the dominant sexual component, and gives rise to the formation of superego. The success and strength of her identifications affect the direction of sexuality in later years, as well as the nature of interpersonal relationships. If the Oedipus complex is resolved successfully, the cathexis for the mother is preserved.

The Latency Stage. From the age of six to puberty, there is a period of emotional quiescence during which Freud assumed the sexual and aggressive instincts are in a relatively repressed or sublimated state. Libidinal energy is sublimated in school activities of learning, participating in games, sports, hobbies, and friendships of the same sex. Latency, then, is a period of acquiring skills. Assuming that personality is largely formed in the first five years of life, and that radical change thereafter is extremely difficult, Freud paid little attention to the latency period.

The Genital Stage. The genital stage, the goal of normal development, emerges with the advent of puberty when the energy of the sexual instincts is again dramatically heightened and the aims of sexual instincts are no longer autoerotic. This stage, along with the physiological changes of the reproductive systems characteristic of the adolescent years, brings an awareness of sexuality and creates stress and conflict that require numerous new adaptations and adjustments—displacements and sublimations. If there are no libidinal fixations, the genital stage culminates in the stabilizing of the personality. Here again, convinced that the first five years are the critical years of personality formation, Freud gave neither the latency stage nor the genital stage much attention.

Fixation and Character Typology   Failure to progress satisfactorily through any of the critical pregenital stages of psychosexual development assumes fixation of libido at that particular erotogenic zone, and the fixated personality can be marked by characteristics of that pregenital stage. Excessive amounts of libido become fixated through severe frustration resulting from deprivation or overindulgence resulting from intense gratification. When excessive amounts of libido have become fixated, the fixated person has the tendency (1) either to act in an infantile manner or to regress to infantile behavior when under stress; (2) to choose compulsively those objects on which he or she is fixated; and (3) to experience a loss of libido when too much of it remains attached to the past object cathexis. Each of the pregenital stages involves bipolar traits, the extremes of which are considered to indicate fixation.

The Oral Character. Bipolar characteristics of the oral character type include optimistic/pessimistic, gullible/mistrustful, manipulative/passive, admiring/ envious, and arrogant/self-depreciating. The bipolar traits of the oral personality are rather direct expressions of the attitudes emerging from defensive interactions on the oral level with parents.

The Anal Character. The anal stage is generalized as a stage of giving and withholding. When parents are either too strict or too indulgent with the child during this stage, the child's adult personality may be characterized as anal in nature. Freud (1960a, 1960b) was fairly clear about the bipolar traits of the anal character type: miserly/overly generous, constricted/expansive, stubborn/acquiescent, tidy/messy, rigidly punctual/constantly tardy, meticulous/slovenly, and explicit/vague. Again, these bipolar traits of the anal character type express the instinctual impulses of giving and withholding or anal expulsiveness and anal retentiveness.

The Phallic Character.   The bipolar traits of the phallic personality are: vain/self-contemptuous, proud/humble, recklessly courageous/meek, brash/bashful, gregarious/solitary, stylish/plain, flirtatious/shy, virtuous/promiscuous, and happy/sad. Characteristics of the phallic type are largely determined by the defense processes employed to resolve the Oedipus complex.

Subjective versus Objective Reality

Our survival depends on our ability to adapt to experiences in reality, but the world we live in is privately constructed from individual perceptions and interpretations. Considering the dynamics of Freud's personality structure, our personal reality is both a function and a product of the distribution of psychic energy

---

BOX 2-2 Freud's Character Typology Difficult to Prove or Disprove

Kline (1972) and Tribich and Messer (1974) conclude that, while there appears to be evidence supportive of the oral receptive and anal retentive character types, the phallic character type is not supported. However, Liebert and Spiegler (1987) note there are formidable problems in interpreting the findings of the character type studies, for Freud's hypothesis can be stretched to cover conflicting outcomes. For example, if a study of oral character types shows dependency, the hypothesis is supported. The hypothesis is also supported if the study of oral character types shows independence, for "independence can be a defense—reaction formation—against independence" (Liebert & Spiegler, 1987, p. 147). It is just as possible with Freud's theory for the oral character type to behave both dependently and independently, for fluctuating behavior may be a compromise between a drive and its defense. In short, hypotheses that explain and predict contrasting and conflicting behaviors are impossible to prove or disprove.

---

among the three major personality systems. Reality testing requires the secondary processes and is therefore an ego function. Only when ego controls the bulk of psychic energy are our perceptions and interpretations of reality likely to be congruent with actual reality. But even then, perceptual reproductions are corruptible.

Even with ego in control and our perceptions closely linked to the sensory stimuli from the outer world, our emotionally toned realities often differ significantly from the realities of others. Reality is a subjective creation, a product of imagination and memory. We naturally endeavor to fill the gaps in our sensory perceptions with plausible inferences and then to translate our inferences into conscious material. We are phenomenological beings. Ego learns to scan the stimuli of the outer world and to select only those features of the environment relevant to the problem it is attempting to solve or the defense it is constructing. Further, ego will summon memories and ideas from the preconscious to assist in decision making or to adjust to the confronting situation.

Our perceptions and interpretations of reality will be influenced unconsciously by the defense mechanisms of ego. Inner feelings, for example, can be projected outward to other people or things, even the world in general. Repression can keep us from becoming aware of important stimuli in the outer world. Displacement can cause us to focus on or attend to something other than what requires our attention. Reaction formation can cause us to act exactly the opposite the way we feel.

Number and Weight Assigned to Motivational Concepts

According to Freud (1940/1964, 1923/1925), all behavior is motivated. We are impelled to act when psychic energy, aroused by bodily needs or impulses seeking expression and the release of tension, is reflected in the form of an instinctual object choice or wish. Freud believed that motivational strength is determined by the impetus of the life instincts and the id's desire to remove immediately the excitation they create. In addition, Freud (1960, 1962) believed we are motivated by death instincts, a compulsion to reestablish the inanimate state out of which we were formed.

Since both life and death instincts reside in the id, we are motivated to act by instinctual urges and drives that are persistent, irrational, conflicting, nearly uncontrollable, and most important, largely outside our consciousness. The aim of every instinct is the cessation of tension and the resultant sense of gratification. All behavior aims at maximizing instinct gratification while minimizing punishment and guilt.

We are motivated, also, to identify with the ethical choices of the ego ideal and the mandates of the conscience. Superego confers pride on the ego for following its decrees and being virtuous. Conversely, it uses its energy to punish ego for behavior that runs counter to its demands.

Explanation of the Learning Process

For Freud, learning is an ego function situated in the defensive postures we assume as we encounter the internal conflicts and external frustrations of living. Ego is an achievement of living, an organization of experience with reality. In our efforts to avoid pain and experience pleasure, we form identifications, displacements, rationalizations, sublimations, compromises, and compensations that involve new object cathexes for instinctual object choices, hence, learning. In short, pleasure and pain are the necessary and sufficient conditions for learning, and cathexis is the equivalent of learning. We learn what is positively cathected and avoid what is negatively cathected.

When it is efficient in gratifying the instinctual needs of id and adhering to the constrictions of superego, ego attracts and binds surplus psychic energy which can then be diverted to the secondary or cognitive processes required for learning. Examples of the secondary processes of ego are perceiving, attending, discriminating, remembering, reasoning, imagining, judging, and deciding. As we mature, develop language and memory systems, and repeatedly invest surplus psychic energy in the secondary processes of ego, our perceptions become more acute, our discriminations more precise, our defense mechanisms more elaborate and complex, and our judgments and decisions more astute.

With ever-increasing knowledge of our world, we are better able to manipulate and control the environment to suit our purposes. Our ego is able to gratify instinctual needs with greater economy. Thus, as we mature and learn, we develop greater skill in resolving conflict and coping with frustration and anxiety.

Determinism versus Freedom of Choice

From the beginning, Freud's stance on this issue is clear. While he recognized that we experience a strong illusion of freedom, Freud began as a strict biological determinist. In Freud's early theory we are governed by the natural laws that apply to all living organisms. There is no place in psychoanalytic theory for concepts such as free will, choice, spontaneity, self-determinism, or self-actualization. Later, Freud shifted his determinism from a physical reality, which he considered inadequate for the description of mental life, to a psychical realm of explanation (Freud, 1960b, 1961a). *The shift was no less deterministic.* There are no purely capricious actions in mental (psychic) activity; all actions are caused by prior mental events. All causes have their effects and all effects their causes. For Freud, true psychic spontaneity, chance, and freedom are illusions—simply wishful thinking.

Like all theorists who postulate determinism, Freud was forced because of his postulate to seek causes and to predict their outcomes. All impulses, thoughts, feelings, aspirations, dreams, and actions are events in a chain of causally related phenomena determined largely by unconscious instinctual forces. Anything one considers "uncaused," according to Freud, simply reflects ignorance of cause. Our experience of freedom is a deception. Even our highest motives are disguised forms of libido. We are biologically incapable of choosing between alternative courses of action. Id, not reason, is ultimately in control. Our cognitive capacities operate only to serve our primal desires. Our primary aim is the fulfillment of perpetual life and death instincts and the resultant homeostatic balance, thus precluding either choice or self-actualization.

Every successful case served as evidence and encouraged his further search for additional proofs. When any case failed to provide the evidence he sought for verification of his observations, Freud was forced to check and recheck his methods of observation and to look for additional data.

Conscious versus Unconscious Determinants

Freud's early topographic theory was cast on three strata: the base and deepest level was the **unconscious** (later named the id); the second or middle level, the **preconscious;** and the third or upper level, the **conscious** (later named ego). His construct of the unconscious conflicted with the established sciences of the era. Psychology had only recently separated from philosophy, and psychologists were determined to model their new science after chemistry, physics, and biology. They were interested only in rational, conscious determinants. There was no place in their science for an inaccessible unconscious that could not be observed by either external evidence or introspection. Further, Freud's (1960a, 1965) assertion that the unconscious plays a major role in determining human behavior was totally contradictory to their view that human behavior was the result of conscious, rational, and moral motivations. Today, however, many personologists consider Freud's topography of the mind, along with his constructs of primary and secondary processes, his greatest contribution to the field of personality.

The Unconscious Stratum Early in his career, Freud's clinical experiences, particularly his experiences with hypnosis (later free association), his patients' dreams, amnesias, and symptom formations, and their resistance and transference in treatment convinced him of the existence of unconscious phenomena. Even though the unconscious was unavailable to awareness, Freud (1965) was certain that the existence of the unconscious could be proven indirectly. The mental processes of dreams and their latent meanings; discoverable reasons for common, involuntary errors or slips made while speaking, reading, or writing; and certain kinds of forgetting (repressed memories) could, Freud (1954, 1965, 1977) believed, only be explained by an unconscious stratum of the mind.

Freud's early view of the unconscious, later incorporated into his theoretical construct of the id, was that of a repository for primitive, animalistic impulses, sexual and aggressive instinctual drives, and repressed psychic material. Moreover, Freud claimed, of the three levels of the mind (unconscious, preconscious, and conscious), the unconscious was by far the most influential determinant of human behavior.

Ewin (1988) cites a survey of empirical research of the unconscious conducted by Shevrin and Dickman (1980) that concludes: "Although the results by no means always agree with Freudian thought . . . no psychological model that seeks to explain human knowledge, learning, or behavior can afford to ignore the concept of unconscious processes" (pp. 72–73). In contrast, Bandura (1986), who points out that "each psychodynamic approach has its own favorite set of inner causes and its own brand of insight," states: "Gaining insight into one's underlying motives, it seems, is more like a belief conversion than a self-discovering process" (p. 5).

The unconscious embodies psychic elements that were never conscious or that, though once conscious, were repressed. Limited to primary process, the unconscious consists of nonverbal ideas and conceptions, along with their related affects (emotions and feelings), and a variety of instinctive impulses or urges that seek immediate gratification.

The Preconscious Stratum   Freud's concept of the preconscious lies somewhere between the unconscious and the conscious and contains perceptions and thoughts that were once conscious. Because preconscious perceptions and thoughts are not repressed, they are readily available to conscious recall by associative processes. The preconscious also contains some material from the unconscious that has eluded the primary censor by disguising itself as non-threatening experiences.

The Conscious Stratum

> *Now let us call "conscious" the conception which is present to our consciousness and of which we are aware, and let this be the only meaning of the term "conscious" (Freud, in Rickman, 1957, p. 47).*

Freud's simple definition of the conscious becomes somewhat more complex as its implications are examined. Only a single conception is present in conscious-

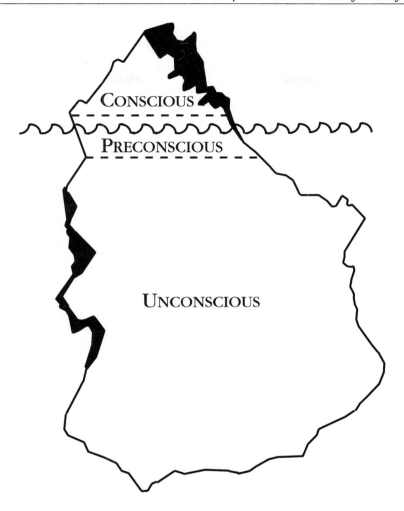

FIGURE 2-2 **Freud's view of the unconscious is represented by the iceberg; the unconscious is by
far the greatest determinant of human
behavior**

ness at any particular moment, and at that moment, all other conceptions, though
once conscious, are unconscious. Conscious material, then, is temporary and
dependent on what the conscious is attending to in the moment. It is also **transitory** (capable of moving instantaneously in and out of awareness).

The content of the conscious stratum, always shifting and changing, varies
with the activities of the person. This swift transition of a conception from conscious to preconscious (which is, so far as conscious is concerned, unconscious)
requires that conscious mental activity act in accordance with the rules of the

secondary process. *"Secondary process thinking* obeys the laws of grammar and formal logic, uses bound energy, and is governed by the *reality principle"* (Rycroft, 1968, p. 124, emphasis in original).

In his mature theory, about 1920, Freud (1960b) renamed the conscious stratum the ego, and increased the role of ego (which was now partly conscious, partly unconscious, and partly preconscious) in normal or healthful personality development. The unconscious or id, however, retained its dominate role in the structure of personality.

Role Assigned to the Self-Concept

While self-concept is implicit in the functional interactions of ego and the ego-ideal of superego, Freud did not grant much importance to the self as a dynamic psychic system or theoretical concept. By stressing the necessity of successfully repressing and redirecting the instinctual drives of the id, particularly sexual desire and aggression, he conferred far greater importance on ego functions and social adaptations than on any notion of being or becoming one's self. The maneuvers of ego are defensive rather than self-actualizing.

As pointed out earlier (see Early versus Continuous Development and Subjective versus Objective Reality), we begin in infancy to differentiate various aspects of our body imagery from objects (persons and things) in the outer world of reality. These perceptual differentiations, along with the accumulation of identifications of the ego and the developmental changes in superego, gradually integrate to form a relatively stable concept of self. Consciousness entails self-perception. Both ego and superego functions serve, however indirectly, to give us a sense of personal identity, a sense of being an individual separate and distinct from all others.

The self in Freud's theory, then, is not synonymous with the total personality that, as an entity, remains somewhat vague and hence difficult to define. Self also does not play a highly significant role in personality development as, for example, do the dynamic systems of id, ego, and superego. Rather, our sense of identity or self-perception is a complex pregenital developmental concept emerging from multiple self-presentations and identifications and gradually achieving constancy.

Centrality of Reinforcement

While Freud did not focus directly on the importance or role of external reward as a behavioral determinant or grant it great significance in personality development, internal reinforcement is implicit in his concept of the pleasure principle as well as in the reciprocal relationship of the three major systems of the psyche. We may, then, reasonably infer that gratification of id's instinctual wishes or, perhaps more accurately, the relief of tension (pleasure) that accompanies instinctual gratification is inherently reinforcing.

An efficient ego is free from the pressure to spend its limited energy on serving id, and an effective ego is rewarded by being in position to bind surplus energy for its own purposes. Ego efficiency is also rewarded by feelings of competence and being in control. Conversely, fear and anxiety are the constant companions of an inefficient ego. Id will not long tolerate ego inefficiency and retains the psychic energy ego needs to operate.

Superego is also in a position to reinforce or punish ego. On the one hand, ego is reinforced with feelings of self-satisfaction and virtuousness when it manages to locate instinctual object choices in a manner that complements the ego ideal of superego. On the other hand, thoughts and behaviors that run counter to ego-ideal are negatively reinforced by superego with painful feelings of guilt, shame, and remorse.

Uniqueness versus Universality

As biological beings, we have much in common with others of our species. For example, we are all, according to Freud, closed energy systems, unconsciously motivated by the same irrational id forces or impulses. We must experience the same psychosexual stages of early development. Our ego and superego functions are the same. And we are all defensive creatures. However, despite our many commonalities, Freud asserts that we are truly unique beings.

While instinctual id impulses derive from our biological nature, their expression must await life experiences. Experience, Freud asserts, is always modified by the social milieu. We pass through the same psychosexual stages of early development, but our experiences during each stage vary significantly from family to family. Indeed, because we are each influenced by a unique set of family interactions and relationships, experiences will differ even among siblings in the same family. No two of us will perceive our experiences precisely the same way. While ego and superego perform the same functions for all of us, their content or nature produces numerous variations; hence, ego and superego differ from one person to another.

Usually by the age of five we have developed a personal set of character attributes, a unique and consistent *schema of apperception* and behavior that defines us as individuals. We are then, according to psychoanalytic theory, unique beings.

Importance of Group Determinants

Although we are biological beings driven by the force of our ids' needs, the social milieu, the people and objects we encounter in living, and the limits and restrictions imposed by authority and society have a significant impact on the expression of our instinctual drives. An important part of our social milieu, particularly during the critical formative years, is the family. Few theorists assign greater importance than Freud to the family (see Early versus Continuous Development), and he assigns special importance to the parents or parent surrogates.

Group affiliations provide us with a sense of security, but always at a cost— namely, the inhibition or sublimation of our instinctual discharges. We must gratify our desires in a sublimated manner if we are to remain members of the group. There is an independent autonomy with laws, customs, and conventions, along with rewards and punishments. Restrictions and renunciations are the dues paid for the security of the group. We are expected to introject a collective psyche, a common ego-ideal created by the group (Freud, 1961c).

The impact of the group as a behavioral determinant can be great, especially when the individual members have become bound to or identified with a strong group leader, giving up their individuality by sharing certain superego elements. The leader's commands and precepts then become the moral laws of the group. Moreover, remorse or guilt is less acute when one follows the leader's conscience. Even the most inhuman acts can be carried out with little self-incrimination when they can be attributed to a leader-dominated conscience (Freud, 1961c). In contrast, this same principle can lift the individual beyond him- or herself to acts of bravery, dedication, justice, and altruism. We become, in essence, comrades in arms, children of God, fellow advocates for justice, friends united for peace.

Note to Reader: A schematic analysis of the theorist's stance on the eleven basic issues appears at this point in each of the theory chapters. These schematic analyses are graphic representations of the theorist's positions on the six polar issues and brief summary statements of the theorist's resolutions of the remaining five issues. Readers should find the schematic analyses helpful as summary reviews, or, if any one graphic representation or summary statement appears unclear, as a reason to return to reread the author's presentation of the theorist's resolution of the issue.

Psychological Health and Psychopathology

Psychology and Health

Classical psychoanalysis, which presents all humans as basically neurotic, does not directly address the healthy personality and the good life. Vinacke (1984) lists only two differences between Freud's "ideal or normal neurotic" and the neurotic: (1) "The structural systems in personality are for the normal person better balanced" (p. 292); and (2) "Defense tactics differ between neurotic and normal people" (p. 293).

By a better balanced structural system, Vinacke (1984) is referring to an appropriate distribution of psychic energy among id, ego, and superego so that each of the three systems has an adequate amount of energy to complete its special functions. By difference in defense strategies, Vinacke (1984) is referring to a greater store of sublimated energy in the ego of the normal person.

Although they would be difficult to measure, characteristics of healthy personality and the good life are inferred in Wallace's (1986) assessment of client progress in therapy:

Heredity	■			Social Determinants
Conscious Determinants			■	Unconscious Determinants
Early Development	■			Continuous Development
Subjective Reality	■			Objective Reality
Determinism	■			Freedom
Uniqueness		■		Universality

Role Assigned to Group Determinants	The primary group (parents or parent surrogates) is especially important in early personality development. The primary group provides security, but expects inhibition and sublimation of instinctual drives in exchange. Children are expected to introject the group's collective ego-ideal.
Explanation of Learning Process	Learning is a function of ego, a defensive posture assumed as internal and external conflicts are encountered. Pleasure and pain are the necessary and sufficient conditions of learning. As id is gratified, ego binds and uses surplus energy for secondary or cognitive processes.
Number and Weight Assigned to Motivational Concepts	Psychic energy motivates. Instinctual drives of the id impel object choice. The goal is relief from tension and subsequent gratification. We are also motivated to identify with ego-ideal and conscience mandates to minimize punishment and guilt.
Centrality of Reinforcement	Internal reward is implicit and comes with relief of tension accompanying instinctual gratification (pleasure). Reinforcement is also experienced as feelings of competence by the efficient ego utilizing surplus energy for itself and as self-gratification and virtuousness by the ego making instinctual object choices congruent with superego.
Role Assigned to Self-Concept	Self-concept is implicit in the interactions of ego and superego's ego-ideal; however, strategies of ego and superego are defensive rather than self-actualizing. Perceptual differentiations, ego identification, and superego developmental changes integrate to form a sense of personal identity.

FIGURE 2-3   Schematic Analysis of Freud's Stance on Basic Issues

1. Extending the unconscious into consciousness, evidenced by insight into repressions and defensive behaviors and increased understanding of self;
2. Giving ego a greater grasp of reality, evidenced by improvements in reality testing and finer discriminations in perceptions of self and others;
3. Renouncing infantile demands, evidenced by more rational behavior;

4. Exchanging pathogenic conflict for normal conflict, evidenced by the obviation of symptom formation;
5. Increasing effort to function autonomously, evidenced by giving up the need for parental figures and transference, especially in the final stages of therapy;
6. Achieving life tasks, evidenced by an increasing ability to love and work (p. 44).

Ego strength is an indication of mental health, for the stronger the ego, the greater its tolerance of stress and tension and the greater its capacity to control emotional reactions. In healthy individuals, ego is the master of id; it thwarts the irrational demands of id and superego, and serves the organism's life-supporting and life-enhancing needs.

Psychopathology

There is no *clear* distinction in Freud's Theory of Psychoanalysis between the categories of normality and abnormality or neurosis and psychosis. Such differences, Freud observed, appear to be quantitative rather than qualitative, and to be dependent on the time, amount, and nature of libidinal fixation. This being the case, neurosis and psychosis can only be explained in terms of the individual's personality and life history.

In his mature theory, Freud (1965) did say that a neurosis is an individual's expression of an unresolved infantile conflict between ego and id, while psychosis is an individual's expression of an unresolved infantile conflict between ego and the outer world of reality. The major symptomatic difference between a neurosis and a psychosis is that, in neurosis, ego's reality testing is unimpaired, while in psychosis, there is a loss of reality and that loss is replaced by delusion and hallucination.

Neurosis. Freud (1960a, 1960b) is convinced that *all* adult neuroses emerge in early childhood as the result of repressed infantile conflicts, typically an unresolved Oedipus complex. Though adults, individuals suffering a neurosis are reenacting, with contemporary figures, those early family experiences that conflicted with their instinctual urges which they have never been able to resolve properly (sublimated or anticathected).

The neurotic's past is confused with the present because the repression of deeply rooted infantile conflicts does not eliminate the effects of conflict on adult perceptions, thoughts, feelings, or behavior. The original internal struggle, when left unresolved, continues into adulthood, and is likely to resurface in a disguised or symbolized form, especially during periods of intense stress and frustration. Indeed, while the neurotic's capacity for fantasy and symbolization makes the unconscious disguising of masked unresolved conflict possible, the distortion of a disguised emotional conflict often exacerbates the neurosis.

Psychosis. In a psychosis, the repressed unconscious of the id commands satisfaction and overwhelms ego, or reality becomes so unbearably painful that a paralyzed ego, no longer able to fulfill its reality function, surrenders to id. The price of ego's surrender is severe. All secondary processes (perceiving, thinking, feeling, and speaking) are seriously regressed. Reality testing and object cathexis are lost. And with id in command, delusion and hallucination replace reality, for id lives by the narcissistic pleasure principle and is limited to primary process (wishing and imaging).

Unlike neurotics, for whom the goal of therapy is to remove the defense mechanisms of ego, the goal of therapy with the psychotic is ego readaptation and the support of neurotic defenses. Freud restricted his practice to neurotic patients, for he believed that a transference relationship, necessary to successful psychoanalysis, could not be established with the psychotic patient.

While Freud (1961b, 1961c) recognized the role of the social milieu, he steadfastly believed that humans are primarily biological beings motivated by instincts that constitute the total psychic energy available to operate all mental processes and functions. The dynamics of personality, an interaction and blending of urging (cathexis) and checking (anticathexis) forces, are determined by the distribution of psychic energy. Human behavior, then, is an expression of the dominant system or principle controlling the bulk of psychic energy available at any particular time. When id retains its energy, behavior is impulsive, irrational, sensual, and indiscriminate.

When psychic energy is relinquished to and bound by ego, behavior is realistic, rational, and goal directed. And when superego controls the bulk of psychic energy, behavior is rigid, moralistic, compulsive, and fearful. Although an individual's instinctual drives emanate from a biological nature shared by all humans, the expressions of instinctual drives are always influenced by the people, objects, and situations encountered and the restrictions and limitations imposed by society and superego.

Heuristic Influences: Research Methods and Techniques

If the heuristic value of Freud's Theory of Psychoanalysis is based solely on its value as a stimulant to other theorists, its heuristic influence must be granted the highest rating. The impact of Freud's provocative views on the nature of being human was so great that few disciplines touching human lives, thought, values, and ethics were unaffected (see "Introduction" and "Extended Applications," this chapter). This achievement alone is enough to assure high marks in heuristic influence.

Regardless of how interesting, persuasive, or provocative it is, every theory must eventually meet the test of empirical validation. Yet fifty years after his death, Freud's theory is still open to question. Freud's observations cannot be repeated, for there is no way of knowing exactly what he did in collecting his data or exactly what analytic procedures he followed to arrive at his hypotheses and generalizations (see "Critique," this chapter).

With his medical background in neurological research, Freud was both knowledgeable and skilled in the research methods of his day. His approach to theory construction was to formulate a hypothesis, gather relevant data from the observations of his patients' free associations, dreams, parapraxes, and transference, and then modify his hypothesis to fit these new data. For Freud, who believed the "law of internal consistency" was the test of all knowledge, the data gathered during psychoanalytic treatment were both *necessary* and *sufficient* for the testing of his theory.

He believed also that only those individuals who were trained in psychoanalysis and who had personally undergone analysis were qualified to collect the data necessary to judge the scientific merit of his work. It is not surprising, then, that Freud was unimpressed with the methods and procedures of the experimental psychologists and that he placed little value on their research findings. He held little value for those findings which appeared to confirm or refute his theoretical constructs. Freud was fully convinced that the psychoanalytic method and the data on which his theoretical constructions were based were "indisputable," hence independent of experimental verification.

While the case study approach is certainly an acceptable method of scientific investigation, there are unquestionably inherent weaknesses in its exclusive use in theory construction (see "Critique," this chapter). Today's psychologists, counselors, and therapists question both the nature of Freud's methodology data and the empirical validation of his theory. Unlike Freud, they do not accept psychoanalysis as an indisputable method of science; indeed, they believe that, even though the language of Freud's theory is relatively vague, it is nevertheless possible to derive hypotheses for empirical testing.

There was never any doubt in Freud's mind that he was a scientist or that his theory construction was scientific. For Freud, objective and verified observation was the source of all knowledge. After thousands of personal observations, and thousands more by other psychoanalysts, Freud felt no need for statistical or experimental studies to back the assumptions and generalizations of his theory. When presented with an empirical study that supported his theory, he wrote the researcher that he found the study "interesting" but "unnecessary" (Gay, 1988). Proof, for Freud, was a matter of internal consistency.

Applications To Psychotherapy

Therapeutic Goals

While at first glance the goals of psychotherapy may appear incautious, even grandiose, closer inspection reveals that they reflect the spirit rather than the letter of the psychoanalytic approach to therapy. They are goals for which the analyst strives, knowing full well they will never be totally realized. It is undesirable—indeed impossible—to uncover *all* repressed material. Nevertheless, bringing repressed material into consciousness is a goal of the analyst. Working through analysis is a lifelong process—hence, not achievable within the therapeutic tenure of the client. Insight, integration, and psychic organization are accepted as both means and ends, processes and products of psychotherapy. Still, while emphasis is on means and processes, they remain no less ends and products.

Freud made rather modest claims for his therapy. He never presented it as a panacea for all psychic ills or offered it as a modality to perfection. Further, he never guaranteed that the benefits gained were permanent or beyond reversal. For a carefully selected group of patients, psychoanalysis offers only the promise of helping those who are willing and able to endure a lengthy, arduous, and often painful process to achieve a resolution of some intrapsychic conflicts so they might encounter the normal conflicts of life's tasks in a mature—hence, responsible and pleasant—way. As expressed earlier, promises made and goals attempted can differ significantly.

The ultimate goal of psychoanalysis is **reorganization,** a form of ego development that promotes the integration of dissociated psychic material and results in a basically changed, firmly established new structure of personality. Subgoals of psychoanalysis include:

1. Establishing a therapeutic relationship that will facilitate the psychoanalytic approach to therapy (see "Therapeutic Relationship," next section);
2. Teaching the process of free association;
3. Extending the unconscious into consciousness, thereby elevating repressed material, abolishing symptom formation, and exchanging pathogenic conflict for normal conflict;
4. Strengthening ego so behavior is more reality based;
5. Helping the client to gain insight into and work through the transference process, becoming more responsible and independent than before in relation to life tasks.

Therapeutic Relationship

In the psychoanalytic approach to therapy, the analyst-and-analysand relationship is conceptualized in conjunction with the induced transference neurosis. The nature of the transference process calls for an analyst–analysand relationship in which the analysand can resurrect and relive the highly emotional conflicts initially encountered with significant others in early childhood and then transfer these emotions to the analyst. Because the analysand's early conflicts originated from difficulties during the psychosexual stages of development—particularly the Oedipal stage—the feelings directed toward the analyst during transference, while displacements, are nevertheless often intense and of a sexual or hostile nature. The therapeutic alliance must be not only strong enough to withstand this level of emotional intensity but also sound enough to ensure that the client's emotions are only expressed verbally.

Freud (1949, 1977) consistently asserted that a compassionate neutrality was the proper attitude for the analyst to convey in the psychoanalytic session. While attentive, accepting, and nonjudgmental, the analyst is a neutral observer of the free association and transference processes, intervening only occasionally to offer interpretations of the significance of the analysand's past experiences and distorted displacements. Objectivity demands that the analyst protect the relationship from becoming contaminated with the subjective feelings normally associated with interpersonal relationships. In fact, should the analyst begin to experience transference, collegial consultation is sought so the countertransference can be worked through and resolved. The analyst neither offers advice nor extends sympathy. Interpretations and explorations that are empathic—hence, emotionally significant and personally meaningful to the analysand—enhance the psychoanalytic relationship by providing support, understanding, and stability.

Initial Procedures and Strategies

Initiating Therapy   The analytic situation begins with the first contact between the prospective analysand and the analyst. Literally everything analysands say and do in their initial approach has potential significance, not only for the analyst's assessment of the analysand's emotional, circumstantial, and psychic readiness for therapy but also for analysis proper should the analyst agree to accept the analysand for treatment. Data for the acceptance decision include the manner and style of the analysand's self-presentation, the nature and onset of the problem or crisis, all analysand reactions and responses to the early structuring of the analytic contact, and any disclosures of the client's current life situation, family background, developmental history, interpersonal relationships, and accomplishments (see Box 2.3).

Course of Psychoanalysis

While there have been modifications, elaborations, and additions to the early methods and techniques of psychoanalysis, the five basic techniques established by Freud remain critical to the psychoanalytic approach today. In his attempt to uncover the contents of the unconscious, Freud's major tools were (1) free association, (2) interpretation, (3) dream analysis, (4) analysis of resistances, and (5) analysis of transference.

Free Association   Often referred to as the *rule* of psychoanalysis and based on the hypothesis that repressed material constantly seeks discharge, free association is an analytic technique designed to facilitate emotional regression and recall of early childhood memories. Reclining on the analyst's couch with the analyst seated out of view, the analysand is encouraged to abandon his or her normal censoring activities, to flow freely with his or her feelings and thoughts, verbalizing immediately and spontaneously *everything* that comes to mind, regardless of

BOX 2-3 Freud's Rules of Psychoanalysis

Freud believed it essential that every person desiring to undergo psychoanalysis understand fully the structure of the analytic process. Certain rules, therefore, were carefully explained and agreed to at the outset. Indeed, the patient's willingness and capacity to follow these rules were often put to the test of a trial period, with acceptance for treatment resting on the outcome.

The fundamental rule of psychoanalysis is free association. The patient develops the ability to free associate (discussed in the next section)—no small accomplishment for the average client but crucial to the analytic process. Freud's second rule of psychoanalysis was the rule of abstention. Freud's patients were expected to suspend all major life decisions for the term of analysis. This included decisions such as marriage or divorce, new business ventures or sizable investments, career choice or change. To avoid outside interference that might hinder the analytic process, Freud never accepted patients who were not independent in all life relations. Further, because psychoanalysis requires lengthy, intensive, and exhaustive self-study, Freud accepted only patients who expressed a willingness to commit themselves to fixed appointment hours and an agreed-upon fee and payment schedule. Freud usually scheduled his patients for one-hour sessions, three to five days a week, and analysis was seldom completed in less than two years and often required as many as five years.

In addition to these rules, Freud restricted treatment to those individuals he subjectively thought would benefit from the psychoanalytic process. His patients were expected to be of at least normal intelligence, to possess a certain degree of ethical development, and to be under the age of fifty, the point of life at which Freud believed the ability to undo psychic processes begins to diminish.

how trivial, ludicrous, preposterous, irrelevant, or painful the feeling or thought might seem. During the free association process unconscious material is permitted to enter consciousness. However, as in dreams, it enters in disguise or in symbolic form and must be interpreted by the analyst.

Initial resistance to free association is usually met with assurance from the analyst that every thought and feeling is significant and relevant. Further, the analyst assures the analysand that his or her memories of the past, whether pleasant or painful, will return once he or she manages to relax and flow with the process. Later resistances (blocks, pauses, censoring, etc.) serve as cues to the analyst that the analysand is avoiding anxiety-arousing material. As the regression of free association progresses, unconscious wishes, dreams, fantasies, conflicts, and motivations emerge and the analyst attempts to reconstruct the original conflict, uncover the developmental sources or fixations, and interpret these to the analysand when it seems to the analyst to be appropriate and timely.

Interpretation Interpretation is an important psychoanalytic technique that requires a great deal of skill and experience on the part of the analyst. It is a major goal of the analytic process. Further, it is an integral part of each of the other four basic techniques and as such is employed complementarily with the analysis of free associations, dream symbols, psychosomatic symptoms, defensive postures, and resistance and transference behaviors.

Client readiness and involvement are crucial to successful analytic interpretation. Correct timing is essential, and analyst insights may be withheld until the climate is right. The manner in which an interpretation is expressed may alone determine whether or not client insight occurs. Interpretations are effectively communicated only when analysands are prepared to recognize and accept them. Expressed too soon, interpretations evoke resistance or further repression and can, if anxiety becomes too great, result in premature termination of analysis.

Dream Analysis Freud (1965) considered dreams to be symbolic gratifications of id's instinctual demands, designed to promote and realize wish fulfillment. When the individual sleeps, ego is relatively inactive; it is not expending its bound energy for reality testing, and it is released from decision making. The id, no longer under such tight corrective control from ego and superego and their immediate concern for reality and morality, is more free to express its unconscious wishes in the form of dreams. Even in sleep, however, there is always the ego censor. Direct expression of the id's unconscious wishes is censored. Through dream work (condensation and displacement) and symbolization, the repressed instinctual urges of the id are heavily disguised in acceptable form and hidden in the manifest content of the dream. Anxiety is not generated, and the individual's sleep is not interrupted.

Freud (1965) believed dreams had three functions: (1) wish fulfillment, (2) discharge of unconscious tension, and (3) preserving sleep. He believed, too, that it is possible to distinguish between two types of dream content—**manifest content** (the apparent and evident content recalled and reported by the dreamer), and **latent content** (the disguised or hidden potential meaning of the dream).

Unlike Adler (Chapter 3), Freud found little value in and paid little attention to the manifest dream content, which he referred to as **day residues** (thoughts of the day's events preceding the night's dream). Latent content, in contrast, Freud (1965) believed to be the product and expression of the unconscious, hence, a critical focus during psychoanalysis. Moreover, Freud was convinced that an experienced, skilled analyst who was familiar with the language of the unconscious, and who possessed the ability to discern psychodynamic structure from few and seemingly unrelated fragments, the knowledge of the dreamer's history and manner of reacting, and the dreamer's associations with the dream material, could uncover and interpret the **latent dream content** (meaning) of the patient's dream.

Although Freud (1965) consistently recommended extreme caution in the overreliance on dream symbols and warned that they are ambiguous and idiosyncratic, he did reveal a number of common or typical dream symbolizations. While far too numerous to deal with in depth in a single chapter, a few of his more common and typical dream symbols included:

1. Emperor or Empress, King or Queen—the dreamer's parents.
2. Prince or Princess—the dreamer.
3. All elongated objects (e.g., sticks, umbrellas, etc.) and all sharp weapons (e.g., knives, daggers, etc.), and reptiles (e.g., snakes, lizards, etc.)—the male sex organ.
4. Boxes, cases, chests, cupboards, ovens, and hollow objects (ships, vessels, etc.)—the vagina or uterus.
5. Baldness, hair-cutting, teeth falling out—castration.
6. Buildings—people (smooth buildings = males; buildings with balconies, awnings, porches = females).
7. Small animals—children.

(Freud, 1965, pp. 385–399)

After his patients related a dream, Freud instructed them to free-associate the manifest dream material. Their associations, along with supplementary material (e.g., histories, manner of relating and reacting, other associations, and early childhood memories) helped Freud recognize latent content and uncover the meaning of the dream for later interpretation to his patients.

Fisher and Greenberg (1977), after reviewing a substantial amount of research related to Freud's theory of psychoanalysis, conclude that Freud was correct when he said that dreams provide an outlet for internal unconscious tensions. However, they found that research does *not* support many of Freud's assumptions about dreams. For example, recent evidence gathered from REM studies does not substantiate Freud's contention that dreams are sleep protectors. Neither is there evidence, according to Fisher and Greenberg (1977), to support Freud's contention that the manifest content of a dream is meaningless. While dreams may function defensively at times, manifest content also contains important information about the dreamer's personality and success in coping with troublesome life problems.

Analysis of Resistances In psychoanalysis, analysand behaviors that interfere with or hinder the analytical process are considered a form of resistance. All forms of analysand resistance are significant, and they are viewed by the analyst as opportunities to gain insight into his or her patients' unconscious motivations, intentions, desires, attitudes, and avoidance or defensive styles. Furthermore, client resistances can be used by the analyst, through interpretation or confrontation, to facilitate insights into the hidden or disguised purposes for clients' feelings and actions.

Some of the common forms of resistance to the analytic process are not attending sessions, arriving either early or late, or constantly attempting to change the agreed time for appointments; complaining about, supposedly forgetting, or refusing to meet fee payments; blocking, censoring, or disrupting the free association process; and either not recalling dreams or developing a fascination for them and dwelling almost exclusively on dreams for entire sessions. Transference, dealt with here as a separate psychoanalytic technique, is also a form of resistance, and unless treated as unreal and interpreted it will impede analysis.

Analysis of Transference   While transference is a form of resistance to therapy, analysis of the transference neurosis is considered a major technique of the analyst. Transference, therefore, can be neither satisfied nor ignored by the analyst; it must be treated as distorted displacement of significant relationships in the client's past, hence unreal and inappropriate. In Freud's approach to the therapeutic relationship, the analyst–analysand relationship is conceptualized in conjunction with the induced **transference** neurosis. The nature of the transference process calls for an analyst–analysand relationship in which the analysand can safely resurrect and relive the highly emotional and unresolved conflicts initially experienced with significant others (usually the patient's parents) during early childhood. The analyst then serves as a substitute for the analysand's parents, an object of his or her libidinal cathexis and aggressive tendencies.

Freud identified three types of transference: (1) negative, (2) erotic, and (3) sensible. In the negative transference, the analysand directs displaced feelings of aggression and hostility toward the analyst. When the transference is erotic, the analysand views the analyst as an object of passionate love. Sensible transference occurs only when the analysand is prepared to gain insight from the analyst's interpretations. Sensible transference may not be stable and can revert quickly to erotic or negative transference. Both negative and erotic transference are forms of resistance that obstruct the analysis; however, they are also valuable sources of unconscious conflicts and fixations.

The only proper response of the analyst to a patient's transference is the cool, patient work of analysis. A transference must be recognized and understood by the analysand for what it is, a distorted displacement and an unconscious form of resistance, if it is to be resolved successfully.

Extended Applications

Any attempt to assess objectively the extended applications of Freud's ideas and theoretical constructs must overcome the distortions of the Freud legend (Sulloway, 1983), as well as the many extensions, adjunctions, interpretations, distortions, and vulgarizations (Ellenberger, 1970). This is far too great a task even to consider in a single summary chapter. In addition to offering those who followed him a solid ideological theory and methodology of treatment to build on, Freud's ideas and theoretical constructs reached beyond personality and psychopathology to other areas. Disciplines such as philosophy, religion, biology, history, political science, sociology, criminal justice, education, psychography, and the arts (painting, poetry, theater, and literature) were also recipients of psychoanalytical notions. Indeed, one could not be accused of overstatement to assert that Freudian thought has touched nearly every aspect of twentieth-century life.

Freud's terminology has literally invaded the languages of many countries, particularly the English language. He awakened interest in early childhood development and child-rearing practices. Writers incorporated his character typology into their novels and plays. Historical figures (including Freud himself) were studied in a process that has become known as psychography. Psychoanalysts became expert court witnesses (for both sides) in criminal trials. The list seems endless. While we may accept or reject the extended applications of Freud's ideas, it is impossible to dismiss his influence or to deny his impact. He has earned his place in history.

Critique

Few if any theories of personality since Freud are as broadly inclusive as his Theory of Psychoanalysis. With the possible exception of Adler (Chapter 3), none have had a greater influence on other personality theorists. And certainly, no single personality theorist has exerted a greater impact on or caused greater controversy in the thinking of Western civilization. Not only does Freud's Theory of Psychoanalysis have profound implications for the mental life of the individual, but it has much to say about the progress of civilization as well. Finally, Freud's theory has passed the test of time. While others since Freud have contributed to the field of psychoanalysis, Freud's ideological framework and methodology of treatment remain essentially as he presented them nearly five decades ago. All of this, of course, does not mean that Freud was without his critics.

Developmental psychologists question both the data and the sample group of Freud's critical, psychosexual stages of early (pregenital) development. Rather than from the direct observation of children (infants to age four), Freud's data for early childhood experiences were gathered exclusively from self-reported childhood memories by *adult*, middle- and upper-class neurotic patients who lived in late nineteenth century Victorian Europe. From these data, Freud then reconstructed his adult patients' psychosexual histories. Not only is the accuracy of self-reported adult memories of childhood in question, there is also reason to question whether this particular atypical sample group should be considered representative of humans in general.

Experimental psychologists are quick to point out a number of methodological faults in Freud's research. Liebert and Spiegler (1987), for example, fault Freud for not always distinguishing between observation and inference. They point to the Oedipus complex as a prime example. It is one thing to say that "four-year-olds show behavior consistent with the Oedipus complex" (an observation), but to say that four-year-olds *experience* an Oedipus complex is "to replace the observation with the inference" (Liebert & Spiegler, 1987, p. 143). They also fault Freud for confusing correlation and cause (Liebert & Spiegler, 1987). To report that children during the first year of life engage in many behaviors involving the mouth, and that they also are dependent on others for their survival, means only that oral behavior and dependency are *correlated*. This correlation, however, does not prove that dependency is *caused* by fixation. Yet Freud does just that. Liebert and Spiegler's criticism could be leveled at each of Freud's pregenital stages of development and the resultant character types. While there are correlations, cause has not been demonstrated. Indeed, there is always the possibility that a third, unknown variable caused both orality and dependency.

As with the other psychoanalytic theories, Freud's Theory of Psychoanalysis is assembled on numerous vague concepts cloaked in a picturesque language that would require operational redefinition for empirical research. Freud's concept of unconscious is but one of many examples—"referring to mental processes of which the subject is unaware" (Rycroft, 1968, p. 172).

Many personologists (Adler, Chapter 3; Skinner, Chapter 13, for example) are critical of Freud's unwavering and total commitment to an evolutionary-biological position. They believe it is a serious error on Freud's part to ignore completely social and situational influences on human behavior.

Beginning with Adler (Chapter 3) and Horney (Chapter 7), and continuing today (Freeman & Strean, 1981; Masson, 1984; Travis, 1984; Gay, 1989) Freud has been accused of formulating a theory of human personality that is blatantly sex biased and offensive to women. Examining Freud's unresolved and ambivalent relationship with his mother, Gay (1989) reports that in the early 1920s, Freud's general view of woman was that the little girl is a failed boy and the mature woman a castrated man. Modern feminists, when they recover from their anger and frustration over Freud's patriarchal theory, find his concept of penis envy ludicrous.

Other criticisms directed at psychoanalysis include: overemphasis on sexual and aggressive instincts, too great a focus on insight and too little concern for life-change strategies, the inherent potential for observational and interpretational bias, and the closed, even cultish, position of the psychoanalytic institutes and professional organizations. The length and cost of treatment are also points of criticism, for they are considerations that limit psychoanalysis to the affluent. Critics also point out that psychoanalysis is not conducive to groups or useful in crisis situations.

Annotated Bibliography

For students who wish to add Freud to their personal libraries and who cannot afford to purchase the twenty-four-volume Standard Edition, Peter Gay's recent book, *The Freud Reader* (1989), offers an overview of Freud's writing that covers more than forty years and includes papers, case histories, psychoanalytic techniques, dream interpretations, human sexuality, anxiety, mental structure, essays in biography, cultural criticism, society, and letters.

C. Brenner's *An Elementary Textbook of Psychoanalysis* (1955) and C. S. Hall's *A Primer of Freudian Psychology* (1954) are two excellent, concise volumes that offer the new student of psychoanalysis condensations of Freud's theory. Again, both of these books are available in paperback and relatively inexpensive. The first is published by Doubleday and the latter by The New American Library.

W. W. Norton, the publisher of *The Standard Edition,* has also published many of Freud's works in paperback. This writer recommends *as a minimum* Freud's first and last major works:

Freud considered his first major work, *The Interpretation of Dreams* (1965, originally published 1900), his most significant book. Certainly, with this volume Freud marked the beginning of psychoanalysis. Dreams, for Freud, were "the royal road to the unconscious."

The Ego and the Id (1960) is Freud's final major work and is recommended highly to students interested in Freud's mature theory. Because the evolution in Freud's writings can cause confusion, many professors of personality courses suggest to their students that they *begin* their reading of Freud with this small volume.

Many new students of psychoanalysis find Freud's case histories fascinating to read, particularly "The Wolf Man" and "The Rat Man." Both these studies can be found in the *Standard Edition*.

Two recent and scholarly secondary sources on Freud and the Theory of Psychoanalysis are: P. Gay's *Freud: A Life for Our Time* (1988), W. W. Norton, and F. Sulloway's *Freud, Biologist of the Mind* (1983), Basic Books. A most highly regarded and often quoted secondary source on Freud is H. F. Ellenberger's *The Discovery of the Unconscious* (1970), Basic Books.

References and Suggested Readings

Bandura, A. (1986). *Social foundations of thought and action: A social cognitive theory*. Englewood Cliffs, NJ: Prentice–Hall.

Blacha, M. D. (1981). The inventory of defenses: A new instrument for the measurement of psychoanalytic defense mechanisms. *Dissertation Abstracts International, 42*(07).

Brenner, C. (1955). *An elementary textbook of psychoanalysis*. New York: Doubleday.

Eidelberg, L. (Ed.). (1968). *Encyclopedia of psychoanalysis*. New York: The Free Press.

Ellenberger, H. F. (1970). *The discovery of the unconscious*. New York: Basic Books.

Ewin, R. B. (1988). *An introduction to theories of personality* (3rd ed.). Hillsdale, NJ: Lawrence Erlbaum Associates.

Fisher, S., & Greenberg, R. P. (1977). *The scientific credibility of Freud's theories and therapy*. New York: Basic Books.

Freeman, L., & Strean, H. S. (1981). *Freud and women*. New York: Ungar.

Freud, S. (1949). *An outline of psychoanalysis*. (J. Starchy, Trans.). New York: W. W. Norton. (Originally published 1938)

Freud, S. (1952). *An autobiographical study*. (J. Starchy, Trans.). New York: W. W. Norton. (Originally published 1925)

Freud, S. (1954). *The origins of psychoanalysis, letters to Wilhelm Fliess, drafts and notes: 1887–1902*. (M. Bonaparte, A. Freud, & E. Kris, Eds. E. Musbacher & J. Starchy, Trans.). New York: Basic Books.

Freud, S. (1960a). *Psychopathology of everyday life*. (A. A. Brill, Trans.). New York: The American Library. (Originally published 1901)

Freud, S. (1960b). *The ego and the id*. (J. Riviere, Trans., & J. Starchy, Ed.). New York: W. W. Norton. (Originally published 1923)

Freud, S. (1961a). *Beyond the pleasure principle*. (J. Starchy, Trans. & Ed.). New York: W. W. Norton. (Originally published 1920)

Freud, S. (1961b). *The future of an illusion*. (J. Starchy, Trans. & Ed.). New York: Anchor Books. (Originally published 1927)

Freud, S. (1961c). *Civilization and its discontents.* (J. Starchy, Trans. & Ed.). New York: W. W. Norton. (Originally published 1930)

Freud, S. (1963). *The sexual enlightenment of children.* New York: Collier Books.

Freud, S. (1965). *The interpretation of dreams.* (J. Starchy, Trans. & Ed.). New York: Avon Books. (Originally published 1900)

Freud, S. (1966). *On the history of the psycho-analytic movement.* (J. Riviere, Trans., & J. Starchy, Ed.). New York: W. W. Norton. (Originally published 1914)

Freud, S. (1977). *Five lectures on psychoanalysis.* (J. Starchy, Trans. & Ed.). New York: W. W. Norton. (Originally published 1910)

Gay, P. (1988). *Freud: A life for our time.* New York: W. W. Norton.

Gay, P. (Ed.). (1989). *The Freud reader.* New York: W. W. Norton.

Hall, C. (1954). *A primer of Freudian psychology.* New York: The American Library.

Holt, R. R. (1989). *Freud reappraised: A fresh look at psychoanalytic theory.* New York: Guilford Press.

Horney, K. (1939). *New ways in psychoanalysis.* New York: W. W. Norton.

Jones, E. (1953–1957). *The life and work of Sigmund Freud.* (Vols. 1–3). New York: Basic Books.

Kline, P. (1972). *Fact and fantasy in Freudian theory.* London: Methuen.

Koller, P. S. (1982). Depression as an ego defense mechanism. *Dissertation Abstracts International, 43*(07), DA8229843.

Liebert, R. M., & Spiegler, M. D. (1987). *Personality, strategies and issues* (5th ed.). Chicago: Dorsey.

Marshall, J. B. (1983). Psychometric and validational studies of an objective test of Freudian defense mechanisms. *Dissertation Abstracts International, 44*(07), DA8326234.

Masson, J. (February, 1984). Freud and the seduction theory. *The Atlantic, 253*(2), 33–60.

Narov, D. (1983). The relationship of gender self-esteem and cognitive style to ego defense mechanism. *Dissertation Abstracts International, 44*(8), DA8327270.

Perls, F. (1969). *Ego, hunger and aggression, the beginning of gestalt therapy.* New York: Vantage Press. (Originally published 1947)

Perls, F. (1972). *In and out of the garbage pail.* New York: Bantam Books. (Originally published 1967)

Rickman, J. (Ed.). *A general selection from the works of Sigmund Freud.* New York: Doubleday Anchor Books.

Rychlak, J. E. (1981). *Personality and psychotherapy* (2nd ed.). Boston: Houghton Mifflin.

Rycroft, C. (1968). *A critical dictionary of psychoanalysis.* New York: Basic Books.

Seegert, C. R. (1984). Group stress management treatment and the relationships between anxiety, coping styles, and ego defense mechanisms in a military setting. *Dissertation Abstracts International, 45*(05), DA8416146.

Shevrin, H., & Dickman, S. (1980). The psychological unconscious: A necessary assumption for all psychological theory? *American Psychologist, 35*, 421–434.

Sulloway, F. (1983). *Freud, biologist of the mind.* New York: Basic Books.

Travis, C. (March, 1984). The hundred year cover-up: How Freud betrayed women. *Ms,* 78–80.

Tribich, D., & Messer, S. (1974). Psychoanalytic character type and status of authority as determiners of suggestibility. *Journal of Consulting and Clinical Psychology, 42*, 842–848.

Vinacke, W. E. (1984). Healthy personality: Toward a unified theory. *Genetic Psychology Monographs, 109*, 279–329.

Wallace, W. A. (1986). *Theories of counseling and psychotherapy: A basic issues approach.* Boston: Allyn and Bacon.

Chapter **3**

Adler's Theory of Individual Psychology

Chapter Overview

Introduction

Biographical Sketch of the Theorist

Adler's Resolutions of the Eleven Basic Issues
  Heredity versus Social Determinants
  Number and Weight Assigned to Motivational Concepts
  Early versus Continuous Development
  Role Assigned to Group Determinants
  Subjective versus Objective Reality
  Conscious versus Unconscious Determinants
  Uniqueness versus Universality
  Explanation of Learning Process
  Determinism versus Freedom to Choose
  Role Assigned to Self-Concept
  Centrality of Reinforcement

Psychological Health and Psychopathology
  Psychological Health
  Psychopathology

Heuristic Influence
  Consensual Validation
  Empirical Validation

Applications to Psychotherapy
  Therapeutic Goals
  Therapeutic Relationship
  Initial Procedures and Strategies
  Course of Psychotherapy
  Additional Methods and Techniques

Extended Applications

Critique

Annotated Bibliography

References and Suggested Readings

Introduction

Alfred Adler (1870–1937) first presented his theory of Individual Psychology in 1912. Because he was an early colleague of Freud (Chapter 2) and a leader of the emergent psychoanalytic movement, many mistakenly assumed that Adler's theoretical formulations were only minor modifications of those offered by Freud. Thus, much of his work was ignored. Others blamed Adler for the dissension in the Vienna Psychoanalytic Society and joined Freud in attacking both Adler and his ideas.

Adler responded to the ridicule of his critics by expanding his ideas about human nature into a personality theory and a psychotherapeutic system that were in marked contrast to the prevailing views of psychoanalysis. Indeed, as Individual Psychology evolved into a mature theory of personality, points of theoretical difference between Adler and Freud continued to increase, in both number and intensity.

While Freud's theory was biologically based, Adler based his theory on the "law of social interest." Freud looked to the individual's unconscious and to past experiences for causal linkages. Adler believed *all* human behavior to be characterized by subjectively determined directions and purposes and looked to the individual's present and conscious perceptions of the future. Freud's theory was analytical and reductionist. Adler viewed the individual as an indivisible, unified whole. Freud's personality was intolerant of tension and stress, hence, motivated by a need for homeostasis. Adler conceived a personality that actively sought experiences which were perceived as goal enhancing or, when such experiences were not perceived, created them. Freud viewed both human personality and society as antagonists; Adler believed humans were inherently social beings and found compatibility between social and individual development.

Over the years, Adler's ideas and theoretical concepts were assimilated into numerous other personality theories and psychotherapies, as well as into parental and educational practices, with surprisingly little mention of their origin. During much of this time, Adler's influence on other theorists was minimized and undervalued. The scholarly works of such writers as Ansbacher and Ansbacher (1956/1964), Ellenberger (1970), and Mozak and Dreikurs (1973) have reversed the tendency to treat Adler's original theoretical conceptions as public domain. Mozak and Dreikurs (1973) cite acknowledgments of Adler's work by many of today's theorists, including the Existentialists Rollo May and Victor Frankl (Chapters 11 and 12); the Rational-Emotive theorist Albert Ellis (Chapter 15); the Humanist Abraham Maslow (Chapter 10); and the founder of Transactional Analysis, Eric Berne (1961). Adler's theoretical concepts also appear in a number of the social theories, such as those of Karen Horney (Chapter 7) and Eric Fromm (Chapter 6). Many of Adler's ideas reemerge in William Glasser's Reality Therapy (1965, 1981), and there are certainly similarities in the ideas expressed by Adler and the theories of Carl Rogers (Chapter 9), Fritz Perls (1971), and Julian Rotter (1981).

In addition to contributing to current personality and counseling theories, Adler increased awareness of parenting and educational practices that facilitate the healthy growth of children. Further, he heightened awareness of the need for social justice and institutional change. His insights into and concern for the plight of women in a biased society preceded the feminist movement in the United States by nearly five decades. Adler was one of the first to defend in front of large audiences made up of physicians, teachers, and parents, the practice of group and family consultation. Certainly many of Adler's ideas were in advance of their time.

Individual Psychology stresses consciousness, cognition, encouragement, social feeling, responsibility, freedom of choice, and action. Adlerian therapy is an endeavor in which counselor and client cooperatively work as equals through an educative or reeducative process. It is not only for the discouraged (those individuals who have lost courage), but also for normal people experiencing normal problems with life tasks. There are individuals today who elect Individual Psychotherapy to improve their understanding of themselves and to actualize themselves.

Biographical Sketch of the Theorist

It is not unusual to discover that many of the ideas and concepts that make up a theory of personality can be unveiled in the theorist's biography. However, the significantly high number of theoretical concepts that can be traced directly to Adler's perceptions of early childhood experiences is surprising.

In addition to the autobiographical material appearing throughout Ansbacher and Ansbacher's (1964) edited work, much of the biographical data for this chapter were found in Orgler (1963), a psychoanalyst and early follower of Adler; Bottome (1957), a novelist and friend of Adler; and Ellenberger (1970), a psychiatrist and historian. In this writer's view, Ellenberger's account is the most neutral and scholarly of the three secondary sources.

Early Years

Alfred Adler, born February 7, 1890, was the second son and third child of six children in a middle-class Hungarian-Jewish family living in Penzig, Austria, a suburb of Vienna. His close relationship with his mother abated drastically with the arrival of a third child, and the sickly and pampered Adler, feeling dethroned, turned to his father for encouragement and support (see "Impact of Ordinal Positions in the Family Constellation," this chapter).

As a child, Adler experienced a strong sense of inferiority. Not only did a deficiency of vitamin D lead to rickets, which made him feel ugly and awkward, but his older brother, Sigmund, whom he viewed as a rival, was both stronger and more athletic. At the age of three, Adler suffered from spasms of the glottis (vocal chords and the opening between them) that placed him in danger of suffocation when he cried. That same year, he witnessed the death of his younger brother, Rudolf, in the bed adjacent to his. When five years old, Adler developed pneumonia and overheard his physician tell his father: "Your boy is lost." It is little wonder that Adler's earliest memories were of jealousy and illness. Nor is it surprising that his early years marked the beginning awareness of an intense sense of inferiority whenever confronted with death, a feeling that was to remain with Adler throughout life.

As Adler grew older, his health improved, and because sun, fresh air, and exercise had been ordered as treatment for rickets, he spent a great deal of time outdoors playing with neighborhood children. To compensate for his physical disabilities, he intentionally cultivated the qualities of leadership and formed friendships with a large number of playmates. His social skills and the pleasure he felt in being in the company of others became an essential part of his lifestyle.

Education

Adler loved music and had, by the age of four, memorized many operettas. Attending the opera with his family was one of the few pleasant memories he could recall of his elementary school years. At the secondary level, Adler performed so poorly in mathematics that he failed and his teacher recommended that his father remove his son from school and have him become an apprentice to a shoemaker. Determined to overcome his deficiency in mathematics, Adler studied diligently at home until he not only managed to repeat the subject successfully but also become one of the best students of mathematics in his class.

After passing his examinations, Adler began the study of medicine at the University of Vienna. He was graduated in 1895. In 1897, Adler married Raissa Epsteina, a Russian student and ardent socialist who had come to Vienna to study at the university. Adler entered private practice as an ophthalmologist in 1898, and later became a general practitioner. As diabetes took the lives of his younger patients, the fear of death and the sense of utter helplessness became more than he could tolerate, and he turned to neurology.

Convinced of the need to understand the total personality of his patients, Adler worked to gain knowledge of their psychic and physical processes and the influence of social situations. His practice flourished, and he established an excellent reputation as a highly skilled diagnostician and therapist.

Emergence of Individual Psychology

In 1902, at Freud's invitation, Adler, then a young practicing physician, joined Freud's Wednesday night discussion group that was to become the matrix of the Vienna Psychoanalytic Society. Often referred to by Freud as *der Adler*, German for "The Eagle," Adler soon became a valued member of the circle and, in 1910, was named Freud's successor as president of the Vienna Psychoanalytic Society. Along with Freud and Wilhelm Stekel, the vice president, he edited the Society's journal, *Zentralblatt für Psychoanalyse.*

Adler began his theoretical formulation in 1908, with the concept of **organ inferiority** (under stress the weakest organ of the body is the first to react). In 1910, he introduced the concept of **masculine protest** (the need to be a "real" man), establishing a distinct shift from biological drives to subjective feelings as the primary motivating force. It was immediately obvious that the differences between Adler and Freud were acute. So they could discuss these differences at length, the Society asked Adler, then president, for a comprehensive presentation of his theories. Adler complied and read three position papers under the title, "Critique of Freud's Sexual Theory of Psychic Life." A heated discussion continued for three meetings following his presentations. When the Society determined that Adler's position was in direct opposition to Freud's, Adler voluntarily resigned from the presidency and the editorial board and, along with nine of the thirty-five members, withdrew to form the Society for Free Psychoanalytic Research. The following year Adler and his followers renamed this affiliation the Society of Individual Psychology, and, in 1914, Adler founded the Society's journal, *Zeitschrift für Individual Psychologie.*

As mentioned earlier, the momentum generated by Adler for his theory was slowed significantly during World War I, when Adler served as a physician in the Austrian army near the Russian front at Cracow and Brunn. After the war, Adler worked for school reform and established the first group of child guidance clinics in the Viennese school system. He also worked to reestablish his theory of Individual Psychology and managed to make great gains in adherents until the rise of Hitler and World War II.

Beginning in 1925, Adler visited the United States regularly. He lectured at Columbia University in 1927. In 1932, he was appointed to the first chair of medical psychology in the United States at the Long Island College of Medicine. In 1935, Adler fled Europe and settled in the United States. He continued his private practice, and his clinics became very popular. On May 28, 1937, Adler died at the age of 67 years of a heart attack while on a lecture tour in Aberdeen, Scotland. He was survived by his wife, son, and two daughters. His daughter, Alexandria, and son, Kurt, were practicing Adlerian psychiatrists in New York City.

Accomplishment and Awards

Beginning with his first paper, "The Physician as Educator," published in 1904, Adler published some ten books and 300 articles and founded a professional journal. A renowned speaker, Adler received frequent invitations to lecture throughout Europe and the United States.

In 1923, Adler delivered a paper to the International Congress of Psychology, and the president of the Oxford University Psychological Society later invited him to lecture before that distinguished body in 1926 and again in 1936. In 1932, the Long Island College of Medicine created the chair of medicinal psychology especially for Adler. The Psychogogic Society in Geneva and the Psychological Society in Leningrad awarded Adler honorary memberships. The Institute for Scientific Treatment of Delinquency in London elected Adler vice president. Wittenberg College of Springfield, Ohio, awarded Adler the title Doctor Honoric Causa. In recognition of his scientific achievements, Vienna bestowed on Adler the highest honor that can be accorded one of its sons, the Freedom of the City.

Perhaps the greatest recognition of Adler's theory is the fact that, years after his death, Individual Psychology is still the theory of choice for many counselors, psychotherapists, and educators. The International Association of Individual Psychology meets every three years. The American Society of Adlerian Psychology meets annually, publishes the *Journal of Individual Psychology,* and reports a growing membership. Adlerian training institutes offering certification programs in Individual Psychotherapy are located in New York, Chicago, Minneapolis, Berkeley, and Toronto. Special courses, workshops, and programs are offered at many universities and colleges in the United States.

Adler's Resolutions of the Eleven Basic Issues

In the attempt to uncover Adler's resolutions of the eleven basic issues, three major difficulties were encountered. The first, and initially most obvious, was the lack of systematization in Adler's writings. Because of this, it was often necessary to search through numerous sources for his response to an issue. The second and greatest difficulty experienced was the major modifications in Adler's resolutions from his early to later writings. When viewed from a basic issues framework, Adler's resolutions underwent considerable evolution during the three decades that he developed his theory. Therefore, Adler's resolutions of the eleven basic issues are those that appear in his final theory.

Although Adler's earlier works are not ignored, they are discussed only when they are considered necessary to a fuller understanding of a particular resolution. Fortunately, Heinz and Rowena Ansbacher (1964) not only have organized Adler's writings but also have explained the major changes in his thinking over the years. Many books and articles were reviewed in preparation for writing this chapter, but their book proved most helpful.

Finally, separating and weighing Adler's resolutions of the eleven basic issues so they could be presented in hierarchical order proved especially difficult. Adler used only a few global constructs to explain all human behavior in all its complexity. Although this might be considered a testimony to the parsimony and holism of Adler's theory, it does make repetition in this presentation impossible to avoid.

Heredity versus Social Determinants

According to Adler, we have evolved as a species to the point where we have subdued most of the basic animal instincts. Drives and urges, once instinctual and characterized by fixed or predetermined directives and objectives, have been supplanted by or subordinated to innate possibilities or predispositions. Although inevitable and ubiquitous, innate predispositions need not always be followed and in some instances may require conscious development.

For Adler, we are victims of neither our biology nor our past environments. Adler introduced the concept of the **creative self** (a subjective power to transform objective facts into personally meaningful events (see "Subjective versus Objective Reality," this chapter). In doing so, he granted us autonomy with our environments. We inherit cerebral potential that permits us to hope, dream, aspire, plan, form attitudes, draw conclusions, and set goals—that is, to be creative and self-directing. We analyze and interpret life's events. All our behavior, according to Adler, is purposive. In short, while Adler did not deny the principle of causality or the impact of heredity and environment, he was convinced that our values and goals exert far greater influence.

Number and Weight Assigned to Motivational Concepts

Underlying nearly every personality theory that attempts to substantiate the uniqueness and self-consistency of individual personalities is an innate, paramount, dynamic motivating force that drives or at least predisposes movement in a particular direction. Adler's Individual Psychology is no exception. However, as Adler developed his theory, originally to explain the behavior he observed in his patients and later to account for the motivation of the normal or healthy personality, his motivational concepts underwent a number of transitions.

In 1907, Adler hypothesized that we are likely to compensate for a weak or damaged organ by centering our attention on the area of that organ's functioning. At this early stage of his theorizing, Adler proposed an inherent, superordinate aggression drive that directed the drive constellation. He then asserted that we strive to be aggressive, to dominate others, and to control the world. He believed then that we were hedonistic and concerned with our self-esteem and self-aggrandizement.

In 1912, Adler referred to the innate striving process as the masculine protest. Aggression, domination, and power still played major roles in human striving, but the masculine protest was a pure psychological drive. Adler then moved from a drive psychology to a socially oriented subjective psychology of attitudes as the governing force of healthy behavior. That same year, Adler posited the **fictional goal** (the ideal of perfection and completion), and striving toward that goal became the motivating force of all humans. The difference between normal or healthy striving and abnormal or unhealthy striving is, according to Adler, the individual's degree of **social interest** (a developed, innate interest and concern for all humanity). For Adler, pathology begins where social interest ends.

It is important to note that Adler never relinquished or contradicted his earlier concepts of motivation (the aggression drive and the masculine protest). Rather, he subordinated his earlier motivational concepts to a newer and higher principle of striving for perfection and completion, which he reserved for the healthy personality. In a sense, Adler was the first to suggest a **hierarchical conceptualization of motivation.** Unlike Maslow's hierarchy (Chapter 10) in which we strive *to become* by actualizing our innate potentials, Adler's hierarchy is based on feelings of inferiority that we strive *to overcome* by compensating for either real or imagined weakness. Adler believed that rather than striving to express inherited potentials, we strive toward unique, ideal, fictional goals created during our earliest years of life. He chose the term **perfection** as the ultimate goal of human striving because he believed it to be the most abstract and general ideal or fiction characteristic of this unique striving tendency. Perfection is never fully achieved, because as soon as we attain one goal the next goal beckons. Whatever our present position, it is always inferior to what might be reached with greater striving.

Human motivation, in Adler's (1973) final theory, is tied unalterably to an innate, never-ending striving for perfection and completion. For Adler (1965, 1969, 1973), to be human means to feel inferior. Feelings of inferiority are a natural product of human evolution and a necessary phenomenon of living. When moderate, sensed inferiorities incite our striving and strengthen our motivation to attempt difficult **life tasks** (work, friendship, and love) and purposeful self-discipline required for forward movement and growth. "They [perceived inferiorities] are the cause of all improvements in the position of mankind" (Adler, in Ansbacher & Ansbacher, 1964, p. 117). We naturally strive to overcome our perceived realities and to move forward and upward toward dimly perceived and personally construed Utopian goals—our idiosyncratic idealizations or **final fictions** of life that were formulated during early childhood (see "Early versus Continuous Development," this chapter).

When healthy, we employ perceived inferiorities to our advantage. However, when we perceive our inferiorities as impossible to overcome, we lose courage; view life tasks as impossible; and experience anxiety, helplessness, and low self-esteem. Our unhealthy striving (see "Psychopathology," this chapter) is no longer an expression of social interest, but rather expressions of self-interest, self-esteem, and self-aggrandizement. Rather than striving to complete life tasks, we strive to avoid them.

Early versus Continuous Development

In the last decade of his work, Adler presented a holistic theory of personality and psychotherapy that does not hold with any arbitrarily defined critical or divisible life stages. He firmly believed that human development, including the rapid development that occurs during the early years, is a unified, continuous process of unique, gradual, holistic emergence. Furthermore, because Adler believed that humans possess a free creative power, even the earliest experiences function only as possibilities, opportunities, and limitations. Experiences, regardless of chronology, are **telic** (expressing purpose), not causal; significant, not critical. Even as infants, we are not simply passive receptors of early family influences. In fact, Mozak and Dreikurs (1973) write that we are actively and creatively busy as infants, modifying our environment, training our siblings, and "raising" our parents (p. 46).

and
practice practice practice

Striving for completion and perfection:
Life goals develop in infancy and life styles
emerge as strategy for reaching those goals.

FIGURE 3-1   Striving for Perfection and Completion

We, then, do not just become; we actively and courageously create our own distinctive personalities. It is not the events in our lives that shape our personalities, our goals, and our striving, but rather our unique perceptions and interpretations of those events. When attempting to understand behavior, Adler advises us to seek purpose rather than cause. At the same time, he warns us to hold all answers loosely, because there is always the possibility that *everything could be different* (Adler, in Ansbacher & Ansbacher, 1964, pp. 194, 363).

Although Adler refutes the idea that early childhood experiences are critical, in the sense that they function as permanent determinants of future behavior, he certainly considers the first four or five years as extremely important. It is during our first years in the **family constellation** (the infant's perceptions of the dynamics of the family group) that we first experience the natural human phenomenon of feeling inferior, formulate ultimate life goals, and design a distinctive style of living.

Feelings of Inferiority   We are totally dependent on others for our survival when we enter this world and remain dependent long after we become aware of our helplessness. It is only natural that we become aware of strong general feelings of inferiority very early in our lives, particularly in regard to our interactions with the larger, stronger, and more competent members of our families. However, for Adler, **feelings of inferiority** are far more than an inescapable sense of inadequacy. Our sense of inferiority is the necessary, constant, and vital motivating force behind all our growth and development. All our striving, whether healthy or unhealthy, is a manifestation of our attempts to overcome or compensate for our feelings of inferiority. Adler believed that our innate sense of inferiority may well account for our survival in the evolutionary process while numerous other species, seemingly far better equipped physically, became extinct.

Constructing a Life Goal   Our early feelings of inferiority lead us to subjectively and creatively construct ultimate **life goals** (expressions of our ultimate desire for a perfect and complete life) and then act as if the achievement of that personal construction will give us our place in the world, provide us with the security we believe we lack, and guarantee us the self-esteem we believe we need. Thus, our life goals represent the final meaning of our existence and our ultimate guiding fiction. Our actions can only be understood fully when we become aware of our personally constructed Utopia, since it is the underlying purpose of all our behavior and we are perpetually responding to the necessity of moving in the direction of completion.

Unfortunately, this process takes place during our earliest years of childhood. Not only are our perceptions limited, but also our interpretations of them are often faulty. Furthermore, we construct our life goals before we have the language to symbolize them. Thus our life goals, our portentous promises of superiority and perfection, are constructed from partial truths and fictions. Because they have not been symbolized, our guiding fictions remain subjectively within us, hidden from our immediate awareness.

Developing a Style of Life Once our life goals are formulated, our thoughts, emotions, and actions are directed toward their achievement. We move toward developing unifying, unique sets of convictions, individual strategies for reaching our goals that, in turn, govern our beliefs about ourselves, others, and the world and become our personal styles of living.

According to Adler, our unique **life styles** (a synonym for personalities or selves—our whole attitude toward and movement in life) are fairly well concerted and crystallized by our fifth year, only to become more complex and fixed as we mature. Our individual perceptions about ourselves, others, and the universe combine to form a resolute "schema of apperception" through which we filter our interpretations of all future experiences. We are, then, according to Adler, truly unique beings—self-created, self-defining, self-expressive.

Cultivating Social Interest According to Adler, we are naturally predisposed to **social interest** (an inherited concern for all of humanity); however, that natural predisposition must be consciously developed if it is to flourish. We inherit only the possibility of social interest. Adler warns us that the aggressive aspects of superiority become socialized only with continuous conscious effort.

To Adlerians, the definitive characteristic of healthy lifestyles is social interest. Lifestyles that do not exhibit an interest in and concern for the welfare of others are deficient and pathogenic. Social interest remains the most important quality necessary to health. In contrast, pathogenic lifestyles are characterized by striving that is self-centered, exploitive, demanding, uncaring, and often hostile and aggressive.

Family Constellation Adler credited Freud for recognizing the influence of early childhood experiences in personality development. However, rather than attributing these influences to psychosexual developmental stages, as Freud had, Adler focused on the child's perceptions and interpretations of the dynamics of the family constellation, as the child strives to create a meaningful and significant place in it.

The infant's relationships with both parents are crucial for encouraging the development of a healthy lifestyle; however, the infant's first and, to Adler, most important social interaction is with the mother. For Adler (1974), the infant–mother relationship holds the greatest potential for the enhancement of the infant's innate possibility for social interest, the singular path to a healthy lifestyle. It is the mother who first interprets society to the child, and it is her function to develop a warm, loving relationship based on affirmation, encouragement, and cooperation. She then encourages the child to extend this attitude first to other members of the family and finally to all humankind. When mothers perform their function well, children learn early that interpersonal relationships require a reciprocity based on mutual respect, trust, and cooperation.

It is in the family that we are first taught and tested in cooperation and mastery. It is here, too, that we discover personal strengths and weaknesses, abilities and deficiencies, courage and fears. During our early years in the family, we develop the cerebral potential that permits us to be interpreters of life; we hope, dream, aspire, plan, form attitudes and alliances, draw conclusions, and set goals. It is in the family constellation that we learn to direct the impact of our environments on our attitudes and our lives.

Role Assigned to Group Determinants

Impact of Ordinal Positions in the Family Constellation   In addition to our early relationships with parents, interactions with other family members, and the particular feelings of inferiority experienced, we are influenced by our ordinal positions in the family. Our order of birth may present special problems and encourage the formation of complex rivalries and alliances—all grist for the milling of our unique styles of living. Five ordinal positions are emphasized in the literature: the firstborn, the secondborn, the middle child, the youngest child, and the only child (Adler, 1954, 1964; Dinkmeyer, Pew, & Dinkmeyer, Jr., 1979; Dreikurs, 1950, 1957, 1964; Sweeney, 1981).

Firstborn.   It is only natural that inexperienced parents lavish an inordinate amount of time, concern, and attention on their first child. Indeed, Adler (in Ansbacher & Ansbacher, 1964) refers to the firstborn as the "reigning monarch." With the arrival of a second child, however, the monarch is dethroned and experiences the sudden loss of his or her unique, enviable, and secure position in the family group. Parental time and attention, once exclusively his or hers, must now be shared with an intruder, and the former monarch suffers the indignity of waiting to be served. Resentment builds, inferiority feelings intensify, and the battle is on to regain the once-privileged position.

According to Adler (1965, 1973), all firstborn children experience the loss of their singular positions, but those who were excessively **pampered** (for Adler, the most serious of three major parental errors) by their parents feel most discouraged and express greatest resentment, even hatred, toward the interloper. The degree of the firstborn's discouragement is affected by numerous factors (the age when displaced or the amount of parental preparation for the new arrival, for example), but the firstborn's place in the family will never be the same, regardless of the effort to make it so. Suddenly, the only child is the elder child, and inherent in the new position is the expectation of responsibility, cooperation, and accommodation.

Adler claims that the firstborn understands best both the significance and the exercise of power. Moreover, the eldest child is most likely to become conservative in attitudes, nostalgically oriented, and inordinately interested in organization, tradition, and maintenance of the status quo. Adler also found that as adults firstborn children may become highly organized, responsible, conscientious, and excellent with order and detail; or when deficient in social interest, extremely insecure, suspicious, and hostile toward others and society.

Numerous studies (i.e., Farley, Smart, & Brittain, 1974; Herrill, 1983; Mellilo, 1983; Schacter, 1959, 1963, 1983) provide substantial empirical support for Adler's assumption that, due to the experience of being dethroned, firstborn children are motivated to achieve and are often characterized as ambitious. In a survey of the military power structure, Herrill (1972) reports that the numbers of firstborn children among Army generals and Navy Admirals "far exceed the probabilities to be found in the general population" (p. 66). In the same study, he discovered that 67 percent of the superior Navy jet pilots and 80 percent of the Air Force "achiever" pilots were also the eldest children in their families (pp. 33–38).

To illustrate further support for Adler's birth order influence, consider a recent article for *Bottom Line.* Leman (1987) found firstborns "consistently over-represented among Rhodes scholars, SAT high scorers, corporate executives, and university professors;" further, he notes that of the U.S. presidents, 53 percent were firstborns, and of the twenty-three original astronauts, twenty-one were firstborns (pp. 198–206). Leman (1987) also uncovered an overrepresentation of firstborns in those who suffer stress ailments, ulcers, colitis, migraine headaches, and asthma.

On the basis of earlier studies, Schachter (1963) concluded that firstborn children are more likely to achieve eminence. He found 50 to 65 percent of the students enrolled at many colleges in the United States were firstborns. His survey revealed as well an overrepresentation of firstborns among graduate students and professors. Schachter (1959) found that ambition in firstborns is not a corollary of independence. While it would appear that as adults many firstborn children tend to be ambitious and more likely to achieve eminence than children born later, it appears also that firstborns tend to be more dependent on and more easily influenced by others than are children who were born later, particularly when they are performing under stress (Schachter, 1959, 1964).

Investigating the effects of birth order and family size on self-actualization, Nystul (1981) found significant birth order effects for males from a three-child family. He concluded that the oldest male in such a family is in the least favorable position. After reviewing five studies with similar findings, Maddi (1980) suggests ". . . the apparent ambition of firstborn children is dependent enough to constitute a wish for approval rather than success in personal terms" (p. 526).

Secondborn. The secondborn never knows the experience of being the only child, of being the focus of full and undivided attention. Neither will the second-born be forced to suffer the shock of dethronement. The secondborn has always had to share parental time and attention, and has always had the model or threat of an older sibling. Unconcerned with the loss of power and authority—indeed, convinced "that there is no power in the world which cannot be overthrown"—many secondborn children are optimistic, competitive, and ambitious (Adler in Ansbacher & Ansbacher, 1964, p. 380). They are likely to view their older siblings as pacesetters to be overtaken and, if at all possible, surpassed (see "Biographical Sketch," this chapter).

If the older child is supportive, encouraging the secondborn's efforts to excel, growth is more likely to be in a healthy direction or, from an Adlerian viewpoint, "toward the useful side of life." Conversely, should the secondborn continually experience only strong resentment and malicious treatment by the older sibling, or should the firstborn excel in almost every area, the second child may mistakenly set irrationally high goals that ultimately lead to failure and discouragement. In such cases, the secondborn may decide that it is impossible to compete successfully, and give up. Typically, however, secondborn children strive in directions opposite to those of the firstborn. All depends on the child's interpretation of the family situation, and children of the same family perceive their situations differently.

Middle Child. As the position implies, middle children often believe that they are in an extremely unfair and difficult position, that they are under constant pressure from both above and below. They are denied many of advantages they once received as the baby of the family. This evaluation is confirmed if, as is often the case, the firstborn helps to care for and becomes an ally of the youngest child. Because middle children feel squeezed in the family constellation, they often seek to establish themselves outside the family and thrive on personal relationships.

So-called squeezed children may be defeated by their older and younger siblings or surpass them. In either case, they often develop a keen awareness of family politics and learn the skills of manipulation and negotiation. Not only will their personalities be different from their older siblings', but they will usually strive in directions opposite those of the firstborn, directions in which the firstborn shows little interest or is unable to master. This is especially likely to occur when the siblings are near in age and of the same sex.

Youngest Child. Youngest children, particularly in large families, are often overindulged by most family members. In addition to their parents, they have older siblings to entertain them and to serve their needs. Further, they usually have an older ally in the sibling group to protect them when they get into difficulty. They may become the family pet and be considered cute, a charmer, *the baby*.

On the one hand, with so many role models, youngest children may be encouraged to excel over all others to establish their place in the family. Youngest children with a competitive orientation and the assurance that there is no younger child to overtake them often develop at a surprisingly rapid pace and become high achievers at the tasks they undertake. On the other hand, youngest children who are pampered may learn to expect others to tend to their needs. They may become helpless and dependent or reliant on their charm or wiles and thus find life tasks difficult to cope with as adults.

Only Child. As with all the ordinal positions, the position of the only child has both advantages and disadvantages. Only children are the firstborn who are never dethroned. They spend most of their early years with adults. They mature early and introject adult manners, behaviors, and attitudes. They are likely to experience both surprise and disappointment when they discover they are not the center of attention or universally admired outside the family setting. Kindergarten can be a rude awakening and a difficult adjustment for the only child.

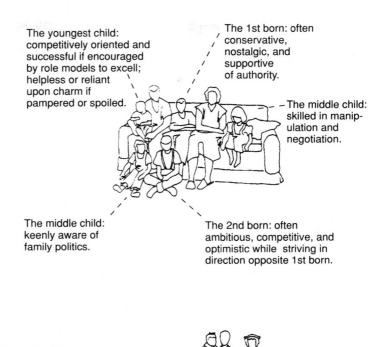

The youngest child: competitively oriented and successful if encouraged by role models to excell; helpless or reliant upon charm if pampered or spoiled.

The 1st born: often conservative, nostalgic, and supportive of authority.

The middle child: skilled in manipulation and negotiation.

The middle child: keenly aware of family politics.

The 2nd born: often ambitious, competitive, and optimistic while striving in direction opposite 1st born.

The only child: matures early, quickly introjecting adult attitudes and behaviors; generally pampered and deficient in social interest.

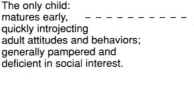

FIGURE 3-2 Family Constellation

Because only children spend more time alone than children with brothers and sisters, they may develop rich imaginations and learn to be highly creative. However, without either sibling models or rivals, only children seldom learn to share or to compete for attention and if, as adults, their efforts receive little acclaim or recognition, they may become easily discouraged. Adler found that only children were likely to be pampered children and, thus, deficient in social interest.

Influence of the Family Constellation   Although typical, the ordinal positions described above are not to be taken as explanations for the development of particular lifestyles or as the single means of understanding individuals. Birth order, alone, is meaningless. It is the child's creative and subjective interpretations of his or her place and significance in the family constellation that can influence his or her unique style of living. A myriad of factors must be considered for any dynamic understanding of the family constellation; the order of birth is but one, and, at best, exists "only as a statistical possibility" (Mozak & Dreikurs, 1973, p. 47).

While it is possible to make some inferences about an individual's personality when his or her ordinal position is known (for example, "Firstborn children are . . ." or "Secondborn children tend to . . ."), it is wise to do so knowing that the actual case may be entirely different, depending on the individual's perceptions, interpretations, feelings, and actions. The relationship between ordinal position and character traits is *not* causal.

Subjective versus Objective Reality

From an Adlerian perspective, we live in worlds privately created by our personal perceptions and interpretations, individual worlds that we can never know fully since parts were created before we mastered language. An objective reality, then, cannot exist. Rather, there are individual realities, and no two are identical. One of the early phenomenologists, Adler (in Ansbacher & Ansbacher, 1964) tells us that to understand another individual it is necessary "to see with his eyes and listen with his ears" (p. 14).

Adler believed that from the moment of birth we think, feel, and act in accordance with our subjective perceptions and interpretations of our experiences, including all inherited possibilities, bodily sensations, and environmental influences. Further, he believed that even as infants, we have unique creative power that enables us to mold and shape all situational influences and, thus, our realities. What we are does not determine our behavior but rather what we *think* we are.

No event determines our behavior, but what we think about that event influences what we feel and do in given circumstances. Moreover, as we form life goals and lifestyles, our perceptions and interpretations are shaded by our striving. We view our worlds through the prejudice of our interests and, in a very short period of time, through a relatively firm and constant **schema of apperception** (style of living). We develop expectations that tend to become self-fulfilling prophecies. Our future, after all, is only our present perceptions of what we believe to be ahead of us. Our past, likewise, is a matter of present attitudes. Our style of living, that unique, unifying set of convictions developed during our first years of life, provides the reference point from which we work, play, celebrate, and cooperate with all persons and events.

Conscious versus Unconscious Determinants

Although we may perceive the polarities of consciousness and unconsciousness and act *as if* conscious and unconscious determinants were responsible for moving us in different, even opposing, directions, Adler reminds us that this is only subjective experience. Conscious and unconscious are not separate and antagonistic entities with discrete functions and qualities. Our unconscious is only what we are unable or unwilling to formulate clearly, what we either do not understand or withhold from understanding (e.g., our life goals).

Once we form a style of life, the function of our memories, according to Adler, is to fit our perceptions, thoughts, feelings, and actions into our striving. Those that fit, we understand and remember. Those that are determined unfit, we reject and forget. The issue of consciousness is settled by our individual lifestyles. The unconscious is not some deep, guarded recess of our psyche. It is not actuality. Adler's concept of the unconscious is simply that it is a convenient term used to cover what we fail or refuse to understand. According to Adler (in Ansbacher & Ansbacher, 1964), "as soon as we understand an unconscious tendency it has already become conscious" (p. 232).

Uniqueness versus Universality

Although we share the common biological needs of our species (air, water, food, shelter, and warmth) and the same basic physiology and body structure, our innate potentials differ from those of every other person. Though we share a vast number of similar experiences, our perceptions are open to an infinite variety of interpretations. We share our distinctive and unifying source of direction and movement with no other person.

Our world views are extensions of our lifestyles. We project our unique styles of living on all we encounter. We are neither predictable nor typical. We pursue our own goals and choose our own actions.

As the name Individual Psychology clearly implies, our singular styles of living define each of us as unique, and we define our uniqueness through the individual choices we make. In all our encounters with others, we must remain conscious of individual nuances and variations because, as humans, we are each unparalleled with potentials, perceptions, attitudes, characteristics, and values.

Explanation of Learning Process

While Adler affirms the value of learning in our growth and development, particularly in the formation of our lifestyles, his explanation of *how* we learn is both general and limited. Apparently, he was more interested in *what* and *where* we learn than in any explanation of the exact learning process. He focused on the early acquisition of social interest, the necessity of the democratic process, and the desirability of permitting natural and social consequences to prove their value in the learning process. He stressed the importance of understanding, patience, praise, cheerfulness, cooperation, and optimism. In brief, since Adler was convinced that we learn only what we believe is useful to us, the primary goal of the parent, teacher, or therapist is to encourage.

As indicated earlier, we strive toward personally formulated fictions or life goals that we believe will lead us to our idea of perfection and completion, our personal concept of Utopia. We subjectively and creatively form associations, discriminations, generalizations, and definitions that fit our lifestyles. We elect to learn only from those experiences that promise us success in our striving, that assist us in overcoming or compensating for our perceived inferiorities, and that help us to gain control of our lives. Conversely, we elect not to learn from those experiences that do not offer the promise of success. In summation, we choose to learn whatever serves our purposes and the meanings we give to life, then act as if this were the only relevant and useful learning for our striving.

Adlerians (Dreikurs, 1950, 1964; Dinkmeyer, Pew, & Dinkmeyer, Jr., 1979; Sweeney, 1975, 1981) believe reality is our most effective teacher. Specifically, we learn best from the natural and social consequences of our actions. Very early in life, we learn that nature has its own recourse for those who choose either to ignore or to violate its laws. The natural consequences of our behavior can teach lasting, sometimes painful, lessons. When we consume more calories than we burn, we gain weight. In a natural consequence, the intervention of others is not required.

Social consequences of our actions prove equally effective in our education. Here too we learn in our early years that every group has expectations, rules, and regulations regarding the behavior of its members, and when our actions exceed the limits or break the rules, we risk and must accept the consequences. If the family agrees that only the clothes in the hamper are washed on washday, then the only consequence of not placing dirty clothes in the hamper is that they will not be washed until the next washday. Warnings, admonishments, and punishments are not involved; in fact, the question of power and the issue of punishment do not arise if the social consequence of an action is to be effective. The goals of learning are encouragement and cooperation, to teach the logic of social living.

Determinism versus Freedom to Choose

It should be remembered that the resolution of this issue emerged from Adler's final theory. As pointed out earlier (see "Heredity versus Social Determinants" and "Subjective versus Objective Reality," this chapter), Adler's theory underwent considerable development and elaboration over the years, especially in response to the issue of freedom. Adler moved from an absolute causality, or hard determinism, to a limited freedom to choose, or soft determinism, when he expanded his theory of personality to include the normal or healthy personality. In his mature theory, Adler subordinated causal determinants of behavior to a **creative self** (that "free creative power" that resides in each of us and enables us to choose the opinions and attitudes we hold toward our heredity and environments and thus to transcend nearly any situation or circumstance).

We apply our creative freedom by choosing to accept those experiences that fit our schema of apperception. We view what we experience through the unique doorways of our styles of living. Because it matters to us that the perceptions we accept affirm our life goals and lifestyles, we are actively and creatively determining how much and in what ways others and our environments influence us. Even as infants we develop skills and strategies to manipulate those around us to gain our own ends. We are the animated extension of our individual lifestyles.

By choosing our lifestyles, we are constructing a unique base that guides our singular law of movement. Our behavior is purposive and therefore predictable only in terms of probabilities. It is best, according to Ansbacher (in Burton, 1974) to "regard man *as if* nothing in his life were causally determined and *as if* every phenomenon could have been different" (p. 12, emphasis in original). Reality is an individual comprehension. Psychological phenomena are not simply reactions but rather individual creative responses carefully tailored to fit our styles of living. By interpreting and giving personal meaning to our experiences, we are self-determined. Our choice to act or not to act is based on the purpose and the function our action or inaction serves.

Role Assigned to Self-Concept

For Adler, the self is a unifying set of convictions or beliefs, the personality conceived as an integrated whole. Our lifestyles define us as unique individuals both to ourselves and to others. Our unique styles of living are responsible for our sense of unity and self-consistency. The self gives us our creative power, freedom to choose, and self-determinism, because not only are we each a representation of a unified self, but also we actively and creatively shape that unity. We manage this by the meaning we choose to give our encounters with others and the world.

> *All inherited possibilities and all influences of the body, all environmental influences, including educational applications, are perceived, assimilated, digested, and answered by a living, striving being, striving for a successful achievement in his view (Adler, in Ansbacher & Ansbacher, 1964, p. 178).*

The self, with its creative power, is the prime mover, the significant intervening variable in the structure of our personalities. The self keeps us from becoming the products of our biology and environments.

Adler also introduced the concept of a guiding **self-ideal** (a personal and unifying concept of our forward movement) that he used interchangeably with the fictional goal (see "Number and Weight Assigned to Motivational Concepts," this chapter). From our private construction of perfection and completion emerges a guiding self-ideal. With our self-ideal we are able to differentiate between useful and meaningful striving. We feel a sense of security and support even as we are compensating for our previously perceived inferiorities. We create and build a model or an image of the self we want to become, and we move toward making that image a reality. The fact that our idealized image of a future self is fiction makes no difference; we act as if our subjective self-ideal were objective and strive for its successful completion.

Of the three terms, *self, creative self,* and *self-ideal,* Adler's concept of the creative self is the least specific. Though it appears to be synonymous with lifestyle, it also implies a freedom of choice. Adler usually defines the creative self as our way of affecting our perceptions, cognition, emotions, and behavior; however, he does on occasion seem to endow the creative self with a mystical power similar to a quality of the healthy self-concept proposed by Rogers (Chapter 9).

Centrality of Reinforcement

Except to point to the fallacy of using an extrinsic reward system as an incentive in child training, the terms *reward* and *reinforcement* seldom appear in the literature of Individual Psychology. According to Dreikurs (1964, 1972), reward, like punishment, emphasizes superiority and power, teaches favorable behavior only under coercion, restricts the healthy development of social interest, denies the sense of intrinsic satisfaction that comes from cooperation and participation, and stifles free and creative movement or striving. Encouragement, in contrast, is strongly emphasized in the literature (Adler, 1965, 1969, 1973; Dreikurs, 1957; Dreikurs et al., 1959; Dreikurs & Soltz, 1964).

Dreikurs, et al. (1959) tell us that "the child needs encouragement as a plant needs water" (p. 23). If this statement seems strong, we need only recall that, from an Adlerian viewpoint, *all* forms of abnormal behavior are rooted in discouragement, the loss of courage that can occur when we are confronted with life tasks for which we feel unprepared. Deliberate encouragement, according to Adlerians, is the only counteractant for discouragement and, as such, is an essential element in every phase of the therapeutic process. Any genuine affirmation of our inherent abilities, our physical and mental strengths, or our positive attitudes and expectations have the intrinsic capacity to renew our self-confidence and self-esteem, hence, to motivate us to risk change and attempt novel life tasks. In brief, we regain our courage. We are encouraged by the understanding and caring of others, for these are indications of their faith in our abilities and competencies. Success of any kind encourages us: completing tasks, approaching problems as challenges rather than threats, setting and achieving goals, establishing attitudes, and developing skills that lead to mastery and independence.

Heredity		Social Determinants
Uniqueness		Universality
Determinism		Freedom of Choice
Early Development		Continuous Development
Subjective		Objective Reality
Conscious Determinants		Unconscious Determinants

Importance of Group Membership	We are social beings, born dependent on our family group. Feelings of inferiority and a need to belong facilitate formulation of a life plan and subsequently a lifestyle. Our schemas of apperception may be influenced by our ordinal positions within the family constellation. The quality of infant–mother relationship is particularly crucial to the development of our social interest.
Explanation of Learning Process	We learn only what serves our purposes, creatively and subjectively forming associations, definitions, discriminations and generalizations that fit our life styles. The natural and social consequences of our behaviors shape our learning; and the primary goal of the parent, teacher or therapist is encouragement.
Number and Weight Assigned to Motivational Concepts	Adler presents a hierarchical conceptualization of motivation based on feelings of inferiority: We strive to overcome, to compensate for weaknesses. A fictional goal represents our desire for completion and perfection, and striving for that goal represents the primary motivating force behind every action. Healthy striving reflects social interest.
Centrality of Reinforcement	Extrinsic reward inhibits free, creative, and courageous striving. Intrinsic reward, however, facilitates a healthy lifestyle. Inner satisfaction comes with the courage to risk change and attempt new tasks, the experience of success, and through cooperative participation with others. Genuine affirmation and encouragement bolster efforts to develop healthy intrinsic lifestyles.
Role Assigned to Self-Concept	Our self is our lifestyle, a unifying set of convictions, and with its creative power (freedom of choice), our self guides our striving. Our guiding self-ideal (fictional goal) represents the personal and unifying concept of our forward movement and propels us toward completion.

FIGURE 3-3   Schematic Analysis of Adler's Stance on Basic Issues

To summarize, encouragement for the Adlerian therapist is both goal and strategy and, for the therapeutic process, both means and end. Encouragement is fundamental to the development of a healthy lifestyle and primary to therapeutic intervention in a mistaken or unhealthy lifestyle.

Psychological Health and Psychopathology

Psychological Health

In Individual Psychology, the healthy personality—and indeed, all desirable human qualities—emanate from an optimal union of social interest and lifestyle choices as we strive to achieve the goal of perfection and completion. When social interest, the definitive characteristic of a healthy lifestyle, is fully developed, we experience a strong sense of communal relatedness to and a genuine concern for all of humanity. When social interest is present, we naturally want to contribute, to share, to participate, and to grow with humankind.

Social Interest and Psychological Health   For Adler, (in Ansbacher & Ansbacher, 1964), the value of an increase in social interest is almost impossible to exaggerate:

> *The mind improves, for intelligence is a communal function. The feeling of worth and value is heightened, giving courage and an optimistic view, and there is a sense of acquiescence in the common advantages and drawbacks of our lot. The individual feels at home in life and feels his existence to be worthwhile just so far as his is useful to others and is overcoming common instead of private feelings of inferiority (p. 155).*

According to Adler (in Ansbacher & Ansbacher, 1964), healthy compensation for the natural feelings of inferiority is evident in those choices and actions that result in useful contributions to the community and evolution of humankind. While motive is clearly implied in social interest, the final criterion of healthy choice and action is the *effect* or *consequence*. Adler's (in Ansbacher & Ansbacher, 1964) stance is clear: "We are not speaking here of professed motives. We are closing our ears to professions and looking at achievements" (p. 153). Further, Adler asserts, the effect of healthy choice and action reaches beyond the immediate:

> It must be viewed "under the aspect of eternity. It means striving for a form of community which must be thought of as everlasting, as it could be thought of if mankind had reached the goal of perfection" (pp. 34–35).

Healthy individuals, then, are future oriented. They possess a sense of dignity and worth that gives them both the courage and the optimism to risk failure, to be imperfect, to choose and act when the outcome of their choice and action is unknowable and unpredictable. They are active, creative, optimistic participants in an optimum social evolution of humankind.

Social Interest and Human Progress   By defining human progress as a "higher development of social interest," Adler's (1974) view of the distant future of humankind is optimistic (p. 15). With social interest "rooted in the germ cell" of the human species, human progress is inevitable, for this unique inherited human potential will, according to Adler (1974), most certainly continue to press and to grow as long as humans exist. Over the long-range scheme of things, Adler is assured of the higher development of both the individual and the species. For Adler (1974), social interest is the eventual solution to all human problems, regardless of how difficult these problems may presently appear. Taking the social interest perspective to its ultimate conclusion, Adler (1974) asserts: "In the holistic relationship between man and cosmos progress will rule until the decline of the human family" (p. 17).

Psychopathology

If, as Adler believed, social interest is the primary requisite for health, it follows that any diminution of social interest is pathogenic—life itself becomes the enemy to those who ignore the "law of social interest." According to Adler (in Ansbacher & Ansbacher, 1964), *all* forms of mental illness or social deviancy are failures to develop social interest. The difference between pathological states is not a difference in kind but rather a difference in degree.

Social Interest and Psychopathology

All failures—neurotics, psychotics, criminals, drunkards, problem children, suicides, perverts, and prostitutes—are failures because they are lacking in social interest. They approach the problems of occupation, friendship, and sex without the confidence that they can be solved by cooperation (Adler, in Ansbacher & Ansbacher, 1964, p. 156).

Without social interest, reality is intolerable and the striving of the disturbed individual reaches for an elevated and precarious image of self-esteem and self-aggrandizement that both ignores the needs of others and is beyond the disturbed individual's ability to control. Life's tasks demand cooperation and fellowship with other beings, qualities missing in those who lack social interest.

The Neurotic The etiology of neurosis, Adler (1964, 1965, 1974) asserts, can always be traced back to the early years of childhood when the child (influenced by mistaken ideas from such factors as pampering, neglect, organ inferiorities, or birth order) experiences exaggerated feelings of inferiority and selects a lifestyle that precludes the development of a healthy interest in others. Neurotic lifestyles are idiosyncratic expressions of highly creative strategies designed to cover painful feelings of inferiority and discouragement with the neurotic's mistaken or fictional belief that he or she is, in some significant way, superior to other people. The purpose of neurotic striving is the enhancement of self-esteem. Neurotic individuals call attention to what they *are* rather than to what they *do*.

Perceiving themselves as superior beings, neurotics believe they have the *right* to impose their ideas and beliefs on others, to delegate their responsibilities to others, to blame others—society, fate, or the gods—for their mistakes and shortcomings, to take everything and give nothing, to be so preoccupied with personal goals that they should not be bothered by the mundane problems of everyday living, and to be intolerant and hypersensitive.

Teichman and Foa (1972) conducted two studies (one in the United States, the other in India) to demonstrate that neurotics engage, more than normal individuals, in depreciating and accusing their parents. The neurotic subjects in both cultures did demonstrate greater depreciation and accusation tendencies; however, the target parent differed in the two cultures. In the United States it was the mothers; the fathers were the targets in India.

> *Pathogenic life-styles are characterized by striving that are self-centered, exploitive, demanding, uncaring, and often hostile and aggressive. Furthermore, in nearly every case of a pathogenic lifestyle there is a victim or, when families are involved, victims (Wallace, 1986, p. 58).*

The neurotic approach to life's demands is: "Yes, but . . ." (Adler, in Ansbacher & Ansbacher, 1964, p. 157). The "yes" is the neurotic's limited recognition of social interest; the "but" is the neurotic's rejection of the recognition and his or her excuse for maintaining and justifying an evasive lifestyle. Living a life lie is painful but highly preferable to the excruciating misery that full awareness of the deeply embedded inferiority complex would bring.

The Psychotic   As noted earlier, differences between pathologies are a matter of degree rather than of kind. Like the neurotic, the psychotic experiences feelings of inferiority, but the psychotic's feelings of inferiority are much more intense and exaggerated. Again, like the neurotic, the goal of the psychotic is superiority over others, but the psychotic's goal is far loftier, godlike, and absolute. Social interest in the neurotic is limited: The psychotic may be completely devoid of any communal feeling. While the neurotic continues to meet a few of life's tasks, the psychotic's imaginary goal becomes his or her reality. The psychotic's goal can only be achieved in fantasies, dreams, delusions, and hallucinations. While neurotics attempt to avoid the challenges of the life tasks, psychotics totally withdraw from the reality of the real world. They much prefer their imagined world, in which they have a better chance of accomplishing their individually created, fictive purposes.

Superiority is the goal of both the neurotic and the psychotic. The lifestyles of both are personally created to compensate for perceived deficits. Both the neurotic and the psychotic, Adler (1950, 1964) asserts, are striving toward the "useless side of life."

The Criminal   It should be noted before beginning this section that Adler's view of criminals, though advanced in his day, will appear stereotypical in light of present knowledge. Adler's observations and studies of faulty lifestyles led him to a greater interest than most personologists in the criminal personality. As his views of criminal lifestyles developed and became clearer, Adler's interest expanded to include other areas of criminal justice, such as the treatment and rehabilitation of imprisoned criminals, juvenile delinquency, and crime prevention. And because his findings differed significantly from those extant in the fields of psychiatry, psychology, and sociology, he felt the need to express his ideas in his writings and lectures (Adler, 1965, 1973, 1974; in Ansbacher & Ansbacher, 1964, 1973; Ogler, 1963).

Adler found the prevalent causal theories of criminality (heredity, environment, organic defects) unacceptable. Neither could he accept the explanation that the criminal was driven by an undeniable instinctual drive of aggression. Rather, Adler asserted, all criminals share a common failure during their early years—they failed to develop social interest. Tracing the criminal's life back to early childhood will uncover one of the major sources of an inferiority complex: organ inferiority, pampering, or neglect. For Adler, the most common and dangerous source of inferiority in the lives of criminals is a neglected or pampered childhood.

Unprepared when confronted with early social developmental life tasks (all of which require cooperation), children who turn to crime evade problems they do not feel capable of solving, then hide their inordinately strong feelings of inferiority behind the compensating facade of a **superiority complex** (a pathological, mistaken sense of power and security that invariably conceals an underlying inferiority complex). They strive to appear strong and heroic, but it is only an appearance, a faulty style of life filled with alibis contrived to preserve their mistaken feelings of superiority. If they cannot succeed at life tasks, they perceive themselves as victims and strive to make their marks by waging war against society and its representatives.

Reimanis (1974) tested the hypothesis that male youths convicted of a crime will recall more childhood memories that interfere with the process of development of social interest than will other youths (p. 53). The study supported his hypothesis. The youth offenders did show a higher level of **anomie** (a state in which standards of conduct and belief are weak or lacking) and remembered more experiences that would be opposed to the development of social interest than did the youths in the two comparison groups.

Adler assumed that criminals without social interest are without scruples. Any means to achieve personal superiority over others and the community is justified. They lack any consideration for the feelings of others; indeed, others' lives mean nothing. With only themselves to consider, they set out to prove that they are stronger and more intelligent than any person or system. As superior beings they are above the law and take great pride in outwitting the police. Committing crimes without being caught confirms their superiority. Further, because they assume they are far too superior ever to be caught, the threat of punishment, including capital punishment, is not a deterrent.

Arrest, conviction, and imprisonment seldom result in changing criminals' lifestyles. Indeed, all too often such deterrents only strengthen the criminals' belief that they live in a hostile world and that all others are enemies. For many criminals, punishment only adds to the challenge. Rather than examining their lifestyles for faulty thinking and mistaken social values, they retain their sense of superiority by convincing themselves that their arrest was due to some insignificant error on their part or some accidental discovery by the police. Their only concern is to correct the mistake or to avoid the accident so that their next crime will be perfect. Separated from common sense, the criminal's logic is a private, erroneous sense that interferes with social functioning and stifles healthy growth.

Heuristic Influence

Before reviewing the heuristic value of Adler's theory of personality, readers may wish to consider a caution issued by Ellenberger (1970):

> *Adlerian psychology belongs neither to the traditional academic psychology nor to experimental psychology, and it radically differs from Freudian psychoanalysis. It is unfair to Adler to evaluate his system with the yardstick of academic, experimental, or Freudian psychology (p. 608).*

Just how radically different Adler's theory is from the academic, experimental, and psychoanalytic theories of personality might best be demonstrated by Adler (1973) himself, as he addresses the impossibility of understanding an individual on the basis of object causation:

> *For all the causalities in the world would not suffice to conquer the chaos of the future nor obviate the planlessness to which we would be bound to fall a victim. All activity would persist in the stage of uncontrolled groping; the economy visible in our psychic life unattained; we should be unintegrated and in every aspect of our physiognomy, in every personal touch, similar to organisms of the rank of the amoeba (p. 3).*

For Adler (in Ansbacher & Ansbacher, 1964), the self-created goal of an individual's life marks the direction for all his or her acts and movements. All psychological processes—thinking, feeling, willing, or acting—are impossible without the perception of some goal. Adler's Individual Psychology is a psychology of use, a psychology of practical value and advantage. He sought understanding rather than explanation, purpose and goals rather than cause. "As a consequence, Adler's psychology is essentially a dynamics of interpersonal relationships. It never considers the individual an isolated and static situation, but rather sees him in the light of his actions and of the reactions of his environment" (Ellenberger, 1970, p. 610).

Consensual Validation

With Adler's death in 1937, interest in his theory declined noticeably. However, serious scholars of Individual Psychology (e.g., Ansbacher & Ansbacher, 1956/1964; Ansbacher, 1983; Dreikurs, 1950; Ellenberger, 1970; Mozak, 1973; Mozak & Dreikurs, 1973) became aware that over the years many of Adler's ideas had been assimilated into numerous current theories of personality, psychotherapy, education, teacher and parent training, social work, and criminal justice and prison reform. Moreover, they noticed that in most instances Adler had not been credited for his ideas. Concerned over the "massive rejection of person and work" this entailed, Ellenberger (1970) wrote:

> *It would not be easy to find another author from which so much has been borrowed from all sides without acknowledgment than Alfred Adler. His teaching has become, to use a French idiom, an 'open quarry'* (une carrière publique), *that is a place where anyone and all may come and draw anything without compunction (p. 645).*

Ansbacher (1965, 1983) presents a strong case for consensual validation of Individual Psychology by documenting the breadth of Adler's pioneering work and its influence on current theorists of personality and psychotherapy.

In retrospect, it is easy to see that Adler was years ahead of his time. His theory of personality and psychotherapy is social, teleological, phenomenological, holistic, and humanistic—all theoretical constructs that have been rediscovered by later theorists, in particular by the ego psychologists, the humanists or Third Force psychologists, and more recently, the social and cognitive psychologists. It would seem that Ansbacher (1983) was justified in his claim of consensual validation for Adler's theory.

Empirical Validation

Early proponents of Individual Psychology relied almost exclusively on an idiographic or case approach to their research. Not only did they appear to mistrust a nomothetic or statistical approach, they were convinced such an approach was antithetical to the concepts of Individual Psychology and, thus, would contribute little to the understanding of the individual. There was, then, neither interest nor effort to seek empirical validation of Adler's theory during its early history. A reminder seems appropriate at this point: Adler lived during the beginning of this century, when theories of human personality were in their infancy and when followers of the various theoretical schools were motivated more to establish their theoretical systems and recruit new members than they were to formalize and research them.

A sudden resurgence of interest in the Individual Psychology of Adler in the sixties and seventies was accompanied by a marked increase in published research. Various explanations are offered for this. One possible explanation for the sudden renewal of interest might be the publication of the Ansbachers' (1956/1964) book. Their work, along with the publications of Dreikurs (1950, 1957) and Ellenberger (1970), forced an awareness of Adler's many contributions to the fields of personality and psychotherapy. Maddi (1980) credits the pathbreaking study of Schachter (1959), which was followed by a "virtual flood of related studies" (p. 525). Watkins (1982) points out that the development of new instruments to measure and analyze Adlerian concepts had a significant impact on the progress of statistical and experimental research in the seventies. Whatever the reasons, Watkins (1982) reports that more research was done to test Adler's theory in the 1970s than in many of the preceding years.

Applications to Psychotherapy

Therapeutic Goals

Although it would be relatively easy to compile a lengthy list of goals for Adlerian therapists, writers and practitioners in this field (Ansbacher & Ansbacher, 1956/1964; Corey, 1982; Dinkmeyer, Pew, & Dinkmeyer, Jr., 1979) specify four major therapeutic goals for most Adlerians:

1. To establish collaborative relationships with clients, based on genuine interest, respect, acceptance, empathic understanding, equality, and encouragement.

2. To gain a comprehensive understanding of clients' lifestyles, which includes: (a) earliest memories or recollections, (b) the dynamics of their family constellations, (c) childhood disorders, (d) day and night dreams, (e) the **exogenous factor** (the tasks, occasions, or situations present at the onset of their symptoms, problems, or difficulties), and (f) the **basic mistakes** (irrational ideas) included in their styles of living.

3. To interpret or explain clients' lifestyles in a manner acceptable to clients so they will recognize, question, and alter the motivations and goals that are the purposes of their mistaken perceptions and interpretations and the resulting dysfunctional behaviors.

4. To assist and support clients as the clients consider available options or alternatives (beliefs, feelings, goals, and behaviors) and experience new or different courses of action.

As discussed in later sections of this chapter, Adlerian therapists are concerned that when these goals are accomplished satisfactorily, their clients' feelings of inferiority are decreased, discouragement is replaced with courage, perceptions and goals are positively modified, and social interest becomes increasingly evident. Psychological distress may be decreased or cease to exist; however, this is not the primary purpose of therapy. Adlerian therapists are working with their clients to change goals, concepts, and attitudes, to unmask their life plans. Purpose, *not cause,* is the primary goal of therapy.

Therapeutic Relationship

Convinced that all human behavior is purposive, all human purpose is a personal creation, and all humans strive only for what serves their purposes, Adlerians regard the therapeutic process a collaborative effort of equal and active participants and the therapeutic relationship a partnership based on respect, parity, trust, and cooperation. All therapeutic endeavors are, of necessity, mutual endeavors, including the alignment of therapeutic goals and the assessment of therapeutic progress. Without cooperation, therapy cannot occur.

Convinced, too, that clients are discouraged when they enter therapy, Adlerian therapists work to develop and maintain a supportive relationship. **Support** (a synonym in Adlerian therapy for encouragement) can be expressed in a variety of ways. Accepting clients as persons of equal worth is supportive. Accurately reflecting their clients' feelings, or, to Adlerians an even higher form of empathy, communicating a deep understanding of their client's lifestyles, is supportive. It is therapeutic for clients to learn that their lifestyles are logical in light of the goals they pursue, and the therapists' ability to understand and explain their clients' styles of living in a genuinely accepting and caring manner results in more meaningful and cooperative, hence supportive, relationships.

Accurate understanding and interpretation of their client's lifestyles are expressions of therapists' faith in their clients, their belief in their clients' creative power to choose and ability to change. Furthermore, expressions of faith by therapists encourage their clients to consider available options and, then, to risk change.

Just as the infant–mother relationship facilitates the awakening, development, and expansion of the infant's innate possibility for social interest, it is the function of Adlerian therapists to establish a therapeutic relationship that encourages their clients to develop an active concern for the well-being of others. The therapeutic relationship forms a realistic model of social interest; it is an experience in cooperation. By relating to therapists who genuinely care and who through their actions demonstrate an interest in others, clients are encouraged to form similar relationships outside therapy.

Initial Procedures and Strategies

It is important to understand that while therapeutic goals, therapeutic relationship, and procedures and strategies of therapy are presented under separate headings in this chapter, it is an artificial separation for the convenience of discussion. Therapeutic goals, relationship, procedures, and strategies are not phase specific—rather they are overlapping and continuous processes and are integrated throughout therapy. The client–therapist relationship does not end with the initial establishment of rapport, nor is it less important when framing goals or interpreting the client's lifestyle. Goal alignment is not a one-time operation occurring early in therapy, for clients often modify their goals and expectations as therapy progresses. Certainly, assessment is a continuous process, beginning with the initial contact of the therapist and client and proceeding through the investigation of the family constellation, the analysis of the earliest memories, the interpretation of dreams, disputation of mistaken ideas and attitudes, and the systematic investigation, evaluation, and interpretation of the client's lifestyle.

Adlerians are committed to the idea that the unique lifestyles of both the therapist and the client must determine the approach to therapy. Ultimately, therapeutic skills, strategies, procedures, and techniques will be integrated into the therapist's lifestyle, along with those essential qualities of genuineness and spontaneity that already exist.

Initiating Therapy   For Adlerian therapists, the importance of the initial phase of therapy cannot be overemphasized. A keen observer, Adler began the work of therapy the instant his clients entered his office and, in many cases, formed tentative hypotheses or educated guesses about his clients' lifestyles in the first few minutes of the initial interview. During the early phase of therapy, he relied primarily on unobtrusive observation, empathic listening, intuition, guessing, and patience.

Adler found his insights into the nonverbal behavior of his clients especially useful. When his clients entered the room, he concentrated on their slightest actions, including their manner of dress, posture, gait, approach, facial expressions, tone and pitch of voice, eye contact, handclasp, and the distance they maintained. He intentionally did not indicate which of the three or four chairs, purposefully arranged at various distances and angles from his own, that his clients were to take because their selections helped reveal their lifestyles.

Adler believed all clients introduce themselves according to their specific law of movement. Because behavior is purposive, each movement, each action or reaction, is indicative of the clients' lifestyles. Because everything has some degree of significance, Adlerians work diligently to develop their observation and listening skills.

Subjective and Objective Conditions   Adler learned of his clients' subjective conditions by letting them talk about the situations, symptoms, problems, feelings, thoughts, and behaviors they believed brought them to therapy. He learned about their objective conditions by inducing them to discuss their life tasks—their work and interpersonal relationships.

The Question   At the appropriate time, usually before ending the first session, Adler asked **The Question:** "What would be different if you were well?" Not only would his clients' responses indicate whether or not their symptoms or conditions had psychological (as opposed to physiological) significance, they also would reveal the *purpose* of their symptoms or conditions—the very thing that they were attempting to avoid. For example: "I would be a better husband." "I would quit this job and start a new career." "I would be successful." "I would be able to accept the promotion that was offered to me." If, however, they responded: "Nothing, I just wouldn't have this headache," referral for a thorough physical examination would seem justified.

Structuring   Without structuring, or goal alignment, a proper therapeutic relationship is impossible. Clients should leave the initial interview with a clear understanding that therapy is a collaborative effort, that they are expected to be active participants in the therapeutic process, and that although there certainly is reason to hope, there is no promise of success.

Like the therapeutic relationship, structuring is not limited to the initial phase of therapy but is returned to many times throughout therapy. **Resistance** in Adlerian therapy is a sign of incongruence in the goals of the therapist and those of the client and signals a need for further structuring.

Discouraged when entering therapy, clients are prone to place the therapist in a position of leadership or authority. Clients' displacement attempts must be consistently thwarted. The therapeutic alliance formed in Adlerian therapy is one of equality. Clients are encouraged to recognize their strengths because this recognition marks the beginning of success.

Course of Psychotherapy

Very early in the course of therapy, usually after rapport is established, Adlerian therapists begin to work toward a comprehensive understanding of their clients' unique styles of living by assessing their clients' family constellations and earliest memories. In recent years, both the formulation and the assessment processes for these two important areas have been standardized. Many Adlerian therapists today employ *The Family Constellation Questionnaire* to gather pertinent information about their clients' perceptions of early family experiences (Sweeney, 1981) and follow formalized interview and assessment procedures for the interpretation of earliest memories (Dinkmeyer, Pew, & Dinkmeyer, Jr., 1979).

The Family Constellation Questionnaire Adlerian therapists, especially those with limited experience, should find this questionnaire helpful when investigating the lifestyles of their clients. Both experienced and inexperienced therapists may wish to use the questionnaire as a time-saving device when exploring their clients' perceptions of relevant conditions at the time their clients were forming personal lifestyle convictions.

The initial section of the questionnaire focuses on the client's parents and includes both factual data (names, ages, vocations, etc.) and subjective data (major personality traits, favorites, ambitions for the children, siblings most similar and dissimilar, etc.). The second section of the questionnaire deals almost entirely with subjective information. For example: Who fought and argued the most? Who played together? Who among the siblings took care of whom? The emphasis of the questionnaire then shifts back to the client: Indicate outstanding or unusual traits, ambitions, accomplishments, perceptions of physical development, strengths, and weaknesses. In the final section, clients are asked to rate themselves and their siblings on twenty-four characteristics or attributes, indicating who least exemplified and who most exemplified each characteristic—that is, greatest sense of humor and least sense of humor, most intelligent and least intelligent, most responsible and least responsible, and so on.

Because an infinite variety of lifestyles does seem possible from even a single family, skilled analysis of the client's responses to *The Family Constellation Questionnaire* requires both knowledge and intuitive abilities. The Adlerian therapist acknowledges and understands fully the many factors considered influential in the development of personality, as well as the common styles of living identified by the theory. In addition, the skilled therapist can recognize and understand patterns and trends to discern their similarities and differences, to see relationships, and to uncover implications, however subtly or elusively presented, as their clients describe their perceptions of family members.

Similarities signal alliances, and differences may indicate rivalries or competition. Basic mistakes are implied in clients' perceptions and striving. Integration and summarization are important parts of the analytic task of the therapist. And since encouragement is essential in therapy, the client's strengths are a significant part of any interpretive summary.

Earliest Recollections (ERs)   Adlerians are confident that when asked to relate their earliest memories, their clients will remember only those incidents that are consistent with their present perceptions of self, others, and the world. Furthermore, Adlerians are convinced that it is unnecessary to determine the validity of their clients' earliest memories because whether actual or imagined, genuine or manufactured, their clients' selections can never run in opposition to their lifestyles. Moreover, because their clients think of their earliest memories as facts and are unaware of the meaning of their memories, they freely and openly reveal self-defeating perceptions, attitudes, and goals—their "overriding law of movement." Adlerian therapists view their clients' earliest memories as projections, consistent with the intent of their present striving and their anticipations regarding the outcomes of their striving. And while memory content is given first consideration by Adlerian therapists, consistent themes and unifying patterns offer more coherent understanding of their clients' lifestyles. The earliest memories of clients also contain hints as to the degree of social interest, optimism, and courage present in their lifestyles.

Again, as with the family constellation, the analysis and interpretation of earliest memories require the ability of therapists to elucidate implications, relationships, patterns, and consistencies and to integrate these discoveries into the clients' present circumstances.

Day and Night Dreams   While Adler (in Ansbacher & Ansbacher, 1964) credited Freud "for laying the foundation of the science of dream interpretation," he found Freud's basic assumption of unconscious "wish fulfillment" inadequate (p. 357). For Adler, an adequate dream interpretation must consider the dream's *intention*—it must express and support, in figurative, metaphorical form, the dreamer's style of life. As with all human behavior, dreaming is purposive. Adlerians believe dreams train or prepare dreamers to solve present problems or to overcome present circumstances by rehearsing them for possible future actions.

The dream mode, then, is present and future, and the dream function is to connect present problems or conflicts to future goal attainment.

Rather than as a door to the unconscious, as Freud contended, Adler (in Ansbacher & Ansbacher, 1964) saw the dream as "a bridge that connects the problem which confronts the dreamer with his goal of attainment" (p. 359). As a kind of rehearsal for an imminent life problem, the dreamer draws strength from the dream's arousing emotions and arrives at a solution that preserves and elaborates his or her lifestyle, even when the lifestyle is faulty and requires self-deception.

Recalled childhood dreams and recurrent dreams are of particular interest to the Adlerian therapist when seeking clues to the dreamer's lifestyle and **basic mistakes** (faulty and irrational beliefs and attitudes). Recent dreams can reveal current problems that test social interest and suggest possible courses of action for the future. All dreams contain hints that may be useful in an assessment of the dreamer's priorities.

While some dreams are common, Adler warned repeatedly that dreams are individual creations based on personal mythologies and that the therapist should avoid becoming too involved in uncovering universal dream symbols. To Adlerian therapists, the symbols of one client's dreams may represent something entirely different when present in the dreams of another client. Nevertheless, he did refer to a few common dream symbols such as flying (moving or striving from below to above), falling (moving or striving from above to below), being chased (an experience of inferiority or weakness in relation to others), and being unclothed in public (fear of disclosure or of being found out). Adler warned, too, that the emotional tone of the dream may be far more significant and revealing than the dream symbols involved.

Inferences from a client's reported dreams should not be accepted or explained before validating their relationship with information gathered from other sources. Interpretations of dreams are valid only when they can be documented and integrated with the client's present problems, the family constellation, and earliest recollections. Since everything could be different, caution seems the key.

Interpretation   The third phase of therapy, the insight phase, involves interpretation of the client's beliefs and purposes. Not only is interpretation a major goal of Adlerian therapy, it is also a major therapeutic method or technique that requires both skill and experience. Interpretation in Adlerian therapy is holistic and telic. It is concerned with the total movement of the client and calls attention to the direction, expectation, and consequences of that movement, enabling the client to understand both the movement and its meaning. When an interpretation is accurate, well timed, and communicated in a manner the client can understand and accept, it provides the client with insight into the purpose of a particular feeling, belief, symptom, or behavior.

To help make the interpretation palatable and avoid an authoritarian stance, the therapist usually presents it only as a possibility to be considered. "Is it possible . . . ?" "Do you think it might be . . . ?" An accurate interpretation encourages the client to view behavior from a fresh perspective. The client is free to recognize its validity, deny it outright, or offer an alternative explanation. Although presented tentatively, usually in the form of a question, the interpretative statement should be direct, clear, and specific.

The client who accepts and learns from the therapist's interpretation usually responds, if not verbally, with some **recognition reflex** (such as a quick smile, glance, or nod of the head). Adlerian therapists are alert for this signal, particularly from the shy, reluctant, or resistant client. In the early stages of therapy, it tells the therapist his or her **guesses** (a term used by Adler for early, unconfirmed interpretations) are on the right track. Client involvement is crucial during interpretation. Since every reaction to an interpretative statement has purpose, it is the function of the therapist to read the client's meaning.

Additional Methods and Techniques

Although Adler believed interpretation and encouragement were the major methods of therapy, he did mention a number of specific techniques in conjunction with interpretation and encouragement in his attempts to facilitate his clients' awareness and understanding of their mistaken perceptions, beliefs, attitudes, and dysfunctional behaviors. Some of these techniques will be described.

The Surprise Tactic   When Adler determined that a session was no longer moving and he wanted to jar the client into listening or becoming more receptive, he occasionally employed the element of surprise by doing the unexpected. He might, for example, suddenly side with or express appreciation of his client's defensive stance. When the surprise tactic is effective, the client stops to consider the reason for the therapist's sudden shift in attitude or, better still, changes roles and views the situation from a different perspective. Caution is advisable when using the surprise tactic since the client may feel ridiculed and become defensive.

Antisuggestion or Paradoxical Intention   This technique appears most effective in **function behaviors** (stuttering or facial tics, for example); however, it may also be employed successfully in other instances. In antisuggestion or paradoxical intention, therapists encourage their clients to exaggerate, practice, or perform on a schedule the symptoms or behaviors they are attempting to avoid or overcome. Constant nail biters, for example, may be instructed to stop once every two hours during the day and intentionally bite their nails, right hands in the morning and left in the afternoon. Each evening they are instructed to spend at least three minutes biting their nails in front of a mirror. Clients who complain of being unable to sleep may be instructed to stop trying; the next time they have difficulty sleeping they are to try not to sleep, to concentrate fully on remaining awake. Antisuggestion, like telling someone that he or she is not, under any circumstances, to think of an elephant in the next hour, often works in reverse. Moreover, by practicing a behavior, clients become overtly aware of the behavior and may gain some insight into the purposes it serves or the gains they derive from it. Fighting a behavior often only acts to strengthen it.

Avoiding the Client's Hidden Agenda   This technique amounts to avoiding traps set by the client so the therapist will confirm a faulty assumption or mistaken attitude. As explained earlier, clients often form opinions and attitudes and then behave in a manner that invites confirmation; indeed, they often go to great lengths to fulfill their own prophesies. Examples of hidden agendas are playing stupid to trap the therapist into being more explicit or taking the responsibility for therapy, seductive behavior from clients who believe all members of the opposite sex want them only for their bodies, and working to fail at therapy because they are convinced they are failures or because they want to convince themselves and others that they have tried everything to get well and just cannot. Not only is it important that these clients' mistaken assumptions and private logic be challenged, but also it is important that, by not becoming entrapped in their clients' snares, therapists break their clients' self-fulfilling prophesies.

Confrontation   Confrontation is closely related to interpretation. However, confrontation forces clients to face their private logic and stimulates an immediate response. While interpretation is presented in a tentative manner, confrontation is much more intense, direct, and evocative. Confrontation may be descriptive of the clients' feelings, beliefs, and behaviors, the purposes of which clients are unaware, and may be in the form of a question: "What were you telling yourself just before you became afraid?" Or it might take the form of a statement: "Although you are talking about how afraid you are, you are smiling."

Spitting in the Client's Soup   Adler borrowed this phrase from a practice he witnessed in a private school dining hall. By spitting in their neighbors' soup, boys often obtained second helpings. The intent of this therapeutic technique is similar. By revealing awareness of the hidden purpose of a symptom or behavior, therapists deprive their clients of the personal satisfaction they receive from the secondary gains their symptoms or behaviors bring them. Private arena perceptions and thoughts are brought into the public arena of therapy and are de-energized as sources of client resistance or displacement. Like the boys in the dining hall, clients may continue to eat the soup, but it will never taste the same, and they can never enjoy it as much.

Encouraging the Client to Act as If   Clients who claim they would do thus and so *if only* they had this quality or that trait are encouraged to act *as if* they possessed the quality or trait they believe they lack and to do the thing they wish to do. This technique is based on the assumption that when clients change their behavior they elicit different responses from others and learn that change is not only less risky than they thought but also rewarding. For example, the college freshman who would ask a woman for a date *if only* he had more self-confidence might be instructed to act *as if* he possessed self-confidence and for the next week to approach at least three women he liked and invite them to dinner and a movie. At the very least he would learn that he could ask a woman for a date, that it was not nearly as terrible as he thought it would be, and that he must possess at least some degree of self-confidence or he would not have accomplished the task agreed to in therapy.

Final Phase   As clients gain insight into their mistaken perceptions and beliefs, they often begin to experience dissatisfaction and discomfort with their lifestyles. At this point they usually discover that insight alone is not enough, that insight, however clear, must be translated into actions consistent with their newly formed and more rational perceptions and beliefs. Only when clients are thoroughly convinced that change is in their best interest is it possible to initiate the reorientation phase of therapy. Only when clients are committed and willing to face the risk of change is it possible to enter the final phase, the real purpose of the therapeutic process. Everything to this point has been preparation.

Dinkmeyer, Pew, and Dinkmeyer, Jr. (1979) believe that the first step in reorientation is the clear establishment of the client's goals and the determination of their realism because unrealistic goals serve only to discourage. Once clients decide on the kind of person they want to be and the kinds of relationships they want to establish, they can begin the serious investigation of alternatives that promise success in the achievement of their goals.

In the reorientation phase of therapy, therapists help their clients not only in the search for new and more appropriate meanings, purposes, and behaviors but also to understand how their beliefs and goals are related to their feelings and actions, as well as to assist their clients to determine and evaluate the possible consequences of any changes being considered.

Action is encouraged in the final phase of therapy. Clients are instructed to act as if they were already the persons they want to become and to act as if they possessed the courage to live differently. Realistic alternatives are selected and acted upon.

Successful change of behavior is, of course, the measure of therapy. However, it is possible to assess progress along the way. Earliest memories change as mistaken beliefs and attitudes change. They reflect corrections of a faulty lifestyle. Dreams are also expressions of the dreamer's lifestyle. Because dreams are forward looking and rehearsals for future action, they can be especially helpful in progress assessment. For example, short dreams with little or no action may indicate little change. Inability to recall dreams may indicate the desire to postpone action. And frightening dreams or nightmares may indicate the wish to avoid action.

Extended Applications

The application of Adler's theory in one-to-one therapy has declined somewhat over the years, but there has been a marked increase during the last two decades in the application of Adler's theory in the classroom at all educational levels, marriage and family counseling, child-rearing practices, crime prevention, and the feminist movement to bring equality of the sexes.

Critique

Any critique of Adler's personality theory would be remiss if it did not recognize Adler's many contributions. In addition to his tremendous influence on subsequent personologists, Adler was a man of many firsts. Adler's Individual Psychology was the first major deviation from the Freudian psychoanalytic movement. He was the first personologist to emphasize the importance of the social element in the life and psychological health of the individual. He was the first to view consciousness as the center of human personality. With his concept of organ inferiority, he was the first to delineate psychosomatic issues in medicine. He was the first psychiatrist to hold open public demonstrations of his therapy sessions and to hold group consultations with teachers and parents. There are some who consider Adler the first milieu therapist. Adler's child guidance clinics, which took therapists to schools to treat children as functioning members of the social milieu, may be considered a pioneer effort of today's community mental health centers.

By pointing out that children are embedded from birth in a social matrix and are thereafter involved in interpersonal relationships that provide the raw material for their striving for perfection and completion, Adler helped to foster the growth of social psychology.

Without some preparation and guidance, students of Individual Psychology may become confused as they first attempt to read Adler's published writings. Early in their reading they discover that Adler's works lack organization and systematization. With a theory of personality as complex as Adler's, such a shortcoming can discourage the new reader.

Students discover, too, that while there is consistency in the development of Adler's theory, there is also a great deal of evolution during the three decades he developed his theory. Indeed, some of Adler's conceptual changes are so drastic that his final stance appears in direct opposition to his initial position (e.g., masculine protest, striving for superiority over others, striving for completion and perfection). For the inexperienced Adlerian, an evolving idea can be perceived as a series of contradictions and can lead to misunderstanding. Ansbacher and Ansbacher (1964, 1973) found that it is "often best to start with Adler's latest writings which present his theory most comprehensively, and to fit the earlier writings into the framework provided by the later views" (p. xviii).

Many new readers are discouraged by the repetition they find in Adler's writings. Because many of Adler's publications are the numerous speeches he delivered to lay audiences in Europe and the United States, he repeatedly reviewed the basic theoretical constructs of his theory. Today, largely through the efforts of such Adlerians as Ansbacher and Ansbacher (1964, 1973), Dinkmeyer,

Pew, and Dinkmeyer, Jr. (1979), Mozak (1973, 1989), and Lundin (1989) these particular shortcomings of Adler's publications have been corrected.

As a scientific theory of personality, Adler's Individual Psychology shares many of the criticisms directed to the theories of Freud and Jung. Two major limitations of Adler's theory are:

1. Adler's theoretical constructs do not lend themselves easily to controlled experimentation.

2. Adler's terminology is global and lacks precise operational definition (i.e., creative power/creative self, fictional finalism, social interest, style of life, goal of perfection and completion).

Feist (1985) contends: "Adler's sweeping statement, that 'Everything can also be different' and his claim that present perceptions shape style of life, pose important problems to the researcher" (p. 88). How is it possible to develop a testable hypothesis when the possibility that "everything might be different" always exists?

While the numerous studies show that a person's order of birth may create experiences that can influence personality development, there are conflicting studies also. One explanation is that Adler referred to an individual's *psychological ordinal position* rather than to an individual's *actual order of birth*. Only the child can define his or her position in the family constellation, for the child's place in the family is a matter of individual perception and interpretation. The youngest child, for example, may perceive him- or herself as an only child. A second child may view his or her role in the family as similar to that perceived by most firstborn children. A middle child may not feel squeezed.

In addition to the difficulties encountered by those who would test Adler's birth order constructs, Gilliland, James, Roberts, and Bowman (1984) warn of the danger of stereotypes: "Adlerians maintain that they do not stereotype by birth order. Yet, the stereotype still exists" (p. 63).

Many of Adler's terms are not amenable to empirical definition; indeed, some of his critics have accused him of being more a religious mystic than a scientist when they attempt to "operationalize" his terminology. For example, the term "creative power" is for Adler the force possessed by all humans that transforms the facts of heredity and environment into a personality that is holistic, unified, dynamic, and subjective.

Similar problems arise for researchers when they attempt to investigate such Adlerian concepts as social interest, fictional finalism, and lifestyle. For the researchers, Adler's definitions of these terms are inherently subject to difficulties, and many become discouraged from attempting further investigative studies of his theory. Ackerknecht (1988) suggests that Adler was "so far ahead of common thinking that the respective vocabulary had not yet been invented;" she then recommends: "Adler had to be read more by meaning than by precision of expression" (p. 455).

Adler has also been criticized for an oversimplified view of the etiology of psychopathology, particularly in light of recent evidence that appears to link certain psychopathologies with such physiological variables as chemical imbalance and faulty genetic structure. Explaining all forms of psychoses as only a more severe expression of a superiority complex that is completely devoid of social interest does appear a bit simplistic.

Adler has also been accused of ignoring the parameters of situational stimuli by focusing exclusively on the subjectivity of the individual. Is it possible that *all* behavior is purposive and determined solely by the individual's perceptions and interpretations of events?

Annotated Bibliography

Students are always encouraged to read the theorists' own works. Because Individual Psychology was an evolving theory, Adler's (1974/1929) *Social Interest: A Challenge to Mankind* will acquaint the reader with Adler's final theory. This book is both easy to understand and informative; indeed, some professors recommend to their students that they begin their reading of Adler's works with this book.

Serious students of Individual Psychology will find Heinz and Rowena Ansbacher's (1964) edited and annotated volume, *The Individual Psychology of Alfred Adler*, a most valuable resource; indeed, it may prove the best single source of Adler's work. Not only did the Ansbachers organize Adler's writings (a task that Adler never seemed inclined to undertake), their selection and systematic presentation of Adler's writings, along with their commentary, are most helpful for those students seeking a full understanding of Adler's theory. In addition, the Ansbachers' comparisons of Freud's and Adler's major theoretical constructs show clearly how great is the variance between these two theorists.

Both experienced and inexperienced practitioners of Adlerian psychotherapy will find Mozak and Maniacci's (1989) "The Case of Roger," in Wedding and Corsini's *Case Studies in Psychotherapy*, interesting and helpful. This case history brings the process, methods, and techniques of Adlerian psychotherapy alive for the reader.

References and Suggested Readings

Ackerknecht, L K. (1988, December). Reconsidering some Adlerian concepts. *Individual Psychology, 44*(4), pp. 453–465.

Adler, A. (1958). *What life should mean to you.* New York: Capricorn Books. (Originally published in 1931)

Adler, A. (1965). *Understanding human nature.* (W. B. Wolfe., Trans.). Greenwich, CT: Fawcett. (Originally published in 1927)

Adler, A. (1969). *The science of living.* (H. L. Ansbacher, Ed.). New York: Anchor Books.

Adler, A. (1973). *Individual psychology.* (P. Radin, Trans.). Totowa, NJ: Littlefield Adams. (Originally published in 1914)

Adler, A. (1974). *Social interest: A challenge to mankind.* (J. Linton & R. Vaughn, Trans.). New York: Capricorn Books.

Adler, A. (1972, March). The progress of mankind. *Journal of Individual Psychology, 38*(1), pp. 3–24.

Allen, T. W. (1971). The individual psychology of Alfred Adler: An item of history and promise of a revolution. *Counseling Psychologist, 3*(1), pp. 3–24.

Altman, D. E. (1973). *The relationship between social interest dimensions of early recollections and selected counselor variables.* Unpublished doctoral dissertation, University of South Carolina.

Ansbacher, H. L. (1974). Goal-oriented individual psychology: Alfred Adler's theory. In A. Burton (Ed.), *Operational theories of personality.* New York: Brunner/Mazel, pp. 99–142.

Ansbacher, H. L. (1983). Individual psychology. In R. J. Corsini & A. J. Marsella, (Eds.). *Personality theories, research, and assessment.* Itasca, IL: F. E. Peacock, pp. 69–123.

Ansbacher, H. L., & Ansbacher, R. R. (Eds.). (1964). *The individual psychology of Alfred Adler: A systematic presentation in selections from his writings.* New York: Harper & Row. (Originally published 1956)

Ansbacher, H. L., & Ansbacher, R. R. (Eds.). (1973). *Superiority and social interest* (3rd ed.). New York: Viking Press.

Barret, D. (1981). Early recollections of anorexia nervosa patients: Reflections of life style. *Journal of Individual Psychology, 37*(1), pp. 5–14.

Barry, H., & Blane, H. T. (1977). Birth order and alcoholics. *Journal of Individual Psychology, 62,* pp. 62–79.

Berne, E. (1961). *Transactional Analysis in psychotherapy.* New York: Grove Press.

Bickhard, M. H., & Ford, B. L. (1976). Adler's concept of social interest, a critical explication. *Journal of Individual Psychology, 34,* pp. 27–49.

Boone, K. B. (1984). A reevaluation of the reliability and construct validity of holistic assessment as an Adlerian lifestyle measure. *Dissertation Abstracts International, 44*(11). DA8405230.

Bottome, P. (1957). *Alfred Adler: A portrait from life.* New York: Vanguard Press.

Buda, E. M. (1981). Adolescents' perceptions regarding their parents' use of selected Adlerian/Dreikursian childrearing principles and expression of social interest. *Dissertation Abstracts International, 42*(5). 8124406.

Burton, A. (Ed.). (1974). *Operational theories of personality.* New York: Brunner/Mazel.

Corsini, R. J., & Wedding, D. (Eds.). (1989). *Current psychotherapies* (4th ed.). Itasca, IL: F. E. Peacock.

Crandall, J. E. (1975). A scale for social interest. *Journal of Individual Psychology, 30,* pp. 187–195.

Crandall, J. E. (1981). *Theory and measurement of social interest.* New York: Columbia University Press.

Croake, J. W., & Hayden, D.J. (1975). Trait oppositeness in siblings: Test of Adlerian tenet. *Journal of Individual Psychology, 31,* pp. 175–178.

Dinkmeyer, D. C., Pew, W. L., & Dinkmeyer, D. C., Jr. (1979). *Adlerian counseling and psychotherapy.* Monterey, CA: Brooks/Cole.

Dreikurs, R. (1950). *Fundamentals of Adlerian psychology.* Chicago: Alfred Adler Institute.

Dreikurs, R. (1957). *Psychology in the classroom* (2nd ed.). New York: Harper & Row.

Dreikurs, R. (1972). *The challenge of child training: A parents' guide.* New York: Hawthorne Books.

Dreikurs, R., with Soltz, V. (1964). *Children: The challenge.* New York: Hawthorne Books.

Dreikurs, R., Grunwald, B., & Papper, F. (1971). *Maintaining sanity in the classroom: Illustrated teaching techniques.* New York: Harper & Row.

Dreikurs, R., Corsini, R., Lowe, R., & Sonstegard, M. (Eds.). (1959). *Adlerian family counseling: A manual for counseling centers.* Eugene, Oregon: University of Oregon Press.

Ellenberger, H. F. (1970). *The discovery of the unconscious.* New York: Basic Books.

Farley, F. H., Smart, D. L., & Brittain, C. Y. (1974). Birth order, rank, and branch of service in the military. *Journal of Individual Psychology, 30*(2), pp. 227–231.

Feist, J. (1985). *Theories of personality.* New York: Holt, Rinehart and Winston.

Gilchrist, L. A. (1984). Use of the revised Self-Administered Lifestyle Inventory in distinguishing between runaway and nonrunaway adolescents. *Dissertation Abstracts International, 45*(10). DA8429712.

Gilliland, B. E., James, R. K., Roberts, G. T., & Bowman, J. T. (1984). *Theories and strategies in counseling and psychotherapy.* Englewood Cliffs, NJ: Prentice–Hall.

Glasser, W. (1965). *Reality therapy: A new approach to psychiatry.* New York: Harper & Row.

Greever, K. B., Tseng, M. S., & Friedland, B. U. (1973). Development of the Social Interest Index. *Journal of Consulting Clinical Psychology, 41,* pp. 454–548.

Herman, I. (1971). *Adlerian psychology: A review of therapy and counseling methods of Rudolph Dreikurs and Manford Sonstegard.* Chicago: Alfred Adler Institute.

Herrill, J. M. (1972). Birth order and the military: A review from the Adlerian perspective. *Journal of Individual Psychology, 28,* pp. 38–44.

Horney, K. (1939). *New ways in psychoanalysis.* New York: Norton.

Jones, M. B. (1982). An empirical test of the Adlerian assumption regarding the psychodynamic unity of certain diverse descriptive categories through common central lifestyle themes and opinions of self and not-self. *Dissertation Abstracts International, 43*(6). DA8226324.

Lantz, J.E. (1981). Depression and social interest tasks. *Journal of Individual Psychology, 37*(1), pp. 113–116.

Leman, K. (1980). The truth about firstborns, lastborns and middle kids, too. *Bottom Line, 8*(3), pp. 198–206.

Lord, D. B. (1982). On the clinical use of children's early recollections. *Journal of Individual Psychology, 38*(3), pp. 198–206.

Lundin, R. W. (1989). *Alfred Adler's basic concepts and implications.* Muncie, IN: Accelerated Development.

Maddi, S. R. (1980). *Personality theories: A comparative analysis,* (4th ed.). Homewood, IL: Dorsey Press.

Manaster, G. J. & Perryman, T. B. (1974). Early recollections and occupational choice. *Journal of Individual Psychology, 30,* pp. 232–237.

Mellilo, D. (1983). Birth order, perceived birth order, and family position of academic women. *Journal of Individual Psychology, 39,* pp. 57–62.

Mozak, H. H. (Ed.). (1973). *Alfred Adler: His influence on psychology today.* Park Ridge, NJ: Noyes Press.

Mozak, H. H. (1989). Adlerian psychotherapy. In R. J. Corsini & D. Wedding, (Eds.). *Current psychotherapies* (4th ed.). Itasca, IL: F. E. Peacock.

Mozak, H. H., & Dreikurs, R. (1973). Adlerian psychotherapy. In R. Corsini, (Ed.). *Current psychotherapies.* Itasca, IL: F. E. Peacock.

Mozak, H. H., & Fletcher, S. J. (November, 1972). Purpose of delusions and hallucinations. *Journal of Individual Psychology, 29*(2), pp. 176–181.

Nystul, M. (1981). The effects of birth order and family size on self-actualization. *Journal of Individual Psychology, 37*(1), pp. 107–112.

Orgler, H. (1963). *Alfred Adler, the man and his work: Triumph over the inferiority complex.* New York: The American Library.

Perls, F. (1971). *Gestalt therapy verbatim.* New York: Bantam Books. (Originally published in 1969).

Reimanis, G. (1974). Anomie, crime, childhood memories, and development of social interest. *Journal of Individual Psychology, 30*(1), pp. 53–58.

Rotter, J. B. (1981). The psychological situation in social learning theory. In D. Magnusson, (Ed.). *Toward a psychology of situations: An interactional perspective.* Hillsdale, NJ: Erlbaum.

Rule, W. R. (1972). The relationship between early recollections and selected counselor and lifestyle characteristics. Unpublished Ph.D. dissertation, University of South Carolina.

Schachter, S. (1959). *The psychology of affiliation: Experimental studies of the sources of gregariousness.* Stanford, CA: Stanford University Press.

Schachter, S. (1963). Birth order, eminence, and higher education. *American Sociological Review, 28,* pp. 757–767.

Schachter, S. (1964). Birth order and sociometric choice. *Journal of Abnormal and Social Psychology, 68,* pp. 453–456.

Sullivan, H. S. (1953). *The interpersonal theory of psychiatry.* New York: Norton.

Sweeney, T. J. (1975). *Adlerian counseling,* (Series 8), Guidance Monograph Series. Boston: Houghton Mifflin.

Sweeney, T. J. (1981). *Adlerian counseling, proven concepts and strategies* (2nd ed.). Muncie, IN: Accelerated Development.

Teichman, M., & Foa, U. G. (1972). Depreciation and accusation tendency: Empirical support. *Journal of Individual Psychology, 28*(1), 45–50.

Vaihinger, H. (1925). *The philosophy of "as if."* New York: Harcourt, Brace, & World.

Vockell, E. L., Falker, D. W., & Miley, C. H. (1973). Birth order literature 1967–1971: Bibliography and index. *Journal of Individual Psychology, 29,* pp. 39–53.

Wallace, W. A. (1986). *Theories of counseling and psycho-therapy: A basic issues approach.* Boston: Allyn and Bacon.

Watkins, C. E., Jr. (1982). A decade of research in support of Adlerian psychological theory, 1970–1981. *Journal of Individual Psychology, 38*(1), pp. 91–97.

Watkins, C. E., Jr. (1983). Some characteristics of research on Adlerian psychological theory, 1970–1981. *Journal of Individual Psychology, 39*(1), pp. 99–110.

Watkins, C. E., Jr. (1984). An examination of the relationship between social interest and self-management effectiveness. *Dissertation Abstracts International, 45,* DA8429629.

Chapter 4

Jung's Analytic Theory of Personality

Chapter Overview

Introduction

Biographical Sketch of the Theorist
Emergence of Jung's Theory
Recognition, Awards, and Tributes

Jung's Resolution of Eleven Basic Issues
Heredity versus Social Determinants
Conscious versus Unconscious Determinants
Subjective versus Objective Reality
Early versus Continuous Development
Number and Weight Assigned to Motivational Concepts
Determinism versus Freedom of Choice
Explanation of Learning Process
Role Assigned to Self-Concept
Uniqueness versus Universality
Role Assigned to Group Determinants
Centrality of Reinforcement

Psychological Health and Psychopathology
Healthy Personality and the Good Life
Psychopathology

Heuristic Influences: Research Methods and Techniques

Applications to Psychotherapy
  Therapeutic Goals
  Therapeutic Relationship
  Initial Procedures and Strategies
  Course of Therapy

Extended Applications
  Education
  Aging and Human Development
  Criminology and Biofeedback Research
  Anthropology and Folklore Studies

Critique

Annotated Bibliography

References and Suggested Readings

Introduction

Though publicly overshadowed by the dominating presence of Freud at the time he formulated many of his theoretical constructs, Carl Gustav Jung (1875–1961) is recognized as a major personologist and an early pioneer of the psychiatric movement. Of all the personality theories, Jung's Analytic Theory is possibly the most complex, unorthodox, and controversial. His concept of the human psyche is "embedded in the past, present, and future; it consists of conscious and unconscious elements, masculine and feminine traits, rational and irrational impulses, spiritualistic and animalistic tendencies, and an innate predisposition to bring all these contradictory tendencies and impulses into harmony with each other" (Herginhahn, 1984, p. 58).

A personality theory as articulate and intricate as Jung's cannot be grasped, much less understood, through a brief introduction, nor can its significance be revealed to any but a receptive and persevering mind. Those who can approach Jung's analytical psychology with a fair degree of openness and a willingness to learn may find, as did Hall and Lindzey (1978): "The originality and audacity of Jung's thinking have few parallels in recent scientific history, and no other person aside from Freud had opened more conceptual windows into what Jung would choose to call 'the soul of man' " (p. 149).

Jung's interests were diverse. Convinced that personology was not the special right or privilege of any single discipline, he pursued knowledge and understanding of human personality across the boundaries of numerous disciplines. In addition to an in-depth self-analysis, extensive clinical experience with neurotic, borderline, and psychotic patients, and the analysis of dreams, visions, and fantasies of both normal and abnormal people, Jung's theoretical concepts of the collective unconscious and the archetypes led him to the study of philosophy, history, literature, the arts, anthropology, the religions (Eastern and Western), mythology, astrology, parapsychology, and even the symbolism of medieval alchemy. The force and influence of Jung's thinking on many of the disciplines listed above cannot be denied. Writers in these areas, including the historian Arnold Toynbee, the writers Philip Wylie and Hermann Hesse, and the author and critic Lewis Mumford, have publicly acknowledged their indebtedness to Jung (Hall & Lindzey, 1985, p. 138). Neither can it be denied that Jung's idea of the individuation process is reflected in many of the humanistic theories (e.g., the theories of Allport, Rogers, and Maslow; Chapters 8, 9, & 10), or that the idea that human development proceeds from a global to a differentiated state is present in the developmental theories (e.g., Erikson, Chapter 5). Further, Jung's focus on the middle years not only extended personality development, but also anticipated contemporary concern for the existential crisis that strikes so many during the second half of their lives (a mid-life crisis).

Biographical Sketch of the Theorist

In addition to the data that emerged during analytic sessions with his patients and a lifelong study of symbolism, Jung (1963/1961), like Freud (Chapter 2), incorporated the insights he gained from a continuous and deep self-analysis into his theoretical formulations. Understanding Jung's theory, therefore, requires a greater understanding of his life, particularly his unconscious life, than is the case with most of the theories appearing in this book. Allotting more space than usual for Jung's biographical sketch is not only justified, it is necessary.

Unlike some of the theorists presented in this book for whom biographical data are sparse, there are, in addition to Jung's autobiography, *Memories, Dreams, Reflections* (1963/1961), a number of biographical accounts, two volumes of letters (in G. Adler, 1973), and a book comprised of a series of recorded interviews (see "Annotated Bibliography"). Unfortunately, the commentaries on Jung's life are divided into two opposing camps. The first group, represented by Brome (1978), Hannah (1976), and Jaffé (1971), accept Jung's view of that stormy period of his life following his break with Freud and describe a deliberate, courageous, and creative period of exploration into the unconscious. The personality that emerges from their writings is brilliant and sensitive—the archetypal image of the Wise Old Man. By contrast, the second group, represented by Glover (1950), Munroe (1955), and Stern (1976), views the years 1913–1917 as a period marked by involuntary psychotic episodes filled with hallucinations and delusions. As extremes, both modes contribute to the mystery that envelops Jung's life, a mystery his autobiography, speaking from the inner direction that guided his life and focusing on dreams, myths, and paranormal experiences, fails to clear.

Childhood Except for a few brief, selected glimpses in *Memories, Dreams, Reflections* (1963/1961), little is known of Jung's childhood years. Unfortunately, these glimpses are the memoirs of a man in his eighties who was convinced that a child's psyche is merely a reflection of the parents' psyches. When Jung was faced with a troubled child, he looked to the child's parents, for he was convinced that when parents attended to their own problems, the child's problems were automatically solved (Jung, in Fordham, 1953, p. 124).

One of Jung's earliest recollections was the bitter sense of abandonment he experienced at the age of three, when his mother was hospitalized for several months. This traumatic experience, he believed, led to a general distrust of women (his mother in particular) that remained with him for many years, even after he realized that his mother's depression was probably due to marital difficulties.

An only child for the first nine years of his life (one older child died a few months after birth, and his sister, Johanna Gertrude, was born in 1884), Jung (1963/1961) recalls the loneliness he felt as a child. It was during this period that Jung imagined that he was really two persons: the unsure child he was, and a wise and powerful old man of authority and knowledge who had lived during the previous century. While the second personality sometimes frightened the first, Jung (1963/1961) found comfort in a private source of wisdom that was available only to him through the second personality.

Jung (1963/1961) was ten years old when he carved a small mannequin from a wooden ruler, dressed it in a black frock coat, boots, and high hat; placed it, along with a black oblong stone, in his pencil case; and secretly stashed it under one of the roof beams in the attic. He would sneak to the attic to talk with his mannequin, and occasionally he would leave secret messages written on tightly rolled scrolls. The knowledge that his mannequin was safely hidden away gave Jung a feeling of security, quelling some of the fear over possessing two personalities (Jung, 1961/1963; Monte, 1980). Recalling this incident more than seven decades later, Jung concluded that the second personality of the Wise Old Man was his first encounter with the collective unconscious (Jung, 1963/1961; Monte, 1980, & Jaffé, 1971).

The label "PK" (Preacher's Kid) can indelibly mark a child; with this label there is no escaping the **persona** (mask or image presented to the public) of the father. Both in school and the small Swiss village near Basel, Jung was never called by his name; he was always the "Parson's Carl" (Hannah, 1976, p. 27). The tradition of the ministry was rooted deeply in both parents' families—there were six parsons in his mother's family and, in addition to his father, the Reverend Dr. Paul Jung (1848–1896), two of his father's brothers were parsons.

Looking back on his childhood, Jung assumed that his father's depression and hypochondria were due to a religious crisis and strained marital relations. From the vantage point of his analytic experience years later, Jung (1963/1961) believed that his father, unable to attain his aspiration to become a university professor of classical and oriental languages, suffered a mid-life crisis because he had to settle for the ministry and harbored serious doubts about the religious beliefs of his church. When, as a child, Jung approached his father with personal doubts and questions about religion, he learned that his father was either unable or unwilling to discuss them. "You think too much!" was always his father's response (Jung, 1963/1961). For a two-year period (1892–1894), most discussions with his father on the subject of religion turned to open quarrel, adding to the stress already present in the Jung household. Brome (1978) reports: "Jung associated the word 'father' with reliability but also with powerlessness" (p. 30).

Jung's mother, Emile Preswerk Jung (1848–1923), was far more powerful and dynamic than her husband, but she was also inconsistent and problematical. A stout woman with "hearty animal warmth," she could be both nurturing and companionable; however, she could suddenly become imposing, unassailable, and for Jung as a child, unpredictable, hence unreliable. Her second personality, which Jung (1961) described as uncanny and frightening, would stun Jung into silence (p. 50). Jung (1963/1961) reports also that his mother kept a diary, noting all the premonitions, "spookish" phenomena, and strange occurrences she experienced (see also Jaffé, 1971, p. 2).

Consciously striving to include both the inner and outer experiences that influenced his life and work, it is natural that Jung (1963/1961) should choose only those facts about his parents and his childhood that fit with his purpose. It is evident, also, that in childhood, the symbolic was as real as the physical for Jung. Indeed, even as an adult, he often preferred to work with "psychological reality" (Jung, 1963/1961).

Education   The transition from a small village school to the large city gymnasium in Basel introduced Jung to a different world. For the first time, Jung realized the poverty expected of a country parson and felt some compassion for his father. His classmates were the sons of affluent parents, who lived in stately mansions, spoke refined German, and rode in fine carriages. They were accustomed to fashionable clothing, and they always seemed to have money in their pockets. Perhaps most enviable to Jung, they discussed family vacations in places that he longed to see, but knew only from reading.

Jung soon became bored with his classes in the gymnasium; they took time from reading about subjects that were of far greater interest to him. Divinity classes offered no answers for his questions on God and religion. He found mathematics confusing and gymnastics disgusting. Still, after a six-month bout with fainting spells, occurring after a minor head injury during a scuffle with another student, Jung managed to become the highest achiever in his class.

Although Jung became friends with some of his classmates, his interests varied so from theirs that he continued to feel he was an outsider. It was during this period, after personally experiencing a number of unexplainable events, that Jung became engrossed with the occult. He participated in séances and read everything he could find on parapsychology (Ewen, 1984).

As is often characteristic of the intelligent young man or woman capable of success in many fields, the choice of a profession proved difficult for Jung. He felt equally drawn to the sciences and to religion and philosophy. For a brief period, he thought he would enjoy archeology, but this was not a course of study offered at the University of Basel, the only school he could afford to attend. Shortly before he was graduated, Jung chose science and the study of medicine. He entered the University of Basel in 1895.

Jung's father died in 1896, just as Jung completed his first year at the university. As the eldest son, Jung suddenly found himself responsible for the support of his mother and sister. Were it not for sympathetic relatives, offering to care for his family and lending him enough money for tuition, Jung would not have been able to continue his education.

Jung's performance in an anatomy course netted him the appointment of junior assistant, and the following semester he was asked to teach the histology course. During his senior year Jung received a coveted invitation to specialize in internal medicine, but to the dismay of his professors and his friends, he elected instead to enter the field of psychiatry. Jung was aware that psychiatry was a new field, held in low esteem by the practitioners of the more established medical specialties. However, after reading a textbook by a German neurologist, Krafft-Ebing (1849–1902), he was convinced that psychiatry was the one area of medicine that could complement both his interests and his aspirations. Here, too, was a field that promised Jung some answers to the dreams, fantasies, and paranormal phenomena he had experienced.

Emergence of Jung's Theory

In December, 1900, under the direction of Eugen Bleuler (the Swiss psychiatrist noted for his conception of schizophrenia), Jung began his career in psychiatry as an assistant staff physician at the Burgholzli Mental Hospital. After publishing his dissertation, *On the Psychology and Pathology of So-Called Occult Phenomena* (1902), and conducting research on the technique of word association at the hospital, Jung studied theoretical psychopathology at the Salpetriere in Paris, under Piere Janet (the director of the psychological laboratory). Years later, Jung stated that during his life's studies he had "only two teachers—Bleuler and Janet" (Campbell, 1971, p. xi).

Jung first met Emma Rauschenbach (1882–1955) when she was a girl of fifteen or sixteen: "I saw her on top of a staircase and I knew: 'That is my wife' " (Jung, in Bennet, 1962, p. 153). They were married in 1903; she was twenty-one and he thirty-eight. Together they raised five children, four daughters and a son. Emma Jung, also an analyst, became a collaborator and worked closely with Jung until her death in 1955.

In 1905, recognized for his work with word association and with a flourishing private practice, Jung was promoted to senior staff physician at Burgholzli and appointed lecturer in psychiatry at the University of Zurich. Impressed with Freud's work in *The Interpretation of Dreams* (1900), Jung initiated contact by sending Freud copies of his articles and his first book, *The Psychology of Dementia Praecox* (1907), a psychoanalytic study of schizophrenia. In February, 1907, at Freud's invitation, Jung went to Vienna to meet Freud. Their first meeting is reported to have lasted thirteen continuous hours (Storr, 1973). Their relationship developed through weekly correspondence, and when both received invitations to speak at Clark University, they spent seven weeks traveling together.

At Freud's insistence, Jung became the first president of the International Psychoanalytic Society. Freud viewed Jung as his heir apparent; Jung was to carry the standard for the psychoanalytic movement. Jung, however, viewed the relationship differently. He did not see himself as an uncritical disciple, but rather as a collaborator, free to pursue his own ideas. He was certain that his book, *Symbols of Transformation* (1911), with its unique view of the unconscious, would place stress on his relationship with Freud. Storr (1973) summarizes the three years leading to Jung's break with Freud succinctly: "It was foreshadowed in 1911, overt in 1912, and final in 1913" (p. 13). With Jung's resignation from the Congress of Psycho-Analysis International in 1914, his break from psychoanalysis was complete.

While severing the relationship was difficult for both men, it was especially traumatic for Jung. In his autobiography, Jung (1963/1961) writes of this period in his life as one of "inner uncertainty" and describes it as being in a "state of disorientation" in which he could neither read nor write. He later recalled conversations with voices that he identified as his anima, a wise old man, and a number of "souls returning from the dead" (Ewin, 1984). Recognizing that he was menaced by a psychosis, Jung resigned his lectureship at the University of Zurich and, limiting all outside contacts to a few private patients and the members of his immediate family to keep a grasp on reality, he began an intensive five-year self-analysis, along with an equally intensive preoccupation with images of the unconscious.

Again, students of analytic psychology vary considerably in their views of this period in Jung's life. Ellenberger (1970) described it as a "creative illness." Stein (1985) notes the similarities in Jung's relationships with his father and with Freud. Brome (1978) and Jaffé (1971) emphasize that all major changes in Jung's life were precipitated by dreams. Whatever the explanation, Jung experienced a serious crisis.

Most sources agree that by 1919 Jung was again functioning effectively (Brome, 1978). Emerging from his self-imposed exile, Jung wrote *Psychological Types* (1921), in which he not only discussed his theoretical differences with Freud and Adler, but also presented a comprehensive taxonomy of character types that offered challenging hypotheses about individual differences derived from unconscious dynamics (see "Attitudinal Dimensions and Functions of Ego," this chapter).

Hypothesizing that primitive people lived closer to the **collective unconscious** (inherited ancestral memories) than people in modern cultures, Jung began a series of trips in 1920 to confirm his theory. His travels included stops in Algiers, Tunis, and the Sahara Desert (1920); Tabs Pueblo, New Mexico (1924); a safari to Kenya and Mount Elgon and a return from Africa by way of Egypt (1925–1926); and a journey to India (1937–1938). Jung learned much from all his travels, but the safari through Africa was an especially profound experience for him. It was in Africa that Jung found a people in the lowest levels of the collective unconscious. Jung was now convinced that insight into individual development could be acquired from knowledge of human evolution and the development of human society.

In addition to his work with people in primitive cultures, Jung became deeply involved in studies of eastern religions and mythology. A friendship with Richard Wilhelm, a recognized authority of Chinese culture, led Jung to become a student of the *I Ching*, an ancient Chinese text in which Jung discovered many insights into mandala symbolism (the mandala was Jung's archetype of the Self).

Recognition, Awards, and Tributes

A prolific writer for six decades, Jung compiled an impressive list of publications. The recently published English language edition of Jung's *Collected Works* (1953–1978) numbers twenty volumes.

Although professional recognition of Jung's contributions to psychology and psychiatry dropped significantly in 1914 (when he resigned from the office of president and withdrew his membership from the International Psychoanalytic Association), Jung became a prominent world figure. In 1930, Jung was elected vice president of the General Medical Society for Psychotherapy; three years later he held the office of president. In 1934, Jung was founder and first president of the International General Medical Society for Psychotherapy.

The city of Zurich awarded Jung the Literary Prize in 1932. Jung was awarded eight honorary doctorates, including honorary degrees from Harvard University in 1936, Oxford University in 1938, and the University of Geneva in 1945.

In 1937, Jung was invited to deliver the Terry Lecture at Yale University. His topic was "Psychology and Religion." The following year in London, he was named Honorary Fellow of the Royal Society of Medicine. In 1943, Jung was named an Honorary Member of the Swiss Academy of Sciences. And in 1944, the University of Basel established the Chair of Medical Psychology for Jung.

The first C. G. Jung Institute was founded in Zurich in 1948, an action soon followed by the founding of the International Analytical Psychology Association. Today, Jungian analytic training institutes are established in many countries, including Denmark, England, France, Germany, Israel, Italy, the Netherlands, Sweden, Switzerland, and the United States.

Final Years Jung's opening sentence in *Memories, Dreams, Reflections* (1963/1961): "My life is a story of self-realization of the unconscious," is a most succinct and accurate summary of his life. Jung died in his home in Zurich, June 6, 1961, the year his autobiography was published.

Resolutions of Eleven Basic Issues

Before examining Jung's resolutions of the eleven basic issues, we might avoid misunderstanding by looking at Jung's definition and structure of personality.

The literal meaning of Analytical Psychology, the name Jung chose for his theoretical approach, is the analytic study of the human psyche. For Jung, **psyche** is "the infinitely varied composite of *all* human nonsomatic capacities, both conscious and unconscious" (Mattoon, 1981, p. 21, italics added). In analytic psychology, the term psyche embraces the *whole* human personality—*all* human thought, feeling, and behavior, whether conscious or not.

While Jung finds it necessary to make use of conceptual components to describe the structure and dynamics of the psyche, it is not his intention to imply that the psyche is an assemblage of parts acquired through either maturation or learning. Neither is it his aim to imply that the components of the psyche are physical entities. Wholeness of the human psyche is inherent in Jung's theory; *its possibility exists at birth.*

It is important to understand also that analytic psychologists define the term *libido* differently than the classical psychoanalysts. For Jung (in de Laszlo, 1959), **libido** "is synonymous with *psychic energy*" (p. 265, italics in original). It is the *intensity* and *value* of all psychic processes, the *determining power* manifested in all psychic operations. The libido is *not* a psychic process itself; neither is it limited solely to sexual energy as Freud postulated.

Heredity versus Social Determinants

Jung's stance on the issue of heredity versus social determinants leans heavily in the direction of heredity. He, like Freud, recognizes the determining power of instinctual urges and drives that serve the purposes of survival and reproduction and the tension that can be produced by physical deficiencies. Jung's collective unconscious is part of our universal heritage also, and it is responsible for many of our words, ideas, actions, memories, prejudices, preferences, interests, fears, dreams, and fantasies. Because we share the biology and evolutionary history of our species, our similarities with other human beings far outnumber our differences.

Jung does, however, grant us limited capacity to decide our destiny, at least for the more courageous of us. If we can accept the dark aspects of ourselves as both present and real (the **Shadow**), become at least partially conscious of our feminine and masculine sides (the **Anima** and **Animus**), refuse to concentrate on the development of but a single function (thinking, feeling, sensing, intuiting), and replace our ego with the Self as the center of personality, we may realize our innate potential and find some meaning and purpose in life.

Conscious versus Unconscious Determinants

Further misunderstanding might be avoided by pointing out that Jung defines *conscious* and *unconscious* differently than most other personality theorists. For Jung (1968), only that psychic content under ego's control is **conscious;** conversely, all psychic content not under control of ego is **unconscious.** Because ego's control of psychic contents is momentary and fragmentary, most of the contents of our psyche are unconscious, hence invisible and unknowable. Indeed, the presence of psychic contents can only be revealed through symbolic manifestations in observable behaviors, and projections of emotions, and attitudes (**introversion** and **extraversion**).

For Jung (1968, 1971), the human psyche or personality is comprised of three major interacting components or levels: the *ego* (or conscious mind), the *personal unconscious* (and its *complexes*), and the *collective unconscious* (and its archetypes).

Consciousness. In analytic psychology, **ego** is the center of our consciousness, wherein the psyche emerges from an enveloping collective unconscious after making contact with the environment. Ego is comprised of conscious perceptions, active memories, current thoughts, sensations, evaluations, and feelings, hence known directly by the individual. "Nothing," according to Jung (1968), "can be conscious without an ego to which it refers" (p. 10). To keep from being overwhelmed by the deluge of psychic material that would thrust itself into consciousness and, by sheer mass, render us helpless, our ego is highly selective about what it admits to consciousness.

The Personality or Psyche =

Conscious Ego
    Perceptions
    Memories
    Thoughts
    Feelings +

Personal Unconscious and Complexes +

    Collective Unconscious and Archetypes
        Persona
        Anima
        Animus
        Shadow +

    Attitudes
        Introversion
        Extraversion +

    Functions +

    Self

FIGURE 4-1 Jung's Structure of the Personality or Psyche

Unconsciousness. The function of our ego (consciousness) is crucial to our personality; however, by itself, ego is but a small part of our psyche. It is our unconscious, Jung asserts, that adds depth, richness, and vitality to our unique personalities. There are numerous unconscious psychic processes unrelated to ego that we must balance and integrate to give our personality completeness and wholeness. Jung divided the unconscious into two levels: the personal unconscious and the collective unconscious.

The Personal Unconscious and Complexes The second level or component of our psyche, immediately adjacent to our ego and just below the threshold of our consciousness, is our **personal unconscious.** This, the upper region of the unconscious, Jung labels "personal" because it is **idiosyncratic** (uniquely our own). Our personal unconscious owes its existence to our personal experiences. The psychic material contained here, though once conscious, was repressed, suppressed, forgotten, ignored, or too weak to make a conscious impression, and thus is only subliminally perceived. In short, the psychic material of our personal unconscious is relatively unconscious; hence, much of it can, with varying degrees of effort, be reclaimed to our consciousness by ego. Since the contents of our personal unconscious are accessible to consciousness, there is a great deal of reciprocal action and interchange between our ego and our personal unconscious.

Complexes. The contents of our personal unconscious are grouped into organized, emotionally toned clusters or constellations centering on a common nucleus, a common theme, or a recurrent motif. The stronger the psychic energy or emotion radiating from the nucleus of a constellation, the greater its valence and the more related experiences the constellation will draw toward itself. Jung refers to these functionally organized constellations as **complexes.** A complex, along with its energy or emotion, has the tendency to form a fragmented personality of itself. In dreams, for instance, a complex can appear in personified form (Jung, 1968, p. 81).

If continually repressed and allowed to gain strength, a complex can become autonomous, overwhelm ego, and control our personality for its own ends. At the point where we can no longer control a complex by conscious intention, it enters the realm of psychopathology in the form of compulsive thought, disturbed memory, hallucination, illusion, or delusion. Hitler's lust for power serves as an example of a complex that has overwhelmed ego. From Jung's viewpoint, we do not have a complex: The complex has us. We then experience the frightening sense of being out of control, of being beside ourselves, an experience that is common in borderline personality disorders.

Complexes are personal, but they also hook into a **collective archetype** (inherited ancestral memories). They link our personal unconscious, along with its repressed contents, to the collective unconscious and its archetypes. For example, the **Shadow** *is* the personal unconscious, insofar as it consists of all that the individual prefers not to know, tries to forget, or represses (i.e., personal weaknesses and uncivilized desires, thoughts, and emotions). The shadow complex is incompatible with and threatening to our habitual attitude of consciousness (extraversion or introversion). But the shadow is more than a complex; it is also a collective phenomenon, represented as an archetype, residing in the collective unconscious where it is inaccessible to consciousness. According to Jung (1964, 1968), then, whether partially conscious or unconscious, every complex has an archetypal core.

The Collective Unconscious and Archetypes While the idea of the collective unconscious did not originate with Jung, he was the first to tie the collective unconscious to the evolutionary process, to describe its function, and to define a number of the more common archetypal contents. Unlike our personal unconscious, which lies near the threshold of ego consciousness and is comprised of personal experiences, the collective unconscious is at the deepest level of the unconscious and is transpersonal. For Jung, "though the personal unconscious is the stuff of neurosis, the collective unconscious permits a valuable identification with what is universal and eternal" (Maddi, 1980, p. 74; see also Jung, 1954, 1957, 1959b).

The contents of the collective unconscious, the archetypes, are inherited, hence universal, with roots that extend back in the process of evolution to the earliest development of the human psyche. Within each of us, then, resides an accumulated psychic culture of an evolved humanity. "In us live the battles they fought, the fears they experienced, the loves they nurtured" (Maddi, 1980, p. 72). The collective contents of the unconscious have never been conscious in the life of any one of us; yet these predisposed, typical modes of apperception bind us as a species to a common origin and development.

In addition to the archetypes, the collective unconscious houses the instincts. Jung agreed with Freud (Chapter 2) that instinctual drives (i.e., hunger and sex) are behavioral directive. For Jung, however, both archetypal and instinctual contents of the unconscious are expressions of the same psychic energy (**libido**, a term Jung [1964, 1978] used to describe all psychic energy) in the unconscious.

The Archetypes Before presenting examples of the more common archetypes, it is important to emphasize that archetypes, for Jung, are not fixed images. Rather, they are uniform modes of apperception; that is, they are possibilities or predispositions to images that shape a variety of specific image-projections. Mattoon (1981) makes this distinction: "the concept would be understood better if the adjective *archetypal* were always used rather than its noun; images may be archetypal but are not in themselves archetypes" (p. 39, italics in original). Archetypal predispositions of the unconscious are innate in humans, but the images they produce, along with their effects, are shaped by our individual conscious experiences in the context of our own culture. Individuals or cultures may have different cultural-specific images of the Great Earth Mother, but the archetypal predispositions that generate those images are inherited, thus the same in all humans regardless of culture.

Archetypes are as numerous as the typical situations in the human condition; however, some are more commonly experienced than others. Over the years Jung

(1954, 1957, 1959b, 1963) referred to such archetypes as Life, Death, the Hero, the Dragon, the Wise Old Man, the Divine Child, the Great Earth Mother, and Christ, as well as those described below, the Persona, the Shadow, the Anima and Animus.

The Persona. The **persona** is the mask or the public facade most of us exhibit in our daily relations with others. It is a compromise between our inner self and the external demands of the environment. Our persona is our personally constructed response to the social pressures to act in an acceptable manner, a projection of an expected image, a model of a prescribed role. It is a mask for the world to see. Just as ancient actors donned masks to signify the roles they were playing, we wear our personas to assist us in our socially prescribed roles. The minister, priest, and rabbi are each expected by the people they serve to behave in a particular way. Patients expect a reassuring bedside manner from their physicians. The police officer is expected to project an image of calm strength, even in potentially dangerous and trying situations. When the persona we adopt fits the role expected by society, it assists us to relate successfully with others; however, should we stray too far from the accepted role, we and others experience confusion; indeed, antagonism results. It is always a shock when our masks fail to be convincing. To be stripped suddenly of our persona leaves us feeling naked and helpless.

Archetypes, like the complexes, are **bipolar;** that is, they hold the potential for both positive and negative valence and are always growth producing or growth inhibiting. Adopting a persona is necessary for successful relations. Those of us who either do not or cannot put on a public face to fit the circumstances of different social situations are judged socially inept. Our behavior is considered insensitive and gauche by those with whom we must relate, and they judge us unreliable and incompetent.

There is potential danger, also, in identifying with the persona. With persona identification, the desire to conform to social pressures becomes inordinately strong, and much that rightly belongs to the personality is repressed (Jung, 1959b). When there is no longer any distinction between our mask and the ego, the mask is fixed, and we are limited to a single rigid role through which the collective unconscious projects itself. The minister, for example, may be unable to discard the persona when at home with the family, thus finding himself or herself unable to relate to the spouse as a husband or wife, or to the children as a father or mother. In short, authenticity is impossible. Considerable psychic energy is invested in the actualization and maintenance of the persona rather than in self-actualization. With our genuine self repressed to the unconscious, our interpersonal relationships suffer, and our conscious ego is open to invasion from the unconscious. The greatest enemy of our persona is the shadow.

The Shadow. Often referred to as the dark and sinister side of our psyche, the **shadow** is comprised in part of idiosyncratic qualities, all the uncivilized desires and emotions that we prefer not to show or to know and therefore suppress or

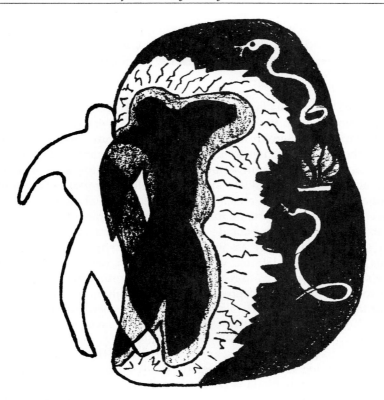

FIGURE 4-2   The Shadow

repress to the collective unconscious. In addition to the idiosyncratic qualities, the shadow contains collective qualities; that is, it is linked through the collective unconscious to a universal archetypal shadow—the animalistic and instinctive side of humanity inherited from an evolutionary process that extends back to a prehuman history. The shadow is always in opposition to the persona.

The more rigid and restrictive the society and the more we identify with our persona, the larger is the shadow. The more repression of shadow contents to the unconscious, the stronger and more dangerous is the shadow. In the unconscious and out of ego's control, the shadow can acquire strength "so that when the moment comes (as usually happens) when it must appear, it is more dangerous and more likely to overwhelm the rest of personality, which otherwise could have acted as a wholesome check" (Fordham, 1953, p. 51). An example of a sudden, unchecked invasion of the shadow is the rioting mob, where civilized people turn savage and behave in animalistic and destructive ways; in modern psychiatric disorder classification, "the explosive disorder" of impulse control disorders.

The Anima. During one particularly difficult period of self-analysis, when Jung found himself arguing with a feminine voice from within as to whether his exploration of his unconscious was art, science, or something different than either, Jung (1963/1961) became convinced that an internalized feminine image was an integral part of every man's psyche. Just as a man's biology consists of both male and female hormones, Jung (1959b) insisted that every man's psyche consists of both masculine and feminine traits.

According to Jung (1959b, 1963/1961), every man has within his unconscious a complex of feminine elements and attitudes that he denied to consciousness because he viewed them as weaknesses, and an archetypal feminine image based on the collective experiences of men with women throughout history. Jung named the unconscious and complementary feminine image the **anima.** For Jung, it is the anima in man that assists with the understanding of women in general, and that permits men to show such traits and feelings as tenderness, sympathy, and empathy. In brief, the anima, like the shadow, contributes to the completion of the male personality by adding a dimension of humanness to the masculine side of his personality. Further, Jung (1959b, 1963/1961) asserts that every man projects his anima onto the women who attract him. He then sees the projection, the powers and attributes of the anima, rather than the actual woman. Complications and discord arise when the anima and the woman onto whom the anima is projected are different.

The Animus. The **animus** in women is the counterpart of the anima in man. The animus appears to be derived from three sources: the inherent, collective image of man; personal experiences with the masculinity in men (especially with father and brothers); and the latent masculine elements in the woman herself (Jung, 1959b).

In the course of life and living, the animus is projected on significant male figures, and these men are perceived through the guise of the animus rather than as they actually are. Through the projection of the animus, a man can be viewed as seducer, conquering hero, knight errant, or mystical seer. Misunderstandings arise when the man fails to conform to the animus projection.

Like the anima in man, the animus, when recognized, helps to complete the woman's self-understanding. Also like the anima, the repressed animus can gain strength in the unconscious and invade ego consciousness. On the positive side, Jung informed us, the animus can give the woman courage and assertiveness when she needs these qualities, help her to better appreciate and understand the role of men, and stir her to strive competitively toward her goals.

Both the anima and the animus, according to Jung (1953), act as mediators between the conscious and the unconscious mind. "When they become personified in fantasies, dreams, or visions, they present an opportunity to understand something that has hitherto been unconscious" (Fordham, 1953, p. 58).

Subjective versus Objective Reality

When operating effectively, ego perceives reality accurately and differentiates between the exogenous world of experience and the endogenous world of im-

FIGURE 4-3   The Anima and the Animus Archetypes: Animus and Anima

ages. Additionally, ego is responsible for a continuous quality of coherence and for developing a distinct and unique sense of identity—that personal and continual sense of an *I* or *me* that provides continuity in personal reference from day to day.

Ego, Jung asserts, is influenced and characterized by the dominate one of two **attitudes** (introversion and extraversion) and one or two of the four **functions** of consciousness (thinking, feeling, sensing, and intuiting). The dominate and characteristic attitude and functions are expressed consciously by ego. The uncharacteristic or inferior attitude and functions—those that are underdeveloped—are part of the unconscious and, if ignored, are in position to threaten ego.

Attitudinal Dimensions and Functions of Ego Too distressed to be objective about his schism with Freud and the Vienna psychoanalytic group, Jung examined the circumstances surrounding Adler's earlier withdrawal from Freud's circle (Chapters 2 and 3). A critical comparison of Freud and Adler led Jung to hypothesize that the two men held opposing perceptual predispositions that led them to perceive humanity and the world in a totally different manner. Further, he hypothesized that their opposing perceptual modes explained their theoretical as well as their personal differences. In short, the habitual attitudes of Freud (introversion) and Adler (extraversion) were so different and presented such striking contrasts that their separation was almost certainly inevitable. Jung labeled *attitude* their perceptual predispositions to act or react in a habitual or characteristic direction, and identified two attitudinal dimensions, *extraversion* and *introversion*. Here, for Jung, was not only an accounting for the personality differences of Freud and Adler, but an explanation for personality differences that could be generalized.

Attitudes Holding an attitude is, for Jung, holding a psychic readiness to act or react, selectively and automatically, in a particular direction. What is perceived as relevant is already decided, whether consciously or unconsciously, by a subjective, idiosyncratic constellation of a priori psychic contents. Being subjective, an attitude clouds judgment. According to Jung (in de Laszlo, 1959), "having an attitude is synonymous with an a priori direction toward a definite thing, whether that be present in consciousness or not" (p. 242).

Extraversion. When extraversion is the dominant or superior attitudinal dimension of the psyche, the individual's psychic energy (the libido) is invested primarily in the objective world—people, objects, and events of the environment. The extravert is primarily oriented to and influenced by the accumulation of objective data. The extravert is pragmatic; indeed, personal tendencies toward the subjective are largely suppressed or repressed, hence unconscious.

On the positive side, extraverts generally have a firm grasp on reality. They are typically personable, optimistic, enthusiastic, and socially adept. They are comfortable in a wide variety of social settings. They attract many friends. Their moral standards coincide with the standards set by society. In short, they fit into the existing conditions of their environment and their society with relative ease.

On the negative side, there is danger in excessive extraversion. Focusing continually on outer reality, extraverts may lose touch with their inner subjective needs, emotions, and intentions, even to the point where they become alienated from their own personhood. When dependent upon the impressions they make, extraverts may only be able to develop superficial friendships. Extreme extraversion may create intolerable misunderstandings in interpersonal relations with introverts. When suppression of subjective factors becomes pathological, hence injurious, extraverts may experience a morbid intensification of fantasy activity. It occurs because the unconscious is thought to be compensatory, and "whenever an exaggeration of the conscious standpoint takes place, the unconscious also comes to light in a symptomatic form" (Jung, in de Laszlo, 1959, p. 198).

Introversion.   When introversion is the most highly developed of the attitudinal dimensions, psychic energy centers inward, with a subjective orientation. The introvert lives in a psychological world of ideas, individualized perceptions, and inner responses. Solitude is preferred and actively sought. Friendships, though few, are often intense, and loyalty to one's friends is valued highly.

Introversion also has its negative side. Introverts are uncomfortable and clumsy in most social situations. They tend to be overconscientious, pessimistic, critical, and either too outspoken or ridiculously polite when confronted with situations requiring extraverted behavior. In a pathological stage of introversion, introverts may attempt to sever themselves so completely from the objective that they expend much of their psychic energy in defensive measures, fighting their fear and distrust of the objective world. For the psychologically disturbed introvert, change becomes disturbing, even terrifying. Objects take on magical qualities, and there is the constant dread of falling under their influence.

The Functions (Rational and Irrational)   It did not take Jung long to realize that, as an explanation for personality differences, a basic attitudinal stance (either extraversion or introversion) was insufficient. Alone, the concept of attitude offered little more than a general discrimination. Jung (in de Laszlo, 1959) then developed the four functions of consciousness: thinking, feeling, sensing, and intuiting (p. 187). Perhaps the most succinct definitions of the four functions are to be found in *Man and His Symbols* (Jung, 1964): "*Sensation* (i.e. sense perception) tells us that something exists; *thinking* tells you what it is; *feeling* tells you whether it is agreeable or not; and *intuition* tells you whence it comes and where it is going" (p. 61, italics in original).

By expanding his explanation for personality differences to encompass the expression of each of the two attitudes through one or more of the four functions, Jung greatly increased the level of discrimination in his theory of personality types. Rather than two general divisions, his theory now provided eight combined attitude-function types.

Eight personality types still seem a simple few considering the complexities of human nature; however, Jung (1964, 1968) repeatedly emphasizes that these eight types rarely exist in pure form. Consideration must be granted to the nearly infinite variety of personality differences that degree of expression can add. Further, the functions are hierarchical. Typically, one function of the rational pair is held in a superior or dominant position in the hierarchy; that is, one function is more highly developed than the others. Another function occupies a secondary or auxiliary position and, while not as highly differentiated as the first, can nevertheless modify the nature of the superior function and, through it, the expression of the major attitude. Not to be ignored are the third and fourth functions that occupy inferior positions in the hierarchy. In opposition to the superior and secondary functions, the third and fourth functions are suppressed, thus, unconscious. Jung views the relationship of the conscious and unconscious as compensatory; therefore, under certain conditions (extreme stress, for example) the inferior functions can invade consciousness and endanger conscious ego.

The Thinking Function (Rational) Thinking, an intellectual function, combines perception and judgment to arrive at a general concept or solution. The thinking function categorizes and assigns meaning, analyzes cause and effect, defines alternatives, and determines truth or falsehood.

The Extravert Thinking Type. When thinking is the superior function of extraverts, thought focuses primarily on objective data that are then utilized to assist in the ordering of the external world. While most extraverted thought relies on objective data, abstract ideas are acceptable to the extravert, provided they are transmitted from without (i.e., the ideas of authority figures—parents, teachers, pastors, political leaders, etc.). Scientists, engineers, and mathematicians serve as examples of extraverts making frequent use of the thinking function in their work.

FIGURE 4-4   Four Functions of Consciousness

Not all extraverted thinking is productive. Without interpretation, extraverted thinking may lead only to an accumulation of data. Because extraverted thinkers are searching for absolutes, for universal truths, they can become intolerant of exceptions and ambiguities. Their lives can be ruled by self-imposed "oughts," "musts," and "have tos," and they are often described as cold, rigid, indifferent, and impersonal.

The Introvert Thinking Type.   When thinking is the most differentiated function of the introvert, it is always oriented at decisive points to subjective data. Introverted thinkers are concerned with abstractions, the formulation of questions, and the creation of theories, often without practical purpose. While there is the tendency for introverted thinkers to ignore facts that do not fit their schema, they may use objective data as evidence for their ideas, or at least give others the impression they are doing so.

At their best, introverted thinkers react to an objective world in a highly subjective and creative way. They can visualize the novel from new interpretations of old data. Inventors and philosophers are representative of the introverted thinking type. When thinking becomes too introverted, however, there is the tendency to ignore objective data that conflict with a fascinating theory. Both time and energy may be wasted on the impractical. At the pathological level introverted thinkers may move from the realm of ideas to the realm of mystic thought and imagery so individualized as to be meaningless to all but themselves.

The Feeling Function (Rational)   The feeling function in Jung's typology is the process of determining value or worth of an object, idea, or event. It is not to be mistaken for emotion or affective value. Like the thinking function, the feeling function is a rational function—both the thinking and feeling functions involve a valuative process and are independent of external stimuli. Unlike emotion, which emerges from the unconscious (e.g., "I feel pity for that child"), the feeling function is a function of conscious ego. It is responsible for judging an object desirable or undesirable, important or unimportant, valuable or worthless.

The Extravert Feeling Type.   When the feeling function is paired with extraversion, it is subject to traditional or generally accepted standards of value. Concerned with interpersonal relations and the impressions they engender, the values extraverts place on objects are highly influenced by the present social standards and can be characterized as fitting, fashionable, or politic. In short, they will fulfill aesthetic expectations. A painting, for example, may be enthusiastically judged beautiful by the extravert's feeling function if: (1) the "top" critics from the "best" papers have deemed it so; (2) it just brought seven figures at an exclusive art auction; (3) it hangs on the wall of an influential person's home in which the extravert is a guest; or (4) it would be in poor taste (not "fitting") to say otherwise because of the setting or the particular social gathering. While the feeling function of extraverts is somewhat capricious and adaptable to the current fad and fashions, these individuals are, when at their best, likeable, fun to be with, and valued guests at nearly any party or social gathering.

Should the feeling function become exaggerated in extraverts, however, they may be perceived as insincere, materialistic, calculating, and untrustworthy. Their niceness can wear thin and their intense, effervescent, sociable affectations can swiftly become irritating.

The Introvert Feeling Type. Introverted feeling is determined principally by subjective factors and controlled by subjective preconditions. For example, a painting will be valued by the introverted feeling type only if it stimulates the feeling process of the introvert to see his or her own subjective vision. The painting itself is never clearly perceived. When the introvert is viewing the object (the painting), his or her feeling function is operating from a subjective precondition of a beautiful painting, and it is this subjective precondition that sets the criteria against which worth is determined. The painting itself is secondary.

As the extravert with a highly differentiated feeling function is prone to overvalue, the introvert is prone to undervalue. Working from the subjective, the introvert's feeling function is unable to conform to current style and fashion. When the feeling function is magnified in the introvert, there is the penchant toward egoism and a strong defensive posture toward any outside aesthetic expectations. There is also the danger of a wounded ego in the matter of judgment, and value (if it is expressed at all under these circumstances) is likely to be stated passively and negatively. Further, just as thinking types tend to suppress the feeling function, feeling types tend to suppress the thinking function.

The Sensing Function (Irrational) The existence of things is determined by the sensing function, a function of conscious perception. The sensing function encompasses all conscious experiences of the five senses, as well as all conscious physiological sensation from within the body. In addition to the five senses, the sensation function implies source, for perception can always point to a source.

The Extravert Sensing Type. When sensation is the major or superior function of the extravert, the individual is interested in the objective facts and materials of the universe. Sensates seek to discover the specifics of the here and now in their worlds, and they are attracted to the unknowns in their environment. Tied to the concrete by their fascination with objective data, extraverted sensates repress intuition, the function of unconscious perception, and they experience difficulty with the abstract and people who deal with the abstract. The extraverted sensate is typically characterized as a hardheaded, pragmatic realist with little feeling or concern about the meaning of the data he generates and uses. For many scientists the sensing function is often the most highly differentiated of the four functions. Proofreading and wine tasting serve as other examples of occupations that require discriminating sensory perception.

In the extreme, extraverted sensation types are too easily bound to the concrete. They are prone to ignore or discount the advantages and contributions of abstract thinking. In addition, they are susceptible to addictions, perversions, and compulsions, particularly for those objects in their environments that release a pronounced sensuous hold on them and are, thus, accepted fully into their consciousness.

The Introvert Sensing Type.   Of primary importance to sensation introverts are their personal reactions to the objective sensory events in their lives. Individuals of this type think and feel on a primitive level; that is, their unconscious alters their sense perceptions at the source. The sensory perceptions of the sensation introverts, then, do not coincide with consciousness, but rather with the predispositions of the collective unconscious. Jung (in de Laszlo, 1959) claims that the intervention of the collective unconscious predisposes sensory introverts to sense the objective events of their world through a psychic mirror: "It is a mirror, however, with the peculiar capacity of representing the present contents of consciousness not in their known and customary form but in a certain sense *sub specie aeternitaitis*, somewhat as a million-year-old consciousness might see them" (p. 232).

Introverted sensory types are often overwhelmed by their sensory impressions. They can become preoccupied with the images of the collective unconscious—a jetliner can remind them of a flying dragon; clouds take on human or animal forms; inanimate objects are personified; they may "see" people who have been dead for some time. The introverted sensory types experience difficulty in finding ways to express themselves in a society that rewards logic and reason. The arts, particularly contemporary art and music, may serve as an outlet for individuals functioning from the introverted sensation level of consciousness.

The Intuiting Function (Irrational)   Possibly the most difficult of Jung's four functions to describe or explain, the intuitive function is sometimes referred to as the sixth sense. It is comprised of perceptions that appear from out of nowhere, require no reason or judgment for their origin, and are of an untraceable source in the unconscious.

The Extravert Intuitive Type.   The intuitive extravert represses sensation, the greatest distraction to the clear, naive images of intuition. For the intuitive extravert there is always an unconscious, expectant attitude toward new possibilities of objective situations that are only subliminally perceived. Ordinary living appears to be a mystery that intuition must unravel. Fresh possibilities are compelling motives when the intuitive function is primary; there are always new worlds to conquer.

While the intuitive function may outwardly resemble the sensation function, it is far more imaginative and creative, and it is guided by hunches. Inventors, politicians, entrepreneurs, gamblers, and speculators are examples of the extraverted intuitive function in action.

The Introvert Intuitive Type. The intuitive introvert is of two natures: the mystical, prophetic dreamer or the seer and the perceiver of visions, exotic fantasies, and extrasensory perceptions. Valued and respected in primitive cultures, intuitive introverts who are unable to find a productive way of expressing their perceptions in the complex societies of today are often thought strange or mad. Made to feel their perceptions are inferior to rational perceptions because they are unable to explain their source, they either withdraw, keeping their perceptions to themselves, or become fanatics or martyrs, willing to die for a cause engendered by some inner vision. Fordham (1953) points to William Blake as a good example of an introverted intuitive who found a way to shape his perceptions in his art and poetry.

Early versus Continuous Development

Personality development, according to Jung, is a continuous, lifelong process of individuation. Moreover, because "the collective unconscious provides a basis whereby each modern person stands on the shoulders of predecessors" and is thus "able to see a little further," the human species is "constantly evolving more differentiated and conscious forms of existence" (Maddi, 1980, p. 84).

Unlike Freud and Erikson (Chapters 2 and 5), Jung does not emphasize specific, sequential, health-dependent life stages, though he clearly distinguishes between the first and second halves of life. While Jung believes our personality types are formed early in life and clearly influence behavior through young adulthood, he views mid-life (between thirty-five and forty years of age) as our opportunity for transition from a personality type to selfhood. A successful transition is characterized by a shift in psychic energy toward introspection and rumination that marks a new beginning of further psychological development.

Entering this world with a collective unconscious, each of us is born with a natural predisposition to move from a state of undifferentiated wholeness to a fully differentiated, balanced, and unified personality. This striving for individuation, or selfhood, is **archetypal.** "No one can avoid the powerful influence of this unity archetype" (Hall & Nordby, 1973, p. 82). Although Jung did not identify specific stages in the journey toward selfhood, four transitional periods can be inferred from his writing—infancy and childhood, youth and young adulthood, middle age, and old age.

Infancy and Childhood (birth to adolescence) For the first year or two of life we are bonded to the collective unconscious and guided by its instincts and archetypal contents, primarily in terms of parental images. That bonding must be transferred to the actual parents (particularly the mother) if we are to relinquish the hold of the archetypal parents and begin the development of a conscious ego.

As infants, we consciously perceive our world, but until we develop a conscious ego, our perceptions lack order and our memory is highly transient. Indeed, even when we identify with our parents, we maintain contact with the archetypal world through fantasy (i.e., the imaginary playmate) until approximately five years of age. For some of us during this period, especially those of us whose parental identification may be weak, fantasy contact with the collective unconscious may last longer (i.e., Jung's secret dialogues at the age of ten with a carved mannequin of the Wise Old Man, see "Biographical Sketch").

For Jung (1933), the psychology of the child reflects the problems of the parents. Indeed, he would only work with children through their parents, and then only after both parents expressed a willingness to put their own house in order.

As children, our ego begins to form once we begin to differentiate between ourselves and others. Ego as perceiver is first manifested in our use of the pronouns "I," "me," and "mine" in reference to a personal and separate self. However, it is not until puberty, a period accompanied by physiological change, that our psyche assumes definite form and content. For Jung, puberty equals psychic birth.

Youth and Young Adulthood (adolescence to age 35 or 40) The beginning of this rather stormy period is marked by rapid physiological changes and the eruption of sexuality. It is a period of pressing decisions, adaptations, and new responsibilities. There is the pain of relinquishing childhood fantasies and illusions, and the clash of unrealistic expectations and existing realities. Conscious differentiation from the parents is experienced and expressed. It is a period of learning a vocation or profession, becoming financially independent, finding a mate, raising children, and accepting a responsible role in the community.

Jung believed that the transition to a vocation or profession occurs fairly smoothly for those of us who, as children, were adequately prepared; however, he warned that those who of us who continue to cling to childish illusions were most certainly going to experience problems. He also hypothesized that cultures demanding an inordinate degree of extraverted adaptation make this period of development especially difficult for youth with introversive attitudes.

Middle Age (age 35–40 to age 65–70) Jung (1933) was one of the first psychiatrists to recognize the middle years—"the noon of life"—as a significant developmental period and to give it full attention in his theory (p. 109). Indeed, he anticipated today's concern with the phenomenon of the mid-life crisis by at least three decades.

While there is no way to be certain, it is possible that Jung's interest in this period can be traced to the traumatic emotional crisis he experienced at about forty years of age (see "Biographical Sketch"). In addition, most patients whom Jung saw in private practice were at the mid-point of their lives when they requested treatment, and many, Jung discovered, were experiencing some kind of existential crisis.

By ordinary standards, many of Jung's patients were successful people. They were well established in their professions; indeed, some were highly recognized and honored. They were married and the parents of grown children. They were active participants in their communities. Yet in spite of the outward appearance of success, they were dissatisfied with life and living. They no longer had the time they would need to accomplish all the goals they had set in their youth. Looking back through their existential dread of life and time wasted, they discovered that much of life had passed unlived, numerous opportunities had been overlooked, and a myriad of potentials had gone unfulfilled. The intensity of their feelings varied significantly, running from a vague sense of uneasiness to deep depression and thoughts of suicide.

Jung (1933) viewed the middle years as an opportunity for growth. It was for Jung a time for introspection and self-exploration, a time to experience archetypal predispositions, and, finally, a time to consider new values and new life goals. Jung called this introspective growth process **individuation,** and looked to certain areas of experience as especially conducive to the individuation process, primarily "the quest for an adequate religious perspective, personal relationships, and analytic therapy" (Mattoon, 1981, p. 188; see also "Applications").

Old Age (age 65–70 to death)   In "The Soul of Death," Jung (1959) viewed death as the "goal of life . . . . a state of rest" and "wholeness," rather than the conclusion of life (pp. 4–5). For Jung, life is a process, and the end of every process is its goal.

Number and Weight Assigned to Motivational Concepts

Jung, like Freud, viewed us as complex, dynamic energy systems. Similarly Freud and Jung believed that all energy (whether physical or psychic) originated from the metabolic processes. Unlike Freud, who used the term libido in reference to sexual energy, Jung's libido encompassed *all* energy. Although Jung saw the human energy system as partially closed, he hypothesized that it functioned as a closed system, regulated by two principles that originated from the science of physics—the **principle of equivalence** (in a closed system energy is neither gained nor lost) and **entropy** (redistribution of energy throughout the system tends toward equilibrium or balance).

When applied to personality, the principle of equivalence means that an increase of physical energy results in a decrease of psychic energy or that energy lost in one of the subsystems of personality must reappear in another. Subsystems in Jung's theory are the conscious psyche (ego), the personal unconscious and its complexes, the collective unconscious and the incorporated archetypes, the attitudes, and the functions. We are, then, motivated by the interactions and diverse polar tendencies of the psyche's subsystems. Motivation may occur in compensation (a high investment in extraversion tends toward a redistribution of energy to introversion, or when energy is concentrated in the thinking function, it will tend to be redistributed toward the opposing functions [e.g., the sensing or intuitive function]).

According to Jung (1959b), the subsystems of the psyche are polarities (conscious–unconscious, persona–shadow archetypes, the attitude of introversion–extraversion, the rational [thinking, feeling]–irrational [sensing, intuiting] functions serve as but a few examples). In addition, there are the polarities of physical and psychic energy, the directives of causality and the aspirations of teleology, and the movement of progression and regression. For Jung (1959b), opposition of the polar tendencies and the redistribution of energy are necessary, for they lead to unification and wholeness. Polarities have the power to attract as well as to oppose. The uniting of polar opposites motivates the individuation process, integrates the psyche's subsystems, and replaces ego with the self as the center of personality.

Determinism versus Freedom of Choice

With the emphasis Jung placed on the unconscious and the racial and phyloge-netic foundations of the human psyche, there is little doubt that his stance on this issue is largely toward determinism. However, Jung was unable to accept Freud's totally causal explanation for all of our complex behavior. He was convinced that our individual views of the future, our personal hopes, goals, and aspirations also influence how we perceive and interpret present experiences and, consequently, how we act in the present. There is a place in Jung's theory for at least limited **teleological** (future-oriented) influences in our search for personal development and our striving for a unified, whole, and complete selfhood.

Explanation of Learning Process

As indicated earlier (see "Early versus Continuous Development"), Jung viewed learning as a dynamic, evolving process, an interaction of progression and regres-sion, that occurs throughout the entire life span. However, it appears that Jung was more interested in *what* must be learned for movement toward wholeness and completeness than he was in an explanation (the *how*) of the learning process.

Jung strongly emphasized that we must do as much as possible to make the unconscious conscious. We must, he insisted, become conscious of our shadow and experience it both intellectually and emotionally. Individuation is impossible until this feat is accomplished. It is also necessary, according to Jung, to rid ourselves of the persona—to become authentically who and what we are. Achiev-ing these most difficult tasks releases the psychic energy we used to keep the shadow unconscious and to maintain the facade of the persona. Once released, the energy can then be focused on the collective unconscious and permit the archetypal images of the Wise Old Man and the Earth Mother to emerge.

As we mature and gain necessary knowledge of the inner world of our own psyche, we gain greater skill in resolving the conflicts that emerge from the polar opposites of the various elements of our psyche. With greater knowledge of the archetypal Self, our perceptions are closer to reality, our discriminations are more exacting, our evaluations are more rational, and our decisions are more intelli-gent.

Jung also discussed in some depth the experiences that can impede or block learning. In early childhood, for example, the wholeness and adjustment of the child's parents and teachers are crucial. It was Jung's conviction that parents and teachers are responsible for making a child neurotic. The child, who has not yet developed a psyche of his or her own, adopts the psyche projected by his or her parents. Teachers who are neurotic project their neuroses onto their students, then relate to them as though they (their students) were neurotic or disturbed. Jung therefore recommended that both parents and teachers learn as much as possible about child development. Even more important, he recommended that they learn about themselves. Most school curricula and teachers, Jung argued, encourage students to memorize facts they can recall when tested rather than to explore their own psyche, to become aware of their universal ties and personal weaknesses, and to avoid one-sided development of their attitudes and functions.

Role Assigned to Self-Concept

To avoid the usual misunderstandings of Jung's concept of the Self, it is necessary to discard all present personal meanings and connotations of this term. For example, Jung's Self is not a phenomenological accumulation of perceptions of the "me–not me." Jung's Self must be viewed as both the beginning and the end in our lives (Progoff, 1956). Jung's Self is already present as an inherent propensity when we enter this world. Indeed, as an archetypal or psychoid **proto-image** (an image that contains the latent purpose of human nature), Jung's concept of the Self represents both a reality and a symbol (the **mandala**) and it is intimately involved in *all* stages of our psychological development. Jung also views the Self as the culmination of our development, the end result of an unconscious psychological process that Jung named "Individuation." For Jung, the individuation process encompasses all phases of development and leads ultimately to integration of the psyche's subsystems and the unity and wholeness of the personality. The Self, then, when viewed from a Jungian perspective, is the final goal of the individuation process.

As an archetype, the Self conceived by Jung is universal, but it also represents the quintessence of each of us. While it is a psychological term, it is more than psychological, "for its function is to direct the modern mind by means of consciousness to levels of experience that transcend the ordinary range of intellectual understanding" (Progoff, 1956, p. 187).

Individuation or the realization of the Self is a goal seldom reached. The Self cannot be realized fully so long as the shadow is repressed. However, finding some way to meet and live with the shadow not only requires tremendous moral effort, it also involves a restructuring of ideal standards and values.

Uniqueness versus Universality

We hold much in common with all members of our species, including a universal collective unconscious that contains the pattern of our ultimate destiny in the archetype of the Self and that predisposes us to relate to our world in similar ways. Still, we are unique. Our personal unconscious, for example, is based on personal experiences, and while we share similar experiences, in no two of us are these experiences identical. For Jung, our individual differences **(uniqueness)** in personality spring from the characteristic direction of libido movement toward introversion and extraversion and the typical way in which we understand the world (thinking, feeling, sensation, or intuition).

Role Assigned to Group Determinants

Jung did not express his stance on this issue in any single source. Rather his views are dispersed throughout his publications. The most helpful primary source was Jung's (1957) book, *The Undiscovered Self.* A secondary source that proved helpful was Odajnyk's (1976) *Jung and Politics: The Political and Social Ideas of C. G. Jung.* Readers who wish to pursue Jung's resolution of this issue further may profit from reading these two sources.

The emphasis to this point has been the impact of the collective unconscious on the individual, for that is Jung's major emphasis. However, given the collective nature of the unconscious and its archetypal propensity for unity, elements of the collective unconscious can be projected to groups and significantly influence group determinants of individual behavior. Archetypes hold a collective character: "... the group united, the group in action, and the group in submission to a leader, for example, are complements of the more individual archetypes of the family, the medicine-man, and the ruler" (Odajnyk, 1976, p. 30).

Jung's example of an individual's identification with elements of the collective unconscious is the way an individual identifies with a position or job title, often at the expense of his or her own personal identity. The facade or mask of the position or title may contain collective as well as personal elements. In short, Jung contends that not only does the individual's identification with a persona enlarge his or her personality, but the position or title itself attracts the individual and seduces him or her to exchange his or her personal identity for the collective identity (transpersonal qualities of the position or the title). Such an identification not only halts personal development, but also offers easy compensation for personal deficiencies.

For example, identification with a minority group may lead to an identification with a socially defined inferior status and role which, in turn, can result not only in the atrophy of individual personality but also compensation, or even justification, for personal deficiencies and the accompanying sense of impotence and inferiority.

Jung also describes submersion in mass emotions and behavior when under the influence of the collective unconscious (e.g., mob violence—the psychic inflation brought on by archetypal influence can lead the group to do things that individual members would not do were they not part of the group). Members of a group can become instruments for the forces of the collective unconscious.

Jung was extremely wary of groups—indeed, he feared that the morality of any group, including any society, decreases as the size of the group increases. The larger the group, the more unavoidable its immorality. In *The Undiscovered Self,* Jung stands strongly against the submergence of individual personality in any collective, whether psychological or social. He believed that until an individual recognized, understood, and began to resolve the polar forces of his or her unconscious, he or she would continue to be susceptible to mass movements, taken in by charismatic and powerful politicians, and serve as a blind follower in confusing political and social upheavals (Odajnyk, 1976).

Centrality of Reinforcement

Reinforcement is not a term that appears in Jung's writing. Indeed, it would seem that reinforcement (at least when given a behavioristic definition) has no place in Jung's theory.

Psychological Health and Psychopathology

Healthy Personality and the Good Life

Jung (1963/1961; see also Fordham, 1953; Hall & Nordby, 1973; and Maddi, 1980) believed there is an innate, continuous, archetypal will to health that develops gradually and becomes more pronounced during the second half of life. He called this natural direction toward healthful growth *individuation* or *self-realization,* and made it the "central concept" of his theory (Jung, 1963/1961, p. 209). While avoidance of the individuation process and the **unity archetype** (the Self) is impossible, the actualization of the individuated self, Jung asserted, is life's ideal. Seldom if ever is wholeness of the Self achieved. Indeed, he states:

> *There is little hope of ever being able to reach even approximate consciousness of the self, since however much we may be conscious of the self there will always exist an indeterminate and indeterminable amount of unconscious material which belongs to the totality of the self (Jung, 1963/1961, p. 398).*

The path to individuation, Jung emphasized, is not a smooth one, and advancement is marked by progression and regression, flux and stagnation, with only occasional glimpses of the Self to make the trip bearable. Further, there are numerous conditions that may either foster or hinder an individual's striving toward greater differentiation and a unified wholeness. Among these are heredity, early childhood experiences with parents, education, religion, society, and age.

Heredity may endow some individuals with an inordinately strong attitude toward life (see introversion and extraversion). Certain archetypes (i.e., anima and animus, the persona, and the shadow) by nature may be especially strong or weak. Childhood experiences with parents can influence either positively or adversely (i.e., early adoption of the parents' psyches, early family role or persona, the anima of the mother for her son or the animus of the father for his daughter, neglect or overprotection, etc.). Society, particularly modern society, provides few opportunities for the individuation of the shadow archetype. And

Heredity		Social Determinants
Conscious Determinants		Unconscious Determinants
Subjective Reality		Objective Reality
Early Development		Continuous Development
Determinism		Freedom
Uniqueness		Universality

Number and Weight Assigned to Motivational Concepts	All energy (physical or psychic) originates from the metabolic processes. The term libido encompasses all energy. The human energy system functions as a closed system regulated by the principle of equivalence and entropy. We are motivated by the interactions and diverse polar tendencies of the psyche's subsystems.
Explanation of Learning Process	Learning is a dynamic evolving process, an interaction of progression and regression, that occurs throughout life. We must do as much as possible to make the unconscious conscious. Experiences can impede or block learning.
Role Assigned to Self-Concept	Self is present as an inherent propensity when we enter this world. Self is an accumulation of our development. The Self is the final goal of the individuation process, a goal seldom reached.
Role Assigned to Group Determinants	Elements of the collective unconscious can be projected to groups and significantly influence group determinants of individual behavior. Members of a group can become instruments for the forces of the collective unconscious. The morality of any group decreases as the size of the group increases.
Centrality of Reinforcement	Reinforcement is a term that does not appear in Jung's writings.

FIGURE 4-5   Schematic Analysis of Jung's Stance on Basic Issues

finally, not all individuals are able to make the necessary transition to introversion when they reach the second half of life.

Although Jung considered individuation an ideal state, he did on occasion describe some of the characteristics of the individuated person. Note the similarities of his descriptions with those of later humanists, for example, Allport, Chapter 8; Maslow, Chapter 10; and Rogers, Chapter 9.

1. Completed individuation "... signifies detachment from valuations and from what we call emotional ties" (Jung, 1963/1961, p. 296; see also Maslow's Taoistic stance, Chapter 10).

2. Acceptance of reality is ". . . an affirmation of things as they are: an unconditional 'yes' to that which is" (Jung, 1963/1961, p. 297).

3. Acceptance of self is ". . . acceptance of my own nature, as I happen to be . . . . to affirm one's own destiny" (Jung, 1963/1961, p. 297; see also Rogers, Chapter 9).

4. Acceptance of weaknesses as well as strengths: "One must take mistakes into the bargain; life would not be complete without them" (Jung, 1963/1961, p. 297; see also Rogers and Maslow, Chapters 9 and 10).

5. Openness to experience means ". . . to become conscious of the contents that press upward from the unconscious" (Jung, 1963/1961, p. 326).

6. Identification with humankind and all living things.

For Jung, the mandala, or the magic circle, is an archetypal image-occurrence that signifies wholeness and is expressive of the self archetype. He adopted this symbol (from Sanskrit writings) for both the principle of individuation and the archetype of orientation and meaning, noting that through the centuries, the mandala appears in many religions, dreams, and works of art, and in alchemical symbolism.

Psychopathology

Far more concerned with psychotherapy than with pathology, Jung expressed little interest in the development of any comprehensive systems for identifying and classifying different forms of mental illness. Indeed, he found existing classifications of neuroses highly unsatisfactory, and thus, meaningless. In those cultures placing high value on the extraverted personality, for example, there is a natural tendency to diagnose the individual with an introversive attitude a neurotic or, in certain instances, a psychotic. A specific diagnosis of psychoneurosis, Jung (1933) asserted, meant simply that psychotherapy was indicated—nothing more. For Jung, then, the general and broad diagnostic classifications of neurosis and psychosis were usually sufficient for therapeutic purposes.

Neurosis A psychoneurosis exists, in Jung's view, when a complex grows so powerful and dissociated that it overwhelms ego and gains control of personality. Most often the *cause* of neurosis is a conflict between the neglected or repressed attitude or function that is confined to the personal unconscious and the superior attitude or function that is consciously expressed by ego. Left unattended, the repressed elements of an attitude or function can constitute a complex and draw enough psychic energy to act autonomously in the form of pathological symptoms (delusions and hallucinations, for example) and invade conscious ego. Although a neurosis is rooted in the existence of complexes and is, in this sense, regressive, the *aim* of a neurosis is to call attention to the neglected attitude or function. Neurosis is purposive.

When viewed as a compensation for a single-sided attitude to life, a neurosis is a reflection of the psyche's innate individuation process, an expression of the

FIGURE 4-6   The Mandala

integrating and unifying archetype, the Self. Jung attributed positive as well as pathological elements to a neurosis. Indeed, Mattoon (1981) reports that Jung believed many neurotics hold greater potential for development than "normal" people: "The neurosis may force the person to face a responsibility that has been dodged and, hence, use capacities that are needed for his or her development" (p. 155). Through a regression, in this instance a neurosis, a person may uncover useful knowledge and wisdom in the unconscious that will enable him or her to overcome stress and frustration.

Psychosis In Jung's view, both neurosis and psychosis are expressions of repressed or neglected unconscious forces; they are separated only by their intensity and their consequent damage to ego consciousness. The unconscious forces of psychosis are archetypal, hence violent. When unleashed, archetypal contents may overwhelm ego in the form of pathological symptoms (i.e., hallucinations and delusions).

With a neurosis, ego consciousness is still relatively intact. Perceptions, while not always accurate, are still reality based. With a psychosis, however, the injury to ego is extensive. Ego is so violently overwhelmed by archetypal contents that ego consciousness is fragmented. A dissociation of personality results, marked by incoherence of association and thought disorders. It becomes impossible for ego to differentiate between reality and the archetypal projections.

Heuristic Influences: Research Methods and Techniques

Jung insisted his theoretical constructs were based on facts, supported by research. He further insisted that personality research should not be limited to the methodology arbitrarily imposed by empirical science. Consequently, most of his theoretical data were not controlled for bias or chance factors; neither were they amenable to systematic quantification and statistical analysis.

With the exception of his work on the *Word Association Test* (WAT), replication of his work is virtually impossible. He did not, for example, keep verbatim records of his analytic sessions with his patients; hence, he was forced to rely totally on his memory for his case studies. The data he used to validate the existence of the collective unconscious and the archetypes were gathered from the analysis of hallucinations, delusions, visions, dreams, and fantasies and from the comparative studies of primitive life, mythology, religion, alchemy, and the occult. While Jung demonstrated vast knowledge in each of these areas, the more scientifically oriented psychologists find both his sources and his methodology unacceptable and consider his facts highly speculative. Indeed, some label Jung a mystic and dismiss his work entirely. The heuristic influence of Jung's analytic theory on psychology, then, is minimal.

Psychologists have attempted to investigate Jung's (1953/1920) conceptualizations of the attitudes and functions. Early research efforts were rather crude, involving little more than demographic and correlation studies of the relative degrees of extraversion and introversion in relation to such variables as sex, age, and occupation. However, with the development of instruments that yield scores on all the variables of Jung's typology, research became more sophisticated.

Five of the instruments that proved useful in studies of Jung's psychological types are:

1. The *Maudsley Personality Inventory* (Eysenck, 1947, 1978).
2. A variant of the Q-sort technique developed by Stephenson (1950, 1953).
3. The *Sixteen Personality Factor Questionnaire* (Cattell & Stice, 1957).
4. The *Gray–Wheelwright Questionnaire* (Gray & Wheelwright, 1946, 1964).
5. The *Myers–Briggs Type Indicator* (MBTI) (Myers, 1962).

The *Myers–Briggs Type Indicator,* which yields scores on both the attitudes (introversion and extraversion) and the four functions (thinking, feeling, sensing, and intuition), is the more popular of the instruments listed above and has been used in "some 400–500 studies" (Potkay & Allen, 1986).

As predicted by Jung, Cattell and Stice (1957) found that creative workers in the arts and sciences (e.g., researchers, artists, and planning engineers) scored high in introversion as measured by the *Sixteen Personality Factor Questionnaire.* Conversely, subjects scoring high in extraversion were found in occupations requiring mechanical skill (e.g., engineering) and alertness (e.g., cooks, truck drivers, fire fighters).

Support for Jung's typology is reported also by Striker and Ross (1962). Here again there was a close relation to Jung's personality types when scores on the *Myers–Briggs Type Indicator* (MBTI) were compared with the job interests of college students. As predicted, subjects who scored high in introversion expressed interest in occupations that involve little contact and interaction with other people (e.g., technical and scientific work). In direct contrast, subjects with high scores in extraversion were interested in jobs that promised the highest levels of social interaction (e.g., sales, public relations).

Hanewitz (1978) administered the MBTI to 1,282 veteran and police recruits, ninety-six undergraduate social work students, 946 dental students, and eighty-eight public school teachers. This study revealed, also, that Jung's personality types (as measured by the MBTI) significantly influenced the valence of different occupations. The police recruits, for example, were found to be sensation, thinking, and judging, coupled most often with extraversion.

With evidence that Jungian typology influences a person's occupational selection and retention, some researchers set out to test Jung's assertion that an individual's personality type also influences an individual's cognition, hence performance, on different job tasks. Exploring the relationship of rating error to the personality characteristics of the MBTI, Holmes (1984) found that the ratings of Sensing/Judging style managers were consistently more severe than the ratings of the Intuitive/Feeling managerial style. Moreover, Holmes discovered, when rating Unconditional Positive Regard, the frequency of errors was higher for Sensing/Judging types than for Intuitive/Feeling types. It should be noted, however, that Holmes found no difference between types when rating Accurate Empathy.

In a study designed to explore the relationships of problem-solving behaviors and Jungian personality types, Hunter and Levy (1982) found that the typological grouping of the MBTI differentiated the performance patterns in various performance tasks. Of interest also, neither the subjects' sex nor the interaction of the subjects' sex and personality types showed a significant effect in any of the performance measures.

Using the MBTI with a sample of female college students to study the relation of Jungian typology to memory, social perception, and social action, Carlson and Levy (1973) found that female college students who were Introverted/Thinking types performed best on memory tests involving neutral or impersonal stimuli, such as numbers. Extraverted/Feeling types demonstrated better memory for human stimuli with emotional overtones, facial expressions for example.

Maddi (1980) finds Stephenson's unique Q-sort approach to the study of Jung's typology of special interest "because it employs a theorist's own words in measuring the peripheral considerations he or she is defining" (pp. 501–502). Further, Maddi (1980) believes that, despite "a very small sample," Stephenson's study "does raise questions as to whether it is personality types which differ that misunderstand each other" (p. 502).

Duckworth (1975) devised a study to test the idea that introverts were naturally superior to extraverts in judging the feelings of others. Using Eysenck's test, Duckworth found that introverts were, in fact, better judges of others' feelings *when they were also low in anxiety*. There was no difference in judgments between introverts and extraverts, however, when both groups scored high in anxiety.

Not all studies agreed with Jung's typology. There are many studies yielding negative or conflicting results.

Applications to Psychotherapy

Despite the fact that Jung's contributions may have been undervalued by psychologists, current psychotherapies have benefited greatly from the applied value of his ideas. Limiting examples primarily to the theorists presented in this book, Jung's novel theoretical formulations can be found in original, modified, or extended form in the theories of Erik Erikson (Chapter 5), Erich Fromm (Chapter 6), Carl Rogers (Chapter 9), Abraham Maslow (Chapter 10), Rollo May (Chapter 11), and Gordon Allport (Chapter 8).

Therapeutic Goals

For Jung, the individuation process, that innate, future-oriented, human drive for self-realization, unity, and wholeness, is the ultimate aim and goal of life, and hence, analytic psychotherapy. While Rogers (Chapter 9) and Maslow (Chapter

10) have elaborated on and creatively extended the concept of self-actualization as a master motive in human behavior, credit for the original formulation belongs to Jung. Differences between Jung and the actualization theorists center more on means than on end; that is, while Rogers and Maslow may disagree with many of Jung's analytic methods and techniques for enhancing the actualization process in his clients, their ultimate therapeutic aims are nearly identical with the aim presented years earlier by Jung.

Therapeutic Relationship

If the inevitable difficulties encountered by both client and therapist in the analytic process are to be overcome, Jung reasoned, a strong, bonding, client–therapist relationship must develop. For Jung, an effective therapeutic relationship begins with mutual liking and respect, then builds to a point where each participant can perceive and accept the other realistically; that is, as a person rather than as an embodiment of either's projected complexes. Here again, it seems Jung anticipated Rogers's conditions of an effective therapeutic relationship—"genuineness, acceptance, and empathy" (Chapter 9).

Unlike classical Freudian therapists, who viewed their role primarily as objective observers, Jung believed therapists must be genuinely and immediately present and accessible in the therapeutic relationship. He moved the couch out of his office and became an active participant in the therapeutic process. Stressing the significance of the client–therapist relationship in analytic psychotherapy, Mattoon (1981) states: "The analyst is not a doctor who treats a patient but, rather a companion on the way" (p. 224). As companions in the individuation process, Jung warned, therapists are not immune to the power of the relationships they establish with their clients; moreover, he added, they are subject to the adverse effects of their clients' archetypal projections.

For Jung, then, the personality or the psyche of the analytic therapist is at least as important to the analytic process as methodology and technique. However, even more important to therapist effectiveness is the wholeness or health of the therapist. Jung did not believe it possible for a therapist to take a client beyond the therapist's own level of wholeness. Consistent with this conviction, he was one of the first to insist that all prospective analysts undergo a lengthy personal-training analysis as part of their formal preparation.

Attempts have been made, also, to apply Jung's character typology to the therapeutic relationship. Similar character typology of client and therapist may enhance the initial relationship—becoming acquainted and feeling comfortable in the office or hospital setting. Opposite typology, however, can stimulate a therapeutic relationship, so long as the therapist is aware of and guards against client dependency. Mattoon (1981) suggests: "It may be, as in other relationships, that in the optimal combination one dominant function is common, the other different" (p. 234).

Initial Procedures and Strategies

Jung was the first of the psychoanalysts to adopt an open stance in his approach to therapy. Indeed, he was adamantly opposed to the exclusive use of any single psychotherapeutic procedure or technique. For Jung (see "Psychopathology"), the form of a particular neurosis or psychosis is influenced significantly by the client's age and degree of psychological development, and by the nature and severity of pathology. In addition, analytic therapists believe the client's and the therapist's character typologies (see "Attitudinal Dimensions and Functions of the Ego") are necessary considerations in any decision regarding the selection of clients and the procedure and methodology of therapy. Techniques that are right for the extraverted client may be totally wrong, even harmful, for the introverted client.

As a practicing psychiatrist and analyst, Jung originated a number of techniques designed specifically for analytic psychotherapy. A review of current therapeutic techniques, however, reveals that theorists and therapists of other schools have either added or adapted Jung's techniques to their own brand of therapy, or they have independently arrived at techniques very similar to Jung's. Unfortunately, when the latter is the case, Jung is not identified as their author, and his contributions remain undervalued.

Dream Work and Dream Analysis. Both Freud and Jung view the dream as a window to the unconscious. They differ considerably, however, on the view that window provides. Unlike Freud, who saw the dream as a disguised gratification of id's instinctual demands, Jung believed the dream to be a symbolic revelation of the psyche's present reality. For Freud, the dream's primary purpose is to conceal; for Jung, the primary purpose of the dream is to reveal. Viewed from this perspective, dream functions are adaptive, healing, and synthesizing. Consequently, while both Freud and Jung considered the analysis of dreams necessary for in-depth psychotherapy, their approaches to the analysis and interpretation of their patients' dreams differed radically.

Convinced that any dream interpretation must make sense to the dreamer, Jung developed two techniques that require the dreamer's active participation in the interpretation of dream images. The first technique he called *amplification*, the second, *active imagination.*

Amplification. Amplification is an analytic technique devised by Jung to elicit the dreamer's personal associations to dream images. Like his Word Association Test, amplification is a projective technique used to uncover the personal experiences of the dreamer that are related, directly or indirectly, to images in the dream. While amplification works well when the dream images are projections of the client's complexes, it is unsuccessful when the dream images are archetypal projections of the collective unconscious, and thus, beyond personal association.

Active Imagination. Applied to both dreams and fantasies, Jung's technique of active-waking imagination is designed to generate a dialogue between the client's ego and the projected images of the unconscious. The purpose of this technique is twofold: First, it gives form to the complexes and the emotions associated with them, and second, it provides the client's ego a way to confront and understand the compensatory contents of the unconscious. When successful, the technique involves the client directly in the interpretation process. "To listen to the therapist's interpretations is to hear the therapist's projections, which can only interfere with and mislead the dreamer's discovery and integration" (Wallace, 1986, p. 156).

Homework Assignments. While he may not ever have used the term "homework," Jung was the first to recognize the value of the outside assignment as a therapeutic technique, a view held and supported not only by analytic psychotherapists but also by rational-emotive therapists (Ellis, Chapter 15). It was not unusual for Jung to ask his clients to read specific books or articles; keep a diary of dreams or a personal journal; write reports; devise plans for behavioral change; draw, paint, or sculpt; sing, act, or model. For his creative use of art as a therapeutic technique, Jung is credited as the precursor of modern art therapy (Ellenberger, 1970; Maduro & Wheelwright, 1977).

Course of Therapy For Jung, the course of therapy could vary considerably from one patient to another. If, for example, the client's pathology was sexual, Jung might elect a Freudian approach. Should the patient's problem presentation be one of striving for power, Jung might decide to follow an Adlerian approach. It is therefore difficult to describe a typical course of therapy for Jung. With that understanding in mind, Jung did, on occasion, discuss four stages of analytic therapy:

Stage One. On different occasions Jung referred to the first stage of therapy as "catharsis," "emotional cleansing," and "confession." At the initial stage of therapy the therapist must establish an empathic, compassionate relationship with the patient (see "Therapeutic Relationship," above) that facilitates a therapeutic climate in which the client can reveal his or her "pathogenic secrets." The cathartic stage of therapy often initiates transference. This leads to the second stage of therapy.

Stage Two. Jung usually referred to the second stage of therapy as the "elucidation" or "treatment" stage. During the second stage, the patient is encouraged to investigate the shadow, the persona, and the personal unconscious and its complexes. The therapist interprets the childhood origins of the patient's neurosis or psychosis and the patient's symptoms and behavior (see "Initial Procedures and Strategies," above).

Stage Three. For Jung, this stage is described as "education." Here, the therapist helps the patient understand and deal with the inevitable gaps in knowledge caused by his or her pathology (again, see "Initial Procedures and Strategies").

Stage Four. Jung's final stage of therapy is referred to as "transformation," a term he also applies to the individuation process (see "Role Assigned to Self-Concept," this chapter). This stage only begins when the client has dealt successfully with his or her persona, personal unconscious, and shadow. It is only when this level of consciousness has been reached that the deeper levels of the unconscious and archetypal symbols are more accessible. The goals of the fourth stage of therapy are continued individuation and differentiation of the Self.

Throughout the entire process of therapy, Jung believed the therapist must model wholeness to the client. The therapist's level of individuation was far more important to Jung than were techniques and strategies. For this reason, Jung strongly advocated that all analytic therapists undergo analysis as part of their preparation to help others.

Extended Applications

Other disciplines also have profited from the application of Jung's ideas. In his search for data, Jung looked beyond the experience of therapy; hence, applications of his theoretical constructs are found in such diverse areas as education, history, comparative anthropology, religion, art, literature, politics, and criminology.

Space prohibits a comprehensive presentation of Jung's applied value on all the theories and disciplines just listed. However, brief descriptions of those areas that have benefited most from the application of his innovative thinking follow.

Education

Jung did not address the subject of education at any length or depth. Nevertheless, he did recognize the significant influence of teachers on the personality development of the students in their classrooms. Whether that significant influence is positive or negative, Jung contended, depends to a large degree on the wholeness and adjustment of the individual teacher. Accordingly, what teachers model is far more important than what teachers say.

Maladjusted teachers, Jung contended, enter the classroom with all their complexes and problems, then proceed, unconsciously, to project them on their students. Just as the problems of very young children are a reflection of the problems of their parents, many school-age children and adolescents reflect the problems of their teachers. Jung, then, was convinced that concern for the teacher's psychic health and adjustment should equal concern for the teacher's knowledge of subject matter. Holding to his bias, he advanced a number of proposals for teacher education.

Because they are in an ideal position to recognize troubled children, Jung believed teachers should possess an understanding of child pathology. Further, he stressed that the education of prospective teachers should include an in-depth background in the humanities, history, literature, and mythology. Knowledge and experience in these areas are necessary, Jung believed, if teachers are to be prepared later to enhance the consciousness of their students.

Reacting, perhaps, to the adverse experiences he had as a child in school when his teachers did not understand him (see "Biographical Sketch"), Jung also pointed out that teachers, like most adults in the Western culture, overvalue extraversion and need to develop a greater awareness of the inclinations of the inherently introverted child.

Aging and Human Development

Jung was one of the first of the personality theorists to insist that the process of human development persists throughout an individual's life. Indeed, he was convinced that inner growth and transformation could proceed at an accelerated pace for individuals with the courage to accept the individuation process in the second half of life. This position also predates similar concepts held by contemporary self-actualization theorists, particularly Abraham Maslow (Chapter 10).

Criminology and Biofeedback Research

Jung's work on the Word Association Test as an instrument to measure the projections of the unconscious continues to be applied to and researched by criminologists and biofeedback therapists who use galvanic, respiratory, and pulse-rate responses to monitor an individual's subjective psychosomatic processes.

Anthropology and Folklore Studies

Jung's methodology and research techniques continue to be applied in anthropology and folklore studies. His comparative analysis of rituals, myths, and symbols is an accepted contemporary anthropological approach to research.

Critique

Readers of Jung's works will discover that there are a number of obstacles to be overcome. Not only is Jung's theory dispersed throughout his writings, but readers have criticized his elusive writing style. Laden with frequent and lengthy references to obscure philosophical, historical, and mythological sources, Jung's writing places great demands on his readers. His language is often metaphorical. His idiosyncratic definitions of common terms tend to confuse rather than to clarify, and his facts are oftentimes highly speculative.

Jung (1963/1961) seemed aware that he presented obstacles to his readers: "I am a solitary, because I know things and must hint at things which other people do not know, and usually do not even want to know" (p. 42). He regularly proclaimed that his work could only be understood in the personal experience of analytic psychotherapy, and as Farau (1961) points out, this response neither encouraged his readers' understanding nor soothed his critics. Despite these difficulties, students willing to make the effort necessary to understand Jung will find that analytic psychology is unrivaled in complexity and comprehensiveness. No other theory covers such a wide diversity of phenomena.

Of all who broke from Freud's classical theory of psychoanalysis, it was Jung, with his range of ideas and force of influence, whom Freud feared most (Brome, 1978). It was Jung who stimulated Freud (1913/1950) to write *Totem and Taboo.*

The strongest criticisms of Jung are focused on his disregard for the rigors of objective science in his approach to theory construction. The data for his theory were not gathered in controlled or objective fashion; hence, his work cannot be replicated. With the exception of Jung's *Word Association Test* (WAT) and his character typology, there is little in his theory to generate experimental testing. For Jung, the word "research" was often synonymous with the comparative study of symbols.

While these criticisms appear justified, Jung's contributions must not be ignored. Historians of the psychoanalytic movement are discovering that contemporary psychotherapies are ultimately rooted in the theoretical concepts of Freud, Jung, and Adler. In Madura and Wheelwright's (1977) assessment: "A great deal of what passes today for 'neo'-Freudian theory (e.g., 'regression in the service of the ego') turns out . . . to be recently *rediscovered,* extended, or modified Jung and Adler" (p. 117, italics in original). As noted throughout this chapter, Jung's influence is not limited to the analytic schools. Indeed, many of the central concepts of current psychotherapies were first proposed by Jung: Erikson's life stages, which covered the adult years; the concept of an innate self-actualization process similar to those found in the theories of Allport, Rogers, and Maslow; an adult transformation process that can only occur in the second half of life and a concern for the spirituality and religious needs of humans, again similar to ideas later expressed by Maslow.

While many psychologists appear somewhat reluctant to recognize an indebtedness to Jung, other disciplines are less hesitant. The invitation to Jung from Yale University, in 1938, to deliver the Terry lecture is an indication of the high esteem accorded Jung by the religious leaders of that period. In addition, Jung received acknowledgements from respected scholars in anthropology, art, criminology, history, and literature.

Annotated Bibliography

Published the year of his death, *Memories, Dreams, Reflections* (1961/1963) is Jung's unorthodox autobiography and final exploration of the forces and influences that he believed molded his intellectual development. In his life, as in his theory, Jung focused on the unconscious—the private inner world of dreams, visions, fantasies, and spiritual experiences. Whenever faced with difficult problems or choices, Jung turned inward for guidance. He followed this same path when writing about his life.

More traditional biographical accounts of Jung's life may be found in Brome's (1978) *Jung: Man and Myth;* Hanna's (1976) *Jung: His Life and His Work;* and Jaffé's (1971) *From the Life and Work of C. G. Jung.* In addition, a unique view of Jung's life and ideas can be acquired through his letters in a volume edited by G. Adler (1973), *C. G. Jung Letters, I: 1906–1950.*

Students attracted to Jung's theory of analytic psychology are encouraged to advance their understanding by reading primary sources, preferably Jung's last works, since these constitute his final theoretical statements. Rather than reading at random from the collected works of Jung, Hall and Nordby (1973) suggest an introductory reading approach that assumes no previous experience with Jung and includes inexpensive paperback editions when they are available (pp. 132–133). Selections from Jung's works are presented in Campbell's *The Portable Jung* (1971), and de Laszlo's *The Basic Writings of C. G. Jung* (1959).

References and Suggested Readings

Adler, G. (Ed.). (1973). *C. G. Jung letters, I: 1906–1950.* Princeton, NJ: Princeton University Press.

Bennet, E. A. (1962). *C. G. Jung.* New York: E. P. Dutton.

Bradway, K. (1971). Jung's psychological types: Classification by test versus classification by self. In H. J. Vetter & B. D. Smith, (Eds.). *Personality theory: A source book.* New York: Appleton–Century–Crofts.

Brome, V. (1978). *Jung.* New York: Atheneum.

Brown, S. R., & Hendrick, C. (1971). Introversion, extraversion and social perception. *British Journal of Social and Clinical Psychology, 10,* pp. 313–319.

Campbell, J. (Ed.). (1971). *The portable Jung.* (R. F. C. Hull, Trans.). New York: Viking Press.

Cattell, R. B., & Stice, G. F. (1957). *Sixteen Personality Factor Questionnaire* (Rev. ed.). Champaign, IL: Inst. Personality Ability Test.

Cox, D. (1968). *Modern psychology: The teachings of Carl Gustav Jung.* New York: Barnes & Noble.

Crooks, T. G., & Pearson, P. R. (1970). The relationship between EPI scores and 16PF second order factors in a clinical group. *British Journal of Social and Clinical Psychology, 9,* pp. 189–190.

de Laszlo, V. S. (Ed.). (1958). *Psyche and Symbol: A selection from the writing of C. G. Jung.* New York: Doubleday.

de Laszlo, V. S. (Ed.). (1959). *The basic writings of C. G. Jung.* New York: Modern Library.

Duckworth, D. H. (1975). Personality, emotional state and perception of nonverbal communication. *Perceptual and Motor Skills, 40*, pp. 325–326.

Edinger, E. F. (1985). *Anatomy of the psyche: Alchemical symbolism in psychotherapy.* LaSalle, IL: Open Court.

Ellenberger, H. F. (1970). *The discovery of the unconscious.* New York: Basic Books.

Evans, R. I. (1964). *Conversations with Carl Jung and reactions from Ernest Jones.* New York: Van Nostrand.

Ewin, R. B. (1984). *An introduction to personality theories* (2nd ed.). New York: Academic Press.

Eysenck, H. J. (1947). *Dimensions of personality.* London: Routledge & Kegan Paul.

Eysenck, H. J. (1976). *Sex and personality.* London: Open Books.

Eysenck, H. J. (1978). The structure of personality. In R. J. Corsini, (Ed.). *Readings in current personality theories.* Itasca, IL: F. E. Peacock.

Farau, A. (1961). C. G. Jung: An Adlerian appreciation. *Journal of Individual Psychology, 17*(2), pp. 135–140.

Fling, S., Thomas, A., & Gallaher, M. (1981). Participant characteristics and the effects of two types of meditation vs. quiet sitting. *Journal of Clinical Psychology, 37*, pp. 784–790.

Fordham, F. (1953). *An introduction to Jung's psychology.* Baltimore: Penguin.

Freud, S. (1950). *Totem and taboo.* (J. Starchey, Trans.). New York: Norton. (Originally published 1913)

Glover, E. (1950). *Freud or Jung.* London: George Allen & Uwin.

Gray, H., & Wheelwright, J. B. (1946). Jung's psychological types, their frequency and occurrence. *Journal of General Psychology, 34*, pp. 3–17.

Gray, H., & Wheelwright, J. B. (1964). *Jungian type survey.* San Francisco: Society of Jungian Analysts of Northern California.

Hall, C. S., & Lindzey, G. (1978). *Theories of personality* (3rd ed.). New York: John Wiley & Sons.

Hall, C. S., & Nordby, V. J. (1973). *A primer of Jungian psychology.* New York: New American Library.

Hanewitz, W. B. (1978). Police personality: A Jungian perspective. *Crime and Delinquency, 24*, pp. 152–172.

Hannah, B. (1976). *Jung: His life and work.* New York: G. P. Putnam's Sons.

Helmes, T. R. (1984). The relationship of rating error to personality characteristics of the Myers–Briggs Type Indicator. (Doctoral dissertation, Michigan State Univ., 1983). *Dissertation Abstracts International, 44*,12. 3918B

Helson, R. (1983). Critics and their texts: An approach to Jung's theory of cognitive and personality. *Journal of Personality and Social Psychology, 43*(2), pp. 409–418.

Hergenhahan, B. R. (1984). *An introduction to theories of personality* (2nd ed.). Englewood Cliffs, NJ: Prentice–Hall.

Hunter, F., & Levy, N. (1982). Relationship of problem-solving behaviors and Jungian personality types. *Psychological Reports, 51*(2), pp. 379–384.

Jacobi, J. (1976). *The psychology of C. G. Jung: An introduction with illustrations.* New Haven, CT: Yale University Press. (Originally published in 1940)

Jaffé, A. (1971). *From the life and work of C. G. Jung* (R. F. C. Hull, Trans.). New York: Harper Colophon.

Jung, C. G. (1933). *Modern man in search of a soul* (W. S. Dell & C. F. Baynes, Trans.). New York: Harcourt Brace Jovanovich. (Originally published in German, 1931)

Jung, C. G. (1953–1978). *Collected works.* H. Read, M. Fordham, & G. Adler. (Eds.). Princeton, NJ: Princeton University Press.

Jung, C. G. (1953). Psychological types. In *Collected works* (Vol. 6). Princeton, NJ: Princeton University Press. (Originally published in 1920)

Jung, C. G. (1957). *The undiscovered self* (R. F. C. Hull, Trans.). New York: Mentor Books.

Jung, C. G. (1959). The soul and death. In H. Feifel, (Ed.). *The meaning of death.* (Pp. 3–15). New York: McGraw–Hill.

Jung, C. G. (1963). *Memories, dreams, reflections* (Rev. ed.). A. Jaffé, (Ed.). (R. Winston & C. Winston, Trans.) New York: Pantheon Books. (Originally published 1961)

Jung, C. G. (1964). *Man and his symbols.* New York: Dell.

Jung, C. G. (1968). *Analytical psychology: Its theory and practice.* New York: Vintage Books.

Jung, C. G. (1973). *Synchronicity.* (R. F. C. Hull, Trans.). Princeton, NJ: Princeton University Press.

Jung, C. G. (1978). Phenomena resulting from the assimilation of the unconscious. In R. S. Corsini (Ed.), *Readings in current personality theories.* Itasca, IL: F. E. Peacock.

Krippner, S. (1983). A systems approach to creativity based on Jungian typology. *Gifted Child Quarterly, 27*(2), pp. 86–89.

Kutash, I. L., & Wolf, A. (Eds.). (1986). *Psychotherapist's casebook: Theory and techniques in the practice of modern therapies.* San Francisco: Jossey–Bass.

Leichtman, R. R. (1979). *From heaven to earth: Jung and Freud return.* Columbus, OH: Ariel Press.

Maddi, S. R. (1980). *Personality theories: A comparative analysis* (4th ed.). Homewood, IL: The Dorsey Press.

Madura, R. S., & Wheelwright, S. B. (1977). Analytical psychology. In R. J. Corsini (Ed.), *Current personality theories.* Itasca, IL: F. E. Peacock.

Marshall, I. N. (1967). Extraversion and libido in Jung and Cattell. *Journal of Analytic Psychology, 12,* pp. 115–136.

Mattoon, M. A. (1981). *Jungian psychology in perspective.* New York: The Free Press.

McQuad, J. (1967). A note on trends in answers to Cattell Personality Questionnaire by Scottish subjects. *British Journal of Psychology, 58,* pp. 455–458.

Monte, C. F. (1980). *Beneath the mask: An introduction to theories of personality* (2nd ed.). New York: Holt, Rinehart and Winston.

Munroe, R. (1955). *Schools of psychoanalytic thought.* New York: Holt, Rinehart & Winston.

Myers, I. B. (1962). *Myers–Briggs type indicator manual.* Palo Alto, CA: Consulting Psychologists Press.

Odajnyk, V. W. (1976). *Jung and politics: The political and social ideas of C. G. Jung.* New York: Harper & Row.

Perls, F. S. (1976). *The gestalt approach and eye witness to psychotherapy.* New York: Banton Books. (Originally published 1969)

Potkay, C. R., & Allen, B. P. (1986). *Personality: Theory, research, and application.* Monterey, CA: Brooks/Cole.

Progoff, I. (1956). *The death and rebirth of psychology: An integrative evaluation of Freud, Adler, Jung, and Rank and the impact of their culminating insights on modern man.* New York: Julian Press.

Shapiro, K. J., & Alexander, I. E. (1969). Extraversion, introversion, affiliation, and anxiety. *Journal of Personality, 37,* pp. 387–406.

Stein, M. (1985). *Jung's treatment of Christianity: The psychotherapy of a religious tradition.* Wilmette, IL: Chiron Publications.

Stephenson, W. (1950). The significance of Q-technique for the study of personality. In M. L. Reynert (Ed.), *Feelings and emotions: The Moosehart symposium.* New York: McGraw–Hill.

Stephenson, W. (1953). *The study of behavior: Q-technique and its methodology.* Chicago: University of Chicago Press.

Stern, P. J. (1976). *C. G. Jung: The haunted prophet.* New York: Braziller.

Storr, A. (1973). *C. G. Jung.* New York: Viking Press.

Stricker, L. J., & Ross, J. (1971). Some correlates of a Jungian personality inventory. In H. J. Vetter & B. D. Smith, (Eds.). *Personality theory: A source book.* New York: Appleton–Century–Crofts.

Taft, R. (1967). Extraversion, neuroticism and expressive behavior: An application of Wallach's moderator effect to handwriting analysis. *Journal of Personality, 37,* pp. 570–584.

Toynbee, A. (1956). The value of Jung's work for historians. *Journal of Analytical Psychology, 1,* pp. 193–194.

Wallace, W. A. (1986). *Theories of counseling and psychotherapy: A basic issues approach.* Boston: Allyn and Bacon.

Wankowski, J. A. (1973). *Temperament, motivation and academic achievement.* Birmingham, AL: University of Birmingham Education Survey and Counseling Unit.

Wehr, G. (1971). *Portrait of Jung.* (W. A. Hargreaves, Trans.). New York: Herder and Herder.

Westman, H. (1961). *The springs of creativity.* New York: Atheneum.

Wickes, F. G. (1963). *The inner world of choice.* Englewood Cliffs, NJ: Prentice–Hall.

Wilhelm, R., & Jung, C. G. (1931). *The secret of the golden flower.* New York: Harcourt Brace & World.

Part 2

Analytic and Neoanalytic Theories

The designation "Analytic and Neoanalytic Theories" was selected for its historical significance rather than for any unified theoretical group or school of thought. While there are some similarities, there are also basic theoretical differences among the theorists selected for presentation in Part Two of this book. Many of the theorists whose ideas appear here started their professional careers as classical or Freudian psychoanalysts. However, their clinical observations led them to place greater emphasis on cultural, social, and cognitive determinants. For these theorists, ego becomes more than a slave to id.

Erik Erikson remained loyal to the Freudian camp, but he introduced major theoretical differences, particularly in the life stages of human development. Not only did he extend the stages to the entire life span, his eight life stages were psychological rather than biological, a major modification of Freud's theory. Ego also played a much greater role in Erikson's theory, and a sense of identity became crucial to mature development and psychological health.

Erich Fromm presented a far different view of human nature than that presented by Freud. From Fromm's perspective, evolution severed us from the safety and security provided by our instinctual unity with nature, and we were left with feelings of aloneness, powerlessness, and the need to transcend our animal nature. We must, Fromm asserted, fulfill our need for relatedness, use our intellect to make sense of our world, and choose those experiences that unite us with ourselves, others, and the environment. Further, because he believed sick societies breed sick people, Fromm was convinced that we must learn to cope with societal influences, especially political and economic influences.

Karen Horney found Freud's view of women and human sexuality totally unacceptable. For her, Freud's Oedipus complex was often nothing more than a little girl's wish for the freedom her parents granted her brother. She also introduced the concept of the real self, an inner motivating force and set of potentials that pulled toward realization. Horney was the first to propose self-analysis. She also introduced the "tyrannical shoulds," which, when inordinately strong, inevitably lead to neurosis.

Though many of the neoanalysts fought against Freudian traditions, they consciously or unconsciously borrowed, at times liberally, from Adler, in particular from his concepts regarding the dynamics of the family constellation, lifestyle, creative self, and the importance of social interest. Jung's individuation process also had an impact on their thinking.

The courage of the neoanalysts must be recognized, also. As you will learn, presenting their ideas often cost them the loss of valued professional affiliations and training positions with psychoanalytic societies and institutes. In a very real sense, the three theorists included under this broad and general classification were also pioneers in the fields of personality and therapeutic theory. Their theoretical concepts, or variations of them, are echoed by many of today's personologists and psychotherapists.

Chapter 5

Erikson's Theory of Ego Psychology

Chapter Overview

Introduction

Biographical Sketch of the Theorist

Resolution of Basic Issues
  Heredity versus Social Determinants
  Early versus Continuous Development
  Subjective versus Objective Reality
  Determinism versus Freedom of Choice
  Conscious versus Unconscious Determinants
  Uniqueness versus Universality
  Explanation of Learning Process
  Role Assigned to Self-Concept
  Number and Weight Assigned to Motivational Concepts
  Centrality of Reinforcement
  Role Assigned to Group Determinants

Psychological Health and Psychopathology
  Psychological Health
  Psychopathology

Applications to Psychotherapy
  Therapeutic Goals
  Therapeutic Relationship

Therapeutic Process and Strategies
Course of Therapy

Extended Applications
Dreams and Dream Interpretation
Psychohistory
Play Therapy
Art Therapy

Critique

Annotated Bibliography

References and Suggested Readings

Introduction

Unlike Fromm (Chapter 6) and Horney (Chapter 7), who in time became openly critical of Freud's Theory of Psychoanalysis as their own theories of personality developed in new directions, Erik Homburger Erikson (1902–) declared his acceptance of Freud's tripartite structure of personality and libido theory. However, though Erikson praised Freud's theory and insisted that there were strong ties binding his theory to Freud's, there are also significant differences that are more than simple shifts in emphasis. Indeed, some differences between Erikson's and Freud's theories are radical.

One major difference between Erikson's and Freud's theories relates to the function of ego. For Freud (Chapter 2), ego functions only to serve the unconscious, irrational, and amoral needs of id. Erikson, in contrast, grants ego autonomous needs of its own; moreover, he stresses the strengths and capacities of a rational ego for positive growth over an entire life cycle. A second major difference with Freud, who insisted that society was inevitably a source of conflict for ego, Erikson argued that society often supported ego by providing sanctioned social roles and identities. As will be seen later, *ego identity*, for Erikson (1964a), is a vital need of all humans.

Finally, while Erikson shares Freud's beliefs regarding the early stages of psychosexual development, he expanded Freud's stages to eight **epigenetic** stages that unfold according to an innate plan (much as the growth of the fetus) and span the entire life cycle, and that are subject not only to biological forces but also to a rational and adaptive ego, to societal processes, and to historical factors. In Erikson's view, then, we are more than bodily beings; we are also psychosocial beings tied to historical factors with the lifetime potential for change that may lead either to growth or stagnation.

Along with Anna Freud (Freud's daughter and Erikson's training analyst), Erikson was one of the first psychoanalysts to treat children. With his background in art and elementary teaching, Erikson was also a pioneer in art and play therapy, particularly in the treatment of seriously disturbed children.

Erikson, his wife Joan, and Helen Kivnick (1986), who assert that aging is the only path to wisdom, are responsible for calling the attention of personologists to the elderly as they struggle with the crisis of personal integrity and feelings of defeat and despair during the final stage of life. Nearing their ninth decade, the Eriksons were able to view the final phase of life in a way that was impossible when Erikson first formulated the eight stages in the 1950s. Considering the aging of our society, this may very well prove to be one of Erikson's most valuable contributions.

Erikson's writing, which fills twelve volumes, includes: *Young Man Luther* (1958), *Childhood and Society* (1963), *Insight and Responsibility* (1964), *Identity: Youth and Crisis* (1968), *Gandhi's Truth* (1969), *In Search of Common Ground* (1973), *Dimensions of a New Identity: The Jefferson Lectures in Humanities* (1974), *Life History and the Historical Moment* (1975), *Toys and Reasons: Stages in the Realization of Experience* (1977), *Identity and the Life Cycle: A Reissue* (1979), *The Life Cycle Completed* (1985), and *Involvement in Old Age* (with Joan M. Erikson and Helen Q. Kivnick, 1986).

Biographical Sketch of the Theorist

Early Childhood

Very little is known about Erikson's biological father, with the exception that he was a Danish Protestant who deserted his wife before Erikson was born. Left alone and pregnant, Erikson's mother decided to stay with friends in Frankfurt, Germany, until she delivered her child. Erikson was born June 15, 1902.

Erikson's mother became friends with her son's pediatrician, Dr. Theodore Homburger, and they eventually married. Deciding that it would be best for Erikson, then nearly three years old, the Homburgers decided not to tell Erikson about his biological father and gave Erikson his stepfather's surname. Though well-intentioned, their decision later created problems for Erikson. Even as a child, he sensed that something was wrong. His parents were Jews, but at the temple he was called "goy" (the Yiddish word for gentile). In school, and to his German classmates, he was a Jew. His appearance, tall, blue eyed, and blond, which was very unlike his parents', only added to his confusion, and he began to suspect that he did not really belong to his family. In response to his concern, his mother and stepfather felt obligated to tell him about his biological father and his Danish heritage. He kept the surname Homburger until 1939. He adopted Erikson as his last name when he became a naturalized citizen of the United States, retaining his stepfather's surname as his middle name.

Education

Although elementary school was a fairly pleasant experience for Erikson, the rigid scholastic atmosphere of the Gymnasium was not. Erikson did not do well in his academic subjects, but he discovered that he was talented in art. After being graduated from the Gymnasium (the end of his formal education), Erikson decided against his stepfather's wish that he enter the university to prepare for a medical career. He chose instead to follow the path taken by many German youths who were undecided about a vocational choice and uncertain of their identity. In Germany, *Wanderschaft* (a ritualistic and reflective wandering) was accepted, even encouraged, for restless young men who needed time away from family and friends to consider who they were and what they wanted to do with their lives. Erikson planned only to wander through Europe, sketch the people and scenery, and write notes on his experiences.

After a year, Erikson returned home and completed a year in art school. Dissatisfied, he went to Munich, where he enrolled in a school of art. Still confused and restless after two years in Munich, he moved to Florence, Italy, and spent his time simply wandering about the city, absorbing its cultural history.

In 1927, at age twenty-five, Erikson returned home, fully determined to continue his study while teaching art for a living. However, when contacted by Peter Blos, who offered him a teaching position in a small progressive American nursery school in Vienna that had been established for the children of Sigmund Freud's patients and friends, he immediately accepted. There he met Anna Freud who, impressed with his work with the children, encouraged him to apply for psychoanalytic training in the Vienna Psychoanalytic Institute. She became his training analyst for an unusually small monthly fee. Erikson (in Erikson and Erikson, 1981) later referred to Anna Freud as his analyst, his mentor, and the first model of a child analyst. Without a doubt she made a lasting impact on his life.

In 1929, Erikson and Joan Mowat were married. She was a Canadian citizen, interested and talented in the arts, who also taught at the nursery school. The Eriksons worked closely together. In addition to her own writing, she edited her husband's books and collaborated on some.

Graduating from the institute and fearing the threat of Nazism, the Eriksons and their two sons fled Germany in 1933. They moved first to Denmark, then to the United States, where Erikson began private practice as a child analyst. He was also a research fellow under the guidance and supervision of Henry Murray in the Department of Neuropsychiatry at the Harvard Medical School.

Emergence of Erikson's Theory

Erikson's theoretical constructs on childhood were formulated through research on infantile neurosis at the Yale School of Medicine, where he worked with both normal and emotionally disturbed children. From 1939 to 1950, Erikson was a research associate at the Institute of Child Welfare, and later became Professor of Psychology at the University of California, Berkeley. He left his position there when he resigned rather than sign a loyalty oath that he considered an infringement of human rights.

From 1951 to 1960, Erikson was a senior consultant at the Austen–Riggs Center and a professor at the University of Pittsburgh School of Medicine. In 1960, Erikson was appointed Professor of Human Development and Lecturer at Harvard University.

Honors

Erikson's Theory of Ego Psychology received wide acceptance in psychiatry and in academic programs. In addition, his writings were well received by the general public. Erikson has lived to see his influence spread from child psychiatry to education, social work, psychiatric nursing, and vocational and marriage counseling. His theory appears in many of the personality textbooks in psychology and counseling.

Erikson held faculty appointments in a number of the most prestigious universities in the United States, including Harvard, Yale, and the University of California, no small accomplishment when one considers that most universities hold fast to academic credentials for their highest faculty ranks. In 1978, Harvard University awarded Erikson an honorary doctoral degree and the Harvard Medical School announced the creation of an endowed Erik and Joan Erikson Professorship of Human Development at Cambridge Hospital. Erikson's theory of psychosocial development was also recognized by the establishment of the Erikson Institute for Early Childhood Education of Loyola University of Chicago.

Resolution of Basic Issues

As with all the neopsychoanalytic theories, Erikson's theory does not directly address all of the eleven basic issues selected for the structure of this book. For example, the terms reinforcement and self-concept either do not appear in his writings or are mentioned only briefly in passing, and he does not discuss groups as determinants of behavior. Still, Erikson does mention the rewards of society for adaptation; his theoretical construct of ego identity is similar in many ways to the constructs of self-concept in other personality theories, and he does write of the impact of social institutions and groups on personality development. In short, it is possible to find (either directly or indirectly) at least partial or implied resolutions for each of the eleven basic issues.

Heredity versus Social Determinants

According to Erikson (1963), the id is the sole component of personality present at birth. Our id contains our entire evolutionary history and all inherited instincts. Moreover, our id, Erikson (1963) asserts, contains a genetically determined nature that predisposes us to grow and develop to a predetermined **epigenetic** schedule that unfolds in proper sequence as we progress through each stage of life. For Erikson (1963), then, at critical points in the maturational process, there is in each of us:

> *a readiness to be driven toward, to be aware of, and to interact with a widening social radius and . . . that society, in principle, tends to be so constituted as to meet and invite this succession of potentialities for interaction and attempts to safeguard and to encourage the proper rate and the proper sequence of their unfolding (p. 270).*

It is evident from this statement that, while Erikson accepts an unconscious, amoral id, he does not endow it with the all-powerful determining force granted to the id in Freud's theory. Indeed, while Erikson retains Freud's tripartite structural model of id, ego, and superego, he attributes to the ego greater strength and constructive capacities and autonomous functions that were absent in Freud's ego construct.

Erikson's clinical observations and research, particularly his studies of the effects of different cultures on personality, convinced him that social and cultural factors significantly influence the developing ego. Further, while Erikson viewed individual psychological growth as an inner process, he also held that the inner process of psychological growth was impossible without certain supportive environmental conditions.

Whether innate (heredity), in the sense that it is part of our genetically determined nature, or acquired in the course of living (social), Erikson believed that ego identity is a vital need in all of us.

Early versus Continuous Development

From his clinical observations, investigations of child rearing practices of various cultures, and psychohistories of noted historical figures, Erikson, like Freud, came to believe that our personality develops as we progress through a series of life stages that are universal to our species. Unlike Freud, however, Erikson believes that there are eight developmental stages that span the entire life-cycle (as opposed to being virtually complete by the age of five) and operate on the **epigenetic principle** (that is, they unfold in an invariant sequence). Further, rather than basing the developmental stages solely on psychosexual urges and drives, as did Freud, Erikson's (1964a) eight stages are primarily psychosocial:

> *I, therefore, have in recent years attempted to delineate the whole life-cycle as an integrated psychosocial phenomenon, instead of following what (in analogy to teleology) may be called the "originalogical" approach; that is, the attempt to derive the meaning of development primarily from a reconstruction of the infant's beginnings (p. 114).*

In addition, Erikson (1963, 1964a, 1968, 1977, 1980) asserts that a vital human need for identity evolves through all of the eight developmental stages, and each stage is characterized by a psychosocial **crisis** that must be confronted. Erikson did not use the term crisis in the usual sense of catastrophic threat or critical conflict, but rather as a crucial, unavoidable turning point in life that requires a decision and results in either progress toward integration and identity or toward fixation, regression, or stagnation of the developmental process.

Unlike Freud, Erikson maintains that ego, which functions rationally, adaptively, and constructively, need not always be in conflict with social and cultural forces. Indeed, the psychosocial crises can provide new energy for growth and assist the development of ego by providing new opportunities for positive growth, contributing to the strengthening of ego, and increasing the probability of successful adaptation at future stage-crises. Erikson's stance on this issue, then, is that personality development is a continuous process.

Erikson's Eight Stages of Ego Development Before reviewing Erikson's Eight Stages of Ego Development, which he feared were often misunderstood and viewed with more optimism than he intended, it is important to note several points.

Ego strengths (sometimes referred to as virtues or qualities: hope, will, competence, etc.) are *not* to be viewed as permanent achievements. Rather, basic conflicts continue to remain and must continually be resolved throughout the life span. Therefore, though a child in the fourth stage may develop a sense of competence, later experiences (e.g., failure at a major vocational task or failure of a significant relationship) may threaten his or her self-efficacy so severely that he or she feels inferior. In short, all is not lost with a negative resolution of a psychosocial crisis, nor is all gained when a crisis resolution is positive.

Never is ego strength completely achieved. Indeed, there must be a balance of the two poles in every psychosocial crisis. For example, both initiative *and* guilt and fear of punishment must be sensed for the ego strength of purpose to be healthy. Healthy **purpose** is the selection and pursuit of realistic goals. Without some guilt or fear of punishment (the negative pole of the crisis resolution) the goals selected and pursued would be dysfunctional, even destructive. Some sense of guilt and fear must be present if the individual is to weigh the risks involved and limit aggressiveness in the pursuit of his or her goals.

The specific age range of each of the eight psychosocial stages is not to be viewed as inflexible; they are approximations. It was not Erikson's intention, for example, to claim that identity *had* to be achieved by the age of twenty, or that a basic trust in self, others, and the world *had* to be developed by the end of the first year. Some adolescents have selected and become committed to a vocational choice by the ages of twelve or thirteen. Others may not decide with any degree of certainty on their career path until years later and, then their decision may have been the result of a chance encounter or a traumatic event (see "Biographical Sketch," this chapter).

Oral–Sensory Stage: Basic Trust versus Mistrust. Although Erikson's initial stage, the most helpless period of life, is similar to Freud's oral stage, in that focus is on the mouth as the center of pleasure, and the infant first senses the world through contact with the mother, the crisis to be resolved is that of basic trust or basic mistrust. If the infant's mother sensitively and affectionately responds to her baby's needs, that is, if she is loving, consistent, and dependable, the infant is likely to feel secure and develop a sense of **basic trust** in self, others, and the world. For Erikson, basic trust is the cornerstone of the healthy personality.

The first positive sign of the infant's accomplishment of basic trust is its willingness to let its mother out of sight without experiencing great anxiety. This will only occur if the infant has developed an inner certainty that its mother will return and continue to feed and care for its needs, and that it will be able to cope during its mother's absence. The child's inner sense of certainty also contributes to a rudimentary sense of identity and the feeling that people and the world are safe and dependable. Basic trust is a mutual experience for mother and infant and, when present, leads to a relaxed and gratifying relationship for both.

Conversely, if the mother acts in an aloof, inattentive, uncaring, inconsistent, and unreliable way to her child, the child will experience frustration, anger, and fright. Further, its behavior will become more demanding and less predictable. The feeling of being deprived of its needs and wishes leads to a sense of **basic mistrust.**

If the infant develops a sense of basic trust, it also experiences the sense of **hope,** a necessary ego strength for a healthy life (see "Determinism versus Freedom of Choice"). Although the child is born with the capacity to learn to hope, the environment must offer him or her a convincing world view and, within that view, specific hopes (Erikson, in Evans, 1967, p. 30). For Erikson, hope is both the earliest and the most significant ego strength inherent in an individual's life. Indeed, Erikson maintains: Life is impossible without hope.

While a sense of basic trust (or mistrust) is established in the first year of life, it may further develop or diminish at later stages, depending largely on future social relationships. Trust and hope established in the first year can be dashed by a child's perceived betrayal in a significant relationship in any of the developmental stages. Likewise, when basic mistrust is the outcome of the first stage, later experiences can provide a second chance. With every new stage there is a new opportunity for reintegrating the crisis of an earlier stage. No crisis resolution is ever complete or irreversible.

Muscular–Anal Stage: Autonomy versus Shame and Doubt.   Erikson's second stage of ego development is similar to Freud's anal stage and usually occurs during the second and third years of life. During this period, toilet training and the control of sphincter muscles become an issue and can lead to a conflict of wills between parents and child.

In addition to the clash of wills over the child's habits of elimination, the child's ability to move about without assistance and its eagerness for new experiences lead to adventures that, while exciting for the child, inevitably result in conflict (e.g., opening and exploring the contents of cabinets and drawers, sampling the dog's food, reaching for the flowers on the coffee table) that require him or her to submit to being controlled by others and to learn self-control and self-restraint.

While the first stage involves trust, the muscular–anal stage involves the risk of that trust. Confronting the crisis of this stage requires an assertion of independence, some degree of choice, and a beginning sense of autonomy. Gradual and firm reassurance on the part of the parents leads to a child's sense of autonomy, a sense of pride in personal accomplishment, and a warm, positive feeling toward others. The strength of **will** ("unbroken determination to exercise free choice as well as self-restraint," Erikson, 1964a, p. 119) emerges. For ego development, this means an increase in ego's power to exercise judgment and decision, determination and restraint.

In contrast, if parents are too demanding or too permissive, if they express anger and force their will on the child, the child experiences a sense of defeat, often accompanied by feelings of shame and doubt. The defeated child does not feel capable of effective decisions and judgments, nor is the child able to exercise control over his or her life. Feeling defeat, the child may learn to expect defeat in any contest of wills with those who are bigger and stronger, and may resort to compulsive behavior to retain some control in an anticipated defeating encounter.

Erikson's second stage offers the child numerous opportunities for developing muscular control and facility with language. Success leads to self-esteem and feelings of self-efficacy. Sustained failure impairs self-esteem and leads to an inordinately strong sense of inferiority.

Locomotor–Genital Stage: Initiative versus Guilt. Erikson's third stage of ego development occurs during the fourth and fifth years of age, and is similar to Freud's phallic stage. During the third stage of development, children seek more contact with others outside the family circle. They engage in play and other experimental activities with their peers. Their curiosity leads to incessant questioning on practically all topics. They fantasize about being adults and act out adult roles in their play. They become concerned with questions about sex, and they attempt, *in fantasy,* to possess the parent of the opposite sex. They experience feelings of rivalry with the same-sexed parent, and develop a sense of guilt if severely punished by their parents for their questions, advancements, and exploratory behavior.

If, however, their parents are understanding and guide their child's motives and desires to socially acceptable activities, the child develops a sense of purpose (setting major life goals and identifying with parents without fear of punishment or guilt). Through their play activities, they identify with their parents, pretending to be a mother or father, and they identify with adult roles by pretending to be a successful doctor, fire fighter, nurse, teacher, lawyer, judge, dentist, and so on.

It is during this stage, also, that the child develops a conscience (superego). Should a feeling of guilt and a conviction of being essentially bad result from the struggle with initiative versus guilt, initiative could be stifled or moralism could convert to vindictiveness. The difficulty of resolving the crisis of this period may be increased significantly if the child's superego is inordinately restrictive or if the child discovers its parents doing the very things that the child's conscience cannot tolerate in itself.

Latency Stage: Industry versus Inferiority. As with Freud's latency stage, in Erikson's fourth stage there is a lull before the storm of puberty. Interest turns from play to the serious business of learning new skills and to building things. Children in this stage (ages five to eleven) develop a sense of **industry** (the experience of pride in seeing a task or project through to completion).

Teachers are important at this stage of the child's development, for they introduce the child to the technology of the culture. Children need instruction and methodology. When children are successful in this stage, they develop a sense of self-efficacy; when unsuccessful, they feel **inferior** and experience feelings of inadequacy. Parents and teachers are in a position to encourage and reward achievement, to emphasize what the child can do, to give affirmation, and to teach the skills necessary for success in the school environment and the culture, whether the school provided by their particular culture is an academic setting or a jungle and the skill is reading or tracking animals. Instruction in technology will vary in different cultures, classes, and races to fit the culture's version of the universe.

Adolescence: Identity versus Role Confusion.   Adolescence covers the ages of thirteen to nineteen. It is a stage considered especially crucial to Erikson, who, it will be recalled, suffered an identity crisis that lasted nearly five years. When the crises of the earlier four stages are resolved successfully, adolescents experience a growing need for a sense of personal **identity.** They know that they are an integral part of the family and loved. At the same time, they know that they are also individuals. They recognize their competence and know that they have the ability to see a task through to completion. They know, too, that they are now faced with making decisions that will have long-term consequences.

For Erikson (1963), **ego-identity** is accrued experience, an integration of all prior identifications and available, fantasized social roles. Identity also refers to direction and **purpose** (all we are, want to be, and believe we should become). The adolescent with a positive sense of identity is able to make a career choice that is both socially recognized and personally expressive, and that calls for firm

FIGURE 5-1 For Erickson, identity is a most critical life stage, © Frank Siteman, 1992

commitment. The inability to make a career decision is, according to Erikson (1926, 1956, 1963, 1965a, 1966), pathogenic, for it can lead to **identity confusion** (excessive inner fragmentation).

A positive identity leads to a sense of **fidelity** (to be faithful to one's values— "the ability to sustain loyalties freely pledged in spite of the inevitable contradictions of value systems" Erikson, 1964a, p. 125). In contrast, failure to resolve the identity crisis results in excessive inner fragmentation and **role confusion.** Adolescents unable to establish a sense of identity are without purpose, hence, particularly vulnerable to ideologies that promise social confirmation and sanctioned direction (cults, religions, gangs, for example). They need additional time to find their direction and purpose, a psychosocial moratorium. "One could say that adolescents are transitory existentialists by nature because they become suddenly capable of realizing a separate identity" (Erikson, in Evans, 1967, p. 38).

Young Adulthood: Intimacy versus Isolation. This stage spans the ages of twenty to twenty-four. If young adults have successfully established a sense of self-efficacy and a positive identity, they are prepared to enter into intimate relationships with others, to commit themselves to partnerships, and to remain loyal to the commitments, even though their loyalty requires compromise and sacrifice of their individual wishes (Erikson, 1963, 1964a). Intimate relationships are only possible, Erikson asserts, when both partners have clearly established identities and loyalties and are willing to share themselves in trusting, affirming relationships. Mature love involves **mutuality;** that is, a shared identity, a sense of a "combined I."

Young adults unable or unsuccessful in developing intimate relationships experience a sense of **isolation** (the inability to risk a personal identity by sharing true intimacy and love). They become self-absorbed and, threatened by intimacy, they are able to engage only in superficial relationships.

Middle Adulthood: Generativity versus Stagnation. Erikson's seventh stage spans the ages twenty-five to sixty-four—by far the longest of the psychosocial life stages. The crisis of this period centers on whether to be productive or to stagnate. **Generativity** (the successful resolution of the crisis of middle adulthood), includes the birth of children, the guidance of the younger generation, the creativity of ideas, the arts, and the manufacturing of products. **Stagnation** (the result of unsuccessful resolution), involves lack of productivity and boredom and loneliness.

Care (a "widening concern for what has been generated," Erikson, 1964a, p. 131) emerges in those with the capacity for generativity. Concern with helping the younger generation to develop in positive directions is evident in those who successfully confront the crisis of this stage of development. They naturally wish to contribute to society through productive work and to demonstrate their concern for those who are less fortunate. Care and teaching by generative adults protect and preserve the accumulation of knowledge and the traditions of cultures.

Late Adulthood: Ego Integrity versus Despair.   The eighth and final stage of ego development spans age sixty-five to death. Erikson (in Goldman, 1988) describes **ego integrity** at this stage of development as the feeling of those individuals who are functioning well and who can look back on their lives and find both unity and meaning. There is a feeling of interdependence, the knowledge that we need each other. A sense of humor is essential for the elderly if they are to be able to accept without fear the inevitability of physical deterioration and death as a necessary part of the life-cycle.

In contrast, those members of this group who have led selfish, uncaring lives experience **despair.** They are painfully aware that life is now too short to start over or to attempt new directions. They feel the despair of life and time wasted, and lack any hope for change in the little time remaining to them.

Erikson associates **wisdom** with a meaningful old age. For Erikson (1964a, see also 1980) "wisdom is detached concern with life itself in the face of death itself" (p. 133). Self-knowledge precedes wisdom, and knowledge of self at this stage of life is accompanied by **humility**—a realistic appreciation of one's limits and competencies. Life culminates in wisdom to the extent that the crisis of each earlier stage was resolved positively. There is a sense of personal completeness, a wholeness that is great enough to ward off the depression that can come from physical disintegration. Wisdom, according to Erikson, has its roots in each of the earlier life stages.

Research of the Eight Psychosocial Stages of Ego Development   Although empirical research is disappointingly sparse for many of Erikson's theoretical constructs, there are a number of studies that seem to support his view of the eight psychosocial stages of ego development. Examples of some of the more recent are: Munley (1975), Ciaccio (1970), Wallace (1973), Tesch and Whitbourne (1982), and Raft, Smith, and Warren (1986). An excellent overview of the research literature on Erikson's theoretical construct of identity formation is presented by Waterman (1982). Although far too extensive to cover within the limitations of this chapter, it is recommended reading for those interested in the research of Erikson's eight stages of development (see "Annotated Bibliography," this chapter).

Munley (1975) explored the relationship between Erikson's theory of psychosocial development and vocational choice behavior and development. Munley's findings indicated that, in his sample of 123 male college students (eighteen to twenty-one years of age), those who had been more successful in developing positive resolutions of the first six psychosocial stages and stage resolution attitudes also made better-adjusted vocational choices and developed more mature attitudes toward their career choices.

Nicholas Ciaccio (1970) asked 120 children (three age groups of forty children each: four-to-five-year-olds, eight-year-olds, and eleven-year-olds) to tell a story for each of five picture cards. The subjects' taped responses were evaluated by a coding system based on a content analysis of the first five stages as presented in Erikson's writings, and they provided a frequency count yielding a quantitative profile of an individual subject in terms of the five ego stages. The hypotheses of

Ciaccio found preliminary confirmation: The five-year-olds were found to be most concerned with Stages II and III, and the eight-year-olds successfully met the expectations of interest in Stage III. The eleven year-olds were found to be concerned with Stage IV issues, and Stage V concerns were beginning to emerge in their stories.

Douglas Wallace (1973), interested in ways college students articulate and organize their universe of problems, explored the developmental theory of Erikson's clinical and phenomenological descriptions of identity diffusion with fifty subjects who were active as community volunteers. The study concluded that Erikson's conflicts of time perspective versus time diffusion, self-certainty versus identity consciousness, and intimacy versus isolation fit well with discrete clusters of latent categories. The conflicts of role experimentation versus negative identity and anticipation of achievement versus work paralysis seemed to blend together in relation to the cluster of categories suggested be the multidimensional scaling analysis. Recommendations of the study are that colleges should develop ways: 1) in which students' compressed sense of time can be related to manageable tasks; 2) for individuals to become more aware of and confident about their own limitations and abilities; 3) to stimulate role experimentation by exposing students to the widest possible variety of persons and life styles; and 4) in which students can learn to deal more effectively with intimate relationships with others.

Investigating intimacy status of forty-eight men and forty-four women (mean age was twenty-five) in relation to ego-identity status in occupation, religion, politics, and sex role, Tesch and Whitbourne (1982) found there were no significant sex differences in intimacy status or identity status; in short, their study supported Erikson's theory. Intimacy status was related generally to identity status among males and females, at least for the sample studied.

Raft, Smith, and Warren (1986), investigating the effects of pleasant imagery on the relief of acute and chronic pain, found that the image generated by the experimenter to represent the most successful mastery of Erikson's developmental stages was the most successful in reducing the subjects' reported pain over a three-day period. Warren (1986) also recommended that future studies investigate acute and chronic pain separately, since his study clearly showed that acute pain patients respond more consistently than do chronic pain patients.

Hamachek (1990) suggests behavioral criteria that can be used for assessing the status of self-concept and ego development in Erikson's last three psychosocial stages in three behavioral expressions tables and, in doing so, contributes much to a concept of the healthy personality.

Implicit Attitudes: Stage 6

1. I'm OK and others are, too.
2. Others can generally be trusted.
3. Life can be difficult, but through mutual interdependence we can make it.

Implicit Attitudes: Stage 7

1. What can I give to others?
2. Risks I would like to take include. . . .
3. I enjoy being productive and creative.

Implicit Attitudes: Stage 8

1. I have much to be thankful for.
2. I am in control of my life.
3. I accept myself for who I am, and I accept others for who they are.

Subjective versus Objective Reality

For Erikson (1985), **reality** must be viewed from a developmental perspective and the concept renewed as we progress from one developmental stage to another. Moreover, Erikson's (1985) reality construct is comprised of three indispensable components: 1) **factuality,** perceiving a "minimum of distortion or denial and a maximum of the validation possible at a given stage of cognitive development and at a given state of technology and science" (p. 90); 2) **contextuality,** "a convincing coherence and order that lifts facts into a context apt to make us . . . realize their nature" (p. 90); and 3) **way of life,** "a viable world view . . . at its best an all-inclusive conception that focuses disciplined attention on a selection of certifiable facts; liberates a coherent vision enhancing a sense of contextuality; and actualizes an ethical fellowship with strong work commitments" (pp. 90–91).

From a developmental perspective, then, the individual's perception of reality begins with the narcissistic "I's" needs for a basic space–time orientation and progresses to the limits and boundaries where *outerness* and *otherness* begin. This perception is followed by superego's function as the personality structure for a sense of tradition and a network of prohibitions. At adolescence, one's perception of reality is open, both cognitively and emotionally, to new ideological imageries which alternately confirm or protest existing world images. By adulthood, this adolescent perception, in turn, offers the potentiality of an ethical sense and the necessity for a modicum of mature planning in accord with historical reality.

In summary, Erikson (1964a) describes **reality** as ". . . the world of phenomenal experience, perceived with a minimum of distortion and with a maximum of customary validation agreed upon in a given state of technology and culture" (p. 165). **Actuality,** which Erikson (1964a) differentiates from reality, is ". . . the world of participation, shared with other participants with a minimum of defensive maneuvering and a maximum of mutual activation" (p. 165).

Determinism versus Freedom of Choice

For Erikson (1964a), the issue of Determinism versus Freedom of Choice is directly linked to the evolution of certain human virtues, in particular hope, will, purpose, and competence. Hope and will, virtues which must evolve in early childhood, are necessary preconditions if we are to experience a healthy sense of freedom, for no ego remains intact without these strengths. "**Hope,**" Erikson (1964a) asserts, "is the enduring belief in the attainability of fervent wishes, in spite of the dark urges and rages which mark the beginning of existence" (p. 119). He defines **will** as ". . . the unbroken determination to exercise free choice as well as self-restraint . . ." (Erikson, 1964a, p. 119). Willing is not a matter of being willful; rather, Erikson (1964a) tells us, to will means "to gain gradually the power of increased judgment and decision in the application of drive" (p. 118). Further, he states that we must learn to will what can be, renounce as not worth willing what cannot be, and believe we will what is inevitable (Erikson, 1964a, p. 118).

Purpose is also one of the emergent strengths of childhood. For Erikson (1964a), purpose ". . . is the courage to envisage and pursue valued goals uninhibited by the defeat of infantile fantasies, by guilt and by the foiling fear of punishment" (p. 122).

When hope, will, and purpose evolve healthfully, we feel a sense of freedom to choose from alternative future courses of action. Moreover, according to Erikson (1964a), all cultures offer us instruction in "perfectible skills" leading to practical use and achievement for those of us willing to work and to help "make things work" (p. 127). With the healthy development of hope, will, and purpose, we are in position to develop a sense of **competence** ("the free exercise of dexterity and intelligence in the completion of tasks unimpaired by infantile inferiority" Erikson, 1964a, p. 124). We learn cooperative participation in technologies, and we rely on the logic of tools and skills.

As stated earlier, Erikson views ego as an organ of active mastery. When our development has been healthy, we play an active and freely chosen role in integrating our adaptive powers with the existing possibilities of our environment. We choose those experiences that we decide are meaningful in guarding our identity as hopeful, willing, purposeful, and competent persons. We cannot will without hope, determine meaningful purpose without will, or achieve purpose without competence. For Erikson, then, a strong ego, which includes such constructive functions as identity and mastery, is the necessary precondition for our willing to choose healthy activities in our life-cycle.

Conscious versus Unconscious Determinants

Erikson's stance on this issue is clear. We are largely governed by unconscious forces. Our id, which houses all inherited instincts and which is our sole component of personality at birth, is totally unconscious. Our acquired personality components, ego and superego, are also largely (though not exclusively) unconscious. All ego defense mechanisms are, by definition, unconscious, though unlike Freud's defense constructs, they may be used for adaptive as well as maladaptive purposes.

Erikson's first four stages of ego development closely parallel Freud's oral, anal, phallic, and latency stages, and like Freud's psychosexual stages of development, they are primarily unconscious. While certainly significant, in the sense that failure to resolve the psychosocial crises of these early stages in a positive way is difficult to overcome at later stages, early resolutions are not critical in the way they are in Freud's theory (Chapter 2).

Although Erikson views us as largely unconscious beings, his expansion of the qualities and functions of ego grants us greater consciousness than in Freud's view. If, for example, our resolutions of the psychosocial crises of the early stages are more positive than negative, our ego's rational, cognitive, and adaptive functions are strengthened. Consciousness is increased with the positive development of hope, will, purpose, and competence, and in the last three stages of development we are even more consciously motivated and reality oriented.

Uniqueness versus Universality

According to Erikson (1968, 1974, 1986), the eight stages of life are universal. All humans are confronted by difficult directional choices in the course of life. However, though the eight life stages are universal, Erikson informs us that uniqueness is the inevitable outcome of human development. Our choices (trust versus mistrust, autonomy versus shame and doubt, initiative versus guilt, industry versus shame and doubt, initiative versus inferiority, identity versus guilt, industry versus inferiority, intimacy versus isolation, generativity versus stagnation, and integrity versus disgust) are idiosyncratic and will differ in both degree and direction. No two of us will share identical personalities. Further Erikson (1974, 1986) informs us that our choices are not fixed or permanent. Our original choices can be supported and strengthened or discouraged and weakened at any of our later life stages. Each stage in the life cycle offers a new opportunity to reintegrate the issues of previous stages and to make different choices. No two of us will develop the same degree of hope, will, purpose, competence, fidelity, love, care, or wisdom.

The unconscious synthesizing operations of ego give each of us a personal inner sense of individuality, wholeness, sameness and continuity, and social solidarity. Each of us possesses a conscious sense of being unique and separate—a distinct entity. Each of us strives for a sense of inner sameness and continuity with a unique past, present, and future. Each of us senses a personal inner solidarity with ideals and values of some group—a sense of belonging and being meaningful to the significant others in his or her life.

Explanation of Learning Process

With the emphasis that Erikson places on social, cultural, and historical forces, learning plays a most important role in the formation of our individual personalities. One of the reasons Erikson felt the need to expand the role and functions of ego was to account for behaviors that are more than just ego defenses. He developed the idea of conflict-free ego functions to explain the processes of perceiving, thinking, and learning, which are independent of the instinctual forces arising out of the id, and which are not necessarily at odds with the restrictions of superego and the conflicts of the surrounding environment. Erikson's expanded concept of ego granted ego autonomous, rational, and adaptive processes. All cultures, according to Erikson (1965a), meet the life stages of youth "... with the offer of instruction in perfectible skills leading to practical uses and durable achievements" (p. 123).

Erikson was convinced that we have a basic need to master or transcend the environment. Learning, he argued, must be more than a form of sublimated sexual curiosity. Rather, he asserts that learning has an energy of its own when hope, will, and purpose are acquired strengths of ego. There is an "energizing ... a new sense of movement and a more active sense of 'going at the world' " (Erikson, 1965a, p. 255). There is also a genuine inner sense of joy in learning, activity, and movement.

Erikson does not give us a clear explanation of the learning process. He does, however, offer those responsible for guiding the learning of children some fairly clear advice. All of the ego strengths (hope, will, purpose, competence, fidelity, love, care, and wisdom) must be taught and learned. Children and youth must be encouraged and taught the skills necessary for success in the school environment and the culture. Early learning experiences must be perceived as rewarding and purposeful. For Erikson, all learning is a continuous process and builds upon previous learning. We do not learn and experience a true sense of competence, in Erikson's view, without first learning to hope, to will, and to find purpose.

Role Assigned to Self-Concept

The term "self-concept" does not appear in Erikson's theory. However, Erikson's concepts of ego and ego identity share many similar functions assigned to self-concept by the self-concept theorists (e.g., Rogers). Before looking at these similarities, it is worth noting that a clear definition of Erikson's ego identity is difficult to determine. On one occasion Erikson may equate ego identity with a conscious sense of self-awareness, the inner sense of a unique "I." At another time, he uses ego identity in reference to an unconscious striving for continuity, a personal feeling of having a past, present, and future. At still another time, ego identity refers to ego synthesis. And on other occasions, ego identity may mean the maintenance of solidarity with the ideals of and identity with a group. Because ego identity is continually under developmental refinement through each of the eight life-stages, Erikson purposefully avoids a single restrictive definition. He does say, however, that the healthy ego identity depends on the successful resolution of hope, will, purpose, and competence, as the rudiments of virtue developed in childhood.

As stated earlier, similarities (both in character and in function) can be found in Erikson's concept of ego identity and the concept of self described by the self-concept theorists. For example, Rogers asserts that the need for positive regard must be adequately met for the individual's self-concept to develop healthfully. Erikson, too, states that a positive ego identity relies upon the support the young individual receives from parents, peers, class, nation, and culture. Rogers writes of the need for continuity between self and experience. In a similar vein, Erikson refers to ego identity as the guardian of meaningful existence; that is, the guardian of an individual's unity. Like Adler, Erikson regards the ego, or self, as a creator, and he states that the true ego identity is associated with successful mastery of the eight stages of life as it actively mediates between environmental stimuli and the individual's emotions and behavior. There are similarities, as well, between Erikson's ego identity and Bandura's concepts of self-efficacy (a sense of personal competency) and self-regulation.

Number and Weight Assigned to Motivational Concepts

While Erikson accepted Freud's concept of libido as a psychic energy force that fuels psychic activity (see "Heredity versus Social Determinants"), he granted the libido considerably less emphasis than did Freud, and he focused more on the innate adaptive force and autonomous functions of the ego and the powerful forces of society and culture. We are motivated also by our innate need for a personal sense of **identity**. We cannot tolerate having our sense of wholeness, of centrality, of freedom of choice threatened beyond a certain point. We strive toward such constructive ego goals as mastery of and adaptation to the demands of society and the traditions of culture. We defend against the projected ideals and restrictions of our superego.

We are motivated, too, by the crises encountered at each developmental life-stage. According to Erikson (1964a):

> For it is clear that each stage of development has its own acuteness and immediacy, because a stage is a new configuration of past and future, a new combination of drive and defense, new set of capacities fit for a new setting of tasks and opportunities, a new and wider radius of significant encounters (p. 166).

Each of Erikson's eight stages, if encountered successfully and mastered, adds something to ego's motivation and growth. Each stage is a turning point in our lives which calls for choice and action. Each stage is an indication of a new crisis to be confronted and mastered. And each crisis mastered contributes to ego's strength and identity formation.

We are motivated by environmental conditions, by society's expectations and strictures. Our inner motivations are complemented by social-cultural motivations. For Erikson (1968) "autonomy, history, and **personality**" (ego in its widest sense) combine to form our destinies. With a rational, adaptive, creative ego, we are capable of conscious direction and growth over the entire life span. Therefore, we are not exclusive products of an early personal history. Some measure of free will has the potential to emerge in Erikson's last four stages. We are more influenced and motivated by learning and experience than by heredity.

Centrality of Reinforcement

Although "reinforcement" is not a term found in Erikson's writings, he does discuss the gratifying emotions experienced by the individual who manages to arrive at positive resolutions of stage crises and, thereby, to achieve greater ego strength. While certainly not central to his theory, in the sense that reinforcement is central to Skinner (Chapter 13), the feelings that accompany the acquisitions of ego strengths are, without doubt, reinforcing.

> *In youth, ego strength emerges from the mutual confirmation of individual and community, in the sense that society recognizes the young individual as a bearer of fresh energy and that the individual so confirmed recognizes society as a living process which inspires loyalty as it receives it, maintains allegiance as it attracts it, honors confidence as it demands it (Erikson, 1965a, p. 9).*

Hope is reinforced with the entry of will, will with the promise of purpose, purpose with the promise of confidence, competence with the promise of fidelity, fidelity with the promise of love, love with the promise of care, and care with the promise of wisdom. Each step increases ego strength and ego integrity, both of which are reinforcing in themselves.

Role Assigned to Group Determinants

Erikson is convinced that psychoanalysts tend to lose sight of the fact that people other than parents are important to ego development. It is true that in infancy and early childhood, first the mother, then the parents, then the family group, and later other instructing adults are most influential in our development. However, adolescents in search of identity demand affirmation from others and from groups outside the family, particularly others and groups who "hold to a design of life" with which they can identify. Indeed, when society offers its youth no meaningful place, they will form a separate society, one with their own language, customs, traditions, and values, even their own music, mode of dress, and symbols of prestige and status. When a society withholds adult roles from youth, they may join a gang or cult, or identify with a new movement and live on the edge of the existing society. Erikson asserts that responsibility and independence are not learned when they are withheld from us during early stages of development. Rather, they are learned only from experience. If society does not provide a place for adolescents, they will either find or create peer groups that will.

Adults also need others. They find support in groups, whether groups of other parents, professional associations, unions, religious groups, or any of a broad array of interest groups. The elderly who have managed to acquire a degree of wisdom need to pass on their accumulated knowledge and experience, and groups can provide the means to do this.

Psychological Health and Psychopathology

Psychological Health

By describing the personality traits which Erikson maintains are characteristic of individuals who successfully confront and master the crises inherent in the eight

Heredity			Social Determinants
Early Development			Continuous Development
Subjective Reality			Objective Reality
Determinism			Freedom
Conscious Determinants			Unconscious Determinants
Uniqueness			Universality

Explanation of Learning Process	The expanded concept of ego granted ego autonomous, rational, and adaptive processes. All of the ego strengths (hope, will, purpose, etc.) must be taught and learned. All learning is a continuous process and builds upon previous learning.
Role Assigned to Self-Concept	Erikson's concepts of ego and ego identity share many similar functions assigned to self-concept by the self-concept theorists. Ego identity is continually under developmental refinement through each of the eight life stages. A healthy ego identity depends on the successful resolution of hope, will, purpose, and competence.
Number and Weight Assigned to Motivational Concepts	We are motivated by our innate need for personal sense of identity, the crises encountered at each developmental life-stage, and environmental conditions. We are influenced and motivated more by learning and experience than by heredity.
Centrality of Reinforcement	Feelings that accompany the acquisition of ego strengths (a result of positive resolutions of stage crises) are reinforcing. Each step increases ego strength and ego integrity, which are reinforcing in themselves.
Role Assigned to Group Determinants	For infants and children, mothers, parents, family, and other instructing adults are influential. Adolescents demand affirmation from others, adults find support in groups, and the elderly need groups to pass on their knowledge.

FIGURE 5-2   Schematic Analysis of Erickson's Stance on Basic Issues

stages of the life-cycle, it is possible to construct ideal verbal pictures of the psychologically healthy individual and, to a lesser extent, a utopian society, neither of which exists in actuality (see "Early versus Continuous Development"). Still, the ideal verbal picture of psychological health can prove valuable so long as it is viewed as potential worth striving for, an ideal psychological state of being that is always beyond our reach.

Successful confrontation and resolution of life's crises does *not* mean *perfect* confrontation and resolution. The healthy infant, for example, is the infant who develops a greater degree of trust than mistrust, for trust in self, others, and the world is necessary for hope, and hope is essential to psychological health and the good life. Likewise, the child must develop a greater degree of autonomy than of shame and doubt, for trust and hope must be secure if will and choice are to be realized. Both will and choice are characteristics of Erikson's concept of the healthy personality. Initiative is also a sign of psychological health, as well as a prerequisite for the valued ego strength of purpose, for the psychologically healthy person must possess the capacity to envisage goals and the courage to pursue them. The healthy person, Erikson asserts, has a strong sense of self-efficacy and the industry and determination to complete tasks that are freely chosen. The healthy person must be capable of intimacy; he or she must trust and hope enough to invest the self in close and loyal friendships and in mutual love of and devotion to a partner. The healthy person knows who he or she is and where he or she is going. True caring and wide concern for others are positive characteristics of Erikson's construct of psychological health. In the final stage of the lifecycle, the psychologically healthy person must achieve a degree of wisdom; the integrity of ego transcends despair and the fear of death, and a review of the experiences of life and living, of love and work, brings a satisfying sense of purpose and meaning.

Though we all possess both positive and negative characteristics at every life stage, a psychologically healthy adjustment to life's crises is, in Erikson's view, a preponderance of these positive characteristics. Both positive and negative characteristics are necessary. Total trust in others and the world would leave the person naïve and vulnerable to any who want to take advantage. Hope without any doubt would lead to a complete lack of caution, even manic behavior. With only industry and determination, impossible tasks would be continually pursued. Relying only on will power and free choice could result in ignoring even the good advice of others.

Psychopathology

Just as positive resolutions of the crises emerging with each of the eight psychosocial stages of ego development strengthen the autonomous functions of ego and lead to mental health, unresolved crises or negative crisis resolutions are pathogenic. The infant unable to trust itself, others, and the world is deprived of the rudimentary sense of identity and the ego strength of hope, the first virtues to arise in life. Without hope, the child submits to the control of others, experiences shame and doubt, fears challenges, and does not develop will. By the end of the third year the child may have already developed a lasting sense of insecurity.

Conflict with the inner urges and sexual fantasies during the third stage of ego development may result in a strong sense of guilt and the need to suppress an inordinately strong feeling of rage. Lacking the virtues of hope and will, which usually develop in the first two stages, there is little chance of developing meaningful purpose during the third stage. Both hope and will are necessary for the development of meaningful purpose.

Because ego strengths and ego identity build upon successful resolutions of the crises encountered in earlier stages, the unsuccessful adolescent is more likely to develop identity confusion, the loss of a sense of identity, of sameness, and of continuity. Deprivation of identity results in a feeling of inner fragmentation, little or no sense of direction, and the inability to achieve a satisfactory role or vocation.

Psychopathology, like psychological health, is a matter of degree, for it is an accumulation of past experiences. How severe is the identity confusion? How limited is the person's ability to cope in the world of reality, to trust, to relate to others, to establish a place and role in society? For Erikson, schizophrenia is the result of basic mistrust and identity confusion. Ego is fragmented and the person is unable to establish supportive relationships that are critical for the major life tasks of work and love. Generativity is never achieved and an impoverished life style is filled with mistrust, shame, guilt, boredom, stagnation, depression, and in the final stage of development, despair.

Applications to Psychotherapy

Therapeutic Goals

The goals of Eriksonian analysis are similar to those of classical analysis—to make relevant unconscious material conscious, and by doing so, to achieve important insights (on both intellectual and emotional levels) that will strengthen the patient's rational, ego-directed choices and behavior. Although the goals of classical analysis and ego analysis are similar, the egos referred to in the goals are not. The ego functions in Erikson's theory include adaptive, creative, integrating, and synthesizing functions, and can be relied upon to express significant unconscious material in associations and dreams.

Therapeutic Relationship

Erikson (1964a) views the therapeutic relationship as an encounter of two people: one, the patient who is in need of help, and the other, the analyst who is in possession of professional training and methods. "Their *contact* is a therapeutic one: In exchange for a fee, and for information revealed in confidence, the therapist promises to act for the benefit of the individual patient, within the ethos of the profession" (Erikson, 1964a, p. 51).

Unlike the classical analysts, Erikson takes a more equalitarian, active, and personal stance toward his patients, for he is convinced that his patients can only be helped to the extent that he, the therapist, is perceived by his patients as actual or real. Erikson therefore advocates a **disciplined subjectivity** (empathy) to analyze and understand the patient's problems. He also advocates an examination of the historical events that occurred during and influenced the patient's life.

The neutral stance of Freudian analysts, Erikson contends, is likely to convey hidden, suggestive, or even biasing elements. Patients, then, are prone to rationalize, blaming their parents or past events for their difficulties rather than accepting responsibility themselves and working to correct past resolutions of developmental crises.

Therapeutic Process and Strategies

Erikson, like Freud, used the techniques of free association, dream analysis, and interpretation to uncover and understand the meaning of unconscious material. Erikson (1964a) relied on the synthesizing function of the patient's ego to associate "what belongs together" (p. 58), regardless of the associated items' separateness in history, space, or contradiction in logical terms. Erikson discovered in his clinical experience that a patient capable of free association will, during a series of therapeutic encounters, reveal a sequence of themes, thoughts, and affects that are relevant to and lead to clarification of his or her particular problems. There is a central core or theme that compresses the evidence. The analyst must permit his or her "free-floating" clinical attention and judgment to lead him or her to all possibilities and, eventually, to the association's or dream's condensed unitary theme and meaning.

When working with children, Erikson makes use of various techniques of play therapy (rather than free association) to unravel unconscious material. "Children," Erikson (1963) found, "are apt to express in spatial configurations what they cannot or dare not say" (p. 29).

Course of Therapy

There probably is no better or more succinct a description of the therapeutic process than that given by Erikson (1964a):

> *There usually is a* complaint, *consisting of the description of more or less circumscribed pain or dysfunction, and there are* symptoms, *visible or otherwise localizable. There follows an attempt at an* anamnesis, *an etiological reconstruction of the disturbance, and an* examination, *carried out by means of the physician's naked senses or supported by instruments, which may include laboratory methods. In evaluating the evidence and arriving at diagnostic and prognostic inferences (which are really the clinical form of a prediction) the physician* thinks clinically—*that is, he scans in his mind different* models *in which different modes of knowledge have found condensation: the* anatomical *structure of the body, the* physiological *functioning of body parts, or the* pathological *processes underlying classified disease entities. A clinical prediction takes its clues from the complaint, the symptoms, the anamnesis, and makes inferences based on rapid and mostly preconscious cross-checking against each other of anatomical, physiological, and psychological modes. On this basis, a* preferred method of treatment *is selected" (p. 51).*

Extended Applications

Dreams and Dream Interpretation

Erikson accepts most of Freud's findings related to dreams and dream interpretation. He agrees that unconscious material may be revealed in dreams, that dream symbols may have more than one meaning, and that the patient's free associations may be valuable aids to the interpretations of the meaning of the patient's dreams. He, like Freud, also looks for unifying themes in his patients' dreams.

Erikson did not, however, believe all dreams were expressions of id's wishes or the result of instinctual drives. A healthy ego, Erikson believes, may produce dreams of achievement that result in the awakened dreamer experiencing feelings of self-efficacy and wholeness. Dream symbols are often perceived by Erikson as disguised threats to the dreamer's identity, "...to a dominate trend in the patient's relation to the therapist, to a significant portion of his symptomatology, to an important conflict of his childhood, and to corresponding facets of his work and love life" (Erikson, 1964a, p. 72).

The experienced dream interpreter, Erikson (1964a) asserts, "often finds himself 'reading' a dream report as a practitioner of medicine scans an X-ray," for the "dream often lays bare the stark inner facts" (p. 62). Erikson (1964a) always looked "for the most plausible explanation" of the dream, but he withheld interpretation until his trial formulations merged into a unitary theme.

Psychohistory

In Erikson's theory, social and historical forces play significant roles in personality development. By extending his theory to the study of noted historical figures, Erikson demonstrated a method of understanding the phenomenon in which an historical moment and an individual's life might converge in crisis to affect an entire nation, or even the world. His best-known psychohistories are *Young Man Luther* (1958) and *Gandhi's Truth* (1969) which won both the Pulitzer Prize and the National Book Award.

Erikson's other psychohistorical studies cited throughout his works included Adolf Hitler (1963, pp. 326–358), Maksim Gorky (the pen name of Aleksey Maksimovich Peskov, 1963, pp. 359–402), George Bernard Shaw (1968, pp. 145–150, 185–189), and Thomas Jefferson (1974).

In his psychohistories Erikson hoped for a better understanding of the forces of history on individual personality, and he achieved this. He also learned that understanding important historical events cannot be completed without considering the life histories of the individuals who were closely and intensely linked with the events. Further, Erikson (1973) applied the psychohistorical approach to analyze a conversation with Huey Newton (the leader of the Black Panthers) in the hope of finding common ground.

Play Therapy

Discovering that children attempt to make sense of their experiences through play, Erikson was one of the first child analysts to help his young patients to express their deepest concerns more clearly through structured play activities. As his experience with this procedure grew, he collected a set of toys and blocks that were especially effective in encouraging children to express their feelings and problems. He often had the child construct a scene with the toys and blocks, then tell a story about his or her construction. Rage that a child was unable to own or vent could be expressed by a doll. Feelings of isolation too painful to be symbolized in words could emerge from the construction of a jail or wall made of blocks. For Erikson, play was the "royal road to the unconscious of children."

Art Therapy

From his experience of teaching art to children, Erikson realized that children often revealed more in their drawings or paintings than they could reveal in words. Moreover, when asked to tell a story about their art work, they were better able to express verbally their feelings and concerns. He recognized, too, that the act of producing a drawing or painting was often therapeutic in itself. The child became less tense, less discouraged, more involved, and more animated.

Critique

Erikson's Theory of Ego Psychology was well received. While he did not deny many of the major premises of Freud's Theory of Psychoanalysis (an instinctual and irrational id, a restricting superego, and the libido, for example), he did expand the role of ego to include autonomous, conflict-free, and adaptive functions; offer a sequence of developmental stages that continue for the life span; and acknowledge the influence (positive as well as negative) of social-cultural-historical forces that jointly and reciprocally determine the development of personality. Moreover, unlike Freud's early developmental stages, which were critical and irreversible, Erikson's eight stages, while most significant, were somewhat flexible in the sense that a crisis left unresolved at one stage could be resolved at a later stage or, conversely, achievement at one stage could regress at a later stage.

Erikson was also recognized as a pioneer of child psychiatry. Further, he developed many of the techniques of play therapy to reveal the unconscious material of the emotionally disturbed child.

Erikson was also one of the first psychoanalysts to defend the rights of minority groups and, though many men and women today might fault him for his view of female sexuality, his theoretical concepts on the role of woman were more equalitarian than those of analysts who held to the Freudian tradition.

Not all psychoanalysts, of course, viewed Erikson's theoretical constructs favorably. The Freudian analysts accused Erikson of proclaiming allegiance to Freud's theory at the same time that his writings emphasized pronounced differences. The neo-analysts criticized Erikson for being overly patronizing of Freud, while failing to recognize the contributions of Adler, Fromm, and Sullivan on his thinking.

Many of the criticisms leveled at Freud's Theory of Psychoanalysis ("Critique," Chapter 2) apply as well to Erikson's theory. The case study approach, though an acceptable method of research, is inherently subjective. There is no way to be certain that the insights of one analyst would necessarily be those of another working with the same analysand. Further, case studies are studies of an individual and, therefore, too few in number to be considered an adequate sample and generalizable to humankind.

Experimental psychologists point out that, like Freud, Erikson tends to treat his inferences as facts and then assume testing is unnecessary. Largely due to Erikson's terminology, which cannot be operationally defined (e.g., hope, will, purpose, fidelity, love, care, wisdom), there is relatively little empirical evidence to support Erikson's theoretical constructs, including his eight stages of development.

It should be noted that five decades have passed since Erikson first published *Childhood and Society,* and during those decades research methods have become a great deal more sophisticated. To evaluate a personality theorist of the 1950s with today's empirical standards is hardly fair.

Annotated Bibliography

Students interested in learning more about Erikson's theory should probably begin their study by reading his first book, *Childhood and Society,* (revised edition, 1963). This book is his most comprehensive work, and it includes most of his theoretical formulations and interesting and illustrative case histories, as well as his study of the Sioux and Yurak Indians.

To complete their understanding of Erikson's theory, students are encouraged to follow their reading of *Childhood and Society* with Erikson's (1982) *The Life Cycle Completed,* an extended monograph based on an essay that he was invited to write for the National Institute of Mental Health in their three-volume *The Course of Life, Psychoanalytic Contributions Toward Understanding Personality Development,* edited by S. I. Greenspan and G. H. Pollock. Erikson's contribution to this work outlines the "elements of a *psychoanalytic* theory of *psychosocial* development." Erikson presents in condensed form a review of his now-complete psychosocial theory.

Gandhi's Truth (1969) and *Young Man Luther* (1962) are two outstanding examples of psychohistories and are highly recommended for students or practitioners in the field who wish to know more about the use of analysis and history to study the person in the historical moment.

Vital Involvement in Old Age: The Experience of Old Age in Our Time (1986) will challenge any reader who wants to learn more about the fastest-growing minority group in the United States. The authors spent several years interviewing a large number of octogenarians on whom data had been collected for over fifty years. Two of the authors of this volume, Eric and Joan Erikson, were themselves in this age group at the time the book was written.

Waterman's 1982 article in *Developmental Psychology* is highly recommended to those students interested in learning more about recent research efforts to test Erikson's eight developmental stages of personality. Waterman's review of the research literature is both thorough and thoughtful.

References and Suggested Readings

Caillet, K. C., & Michael, W. B. (1983, Spring). The construct validity of three self-report instruments hypothesized to measure the degree of resolution for each of the first six stage crises in Erik Erikson's developmental theory of personality. *Educational and Psychological Measurement, 43,* pp. 197–209.

Ciaccio, N. V. (1970). Erikson's theory of ego epigenesis: Empirical and theoretical perspective for human development. *Dissertation Abstracts International, 70.* 5252B-5253B

Darling-Fisher, C. S., & Leidy, N. K. (1988). Measuring Eriksonian development in the adult: The modified Erikson Psychological Stage Inventory. *Psychological Reports, 62,* pp. 747–754.

Erikson, E. H. (1939). Observations on Sioux education. *Journal of Psychology, 7,* pp. 101–156.

Erikson, E. H. (1942). Hitler's imagery and German youth. *Psychiatry, 5,* p. 475.

Erikson, E. H. (1951). Sex differences in the play configurations of preadolescents. *American Journal of Orthopsychiatry, 21,* pp. 667–692.

Erikson, E. H. (1960). The problem of ego identity. In M. Stein, A. J. Vidich, & D. M. White, (Eds.). *Identity and anxiety.* New York: The Free Press, pp. 37–87.

Erikson, E. H. (1962a). *Young man Luther: A study in psychoanalysis and history.* New York: W. W. Norton. (Originally published 1958)

Erikson, E. H. (1962b, Winter). Youth: Fidelity and diversity. *Daedalus,* pp. 5–27.

Erikson, E. H. (1963). *Childhood and society,* (35th anniversary ed.). New York: W. W. Norton. (Originally published 1950)

Erikson, E. H. (1964a). *Insight and responsibility.* New York: W. W. Norton.

Erikson, E. H. (1964b). *Insight and identity: Lectures on the ethical implications of psychoanalytic insight.* New York: W. W. Norton.

Erikson, E. H. (1965a). *The challenge of youth.* New York: Doubleday, Anchor Books. (Originally published as *Youth: Change and challenge,* 1963)

Erikson, E. H. (1965b). Youth and the life cycle. In D. E. Hamachek, (Ed.). *The self in growth, teaching, and learning.* Englewood Cliffs, NJ: Prentice–Hall, pp. 325–337.

Erikson, E. H. (1966). Consolidation in adolescence. In J. M. Lee & N. J. Pallone, (Eds.). *Readings in guidance and counseling.* New York: Sheed and Ward, pp. 40–47.

Erikson, E. H. (1967a). Memorandum on youth. *Daedalus, 96*(3), pp. 860–870.

Erikson, E. H. (1967b). Growth and crisis of the healthy personality. In C. Kluckholm, H. A. Murray, & D. M. Schneider, (Eds.). *Personality in nature, society, and culture.* New York: Alfred A. Knopf, pp. 185–225.

Erikson, E. H. (1968). *Identity: Youth and crisis.* New York: W. W. Norton.

Erikson, E. H. (1969). *Gandhi's truth.* New York: W. W. Norton.

Erikson, E. H. (1970). Autobiographic notes on the identity crisis. *Daedalus, 99*(4), pp. 730–759.

Erikson, E. H. (1972). Play and actuality. In M. W. Piers, (Ed.). *Play and development.* New York: W. W. Norton.

Erikson, E. H. (1973). *In search of common ground.* New York: W. W. Norton.

Erikson, E. H. (1974). *Dimensions of a new identity: The 1973 Jefferson lectures.* New York: W. W. Norton.

Erikson, E. H. (1976). Reflections on Dr. Borg's life cycle. *Daedalus, 105*(2), pp. 1–28.

Erikson, E. H. (1978). *Life history and the historical moment.* New York: W. W. Norton.

Erikson, E. H. (1980). *Identity and the life cycle.* New York: W. W. Norton. (Originally published 1959)

Erikson, E. H. (1981, May). On generativity and identity: From a conversation with Erik and Joan Erikson. *Harvard Educational Review, 51*, pp. 249–269.

Erikson, E. H. (1985). *The life cycle completed: A review.* New York: W. W. Norton. (Originally published 1982)

Erikson, E. H.; Erikson, J. M., & Kivnck, H. Q. (1986). *Vital involvement in old age: The experience of old age in our time.* New York: W. W. Norton.

Evans, R. I. (1967). *Dialogue with Erik Erikson.* New York: Harper & Row.

Fitzpatrick, J. J., & Friedman, L. T. (1983, September). Adult development theories and Erik Erikson's life-cycle model. *Bulletin of the Menninger Clinic, 47*(5), pp. 401–416.

Fregeau, D. L., & Barker, M. (1986, Winter). A measurement of the process of adolescence: Standardization and interpretation. *Adolescence, 21*(84), pp. 913–919.

Goleman, D. (1988, June 14). In old age, Erikson expands his view of life. *The New York Times Biographical Services,* 708\710.

Gray, M. M., Ipsa, J. M., & Thornburg, K. R. (1986). Erikson's Psychosocial Stage Inventory: A factor analysis. *Educational and Psychological Measurement, 46*, pp. 979–983.

Gross, F. L. Jr. (1987). *Introducing Erik Erikson: An invitation to his thinking.* New York: University Press of America.

Hall, E. (1983, June). A conversation with Erik Erikson. *Psychology Today,* pp. 22–30.

Hamachek, D. (1985, October). The self's development and ego growth: Conceptual analysis and implications for counselors. *Journal of Counseling and Development, 64*, pp. 136–142.

Hamachek, D. (1988, April). Evaluating self-concept and ego development within Erikson's psychosocial framework: A formulation. *Journal of Counseling and Development, 66*(8), pp. 354–365.

Hamachek, D. (1990, July/August). Evaluative self-concept and ego status in Erikson's last three psychosocial stages. *Journal of Counseling and Development, 68*, pp. 677–683.

Harvard Educational Review. (1981). On generativity and identity: From a conversation with Erik and Joan Erikson, *5*, pp. 249–269.

Knowles. R. T. (1986). *Human development and human possibility: Erikson in the light of Heidegger.* New York: University Press of America.

Lawrence, F. C., & Wozniak, P. H. (1987). Rural children's time in household activities. *Psychological Reports, 61*, pp. 927–937.

Liptzin, B. (1985). Psychotherapy with the elderly: An Eriksonian perspective. *Journal of Geriatric Psychiatry, 18*(2), pp. 183–202.

Massey, R. F. (1986, March). Erik Erikson: Neo-Adlerian. *Individual Psychology: The Journal of Adlerian Theory, Research, & Practice, 42*(1), pp. 65–91.

Miller, P. H. (1989), *Theories of developmental psychology* (2nd ed.). San Francisco: Freeman.

Munley, P. H. (1975). Erik Erikson's theory of psychosocial development and vocational behavior. *Journal of Counseling Psychology, 23*(4), pp. 314–319.

Raft, D., Smith, R. H., & Warren, N. (1988). Selection of imagery in the relief of chronic and acute clinical pain. *Journal of Psychosomatic Research, 30*(4), pp. 481–488. Printed in Great Britain.

Roazen, P. (1976). *Erik H. Erikson: The power and limits of a vision.* New York: Free Press.

Roscoe, B., Kennedy, D., & Pope, T. (1987, Fall). Adolescents' views of intimacy: Distinguishing intimate from nonintimate relationships. *Adolescence, 22*(87), pp. 511–516.

Stewart, A. J., Franz, C., & Layton, L. (1988, May). The changing self: Using personal documents to study lives. *Journal of Personality, 56*(1), pp. 41–72.

Temple, S. (1988, November). Erikson's model of personality development related to clinical material. *British Journal of Occupational Theory, 51*, pp. 399–402.

Tesch, S. A., & Whitbourne, S. K. (1982). Intimacy and identity status in young adults. *Journal of Personality and Social Psychology, 43*(5), pp. 1041–1051.

Viney, L. L. (1987). A sociophenomenological approach to life-span development complementing Erikson's sociodynamic approach. *Human Development, 30,* pp. 126–136.

Wallace, D. (1973). An explanation of the latent structure of pro-social student-defined problems and its relationship to the developmental theories about youth of Erik Erikson and Kenneth Deniston. *Dissertation Abstracts International.* 7011A-7012A

Waterman, A. S. (1982). Identity development from adolescence to adulthood: An extension of theory and a review of research. *Developmental Psychology, 18*(3), pp. 341–358.

Whitbourne, S. K., Jelsma, B. M., & Waterman, A. S. (1982). An Eriksonian measure of personality development in college students: A reexamination of Constantinople's data and partial replication. *Developmental Psychology, 18*(3), pp. 369–371.

Chapter 6

Fromm's Humanistic Social Analysis

Chapter Overview

Introduction

Biographical Sketch of the Theorist

Resolutions of the Eleven Basic Issues
Heredity versus Social Determinants
Determinism versus Freedom of Choice
Conscious versus Unconscious Determinants
Early versus Continuous Development
Role Assigned to Group Determinants
Number and Weight Assigned to Motivational Concepts
Subjective versus Objective Reality
Uniqueness versus Universality
Explanation of Learning Process
Role Assigned to Self-Concept
Centrality of Reinforcement

Psychological Health and Psychopathology
Healthy Personality and the Good Life
Psychopathology

Heuristic Influence

Application to Psychotherapy
Therapeutic Goals
Therapeutic Relationship

Initial Procedures and Strategies
Course of Therapy

Extended Applications

Critique

Annotated Bibliography

References and Suggested Readings

Introduction

Erich Fromm's view of the human condition did not evolve from a single discipline. All his books demonstrated evidence not only of his work as a psychoanalyst, but also his extensive knowledge in such areas as philosophy, sociology, anthropology, history, literature, and religion.

Fromm (1961, 1962) was strongly influenced by Karl Marx and Sigmund Freud. He compared their theories, noted their contradictions, and attempted a synthesis (Fromm, 1962). Hall and Lindzey (1978) concluded that Fromm's comparison (particularly in *Beyond the Chains of Illusion,* 1962) favors Marx as the "more profound thinker" of the two great men, and he drew from psychoanalysis "mainly to fill in the gaps in Marx" (p. 170). They also stated that though Fromm preferred to be thought of as a *dialectic humanist,* he "could be accurately called a Marxian personality theorist" (Hall & Lindzey, 1978, p. 170). Like Marx, Fromm was certain that socioeconomic and political forces exert a significant impact on human personality development.

Convinced that the present path of humanity would eventually lead to destruction, yet impressed with the resilience of individuals in the face of pathogenic social, economic, and political forces, Fromm sensed a strong obligation to use his knowledge and skills as a psychoanalyst to awaken public concern for the survival, growth, integrity, and freedom of humanity. Hoping to reach the greatest number of people in the shortest possible time with his message of the radical social reforms he believed were absolutely necessary for human survival, Fromm intentionally directed his writing to the general public rather than to scholars and professionals in the fields of personality, social psychology, or psychotherapy.

A prolific writer with a popular style and an almost uncanny sense of timing (his interests seemed to anticipate contemporary controversy), Fromm developed a vast appeal as a writer. The most popular of his twenty books, *The Art of Loving* (1956a), was translated into twenty-eight languages and sold 500,000 English-language copies by 1970 (Funk, 1982, p. 7). Indeed, Fromm's books continue to be read widely, both in the United States and in Europe, and many are required reading in a variety of academic disciplines on college and university campuses throughout the world.

Unlike most theorists whose ideas are presented in this book, Fromm did not limit his political activity to writing. In the 1950s, long before being an advocate for peace was popular, Fromm was one of the founders of SANE, an American peace organization that took a hard stance against the nuclear arms race and later, against the Vietnam War.

Although Fromm held little hope for the prospects of a lasting world peace, he firmly believed that as long as there is life, he was obligated to give his last effort to "making people wake up to the reality in which they live" (Fromm, in Wakin, 1980, p. 319). Fromm articulated and lived his love of humanity and in doing so became a participant in human history. His legacy was his faith in life and his humanism.

Fromm defined **personality** as the totality of psychic qualities; that is, the individual's inherited temperament or mode of reaction (slow or swift, weak or strong) and the individual's character or object of reaction (motivation). Since temperament is inherited and therefore fixed, the concept of **character** (viewed by Fromm as a constellation of character traits and referring to an organized orientation of relating to self, others, and the world) is central to Fromm's concept of personality.

Biographical Sketch of the Theorist

As Hausdorff (1972) warns: Fromm ". . . seems to have taken seriously Freud's remark that there is 'a discretion which one owes oneself' " (p. 13). Elkind (1981) also remarks that, while warm and friendly, Fromm "maintained a quiet reserve, a sense of privacy and personal space" (p. 522). Except for a brief introduction to *Beyond the Chains of Illusion* (Fromm, 1962), in which he tried to show which experiences during his adolescence created the conditions for his "passionate interest in the teachings of Freud and of Marx" (p. 9), and a short interview reported in *For the Love of Life* (1986), in which he discussed the impact of growing up in the Orthodox Jewish tradition, Fromm recorded very little about his own life. Unlike Sigmund Freud, Carl Jung, Abraham Maslow, Fritz Perls, and B. F. Skinner, Fromm left no autobiography or personal journal for those who would later seek to learn the details of his life.

Early Years

Erich Fromm (1900–1980), the only child of Naphtali and Rosa Fromm, was born in Frankfurt, Germany, on March 23, 1900. With long lines of rabbinical forefathers on both sides of his family, Fromm's heritage was of the Orthodox Jewish tradition, "a tradition that was certainly more medieval than it was modern" (Fromm, 1986, p. 98). His Jewish heritage was further reinforced by a long and intense study of the Talmud, the works of his favorite writer, the German mystic Meister Eckhart, and the repeated family stories about his ancestors. He later recalls the exhilaration he experienced when reading the stories of Abraham,

Adam and Eve, and Jonah, and especially the promise of the Old Testament prophets Isaiah, Hosea, and Amos that there would come a time of universal peace and harmony (Fromm, 1962).

Even with the little we know of his early family life, it is not surprising that the tradition of Judaism had a greater reality for Fromm than the twentieth century in which he lived. Neither is it surprising, considering his later works, that Fromm (1986) reports that he remained an alien in the business or bourgeois culture for most of his life (p. 99). Hausdorff (1972) comments: "Fromm's evaluation of the impact of Judaism on Sigmund Freud seems equally applicable to Fromm himself" (p. 12).

For many years, Fromm believed that he lived simultaneously in two worlds: an older, Jewish, and traditional world, and a modern, Protestant business and industrial world. Frankfurt was one of the leading business, industrial, and financial centers of Europe, with a Protestant tradition that extended back to 1522. Hausdorff (1972) explains Fromm's need to resolve the dilemma of living a dichotomized existence when he writes: "As both 'stranger' and 'participant' in a dynamic, capitalist society, he felt impelled to create a fresh and viable synthesis for himself" (p. 12).

Fromm's parents must have felt the stress of a dichotomized emotional existence also. Fromm (1962) describes his father, an independent wine merchant, as "over anxious and moody" and his mother as "depression prone." He characterized himself as "an unbearable, neurotic child." In retrospect, Fromm (1962) perceived the atmosphere of his boyhood home as tense and unpleasant.

The death of a family friend, a talented artist and, in the eyes of a twelve-year-old Fromm, a very beautiful young woman, who chose to kill herself so that she might assure burial next to an excessively loved father, was not only incomprehensible but also frightening. Years later, Fromm found some of the pieces to this old and haunting puzzle of a wasted life in Freud's writing. Hausdorff (1982) suggests possible connections between this early painful incident and Fromm's reinterpretation of Freud's Oedipus theory, Fromm's ideas concerning symbiotic relations of dependence, and Fromm's biophilous and necrophilous frames of orientation (p. 2).

The First World War erupted during the summer of Fromm's fourteenth year, and he was nearly overwhelmed by the mass hysteria of hate and the senseless, brutal killing. He observed a teacher who for years had taught the ideal of universal peace suddenly change into a fanatical advocate of war. He felt the losses of older family members and friends. He saw rational German people become highly irrational, and he was haunted by the question: "How could it be possible?" (Fromm, 1941, 1962).

Education

Fromm spent the years 1918 to 1924 in university studies, concentrating on psychology, philosophy, and sociology. During this period, he was introduced to the widely diffused ideas of Buddha, Karl Marx, and Freud. The writings of Marx and Freud, especially, remained central to Fromm's thinking, and as mentioned earlier, he spent most of his professional life attempting to devise a synthesis between the concepts of these two great men.

Fromm completed his doctorate in philosophy at the University of Heidelberg in 1922, and continued his studies at the universities of Munich and Frankfurt. In 1925, without a formal medical education, he began a didactic analysis in Munich. Fromm completed his training in psychoanalysis at the renowned Psychoanalytic Institute in Berlin. It was there that he met, and on June 16, 1926, married, Frieda Reichmann, a physician and psychoanalyst. Until their divorce, the Fromms worked in a small hospital in Heidelberg. Together they also helped to found and manage the Psychoanalytic Institute of Frankfurt. Henny Gurland and Fromm were married on July 24, 1944. His second wife died in 1952. Fromm and Annis Freeman were married on December 18, 1973.

In 1929, under the auspices of the International Institute for Social Research, Fromm assisted in one of the earliest studies of the psychology of Nazism. He became intensely absorbed in the idea of historical change and the impact of socioeconomic and political forces on human behavior.

In the years 1930 to 1932 Fromm was appointed Lecturer at the Psychoanalytic Institute of Frankfurt and Fellow at the Institute for Social Research, University of Frankfurt. He was associated with the International Institute of Social Research, Geneva, from 1932 through 1933. It was during this period that Fromm first published articles that were critical of Freud's theory, particularly Freud's refusal to acknowledge the influence of socioeconomic forces on personality structure.

In 1933, when the political situation in Germany became unbearable, Fromm accepted an invitation from the Chicago Psychoanalytical Institute and emigrated to the United States. Fromm moved to New York City in 1934, where along with Karen Horney and Harry Stack Sullivan, he began his work at the International Institute of Social Research. While Freud encouraged the training of lay analysts, American psychoanalysts viewed psychoanalysis as primarily a medical method of treatment, insisted on medical licensing, and denied clinical practice to lay analysts. The difficulties Fromm encountered during this controversy led to his resignation from the Institute. Along with Sullivan, Fromm helped to found and became a trustee of the William Alanson White Institute.

Emergence of Fromm's Theory

For the first ten years of his practice, Fromm accepted and applied the orthodox approach to psychoanalysis. As he acquired experience, however, he gained awareness that some of his clinical observations were at variance with those anticipated by Freud's theory. Moreover, he grew bored with orthodox psychoanalytic techniques that, he believed, limited the analyst–patient relationship.

Fromm gradually moved away from the methodology of his psychoanalytic training and developed more active and confrontive processes and techniques. He criticized instinct theory, reinterpreted Freud's Oedipus complex by extending the parent–child relationship to a quest for independence, recognized the impact of socioeconomic influences, and encouraged the growth of an authentic self within an authentic relationship. In short, he began the construction of a personal psychotherapeutic theory that he continued to expand and refine for more than three decades.

In addition to his practice as a psychoanalyst, Fromm taught at several universities in the United States, including Columbia, New York, Michigan State, and Yale. In 1949, he joined the faculty at the University of Mexico as professor of psychiatry and was named the director of the Mexican Psychoanalytic Institute. Fromm and Annis Freeman Fromm retired in 1965. In 1976, Fromm and his wife moved to Switzerland. He died of a heart attack at his home in Muralto, Switzerland, March 18, 1980, days before his eightieth birthday.

Awards

Fromm's awards included a fellowship in the New York Academy of Science, delivery of the Terry Foundation Lectures at Yale University in 1950, and participation in the Fourth International Congress on Mental Health, Mexico City, 1951. Fromm was awarded the status of Diplomate in Clinical Psychology by the American Psychological Association. He was also a Fellow of the New York Academy of Science, a member of the Washington Psychoanalytic Society, an honorary member of the Mexican National Academy of Medicine, and Director of the Mexican Institute of Psychoanalysis in Mexico City.

Resolutions of the Eleven Basic Issues

Fromm's primary concern was with human nature and the limiting influences of society. While some of his concerns paralleled the eleven basic issues selected for the structure of this book, others did not. When the latter proved to be the case, the author relied upon logical inferences.

Heredity versus Social Determinants

Fromm (1965/1941, 1947) assumes an inherited animal side to our nature that is common to all members of our species and contributes to our physical survival. However, he grants the animal side of our humanness only minor significance. Far more important, Fromm (1941/1965) asserts, we have acquired through evolution a distinct **human nature** (reason, self-awareness, imagination, and choice).

As we evolved from lower animals and developed a brain with the capacity to reason and imagine, we became self-aware, including the awareness of our limitations and the fact that we are finite. In short, we know that we can never realize all our potentials in the time allotted to us. Freed from our primary ties with nature, we were set apart from other living organisms. We experienced loneliness and alienation. Without the animal instincts that once determined our actions, we were forced, for the first time, to choose our direction and behavior and to accept responsibility for becoming productive citizens. Our alternative is to escape our freedom by submitting ourselves to others or by trying to destroy them.

While we became aware of our expanded possibilities and our unique human potentials, we also became aware of existential dichotomies that result in doubt and anxiety, insecurity and isolation, aloneness and powerlessness. For while we

FIGURE 6-1   Evolution severed our species from nature and animal instincts

are in nature and limited by its laws, we are no longer a part of nature. On the one hand, we strive toward the affirmation of life—to actualize and express as fully as possible our unique human potentials, to realize, in the limited time we have, our innate humanness. On the other hand, we yearn for our lost harmony with nature and the security of a peaceful, instinctual animal existence.

When the terror of being alone and the responsibility of choice become too great, we have a strong tendency to shrink from the expression of humanness and return to a more primitive, though more restricted, way of living in this world. Our natural human impulse, according to Fromm, is the desire to regain our lost unity and balance by submitting to secondary ties, and thus escaping the burden of freedom and movement *toward* some purpose or goal. **Secondary ties,** asdefined by Fromm (1965/1941, 1947, 1962, 1966/1946), might be leaders, clans, tribes, states, or nations; cults, religions, gods, or sciences; corporations, businesses, or academic disciplines; indeed, *anyone* or *anything* in which we mistakenly endow a power greater than our own. While secondary ties provide us with a sense of security and belonging, they require our submission to external agencies and invite the physical and spiritual diminishment of human nature.

We are then, according to Fromm (1947), contradictions, "freaks of nature" (p.49). We are in nature, yet we transcend it. We are driven to affirm life, yet we are aware of the inevitability of death. We strive to actualize fully all our potentials, yet we realize life is far too short to permit the completion of our goal. We desire meaning and purpose, yet we know that there is no meaning except that which we can give our lives in the productive fulfillment of our potentials. Fromm, always a dualistic thinker, placed us on the horns of many a historical and existential dilemma.

Fromm also believed that certain basic psychic or existential needs, like our physiological needs, are rooted in the very essence of our human nature and must be gratified if we are to grow in a healthy or productive direction. In *Sane Society* and *Anatomy of Human Destructiveness,* Fromm (1955, 1973a) identified eight distinct human needs, the needs for:

   1. relatedness/rootedness (the need to unite with other beings, to genuinely belong; see also "Role Assigned to Group Determinants," this chapter);
   2. transcendence (the need to rise above the animal side of one's human nature, to create; see also "Number and Weight of Motivational Concepts," this chapter);
   3. unity (the need to integrate one's animal and non-animal natures through love and work with other beings);
   4. identity (the need for a sense of individuality; see also "Role Assigned to Self-Concept," this chapter);
   5. a frame of orientation (the need to make sense of the world; see also "Explanation of Learning Process," this chapter);
   6. an object of devotion (the need for direction and purpose);

7. excitation/stimulation (the need for challenging, meaningful, and lasting action); and

8. effectiveness (the need to exercise competence to realize one's full humanness).

Determinism versus Freedom of Choice

According to Fromm (1941/1965), we are engaged in a lifelong struggle with freedom. Moreover, he points out that achieving freedom can be a frightening predicament, for we are then faced with the dilemma of what we want to *do* with it. In *Escape from Freedom,* Fromm (1941/1965) discusses the difference between **freedom from** (a move from outside rule that is without purpose and goes nowhere) and **freedom toward** (choosing the constructive use we make of our freedom). Freedom toward some goal or purpose makes us painfully aware that we are ultimately alone and therefore fully responsible for our own growth and development. We become aware, also, of the uncertainties and contradictions of the existential dichotomies that living and choosing force us to face and then alone try to resolve. Moreover, we are aware that we must accomplish this knowing that with each gain in freedom from one form of restriction, we open ourselves to newer (and often more difficult and anxiety-provoking) forms of restraints. The struggle for freedom and **individuation** (actualization of potentials and possibilities) is an endless and personal process, always accompanied by the pain of anxiety. Further, as solitary beings in this struggle, we are each required to martial a great deal of courage, discipline, patience, and self-efficacy.

Fromm's historical analysis of human freedom uncovered its paradoxical power to "deaden the human spirit" and "numb the human will" (Monte, 1980, p. 484). Society will, if it can, bind us to custom and enforce its rules. Indeed, societies tend to make us believe that we willingly act the way it dictates that we ought to act. **Pathological societies** (authoritarian, dictatorial, monolithic, and punitive societies) pervert human nature. Rather than expressing a vigorous humanness, members of sick societies recoil from freedom, submit to an outside power or authority, and conform to the dictates of powerful others (Fromm, 1965/1941, 1947, 1955).

Conscious versus Unconscious Determinants

As Fromm gained experience in psychoanalysis, his ideas of an innate human nature began to change; perhaps the most drastic changes occurred over the issue of conscious and unconscious determinants of human behavior. He rejected Freud's instinctivist concept of an id-driven, pleasure-seeking, determining unconscious. Indeed, he rejected Freud's psychic structure of personality: id, ego, and superego. Personal growth, from Fromm's new perspective, did not result from overcoming unconscious instinctual forces or from adjusting to the demands of society, but rather from relatedness, productive love, and the actualization of unique and basically good human potentials. Adjusting to society's dictates, customs, and rules was, in Fromm's view of human nature, pathogenic. Modern society and human individuality, Fromm asserted, were on a collision course that if left unchecked would lead to the destruction of humanity.

Fromm accepted the importance and influence of unconscious processes (repression and defense mechanisms, for example), and he made use of some of the psychoanalytic strategies for making the unconscious material conscious (e.g., free association, transference, dream interpretation), at least in modified form. Unlike the classical psychoanalysts, however, he did not present human consciousness as irrelevant and immaterial.

Early versus Continuous Development

Unlike Freud (Chapter 2), Fromm did not identify and define specific, critical, or divisible developmental stages. While he recognized the formative powers of early childhood experiences, Fromm reasoned that human personality development may well extend into adulthood.

Drawing a parallel between the developmental history of the human species and the pattern of childhood development, Fromm (1964) concluded that the evolutionary individuation process of the human species is repeated in every individual's childhood. Thus, for Fromm (1964), just as human history begins with the first act of human liberation, the human individuation process begins with the severing of the umbilical cord.

According to Fromm (1964), the human infant enters this world in a state of primary narcissism. Unable to distinguish between the "I" and the "not I" (a necessity for relating to the outside world), the infant's only reality is itself—its bodily sensations, its thirst, its need for sleep and physical contact. Born with minimal instinct to guide its actions, the human infant is helpless. It is totally dependent on its primary ties with parents or parent surrogates for survival. While a dependent relationship on all-providing parents offers the infant security, the child's innate individuation process calls for cutting the primary ties and striving toward freedom and independence.

When writing about human nature, Fromm (1941, 1947, 1964) referred to certain "natural capacities" for growth, but it is apparent also that he believed parents play a highly significant role in the formation and development of their child's innate capacities. Loving contact with **biophilic** (healthy and joyful love of life) parents communicates, without words, the love of life; it is contagious. The biophilic mother or father is impressed with the child's joy, enthusiasm, and accomplishments. Just as contagious, **necrophilic** parents (those with a pathogenic attraction to illness, death, and decay) can destroy the child's faith in growth. Fromm (1973a) warns that by focusing on their child's illnesses and failures, predicting a bleak future, and viewing all change with suspicion and fear, necrophilic parents infect their child with their pathogenic orientation. For Fromm, then, the relationship between child and parents or parent surrogates is a far more significant condition of personality development than any arbitrarily assigned developmental stages.

FIGURE 6-2 **The necrophilic family, Reprinted by permission of Doug Marlette and Creators Syndicate**

In favorable circumstances, the child is introduced to a nurturing society through biophilic parents. The mother, in particular, is the child's sanctuary, from which "... the child can make forays into the novel and strange and return when he (or she) needs reassurance" (Schector, in Landis & Turber, 1971, p. 92). In short, the child is permitted to move freely between **symbiotic** (identification and dependency) and individuated forms of relatedness. For Fromm, a fundamental problem of human development is the courage to deal successfully with the polar tension between the desire for symbiotic unity and the natural striving for individuation. For the child, this means breaking away from the security of primary ties. This major developmental step is difficult. For Fromm (1955), "Mother is food; she is love; she is warmth; she is earth" (p. 43).

Fromm is not always consistent when writing about the child–parent relationship and child development. For example, he seems unable to decide whether children will develop in a manner opposite or similar to the way they were treated by their parents. There are occasions when he argues that societal forces tend to perpetuate classes within a society, which seems to favor similarity. There are other occasions, however, when he suggests that children develop in a manner opposite to the way they were treated. He offers reasons for both positions, but he cites no empirical evidence for either.

Role Assigned to Group Determinants

According to Fromm (1947, 1955), when evolution severed our species from the safety and security provided by our earlier instinctual unity with nature, strong feelings of aloneness and powerlessness emerged in our awareness. A need for relatedness to nature, other beings, and the self became a part of our human nature and, like the physiological needs common to all of our species, becomes pathogenic when not gratified. When unable or unwilling to address our need for productive relatedness, we suffer intellectual and spiritual illness, even psychosis (see "Psychopathology," this chapter).

Without the instincts of lower animals to determine our behavior, we are forced to use our reason and imagination to create forms of relating to our world, other beings, and ourselves. We may choose to relate spontaneously through a genuine expression of our intellectual, emotional, and sensuous capacities. Conversely, we may choose to relinquish our personal freedom and surrender our autonomy and individuality by fusing ourselves, either through submission or dominance, with someone or something (idea, cause, institution, etc.) outside ourselves. The first choice is progressive; the second is regressive. Either strategy is rooted in our individual need for relatedness, but only spontaneous, productive love leaves us whole and healthy. All regressive paths lead to narcissism or self-isolation and ultimately to the pathogenic loss of our sense of self.

Number and Weight Assigned to Motivational Concepts

According to Fromm (1955), by our very nature, we are dissatisfied with the passive role of animals. We naturally strive to fulfill a desire for health and happiness. Unlike the lower animals, we experience a strong need to **transcend** (rise above) our animal nature—to be active, creative, and imaginative.

Those of us unable to transcend our animal nature become destructive. The need for transcendence can be sought through healthy creativity or through malignant aggression and destructiveness. When the latter is the choice, we escape the feeling of helplessness by attempting to destroy the world or, if our outward destructiveness is blocked, by attempting to destroy ourselves. Destructiveness is selected, Fromm (1973a) asserts, when our imagination and creativity are thwarted.

Biophilic and Necrophilic Orientations   Fromm found Freud's idea that *all* human motivation and behavior are rooted in the life and death instincts (Eros and Thanatos) unacceptable. He especially rejected an instinctivist explanation for the human capacities of love and aggression. As early as 1947, Fromm proposed that a drive to actualize all of one's inherent potentials was an essential part of human nature. Further, he argued, when the **primary drive** (toward self-actualization or individuation) is constantly thwarted by the forces of society, it is replaced with a **secondary drive** (a drive toward aggression and destruction). The important difference between Freud's biological life and death instincts and Fromm's biophilic and necrophilic character orientations is that, for Fromm, biophilia is the normal biological impulse inherent in human nature, while necrophilia is only an alternative to biophilia, emerging only when normal human striving toward life and growth is blocked. In short, while not a primary genetic force in human nature, necrophilia is a potential rooted in the human condition, a propensity of character rather than an innate human tendency or a primary motivation.

Extending our primary and secondary drives to their purest forms, Fromm (1966, 1970/1968, 1973a) arrived at two extreme character orientations: biophilia (the love of life and growth) and necrophilia (the love of death and decay). For Fromm (1964): "There is no more fundamental distinction between men, psychologically or morally, than the one between those who love death and those who love life, between the *necrophilous* and the *biophilous*" (p. 37, italics in original). In their purest forms, the biophile is saintly and the necrophile is the "quintessence of evil." The vast majority of us, however, are a blending of biophilic and necrophilic character types, with one orientation being dominant.

The Biophilic Character Orientation.   Because the biophilic character orientation is described elsewhere in this chapter (see "Healthy Personality and the Good Life"), it will not be dealt with in any depth here. It cannot be overemphasized, from Fromm's perspective, that when the demands of society are contrary to human nature (as to some degree all existing societies are), total biophilic character orientations are extremely rare, perhaps nonexistent. Further, Fromm asserts, no society yet exists that can meet *all* the needs of human nature constructively.

The Necrophilic Character Orientation. Necrophilous character types hold a particularly malignant orientation toward self, others, and the world, an orientation that is characterized by a profound sense of alienation and detachment from everything human and alive. Necrophiles have no inclination, therefore, to seek human relationships; indeed, they are unable to enter into a loving relationship with another person —*any other person.*

Five Character Orientations Fromm (1947) identified five character orientations that he believed were common in Western society. While each of the five is comprised of both positive and negative traits, his first four orientations are largely nonproductive adaptations to the demands of society or failures at one of the two basic **life-tasks**—love and work.

Although the first three of Fromm's character orientations (receptive, exploitive, and hoarding) contain traits similar to Freud's oral and anal character types, there are major differences. In Freud's typology, future character types are based on the fixation of libido on certain erogenous zones of the body (Chapter 2). Conversely, Fromm based his character orientations on the different ways people adapt to dehumanizing societal demands. Fromm's marketing orientation, comprised of character traits developed in and common only to capitalist societies, is unlike any character type in Freud's typology. And while Fromm's fifth character orientation has been compared to Freud's genital character type, Fromm's productive orientation represents the ultimate in human health and development, an ideal impossible to achieve fully, at least in any existing society.

The Receptive Orientation Individuals with dominant receptive orientations fully expect all their wishes and desires to be provided by someone or some source outside themselves. They believe they should be recipients rather than earners or creators, be loved rather than loving, be skilled rather than develop a skill through practice, be knowledgeable rather than acquire knowledge through study. Left on their own, they feel quite helpless. Fromm (1947) lists the key character traits of the receptive orientation as: "passive, opinionless, submissive, unrealistic, cowardly, wishful, gullible, and sentimental" (p. 120).

Unable to solve the existential problem of loneliness, receptive types are often indiscriminate in their love relationships, unrealistically expecting love and devotion from all around them. They are careful not to offend and agree to the requests, opinions, and ideas of others without any consideration of the consequences or the responsibilities of their actions. Submission and compulsion rob them of their identity, and their constant requests for reassurance drive others away.

There is a positive side to Fromm's receptive orientation. When receptive character types possess sufficient health and productive motivation, they are sometimes able to transform the negative traits of the receptive orientation into positive traits (Fromm, 1947). Passivity may be transformed into "acceptance," opinionlessness into "responsiveness," submissiveness into "devotion," unrealism into "idealism," cowardice into "sensitivity," and wishfulness into "optimism" (Fromm, 1947, p. 120). For the most part, however, the receptive-oriented character type, much like Freud's oral stage (sucking), lives with the philosophy that all good things are provided for those who wait.

The Exploitive Orientation Similar to Fromm's receptive character types, exploitive-oriented character types also look to sources outside themselves to provide their needs and desires. Rather than expecting to receive, however, they expect to *take* what they want through force, stealth, or trickery. Whether another's material possessions, spouse, friend, ideas, or creations, that which is most valued by others is most envied and coveted by the exploitive character. Furthermore, if they can obtain what they want by force or theft, their pleasure in their gain is increased significantly. Indeed, that which is freely given to them holds no value and brings no pleasure.

Exploitive types approach their problem of loneliness by dominating others. They must be in control of relationships. Interested only in what they can get out of a relationship, they quickly lose interest when their partners expect something in return.

Fromm's (1947) key trait labels for exploitive character types are: "aggressiveness, egocentricity, conceitedness, rashness, arrogance, and seductiveness" (p. 120). Near health and positive motivation in the exploitive orientation can change the quality of these negative traits into more positive qualities. Aggressiveness can change to "self-initiating" behavior; egocentricity to "the ability to make claims;" conceitedness to "pride;" rashness to "impulsiveness;" arrogance to "self-confidence;" and seductiveness to "captivating" style (Fromm, 1947, p. 120). As with the receptive orientation, comparisons of the exploitive orientation have been made with Freud's oral stage (biting).

The Hoarding Orientation Reminiscent of Freud's anal retentive fixation, the chief character trait of Fromm's hoarding orientation is miserliness. Security for hoarder character types is related to their success in accumulating and protecting wealth, power, and love. Wives, husbands, sons, daughters, friends, and employees, like material goods, are considered possessions. For hoarder types, anything less than total possession brings a sense of insecurity. Ownership must be unquestionable and complete; there are no partnerships.

Hoarders struggle to keep what they have by acting as if they and their possessions were surrounded by a protective boundary or wall. Fromm (1947) lists the key traits of the hoarding character type as "unimaginative, stingy, suspicious, cold, stubborn, obsessional, and possessive" (p. 120). However, with sufficient health and productivity, these negative traits can become positive. Unimaginative can become "practical;" stingy can become "economical;" suspicious can become "careful;" cold can become "reserved;" stubborn can become "steadfast;" obsessional can become "methodical;" and possessive can become "loyal" (Fromm, 1947, p. 120).

The Marketing Orientation According to Fromm (1947), the marketing orientation emerged during the twentieth century, particularly in the personalities of those enveloped in a Western industrial culture. Marketing character types measure their personal worth as they measure commodities, by how well they sell themselves on the open market. They package their personalities as they package the goods they produce and sell, by wearing the right clothes, driving the right cars, attending the right schools, marrying into the right families, seeking membership in the right clubs, attending the right church, joining the right political party, being seen with the right people. Unfortunately, when choice is a matter of style and taste, there is no longer the implication of commitment and permanence. Cars, clubs, and churches—even spouses, friends, and careers—are subject to immediate cancellation and replacement. Just as fashion dictates a complete change of wardrobe, a change in management style dictates a completely new personal image. Soon, the superficial qualities of the package receive greater attention than the inner qualities of the self. Identification with the packaged self results in the loss of contact with the real self. Indeed, selfhood and personal identity are problematic.

Genuine interpersonal relationships are impossible for individuals in the marketing orientation, for their packaging alienates them not only from others, but from themselves as well. Like Jung's persona (Chapter 4), the role of the marketing orientation places self-esteem on the whims of societal expectations and the current conditions of the open market, conditions over which the individual has no control. Partners have value to marketing character types *only* if they fit the cultural image.

For Fromm (1947), the key descriptive traits of the marketing character type are "opportunistic, inconsistent, childish, aimless, tactless, and indifferent" (p. 121). Entrepreneurs and powerful politicians rule the majority of people in a marketing society and treat them as commodities.

Again, however, Fromm reminds us that when there is a modicum of health and productivity present in the marketing orientation, these negative traits can be turned into positive qualities. Opportunistic can turn to "purposeful;" inconsistent may become "able to change;" aimless can change to "experimenting;" tactless may become "curious;" and indifferent can change to "tolerant" (Fromm, 1947, p. 121).

The Productive Orientation to Life Fromm's answer to the dilemma of freedom and the individuation process is the **productive orientation:** An ideal, hence never totally achievable, character type, Fromm's concept of the productive orientation represents the ultimate in human health and the ideal in human ethics. In many ways similar to Jung's individuated personality (Chapter 4), Maslow's self-actualizing personality (Chapter 10), Rogers's fully-functioning personality (Chapter 9), and Allport's mature personality (Chapter 8), Fromm's productive personality is able to utilize all his or her capacities to develop and realize all inherent potentialities as fully as possible.

Having met the basic needs of human nature and thus, able to transform the negative character traits of the nonproductive orientations into traits that are positive, Fromm's healthy and productive personality possesses a strong sense of identity, is firmly based in reality, and is actively and intensely involved in the life tasks of love and work (see "Healthy Personality," this chapter). Unlike the nonproductive orientations, there is no set of character traits for the productive orientation, perhaps because the "truly productive person would not be predictable enough so that one could specify fixed traits" (Maddi, 1972, p. 343).

Subjective versus Objective Reality

Individual reality is relative, for it reflects, among other things, our state of consciousness; perceptual inaccuracies, distortions, and repressions; cognition (attitudes, values, and beliefs); imagination and creativity. In addition, Fromm (in Fromm, Suzuki, and De Martino, 1960,) informs us:

> *Every society develops a system of categories which determines the forms of awareness. This system works, as it were, like a* socially conditioned filter. . . . *Experiences which cannot be filtered through remain outside of awareness; that is they remain unconscious (p. 99).*

Each culture also develops its own language system, the purpose of which is to persuade its members of the truth of its own assumptions, especially for those "truths" most important for the survival of the culture. The vocabulary of the culture's language system is used to form beliefs and attitudes that determine what will enter consciousness and hence, what will be ignored, distorted, or repressed. In the more mechanistic or marketing cultures, for example, it is difficult to describe experiential knowledge, for subjective experiences will not fit easily into the cultures' language systems.

In summary, we perceive events in our environment and from our perceptions, attempt to create order, structure, meaning, and relationships. Our realities, Fromm asserts, are individual, private constructions.

Uniqueness versus Universality

Fromm (1941, 1947, 1960, 1964) reminded us repeatedly that we share the history of evolution with all others of our species, and as a result of this history, enter the world with a common human nature. It follows, then, that by virtue of being human, we possess many common biological and psychological needs and processes and the predisposition to an inherited and formative actualizing tendency that prompts us to fulfill our latent potentialities. We share also the anxiety-provoking existential dichotomies intrinsic to human nature and the myriad possibilities of existence. A few examples of the dichotomies that humans must resolve are self-awareness and death awareness; freedom and its accompanying feelings of aloneness and isolation; a desire to fulfill our potentials and the tendency to return to our former peaceful ties with nature and other animals; and the incessant need to balance a complex blend of animal passion and human reasoning.

Despite our commonalities, Fromm's (1941) resolution of this issue is clear: *We are unique beings.* While it is true that we share an inherent tendency to fulfill our potentials, in no two of us are these potentials identical in number, kind, or intensity. Even when our potentials are similar to the potentials of others, given the infinite possibilities of living in the world, our actualization of them will almost certainly occur to a greater or lesser extent. While we all experience some degree of anxiety when we encounter existential dichotomies, our resolutions of the dichotomies are uniquely our own. We select, perceive, interpret, and process experiences and information in our own unique ways, for we live in separate realities (see "Subjective versus Objective Realities," this chapter).

Explanation of Learning Process

Fromm did little to explain *how* we learn. He did, however, help us to understand *why* we learn.

Endowed with the capacity of reason, we must use our intellect to make sense of and to orient ourselves to our world. It is only through an objective frame of orientation and devotion that we can hope to discover our meaning in life, our reason and purpose for being. The need for a frame of reference is so strong in our nature that Fromm (1947, 1973a) was convinced an irrational frame of orientation to the world, backed by rationalizations, was preferable to none.

We each, by our very nature, need a personal philosophy to establish a personal set of values and goals. Healthy development, however, gives rise to questions regarding the truth of the orientation we hold. Objectivity becomes a goal for the healthy personality. The healthy personality's orientation to the world, nature, other beings, and the self must be based on accurate perceptions and evaluations, if it is to result in the realization of distinctive potentialities and a unique position in the overall scheme of things. When truth is veiled or distorted by illusions and rationalizations, our need for a frame of orientation and devotion becomes pathogenic.

Role Assigned to Self-Concept

We experience the need for identity and unity; we need to be able to sense, say, and feel: "I am I, the subject of my actions." Our need for identity and unity, Fromm asserts, is more than a philosophical need requiring intellect and thinking; rather, it involves our whole person and expresses itself in our search for experience of unity with the self and with the environment. The more closely it is tied with any form of conformity, the less satisfied the need. Conversely, the more it is a part of fully developed reason and productive love, the more the need for identity and unity is realized.

Centrality of Reinforcement

The term "reinforcement" seldom appears in the theoretical vocabulary of most humanists, and certainly Fromm must be classified a humanist. He does imply, however, that the fulfillment of human needs, whether physiological or psychological, usually results in at least a momentary sense of satisfaction, however brief. Moreover, he asserts, even partial fulfillment of any one of the human needs contributes to the gratification of others, since the psychic needs are interrelated and an integral part of our inherent human nature. There is a sense of joy in productive love; a sense of self-efficacy in effective work; a sense of security in good and loyal friends; a sense of excitement and strength in meeting life challenges and personal goals; a sense of competence and victory in overcoming the restrictive forces of society. In short, the healthy personality finds life pleasant and rewarding.

Psychological Health and Psychopathology

Healthy Personality and the Good Life

Over the years, Fromm (1976, pp. 173–174; also Fromm, 1947; Chang & Maslow, 1960; Schultz, 1977) developed a clear picture of the healthy personality and the good life. Moreover, like Maslow (Chapter 10), Fromm gave considerable thought to the kind of society that would facilitate positive human growth.

In its ideal form, the healthy personality fulfills all human needs (relatedness, transcendence, rootedness, a sense of identity, and a frame of orientation) and realizes all innate human potentials (Fromm, 1947, 1966, 1976). Fromm first referred to this ideal level of health as the *productive orientation* and later as the *being mode of existence*. In both instances, Fromm was expressing a generalized concept that included *all* human aspects of life and living—all cognitive, emotive, and sensory responses to self, other humans, animals, plants, objects, and events in the person's world. In short, the being mode of existence is a full and vigorous expression of humanness. More than that, Fromm was expressing a dynamic concept, a lifelong process rather than a state of being, a goal rather than an end. As an ideal, Fromm's concept of health was a level of health that was to be strived for rather than achieved, much like Jung's individuation process, Maslow's self-actualization process, or Rogers's process of becoming fully functioning. For Fromm, the fully productive and ideally healthy personality, then, has never been achieved in any society, though a very few exceptional individuals have managed somehow to come close, in spite of the sick or "insane" societies in which they found themselves.

Fromm (1976, p. 173) describes the healthy, biophilous person in the being mode of existence as one who:

- lives fully in the present;
- experiences the joy that comes from giving and sharing;
- loves and respects life in all its manifestations;
- reduces greed, hate, and illusions as much as possible;
- lives without idols;
- develops the capacity for love, together with the capacity for critical, unsentimental thought;

Heredity			Social Determinants
Determinism			Freedom
Conscious Determinants			Unconscious Determinants
Early Development			Continuous Development
Subjective Reality			Objective Reality
Uniqueness			Universality

Role Assigned to Group Determinants	When evolution severed our species from the safety and security provided by our instinctual unity with nature, strong feelings of aloneness and powerlessness emerged. A need for relatedness became a part of our nature and is pathogenic when not gratified. We may choose to relate progressively or regressively.
Number and Weight Assigned to Motivational Concepts	We experience a need to transcend our animal nature. Primary and secondary drives extended to their purest forms produce two extreme character orientations: biophilia (love of life and growth) and necrophilia (love of death and decay). Fromm identified five character orientations common in the Western world: the receptive, the exploitive, the hoarding, the marketing, and the productive.
Explanation of Learning Process	We use our intellect to make sense of and to orient to our world. A need for a frame of reference is so strong that an irrational frame of orientation is preferable to none.
Role Assigned to Self-Concept	We experience the need for identity and unity. Our need for identity involves our whole person and expresses itself in our search for an experience of unity with the self and the environment.
Centrality of Reinforcement	The fulfillment of human needs (physiological or psychological) results in a sense of satisfaction. The healthy personality finds life pleasant and rewarding.

FIGURE 6-3   Schematic Analysis of Fromm's Stance on Basic Issues

- sheds narcissism and accepts the tragic limitations inherent in human existence;
- makes growth of self and others the supreme goal of living;
- knows life's goal requires discipline and respect for reality;
- knows no growth is healthy that does not occur in a structure;
- develops imagination as the anticipation of real possibilities;
- is innocent, but not naïve;
- knows self; and
- senses a feeling of oneness with all life.

While Fromm's *ideal* concept of health is based on a unidimensional frame of orientation and devotion that is possible only when a society's needs and purposes are in perfect synchronicity with the psychological and physiological needs inherent in humans, there is yet no society in which these conditions exist. It is impossible, then, for any personality to be totally productive or totally unproductive. Rather, human personality is a unique blending of different frames of orientation and devotion, with one being predominate. An individual who is productive, loving, charitable, and creative about most things most of the time, may, on occasion, be somewhat narcissistic or power oriented. Likewise, a person who is predominately narcissistic and hoarding oriented may, at times, be kind or charitable.

Though Fromm (1964) believes the ultimate goal of health and the good life remains out of reach, he is convinced that productiveness is an attitude that every human is capable of achieving: "the moral effort consists in strengthening the life-loving side of oneself" (p. 50). What matters in Fromm's theory of character structure is which of the two frames of orientation to life (biophilia and necrophilia, being and having) is dominant.

All humans have an inherent tendency to actualize their potentialities and to affirm life. Well-being, according to Fromm (1970/1960), "is being in accord with the nature of man" (p. 86). This requires the courage of ethical and moral choices to develop awareness, reason, and the capacity to love; in short, to transcend egocentric involvement and to move toward a productive orientation.

Fromm agrees with Freud (Chapter 2) that there are no alternatives to love and work for achieving the good life. Only by loving and working productively can humans move toward self-realization and achieve independence. Those unable or unwilling to strive toward a productive orientation risk becoming subjects to their chronic, neurotic needs and leading dependent or animalistic existences.

Psychopathology

There are a few general observations that may prove helpful in understanding Fromm's view of psychopathology:

1. Excluding congenital psychopathological conditions, the difference between the healthy and the disturbed personality is a matter of degree rather than of kind—the compulsive dynamics that determine the neurotic personality are only accentuated or extreme instances of the same dynamics that determine the normal personality.

2. Adult neurosis can usually be traced back to early childhood experiences, particularly the child–parent relationship.

3. Productive love is the fundamental rule of life; hence, the violation of love is responsible for most human unhappiness and psychological disturbance.

4. All existing societies contain some degree of psychopathology and to that degree, conflict with the basic needs of human nature—neurosis always consists of a conflict between these two opposing forces.

5. The ultimate solution to human psychopathology is a radical remodeling of society; in short, the creation of a sane society.

Parental Influences Convinced that the experiences of infancy and early childhood significantly influence a child's construction of a healthy or unhealthy frame of orientation, Fromm (1967b), like Freud (1960), believed that the root of neurosis is embedded in the failure of the child to resolve satisfactorily an early conflict between child and parent. Unlike Freud, however, Fromm did not think this conflict emerged as a result of sexual rivalry, but rather from the child's fear of and submission to parental authority. Conflict arises, according to Fromm (1967), when the relationship between child and parent is based on irrational authority. Fromm defined irrational parental authority as a power-based child–parent relationship in which the child is subjected to authority, stands in fear and awe of it, and later reciprocates. Irrational authority, Fromm asserts, breaks the child's will, kills the child's spontaneity, and deprives the child of independence.

For Fromm, a pathological frame of orientation occurs when the healthy drives of the child's inherent nature are thwarted and at least partially overcome by parental or societal influences that lead to nonproductive (regressive and compulsive) striving. Viewing psychopathology from this perspective, neurosis is better understood as a nonproductive frame of orientation or the incapacity for productive love and work.

Societal Influences The human infant is psychologically healthy at birth, but the society into which it is thrown is not. Though Fromm argues that it is possible for humans to create a healthy society, he is convinced that all existing societies contain some degree of pathology and to that degree, conflict with basic human needs. A sick society produces a sick people, and they in turn reproduce the pathology of their society.

Some individuals are more successful than others in resolving their conflict with a dehumanizing society, but Fromm (1967) believed most are defeated to some extent and their scars "are to be found at the bottom of every neurosis" (p. 518). Indeed, for Fromm (1941, 1947) the primary question of mental health is not why some humans become insane, but rather why most do not.

Heuristic Influence

Fromm's theoretical formulations were based primarily on the psychoanalytic research strategies advocated in his training (clinical observations and case studies); hence, his critics (most often proponents of experimental strategies) pointed to three logical errors in his evidence. First, Fromm did not distinguish between observation and inference. Second, he often confused correlation and causation. And third, he sometimes cited analogy as proof, a rather weak strategy at best.

Weaknesses of the case study were also presented by his critics. Not only are these data based on a small, atypical sample (thus not representative), they represent the analyst's selective recollections of the case, which may be biased. Further, there is often disagreement within the psychoanalytic community itself on the interpretation of these data. Dreams, for instance, may be interpreted differently by different psychoanalysts.

In addition to the criticisms leveled at the psychoanalytic research strategies just cited, Fromm has been criticized for concepts that are poorly defined—vague, ambiguous, qualitative, non-operational terms that are more literary, philosophical, and religious than they are scientific. Poorly defined concepts defy measurement and are therefore impossible to test objectively.

Like most humanists, Fromm took a strong stance against scientism, deeming it too narrow a conception of science to provide a full understanding of human nature. He was convinced that the psychoanalytic method of investigation, based on many hours of careful observation, was truly scientific. Moreover, he was certain that his theory would be validated with the accumulation of anthropological data necessary for cross-cultural comparisons. Indeed, it was this line of reasoning that led to the Fromm–Maccoby (1947) study of a developing Mexican village.

Fromm's Single Attempt at Empirical Research

Years after Fromm (1947) first published his theory of character types, Fromm and Maccoby (1970) conducted an extensive study of 406 adult Mexican villagers and published evidence that seemed to confirm Fromm's character typology. Over a period of several years (1957–1963), a team of cross-disciplinary specialists (including psychologists, anthropologists, physicians, and statisticians) studied a small isolated village southwest of Mexico City. The instruments used to gather data for the study included questionnaires, interviews, the Rorschach Inkblot Method, and dream analysis.

Fromm and Maccoby (1970) were able to show that with the exception of the marketing orientation (a product of the more highly industrialized societies), the three main types of personality types presented in Fromm's earlier works were present in the village. The largest representation was the nonproductive–receptive character type. The productive–hoarding type ranked second. And the least frequent type was the exploitive character, which consisted of both productive and nonproductive subtypes. An analysis revealed that each of the three character types evolved as a result of psychological and social adaptation strategies to the inescapable conditions of the subject's social niche in a fairly rigid class structure.

The nonproductive–receptive character types emerged from the landless day-laborers who shared a position on the bottom of the socioeconomic hierarchy of the village. Feeling inferior to their employers and the landowners, they behaved passively and dependently. Believing they had little or no control over their own lives, they strived to please those they considered more powerful and in control.

Approximately one third of the subjects of Fromm and Maccoby's study exhibited the character traits of Fromm's productive–hoarding type (Fromm & Maccoby, 1970, p. 117). The villagers who fit this type tended to be more productive, hence, more socially and economically independent and self-reliant. In addition, they owned small plots of land, surviving only through hard work and what they could hoard against lean times.

Unproductive and productive exploitive character types accounted for 10 to 15 per cent of the villagers. Male exploitive character types who were unproductive and marked by destructive tendencies were often responsible for knife and gun fights. Female unproductive–exploitive types were responsible for much of the malicious gossip in the village. Conversely, the productive–exploitive character types were modern entrepreneurs, owned most of the land, and employed others to work for them.

The productive character types were the most democratic. They respected the rights of others and those who worked to help the villagers. They also expressed both love and respect for their children.

Application to Psychotherapy

Whether it was because Fromm directed his writing to the general reader rather than to other psychoanalysts, or because he was more concerned with the limits imposed on human nature than he was with human nature itself, Fromm did not address his personal approach to individual therapy in his many publications. It is possible to assume from his critique of Freud that Fromm accepted many of the doctrines and therapeutic strategies of classical psychoanalysis, including, for example, the need to make the unconscious conscious, the technique of free association (though Fromm was more active than the classical analysts), transference, and a modified and expanded form of dream interpretation (see "Extended Applications" and "Dreams," this chapter).

Therapeutic Goals

The primary goal of Fromm's Humanistic Social Analysis is to assist the client to achieve a fuller expression of his or her inherent human nature. This often entails secondary goals (e.g., helping the client to fulfill the needs inherent in human nature and assisting the client to transcend the pathogenic orientations he or she employs to escape the frightening prospects of freedom and the anxiety of loneliness, isolation, and alienation).

Therapeutic Relationship

Finding the orthodox Freudian analyst–patient relationship both boring and limited, Fromm developed a more authentic, interactive, and confrontive presence in the therapeutic setting. Keeping his patients' psychic needs in mind (relatedness, transcendence, unity, identity, a frame of orientation, excitation and stimulation, effectiveness), Fromm attempted to establish a democratic therapeutic relationship in which he was genuinely and actively present.

Fromm believed the therapist must experience and actively express empathy when working with a client; that is, assimilate the client's internal frame of reference and communicate this empathic understanding to the client. Empathy is necessary, Fromm maintained, to demonstrate to the client that the or she is not alone, that the therapist and the client share a common humanity.

Initial Procedures and Strategies

Fromm's essential focus in his writings was on the reciprocal interaction of the individual and society. Hence, despite his psychoanalytic training and experience, he disagreed with many of the theoretical constructs of orthodox psychoanalysis. Fromm (1951) nevertheless employed a form of free association and placed great emphasis on the interpretation of dreams as an essential part of therapy.

While Fromm was not always clear about the methods and techniques of therapy, he did imply that he was more active in the process of therapy than were most classical psychoanalysts. He did not hesitate to intervene when he thought his intervention would facilitate the client's progress in therapy.

Course of Therapy

As with classical psychoanalysis, Fromm observed facts, drew inferences from his observations, formed hypotheses, considered his hypotheses in the light of additional facts that emerged during the course of therapy, and eventually arrived at a conclusion regarding the validity of his hypotheses. In addition to the therapeutic setting, many of Fromm's insights emerged from such fields as religion, philosophy, psychology, sociology, anthropology, economics, and political science.

Extended Applications

Dreams

Many clinicians credit Fromm for expanding our knowledge of dreams and dream interpretation. Fromm agreed with Freud, who was the first to view dreams as the "royal road to the unconscious," that dreams can serve the purpose of wish fulfillment. He did not, however, believe that dreams necessarily held disguised meanings or that dream symbols necessarily had to be sexual.

For Fromm (1951/1957), dreams were often obvious expressions of the dreamer's current anxieties and misgivings:

> *"We are not only less reasonable and less decent in our dreams, but . . . also more intelligent, wiser, and capable of better judgment when we are asleep than when we are awake" (p. 33).*

In short, Fromm (1951/1953) believed "unconscious knowing" may emerge in our dreams *before* it is accessible to our conscious awareness. For example, a person who impressed us most favorably on first meeting appears in a dream that night as one who cannot be trusted. Later we discover the person presented in the dream was more accurate than our original impression.

Fromm (1951/1957) also considered symbolic language as an important mode of communication in dreams, and he agreed with Freud that some dream symbols were universal. However, he believed the connotations of universal dream symbols were:

> "... *because they are intrinsically related to what they represent, such as the power and vitality of fire, the slow and steady quality of moving water, and the security of a valley enclosed by mountains. In contrast to Jungian archetypes, universal symbols result from these intrinsic meanings rather than from racial inheritances*" (*Fromm, 1951/1957, p. 18*).

Society and Culture

A repeated theme in nearly all of Fromm's published works was the negative impact of societal and cultural influences on the formation of human personality. Fromm (1941, 1947, 1955, 1960, 1967a, 1976) was convinced that all existing societies impose demands that limit fulfillment of needs that are basic to human nature; in short, he believed all societies created to date are, to a greater or lesser degree, pathogenic.

Fromm (1955, 1965) envisioned a utopian society (Humanistic Communitarian Socialism) that he thought would fulfill human nature, and called for drastic spiritual and social reforms that he believed were necessary to make his concept of a healthy society a reality. It is interesting to note that many of these reforms are being echoed by today's scientists and ecologists.

In his last book, *To Have or To Be?*, Fromm (1976) describes still another pair of character orientations: The *being* (being, experiencing, participating) and the *having* (having, consuming, destroying) orientations. According to Fromm (1976, also 1964, 1973a), the biophilic and necrophilic orientations combined with the being and having orientations determine how humans perceive and experience reality, whether in themselves, others, or the world.

The Being Orientation By combining the productive and the biophilous character orientations into the being orientation, Fromm (1947, 1964, 1973a, 1976) provides a rather clear picture of psychological personality traits. Less clear, however, are his suggestions for acquiring these traits, particularly since they are inseparably linked to an elusive set of human values and are largely dependent upon a healthy society. While it is the nature of humans to strive for emotional health and well-being, it is the nature of society to facilitate or inhibit the actualization of human nature.

Unfortunately, each society demands that its members meet its definition of mental health, even to the point of threatening their sanity. Only when the nature of society and the nature of humans are congruent are humans in position to use all their powers to realize fully their inherent potentialities—to perceive and reason objectively, to be imaginative and creative, to love, to experience a strong sense of identity, to be in control of and actively direct the course of their lives. Happiness is, for Fromm, an integral, dynamic element of the being frame of orientation, so much so, in fact, that Fromm believed happiness may be the best single criterion to assess a person's success in living productively in the being mode.

The Having Orientation   Those living in a having orientation define themselves and their success by what they have when compared to others. Further, since security in the having mode rests in ownership, and insecurity is a fact of life, persons in a having orientation always believe that to be secure and happy they must have more. They continue to think this way, even after learning that security and happiness did not magically arrive with the second car, the Caribbean cruise, or the vacation home in the country. Primarily consumers, they pursue possessions. They cannot understand that like all spiritual, mental, and intellectual content, security and happiness are not things to be possessed, but rather a sense of inner-aliveness and well-being to be experienced.

As with all Fromm's nonproductive orientations, the having orientation leads to an unconscious alienation from the self. Having character types often report that they *have* problems, as though their problems were possessions, or worse, as though they were possessed by their problems. Rather than "I am I," having character types identify themselves with their possessions—"I am I because I have this or that." A statement such as: "I have this terrible feeling that comes over me every time I am expected to make a decision" helps having character types avoid the realization that they are experiencing misery because they are unable to make and to take responsibility for their decisions.

Critique

Too Cross-Disciplinary?

It will be recalled that Fromm's study of human personality ranged across the boundaries of other disciplines, including history, economics, sociology, anthropology, philosophy, religion, and political science. Indeed, Fromm's unique interpretation of the interaction between humanity and society could only have resulted from an extensive cross-disciplinary research effort. Such an approach is not without its risks, and certainly not without its critics.

While personologists may welcome data from other disciplines, they are suspicious of inferences drawn from those data, especially when the inferences run counter to accepted theories or when the inferences are qualitative rather than quantitative. And while authorities in the other disciplines recognized Fromm's scholarly abilities, they often questioned his interpretation of *their* data. In short, Fromm's challenge to personologists to think beyond the boundaries of psychoanalysis and psychology drew critical fire not only from certain of his colleagues, but from some authorities of the other disciplines as well.

The Criticism of Psychoanalysts

Classical psychoanalysts were skeptical of any data not derived from the psychoanalytic process and they found Fromm's attempts to revise Freud's major theoretical constructs especially objectionable. When Fromm rejected the instinctivist stance articulated by Freud in favor of a distinctive image of an actualizing human nature, many psychoanalysts simply ignored his reasoning by reminding themselves and others that Fromm did not hold medical credentials. When Fromm suggested that Freud's Oedipus complex was more an authoritarian conflict between the child and the parent than it was a sexual conflict, the classical psychoanalysts responded that considering his background, his explanation could be predicted.

Hausdorff (1972), an advocate of Fromm's theory, admits that it did seem a practice of Fromm's to credit Freud and then negate that credit by offering an immediate revision of the concept. He states: "In *Man for Himself*, his [Fromm's] attempt to formulate a 'scientific' theory of ethics based on human needs and norms, Fromm continually returns to Freudian concepts, and constantly 'revises' them" (Hausdorff, 1972, p. 160).

The Criticisms of Psychologists

Defending the research strategies advocated in his training as a psychoanalyst, Fromm was subject to the many criticisms leveled against psychoanalysis. The strongest criticisms came from American academic psychologists who believed that human behavior should be studied under controlled conditions and that theoretical concepts should be operationally defined and assessed by using quantitative measures that are reliable and valid. Psychologists, in particular, point to Fromm's neglect of the learning process as a major omission in his theory.

A Contributor to Social Psychology

While no single theorist can be credited for the emergence of social psychology, Fromm's humanistic social analysis certainly contributed to the cumulative series of theoretical developments that called attention to the dynamic influence of social forces in the formation of human personality. Fromm grounded his theory in a distinctive image of an actualizing human nature, then analyzed societal, cultural, economic, and political demands that were either liberative (productive) or repressive (nonproductive) to the expression of that nature. Indeed, it was because Fromm wrote so persuasively of his concern over the impact of human (sane) and inhuman (insane) societal demands on human nature that he drew a vast following in the academic community, particularly from among the young.

Appeal to Western Youth

Although many of Fromm's recommendations for radical social reforms proved controversial, they do appear to strike a responsive chord in those individuals who believe contemporary Western society should be held accountable for ignoring dehumanizing social conditions that lead to alienation and loneliness in a technological society. Young people especially are attracted to Fromm's view of a normative human nature with an inner dynamism of its own. Further, they admire Fromm's courage and integrity, his dedication to scholarship, and his commitment to individual freedom and the democratic ideal.

Conclusion

Though Fromm's theory of human nature is without a strong empirical base, thus highly speculative, his ideas continue to stimulate the thinking of others, particularly in the Western world. In addition to the millions who have purchased and read his works, many of Fromm's conclusions are repeated in the works of other personality theorists, especially the humanists and existentialists (for examples, see Rogers, Chapter 9; Maslow, Chapter 10; Allport, Chapter 8). In his journals, Maslow makes numerous references to Fromm—all of them positive.

After considering Fromm's contributions to personality theory, Ryckman (1985) concludes:

> *The primary value of Fromm's theory is its ability to stimulate the thinking of others. It is a complex set of formulations that rests firmly on moral issues that are important to each of us and that Fromm correctly concluded must be grasped and understood if we are to live in a more harmonious relationship with one another (p. 159).*

This writer echoes Ryckman's thinking.

Annotated Bibliography

Students interested in continuing their study of Fromm's personality theory are encouraged to read his works. For most students this presents a dilemma: "Where does one begin?" Fromm was a prolific writer. His publications begin with his dissertation in 1922, and with very few breaks, continue each year until his death in 1980. Unfortunately for the new student, not one of these hundreds of published works contains a complete and systematic presentation of his theory. His ideas and theoretical formulations, along with their modifications and elaborations, appear throughout his works as they were developed. First-time students of Fromm are usually directed to three of his books—*Escape from Freedom* (1941), *Man for Himself* (1947), and *Psychoanalysis and Religion* (1950). Fromm referred to these three volumes as a trilogy of related works.

For Fromm, the desire to be free is a basic part of human nature. In *Escape from Freedom* (1941), Fromm's first major work, he explores the problems inherent in human freedom and the human tendency to surrender freedom in exchange for the protection of a tyrannical leader or for the security of authority. Fromm's insight into the phenomenon of Nazi Germany impressed an American public whose country was about to enter a second World War, and contributed to the book's immediate success in the United States.

Continuing with the major themes introduced in *Escape from Freedom,* Fromm's *Man for Himself* (1947) is a study of humanistic ethics and values. Unlike Freud, Fromm presents a strong argument for the basic goodness of human nature. Here too the reader is introduced to Fromm's formulations of five character types.

In the third volume of Fromm's trilogy, *Psychoanalysis and Religion* (1950), he contends that since the development of human nature is the goal of both psychoanalysis and religion, neither should be perceived as a threat to the other. The positive aspects of both psychology and religion encourage productive growth in humans, hence leaders in both areas are called upon to respond to the challenge of today's society.

Two additional books are strongly recommended before turning the new student loose for independent study: *The Art of Loving* (1956), Fromm's most popular book, and *The Forgotten Language* (1951). In *The Art of Loving,* Fromm not only describes the various kinds of love that humans express, but also insists that there is a direct relation between the culture and a person's ability to love. For Fromm, there is no alternative to productive love and work if humans are to be free and live the good life. In addition, Fromm discusses steps humans can take to enhance their ability to love productively.

With publication of *The Forgotten Language,* Fromm (1951) was acknowledged as a major contributor to the understanding of symbolic language and the interpretation of dreams. In this book, Fromm attempts to prove his belief that the language of symbols is the common language of all humans.

References and Suggested Readings

Chang, H., & Maslow, A. H. (Eds.). (1960). *The healthy personality* (2nd ed.). New York: D. Van Nostrand.

Elkind, D. (May, 1981). Obituary: Erich Fromm (1900–1980). *American Psychologist 36*(5), pp. 521–522.

Evans, R. I. (1976). *The making of psychology: Discussions with creative contributors.* New York: Alfred A. Knopf.

Fromm, E. (1941/1965). *Escape from freedom.* (Avon Library Ed.). New York: Holt, Rinehart & Winston. (Originally published 1941)

Fromm, E. (1946/1966). *You shall be as gods.* Greenwich, CT: Fawcett.

Fromm, E. (1947). *Man for himself.* New York: Rinehart.

Fromm, E. (1950/1976). *Psychoanalysis and religion.* New York: Bantam. (Originally published 1950)

Fromm, E. (1951). *The forgotten language.* New York: Grove Press.

Fromm, E. (1955). *The sane society.* New York: Rinehart.

Fromm, E. (1956a). *The art of loving.* New York: Harper & Row.

Fromm, E. (1956b). Selfishness, self-love, and self-interest. In C. Moustakas, (Ed.). *The self: Explorations in personal growth.* New York: Harper & Row, pp. 58–69.

Fromm, E. (1959). *Sigmund Freud's mission: An analysis of his personality and influence.* New York: Harper & Row.

Fromm, E. (1960). *Psychopathology of everyday life.* (A. A. Brill, Trans.). New York: The American Library.

Fromm, E., Suzuki, D. T., & De Martino, R. (1960). *Zen Buddhism and psychoanalysis.* New York: Harper & Row.

Fromm, E. (1961a). *May man prevail?* Garden City, New York: Doubleday.

Fromm, E. (1961b). *Marx's concept of man.* New York: Ungar.

Fromm, E. (1962). *Beyond the chains of illusion.* New York: Simon & Schuster.

Fromm, E. (1964). *The heart of man.* New York: Harper & Row.

Fromm, E. (Ed.). (1965). *Socialist humanism: An international symposium.* New York: Anchor Books.

Fromm, E. (1967a). Individual and social origins of neurosis. In C. Kluckholm, H. A. Murray, & D. M. Schneider, (Eds.). *Personality in nature, society, and culture.* New York: Alfred A. Knopf, pp. 515–521.

Fromm, E. (1970/1968). *The revolution of hope.* New York: Harper Colophon Books. (Originally published 1968)

Fromm, E. (1970). *The crisis of psychoanalysis.* New York: Holt, Rinehart, and Winston.

Fromm, E. (March, 1971). Mother. *Psychology Today,* 4(10), pp. 74–77.

Fromm, E. (August, 1973). Man would as soon flee as fight. *Psychology Today,* 7(3), pp. 35–39, 41–45.

Fromm, E. (1973a). *The anatomy of human destructiveness.* New York: Holt, Rinehart and Winston.

Fromm, E. (1976). *To have or to be?* New York: Harper & Row.

Fromm, E. & Maccoby, M. (1970). *Social character in a Mexican village.* Englewood Cliffs, NJ: Prentice–Hall.

Fuller, A. R. (1986). *Psychology and religion: Eight points of view* (2nd ed.). Lanham, MA: University Press of America.

Funk, R. (1982). *Erich Fromm: The courage to be human.* New York: Continuum.

Hall, C. S., & Lindzey, G. (1978). *Theories of personality* (3rd ed.). New York: Simon and Schuster.

Hausdorff, D. (1972). *Erich Fromm.* New York: Tyayne.

Landis, B., & Tauber, E. S. (Eds.). (1971). *In the name of life, essays in honor of Erich Fromm.* New York: Holt, Rinehart and Winston.

Maddi, S. R. (1972). *Personality theories: A comparative analysis* (Rev. ed.). Homewood, IL: The Dorsey Press.

Ryckman, R. M. (1985). *Theories of personality.* Monterey, CA: Brooks/Cole.

Schultz, D. (1977). *Growth psychology: Models of the healthy personality.* New York: D. Van Nostrand.

Wakin, E. (1980, April 12). Erich Fromm: Most of all a teacher. *America,* 142(14), p. 319.

Wells, H. K. (1963). *The failure of psychoanalysis, from Freud to Fromm.* New York: International.

Chapter 7

Horney's Theory of Psychosocial Analysis

Chapter Overview

Introduction

Biographical Sketch of the Theorist

Resolution of the Basic Issues
  Heredity versus Social Determinants
  Role Assigned to Self-Concept
  Early versus Continuous Development
  Number and Weight Assigned to Motivational Concepts
  Conscious versus Unconscious Determinants
  Subjective versus Objective Reality
  Determinism versus Freedom of Choice
  Explanation of Learning Process
  Uniqueness versus Universality
  Role Assigned to Group Determinants
  Centrality of Reinforcement

Psychological Health and Psychopathology
  Psychological Health
  Psychopathology

Application to Psychotherapy
Therapeutic Goals
Therapeutic Relationship
Initial Procedures and Strategies
Course of Psychotherapy

Extended Applications

Critique

Annotated Bibliography

References and Suggested Readings

Introduction

Like many psychoanalysts, as Karen Horney (pronounced "Horn-eye") gained clinical experience, she began to doubt the validity of some of the basic tenets of Freud's theory. In particular, she questioned the primacy of Freud's libido theory as the source of motivation, the emphasis that he placed on psychosexual development, and his exclusion of social and cultural forces in the shaping of personality.

Horney's (1939) first doubts emerged when she read Freud's concept of feminine psychology, and they were strengthened by his postulate of **Thanatos,** the death instinct (p. 7). Later, after observing the marked differences between the symptoms and attitudes of her German patients and her patients in the United States, she became aware of the significance of social, cultural, and economic forces on both healthy and pathogenic personality development. She also became convinced that neuroses were the result of the interpersonal relationships of the child with his or her parents and siblings, rather than the result of the physiological forces and fixations at particular psychosexual stages of development, as Freud asserted.

Horney offered an optimistic, holistic view of human nature. Her positive theory of **self-realization** (our capacity, motivation, and obligation to realize our innate potentialities) is a rejection of Freud's instinctivistic and mechanistic approach to personality development (Chapter 2).

Horney's Theory of Psychosocial Analysis also offered the first equalitarian view of women, a view much more acceptable today than at the time she presented it. She challenged Freud's concept of penis envy which, she argued, served as the basis for the stereotypical thinking about women's inferior roles in life. For Horney, Freud's Electra complex was often no more than a little girl's wish for equal status and power to that which parents and society grant freely to little boys.

Horney (1939a) was convinced that "psychoanalysis should outgrow the limitations set by its being an instinctivistic and genetic psychology" and then build upon the foundations of Freud's theory (p. 8). In her attempts to expand

Freud's pioneering efforts, she formulated a theory of personality development that is primarily interpersonal and cultural, makes use of anthropological and sociological methodologies (as well as typologies), presents a liberating and equalitarian view of feminine sexuality and psychology, and offers new ways of understanding the role of the **real self** ("that central inner force common to all human beings and yet unique in each, which is a deep source of growth," Horney, 1950, p. 17), and the constructive forces of self-realization (the actualization of innate potentialities).

Horney (1942) was also the first psychoanalyst to consider the feasibility of **self-analysis** as a self-help procedure for the lay person. She offered her lay readers an in-depth discussion of the possibilities, hazards, and limitations for those wanting to do something about their own problems by systematically analyzing themselves (Horney, 1942). While both Freud (Chapter 2) and Jung (Chapter 4) offered data from their self-analyses in support of their theoretical constructs, neither recommended self-analysis to lay persons who had not undergone analysis by a qualified analyst.

Biographical Sketch of the Theorist

There are rich, though contrasting, sources for Horney's biography, including her early attempts to keep a diary. These include Eckardt's (1984) "Karen Horney: Her Life and Contribution," Quinn's (1987) *A Mind of Her Own: The Life of Karen Horney,* and Rubins's (1978) *Karen Horney: Gentle Rebel of Psychoanalysis.* Rubins's book may be the most objective source, for Quinn is an ardent follower of Horneyan theory and relies heavily on Horney's diaries for much of her material on Horney's childhood years.

Early Years

Karen (Danielson) Horney was born September 15, 1885, in Eilbek, a suburb of Hamburg, Germany. She was the second child of Berndt Henrik Wackels Danielson and Clothilde Marie (Van Roncelen) Danielson. Their firstborn, Horney's brother, Berndt, was four years older than she. Horney's father had four teenage children from his first marriage when he married her mother, who was seventeen years younger than her husband. The number present in the Horney household varied during Horney's childhood. In addition to her parents and brother, there were at times four stepchildren and a grandmother, whom Horney dearly loved and with whom she felt loved and secure.

Wackels Danielson was a Norwegian steamship captain who became a German citizen and later was appointed Commodore of a major North German shipping company. A zealous Lutheran, Danielson was morose, authoritarian, domineering, and to Horney as a child, very intimidating. At the age of twelve Horney decided that she wanted to become a doctor, which was by no means her father's idea of a proper career choice for his daughter. Viewing the role of women as inferior to that of men, Horney's father vehemently opposed her educational goals, while at the same time, showing gross favoritism and granting a great deal of freedom to her brother. Her father often made demeaning remarks about Horney's appearance and intelligence, which led her to believe that she was unattractive, unloved, and unwanted.

The marked differences in the personalities of her mother and father led to numerous arguments and for Horney, a stressful and insecure atmosphere at home. Her father's frequent and lengthy voyages at sea meant only a more peaceful and pleasant life at home. Horney's mother was attractive, vibrant, and an independent thinker. Recognizing her daughter's academic ability, she encouraged Horney to pursue her goal to become a doctor, and she intervened when the tensions between Horney and her father become too great for a child to handle. It is probably safe to speculate that Horney's (1945) concepts of **basic anxiety** ("a terrible feeling of being isolated and helpless in a potentially hostile world," p. 39) and the need for security in children might be traced to her own childhood experiences (see "Early versus Continuous Development," this chapter).

Education

In 1906, Horney was admitted to medical school at Freiburg; she was the only woman in her class. An excellent student, she found the male-dominated atmosphere of the medical school exciting and challenging, though she constantly felt that she had to prove her competence. It was while in medical school that she met and in 1909 married Oskar Horney, a Ph.D. candidate in economics. Oskar Horney became an attorney and was hired by a large investment firm, where he was rapidly advanced to a managerial position.

The next ten years were extremely stressful for Horney. In addition to completing her medical training and psychoanalysis by Karl Abraham (a loyal follower of Freud who was recognized as an outstanding training analyst), Horney became the mother of three daughters (Sonni Brigitte, Marianne, and Renate). She lost her father in 1910, and her mother died the following year. She received her medical degree from the University of Berlin in 1913 and worked at a neuropsychiatric hospital near Berlin while also working privately as a practicing analyst. Horney's husband lost his job in 1923, necessitating a drastic change in their lifestyle. Her brother Berndt died that year. She and her husband separated in 1926. They were divorced in 1937.

Emergence of Theory

Between 1922 and 1935, Horney published a series of fourteen papers on the subject of feminine sexuality and personality development. With each publication, her differences with Freud became increasingly more evident. Also evident, in retrospect, is the fact that these early publications served as a base for her later theoretical formulations.

In 1932, Dr. Franz Alexander, head of the Institute for Psychoanalysis in Chicago, invited Horney to be the associate director of the Institute. After two years in Chicago, Horney made application to the New York Institute of Psychoanalysis. She joined the faculty of the New School for Social Research, which included among others such theorists as Eric Fromm (Chapter 6), Harry Stack Sullivan, Margaret Mead, John Dollard (a personality theorist, who along with Neal Miller integrated the theories of Freud and Pavlov), Paul Tillich (a religious philosopher and existentialist), and Menard Boss (an existential personality theorist). Her lectures attracted large audiences, and along with her earlier publications, were the seeds for her first book, *Neurotic Personality of Our Time* (1937). Her second book, *New Ways in Psychoanalysis* (1939), even more critical of orthodox psychoanalysis, led to disciplinary action by the Education Committee of the Institute, and she was demoted from instructor to lecturer. Incensed by their action, Horney and others who disagreed with the action of the Education Committee walked out of the meeting and broke all ties with the New York Psychoanalytic Association and the Institute.

In 1941, Horney and colleagues of similar ideologies founded the Association for the Advancement of Psychoanalysis (AAP) which, despite the exclusion from the American Psychoanalytic Association, attracted training applicants and was granted professional affiliation with several hospitals. Horney was named Dean, a position she held until her death in 1952.

Shortly before her death, Horney became interested in Zen as a means of transcending the self. She made a pilgrimage to Japan and with the aid of a scholar of Zen Buddhism, was impressed with the focus in Zen on concentration and intuitive understanding. She could see the advantages of greater focus in these areas for the analytic situation and expressed her views in articles that were published posthumously (Horney, 1987).

Honors and Awards

In addition to being one of the founders of the American Association for the Advancement of Psychoanalysis, later renamed the Karen Horney Psychoanalytic Institute and Center, Horney was honored as a fellow of the American Psychiatric Association and served as editor of the *American Journal of Psychoanalysis.* Her publications include five books and numerous articles. She was an M.D., a psychoanalyst, a training analyst, and a major theorist of personality and psychotherapy. Horneyan analysts may be found today in the United States and throughout Europe. Horney's stance on feminine psychology preceded by decades the current feminist movement in the United States. Her theory continues to appear in current textbooks on personality theory forty years after her death. Students in psychiatry, psychology, counseling, and social work are familiar with Horney's theoretical formulations.

Resolution of the Basic Issues

Horney repeatedly stated that it was not her intent to formulate an original theory of personality. Rather, she claimed that her goal was the advancement and development of Freud's work so that it would better fit a different time and culture. Indeed, she believed that had Freud lived, their ideas would be quite similar. Nonetheless, as Horney's theoretical formulations evolved, many grew in direct opposition to those of Freud. These differences will become evident as the reader compares her resolutions of the basic issues with those of Freud (Chapter 2). It will be evident, as well, that Horney borrowed some of her ideas from Adler (Chapter 3) and Fromm (Chapter 6), as well as from other disciplines, in particular sociology and anthropology.

Heredity versus Social Determinants

According to Horney (1950), we have an innate capacity and desire to actualize our particular potentialities. She describes this inherent growth principle as evolutionary constructive forces pressing us to actualize our **real selves**—a central inner force common to all, yet unique to each individual (Horney, 1950, p. 15). We therefore naturally strive toward (though never fully achieve) self-realization.

Like Maslow's hierarchy of needs (Chapter 10), Horney's growth needs can be paralyzed by deficit (**neurotic**) needs, in particular by the overemphasized need for security (see "Early versus Continuous Development," this chapter). Horney's security needs involve both physical and psychological security; the need for security must be adequately gratified before there is sufficient energy to meet our need to realize our possibilities in life. When our security is threatened, our energy is diverted from the weaker biological **growth need** (to actualize the real self) to reduce the stronger cultural threat to our security.

When our psychic and physical energy are directed toward self-realization, our behavior is flexible and we experience a sense of freedom. Conversely, when our behavior is directed toward security, it is inflexible and compulsive and we experience feelings of anxiety, isolation, loneliness, and hopelessness.

For Horney (1967), our individual personalities are ". . . shaped as much (or more) by cultural forces as by certain instinctual demands" (p. 28, parentheses added). She reminded us repeatedly that it is the culture that defines normality and abnormality. So while Horney did not deny biological determinants, she flatly rejected Freud's total emphasis on biology to the neglect of cultural and social factors in personality development. **Neurosis,** Horney asserted, is the result of paralyzing conflicts in our interpersonal and social relationships rather than conflicts between ego and id (see "Psychopathology," this chapter).

Role Assigned to Self-Concept

Before considering Horney's resolution of this issue, we might avoid confusion by first looking at Horney's multiple conceptions of the self, specifically her distinctions between and the roles assigned to our real self, our actual self, our self-image, and our ideal self.

According to Horney (1950), we enter this world with a **real self,** an innate, unique set of intrinsic potentialities that will develop naturally in a facilitating environment (p. 17). Our real self is a deep inner force for growth, and if not blocked by cultural forces, will motivate us to strive for its realization.

The **actual self** is, for Horney, the self we are at any particular time in life. We are not always fully aware of our actual self.

We also enter this world with a brain that gives us the capacity to reflect upon our physical and psychological experiences. From our perceptions of our experiences and our thoughts about them, we form a **self-image** (the self that we *think* we are). Our image of self may or may not coincide with our actual self of the moment or with the potentials of the real self. Nonetheless, regardless of the similarities or variances, our self-image has consequences. Our self-image is comprised of a set of beliefs, values, and attitudes, and these define our personal standards, expectations, aspirations, and the demands we place upon ourselves, others, and the world. Ultimately, we act upon our self-image.

In addition to her concepts of real self, actual self, and self-image, Horney also assigned a significant role to our **ideal self,** the self that we wish to be or, if irrational, the self that we *should* be and *must* become.

If we are to develop healthfully, there must be some degree of congruence among our real self, actual self, self-image, and ideal self. In the healthy individual (see "Psychological Health," this chapter), the actual self is moving toward the real self by actualizing some of the innate potentials of the real self; the distance between the actual self and the self-image is not too great, and the standards, expectations, aspirations, and demands of the ideal self are realistic and attainable.

Horney's multiple self-concepts and the roles they play in our lives are laden with potential for conflict. While movement in the direction of the real self leads toward self-realization (fulfilling the innate potentials of the real self), blockages to the real self are, from Horney's perspective, the essence of **basic anxiety** (the paralyzing threat of insecurity—feelings of isolation, alienation, loneliness, and helplessness, hence at the center of all neurotic processes).

Early versus Continuous Development

Horney rejected the Freudian view of early childhood. She could not accept the notion that we *must* successfully progress through specific psychosexual stages of development that fix our personalities by the age of five. We have the innate capacity for continuous growth as long as we live. For Horney, then, our early childhood experiences are important, but not critical, since the effects of early experiences are reversible.

Our parents can exert significant long-term influence on our personalities. They can either facilitate our self-realization or impede our healthy development.

At birth, human infants must rely totally on their parents, and a strong need for security is a natural phenomenon. If infants' security needs are not met regularly and adequately, they experience basic anxiety. According to Horney (1945):

> *A wide range of adverse factors in the environment can produce this insecurity in a child: direct or indirect domination, indifference, erratic behavior, lack of respect for the child's individual needs, lack of real guidance, disparaging attitudes, too much admiration or the lack of it, lack of reliable warmth, having to take sides in parental disagreements, too much or too little responsibility, overprotection, isolation from other children, injustice, discrimination, unkept promises, hostile atmosphere, and so on and so on (p. 41).*

Indeed, for Horney, *anything* that affects the security of the child in relation to his or her parents may result in the child's feeling the fright and pain of basic anxiety.

Unable to tolerate the feelings of isolation and helplessness that accompany basic anxiety, children learn to employ a variety of defense strategies, including hostile and vengeful actions toward their parents, who they believe reject or mistreat them. Children suffering basic anxiety may become totally submissive to win their parents' love. They may initiate a power struggle with their parents to compensate for their sense of helplessness by controlling their parents. They may resort to threats, bribery, manipulation, or self-pity. They may direct their aggression inward and attempt to be self-effacing or to harm themselves. *Anything* is preferable to the frightening feelings engendered by basic anxiety.

The strategies employed in childhood may achieve drive status and then some degree of permanence in the child's personality. Horney (1942) lists ten neurotic needs that insecure children may acquire. All ten needs are irrational and if neurotic, insatiable, indiscriminate, and compulsive. While we all resort to *some* of these needs *some* of the time, the neurotic holds his or her neurotic needs as absolutes and compulsively strives to fulfill them, unconsciously believing that in doing so he or she will feel safe and secure in a hostile environment.

Horney's Ten Neurotic Needs

1. *The need for affection and approval.* When neurotic, this need becomes an insatiable desire to please others, to meet their expectations, to be, say, and do whatever others are perceived to want, even when meeting the expectations of others means doing things that violate one's moral standards and cause one a great deal of anguish. The need for affection and approval is also marked by an inordinately strong sensitivity to any perceived displeasure, disagreement, or rejection by others.

2. *The need for a partner who will take over one's life.* When neurotic, this need is characterized by an irrational reliance on another person for all needs, wants, or wishes. There is also an extreme fear of being abandoned by the partner, for without this person's constant presence, attention, and love, the neurotic with this need feels inadequate, lost, and helpless.

3. *The need to restrict one's life within narrow borders.* When neurotic, manifestations of this need are inconspicuous behavior, extreme modesty, and a lack of any striving for change. There is a real fear of risk and failure, hence new experiences are avoided in favor of a highly circumscribed life. Routine and orderliness become primary goals.

4. *The need for power.* When neurotic, this is an insatiable striving for power over both self and others, a contempt for weakness in either self or others, and an unshakable belief in the strength of will power. For the neurotic who strives for power, there is the unrealistic belief that *with sufficient willpower* any pain can be tolerated and any task achieved, regardless of the intensity of the pain or the actual difficulty of the task. The ideal image held by the neurotic with a need for power is one of a superior being who *should* be able, with little effort, to master any situation quickly, and one whose decisions and choices are always perceived as superior to those of others.

5. *The need to exploit others.* When neurotic, this need is marked by the use of others to achieve personal gain. Anyone who is perceived as weaker, less knowledgeable, less experienced, or overly trusting is a target for exploitation. The neurotic with the need to exploit others will not hesitate to take credit for another's ideas, steal the wife or husband of a friend, or undermine another for a promotion. *All* others are suspect, for they are thought to hold to the same philosophy. Any indication of friendship from another is viewed as a weakness that can be used to personal advantage.

6. *The need for prestige.* When this need is neurotic, self-worth is determined solely by the recognition received from others. There is a need to live in the best neighborhood, to attend the best schools, hold memberships in the most elite clubs and associations, purchase clothes with only the most prestigious labels, and own the most sought-after automobiles. Everything and everyone is evaluated in terms of prestige value, including the neurotic's spouse, children, and friends.

7. *The need for personal admiration.* When neurotic, this need is characterized by an inflated view of self and the expectation to be admired for this view. Behavior is often pompous and overbearing, for the idealized image of self is usually that of saint or genius.

8. *The ambition for personal achievement.* When neurotic, there is an inordinately strong need to be the best at everything attempted. There is also a constant search for ways to improve personal knowledge, organizational and job-related skills, and time management in order to achieve a competitive edge and take first place. Since neurotics with this need cannot be the best in everything they attempt, they will try to topple those who are successful, to bring them down to an equal or lower level than their own.

9. *The need for self-sufficiency and independence.* When neurotic, there is an inordinately strong desire to prove the complete lack of any need for others. There are no attempts to establish long-term relationships that would require intimacy or obligation. Should others offer assistance or express interest, they are treated coldly or aloofly, and their offer is rejected. Solitary activities that do not involve competition or comparison with other people are preferred, for these activities are less stressful and are less likely to shatter the illusion of the idealized self. Individuals with the need for self-sufficiency and independence much prefer solitude, and are usually viewed by others as loners.

10. *The need for perfection and unassailability.* When neurotic, there is an evident fear of mistakes and an overreaction to criticism, regardless of the intention behind it. There is also a constant search for personal flaws so that they may be corrected, or even more important, hidden from others. Because all humans are fallible, striving for perfection is certain to meet with failure; hence, the neurotic with the self-ideal of perfection equates knowledge of moral values with being moral and the knowledge of a skill as being skillful.

According to Horney, everyone possesses the ten needs just listed, but for the neurotic these needs become absolute needs; that is, they are irrational, generalized, indiscriminate, and compelling needs. Though all are adopted to solve problems created by disturbed relationships, they are irrational solutions and lead to inordinately strong emotions and to grandiose, compulsive, dysfunctional, or even destructive behavior, thus creating more and greater relationship problems.

Roemer (1986) reports a study using Leary's (1957) circle matrix and operational procedures within Horney's (1950) clinical concepts to assess the Type A–B model. He found that Type A subjects were significantly characterized by expansive traits of aggressiveness and control/power, and that Type B subjects were characterized by the self-effacing traits of helplessness/submissiveness and affiliation. He concluded that his study provides empirical validation of the clinical concepts in Horney's model and adds that the key issue of his study is that Horney's clinical insights were tested within an applicable model that prior to his study had never been used.

Perhaps the greatest support for Horney's Ten Neurotic Needs may be found in the research of Albert Ellis and his followers. Ellis's Irrational Beliefs and Horney's Ten Neurotic Needs are quite similar. Two excellent sources for review of this research are available in Ellis and Grieger's two edited volumes, *Handbook of Rational–Emotive Therapy* (1977, 1986).

Number and Weight Assigned to Motivational Concepts

As stated in the issue "Heredity versus Social Determinants," the inner force of the real self is the primary motivating force in all humans. It is the force of the real self that urges us to strive toward the realization of our innate potentials. Given a favorable environment, we are naturally motivated to develop our particular possibilities of living in this world.

Social and cultural forces also exert a motivating force, and all too often their motivating force conflicts with and points to directions away from the directions of the real self. In direct conflict with our real self, for example, is our psychologically acquired idealized image of the self. The intrinsic drive of the idealized self-image blocks the inner drive of the real self (see "Role Assigned to Self-Concept"). In lieu of healthy development (see "Psychological Health"), the idealized image, which becomes an absolute and insatiable need, drives us to seek the neurotic level of perfection. It creates both an insoluble gap between the idealized image and reality and irrational claims of entitlement. Further, because we are fallible, the drive to actualize an image of perfection is doomed to failure from the start.

Although the realization tendency of the real self is made up of a vast number of physiological (internal) and social (external) needs, when living in the immediacy of the present, we identify with, feel intensely about, and strive toward the fulfillment of those needs that we define as essential to continued life. Whether innate or acquired, our needs possess an intrinsic motivating force. When our psychologically acquired needs become inordinately strong and conflict with the needs of the real self, we lose touch with the present, live in fantasy rather than reality, deny our real needs, and function poorly, even abnormally.

Conscious versus Unconscious Determinants

Horney recognized the significance of unconscious forces and emphasized the importance of unconscious motivation; however, her view of the dimension and meaning of unconscious forces was very different from that of Freud. She did not accept conscious and unconscious as separate entities; nor did she conceive the unconscious as a deep, dark recess of our psyche that is forever unavailable to consciousness.

According to Horney, conscious and unconscious motivations vary considerably between individuals. For example, when healthy, the ideal self and real self are fairly congruent, for the ideal self is based on realistic assessments. Further, our innate potentialities are available to consciousness. With the emergence of basic anxiety, however, the real self is repressed and replaced by an idealized image of the perfect self. The powers and potentialities of the real self are no longer available to consciousness. Indeed, in the case of severe neurosis, the real self is abandoned, and all possibilities of growth are blocked in an all-out quest for safety and security (see "Early versus Continuous Development").

Horney recognizes a number of unconscious solutions that may be employed to resolve neurotic conflicts and maintain a sense of wholeness when one suffers any of the three main characteristics of basic anxiety: helplessness, aggressiveness, and detachment. These unconscious solutions are: (1) **moving toward people** (a helpless orientation characterized by an inordinately strong desire for protection and compliance and the neurotic claim: "The world exists to serve me"); (2) **moving against people** (an aggressive orientation characterized by strong wishes for mastery, control, and domination and the neurotic claim: "I am a superior being whose words should be heard and heeded by all"); (3) **moving away from people** (a detachment orientation characterized by the strong desire to avoid all others and the neurotic claim: "I don't need anyone"); and (4) **idealized self** (a glory orientation, masking unconscious self-contempt and characterized by the pursuit of a grandiose image of a perfect self and accompanied by the neurotic claim: "I am a superior being and must be treated as such").

Relating Horney's (1945) neurotic strategies (moving toward people, moving against people, and moving away from people) to adolescent attitudes toward the physically disabled, Norma Jabin (1987) hypothesized that significant correlations would form three distinguishable subgroups: hostility, pity, and repulsion. She found that her subjects (294 adolescents, ages fifteen to eighteen) rejected the disabled to the degree of threat felt and the degree of alienation from interpersonal relationships. Subjects more dependent on the environment for acceptance needs or mobility will tend toward greater attitudes of pity with underlying hostility and repulsion toward the physically disabled. The more alienated subjects expressed more hostility and repulsion, though also harboring attitudes of pity toward the physically disabled.

Subjective versus Objective Reality

Though certainly not pure a **phenomenologist** (one who believes that phenomena are the *only* realities), Horney advocated a phenomenological approach to understanding the worlds of her analysands as they presently are. Our worlds, experienced through our individual streams of consciousness, are reciprocally the process and the product of the impact of psychological and social-cultural influences and our personal sense and interpretation of our relation to these influences. When our world is viewed as potentially hostile, we suffer basic anxiety and take rigid defensive postures to maintain our sense of unity. Defensive postures, in turn, influence subjective perceptions. When extreme, we may view all others as adversaries, inferiors, people to be manipulated for our own gains, providers of our needs, protectors, or annoyances to be avoided. We may view the world as hostile, unfair, existing simply to serve our needs, or to be controlled and used. In short, our defensive perceptions and postures create neurotic conflicts and needs which in turn lead us to move toward people and the world or against people and the world, or to detach ourselves from people and the world.

Determinism versus Freedom of Choice

For Horney, freedom is a matter of psychological health. She views the difference between a healthy striving and a neurotic one as the difference between "I want" and "I must have." Freedom of choice, from Horney's perspective, exists only when we are striving to realize our real self.

There is no freedom in the fulfillment of neurotic needs. The pathogenic "shoulds" are tyrannical; they call for rigid, compulsive thinking and acting. Moreover, they are destructive, for while blindly reaching for the ultimate and the infinite, we abandon the authentic self that we truly are, and we lose the freedom that comes with healthy striving.

Explanation of Learning Process

Horney's holistic approach to personality development did not view learning as a separate or special process, but rather as an intrinsic phenomenon of the inner force of the real self—in brief, a natural human predisposition. Learning, then, like maturation and development, will be constructive and healthy unless blocked or twisted by the individual's pursuit of neurotic needs. The same conditions that promote personality development also promote learning.

Addressing teachers in her article, "Can You Take a Stand?" Horney (1939b) stated:

> *I can merely suggest that in your contact with students you do everything in your power to impress upon the mind of each of them that everyone should consult and express his own feelings and not blindly follow the leadership of others. Show them how imperative it is to take a stand upon all important questions. In a word, try both by precept and by example to be himself (p. 132).*

For Horney, healthy learning involves morality and responsibility. Parents, teachers, and psychoanalysts are advised by Horney (1939b) not to attempt a neutral stance on important issues, not only because morality and responsibility are essential to healthy learning, but because moral neutrality is antithetical to the realization of the real self.

Healthy learning, like the process of self-realization, requires the full, selfless, sensitive presence of others (e.g., parents, teachers, psychoanalysts) that communicates to us the deep caring for our welfare and the continued faith in and respect for our innate, idiosyncratic potentialities. Horney believes that our natural capacity to learn can be blocked or twisted by adverse social and cultural forces that threaten our sense of safety and security (see "Early versus Continuous Development," this chapter).

Uniqueness versus Universality

From the Horneyan viewpoint, we hold much in common with our fellow beings, including, paradoxically, our uniqueness. We share many of the same needs and inhabit the same world, but there are no duplications in our species. Each of us possesses an innate set of potentials at birth that, if not blocked, offers direction and purpose, and in no two of us are these inherited potentials identical.

Certainly, we are physical beings and must obey the laws of nature if we are to survive. Just as certainly, we are embedded in and must interact with and relate to an environmental field if we are to live and grow. As physical beings we need food, water, shelter, and warmth. As psychological beings, we need safe and secure relationships with other beings and with the events in our lives.

Our awareness encourages us to perceive ourselves in both a personal and a social context, and our awareness and the relationships we establish are open to an infinite variety of interpretative shadows. Though we are directed by the inner force of the real self, we are also subject to the impact of environmental forces that are more likely than not to conflict with this direction.

Role Assigned to Group Determinants

We are, as indicated in previous resolutions, biological and social beings. Both physiological and social-psychological needs must be met through relationships with objects, individuals, and groups in our environments. Particularly as infants, we need contact with others as much as we need food and water on the physiological level if we are to live and develop healthfully. Indeed, Horney tells us that our sense of the quality of our relatedness to others, especially as children to our parents or guardians (see "Early versus Continuous Development"), is most important to healthy development.

As infants, our initial group contact is with our families. Not only does our survival depend on the support we receive from the members of this primary group, our sense of the world and our attitudes toward it (safe or hostile) are formed from our relations with this most important group, parents or guardians in particular. If we are fortunate, our early years are filled with genuine warmth, interest, understanding, encouragement, and mutual respect, and we are allowed to grow naturally and unimpeded. Conversely, if we are unfortunate, if our parents or guardians relate to us in pathogenic ways (through domination, overprotection, humiliation, aversive criticism, overindulgence, neglect, indifference, or erratic behavior), we experience basic anxiety and develop in fixed ways that are alien to the inner forces of our real self.

Although Horney viewed our early childhood years as crucial to the initial phase of self-realization, she did not, as did the classical psychoanalysts, believe that these early experiences were fixed and irreversible. Horney allows for change in our relationships with others and with life events.

Centrality of Reinforcement

The term "reinforcement" does not once appear in the indexes of Horney's five books. However, she repeatedly warned that all cultures are highly organized structures governed by a system of values that the culture then holds out to members as a set of prescriptions for conduct, judgment, and benefit. In short, every culture formulates its own version of the ideal self for its members. Cultural versions of the ideal self vary, at times considerably; hence what is considered normal in one culture may be considered abnormal in another.

From our earliest years, we are subjected to daily exposure of our particular culture's values, first by our parents, then from the media and cultural institutions. Furthermore, we are reinforced by our culture for adopting its idealized version of self as our own. From the Horneyan perspective, there is a very real danger when, in pursuit of our culture's idealized presentation of the model self, we abandon the actualization of our real self. For Horney (1950), the abandonment of the real self can only result in a chronically disordered personality.

In the United States, a capitalistic system, the media present us an idealized picture of the good life that stresses such idealized character traits as power, status, wealth, fame, and even glory. Further, we are told that our culture's version of the good life is available to any one of us who is determined and aggressive enough to pursue it, when, in reality, only a very few will succeed regardless of determination and effort. Even those of us who are not drawn to our culture's version of the idealized self and elect instead to actualize our real self will face many of the stresses that are inherent in our culture's prescribed idealistic personality.

Psychological Health and Psychopathology

Psychological health and psychopathology are, for Horney (1936, 1937, 1939c, 1942, 1945, 1950), a matter of degree. Even the healthiest of us have some neurotic tendencies, for self-realization is never fully achieved. Likewise, even the most

Heredity		Social Determinants
Early Development		Continuous Development
Conscious Determinants		Unconscious Determinants
Subjective Reality		Objective Reality
Determinism		Freedom
Uniqueness		Universality

Role Assigned to Self Concept	Multiple conceptions of the self include real self (innate set of potentials), actual self (self of a particular time in life), self-image (self that we think we are), and ideal self (self we wish to be). Healthy development requires congruence among the selves.
Number and Weight Assigned to Motivational Concepts	Inner force of the real self motivates human towards realization of innate potentials. Social and cultural forces exert a motivational force but often away from the real self. Physiological (internal) and social (external) needs possess an intrinsic motivating force.
Explanation of Learning Process	Learning is a natural human predisposition which is constructive and healthy unless blocked or twisted. Healthy learning involves morality and responsibility and the full, selfless, sensitive presence of others (e.g., parents, teachers, psychoanalysts).
Role Assigned to Group Determinants	Biological and social needs must be met through relationships. Early years with families (initial group contact) can result in natural psychological growth or basic anxiety. Early experiences are not fixed and irreversible.
Centrality of Reinforcement	All cultures formulate the ideal self for their members through a system of values. Reinforcement occurs when cultures' members adopt the idealized version of self as their own.

FIGURE 7-1   Schematic Analysis of Horney's Stance on Basic Issues

neurotic of us function normally in some aspects of our lives. Moreover, Horney asserted, the growth process is in constant flux. In short, psychological health and psychopathology are qualitative rather than quantitative classifications.

Psychological Health

Horney (1939a, 1950) saw psychological health as the result of adequate development. For her, the quality of psychological health can be measured by the quality of the individual's relation to his or her real self, for the real self is the full definition of the individual. The healthy person, according to Horney, *knows* and *expresses* his or her real self, then *acts* in accordance with his or her knowledge and expression. To the extent that pure expression of the real self is possible (pure spontaneity), to that extent is the individual psychologically healthy.

The attainment of psychological health is no small task; indeed, it is practically impossible if the forces of society and culture are not conducive to the principle of human growth. For Horney (1936, 1937, 1939a, 1939c, 1950), culture is required for self-realization, but culture can also threaten security needs and block the weaker inner forces of the real self. Security needs, the primary cause of basic anxiety, must first be gratified, for they are proponent and thus take precedence over the growth needs of the real self.

The gratification of security needs brings the highest sense of satisfaction. They are both biologically and psychologically desirable, for when gratified, both physical and psychological energy may then be diverted to the free pursuit of the innate values and potentialities of the real self. The healthy person is free to affirm and experience his or her uniqueness and in doing so, to find his or her purpose and meaning. Individual integrity is maintained and fostered with the affirmation of one's own intrinsic nature.

Horney's (1945, 1950) concept of **wholeheartedness** (to be without pretense, to be emotionally sincere, to be able to put the whole of one's self into one's feelings, one's work, one's beliefs) is only possible after cultural conflicts have been resolved, and are in a constructive interaction of the individual and culture.

Psychopathology

Just as anything that facilitates the affirmation of the real self is healthful, anything (whether internal or external) that alienates the individual from the real self is pathogenic. For Horney, neuroses often originate in early childhood (see "Early versus Continuous Development"). The child who fears being alone or abandoned in a hostile world also experiences conflict between his or her existing dependency on parents and rebellion against them. For the child, this is a defenseless position at best. Because the child must depend on his or her parents for survival, hostile feelings must be repressed, leaving the child feeling helpless. Under threat, behavior becomes rigid. The fluidity and adaptation generally associated with healthy behavior are vastly decreased. Energy is focused on security needs rather than on the needs of the real self. The fear of risk is intensified, and new experiences required for growth are avoided. Defensive postures, either through a personally created idealized image of the self or the culture's version of *the* ideal self (see "Role Assigned to Self-Concept") are erected, and these perfected, seemingly unassailable images are alien to the real self and hence, pathogenic.

All the absolutes ("shoulds," "oughts," "musts," and "have tos") are, in Horney's view, pathogenic. She did not hesitate to assist her patients to free themselves from "the tyranny of the should" (Horney, 1950, p. 67, see also pp. 64-85).

Application To Psychotherapy

Therapeutic Goals

For Horney (1942, 1945, 1946, 1950), the ultimate goals of psychoanalysis are to help the patient: 1) to resolve inner conflicts; 2) to acquire a personal sense of **responsibility** (the feeling that one is the active, responsible force in his or her own life, and that he or she is capable of making decisions and accepting the consequences); 3) to achieve an **inner independence** (establishing a personal hierarchy of values and applying it to whatever experiences life offers); 4) to develop **spontaneity of feeling** (the capacity for the expression of feeling, whether love or hate, happiness or sadness, fear or courage); and 5) to strive for **wholeheartedness** (to be without pretense, to be emotionally sincere, to be wholeheartedly involved in feelings, work, or beliefs) (Horney, 1945, pp. 241–242).

According to Horney (1945): "These goals are not arbitrary;" they "are the elements upon which psychic health rests" and they "follow logically from a knowledge of the pathogenic factors in neurosis" (p. 242). Further, Horney (1945) asserted: "They are ideals to strive for, their practical value lies in their giving us direction in our therapy and in our lives" (p. 242). As ideals, Horney's therapeutic goals are never fully achieved; rather, the analyst and patient can only attempt to become free enough from inner conflicts "to strive for approximations of these ideals" (p. 243).

Therapeutic Relationship

For Horney (1942, 1950), the therapeutic relationship is viewed as a unique encounter between two people, the patient and the analyst. Transference and resistance are considered mechanistic concepts and are not discussed with the patient; rather, the analyst assumes responsibility for the direction of the analytic process, and because talking about resistance places all the responsibility on the patient, discussion is limited to blockage of the patient's growth process, which occurs outside as well as within the analytic relationship. Neither is the patient's past emphasized in Horneyan analysis; rather, the here and now holds priority. Because the analyst and the patient focus on the present, the patient's past cannot serve as an excuse for behavior. Finally, Horney did not believe that the analyst should take a neutral stance in the analytic relationship. First, she believed neutrality is impossible as long as there are two people in the relationship; second, she was convinced that the analyst should serve as model and take a stand on the moral issues that arise in therapy. She believed that a person with the potential for growth and expansion should question whether a particular desire or act is conducive to healthy development or representative of an obstacle to growth.

Horney was far more active in the therapeutic relationship than were the classical analysts of her day. She would often initiate a topic for discussion or offer her personal opinions on specific subjects. She was not hesitant to use dialogue, illustration, humor, dramatization, education, and feedback when she felt they were appropriate, for she believed the analyst should be both genuine and spontaneous in the therapeutic relationship.

Horney (1987) believed also that the critical element of the therapeutic relationship was the understanding of the patient "in a way more than intellectual." The initial purposes of the analytic relationship are to accept and understand the patient *as he or she is.* This quality of understanding requires **empathy** (feeling as the client feels), attentiveness, concentration, and genuine compassion. She reminded her training analysts that all psychotherapy is self-therapy, since no changes can take place without the authentic involvement of the patient and no relationship exists without the involvement of the analyst (Horney, 1987).

Initial Procedures and Strategies

Free Association and Interpretation   Although Horney rejected many of the basic tenets of Freudian psychoanalysis, she continued to rely on the use of free association and interpretation. Like many of the neoanalytic theorists (Fromm, Chapter 6, for example), Horney was a much more directive participant in the analytic process than is usual in the practice of orthodox psychoanalysis.

Horney was convinced that the goals of most patients were in conflict with the goals of therapy. Patients enter therapy wanting to improve the consequences of their neurosis without changing or even recognizing their inner conflicts. In Horneyan analysis, patients must first recognize, at both intellectual *and* emotional levels, their neurotic solution to conflict, discover that it is self-defeating, and then abandon it. Insight alone is not enough.

Horneyan analysts do not accept the orthodox focus on early childhood experiences, for they believe an overemphasis on early childhood events all too often serves as rationalization of their patients' failures and as an excuse for their patients' lack of involvement in the work required in their analysis. Horney was also more likely to stress her patients' moral values than many psychoanalysts who take a neutral stance in the analytic process.

Dreams and Dream Interpretation Unlike Freud, Horney believed that dreams contain the dreamers' true feelings. For example, dreaming of looking into a mirror and seeing no reflection may be an indication of the loss of the dreamer's real self. Dreaming of tenderly nurturing an injured pet suggests self-concern and sympathy. A dream of being trapped in a room with someone bent on killing the dreamer is an indication of self-hatred. The dream of clinging to the ledge of a mountain indicates a person who feels that he or she cannot climb any higher and has decided to hold on where he or she is (Horney, 1950, p. 31). A dream in which the dreamer discovers a room that he or she had not known existed expresses places within the dreamer that he or she is as yet unaware of (Horney, 1950, p. 350). According to Horney (1950): "In dreams we are closer to the reality of ourselves and they represent attempts to solve our problems, in either a constructive or destructive way" (p. 349).

Self-Analysis Horney (1942) often suggested to her patients that they use their time between sessions to work on self-analysis. She encouraged them to make deliberate, accurate, and systematic self-observations and then attempt to arrive at some insight through their own power of reasoning (see "Extended Applications").

Course of Psychotherapy

After warning her readers that any brief outline of the typical course of psychotherapy would involve gross oversimplifications, Horney (1942) attempted just such an outline. She stated that it is characteristic for each neurotic trend uncovered to follow three steps: first, "recognition of a neurotic trend; second, discovery of its causes, manifestations, and consequences; and third, discovery of its interrelations with other parts of the personality, especially with other neurotic trends" (Horney, 1942, p. 82). These three steps, she argued, must be taken for each neurotic trend involved, though not always in the order named, since some understanding of the neurotic trend's manifestations is necessary before the trend can be recognized as such.

The first step, recognizing a neurotic trend, entails recognizing a driving force in the disturbance of the patient's personality. Sometimes the patient's recognition of a neurotic trend is in itself enough to cure a neurotic disturbance. Discovery of a neurotic trend's causes, manifestations, and consequences (the second step in the course of psychotherapy) strengthens the patient's willingness and resolve to conquer the disturbing drive, and increases the patient's acceptance of the need for change. The patient's ability to work through the problem also increases as the manifestations of the neurotic trend continue to come to awareness. As the patient begins to feel less insecure, less isolated, and less hostile, his or her relationships with both self and others improve. The third step, the recognition and understanding of the interrelationships of different neurotic trends, leads to the patient's grasp of the deepest conflicts. At this point, the importance is for the patient to see the *whole* structure. All components of the conflict must be understood and their intensity diminished.

Again, it must be noted that the brief presentation of the course of therapy just given is oversimplification in the extreme. In each step of analysis the sequence lies in the nature of the neurotic trends, *as they become accessible in the analytic process.*

Extended Applications

Feminine Psychology

Horney must be numbered among the personologists who first recognized the impact of social and cultural forces on the development of human personality. However, her greatest legacy may very well be her views on feminine psychology. Few today will contest the assertion that Horney's feminine psychology caused many, both in and outside the field, to reexamine Freud's theoretical constructs on the early psychosexual development of women. Indeed, many of the ideas championed by current feminist organizations echo those presented by Horney in the 1920s and 1930s. And though still disregarded by the classical psychoanalysts, some of her views on feminine psychology have been integrated into the mainstream of psychiatry, as well as into the recent theoretical constructs of cognitive therapists, in particular Kelly (Chapter 14) and Ellis (Chapter 15).

Gently at first but with far greater resolve later, Horney confronted Freud's views of the role of women. Her first disagreement centered on Freud's male-oriented phallocentric conception of the castration complex in women. Not only did Horney find the concept false, she held the thinking behind it responsible for a little girl's feelings of inferiority, resentment, and envy, as well as for the devaluation of her sexuality, continuing search for ways to compensate for nature's unfair treatment, and retreating into a fictitious masculine role. Horney (1967) argued that from birth, the masculine character of societal and cultural forces constantly reminds the little girl of her inferiority, and her masculinity complex develops in response to these forces rather than to libidinal forces.

Horney (1939a, 1967) could not accept Freud's concept of female masochism as the psychic consequence of sexual anatomical differences. This, too, she believed to be the result of interpersonal conflict and social conditioning. For Horney, masochism in women and in men is the result of attempts to attain feelings of security through self-effacement and submission. Unconsciously, this path is a way of controlling others by expressing weakness and hides an expression of hostility from self and others through suffering. Societal and cultural forces present an idealized version of the ideal self for women that reinforces masochistic attitudes in women and encourages them to seek protection and support by looking to family, husband, and children as their only source of fulfillment. In Horney's final theory, women do not acquire masochistic tendencies either by virtue of being female or by virtue of living in a particular society. Masochism, for Horney, is a way of satisfying neurotic needs.

According to Horney, society blocks proper expression of sexuality for women by valuing women only as childbearers, by viewing women as inferior (fragile, emotional, ineffective), and by limiting economic opportunities to the social services, such as nursing, teaching, and social work. Horney (1939b) strongly advised women to take a stand on all important issues in their lives, including political, economic, and career issues, and to pursue their own goals. In Horney's final theory, constructs of the real self and of self-realization are neither masculine nor feminine issues; they are, rather, human issues. The goal is the same for both. Both men and women must learn to assume the natural differences between the sexes, and work toward the realization of their particular potentialities for living in the world—in short, to work toward the realization of the innate potentials of the real self.

Self-Analysis

As stated earlier, Horney (1942) was the first psychoanalyst to suggest the feasibility and the desirability of self-analysis, not only for the patient in analysis but also for the individual who wants to solve his or her own problems and for whom work with a psychoanalyst is impossible, either because of geographical location or because the cost of professional analytical help is prohibitive.

Horney (1942) warns her readers that self-analysis is a strenuous, slow process that is certain to be painful and upsetting at times and should not be undertaken by any but the most highly motivated. Strong incentive is crucial to self-analysis, for "nothing short of ruthless honesty with oneself is helpful" (Horney, 1942, p. 26). As for danger in self-analysis, Horney (1942) states: "I would say that it is constructive if it is used in the service of a wish to become a better, richer, and stronger human being—if it is a responsible endeavor of which the ultimate goal is self-recognition and change" (pp. 28–29).

Horney often recommended self-analysis to her patients as a way to shorten the analytic process. By working at self-analysis between sessions or during periods when their analyst was unavailable, the active and independent work could accelerate their progress and increase their self-confidence and justifiable pride in their own capacity for growth.

Horney (1942) discusses the difficulties of recognizing unconscious motivations and neurotic trends in one's self. She therefore spends some time in her book, *Self-Analysis*, describing the nature and characteristics of neurotic trends. She asks the questions that her patients have asked her, then answers them in some depth. In Chapter 2 of *Self-Analysis*, she discusses the Ten Neurotic Needs.

Chapter 3 focuses on the stages of psychoanalytic understanding. It is also necessary to know something about the sequence in which the work of self-analysis must be done. Usually, the least deeply repressed emerge to awareness first (see "Therapeutic Process," this chapter).

Because self-analysis is an attempt to be both patient and analyst, Horney discusses the tasks of both in relation to free association and dreams. She also reviews a case study of one woman's self-analysis. This is followed by a chapter on the spirit and rules of systematic self-analysis, then dealing with resistances, and finally, a chapter on the limitations of self-analysis.

Critique

Horney's published works were largely ignored by orthodox psychoanalysts at the time of their publication; however, her books and articles received widespread recognition and approval from other psychotherapists and the general public. Horney's greatest contributions center around the four areas on which she concentrated most: neurosis, psychotherapy, feminine sexuality, and human growth or self-realization.

Horney's vivid and empathic descriptions of neurotic suffering and defensive strategies have contributed to an improved understanding of the neurotic personality and the neurotic process. She offered great depth and detail for both the **cause** (social relationships and the impact of complicated social and cultural forces) and **treatment** (specific psychotherapeutic strategies and techniques) for various forms of neuroses.

Horney's theoretical statements on feminine sexuality, though largely disregarded when she made them, have been rediscovered recently by those active in the feminist movement. Her equalitarian stance on the rights and roles of men and women sets well with current thinking.

Horney's growth principle (an innate tendency toward psychological health and self-realization) marks her as a precursor of the thinkers in the humanistic or Third Force movement in the United States (Chapters 8, 9, 10, as examples).

When it became evident that Horney's view of human personality differed significantly from Freud's, she was accused of borrowing too liberally the ideas of Freud and Adler rather than formulating original theoretical constructs. She was accused also of simply elaborating on ideas implied, but not clearly expressed, by Freud.

Certainly Horney's theory of personality is less comprehensive than Freud's, Adler's or Jung's, a limitation resulting from her pronounced emphasis on neurosis. She neglected normal or healthy personality development and structure. She also neglected specific explanations of the learning process.

Horney shares many of the criticisms leveled at the humanists. She provides no evidence for the inherent predisposition to strive for self-realization. Other than her own clinical observations (which were recognized as especially acute), she offered no scientific evidence to support her theoretical constructs. Definitional ambiguities in her terminology make it difficult for others either to repeat her findings or to design empirical tests of her theory. It might be noted, however, that some of the experimental studies conducted by recent cognitive and social psychologists appear to support some of her theoretical constructs, and there is the possibility that additional support for Horney's theory is forthcoming.

Annotated Bibliography

The student interested in the evolution of Horney's Theory of Psychosocial Analysis may want to read her books in the order of their publication: *The Neurotic Personality of Our Time* (1937), *New Ways in Psychoanalysis* (1939), *Self-Analysis* (1942), *Our Inner Conflicts* (1945), *Neurosis and Human Growth* (1950), and *Feminine Psychology* (1967, a posthumous publication, edited by D. H. Ingram). Those interested in her final theory may prefer to concentrate on her last two books. Particularly helpful in the understanding of Horney's theory is *Our Inner Conflicts*. Here Horney (1945) discusses the social and cultural forces that work in opposition to the actualization of the real self and toward the impoverishment of personality.

Students especially interested in the application of Horney's theory will want to read *Final Lectures*. Edited by Douglas H. Ingram, and published thirty-five years after her death, *Final Lectures* (1987) is a small collection of Horney's lectures on psychoanalytic technique. The emphasis is on training and competence. In addition to an improved understanding of the goals and strategies of Horney's theory of psychotherapy, the reader is almost certain to experience Horney's dedication and commitment. More, with little effort it is possible to feel her conviction that her ideas were important and worth sharing with those who were in training to become psychoanalysts.

Of interest to both psychotherapists and the lay public is Horney's book *Self-Analysis* (1942). In this book Horney discusses the possibilities, limitations, difficulties, and hazards of undertaking self-analysis. Her views of the different stages of psychoanalytic understanding are also shared in this book.

References and Suggested Readings

Barcia, D. (1984). Medical anthropology in the work of Karen Horney. *The American Journal of Psychoanalysis, 44*(3), pp. 254–265.

Block, M. (Ed.). (1941). Horney, Karen. *Current Biography 1941.* New York: H. W. Wilson, p. 409.

Brown, M. (1987). Application of Horney theory in the treatment of a traumatized child. *The American Journal of Psychoanalysis, 47*(1), pp. 3–20.

Clemmens, E. R. (1984a). The work of Karen Horney. *The American Journal of Psychoanalysis, 44*(3), pp. 242–253.

Clemmens, E. R. (1984b). Transference and countertransference in the Horneyan system. *American Journal of Psychoanalysis, 44*(3), pp. 311–315.

Danielian, J. (1988). Karen Horney and Heinz Kohut: Theory and the repeat of history. *The American Journal of Psychoanalysis, 48*(1), pp. 6–24.

Dr. Karen Horney, 67, psychoanalyst dies. (1952, December 5). *The New York Times,* p. 27.

Eckardt, M. H. (1984). Karen Horney: Her life and contribution. *The American Journal of Psychoanalysis, 44*(3), pp. 236–241.

Ellis, A., & Grieger, R. (Eds.). (1977). *Handbook of rational-emotive therapy* (Vol. 1). New York: Springer.

Ellis, A., & Grieger, R. (Eds.). (1986). *Handbook of rational-emotive therapy* (Vol. 2). New York: Springer.

Feiring, C. (1983). Behavioral styles in infancy and adulthood: The work of Karen Horney and attachment theorists collaterally considered. *Journal of the American Academy of Child Psychiatry, 22*(1), pp. 1–7.

Hammon, S. A. (1987). Some contributions of Horneyan theory to enhancement of the type A behavior construct. *The American Journal of Psychoanalysis, 47*(2), pp. 105–115.

Horney, K. (1936). Culture and neurosis. *American Sociological Review, 1*, pp. 221–230.

Horney, K. (1937). *The neurotic personality of our time.* New York: W. W. Norton.

Horney, K. (1939a). *New ways in psychoanalysis.* New York: W. W. Norton.

Horney, K. (1939b). Can you take a stand? *Journal of Adult Education, 11*, pp. 129–132.

Horney, K. (1939c). What is Neurosis? *American Journal of Sociology, 45*, pp. 426–432.

Horney, K. (1940). Your psychic security. *Independent Woman, 19*, pp. 113, 125–126.

Horney, K. (1942). *Self-analysis.* New York: W. W. Norton.

Horney, K. (1945). *Our inner conflicts.* New York: W. W. Norton.

Horney, K. (1950). *Neurosis and human growth.* New York: W. W. Norton.

Horney, K. (1967). *Feminine psychology.* New York: W. W. Norton.

Horney, K. (1987). *Final lectures.* D. H. Ingram. (Ed.). New York: W. W. Norton.

Ingram, D. H. (Editorial). (1985). Karen Horney at 100: Beyond the frontier. *The American Journal of Psychoanalysis, 45*(4), pp. 305–309.

Jabin, N. (1987). Attitudes toward disability: Horney's theory applied. *The American Journal of Psychoanalysis, 47*(2), pp. 143–153.

Kelma, H. (1946a). What are your doubts about analysis? In K. Horney, (Ed.). *Are you considering psychoanalysis?* New York: Norton, pp. 93–133.

Kelma. H. (1946b). Who should your analyst be? In K. Horney, (Ed.). *Are you considering psychoanalyst?* New York: Norton, pp. 135–157.

Kerr, N. J. (1977/1988). "Wounded womanhood:" An analysis of Karen Horney's theory of feminine psychology. *Perspective in Psychiatric Care, 23*(3–4), pp. 132–141.

Leary, T. (1957). *Interpersonal diagnosis of personality: A functional theory and methodology for personality evaluation.* New York: Ronald Press.

Lerner, J. A. (1983). Horney theory and mother/child impact on early childhood. *The American Journal of Psychoanalysis, 43*(2), pp. 149–155.

Lopez, A. G. (1984). Karen Horney's feminine psychology. *The American Journal of Psychoanalysis, 44*(3), pp. 280–289.

Manrique, J. F. D. (1984). Hope as a means of therapy in the work of Karen Horney. *The American Journal of Psychoanalysis, 44*(3), pp. 301–310.

Mere, A. G. (1984). Closing remarks. *The American Journal of Psychoanalysis, 44*(3), pp. 334–336.

Ogara, C. R. (1984). The concept of neurosis in Karen Horney. *The American Journal of Psychoanalysis, 44*(3), pp. 316–318.

Paul, H. A. (1984). Horneyan developmental psychoanalytic theory and its application to the treatment of the young. *The American Journal of Psychoanalysis, 44*(1), pp. 59–71.

Quinn, S. (1987). *A mind of her own: The life of Karen Horney.* New York: Summit Books.

Rendon, R. (1984a). Karen Horney's biocultural dialectic. *The American Journal of Psychoanalysis, 44*(3), pp. 267–279.

Rendon, R. (1984b). Clinical work in the Horney tradition. *The American Journal of Psychoanalysis, 44*(3), pp. 320–333.

Roemer, W. W. (1986). Leary's circle matrix: A comprehensive model for the statistical measurement of Horney's clinical concepts. *The American Journal of Psychoanalysis, 46*(3), pp. 249–262.

Rubins, J. L. (1978). *Karen Horney: Gentle rebel of psychoanalysis.* New York: Dial Press.

Rubins, J. L. (1980). On cognition, affects, and Horney theory. *The American Journal of Psychoanalysis, 40*(3), pp. 195–212.

Seeley, E. (1940). Your psychic security. *Independent Woman, 19*, pp. 113, 125–126.

Simon, L. (1982). Other voices: Observations on neurotic traits in the college teacher. *The American Journal of Psychoanalysis, 42*(4), pp. 349–355.

Wassell, B. B. (1980). New frontiers in Horney theory of self-realization. *The American Journal of Psychoanalysis, 40*(4), pp. 333–346.

Organismic Theories

In the third part of this book you will find the personality theories of Gordon W. Allport, Carl R. Rogers, and Abraham Maslow. Again, not all readers will agree to the classification "organismic" as the most descriptive term to classify their theories. "Humanists" or "Third Force Psychologists" are terms often used to describe these theories. Regardless of the term, the three theorists selected for presentation here do hold a number of common views. First, they believe that whatever affects the organism affects the entire organism; their stance is holistic. Second, they subscribe to an innate actualizing tendency as the primary motivating force for most human behavior. Third, they are telic; that is, they believe human movement is future oriented, governed by the individual's plans, hopes, and aspirations. Fourth, they assign significant importance to the role of the individual's self-concept. Fifth, all three take a phenomenological stance on individual reality. Finally, each believes uniqueness and freedom of choice are characteristics of every healthy personality.

For the first time in this book, the theorists presented spent all, or a significant portion, of their lives in academic settings. All three were involved in the education of psychologists and counselors. Their research subjects were, with few exceptions, drawn from the college population. Most important, all three were interested in learning more about psychological health or, as Maslow stated, "the upper reaches of human nature."

All three of these theorists strongly believed, and openly expressed the opinion, that the prevailing scientific approach to the study of human nature, though certainly important, was limited in both methodology and technique. Each held the view that the subjective nature of humans required an idiographic (qualitative) approach to research, as well as a nomothetic (quantative) approach. Further, each had rather strong reservations about generalizing the findings of research on animals, the abnormal, or the immature to healthy, actualizing adults.

Chapter *8*

Allport's Theory of Personalism

Chapter Overview

Introduction

Biographical Sketch of the Theorist

Resolution of Eleven Basic Issues
    Heredity versus Social Determinants
    Number and Weight Assigned to Motivational Concepts
    Uniqueness versus Universality
    Subjective versus Objective Reality
    Role Assigned to Self-Concept
    Determinism versus Freedom of Choice
    Conscious versus Unconscious Determinants
    Explanation of the Learning Process
    Early versus Continuous Development
    Role Assigned to Group Determinants
    Centrality of Reinforcement

Psychological Health and Psychopathology
    Psychological Health
    Psychopathology

Applications to Psychotherapy
    Therapeutic Goals
    Therapeutic Relationship

Therapeutic Process and Strategies
Course of Therapy

Extended Applications

Critique

Annotated Bibliography

References and Suggested Readings

Introduction

Gordon Willard Allport's life work centered on personality theory, particularly on the structure and motivation of personality. His unwavering psychological quest for answers to the major philosophical questions of human nature led him to related areas of interest. He became involved, for example, in the problems of prejudice, the individual and his or her religion, the study of attitudes, the value of personal documents (letters and journals), and expressive behaviors (facial expressions, gestures, posture, gait, and carriage).

Allport's approach to formulating his Theory of Personalism might best be described as an uncompromising systematic and rigorous eclecticism. He drew from the many and varied existing theories, as well as from philosophy, to define the controversial and essentially philosophical questions of human nature: mind–body, nature–nurture, intentionality–determinism, and the concepts of time, consciousness, the self, and subject–object.

At a time when prevailing interests of psychologists seemed to be toward quantitative analysis and control of human behavior, Allport was concerned with the whole personality and the unpredictability of human intentionality. He was convinced from his qualitative studies and observations that normal, healthy adults were governed more by values, choices, and goals than by instincts or reinforcements, more by present and future intentions than by the influences of past experiences or reinforced behaviors. Allport's (1955, 1960a, 1961, 1963, 1964a) theoretical stance was that the mature human being is "a being-in-the-process-of-becoming." That is, he saw humans as relatively free, proactive beings with the capacity to regulate their lives. For Allport, we are active participants in our individual destinies; we are truly unique beings. Because of this stance, Allport expressed serious doubts that quantitative methodology could ultimately provide a complete understanding of the uniqueness and wholeness of human nature.

Needless to say, holding fast to an anti-deterministic view of human nature forced him to cross swords with learning theory, with the reductionists, and with what for Allport was an overemphasis on unconscious processes, projective techniques, and simplified drive theories of motivation. Allport also held to a sharp distinction between animal and human studies and between infantile motivation and adult propensities. Neither did Allport hesitate to express his disappointment with articles appearing in the professional journals: "Our journals show a preponderance of small but empirical studies, elegantly designed methodologically, but having little bearing on the problems which originated the research" (Allport, in Evans, 1971, p. 88). "May it be," he asks, "that the goal to 'publish or perish' encourages swift piecemeal, unread, and unreadable publications crammed with method but scant on meaning?" (Allport, 1968, pp. 37–38)

Biographical Sketch of the Theorist

Early Years

Gordon Willard Allport, the fourth son of Dr. John Edwards Allport and Mrs. Nellie Edith (Wise) Allport, was born November 11, 1897, in Montezuma, Indiana. His three older brothers were Harold E. (nine years older), Floyd F (seven years older), and Fayette W. (five years older).

When Allport was six years of age, his family moved to Cleveland, Ohio. It was in Cleveland that Allport grew up, in a house that he later described as "plain Protestant piety and hard work."

Allport was the editor of the Glenville High School newspaper at the age of fifteen, and independently managed his own multigraph business while going to school. He was graduated in 1915, the valedictorian of his class of 100 seniors.

Education

Allport's brother Floyd, then a graduate student of psychology at Harvard University, encouraged Allport also to apply for admission to Harvard. He received his B.A. degree in 1912 with double majors in philosophy and economics and Phi Beta Kappa honors. Allport then went to Constantinople, Turkey, where he taught English and sociology at Robert College for a year. In 1920, Allport returned to Harvard. He completed his Ph.D. in psychology in 1922; the title of his dissertation was *An Experimental Study of the Traits of Personality: With Special Reference to the Problem of Social Diagnosis.*

Awarded the Shelden Traveling Fellowship, Allport studied two years in Europe, first at the University of Berlin and then at the University of Hamburg, where he studied the then-new Gestalt psychology. He spent the second academic year at Cambridge University, where his reports on the Gestalt school were less than well received by the British psychologists.

Returning to Harvard University as an instructor in social ethics, Allport met Ada Lufkin Gould, a clinical psychologist. They were married June 30, 1925. During the 1924–1925 academic year, Allport taught the first course on human personality. Allport accepted a faculty appointment at Dartmouth College, and taught there for four years.

In September, 1930, Allport again returned to Harvard University, where he remained for forty-three years. He helped to found the Department of Social Relations in 1946, and chaired the Committee on Higher Degrees for eighteen years. This unique department combined degree programs in clinical psychology, social anthropology, social psychology, and sociology.

Emergence of Allport's Theory of Personality

In 1937, Allport published *Personality: A Psychological Interpretation*. He expanded and refined his theoretical formulations in *Becoming: Basic Considerations for a Psychology of Personality* in 1955 and in *Pattern for Growth in Personality* in 1961. Other works include *The Nature of Personality: Selected Papers* (1950) and *Personality and Social Encounter* (1960).

Honors and Awards

Allport received numerous honors and awards. He was the editor of the *Journal of Abnormal and Social Psychology* from 1937 to 1949. He served as president of the American Psychological Association in 1939, and of the Eastern Psychological Association in 1943, and of the Society for the Psychological Study of Social Issues in 1944.

During World War II, Allport was an active member of the Emergency Committee in Psychology, and he was secretary of the Ella Lyman Cabot Foundation, which assisted refugee psychologists escaping from Germany.

Allport's contributions to the area of personality were recognized throughout the world. He was named an honorary Fellow of the British Psychological Society, and awarded honorary memberships in the Deutsche Gesellschaft für Psychologie and Osterreichische Arztegesellschaft für Psychotherapie. He was elected a *membre associé (à 'titre' étranger)* of the Societé Française de Psychologie. An active advocate of international scholarship, Allport was a member of the national commission for UNESCO. During the war years, Allport was also the director of the National Opinion Research Center.

In 1963, Allport was awarded APA's Gold Medal Award for distinguished and long-extended contributions to psychology. That same year, fifty-five of his former doctoral students held a testimonial dinner and presented him with a two-volume set of their publications. The dedication read: "From his students—in appreciation of his respect for their individuality." Allport considered this an "intimate honor," and valued it above all other awards. In 1964, he received the award for distinguished contributions from the American Psychological Association. In 1966, Allport was the first Richard Clark Cabot Professor of Social Ethics.

Allport lived to see his ideas, many of which were unpopular at the time he first presented them, come to fruition as other psychologists followed the path he pioneered. He died in October, 1967, of lung cancer. He was sixty-nine years old.

Resolutions of Eleven Basic Issues

For most personologists, personality constructs are abstractions intended only to help us understand and, if possible, predict human behavior. This is not the case with Allport (1961) who looked at personality as *real*, and who defined **personality** as "the dynamic organization within the individual of those psycho-physical systems that determine his unique adjustments to his environment" (p. 48). Personality, for Allport, is everything the person is: constantly changing and evolving, yet persistent and structured; mind and body, flesh and self, with tendencies to characteristic behavior and thought (Hall & Lindzey, 1978).

While Allport directly or indirectly addressed most of the basic issues selected for the presentation of the personalities in this book, he did so from a different perspective than the great majority of theorists who were also psychotherapists. As an academic psychologist, Allport was primarily concerned with healthy, mature adults. Indeed, he was convinced that studies of animals, infants, and the emotionally disturbed not only should not, but could not, be applied to understanding and predicting the behavior of healthy adults.

Heredity versus Social Determinants

Although Allport accepted as fact that we, like all living creatures, are subject to the laws of heredity, he reminded us that we are only beginning to discover with any certainty what these laws are and how they influence our individual personalities. Further, he noted: "The most important point of scientific agreement is that no feature or quality (of human personality) is exclusively heredity, and none is exclusively environment in origin" (Allport, 1961, p. 68, parentheses added). Until he could find evidence to the contrary, Allport was prepared to accept only the biological drives and the "possibility-of-becoming" as universal, inborn human existence.

According to Allport, the force of culture in the shaping of personality rests in its "ready made, pretested solutions" to many of the problems we encounter in life.

> *". . . out of his own life experiences a child could hardly be expected to invent a language or a scheme of medical treatment; he could not evolve a science, an ethics, or an embracing religion. . . . Culture offers him stored-up solutions—not always accurate but at least available" (Allport, 1961, p. 161).*

The child begins early in life to learn cultural values—at home, in his or her place of worship, in school, and through various media, television especially. For Allport (1961), a **cultural value** is "a way of life deemed desirable by most members of society" (p. 169). Personality is, then, a system within a matrix of sociocultural systems.

Number and Weight Assigned to Motivational Concepts

After discovering that human motives are idiosyncratic (some are transient, others recurring; some momentary, others persistent; some conscious, others unconscious; some opportunistic, others propriate; and some tension reducing, others tension maintaining), Allport (1961, pp. 220–227) arrived at certain necessary requirements of a theoretical construct of human motivation:

1. *It will acknowledge the contemporaneity of motives.* That is, whatever motivates us to think or act does so in the present. Limiting an explanation of human behavior exclusively to the past fails to consider where the person is attempting to go, and is therefore an incomplete explanation. Only when the past can be shown to be dynamically active in the present can the past influence individual motivation.

2. *It will be a pluralistic theory—allowing for motives of many types.* Allport is neither a reductionist nor a seeker of global explanations for complex behaviors. Both deficit motives (thirst, hunger, sleep, safety, comfort) and growth motives (interests, aspirations, goals, plans) must be encompassed by an adequate theory of motivation.

3. *It will ascribe dynamic force to cognitive processes—to planning and intention.* Allport recognizes the dynamic force of human cognition. Cognition enables us to trace the course of motivation in human existence into the future. **Intention** (the individual's hopes, plans, wishes, aspirations) plays a most important role in Allport's Theory of Personalism.

4. *The theory will allow for concrete uniqueness of motives.* The driving desire to become a pianist, the insatiable need for love and recognition, or the intense fear of crowds serve as examples.

All these requirements, Allport (1961) asserts, are fulfilled in his concept of **functional autonomy,** which states that *despite its origin* a motivation can become an end or goal in itself. In Allport's (1961) words: "Functional autonomy regards adult motives as varied, and as self-sustaining contemporary systems, growing out of antecedent systems, but functionally independent of them" (p. 227). It is important to note that Allport's concept of functional autonomy does not refer back to the earlier motive or basic need. Rather, he asserts, though a motive was once a means to an end, it can become an end in itself, even in the absence of the original motive. For example, a student originally motivated to read about the Civil War in order to write an assigned term paper and receive a passing grade in history may continue his research of this period of American history long after he has successfully completed the course, *simply because he enjoys doing so.*

Allport (1961) was convinced, also, that human motivation contributes to the unification of personality. Like Maslow (Chapter 10), Allport believes it is not the attainment of a major goal that motivates us; rather, it is the striving itself—the pursuit. Indeed, Allport (1961) asserts: "The more unattainable the goal the more formative it will be" (p. 391). Motivation of the healthy adult does not stop when a major goal is achieved. Aspiration increases with success in reaching a major goal; new and higher goals are formulated and striving continues.

If we accept Allport's theory of functional autonomy, we must, as Allport (1961) did, also accept the notion "that motives in animals will *not* be an adequate model for motives in men [adult humans]; neither will the motives of adulthood always continue the motives of childhood; and, finally, motivation in a neurotic personality will *not* necessarily define motivation in a normal individual" (pp. 221–222, parentheses added). This notion applies as well to personality constructs other than motivation.

Uniqueness versus Universality

Allport (1961, also Allport in Evans, 1971, p. 54) insisted that individuality is the prime characteristic of our nature, and he argued for uniqueness at every stage of our being. Each of us deviates in thousands of ways from every other member of our species—no two of us are alike. Indeed, "no two human beings (with the possible exception of identical twins) have even the potentiality of developing alike" (Allport, 1961, p. 5, parentheses in original). For Allport, this means that individuality cannot be studied scientifically, for **nomothetic** (quantitative) studies seek universal laws. Rather, he emphasized, individuality can only be studied by history, art, or biography, hence, **idiographically** (qualitatively).

Subjective versus Objective Reality

Not only is our **desire to know** (to understand and find order in the world) one of the primary human motivations in Allport's (1961) Theory of Personalism, the role of cognitive processes in our knowing is raised to a level of primary importance (p. 274). It is through our senses and cognition that we perceive, interpret, and formulate social attitudes which we then use to confront social and somatic stimuli. For Allport, perception is subjective—wholly a personal phenomenon. Society presents the circumstances, but we individually mold, accept, reject, or criticize our perceptions of the world, other beings, and ourselves. We each add our unique personal meanings to our sensory input of the environment, including ourselves (Allport, 1961, p. 274).

By accepting human rationality, Allport accepts subjective experience and self-reports as valid data for understanding human behavior. Adults who know themselves, Allport asserts, are able to give adequate accounts and predictions of their own behavior. In short, if we want to know something about the developed adult, we have only to ask him or her. Projective techniques for healthy adult subjects, then, are not only unnecessary, but quite useless from Allport's perspective.

Role Assigned to Self-Concept

Allport learned early in his studies of human personality that the terms "ego" and "self" varied considerably in definition from one theorist to another and from one point to another in the various stages of growth. To avoid the confusion created by the various definitions, Allport preferred the term **proprium**—the fusion or unity of all the eight stages of development of the self (the bodily self, self-identity, self-esteem, self-extension or identity, self-image, self as rational coper, propriate strivings, and self as knower; see also Early versus Continuous Development, this chapter).

Allport viewed the proprium as the ultimate unification of all intimate, distinct, and personal functions and aspects of our personality. The proprium is, then, our sense of personal importance and strivings, and serves as the unifying core of our personality. The proprium is not to be mistaken for an entity—the proprium does not *do,* nor does it *will.* It is not to be thought of as separate from our personality. It would be in error, therefore, to say that the proprium thought this or needed that.

Allport's concept of proprium is a unification that is never totally achieved, a gradual acquisition and unifying core that includes eight personal aspects of existence.

Determinism versus Freedom of Choice

We are, according to Allport (1955, 1961), proactive beings. However, Allport's systematic, eclectic approach to theory is not exclusionary. To his reactive colleagues he said, in effect: "You have done an excellent job on the mechanical aspects of human behavior, but there is more to human nature than you are able to explore with the exclusive use of your preferred model." Mature, healthy adults, Allport asserts, experience a sense of **relative freedom** (the capacity for planning–striving–hoping, guided by self-image) whenever value is in play. In healthy personalities, cognition is dynamic enough for shaping, directing, orienting, planning, and choosing from multiple possibilities for behavior. Intentionality, a cognitive process, must be considered for a full understanding of Allport's stance on this issue.

Further, Allport argued, there is relatively greater freedom in certain modes of choosing than in others. For example, the act of momentary reflection *before* the act of choosing sets the larger systems of propriate striving into motion, and opens new pathways of decision, thus improving an individual's degree of freedom.

Allport's principle of functional autonomy is also evidence of freedom. The transformation of motives is for Allport the direct consequence of freedom of choice.

Conscious versus Unconscious Determinants

There is some ambivalence in Allport's stance on this issue. On the one hand, he states:

> *Of the whole of our nature we are never directly aware, not of any large portion of the whole. At any given moment the range of consciousness is remarkably slight. It seems to be a little more than a restless pencil point of light darting here and there within a large edifice of personality, focused now within, now without (Allport, 1961, p. 139).*

Initially, this view seems to be in line with that of the psychoanalytic theorists. However, Allport (1961) told us that mature, healthy adult motives are both conscious and concrete, and he argued that the most important aspects of the healthy adult's personality can be understood by simply asking him or her for the information needed.

> *Yet for all its feebleness, consciousness provides each of us with the only sure test of our personal existence and identity. At one moment we think back to some event in childhood; the next moment we have an image of what will happen tomorrow; then immediately we are aware of some present event. Our sense of self, as well as our knowledge of the outside world, is wholly dependent on this crisscross of conscious states (Allport, 1961, p. 139).*

Explanation of the Learning Process

After a thorough examination of the existing theories of learning, Allport was convinced that the learning process for humans was far too vast and complex to be explained fully by any simple theory. An eclectic, Allport accepted some of the findings of the psychoanalytic and learning theorists; however, his acceptance must be described as partial or conditional. For example, though he agreed to the impact of the defense mechanisms and early trauma on the learning of animals and infants and on opportunistic learning, he denied their significance on the learning of mature adults. Similarly, while he accepted the explanations of conditioning, reinforcement, and habit of the learning theorists, he again believed these explanations were inadequate when applied to healthy adults and thus, did not grant them central importance in his theory.

For Allport, a satisfactory explanation of the learning process of mature adults must include functional autonomy and propriate learning:

> *Typically a person learns when he is trying to relate himself to his environment, under the combined influence of his motives, the present requirements of the situation, active participation, and a knowledge of relevant facts, including a memory of his previous success and failure (Allport, 1946, Jan.–Nov., p. 345).*

Cognition, then, plays a significant role in Allport's explanation of the learning process. We absorb anything that we consider personally relevant, subject only "to the limitations of fatigue, intellectual capacity, clear perception, and other similar conditions" (Allport, 1946, Jan.–Nov., p. 346). We are self-aware, self-critical, and self-enhancing. We possess an innate tendency to form structures, including such complex structures as a moral conscience, a conception of self, preemptive traits and interests, a schemata of meaning, and a philosophy of life (Allport, 1955).

Though Allport obviously grants the process of learning great importance, he did not provide us clear explanations of the dynamics and mechanisms of the process. He did introduce the concept of propriate functional autonomy to account for the idiosyncratic motivation behind learning, and the process of becoming to account for the urgent disposition to realize our possibilities of living in the world. In short, like Maslow, Allport offers us more an explanation of the motivation of the learning process than he does of learning methods, strategies, or techniques.

Early versus Continuous Development

Allport rejected Freud's psychosexual stages of early childhood development, as well as the psychoanalytic notion that personality is essentially formed in the first five years of life. Allport (1955) contends that personality development or **becoming** is a continuous (though usually episodic) process from infancy to death. Indeed, in contrast to Freud, who defined the early stages of development as *critical,* Allport (1961) concluded that "... in a sense the first year is the least important year for personality, assuming that serious injuries to health do not occur" (p. 78).

During the first year, the infant functions in relatively reflexive ways, only in accordance to the principle of tension reduction. The beginning signs of consciousness and hence, selfhood in a bodily sense, only begin to appear at the end of the first year. The infant "... has no concept of himself, no lasting memories, and no firm anchorage of habits" (Allport, 1955, p. 78). Self-identity, followed by self-esteem, begin to develop the second and third years. Some self-extension and self-image are possible from four to six years. And some rational coping qualities of the proprium become apparent from six to twelve years of age. Increasing evidence of propriate striving emerges during adolescence and continues into adulthood, which is also normally accompanied by signs of maturity. In short, as the proprium expands and gains strength, **opportunistic functioning** (concerned primarily with tension reduction) recedes.

Role Assigned to Group Determinants

As indicated earlier (see "Heredity versus Social Determinants," this chapter), Allport did not attribute significant influence to external forces on the personalities of normal or healthy adults. They, he asserted, follow conscious, flexible, and functionally autonomous motives that make it possible for them to cope effectively with the difficulties they encounter in life. That is, the normal adult relies on his or her own inner dynamics, rather than on external forces.

A different view of environmental forces emerges, however, when Allport addresses the personalities of children or those adults whose innate tendency for normal development has been thwarted by childhood trauma or pathogenic childrearing practices, the unconscious use of defense mechanisms to avoid life's realities, or the unconscious motives that lead to rigid or compulsive behavior. In addition to psychodynamic factors, Allport (1954/1958) also cited historical, sociocultural, situational, and stimulus object factors as principle causes of prejudice, which incidentally, he, like Adler (Chapter 3) believed to be pathogenic.

Allport (1954) discovered that as early as the age of five we are capable of understanding that we are members of a variety of groups, including ethnic identification, though we may not reach understanding of how one group differs from others until the age of nine or ten. The significance of Allport's findings in his study of prejudice for this issue is:

> *One of the facts of which we are most certain is that people who reject one out-group will tend to reject other out-groups. If a person is anti-Jewish, he is likely to be anti-Catholic, anti-Negro, anti-any out-group (p. 68).*

In short, Allport (1954) learned: "Common prejudices create common bonds" (p. 68).

There is, according to Allport (1954), a separateness among groups. We tend to mate with "our own kind," and to reside, eat, and play in homogeneous clusters. While much of this cohesion is due solely to convenience (it takes much less effort to deal with others who share similar presuppositions), this same sense of cohesion often leads to the identification of out-groups (Allport, 1954, p. 17).

Centrality of Reinforcement

As with many of the humanists, the term "reinforcement" does not appear in his theory. He does, however, state:

> *The first rule of applied psychology is that every child and every adult needs some experience of success and social approval. . . . The* ego *must be satisfied, not the sex drive, nor the maternal drive, however temporarily insistent these segmental tensions may be (Allport, 1943, p. 466, emphasis in original).*

For Allport, the **ego drive** (pride or desire for approval) takes precedence over all other drives.

Like Adler (Chapter 3), Allport asserts that encouragement and approval bring with them a sense of pleasure and hope for the future. Whenever success is viewed as "peculiarly mine," and involves our interests, planning, intentions, values, standards, meanings, judging, wanting, or loving, we experience a personal sense of self-esteem—in short, reward. We are especially rewarded when success results from propriate striving, which, for Allport, is the highest level of motivation.

Reward is idiosyncratic; it is a wholly personal affair. As unique beings, we perceive, interpret, and give meaning to all environmental stimuli. We determine what contributes to and enhances our tendency toward psychological growth. Intentions, planning, striving, and hope are guided by our self-image and personal values. All propriate functioning is rewarding.

Psychological Health and Psychopathology

Addressing the subject of normal and abnormal personality, Allport (1957, Fifth Interamerican Congress of Psychology; reprinted in Chiang & Maslow, 1960) maintained that the usual standards of statistics (average or usual) and ethics (desirable or valuable) were inadequate to determine the difference between normal and abnormal human conduct or to arrive at a concept of psychological health and the good life. He was convinced that a standard for the healthy personality could only emerge from the study of human potentialities. He was

Heredity		■			Social Determinants
Uniqueness	■				Universality
Subjective Reality	■				Objective Reality
Determinism			■		Freedom
Conscious Determinants		■			Unconscious Determinants
Early Development			■		Continuous Development

Number and Weight Assigned to Motivational Concepts	Allport arrived at four requirements of a theoretical construct of human motivation: (1) acknowledge contemporaneity of motives, (2) be pluralistic, (3) ascribe dynamic force to cognition processes, and (4) allow for concrete uniqueness of motives. These requirements are fulfilled in his concept of functional autonomy.
Role Assigned to Self-Concept	To avoid the confusion created by various definitions of "ego" and "self," Allport preferred the term "proprium" (the fusion or unity of the eight stages of development of the self). Proprium is the unifying core of personality—a unification that is never totally achieved.
Explanation of Learning Process	The learning process for humans is too vast and complex to be explained fully by simple theory. An explanation of the learning process of mature adults must include functional autonomy and propriate learning.
Role Assigned to Group Determinants	The normal adult relies on inner dynamics, rather than on external forces. Psychodynamic, historical, sociocultural, situational, and stimulus object factors are principle causes of prejudice. There is a separateness among groups.
Centrality of Reinforcement	For Allport, the ego drive (pride or desire for approval) takes precedence over all other drives. We are especially rewarded when success results from propriate striving. Reward is a personal affair.

FIGURE 8-1   Schematic Analysis of Allport's Stance on Basic Issues

further convinced that the study of human potentialities would require the cooperative effort of both psychologists and moral philosophers, for whom the quest for health and the good life was central.

Allport believed that moral philosophers should be given the freedom to pursue their intuitive, rational approach to the discovery of moral imperatives for living the good life, and encouraged to arrive at ethical solutions to the questions of normal and abnormal conduct. He was equally convinced that the research and analysis of the psychologists could not be ignored. Indeed, it is the psychologists who have gathered the facts of normality and abnormality, and then attempted to integrate these facts into their work with people in clinics, laboratories, schools, business, and industry. Since neither psychologists nor philosophers have been able to arrive at a testable definition of normal and abnormal conduct, Allport suggests that they combine their efforts.

Psychological Health

Rather than wait until better standards were developed, Allport looked to the goals of psychotherapists for his answer to the issue of psychological health and psychopathology. Among others, he reviewed the work of Freud (love and work), Adler (*Gemeinschaftsgefuhl* or social interest), Jung (individuation), Fromm (productive orientation), Erikson (identity), Rogers and Maslow (self-actualization), and Frankl (meaningfulness and responsibility), and from their listings composed his own:

1. *Ego extension*—The ability to transcend self-interest involves projection into the future—to defer momentary needs, pains, pleasures, or desires in favor of reaching a long-term goal. Here Allport accepts the attributes that Fromm (Chapter 6) lists for the productive personality.

2. *Self-objectification*—". . . That particular detachment of the mature person when he surveys his own pretenses in relation to his abilities, his present objectives in relation to possible objectives for himself, his own equipment in comparison with the equipment of others, and his opinion of himself in relation to the opinion others hold of him" (Allport, 1937, p. 214). Self-objectification is always tied to a sense of humor, in particular to insight and the absurdities of the self.

3. *Unifying philosophy*—Mature persons live their lives by a personal set of guiding principles and standards that serve in the search for meaning and finding one's place in the scheme of things (Frankl, Chapter 12). For Allport, religion represents one of the more important sources of a person's unifying philosophy.

4. *Capacity for a warm, profound relating of one's self to others*—For Allport, as for Maslow (Chapter 10), the mature healthy adult is able to relate himself or herself warmly to others, in both intimate and non-intimate contacts. Relationships of the psychologically healthy are free of possessiveness and jealousy.

5. *Possession of realistic skills, abilities, and perceptions*—The ability to perceive, think, and act in a world of reality. A realistic orientation toward self, others, and the world (see Rogers's fully-functioning person and Maslow's self-actualizing person, Chapters 9 and 10). Psychologically healthy individuals generally are aware of what they want, what they are doing, and their reasons for their actions. At the core of their behavior are propriate functions which are enmeshed in their aspirations and goals. When functions are propriate, motivation is telic; that is, it pulls from the future rather than pushes from the past.

6. *A compassionate regard for all living creatures* (Adler's concept of *Gemeinschaftsgefuhl,* Chapter 3)—More than just acceptance and tolerance, though these are certainly present, Allport sees the mature and healthy adult as contributing in a positive way to the future evolution of his or her species, as well as to his or her world.

Allport, like Frankl (Chapter 12), warns us not to equate psychological health with happiness. The psychologically healthy are not immune to the frustrations, disappointments, failures, and tragedies that are part of life in this indiscriminate world. The pursuit of meaningful goals brings both happiness and unhappiness.

Psychopathology

When an individual's development is blocked by pathogenic influences in childhood, healthy growth is stunted. Drives and motives continue to function at an infantile level. Motives do not become functionally autonomous, for they remain tied to their original physiological drives rather than freely emerging from present conscious intentions. The proprium does not develop. Energy remains diffuse and scattered, as it is in infancy. Self-expression is deficient, because the individual is too preoccupied with self-image to be spontaneous or genuine. The ideal self, which is not based on current performance, is unrealistic and unattainable. Goals are grandiose, idealistic, and culturally dependent rather than self-valued.

Allport's view of psychopathology is similar in some ways to that of Adler. Both theorists see a polar difference between the courageous confrontation of reality and the defensive posture of escape and withdrawal. Allport (1957, in Chiang & Maslow) lists catabolic functions that he believes generate psychopathology:

- Escape or withdrawal;
- Repression or dissociation;
- Other ego defenses, including rationalization, reaction formation, projection, and displacement;
- Impulsivity (uncontrolled);
- Restriction of thinking to a concrete level;
- Fixation of personality at a juvenile level; and
- All forms of rigidification (p. 10).

Applications to Psychotherapy

As stated earlier, Allport was not a psychotherapist. Further, he focused primarily on the healthy, mature adult. His discussion of psychotherapy, therefore, was both limited and superficial. Although there is an eclectic acceptance of psychotherapy as a way to bring about behavioral change, Allport did not attempt to integrate methods of psychotherapy into his theory. Hall and Lindzey (1978) remark: "This is a critical omission which seriously curtails the utility of Allport's theory" (p. 243).

Therapeutic Goals

In *Pattern and Growth in Personality*, Allport (1961) does mention therapeutic goals:

> *It would seem wise for the therapist to determine whether the patient's symptoms are to be relieved by "going to the root of the problem" or whether the most that can be hoped for is to reconcile the patient to his own developed style of life. In the first instance he is assuming that the neurosis is not functionally autonomous. In the latter case it is, and can be handled better by re-education than by reliving (p. 241).*

Therapeutic Process and Strategies

For Allport (1968), therapy is still largely experimental. Though therapists manage to give their patients relief, they ". . . are still far from being able to fashion balanced and productive lives. . . ." (p. 146).

Allport is convinced that before we can study or mend a broken personality, we must first gain a deep knowledge of normal personality. No therapist can forcibly enter the client's proprium and plant a functionally autonomous motive. "He can at best open channels of experiencing and, by his *obiter dicta*, sometimes lead the student [client or patient] to see the value-potential in the experience" (Allport, 1968, p. 169, parentheses added).

Extended Applications

Expressive Behaviors

Allport (1961), like Adler (Chapter 3), believed there were two important aspects to all human behavior: *adaptive* (or coping) and *expressive*. Adaptive aspects of behaviors are purposive; that is, they are specifically and consciously motivated and as such, point to a goal. Conversely, expressive aspects of behavior are neither purposive nor specifically motivated. Indeed, expressive aspects of behaviors are generally unconscious, spontaneous, difficult to alter, and often uncontrollable.

For anyone trying to understand the behaviors of another, the expressive aspects of behaviors (posture, gait, hand gestures, voice timbre and tone, facial expressions, and handwriting) are the more significant of the two behavioral aspects (Allport, 1961; Allport & Vernon, 1930). Expressive behaviors, Allport maintained, are reflections of underlying motives and conflicts, often the very dispositions that a person may be trying to hide or repress.

Allport and Phillip Vernon (1930) found a marked consistency in the individual's expressive behaviors, and were in some instances able to judge accurately the individual's personality traits. They strongly recommended additional research in this area, for they believed it held great potential as a method for understanding personality. Studies in body language and by the adherents to National Linguistic Programming have confirmed some of Allport's findings, though much more needs to be done before expressive behaviors become reliable data for diagnostic purposes, as Allport had hoped.

Religion

For Allport (1955), there is a religious sentiment in human nature. Moreover, he reasons, our religious nature is linked to ". . . the most elusive facts of becoming, including propriate striving, generic conscience, and intentionality" (Allport, 1955, p. 93). The developed (mature, healthy) adult attempts to link him- or herself "meaningfully to the whole of Being" (Allport, 1955, p. 94). The religious sentiment of the adult is not, according to Allport (1955), dependency or defense against fear. Neither is it exclusively rational. The mature adult has learned that ". . . to surmount the difficulties of a truculent world" both faith and love are necessary (p. 95). The religious form of propriate striving (see "Number and Weight of Motivational Concepts," this chapter) provides the developed adult ". . . a synthesis of all that lies within experience and all that lies beyond" (Allport, 1955, p. 97).

Allport realizes that the religious nature of the developed adult is far too complex to understand with the present methods of science, but he asserts that as we become more adept, we shall develop methods and theories suited to regions of personality that are currently inaccessible. Further, Allport (1955) is convinced that, when we are able to view the mature adult as ". . . a self-assertive, self-critical, and self-improving individual whose passion for integrity and for a meaningful relation to the whole of Being," we may discover his most distinctive capacities (p. 97).

Prejudice

Allport (1962a; see also 1946, 1967a, Allport & Ross, 1967) maintains that ". . . at least four-fifths of the American population lead mental lives in which feelings of group hostility play an appreciable role" (p. 9). He also asserts that ". . . prejudice, like tolerance, is often imbedded deeply in personality structure and is reflected in a consistent cognitive style" (Allport & Ross, 1967, p. 443). The three attitudes of the prejudiced mind, according to Allport (1945), are "unwarranted, unjust, and insensitive" (p. 24).

In his studies on the subject of prejudice, Allport (1946) found that we begin life without prejudice; indeed, he tells us that we are for the most part "incapable of fixating hostility upon any group" through the preschool years.

Allport (1946) reports that those individuals who attend church are more prejudiced than those who do not. The exceptions to this correlation are those churchgoers with an **intrinsic** (devout, internalized, and genuine) religious orientation.

Allport (1946, 1962a) also discovered that children who introject parental values are more likely to be prejudiced. Conversely, those children who are critical of parental patterns are freer from prejudice.

There is a correlation, also, with a college education. Children of college-educated parents are less prejudiced than are children of parents who are not college graduates.

In summary, Allport finds no single or simple explanation for ethnic, religious, or political prejudice; rather, like the person who is prejudiced, prejudice is a complicated phenomenon with multiple causes and can be explained only in terms of a unique combination of historical factors, sociocultural influences, situational determinants, psychodynamic factors, phenomenological beliefs, and characteristics of the stimulus object.

Like Adler, Allport believes prejudice to be pathogenic, and like Fromm, Allport was not convinced that we will be able to develop an allegiance to humanity as a whole in time to avoid destruction. It was evident to Allport, as it was to Fromm, that psychology has not kept pace with technological advances.

Personal Documents

As discussed earlier (see "Psychological Health," this chapter), Allport presented mature healthy adults as rational beings who consciously formulate long-term goals and plans to achieve them. Understanding an individual personality, then, can be enhanced by the study of **personal documents** (autobiographies, diaries, journals, letters, and published works). To demonstrate this premise, Allport (1965) conducted a study of 300 letters written over a twelve-year period by an elderly woman to a young married couple. Using the method of content analysis, Allport was able to characterize Jenny Masterson (not her real name) in terms of eight personal dispositions: paranoid suspiciousness, self-centeredness, independence, dramatic intensity, artistic appreciation, aggressiveness, cynical morbidity, and sentimentality. For Allport (1961), the study showed that it was possible to design a sound quantitative study of the individual case (pp. 59–62).

Critique

With the publication of *Personality: A Psychological Interpretation* in 1937, Allport not only introduced the study of personality to academia, he made it a respectable part of the curricula of university psychology programs. In addition to formulating a systematic, eclectic, and holistic theory of personality, Allport insisted on discontinuity between child and adult, animal and human, and abnormal and normal or healthy. He was convinced that no theory of adult personality could be considered complete without a full explanation of human motivation. He was further convinced that no explanation of motivation would be complete without acceptance of conscious, rational cognition. Allport was also concerned with the intentionality of healthy adults, whom he viewed as functionally autonomous and moving toward the future.

There is little doubt that his theoretical concepts appealed to and influenced the humanists or Third Force psychologists (Rogers, Chapter 9; Maslow, Chapter 10; May, Chapter 11; and Frankl, Chapter 12). Like Allport, they favored an antideterministic, telic view of human nature over the causal theories of the psychoanalysts and behaviorists. Allport's theory offered them an alternative to those who shared his views of the study of the whole person.

One does not challenge the major tenets of existing theories, as Allport certainly did, without return fire. Robert Holt (1985) expressed the thinking of many personologists who held the view that theory must withstand the validation of empirical studies, when he accused Allport of confusing art with science and referred to Allport's theory as a "romantic personality" that was overly optimistic. Allport, like Adler, Rogers, Maslow, Kelly, and to some extent Jung and Fromm, was convinced that psychology, if it is to approach full understanding of the whole person, must become far more idiographic.

With the exception of his studies of expressive behavior, Allport's theory has not generated a great deal of research, nor indeed has it provided either method or evidence of its predictive value or therapeutic application. Allport has also been accused of placing too great an emphasis on the inner dynamics of the person and too little on the influences of external forces. Those who believed that the purpose of personality theory is to discover general laws of human behavior faulted Allport's insistence on limiting his study to the individual case. Behaviorists and experimental psychologists, especially, criticized Allport's insistence that healthy adult behavior is distinctly different from animal, child, and neurotic adult behavior. They pointed to the information gained from studies of these subjects. Perhaps the strongest criticism of Allport's theory was leveled at his key concept of functional autonomy, which is as yet impossible to demonstrate empirically and which is ineffective in predicting individual behavior.

Annotated Bibliography

The intent of Allport's *Personality: A Psychological Interpretation* (1937) was to give a psychological definition of the field of personality as he viewed it. While he wanted to fashion an experimental science, his chief aim was an image of man that allowed him to test in full whatever democratic and humane potentialities a human might possess. This book, which first presented Allport's concept of *functional autonomy*, stood for twenty-five years as standard reading in the field, and identified Allport as one of the first personologists.

In 1961, Allport undertook a complete rewriting of this text in order to update the material; he titled the revised edition *Pattern and Growth in Personality*. This book is the best single source of Allport's final theory of human personality, and is highly recommended to both the student in training and the practitioner in the field.

Becoming: Basic Considerations for a Psychology of Personality (1955) emerged from Allport's assignment of the Terry Lectures at Yale. Here Allport expresses the need for a psychology of *becoming*—of striving toward human growth and development.

As the title clearly indicates, *The Nature of Prejudice* (1954) is Allport's classic comprehensive study of the psycho-social dynamics of human prejudice. He wrote this book with two groups of readers in mind: college and university students who are concerned with the social and psychological foundations of human behavior and guidance in the improvement of group relations, and the growing population of older citizens and general readers who are of the same mind and who are looking for practical ways to reduce group tensions. It is as relevant today as when it was written four decades ago, particularly for those who wish to learn more about the multiple causes (situational, psychodynamic, and phenomenological) of prejudice.

In *The Individual and Religion,* Allport (1962), unlike many personologists who either avoid the subject of religion or do not find the individual's religious beliefs crucial to psychological health, presents his view of the function of religion in the mature personality. Allport was convinced that intrinsic, sincere religious belief not only fortifies the individual against anxiety and despair, but makes it possible for the individual to relate meaningfully to his or her existence in the total scheme of life. Allport also warns those readers who use religion to achieve their own goals (e.g., to make contacts for business purposes, for political gain, or to achieve esteem in the community) that they do so at risk of their psychological health.

Allport's (1968) book, *The Person in Psychology*, presents his view of the mature adult personality as a being-in-the-process-of-becoming, in "expressive movement." In this book Allport views the healthy individual as a noble, valuable, evolving, unique being, and argues strongly against the use of experimental data derived from the lower animals (pigeons, rats, cats, dogs, and apes), from children, and from abnormal adults to understand normal, healthy adult behavior.

References and Suggested Readings

Acklin, M. W. (1985). An ego developmental study of religious cognition. *Dissertation Abstracts International, 45.* 3926B-2927B. (University Microfilms No. 85-03,-799).

Allport, Gordon Willard. (1960–1963). *The National Cyclopedia of American Biography: Vol. 6.* New York: James T. White & Co.

Allport, G. W. (1921). Personality and character. *The Psychological Bulletin, 18*(9), pp. 441–455.

Allport, G. W. (1924). The study of the undivided personality. *Journal of Abnormal & Social Psychology, 19,* pp. 132–141.

Allport, G. W. (1927). Concepts of trait and personality. *Psychological Bulletin, 24*(5), pp. 284–293.

Allport, G. W. (1929). The study of personality by the intuitive method: An experiment in teaching from the Locomotive God. *Journal of Abnormal & Social Psychology 24*(1), pp. 14–27.

Allport, G. W. (1931). What is a trait of personality? *Journal of Abnormal and Social Psychology, 25,* pp. 368–372.

Allport, G. W. (1937). The functional autonomy of motives. *American Journal of Psychology, 50,* Golden Jubilee Volume, 1887–1937, pp. 141–156.

Allport, G. W. (1940, January). The psychologist's frame of reference. *Psychological Bulletin, 37*(1), pp. 1–28.

Allport, G. W. (1942). Morale and its measurement. In C. J. Friedrich & E. S. Mason, (Eds.) & Patterring, (Assoc. Ed.). *Public policy: A yearbook of the Graduate School of Public Administration, Harvard University.* Cambridge, MA: Graduate School of Public Administration, pp. 3–17.

Allport, G. W. (1943, September). The ego in contemporary psychology. *The Psychological Review, 50,* pp. 451–478.

Allport, G. W. (1945, May). The psychology of participation. *The Psychological Review, 53*(3), pp. 117–132.

Allport, G. W. (1946). Preface. In E. Simmel, (Ed.). *Antisemitism: A social disease.* New York: International Universities Press, pp. 7–9.

Allport, G. W. (1947, January–November). Scientific models and human morals. *The Psychological Review, 54,* pp. 182–192.

Allport, G. W. (1950). *The nature of personality: Selected papers.* Reading, MA: Addison–Wesley.

Allport, G. W. (1953). The mature personality. In A. Walters, *Readings in psychology.* Westminster, MD: Newman Press, pp. 175–176.

Allport, G. W. (1954). *The nature of prejudice.* Cambridge, MA: Addison–Wesley.

Allport, G. W. (1955). *Becoming: Basic considerations for a psychology of personality.* New Haven, CT: Yale University Press.

Allport, G. W. (1960a). *Personality and social encounter.* New York: Holt, Rinehart and Winston.

Allport, G. W. (1960b). The open system in personality theory. *Journal of Abnormal and Social Psychology, 61*(3), pp. 301–310.

Allport, G. W. (1960c). In C. Moritz, (Ed.). *Current biography yearbook* (pp. 6–8). New York: H. W. Wilson.

Allport, G. W. (1961). *Pattern and growth in personality.* New York: Holt, Rinehart and Winston. (Originally published 1937)

Allport, G.W. (1962a). Prejudice: Is it societal or personal? *The Journal of Social Issues, 18*(2), pp. 120–134.

Allport, G. W. (1962b, Fall). Psychological models for guidance. *Harvard Educational Review, 32*(4). (Reprint)

Allport, G. W. (1963). The mature personality. In Sister Annette Walters, (Ed.). *Readings in Psychology.* Westminster, MD: Newman Press, pp. 175–176.

Allport, G. W. (1964a). *Personality and social encounter: Selected essays.* Boston: Beacon Press. (Originally published 1960)

Allport, G. W. (1965). Psychological models for guidance. In R. L. Mosher, R. F. Carle, & C. D. Kehas, (Eds.). *Guidance: An examination.* New York: Harcourt, Brace & World, pp. 13–23.

Allport, G. W. (1967). Crisis in normal personality development. In H. W. Benard, & W. C. Huckins, (Eds.). *Readings in Human Development.* Boston: Allyn and Bacon, pp. 72–81.

Allport, G. W. (1968). *The person in psychology: Selected papers.* Boston: Beacon Press.

Allport, G. W., & Vernon, P. E. (1930). The field of personality. *The Psychological Bulletin, 27*(10), pp. 677–730.

Allport, G. W. & Kramer, B. M. (1946). Some roots of prejudice. *The Journal of Psychology, 22,* pp. 9–39.

Allport, G. W., & Ross, M. (1967). Personal religion orientation and prejudice. *Journal of Personality and Social Psychology, 5*(4), pp. 432–433.

Allport, G. W., Vernon, P. E., & Lindzey, G. (1960). *Study of values* (2nd ed.). Boston: Houghton Mifflin. (Originally published 1931)

Allport, F. H., & Allport, G. W. (1921). Personality traits: Their classification and measurement. *Journal of Abnormal & Social Psychology 16*(1), pp. 6–40.

American Psychological Foundation gold medal award. (1963). *American Psychologist, 18,* pp. 812–813.

Baumeister, R. J., & Tice, D. M. (1988). Metatraits. *Journal of Personality, 56*(3), pp. 571–598.

Burdick, J. A., Kreicker, R. A, & Klopfer, F. J. (1981). Selected values and beliefs of Mensa. *Psychological Reports, 48,* pp. 407–414.

Cantril, H. (1968). Gordon W. Allport (1897–1967). *Journal of Individual Psychology, 24*(1), pp. 97–98.

Costa, P. T., & McCrae, R. R. (1977–78). Age differences in personality structure revisited: Studies in validity, stability, and change. *International Journal of Aging and Human Development, 8*(4), pp. 261–275.

Chiang, H., & Maslow, A. H. (Eds.). (1960). *The healthy personality: Readings.* New York: D. Van Nostrand.

Cumming, C. E., & Rodda, M. (1989). Advocacy, prejudice, and role modeling in the deaf community. *The Journal of Social Psychology, 129*(1), pp. 5–12.

Dunbar, R. E., Smith, P. C., Bearse, L. N., Johnson, S. M., Salick, M. R., Erenkrantz, B. D., & Ironson, G. H. (1981). Multidimensional scaling and standardized testing of value systems. *Perceptual and Motor Skills, 52,* pp. 559–573.

Evans, R. I. (1971). *Gordon Allport: The man and his ideas.* New York: E. P. Dutton. (Originally published 1970)

Fehr, L. A., & Heintzelman, M. E. (1977). Personality and attitude correlates of religiosity: A source of controversy. *The Journal of Psychology, 95* pp. 63–66.

Garvin, B. J., & Boyle, K. K. (1985). Values of entering nursing students: Changes over 10 years. *Research in Nursing and Health, 8,* pp. 235–241.

Ghougassian. J. P. (1972). *Gordon W. Allport's ontopsychology of the person.* New York: Philosophical Library.

Gordon Allport of Harvard dies. (1967, October 10). *The New York Times, 117*(40, O71), p. 47.

Hall, C. S., & Lindzey, G. (1978). *Theories of personality,* (3rd ed.). New York: John Wiley & Sons.

Hater, R. J. (1968). Psycho-philosophy of the human person: (Gordon W. Allport's dynamic theory of human personality, with special emphasis on the philosophical implications derived from the study of his approach to man). *Dissertation Abstracts International, 28*(9). 3712A-3713A. (University Microfilms No. 68-3823).

Hilton, T. L., & Korn, J. H. (1964). Measured change in personal values. *Educational and Psychological Measurement, 24*(3), pp. 609–622.

Holt, R. R. (1985). The current status of psychoanalytic theory. *Psychoanalytic Psychology, 2,* pp. 287–315.

Lunde, D. T. (1974). Eclectic and integrated theory: Gordon Allport and others. In A. Burton, (Ed.). *Operational theories of personality.* New York: Brunner/Mazel, pp. 381–404.

Maddi, S. R. (1963). Humanistic psychology: Allport and Murry. In J. M. Wepman, & R. W. Heine (Eds). *Concepts of personality.* Chicago: Aldine, pp. 162–205.

Maddi, S. R., & Costa, P. T. (1972). *Humanism in personology: Allport, Maslow, and Murray.* Chicago, IL: Aldine–Atherton.

McClain, E. W. (1978). Personality differences between intrinsically religious and nonreligious students: A factor analytic study. *Journal of Personality Assessment, 42*(2), pp. 159–166.

Palmer, D. D. (1982). Personal values and priorities of organizational goals. *Psychological Reports, 51,* pp. 55–62.

Pearman, F. C. (1975). Catholic scaled values according to the Allport–Vernon and Lindzey study of values in relation to the 1970 national high school norms: Grades 10–12. *Adolescence, 10*(40), pp. 499–506.

Pettigrew, T. F. (1969). Gordon Willard Allport. *Journal of Personality & Social Psychology, 12*(1), pp. 1–5.

Plax, T. G., & Rosenfeld, L. B. (1977). Antecedents of change in attitudes of males and females. *Psychological Reports, 41,* pp. 811–821.

Rabinowitz, W. (1984). Study of values: G. Allport, P. Vernon, and G. Lindzey. In D. Keyser & R. Sweetland (Eds.). (1984). *Test Critiques, Vol. 1.* Kansas City, MO: Test Corporation of America.

Rosnow, R. L. (1980). Psychology of rumor reconsidered. *Psychological Bulletin, 87*(3), pp. 578–591.

Zuroff, D. C. (1986). Was Gordon Allport a trait theorist? *Journal of Personality & Social Psychology, 51*(5), pp. 993–1000.

C h a p t e r **9**

Rogers' Person-Centered Theory

Chapter Overview

Introduction

Biographical Sketch of the Theorist

Resolutions of the Eleven Basic Issues
    Heredity versus Social Determinants
    Number and Weight Assigned to Motivational Concepts
    Subjective versus Objective Reality
    Early versus Continuous Development
    Role Assigned to Self-Concept
    Conscious versus Unconscious Determinants
    Determinism versus Freedom of Choice
    Explanation of Learning Process
    Uniqueness versus Universality
    Role Assigned to Group Determinants
    Centrality of Reinforcement

Psychological Health and Psychopathology

Heuristic Influences: Research Methods and Techniques

Applications to Psychotherapy
    Therapeutic Goals
    Therapeutic Relationship

Initial Procedures and Strategies
Course of Psychotherapy

Extended Applications
The Intensive Group Experience
Education
Marriage and Its Alternatives
Recent Efforts to Extend Applications

Critique

Annotated Bibliography

References and Suggested Readings

Introduction

At the mention of the name Carl Rogers, three generations of mental health professionals project an image of the man they recall. Younger members envisage the counselor archetype—a kindly smiling, soft-spoken, bespectacled, fatherly looking gentleman—the father of Person-Centered Therapy. The image in the minds of older members is that of an intellectual revolutionary—an involuntary revolutionary perhaps, but a revolutionary nonetheless. In truth, both images, though far from complete, are accurate.

As a practicing therapist in the late 1930s and early 1940s, Rogers was deeply involved in helping his clients. His pragmatic approach to counseling and research focused more on learning what works than on developing a formal theory of psychotherapy. Consequently, he was unaware that his work was innovative and in conflict with traditional psychological interpretations and practices. He assumed that his book, *The Clinical Treatment of the Problem Child* (1930), was simply a "summarization of the work of *all* practicing counselors and therapists" (Rogers, 1974a, p. 7, emphasis added). Indeed, it was not until he was invited to present a paper to the chapter of Psi Chi (Psychology Honor Society) at the University of Minnesota in December, 1940, that Rogers (1974a) began to think that he might "have some original contributions to make to the field of psychotherapy" (p. 8).

Although he was totally unprepared for the praise and attacks both he and his ideas received following his presentation, he did realize for the first time that his approach to psychotherapy was uniquely his own (Rogers, 1974a, 1980). His theoretical constructs forced him to cross swords with the two major established theories—psychoanalysis and behaviorism. He questioned and in some cases ignored long-standing traditions. He called for radical reforms in many of the nation's major institutions, education and medicine in particular. He refused to use standardized diagnostic categories in his practice, rejecting such accepted diagnoses as neurotic, psychotic, or manic depressive. Further, he dared to propose an expanded and modified philosophy of science for psychology, arguing that presently accepted scientific methodologies actually prohibit significant discoveries of the nature of being human. Rogers was not just a revolutionary, he was a courageous, resolute, and persuasive revolutionary whose time had come.

Rogers soon attracted many ardent followers from a wide variety of disciplines, who much to Rogers's surprise, welcomed his positive and optimistic view of human nature. Equally surprising to Rogers, who always presented his theoretical hypotheses as tentative and subject to empirical investigation, he also attracted heavy critical fire, not only from loyal adherents to psychoanalysis and behaviorism but also from large numbers of academic psychologists and leaders in other disciplines, such as medicine and education.

Emerging primarily from his experiences as a counselor in the therapeutic process, Rogers's theoretical concepts began and remained descriptively centered on the unique, inner-subjective world of the person. Initially applied only to the individual and focused on the one-to-one counselor–client relationship, Rogers's person-centered approach expanded over nearly a half century to encompass an ever-widening philosophy.

> *Person-Centered Theory, today, is applied in teaching, administration, organizational behavior, marriage and its alternatives, parenting, race relations, the building of community, conflict resolution, social action, and international relations in general (Boy & Pine, 1982, p. vii; see also Rogers, 1974a, 1974b, 1980).*

In his 1973 address to the American Psychological Association, where he was the recipient of that organization's first Distinguished Professional Contribution Award, Rogers (1974b) looked back over forty-six years of his work and assessed its impact:

> *It turned the field of counseling upside down. It opened psychotherapy to public scrutiny and research investigation. It has made possible the empirical study of highly subjective phenomena. It has helped to bring some change in the methods of education at every level. It has been one of the factors bringing change in concepts of industrial (even military) leadership, of social work practice, of nursing practice, and of religious work. It has been responsible for one of the major trends in the encounter group movement. It has, in small ways at least, affected the philosophy of science. It is beginning to have some influence in interracial and intercultural relationships. It has even influenced students of theology and philosophy (p. 115).*

While Rogers (1974b) professed "utter astonishment" at this long list of accomplishments, William Kilpatrick (1985) argues that Rogers is "altogether too humble . . . the scope of his impact is much broader and goes much deeper than his assessment would indicate" (p. 22). Kilpatrick (1985) goes on to say: "He [Rogers] is frankly interested in the creation of a new type of human being, a new and better strain of human nature, a person as different from our present race as we are different from Australopithecus Africanus" (p. 22).

Richard Farson (1974), possibly the first to refer to Rogers as "the quiet revolutionary," agrees: "His [Rogers's] approach, though not easy to learn, is so elegant in concept and so dramatically rewarding in practice that it swept not only psychology but almost every other profession as well" (p. 199). Farson (1974) also credits Rogers for bringing science into "a field previously regarded as unknowable on any scientific basis" and for making "psychology the business of normal people and normal people the business of psychology" (p. 199).

It is not often that students of personality theory have the opportunity to witness a single theory of personality evolve and grow over nearly a half century. Rogers continued to change his views and to modify his theoretical constructs. Change was particularly evident in his psychotherapeutic approach as he gained greater confidence in the efficacy of his theory, in its ever-widening application to larger and larger groups.

Biographical Sketch of the Theorist

Convinced that theory should emerge from experience, Rogers recognized that his theory of personality was especially shaped by his life experiences. A clear understanding of his theoretical approach to counseling and personality, then, required that Rogers (1961, 1980) share not only those experiences that related to his professional life but also those personal experiences that he thought might give more context and meaning to his views on the nature of being human. Unlike many personality theorists who preferred not to reveal themselves in any personal way, Rogers (1961, 1980) was quite open about his life. Indeed, self-disclosure played a significant part in his presentations (papers, articles, and books) and was reflected in his informal manner and writing style.

Early Years

Born January 8, 1902, in Oak Park, Illinois, Carl Ransom Rogers was the fourth of six children of Walter A. and Julia (Cushing) Rogers. In addition to rather narrow fundamentalist religious beliefs, Rogers's parents valued and modeled the virtues of the Protestant work ethic. While the Rogers's home was marked by close family ties and the children were confident their parents loved them, Rogers (1961) later reported that his parents were "in many subtle and affectionate ways, very controlling of their children's behavior" (p. 5). Rogers (1961, 1980) recalls that as a child, he assimilated the righteously tolerant, aloof attitudes of his parents toward people outside the immediate family, and through elementary school, believed that he was somehow different from the other children. As a consequence, he led a very solitary life with "no close friend and only superficial personal contact" with other children (Rogers, 1980, p. 29). Books and dreams were Rogers's refuge. He became an incessant reader, hungrily perusing anything in print, including encyclopedias and dictionaries.

When Rogers was twelve, his family moved to a farm (a move which Rogers later suspected was his parents' way to keep their adolescent children from the temptations of suburban living); the boys were encouraged "to have independent and profitable ventures" on their own (Rogers, 1961, p. 6). Rogers's most profitable business venture was egg sales from a flock of chickens. It was during this period also that Rogers (1961) developed "an intense scientific interest in collecting and rearing the great night flying moths" that inhabited the woods near his home (p. 6).

Education

At the age of seventeen, Rogers entered the School of Agriculture at the University of Wisconsin, and for the first time, experienced the meaning and value of good friends (Rogers, 1951). That same year he dated Helen Elliot, the first person with whom he felt he could be fully open and trusting.

In 1922, Rogers was one of ten American students selected to attend the World Student Christian Federation Conference that was held in Peking, China. Traveling for six months with a group of young people with religious views very different from his own forced Rogers to stretch his thinking. Consequently, he broke from the fundamentalist religion of his parents. As his religious commitments matured, he decided to enter the ministry and transferred from the School of Agriculture to the College of Arts and Letters, where he majored in history.

Rogers and Helen Elliot were married immediately after completing their degrees in 1924 so that they could attend graduate school together. They moved to New York, and Rogers was admitted to the Union Theological Seminary. In two years, Rogers learned that he could not remain in a field that would require him to believe in a specific religious doctrine. He sought a career field in which his freedom of thought would not be limited and found it across the street at Teachers College, Columbia University. With little adjustment, he "shifted into the field of child guidance, and began to think of myself as a clinical psychologist" (Rogers, 1961, p. 9). Rogers received his M.A. degree in psychology in 1928, and began his internship at the Institute for Child Guidance in Rochester, New York. He was awarded the Ph.D. degree in clinical psychology in 1931.

During the twelve years Rogers worked at the Society for the Prevention of Cruelty to Children in Rochester, he served as psychologist (1928–1930) and director of the Child Study Department (1930–1938). In 1939, when the agency was reorganized and renamed the Rochester Guidance Center, he was appointed its director. His theoretical views underwent drastic change as he worked to become an effective therapist for the problem children placed in his charge by the courts. From an analytic interest in diagnosis, followed by a series of treatment interviews, Rogers (1961) moved to the conviction "that it is the *client* who knows what hurts, what directions to go, what problems are crucial, what experiences have been deeply buried" (p. 12).

During this same period, the Rogers's children, a son and a daughter, grew through infancy and childhood. According to Rogers (1980): they "taught me far more about individuals, their development, and their relationships, than I could ever have learned professionally" (pp. 12–13).

In 1940, Rogers moved from an agency to an academic setting by accepting a full professorship at Ohio State University. Looking back at this unexpected offer years later, Rogers (1961) was certain that his book, *The Clinical Treatment of the Problem Child* (1939), had much to do with beginning his academic career with the rank of professor. His second book, *Counseling and Psychotherapy* (1942), was Rogers's attempt to crystallize what he had learned from his long experience as a therapist. His ideas about a therapeutic approach were put to the test by graduate students who wanted reasons for the techniques they were learning. Not only did Rogers articulate clearly the therapeutic process, he and his students supported his views with impressive research data.

In addition to teaching, research, and writing, Rogers became an active participant in a number of professional organizations. He was president of the American Association of Applied Psychology from 1944 to 1945. He was president of the American Psychological Association (APA) and the Division of Clinical and Abnormal Psychology from 1949 to 1950.

Rogers joined the faculty of the University of Chicago in 1945, where he continued to research the counseling process and to develop his theory. It was here that he wrote *Client-Centered Therapy: Its Current Practice, Implications, and Theory* (1951). This was his first attempt to formalize a theory of personality. The title of his book became applied to his theory for many years, and it was this book that earned him an international reputation. Before the publication of *Client-Centered Therapy*, Rogers's approach to therapy was mistakenly labeled Nondirective Therapy or simply Rogerian Therapy. It was not until 1974, after extensive scrutiny of the therapeutic value of the close interpersonal relationship—the I–Thou relationship affirming both participants—that Rogers changed the name of his theory from Client-Centered Therapy to the more descriptive Person-Centered Therapy. Holdstock and Rogers (1977) cite five stages that characterize the development of the current person-centered approach:

- Precursor stage
- Nondirective stage
- Client-centered stage
- Experiential stage
- Person-centered stage

Rogers returned to the University of Wisconsin in 1957, accepting joint appointments in the departments of psychology and psychiatry. Rogers and his colleagues organized the Psychotherapy Research Group, which designed and conducted a lengthy study of psychotherapy with hospitalized patients diagnosed as schizophrenics. The results of this group's efforts were published in *The Therapeutic Relationship and Its Impact: A Study of Psychotherapy with Schizophrenics* (1967).

Though Rogers spent twenty-four very productive years on university campuses, he was not always pleased with the academic process. Indeed, he was on occasion extremely critical of traditional university structures, particularly of the pressures and politics of academic departments. He was most unhappy with the restrictions placed upon graduate students, and called for total reform of the graduate program (Rogers, 1969). In an interview, Rogers (in Heppner, Rogers, & Lee, 1984) stated: "I was so naïve about the politics of it when I went to Ohio State" (p. 15). At the University of Wisconsin, rebellion and chaos in a large research team taught Rogers (1980) "a most painful lesson" (p. 40). He followed the release of his criticism of current educational policies with a letter of resignation.

In 1964, Rogers moved to California as resident fellow of the Western Behavioral Sciences Institution. In 1968, he helped to found the Center for the Studies of the Person, in La Jolla, California.

In collaboration with Barry Stevens (a writer who describes herself as a high-school dropout), Rogers wrote *Person to Person: The Problem of Being Human* (1967). *Freedom to Learn* was published in 1969, *Carl Rogers on Encounter Groups* in 1970, *Becoming Partners: Marriage and Its Alternatives* in 1972, *Carl Rogers on Personal Power* in 1977, *A Way of Being* in 1980, and *Freedom to Learn for the 80's* in 1983.

Rogers died unexpectedly in 1988 from a blood clot following hip surgery. Although Rogers's theory of personality is considered strictly an American phenomenon, his books and articles are printed in numerous languages and his theory is taught in universities around the world. Rogers (1980), in his usual quiet manner, stated: "I had expressed an idea whose time had come" (p. 49). We must wait, however, to learn if, as Rogers (1980) believed, current developments and trends will "profoundly transform our concept of the person and the world that he or she perceives" (p. 347) and "will be in the direction of more humanness" (p. 356).

Awards and Honors

During his lengthy career, Rogers was the recipient of a considerable collection of honors and awards. Among them are:

- Resident fellow at the Center for Studies of the Person in La Jolla, California
- President of the American Psychological Association, the American Association for Applied Psychology, and the American Academy of Psychotherapists
- Recipient of the Distinguished Scientific Contribution Award for research in psychotherapy and the first Distinguished Professional Contribution Award from the American Psychological Association
- Recipient of the Award of Professional Achievements from the American Board of Professional Psychology
- Keynote speaker at the 1984 American Association of Counseling and Development (AACD) convention in Houston, Texas, where he spoke on nuclear planetary suicide
- AACD Lifetime Achievement Award, 1986
- Recipient of eight honorary doctorates
- Author and/or co-author of twelve books and hundreds of articles in various professional journals, from 1930 to 1987

Resolutions of the Eleven Basic Issues

Whether or not Rogers would have agreed with the eleven basic issues that structure the theories presented in this book, he has, in the course of developing a theory of personality, addressed them. Further, his resolutions are reflective of his close alliance with the humanistic psychotherapies. The positions of the issues in the hierarchical arrangement presented here are assigned by the present author and, therefore, are open to debate. However, as pointed out in Chapter 1, the advantages of the issue approach far outweigh the risk of disagreement.

It is important to note also that when a theory is based on a relatively few global theoretical constructs, repetition cannot be avoided (i.e., the innate actualizing tendency will influence the resolutions of many of the issues).

Heredity versus Social Determinants

For Rogers (1959, 1961, 1980), the core tendency of all humans, *as of all living organisms*, is to actualize their potentials. He was convinced that we enter this world with an inherent **actualizing tendency** (a biological drive to actualize, maintain, and enhance ourselves). We possess an inner motivation, or will, to become whatever is in our inherited nature to be. Our actualizing tendency is grounded in both the involuntary and voluntary expressions of life itself; it is an innate motivating force to fulfill our individual genetic blueprints. Rogers (1959) argued also that the actualizing tendency endows each of us with a **bodily wisdom** (a "naturalistic value system" that when trusted and followed may be used to differentiate between actualizing and nonactualizing experiences and to select behavioral options that facilitate the development of innate potentials).

Since we possess a natural predisposition to actualize our innate potentials, it would seem that self-actualization should be both simple and easy. In reality, such is not the case. Our actualizing tendency, Rogers (1951, 1961, 1980, 1983) reminds us, requires external stimulation that can be provided only by the physical, social, and cultural environments in which we live. Environmental conditions are not always conducive to healthy growth and development. In fact, we often encounter stimuli that are hostile to the actualization of our potentials. We are born into a world in which we are driven by our actualizing tendency to become what we potentially are. How much we realize our potentials depends to a large extent on how favorable the conditions of our world are to healthy human development.

Rogers's (1961, 1980) response to those who claim his is a deterministic stance is that the inborn forward movement of the actualizing tendency is away from external control toward an **experiential freedom** (an inner sense that we are free to live our lives in the manner we choose). Because we are rational, choosing beings, we can, to the degree that we perceive and experience a sense of freedom, transcend our biological and environmental influences. By recognizing our creative ability, Rogers (1961) stands with the existentialists and moderates on the issue of biological and/or social determinants of behavior. Our sense of being free is an inextricable part of our inherent actualizing tendency that, in turn, can only be initiated by stimuli from our environment.

Number and Weight Assigned to Motivational Concepts

As Rogers's resolution of the previous issue indicated, there is but one all-encompassing master motivational construct: the actualizing tendency—an inherent, sovereign drive to actualize, maintain, and enhance our potentials. The actualizing tendency is rooted in the physiological processes of our bodies and encompasses all our needs from the most basic maintenance needs (such as air, water, food, and shelter) to the most complex and sophisticated enhancement needs (such as autonomy, self-reliance, freedom, and creativity). Rogers sees this forward-moving life force, this tenacity to become, in all living things.

Unlike Freud's instincts, Rogers's actualizing tendency does not seek tension reduction. Rather, the full expression of the actualizing tendency is sought through tension increase. Its direction is forward. Its understanding is in terms of fulfillment of **inherent potentialities** (all capacities and talents that serve to maintain and enhance life). It is tenacious, purposeful, and when not thwarted by too-powerful outside forces, it is positive and constructive. Further, Rogers (1959, 1961, 1980) asserts, the actualizing tendency is to be trusted, for there is nothing inherent in human nature that is evil or pathogenic. All potentials present at birth are innately good.

The degree to which we fulfill our potentials, then, is contingent upon our physical, social, and cultural environments. The actualizing tendency, Rogers reminds us, requires favorable external conditions if it is to flourish. The healthful movement of the actualizing tendency is away from external control and toward an experiential freedom. Only to the degree that we experience a **sense of freedom** ("an inner, subjective feeling that we can think independently, live authentically, determine our own values and direction, and accept the consequences of our choices and actions")—can we transcend our biological and environmental influences (Wallace, 1986, p. 94).

Subjective versus Objective Reality

For Rogers, there is no absolute world—at least not available to human knowledge. Rather, there is a world of multiple private realities: "millions of separate, challenging, exciting, informative, *individual* perceptions of reality" (Rogers, 1980, p. 106, emphasis in original). The worlds we live in and the realities we react to are individual creations, constructed of our individual subjective perceptions and interpretations of personal experience. There are, Rogers asserts, as many worlds of reality as there are people, and while there are many similarities, no two of us ever perceive or experience exactly the same world.

Rogers's stance on the issue of reality is clear; it is radically **phenomenological** (reality that is experienced by the individual at any given moment). Holding to a belief in a reality or in a real world is for Rogers (1980) "a luxury we *cannot* afford, [and] a myth we dare not maintain" (p. 104, emphasis in original). The real world for any one of us is a function of individual perception—it is a private, experiential world that is uniquely our own. Only we can know it fully. Further, because each of us reacts as an integrated whole to a unique world, no one of us can predict the behavior of another with any degree of certainty.

To understand another's behavior, it is necessary to view that behavior from the other's present internal frame of reference. Unlike the psychoanalysts and behaviorists who look to the past for the causative factors of current behavior, Rogers looks for *present* perceptions and interpretations of current conditions, or in the case of ongoing behavior, for *present* anticipations of future conditions.

Early versus Continuous Development

It will be recalled that Rogers's theory emerged from his observations in therapy. Person-centered therapy does not draw upon instinctual urges or drives (i.e., Freud, Chapter 2), it does not focus on a pre-species psychic residue (i.e., Jung, Chapter 4), nor does it relate human development to the history of humankind (i.e., Fromm, Chapter 6). As a therapist first, Rogers was much more interested in learning how he could help his clients lead happier and more effective lives than he was in personality development per se. In short, his early focus was more on *change* than on development, more on the *process of growth* than on any stages or passages of life. It is not surprising, then, that Rogers apportioned little space in his theoretical writings to the early development of human personality.

While Rogers did recognize a number of developmental periods—periods of genetically determined biological changes and culturally determined social growth—he did not identify specific critical life stages. Neither did he propose any developmental timetable (Holdstock & Rogers, 1977). When asked about this, Rogers (in Evans, 1975) said he believed it "somewhat artificial to divide the development of the child into hard-and-fast stages" (p. 8). Human development is continuous and will occur whenever conditions are favorable, regardless of our age or personal history.

Of far more importance to Rogers was the gradual development of the image the child carried of him- or herself and the effect that picture seemed to have on the child's feelings of worth and behavior. Early childhood especially interested Rogers, because he believed it to be the period when the construction of the self-concept begins and when the universal needs for **positive regard** and for **positive self-regard** are first learned (both terms to be discussed later in this chapter).

Role Assigned to Self-Concept

When Rogers (1942) began his clinical practice, he considered the term *self* rather vague and abstract. Seeing it as a scientifically meaningless term, he left the task of defining the self to philosophers and poets. Continuous contact with clients who persisted in relating their problems, feelings, and attitudes in terms of their "selves" and who were motivated to enter and to remain in therapy in hope of becoming more their "real selves" forced Rogers to revise his view. Indeed, as Rogers's (1942, 1951, 1954, 1961, 1980) descriptions of his clients' self-structures became more explicit and organized, in regard to both attributes and functions, he recognized that a person's **self-concept** is a psychological reality, and as such, could be operationally defined and researched (Rogers & Dymond, 1954). Over the years, the self-structure became a major operational construct in Rogers's theory.

Unaware of self as a separate entity, the newborn human infant perceives and evaluates all visceral sensations and interactions with the environment through its **innate organismic valuing system** (one function of the actualizing tendency). All experiences, whether internal or external, are clearly perceived as facilitating or impeding the innate actualizing tendency. By its very nature, then, the infant *organismically knows* what is good and what is bad for its survival and enhancement, and behaves accordingly. Excluding instances of disease, genetic defects, and birth injuries, there is, in Rogers's (1961) terms, a "natural state of congruence" during the neonatal period between the organismic needs of the infant and the infant's experience.

Reacting as an organized, integrated whole to their phenomenal fields and trusting the differentiation process of their actualizing tendency, human infants begin to perceive certain of their experiences as *self-experiences.* In the process of sensing the physical experiences of their bodies and interpreting their interactions with the other people and objects in their environments, they gradually become aware of a feeling of separateness, a subjective sense of being and having a *self.* With maturity, the differentiation process becomes more complex and the self-perceptions form into an organized Gestalt that is perceived as the *I* and *me.* In short, where once there was only a self, an organism, there is now a *self-aware-of-self.*

Following the general laws and principles of perception, **self-concepts** are fluid, growing and changing with experience, but at any given moment they can also be perceived as entities with specific characteristics, traits, values, attitudes, and attributes. The human concept of self is, then, both *process* and *entity,* both *potentiality* and *actuality,* both *subject,* "I," and *object,* "me."

There is a need for congruence between the **actual self** (the organism or self-structure) and the **self-concept** (the perceived and experienced self). Experiences that are congruent with the organismic needs are perceived as enhancing to the self, valued, and assimilated into the self-concept.

There is a need, also, for congruence between the self-concept and experience. Experiences at variance with the self-concept are perceived as threatening to the self and denied symbolization. Though not in awareness, those **subceived** (nonverbalized, nonconscious) experiences that are incongruent with the self-concept are a source of disturbance (see "Psychopathology," this chapter).

The Self-Ideal Along with the development of a self-concept, children begin the construction of a **self-ideal** (the self-concept they believe they ought to have and

FIGURE 9-1   Self and Self-Ideal, ©Jeff Persons/Stock Boston

would most like to possess). In the **fully-functioning** (healthy) person the self-concept and the self-ideal practically merge. For the threatened and anxious person, the gap between the self-concept and the self-ideal widens and can be disturbing. Both the self-concept and the self-ideal are perceptions, hence, both are symbolized and in awareness.

The Need for Positive Regard   With the development of self-awareness and the infant's concept of an "I," there emerges a strong desire for **positive regard** (a basic perceived need for expressions of approval, acceptance, caring, love, and respect from others, especially from those others with the greatest significance in the life of the infant—the infant's parents or parent surrogates). According to Rogers (1951), the infant's need to experience positive regard is so great and so persistent that the infant will do almost anything to fulfill it, including the surrender of its organismic valuing system.

The Need for Self-Regard   The need for positive regard from significant others is accompanied by a need for **positive self-regard** (or self-esteem). When the positive regard received from others is unconditional, it facilitates healthy self-development and the individual is capable of giving positive regard to him- or herself. In short, the child acquires conditions of worth and is capable of becoming his or her own significant other. Capable of giving positive regard to self, he or she is not only less vulnerable to the contingent regard of others, but also more likely to risk the positive regard of others in favor of self-direction.

Conversely, when the positive regard from others is conditional ("I love you when . . ."; "I love you if. . . ."), the child's positive self-regard continues to depend on the evaluations of others. Personal worth and esteem are evaluated in terms of the conditions imposed on the child by others, and discrepancies may develop between the actualizing needs of the organism and the needs of the self-concept for positive regard. There is, then, an incongruence between the self-concept and experience, and psychological maladjustment can occur as a result of the individual's attempts to protect his or her self-concept. Experiences deemed threatening to the self-concept will be denied admission to awareness (subceived rather than perceived) or distorted to fit the self-concept. Feelings do not cease to exist when they are denied. They continue to influence behavior in various ways even though they are not in awareness. Unsymbolized (subceived) material may, for example, result in visceral reactions such as an increase in the heart rate, a cold sweat, and dizziness without awareness of the cause of the anxiety they evoke.

Conscious versus Unconscious Determinants

Determining Rogers's position on this issue proved difficult. Although his existential stance in the 1960s clearly favors conscious determinants of behavior, since the late 1970s it appears that Rogers (1977, 1980) is tempering the importance of the role of consciousness in the functioning of healthy people. Where once he hypothesized that our actualizing tendency could operate *only* when our choices were "clearly perceived" and "adequately symbolized" (Rogers, 1951), in his later years he seemed to think that when we are healthy and functioning well, our actualizing tendency may elicit actualizing behaviors even though our needs are not symbolized (Rogers, 1980). The unconscious processes may serve as dependable, intuitive directives from the actualizing tendencies of healthy persons, enabling them to be wiser than their intellects *if* they trust and act on their intuitions (Rogers, 1980).

Rogers (1980) was reluctant to predict any timetable, but he believed that our evolutionary flow may bring us other sources of self-knowledge, including sources that transcend reason. In *A Way of Being* (1980), he wrote of the possibilities of paranormal or "uncommon" perceptions and experiences and of the possibility of separate and different realities or levels of reality.

Although Rogers may have been in the process of revising his view of consciousness in the 1980s, his concept of the unconscious differs considerably from that of the psychoanalysts. Certainly it is not the animalistic, demonic, impulsive unconscious posited by Freud, nor the collective unconscious of Jung. Rogers's unconscious represents another doorway to self-knowledge. It epitomizes a part of the organismic tendency toward fulfillment, a trustworthy tendency that expresses itself "in the widest range of behaviors in response to a wide variety of needs" (Rogers, 1980, p. 123).

Determinism versus Freedom of Choice

As indicated in the discussion of previous issues, Rogers is well aware of the influences of our biology, environment, and past experiences on our behavior. Nevertheless, his experiences with the therapeutic process convince him that the unitary, motivating force of the actualizing tendency is away from external control and conditioning and toward an **experiential freedom** (an inner sense or subjective feeling that we can think independently, live authentically, determine our own values and directions, and accept the consequences of our choices and actions). Since experiential freedom is an integral part of the actualizing tendency, the more we conquer our inner fears, the more we increase our self-regard by overcoming the conditions of worth introjected during our early childhood years. Further, the more open we are to our experiences in the present, the greater is our realization of the freedom to will and choose, and the more likely we are to choose wisely.

Because Rogers believes we are inherently unpredictable (see "Heredity versus Social Determinants"), it follows that we have some degree of freedom to choose our destinies. It follows, also, that the more we facilitate or enhance our actualizing tendency, the greater the degree of freedom we experience. A healthy self-regard gives us the power to choose our attitude toward nearly any situation and to mediate consciously the influence that situation will have on us. With the freedom to choose our attitudes, we can change both the influence of past experiences and our expectations of the future. In Rogers's view, we have the potential to create our own lives.

Explanation of Learning Process

Rogers's (1969, 1983) consideration of the learning process focuses on significant, meaningful, experiential learning that includes both thinking and feeling. The person-centered learning described by Rogers (1969) is self-initiated, self-directed, self-appropriated, self-evaluated, and self-rewarding. Only this special kind of learning, he believes, gives us a sense of self-discovery and makes a difference in our attitudes, behavior, and personalities.

Rogers (1969, 1983) is sure that certain conditions must exist for person-centered learning to occur. We must experience a sense of freedom—freedom to think, to feel, to believe, to express, to act, and to follow our own paths and purposes. We are able to do this when we believe we are governed by our own curiosity and interest, when we feel trusted and respected, when we perceive and symbolize that significant others genuinely believe in us and in our capacity to learn, when we do not feel that we are being judged and evaluated, and when external threats are at a minimum. In short, we learn best when we can trust and follow our actualizing tendency. Rogers (1969) cautions us, however, that even when these conditions exist, learning may not be easy. In fact, when learning involves a threat to our self-concept, it can be painful, and our natural tendency is to resist. Learning the **process of learning** ("a continuous openness to experience and incorporation into oneself of the process of change") is "the most socially useful learning in the modern world" (Rogers, 1969, p. 163).

Rogers (1969) was convinced that education, "the most traditional, conservative, rigid, bureaucratic institution of our time," is at a crisis point (pp. vi–vii). Indeed, he believed that unless numerous innovative changes were immediately implemented, it would be impossible for education to meet the incredible challenges facing it. In *Freedom to Learn* (1969), Rogers's first book addressed specifically to educators, he called for radical educational reform at all levels. He echoed that call fourteen years later (Rogers, 1983).

It will be recalled that Rogers's person-centered theory proposes an inherent actualizing tendency and supports freedom, trust, and openness. Yet, Rogers (1969) asserts, the pervasive and implicit assumption of most educational systems in the United States is: Students cannot be trusted to pursue their own learning.

> "... it is almost uniformly true that the faculty attitude is one of mistrustful guidance. Work must be assigned; the completion of this work must be supervised; students must be continually guided and then evaluated" (Rogers, 1969, p. 171).

Such an assumption is the polar opposite of the person-centered approach to learning. A learning atmosphere based on such an attitude would damage human development, prevent meaningful learning, and kill curiosity and creativity. Priority is assigned to the curriculum rather than to student needs. Self-assessment is discouraged. There is no collaborative effort between student and teacher, no sharing of responsibility and power. Ambiguity is not tolerated, and multiple truths are not honored.

Viewed from the person-centered approach, learning has a quality of personal involvement, is self-initiated, is pervasive, and is evaluated by the learner; its essence is meaning (Rogers, 1969, p. 5). A prescribed curriculum, similar or identical assignments for all students, lectures, standard tests, and instructor evaluation and grades all make significant learning highly improbable, if not impossible.

Uniqueness versus Universality

We share with others of our species the common biological needs, processes, and predispositions of our inherent and formative actualizing tendency, as well as innumerable common stimuli from our physical, social, and cultural environments. Each of us can recall occasions when our perceptions, thoughts, and emotions were shared by others.

Person-centered theory encourages us to recognize and accept our commonalities. However, it places even greater emphasis on the importance of recognizing and accepting our uniqueness. Holdstock and Rogers (1977) encourage us to "accept that your eyes and ears and brain select, perceive, and process information differently from anyone else" (p. 143). We do not perceive our physical, social, and cultural environments the same way. We are forced to accept the idea that we live in separate realities. Although we share an inherent tendency to fulfill our potentials, in no two of us are these potentials identical. Even when potentials are similar, given the infinite possibilities of living in this world, their actualization will almost certainly occur to a greater or lesser extent.

Rogers's position on this issue might best be summarized by the following statement: "Person-centered theory recognizes the unique individuality of each person as well as the relatedness of each person to the other—the necessity of community" (Holdstock & Rogers, 1977, p. 147).

Role Assigned to Group Determinants

The position of this issue in the hierarchical order of presentation is not a true indication of its importance within Person-Centered Theory. It appears here because the writer decided that the resolutions presented earlier contribute to a fuller understanding of the importance of group membership.

As disclosed earlier, Rogers believes that we are naturally gregarious. He informs us that we need and strive for positive regard from others. Only when that positive regard is unconditional do we develop healthy self-regard. Our sources of unconditional positive regard are limited, or in some cases nonexistent. Therefore, many of us settle for conditional self-regard, thinking of ourselves as worthwhile only when we meet the expectations of others.

Formal groups, associations, and organizations normally offer conditional positive regard to the membership. There are specific conditions, whether explicitly stated or subtly implied, for belonging. Because the needs for positive regard and self-regard are expressions of our actualizing tendency, it is important for us to find at least one group that facilitates the fulfillment of these needs. Rogers (1970) thinks the **encounter group** (a planned, intensive group experience) may be one way to provide us this opportunity. He believes the encounter group offers "psychological growth promoting effects" (Rogers, 1970, p. 129), especially to those of us experiencing difficulty in adapting to change, clarifying values, overcoming feelings of depersonalization or alienation, improving interpersonal relationships, or becoming more self-reliant (pp. 172–182).

Centrality of Reinforcement

A review of the literature of Person-Centered Theory reveals that Rogers is interested in but one kind of reward—self-reward. All experiences that facilitate the inherent actualizing tendency are sought and prized. With self-rewarding activities, we are aware of an inner, subjective sense of satisfaction, as well as an increased sense of self-regard and self-efficacy. Conversely, experiences we perceive as harmful or dysfunctional to our maintenance or enhancement are not valued and are avoided.

Person-centered therapists, because of their strong commitment to self-reward, do not intentionally employ reinforcement to guide or manipulate their clients. Rather, they endeavor to provide an atmosphere in which the actualizing tendency of their clients will naturally unfold and express itself.

Examples of facilitating and rewarding experiences appear throughout this chapter, but a few seem worth repeating here: Sharing close interpersonal relationships in which each person experiences affirmation by the other; experiencing the freedom and the courage to choose and actively pursue our goals, directions, and purposes; expanding our feelings of self-worth or self-regard; and having creative experiences.

Psychological Health and Psychopathology

Psychological Health

For Rogers (1959, 1961, 1980; Chiang & Maslow, 1960), psychological healtn and the good life are concomitant with vigorous expression of the actualizing tendency. Acquiescence and defense play no part in Rogers's view of the healthy personality.

As with so many of the humanists (Maslow, Chapter 10, for example), Rogers's theory of personality emphasized the healthy or fully-functioning personality. Attempting to discover the traits of the person who had successfully completed psychotherapy and could, therefore, be said to be mentally healthy, Rogers (1961, pp. 187–196) found three primary and three secondary characteristics: an openness to experience, an ability to live in an existential fashion, and a trust in his or her own actualizing tendency; no fear of his or her own feelings, not determined, and creative.

Primary Characteristics of Psychological Health Rogers (1960, 1961, 1980) asserts that the primary characteristics of the fully-functioning or healthy person are an openness to experience, an ability to live in an existential fashion, and trust in one's own organism.

Openness to Experience. Fully-functioning persons, Rogers asserts, have no need for defenses, no need for the mechanism of subception—denial or distortion of threatening experiences. They are open to *all* experiences; that is, they perceive and accept all sensory and visceral experiences into a consistent and integrated self-structure. Because there is no breach between their self-concepts and their organisms, there appears to be little deliberation preceding their choices. The nondefensive person intuitively permits the actualizing tendency to reveal itself and quickly converts intuition into action. People who believe they are free and believe their behavior has impact, experience a sense of well-being and operate more holistically.

Ability to Live in an Existential Fashion. Fully-functioning persons live closely in touch with the present, both within themselves and in their activities in their worlds. Each moment is new. They actively reach out to life, seeking those experiences that will expand and enhance their being and acting upon their own sense of what is authentic and true. They are intrinsically motivated to become involved in exploration of the novel. They value deep relationships and strive to achieve close, genuine, fully communicative contact with other beings who are also in the process of becoming.

Choosing to be in the center rather than on the fringe of life, they encounter life in the here and now. Their commitment is to the present rather than to the

Heredity	▓	Social Determinants
Subjective Reality	▓	Objective Reality
Early Development	▓	Continuous Development
Determinism	▓	Freedom of Choice
Uniqueness	▓	Universality
Conscious Determinants	▓	Unconscious Determinants

Role Assigned to Self-Concept	From our total field we differentiate experience, formulating self-perceptions as organized, conceptual Gestalts perceived as I, me, or my. Fluid and subject to change at any given moment, the self is perceived as distinct. Indeed, self is both an entity and a process, an actuality and a potentiality.
Number and Weight Assigned to Motivational Concepts	Rooted in our biology, the actualizing tendency is an innate, sovereign, drive to actualize potential, encompassing both our most basic needs for survival and our needs for self-enhancement. All behavior is guided by this unitary force, which aims for the future and fulfillment of growth-facilitating goals.
Role Assigned to Group Determinants	We are naturally gregarious, and we need and strive for positive regard from others. Our needs for positive regard and self-regard are manifestations of our actualizing tendency, and only when we receive unconditional positive regard do we develop healthy self-regard.
Explanation of Learning Process	Person-centered learning focuses on self-discovery, the personal, meaningful, experiential learning occurring on both affective and cognitive levels. Nonthreatening environments and unconditional positive regard promote the sense of freedom requisite to self-discovery and subsequently to effective learning.
Centrality of Reinforcement	For Rogers, there is but one kind of reward: self-reward. We seek and prize experiences that facilitate our actualizing tendency and bring us a sense of satisfaction and increased self-regard.

FIGURE 9-2   Schematic Analysis of Rogers's Stance on Basic Issues

past. Being here, now, present in one place is a fact of existence and accepted. Life is too precious to the fully-functioning individual to waste dwelling on the past or anticipating the future. Life and the self are continually in flux, and both are to be lived in the immediate moment.

Trust in One's Own Organism. With feelings of self-regard, worthiness, and freedom, fully-functioning people look inward for direction and trust the wisdom of their actualizing tendency. They trust their own feelings as a source of knowledge and as a valuing system. They make their own choices and live with the consequences. As authentic beings, they reject sham and hypocrisy. They are indifferent to authority and status and opposed to inflexibility. Both personal and social values emerge from the natural unfolding of an inherent actualizing process. When in touch with their organismic experiences, they not only enhance self-knowledge and self-direction, but also social interest and social responsibility. Organismic values lead to enhancement of self and others and promote a positive evolutionary process (Rogers, 1969, p. 256).

Secondary Characteristics of Psychological Health Secondary characteristics of psychological health, according to Rogers (1960, 1961, 1980), are an openness to one's own feelings, an inner sense of freedom, and an inherent creativity.

Unafraid of One's Own Feelings. Open to all experiences and committed to live a full and productive life, fully-functioning persons accept the full range of feelings that life brings them. Life is a feeling–valuing process. The release of feelings, whether negative or positive, is both valued and supported. For fully-functioning persons, *all* feelings are a fact of existence—just as joy and elation are considered natural and expected, so are pain and suffering. Risks are an essential part of living if life is to be lived fully, and experiencing occasional disappointment and pain is a natural and accepted consequence of risk.

Not Determined. Convinced that the unitary motivating force of the actualizing tendency is away from external control and conditioning and toward an inner, experiential freedom, Rogers believes that fully-functioning persons experience an inner sense that they think independently, live authentically, and determine their own values and directions. In short, they believe they are free to choose from among the alternatives life offers. A healthy self-regard gives them the power to choose their attitudes toward nearly any situation and to mediate consciously the influence that situation will have on them. With their *perceived* freedom to choose their attitudes, they can change both the influence of past experiences and their expectations of the future. They have the potential to create their own lives and to live with the consequences of their choices and their actions.

Creative. Rogers believes that humans are inherently creative. Creativity is part of the actualizing tendency; hence the process by which the innate human capacity for creativity comes to fulfillment is the same as for the actualization of any of the organismic needs. Being fully open to all experiences is marked by a kind of naïve innocence that enables the fully-functioning person to see new forms, patterns, relationships, and possibilities, both in self and in the environment.

The fully-functioning person has two different kinds of creative resources: first, the mass of learned information, and second, an active and creative actualizing tendency which is used to determine the value of that information. The creative process in motion is one of unfolding, the drive of the innate actualizing tendency concretely and freely expressed. While the behavior of the creative person would be dependable, it would not be predictable.

Psychopathology

If, as Rogers maintained, health is the vigorous expression of the actualizing tendency, then defensively ignoring, distorting, or denying that expression is pathogenic and at the very least leads to an unnecessarily meaningless, compromising, acquiescing, and unsatisfactory life. It will be recalled that for Rogers (see "Early versus Continuous Development," this chapter), psychopathology usually begins in early childhood.

When the positive regard of parents for their children is contingent (conditionally based on their values of what their children *should* be and do, or simply due to the fact that they do not experience their children as equally lovable at all times), the children, in their striving for love and affection, are likely to introject their parents' imposed values. Rather than being guided by the bodily wisdom of their innate actualizing tendencies, as they were in infancy, these children now evaluate their visceral sensations and environmental interactions by the introjected values of others. Being other directed, Rogers asserts, is pathogenic.

By rejecting their organismic valuing systems in favor of the introjected values of others, children are in a state of incongruence and experience feelings of estrangement. The children's self-structures and experiences are no longer in harmony; their self-structures are threatened, and they find themselves ridden by anxieties that they cannot explain and disturbed by feelings they cannot understand.

In defense of their self-concepts, children are no longer open to all experiences. The most threatening of their experiences must be denied, and other experiences, though less threatening, must be distorted before being consciously perceived and admitted to awareness. Only those experiences that are congruent with the children's images of themselves can be permitted free and full perception.

The more conditional the love of the parents, the more selective their children's perceptions and the more psychopathology is likely to develop. While the denial and distortion of incongruent experiences may help children to preserve both their self-concepts and their self-regard, it is a costly defense. An inner contradiction creates a split between the flow of experience and the children's self-concepts. When this occurs, they can maintain their self-concepts only with great effort. Openness is replaced with a cognitive rigidity, often referred to by

Rogers as **intentionality.** Organismic experiences and needs may not be symbol-ized, and when such experiences are acted upon, these children are likely to disown their behavior. Fluidity is lost when experience is interpreted in absolute terms. There is a tendency to overgeneralize. The capacity to create is replaced by a desire to adjust and conform. Feelings of being manipulated by others, or by some outside force, may override experiential freedom.

When the state of incongruence between the children's experiences and self-structures is pronounced and frequent, the children are vulnerable to anxiety and they behave defensively. When incongruent experiences are traumatic, hence impossible to deny or distort, children may experience panic. When incongruent experiences are severe and obviously contradictory, they may suddenly flood awareness and shatter children's self-structures, leaving them in an anxious and disorganized state.

By this time, Rogers's attitude toward the medical model of mental illness becomes evident. Perhaps he expressed it best during an interview with Evans (a biographer):

> *I don't know whether it's quite true that mental illness is a myth, but there certainly is a great deal of mythology about it. I heartily agree with Szasz in his belief that the medical model is totally unsuited to consideration of psychotic states (Rogers, in Evans, 1975, p. 95).*

While Rogers (in Evans, 1975) wanted to remain open-minded on the question of psychosis (particularly regarding the possibility of "some hereditary genetic fac-tors which enter into certain psychoses" or the potential for the discovery of "definite psychological circumstances in which the person grew up"), he held fast to his belief that psychosis "is not satisfactorily dealt with in the doctor–patient relationship" (p. 95). Diagnostic labels, or any labels in Rogers's view, impede the establishment of a person-to-person relationship and the necessary and sufficient conditions of therapy: genuineness, acceptance, and empathy (see "Applica-tions," this chapter).

Heuristic Influences: Research Methods and Techniques

There is no doubting the heuristic value of Rogers's theories of psychotherapy and personality. His hypotheses stimulated vigorous research efforts, not only in his own field, but also in many of the related helping professions. Regarding the importance of the self and the self-concept, his ideas proved especially challeng-ing to researchers and generated a burst of empirical studies during the 1950s. Indeed, much of the research related to the therapeutic process in the 1960s and 1970s focused on the "Rogerian relationship variables"—counselor empathy, warmth, and genuineness (Boy & Pine, 1982; Coulson & Rogers, 1968; Rogers & Dymond, 1954).

Always skeptical of dogma, Rogers believed empirical validation to be the crucial test of any theory. He repeatedly reminded his students and readers that his theory, like the person he attempted to understand, was always in the process of evolving or becoming, and that his hypotheses, by definition, were tentative and subject to investigation. However, while Rogers acknowledged the value of the conventional view of psychology as *one* mode of gaining new knowledge, he insisted that it was not the *only* mode. Before attempting any review of the heuristic influence of Rogers's theories, it will be helpful to look, albeit briefly, at Rogers's (1964, 1968, 1980; Rogers & Dymond, 1954) philosophy of science, a philosophy that had a profound effect on the character of his approach to and methods of research.

Rogers' Philosophy of Science

> *I am no longer talking simply about psychotherapy, but about a point of view, a philosophy, an approach to life, a way of being, which fits any situation in which growth*—of a person, a group, or a community—*is part of the goal* (Rogers, 1980, p. ix, emphasis in original).

Though never claiming credentials as a philosopher of science, Rogers (Coulsen & Rogers, 1968) nevertheless freely expressed his ideas on the nature of science and pleaded for an expanded and modified view of the science of psychology. As early as the 1950s, and for many years thereafter, Rogers (1959, 1964, Coulsen & Rogers, 1968) openly stated his dissatisfactions with the constraints imposed by logical empiricism on the study of the person. Convinced that there was "no room for the existing, subjective person" in traditional research methodology, Rogers (1959) called for new, more appropriate models of science—a plea, incidently, that was echoed by other humanists (Maslow, Chapter 10, this volume).

It will be recalled that one of Rogers's major theoretical constructs is that humans are essentially existential–phenomenological beings who create **individual meaning structures** (internal frames of reference) that determine *and explain* their perceptions (realities), thoughts, feelings, and actions. The implications of this belief for a science of psychology are many and far reaching. For Rogers, his colleagues, and associates, any understanding of human behavior lacking insight into the individual's internal frame of reference is incomplete. As stated earlier, experiencing or perceiving is clearly phenomenological. It follows, then, that in any research of the whole person attention must be paid to subjectivity. Researchers must be committed to incorporating subjective data into their research designs and methodologies. "It implies that qualitative and quantitative strategies may differ as to the types of questions which they address, the kinds of data which they generate, and the forms of analysis they utilize" (Neimeyer & Resnikoff, 1982, p. 76).

In *Man and the Science of Man* (1968), Rogers argued that the science of psychology is unlike the science of other disciplines (e.g., chemistry, astronomy) because the subject of psychology "is man himself" and the "observer is the observed." Such a science, Rogers (Coulsen & Rogers, 1968) asserted, cannot afford to ignore subjective data. Indeed, he believed that the scientific approach taught in most graduate psychology programs in the United States actually purged scientific work of creative, subjective speculation, cutting the psychologist off from any significant discoveries. "In our desire to be rigorous, we so often strangle the newborn idea, rather than nourishing its growth and development" (Coulsen & Rogers, 1968, p. 70).

With the emphasis placed on statistical methodology rather than on meaning, far too many psychologists, Rogers was convinced, select hypotheses because tools exist to measure the observable variables at hand. In short, "the methods of testing hypotheses come to be regarded as dogmas" (Coulsen & Rogers, 1968, p. 67). Selective attention to quantifiable aspects of human behavior necessarily disregards qualitative aspects of experience, hence neglecting much that is meaningful to the practitioner-researcher.

Rogers was an advocate for combining quantitative and qualitative methods to maximize an investigation's external and internal validity, while at the same time reflecting the researcher's appreciation of the dignity, complexity, and multifaceted nature of the human condition. It is not surprising that Rogers's description of the ideal scientist closely resembles his concept of the fully-functioning person. To be fully functioning, according to Rogers (Coulsen & Rogers, 1968) the ideal scientist is open to his or her experiences and is flexible, intuitive, and creative. Furthermore, Rogers was convinced that it is impossible for the creative practitioner-researcher to be a detached observer who views all phenomena objectively. Rather, Rogers argued, he or she must be totally immersed in the phenomena under study.

Science for Rogers (Coulsen & Rogers, 1968) is essentially a human enterprise. It begins when patterns in the phenomena are first perceived, and at this point, according to Rogers, choices of values and direction are intuitive. Without the benefit of evidence, vague, intuitive ideas are nourished until testable hypotheses can be formed. Methodology plays no role in the nature of the research; the questions, the meaning, and the problem take precedence in the formulation of hypotheses.

Research Methods and Techniques

The limitation of space imposed by a single chapter makes it impossible to present an overview of the years of research conducted to confirm the hypotheses of Rogers's Person-Centered Theory of Personality. Fortunately, there is no need to do so. Over the years, several excellent and comprehensive reviews have been published. Readers interested in delving deeper into the heuristic influences of Rogers's theories of person-centered therapy and personality development are encouraged to read Rogers and Dymond (1954), which presents detailed studies of recorded therapy sessions to investigate client change, and includes pre-therapy, post-therapy, and follow-up studies of twenty-five clients; Rogers (1967), a five-year study to test the efficacy of Rogers's "necessary and sufficient" conditions of therapy (see "Applications to Psychotherapy," this chapter) on hospitalized schizophrenic patients; Rogers (1969), a three-year study of the impact of intensive groups on educational institutions; Hart and Tomlinson (1970), *New Directions in Client-Centered Therapy*; and Wexler and Rice (1974), *Innovations in Client-Centered Therapy*.

Transcriptions, Content Analysis, and Rating Scales It will be recalled that Rogers was the first to record actual counseling sessions. Initially, Rogers (Rogers & Dymond, 1954) relied on selected excerpts of client statements (e.g., self-referents) or the reported experiences of counselors to present a qualitative view of the course of therapy. He soon realized, however, that more rigorous and objective research methods were necessary to determine the effectiveness of therapy or to demonstrate change in self-referents. Content analysis and rating scales were the two general methods employed to meet this need. By accumulating sets of exact transcriptions of his recordings and formulating sets of categories or rating scales, empirical studies of the therapeutic relationship, process, change, and outcome were possible.

Most of the research conducted by Rogers and his associates (colleagues and advanced graduate students) was designed to investigate the process and outcomes of person-centered therapy. Rogers (1967) and his associates later selected research instruments that would measure subtle, subjective personality changes as objectively as possible. They chose, for example, such instruments as the Thematic Apperception Test (TAT), the Self–Other Attitude Scale (S–O Scale), the Willoughby Emotional Maturity Scale (E-M Scale), and the Q-technique. Brief descriptions of each follow.

Content Analysis. Consistent with Rogers's phenomenological stance, that the client is the center of perceptions, interpretations, knowledge, emotions, and behaviors, Rogers and his associates developed self-referent categories that were then used to classify and count the client's recorded verbalizations. One of the first to employ content analysis to the transcripts of recorded counseling sessions, Raimy (1948) developed six self-reference categories and found that, as clients progressed successfully in therapy, their self-referents changed from a preponderance of "disapproving" or "ambivalent" referents at the beginning of therapy, to increasing "self-approval" with mounting ambivalence during therapy, to a preponderance of "self-approval referents at the end of therapy." Conversely, the majority of the self-referents of clients whose progress in therapy was not successful continued to fall into the "ambivalent" and "disapproving" categories in all stages of therapy.

Rating Scales. Process rating scales have played a prominent role in client-centered research, particularly those rating scales that can be applied to transcriptions of recorded counseling sessions. Perhaps the most ambitious research project to make use of rating scales is Rogers's (1967) research on the person-centered therapeutic approach with schizophrenic patients. Rogers and his collaborators developed rating scales to measure accurate empathy (Truax, in Rogers, 1967, pp. 555–568), therapists' attitudes (Kiesler, in Rogers, 1967, pp. 581–584), and the manner of relating (Gendlin, in Rogers, 1967, pp. 603–611).

Q-technique. Another rating scale, The Q-technique, developed by William Stephenson (1953), consists of 100 self-referent statements printed on 3-in. × 5-in. cards. Subjects are requested to sort the cards into piles from "most like me" to "least like me," under either "self" or "ideal self." The sorts, thrown by the client into specific categories (either nine or eleven) with fixed distributions, permit specific perceptions about both the self and ideal self to be quantified and compared, making possible a "self-ideal discrepancy score." Moreover, by throwing self Q-sorts at various periods (before, during, and after therapy, for example), it is possible to determine changes in the client's perceived-self over time. For example, clients' perceived-self and ideal-self Q-sorts, thrown before therapy, showed considerably greater self-ideal discrepancies than those sorts thrown after therapy (Rogers & Dymond, 1954).

Applications to Psychotherapy

Therapeutic Goals

Rogers (1951, 1960, 1961, 1980) believes the primary goal of the therapist is to provide a climate that facilitates the innate actualizing tendency of the client. Essentially, a relationship is created in which the client is encouraged to grow, to become fully-functioning. The counselor–client relationship is the essence of the Rogerian therapeutic process. Everything that happens in therapy occurs within this special person-to-person, I–Thou relationship. To the uninitiated or to the therapist accustomed to working in a system in which clear behavioral objectives and outcomes are known in advance, this goal may appear vague, unsystematic, and unscientific. However, those familiar with the basic principles of Rogers's theory realize that person-to-person therapy is an open system of psychotherapy. It deals with the inner subjective lives of people, their perceptions, feelings, attitudes, beliefs, values, hopes, fears, and aspirations.

Person-Centered Therapy is a process of personal exploration and discovery. Specific individualized client objectives or outcomes emerge from the process. The direction of exploration and the specific nature of the client's discoveries are not known by either the client or the therapist at the start of the process. Since the client is in the best position to know which directions best fit his or her needs, the therapist chooses to be a facilitator rather than a director.

The therapist's goals are directly related to the therapist's belief in the actualizing tendency and resulting attitudes toward his or her clients. To facilitate the client's awareness of and trust in his or her inner direction, the person-centered therapist expresses an attitude of uncompromising trust or faith in the actualizing tendency of the client. The therapist believes that the client's innate predisposition to become is a constant therapeutic ally, that the client's will to health is ever present, positive, and predictable. Therapy, then, promotes conditions that facilitate natural growth and development. The therapist's attitudes and intent become the criteria for judging both method and technique.

Therapeutic Relationship

Even a brief review of Rogers's resolutions of the eleven basic issues reveals that he is convinced that an intensely personal and subjective person-to-person relationship is the heart of the therapeutic process. Further, it is evident that Rogers believes that three conditions are directly related to the therapist's attitudes and intent, and all must be present and communicated in the relationship if the therapist is to create a growth-promoting atmosphere for the client. Since these three conditions are considered both *necessary* and *sufficient* for an effective psychotherapeutic relationship, they merit special attention.

Genuineness or Congruence   The first of the necessary and sufficient conditions of psychotherapy Rogers calls genuineness, realness, or congruence. In *A Way of Being,* he writes: "The term 'transparent' catches the flavor of this condition" (Rogers, 1980, p. 115). For the therapist it is the risk of letting the self go, of giving up roles and façades, so that the interaction with the client becomes an encounter with a significant other whose intention it is to be helpful. It is a matter of being genuinely and immediately present and accessible in the relationship so that the therapist is

> *without any conscious thought about it, without any apprehension or concern as to where this will lead, without any type of diagnostic or analytic thinking, without any cognitive or emotional barriers to a complete "letting go" in understanding (Rogers, in Corsini, 1978, p. 65).*

The person-centered therapist literally launches him- or herself into the process, trusting fully the outcome.

The implication of the therapist's self as the instrument of therapy is rather awesome. There is an undeniable obligation of the person-centered therapist to examine his or her attitudes and intent to know, refine, and improve the self as an instrument. The method and techniques of the person-centered therapist are to be without method and techniques, to be therapeutically present and to remain congruent in the relationship.

There can be no contradiction between what the therapist is and what he or she says or does; however, this does not mean that the therapist impulsively shares all feelings with the client. Self-disclosures must be appropriate. The therapist must be genuinely moved to express personal feelings and willing to take responsibility for the feelings being expressed. Disclosure is often reserved for those feelings that are persistent and, if left unexpressed, would block the therapist from being fully present in the person-to-person relationship.

Acceptance or Unconditional Positive Regard   The second necessary and sufficient condition of the therapeutic relationship, according to Rogers, is acceptance or unconditional positive regard. Rogers (1961, 1980) defines acceptance as a deep and genuine caring or prizing, without reservations, conditions, judgments, or evaluations. With a firm belief in the client's innate goodness as a human being, regardless of his or her present values, beliefs, feelings, or behaviors, the therapist communicates a respect for the client's individuality and complexity, and a faith in the client's potential and capacity for growth.

Acceptance cannot be communicated by any learned method or technique. The therapist must move into the client's private phenomenal world and then communicate his or her experiencing of that world to the client so that the client may come to a deeper level of understanding of his or her self than was previously possible. Rogers was convinced that in the person-to-person relationship the attitude of the therapist will be communicated to and eventually perceived by the client, whether genuine or false, positive or negative, constructive or destructive. For therapists to communicate caring they must genuinely care, and to communicate acceptance they must genuinely accept.

If the person-centered therapist should experience negative feelings or attitudes toward a client, making it impossible to offer that client unconditional positive regard, immediate self-examination is required. If after an honest and thorough search of self, these negative feelings persist, authenticity requires that the therapist own and disclose them, or refer the client to a therapist capable of offering the necessary conditions of therapy. For the person-centered therapist to play a role, or to act as if the proper attitudes were present when they are not, is not only unethical but also destructive to both the therapist and the client.

Accurate Empathic Understanding   The third of the three necessary and sufficient conditions of therapy is accurate empathic understanding. Empathy is an accurate sensing of the moment-by-moment feelings and personal meanings of the client. It requires therapists to suspend *temporarily* their own needs, values, meanings, and expectations so that they can immerse themselves fully in their clients' inner subjective worlds. It is, Rogers asserts, *as if* the person-centered therapist were the client, but he warns that the therapist must never lose sight of the *as if* quality of the relationship. Anthony Barton, in *Three Worlds of Therapy* (1974), writes:

> *The highly focused, specialized attentiveness and valuing of the person's feeling-life is an extraordinary transformation of the field of personal interaction. . . . The feeling-self is not blindly affirmed but is developed, fostered, articulated, differentiated, spoken of, and spoken to. Therapist and client together enliven and illuminate that flow of feeling that the client concretely finds within himself (p. 204).*

The therapist's self, therefore, remains the therapist's referent throughout the therapeutic relationship. Again, "the self-as-instrument is as important in the communication of empathy as it is in the communication of genuineness and acceptance" (Wallace, 1986, p. 99).

While the self of the therapist is the therapist's referent, verification of empathic understanding can only be confirmed by client. It is the client who must *feel* understood. Empathy also communicates acceptance and caring. When truly understood, clients feel that they have at last found someone who cares enough to listen, who knows what and how they are feeling, and who accepts them as they are, without judging, evaluating, and rejecting them.

Rogers cautions person-centered therapists that they are not immune to the power of the relationships they establish with their clients. When genuineness, acceptance, and empathy are present, the climate of the therapeutic relationship is growth promoting for both participants. The more involvement person-centered therapists offer in the relationship, the more they benefit from it. Conversely, becoming an ineffective or poor person-centered therapist may indeed be detrimental to both the therapist and the client.

Initial Procedures and Strategies

There is only one procedure in person-centered therapy: the establishment of a facilitative relationship, a therapeutic climate that promotes change and growth in its participants. The therapist's strategy throughout therapy is the communication of the therapist's attitudes and intent, particularly those considered essential to effective therapy: genuineness or congruence, acceptance or unconditional positive regard, and a deep empathic understanding.

Initiating Therapy. In the person-to-person approach to therapy, the therapist usually opens the first session by saying: "This is our first session together; I hope we can use this hour to get to know each other better, to understand one another in some meaningful way." Not only does the therapist hope to establish a here-and-now presence with this statement, he or she also wants to introduce the idea that the relationship is the process of therapy. Further, by expressing an interest in the client as a person, the therapist avoids focusing on the client as a person with a problem or giving the client the impression that the therapist's intent is to solve the client's problems. This is the therapist's first attempt to communicate the attitudes of genuine interest and caring. Thereafter, the direction of therapy is decided by the client.

Client Expectations and Structuring. Person-centered therapists are well aware that their clients' initial perceptions of them and of therapy are influenced significantly by the expectations they bring to the first counseling session. However, rather than attempting to describe the therapeutic relationship or process, person-centered therapists count on the client's direct sensory experiences of the process to structure the person-centered approach. Many practitioners believe that any attempt to describe intellectually the character and purpose of the person-to-person relationship or the process of the person-centered approach is needless and may impede the process of therapy.

Most person-centered therapists agree that therapy is possible only when the client decides personally to enter therapy or, if referred, to remain in therapy. Little can be achieved if the client is forced into therapy, or if the client is there only to please someone else.

Course of Therapy

When the therapist manages to provide the necessary and sufficient conditions of the intensive relationship just cited, and when the client can permit him- or herself to experience these conditions, Rogers (1951, 1961, 1967, 1980) claims that a natural, observable process of client change begins. The client becomes less defensive and more open to perceptions. Experiences once distorted or denied because they threatened the self-concept are permitted accurate symbolization and are subsequently integrated. Integration results in greater congruence between the self and experience for the client. In addition to increased openness to new experience, the client becomes more spontaneous and better able to live fully in the moment.

Experiencing acceptance and unconditional regard from the therapist, the client develops an increasing positive regard for him- or herself as a person of worth. The client develops confidence in his or her ability to form standards and to be self-directing. The client learns to trust his or her decisions, particularly as perceptions become more differentiated and as goals and ideals become more realistic and achievable. The client becomes more objective and rational and less emotional. Finally, the client begins to experience unconditional positive regard for others and, though less likely than before to conform, becomes more tolerant of customs and traditions.

Positive client movement in person-centered therapy is away from façades and the rigid, tyrannical "shoulds" or "musts" and toward greater openness and trust in the inner bodily wisdom of the actualizing tendency. Client growth in the course of therapy is best summarized by Rogers (1961): "This openness of awareness to what exists at *this moment* in *oneself* and in *the situation* is, I believe, an important element in the description of the person who emerges from therapy" (p. 116, emphasis in original).

The Process Scale in Individual Therapy Rogers (1961, pp. 132–156) developed a process scale of seven behavior stages that has been used to assess client change in the course of therapy. Client behavioral stages covered by the process scale are:

1. Feelings and personal meanings,
2. Manner of experiencing,
3. Degree of incongruence,

4. Communication of self,
5. Manner in which experience is constructed,
6. Relationship to problem, and
7. Manner of relating.

With the process scale, Rogers and his colleagues were able to determine the current behavior stage of a client by analyzing the content of a taped therapy session. Periodic analysis of the seven process stages assists the therapist in assessing both the amount and the rate of client growth during therapy.

Extended Applications

A remarkable characteristic of Rogers's person-centered approach, especially when viewed over nearly four decades, is its ever-widening scope of applicability. Initially client-centered therapy was formulated as an individual therapeutic approach (Rogers, 1942, 1951); its basic concepts and methods were later demonstrated to be relevant to all levels of education (Rogers, 1969, 1983, in Robinson, 1985). Still later, the application of Rogers's theory was expanded to intensive small-group experiences, specifically T-groups and encounter groups (Rogers, 1970). Rogers (1972, 1974a, 1974b, 1977, 1980) eventually came to believe that his person-centered approach could also be applied to nearly every aspect of the human condition, including marriage and family life, administration, social work, the problems of minority groups, and interracial and intercultural relationships. Moreover, Rogers (1974a, 1974b, 1980, 1984) believed and set out to prove that his person-centered theory would, in time and to a greater or lesser degree, effect needed changes in social conditions at national, international, and even global levels.

The Intensive Group Experience

For Rogers (1980), the need for interpersonal relationships is a human imperative that is firmly rooted in the inherent actualizing tendency of the species. Biologically and psychologically, there are organismic needs that can be satisfied *only* through positive, healthy interactions with other humans. Both personal and species survival depend on the ability to initiate, develop, and stabilize interpersonal relationships.

It will be recalled (see "necessary and sufficient conditions of counseling and psychotherapy" above) that Rogers believed the kind of persons humans become depends to a large degree on the manner in which they relate to others and the nature of the relationships they experience and maintain. To the extent that their relationships reflect genuineness, acceptance, caring, and empathic understanding, they become more actualized, for healthy human relationships are affirmations of humanness. It will be recalled, too, (see "The Need for Positive Regard," this chapter) that with the emergence of self-awareness, humans desire and strive for the positive regard of others. Further it was noted that the ability to give oneself positive regard is achieved only when the positive regard received from others is perceived as unconditional.

The quest of the actualizing tendency to become fully functioning never ends; as a continuous process there are always potentials awaiting fulfillment and possibilities that are as yet untried. Conceptualizing growth as a continuous process, Rogers did not limit the application of his theory of therapy to the emotionally disturbed. Indeed, the actualizing tendency, by its very nature, especially drives the healthy person to seek further growth and development. Rogers (1969, 1970, 1977, 1983) was certain that when his theoretical constructs for therapy were applied to the intensive group experience by a skillful group facilitator, the experience held great promise for filling the void created by a dehumanizing technological society. This is particularly so for relatively healthy persons. In brief, the necessary and sufficient conditions of therapy mentioned above are the same conditions that must be present in all healthy human relationships, whether these are relationships between husband and wife, parent and child, teacher and student, employer and employee, management and labor, minister and parishioner, politician and constituent, as well as racial or intercultural groups and even the diplomats of hostile nations.

Trusting the Group Process   As the person-centered therapist trusts in the actualizing tendency of the client, the person-centered group facilitator trusts in the intensive group experience. Whether the client is an individual or a group, positive growth will naturally occur when certain conditions are present and experienced. It is a matter of being genuinely present, accepting, and prizing. There is no need to teach or explicitly to foster group growth. The group facilitator focuses completely on the immediate feeling-sensing selves of the group members. By not taking charge or accepting the responsibility of leadership, the group facilitator not only does not interfere with the natural unfolding of the intensive group experience, but also expresses a strong faith in the capacity of the group to discover its own direction and purpose and to assume responsibility for its own decisions and actions.

Stages of the Group Process   The group process is similar to the therapeutic process of individual therapy; however, rather than seven stages, Rogers (1970) lists fifteen stages for the group process. These are:

1. Milling around,
2. Resistance to personal expression,
3. Expression of past feelings,
4. Expression of negative feelings,
5. Expression and exploration of personally meaningful material,
6. Expression of immediate interpersonal feelings,
7. Development of a therapeutic or healing capacity,
8. Self-acceptance,

9. Breaking down of façades,
10. Honest feedback,
11. Confrontation,
12. The basic encounter,
13. Helping one another outside the group,
14. Expression of positive feelings and closeness, and
15. Behavior change.

Education

Concerned with the traditional programs and teaching–learning approaches in counseling psychology that centered almost exclusively on intellectual processes, Rogers (1969, 1980, 1983) first extended the application of his theory to education. The changes he advocated for education at all levels were revolutionary and entailed "turning the politics of education upside down" (Rogers, 1980, p. 306).

> *I have days when I think the educational institutions at all levels are doomed and perhaps we would be well advised to bid them farewell—state-required curricula, compulsory attendance, tenured professors, hours of lectures, grades, degrees, and all that—and let true learning begin to blossom outside the stifling hallowed walls (Rogers, 1980, pp. 268–269).*

Rogers viewed most of the prevalent practices in education as antithetical to meaningful learning; indeed, he was convinced that should these practices be permitted to continue they would damage human development and kill curiosity and creativity (see "Explanation of Learning Process," this chapter).

Rogers (1980) was well aware that attempting the changes he advocated (or even tentative steps toward them) would polarize both faculty and students and create turbulence both within and outside the educational institution. He knew he was proposing radical reforms of prevalent practices with long traditional histories. And he knew resistance would be great.

Marriage and Its Alternatives

For Rogers (1972), conventional marriage as we know it in the United States is also at a crisis point. Divorce statistics provide ample evidence that many couples are ill prepared for coping with the complexities of marriage and family life. Convinced that an important contribution of person-centered theory was the ethical base it offered to people living together and raising a family, Rogers (1972) explored various forms of couple unions in the United States in the 1970s and concluded that the impact of person-centeredness held particular relevance for the special risks of intimacy and partnership with another person.

In *Becoming Partners*, Rogers (1972) proposed that the answer to a successful relationship would be found in the couple's commitment to the *process* of living together; that is, the process of an open, considerate, and courteous struggle that is essential to any long-term relationship. Such a relationship, Rogers asserts, offers a great deal of freedom for both partners. While there is commitment to the union, there is also commitment to "separate but intertwined pathways of growth." Each partner facilitates the growth of the other.

Recent Efforts to Extend Applications

As Rogers's confidence in the impact of applying the principles of person-centered theory grew, he limited his activity to encounter groups that promised significant social impact. In his seventies, Rogers (1974b) wrote that he was involved in a program with more than 200 medical educators for the humanizing of medical education (p. 122). In that same article, he reported that he helped to sponsor and take part in interracial and intercultural groups, the most difficult composed of Catholics, Protestants, and English in Belfast, Northern Ireland. He worked with a group involved in the drug culture that included narcotics agents, individuals addicted to drugs, and a convicted pusher. "There were blacks and whites, young and middle-aged, ghetto products and members of the middle class" (Rogers, 1974b, p. 121). In 1978, Rogers was involved in a workshop in Spain that included 170 people from twenty-two different nations. He served as a group facilitator for workshops in the State Department to improve communication between staff members to enhance the possibility of communication between ambassadors and staff members and the natives of the host countries.

Rogers viewed the encounter group approach as a growing counterforce to the dehumanization of our culture. Moreover, he saw it as a way to help people adapt to change, particularly institutional change. And he found the encounter group approach especially helpful in the merger of two large industries.

In his later years, Rogers (in Heppner, M. E. Rogers, & Lee, 1984) was involved in encounter workshops in South Africa, Brazil, Japan, Switzerland, Germany, and England. Shortly before his death he toured the Soviet Union, "where he demonstrated client-centered therapy and led encounter groups with English-speaking Russians" (*New York Times, 136,* 47,042, p. 12).

Critique

Rogers was accused repeatedly of being antiintellectual, naïve, overly religious, and simplistic. The most vocal of his critics seemed to come from his own profession. The accolades Rogers received for being the first to take audio-taping equipment into the counseling session, then using the tapes for empirical investigations and teaching were accompanied by disproving criticisms because much of his research was based on his clients' self-reports, a notoriously unreliable data source. Academic experimental psychologists, especially, pointed to methodological errors in Rogers's research: lack of control groups or the use of control subjects who were not candidates for therapy, failing to control for placebo effects, inappropriate statistics, heavy reliance on correlational studies, limited research instruments, and lack of follow-up studies for recidivism.

The initial defensive strategy of the medical profession was simply to ignore him. When this proved ineffective, they attempted to withhold the title of psychotherapist from psychologists on the grounds of credentials, specifically medical training. Educators accused Rogers of crossing disciplinary boundaries without adequate training, background, or understanding of teaching and learning processes.

Some of the strongest criticisms, and perhaps those most justified, were:

1. That Rogers ignored the unconscious, despite the evidence accumulated over a period of eighty years by the psychoanalysts that unconscious determinants motivate human behavior;

2. that his theory could not explain how some people who had not experienced unconditional positive regard managed to become fully-functioning; and

3. that although Rogers assumes a phenomenological stance, which in the extreme is deterministic, he grants the individual both the will and the freedom to choose—in brief, to become self-directing.

While the first criticism (ignoring the unconscious) may have been justified at one time, it seems less so today. In *A Way of Being* (1980), Rogers changed his view of the unconscious. Where once he hypothesized that the actualizing tendency could operate only when choices were "clearly perceived" and "adequately symbolized" (Rogers, 1951), at this point in his life Rogers seemed to think that when the individual is healthy and functioning well, the actualizing tendency may elicit actualizing behaviors even though organismic needs are not symbolized. Unlike Freud, who viewed unconscious forces as impulsive, asocial, and in conflict with conscious forces, Rogers believed unconscious processes can serve as dependable, intuitive directives, enabling healthy individuals to be wiser than their intellects if they trust in and act on their intuitions. In short, Rogers's unconscious represents another doorway to self-knowledge. It epitomizes a part of the organismic tendency toward fulfillment, a trustworthy tendency that expresses itself "in the widest range of behaviors in response to a wide variety of needs" (Rogers, 1980, p. 123).

The third criticism (the determinism of phenomenology versus freedom of choice) addressed briefly by Wallace (1986) who points out that "[F]rom a phenomenological stance, when the freedom to choose is perceived and experienced by the client, it is, for that client, reality" (p. 106). He goes on to say: "Freedom to choose may be a reality only when perceived and experienced, and when it is thus, that individual can, at least to a limited degree, transcend the determinism of conditioning" (p. 106).

Rogers's legacy, then, is an innovative, organismic growth psychology that is anchored firmly in a philosophy of life and pervades every aspect of human relations, whether between individuals, groups, communities, or nations. Deceptively simple, his theoretical concepts are loaded with radical implications that become apparent only when carried to their logical extreme (Farson, 1974). Rogers founded a new and revolutionary approach to counseling, personality development, and education that helped to establish Third Force Psychology. In addition to counselors, psychotherapists, and educators, Rogers's theoretical constructions have been incorporated and applied by administrators, social workers, nurses, psychiatrists, parents, religious leaders, and law enforcement and correctional officers. The encounter group movement of the 1960s and 1970s was based on Rogers's work and example. Most recently, diplomats, the military, and political leaders are applying Rogers's ideas.

Annotated Bibliography

Rogers introduced his revolutionary therapeutic techniques in *Counseling and Psychotherapy* (1942). With its emphasis on the actualizing and formative tendencies of humans, many considered this book to be the first viable alternative to psychoanalysis. It was also the first book to present typescripts of actual recorded counseling sessions, dispelling many of the myths of the therapeutic process.

Considered by most to be Rogers's major theoretical work, *Client-Centered Therapy: Its Current Practice, Implications and Theory* (1951) is Rogers's first attempt to present his theory of human personality and behavior. His nineteen basic propositions have remained fundamentally unchanged over the years, though the applications of these propositions have changed significantly.

Undoubtedly Rogers's most popular book, *On Becoming a Person* (1961) soon established Rogers as a major spokesman for the humanistic movement. In addition to his personal experiences as a therapist, Rogers gives the reader his view of the fully-functioning person. Included also is Rogers's critique of B. F. Skinner's theory of operant conditioning. Daniel Goleman, a writer for the *New York Times* (36, 47,042, p. 12) writes: "the book was to become the bible of the humanistic psychology movement." Though Rogers might have found this a bit strong, *On Becoming a Person* is a classic in the literature of humanistic psychology and a good introduction to Rogers's thinking.

Freedom to Learn (1969) represents Rogers's application of person-centered theory to the classroom. In this book Rogers explains the person-centered learning process and emphasizes the educator's role in creating a facilitative learning atmosphere. The book is addressed to educators, but students interested in personality development will find it most helpful. Students who find this book challenging are directed to *Freedom to Learn for the 80's* (1983).

In *A Way of Being* (1980), Rogers has become more conscious of the wide applicability of the person-centered approach. His interests cover a much wider social context, including institutional change, labor–management disputes, and interracial and intercultural struggles on community, national, and even global levels. There is an especially interesting chapter on Rogers's description of the person of the future, and the book represents Rogers's shift to a philosophical approach to life. It is here that Rogers introduces a revised view of the unconscious, particularly the role of the unconscious in determining the behavior of the healthy individual.

References and Suggested Readings

Barton, A. (1974). *Three worlds of therapy: Freud, Jung and Rogers.* Palo Alto, CA: Mayfield.

Boy, A. V., & Pine, G. J. (1982). *Client-centered counseling: A renewal.* Boston: Allyn and Bacon.

Cartwright, D. (1957). Annotated bibliography of research and theory construction in client-centered therapy. *Journal of Counseling Psychology, 4,* pp. 82–100.

Chiang, H. & Maslow, A. H. (Eds.). (1960). *The healthy personality: Readings* (2nd ed.). New York: D. Van Nostrand.

Coulson, W. B., & Rogers, C. R. (Eds.). (1968). *Man and the science of man.* Columbus, OH: Charles E. Merrill.

Devine, E., Held, M., Vinson, J., & Welsh, G. (Eds.). (1983). *Thinkers of the twentieth century: A biographical, bibliographical and critical dictionary.* (pp. 483–484) Detroit: Book Tower.

Evans, R. I. (1975). *Carl Rogers: The man and his ideas.* New York: E. P. Dutton.

Farson, R. (1974). Carl Rogers: Quiet revolutionary. *Education, 95*(2), pp. 197–203.

Frick, W. B. (1971). *Humanistic psychology: Interviews with Maslow, Murphy, and Rogers.* Columbus, OH: Charles E. Merrill.

Goleman, D. (1961). On Becoming a Person, Carl R. Rogers. *The New York Times 36,* 47,042, p. 12.

Hart, J. T., & Tomlinson, T. M. (Eds.). (1970). *New directions in client-centered therapy.* Boston: Houghton Mifflin.

Heppner, P. P., Rogers, M. E., & Lee, L. A. (1984). Carl Rogers: Reflections on his life. *Journal of Counseling and Development, 63*(1), pp. 14–20.

Holdstock, T. L., & Rogers, C. R. (1977). Person-centered therapy. In R. Corsini (Ed.), *Current personality theories* (2nd ed.). Itasca, IL: F. E. Peacock.

Kirschenbaum, H., & Henderson, V. L. (Eds.). (1989a). *The Carl Rogers reader.* Boston: Houghton Mifflin.

Kirschenbaum, H., & Henderson, V. L. (Eds.). (1989). *Carl Rogers: Dialogues.* Boston: Houghton Mifflin.

Kilpatrick, W. K. (1985). Carl Rogers's quiet revolution: Therapy for the masses. *Christianity Today, 29*(16), pp. 21–24.

May, R., Rogers, C., Maslow, A., & others. (1986). *Politics and innocence.* Dallas, TX: Saybrook.

Meador, B. D., & Rogers, C. R. (1979). Person-centered therapy. In R. Corsini (Ed.). *Current psychotherapies* (2nd ed.). Itasca, IL: F. E. Peacock.

Moritz, C. (Ed.). (1962). *Current biography yearbook.* New York: H. W. Wilson, pp. 357–358.

Neimeyer, G., & Resnikoff, A. (1982). Qualitative strategies in counseling research. *The Counseling Psychologist, 10*(4), pp. 75–85.

Patterson, C. H. (1980). *Theories of counseling and psychotherapy* (3rd ed.). New York: Harper & Row.

Raimy, V. C. (1943). The self-concept as a factor in counseling and personality organization. Unpublished doctoral dissertation. Ohio State University.

Rogers, C. R. (1939). *The clinical treatment of the problem child.* Boston: Houghton Mifflin.

Rogers, C. R. (1942). *Counseling and psychotherapy: Newer concepts in practice.* Boston: Houghton Mifflin.

Rogers, C. R. (1951). *Client-centered therapy: Its current practice, implications, and theory.* Boston: Houghton Mifflin.

Rogers, C. R. (1959). A theory of therapy, personality, and interpersonal relations as developed in the client-centered framework. In S. Koch (Ed.), *Psychology: A study of a science,* Vol. III, pp. 184–256. New York: McGraw–Hill.

Rogers, C. R. (1960). My philosophy of interpersonal relationships and how it grew. In H. Chaing and A. H. Maslow (Eds.). *The healthy personality, readings* (2nd ed.). New York: D. Van Nostrand.

Rogers, C. R. (1961). *On becoming a person.* Boston: Houghton Mifflin.

Rogers, C. R. (1964). Toward a science of the person. In T. W. Wann (Ed.). *Behaviorism and phenomenology: Contrasting bases for modern psychology.* Chicago: University of Chicago Press.

Rogers, C. R. (Ed.). (1967). *The therapeutic relationship and its impact: A study of psychotherapy with schizophrenics.* Madison, WI: University of Wisconsin Press.

Rogers, C. R. (1969). *Freedom to learn: A view of what education might become.* Columbus, OH: Charles E. Merrill.

Rogers, C. R. (1970). *On encounter groups.* New York: Harper and Row.

Rogers, C. R. (1972). *Becoming partners: Marriage and its alternatives.* New York: Delacorte.

Rogers, C. R. (1974a). Remarks on the future of client-centered therapy. In D. A. Wexler and N. Rice. (Eds.). *Innovations in client-centered therapy.* New York: John Wiley & Sons.

Rogers, C. R. (1974b). In retrospect: Forty-six years. *American Psychologist, 29*(2), pp. 115–123.

Rogers, C. R. (1977). *Carl Rogers on personal power: Inner strength and its revolutionary impact.* New York: Delacorte.

Rogers, C. R. (1978). Persons or science? A philosophical question. In R. J. Corsini. (Ed.). *Readings in current personality theories* (pp. 64–79). Itasca, IL: F. E. Peacock.

Rogers, C. R. (1980). *A way of being.* Boston: Houghton Mifflin.

Rogers, C. R. (1983). *Freedom to learn for the 80's.* Columbus, OH: Charles E. Merrill.

Rogers, C. R. (1985). Toward a more human science of the person. *Journal of Humanistic Psychology, 25*(4), pp. 7–24.

Rogers, C. R. (1987). Rogers, Kohut, and Erickson: A personal perspective on some similarities and differences. In J. K. Zeig. (Ed.). *The evolution of psychotherapy.* New York: Brunner/Mazel.

Rogers, C. R., & Dymond, R. F. (Eds.). (1954). *Psychotherapy and personality change: Coordinated studies in the client-centered approach.* Chicago: University of Chicago Press.

Rogers, C. R., & Stevens, B. (1967). *Person to person: The problem of being human.* Lafayette, CA: Real People Press.

Stephenson, W. (1953). *The study of behavior: Q-technique and its methodology.* Chicago: University of Chicago Press.

Wallace, W. A. (1986). *Theories of counseling and psychotherapy: A basic issues approach.* Boston: Allyn and Bacon.

Wexler, D. A., & Rice, L. N. (Eds.). (1974). *Innovations in client-centered therapy.* New York: Wiley.

Chapter 10

Maslow's Metamotivational Theory of Personality

Chapter Overview

Introduction

Biographical Sketch

Resolution of the Eleven Basic Issues
    Heredity versus Social Determinants
    Number and Weight Assigned to Motivational Concepts
    Subjective versus Objective Reality
    Early versus Continuous Development
    Determinism versus Freedom of Choice
    Uniqueness versus Universality
    Explanation of Learning Process
    Role Assigned to Self-Concept
    Conscious versus Unconscious Determinants
    Role Assigned to Group Determinants
    Centrality of Reinforcement

Psychological Health and Psychopathology

Heuristic Influences: Research Methods and Techniques

Application to Psychotherapy
    Therapeutic Goals
    Therapeutic Relationship
    Initial Procedures and Strategies
    Course of Psychotherapy

Extended Applications

Critique

Annotated Bibliography

References and Suggested Readings

Introduction

Abraham Maslow's mission—"discovering a psychology for the peace table" and restructuring science "so that it is adequate for the salvation of the human being"—led ultimately to the exploration of the "growing tip" of humanity, that fraction of one percent of the population responsible for "all the growth for the whole human species" (in Hall, 1968, pp. 54–66). Following his conviction that "human beings are capable of something grander than war and prejudice and hatred" (in Hall, 1968), Maslow (1970) looked to the healthiest and best of humanity, those rare individuals who have achieved a state of exemplary personality integration in the process of becoming fully human.

By focusing on the upper limits of human motivation and functioning, Maslow (1970) discovered a transcendent human nature that becomes perceivable at the higher level of personality development, an optimistic alternative to the views offered by then-extant theories of personality with a history of concern for deviance. He called his approach **Third Force Psychology** (a term since adopted by personologists to describe a third general school or movement, the first being psychoanalysis and the second behaviorism).

Convinced that "human life will never be understood unless its highest aspirations are taken into account," Maslow (1970, p. xii) risked professional censure and ridicule to reveal his schematic representation of the intrinsic values of humanity. He hypothesized that humans have innate potentials and capacities that are species specific. The potential to be noble, loving, and creative, Maslow asserts, is within human nature. Indeed, all the higher virtues are part of an inherent **actualizing tendency** (an innate predisposition to actualize innate potentials) toward positive growth and health. Maslow (1943) offered a theory of personality that is "holistic rather than atomistic, functional rather than taxonomic, dynamic rather than static, dynamic rather than causal, purposive rather than simple–mechanical" (p. 519).

Maslow (1970) undoubtedly conceived a brighter and more optimistic view of humanity; however, it remains to be seen whether, as he predicted, future studies ". . . will change our philosophy of science, of ethics and values, of religion, of work, management and interpersonal relations, [and] of society" (p. xxii). Undaunted by his critics, who accused him of being more inspirational, philosophical, and speculative than he was scientific, Maslow was convinced that his ideas would surface and become validated in the works of other scientists, not only in psychology but in related disciplines as well. This, to some extent, has happened; Maslow's need-hierarchy theory of motivation is widely taught and applied in many disciplines.

Biographical Sketch of the Theorist

Like most theories, personality theories are shaped to some degree by the personal histories of the theorists. Maslow's metamotivational theory is no exception. Consider, for example, his lifelong interest in dominance, his deliberate search for and attachment to eminent and successful personalities, his inordinate fear of criticism and strong desire for recognition, his feeling of inadequacy for not conducting rigorous experimentation in support of his theoretical constructs, and his visions of **Eupsychia** (a psychological Utopia in which humans would become fully actualized).

Childhood

The first of seven children of uneducated Russian immigrants, Abraham H. Maslow was born April 1, 1908, in a Brooklyn slum. His father, a vigorous man and a cooper by trade, had hitchhiked across Europe from Kiev at the age of fifteen to come to the United States. Soon after he was established, he sent for and married a cousin from his hometown.

Maslow (in Leonard, 1983) described his early childhood as the most miserable period of his life. He was alienated from his superstitious and religious mother and, while he identified with his father, an avowed freethinker, he felt their relationship was strained. Worse still, as his father's business prospered and the family moved to new neighborhoods and improved housing, an "extremely thin and peculiar looking" Maslow found himself the only Jewish student in the school and a victim of anti-Semitism (Lowry, 1973, p. 13). The library became Maslow's refuge, and reading became his escape.

Education

Accepted and successful at Brooklyn Borough High School, about an hour and a half from his home, Maslow was elected to the honor society, became a member of the chess club, and edited both the Latin and the physics magazines. He entered the City College of New York at age eighteen and, as his father wished, registered for pre-law classes. Because he was unable to muster interest in the required courses, his class attendance and scholastic performance were poor. He was placed on academic probation for the second semester.

Although Maslow found his classes dull, he was stimulated by the many intellectual opportunities available in New York City. He managed to attend two concerts a week at Carnegie Hall by selling peanuts for admission. He also attended the lectures of such notables as Will Durant, American historian and philosopher; Bertrand Russell, British philosopher and mathematician; and Reinhold Niebuhr, American theologian and penetrating critic of society. It was during this period of his life that Maslow became a confirmed atheist, and though he never joined the party or became politically active, turned to a socialist philosophy.

At age nineteen, and hopelessly in love with Bertha Goodman, a distant cousin of whose family his parents disapproved, a frustrated Maslow fled home to attend a semester at Cornell University. His law classes at Cornell were no more interesting to him than those at CCNY, and Maslow was forced to tell his father that he wanted to change his major course of study. Although his father was disappointed, he wanted his son to have the advantages of an education, and reluctantly agreed that Maslow could transfer to the University of Wisconsin.

At Wisconsin, Maslow discovered the works of John B. Watson, the father of American behaviorism. Because of Watson's influence, he began a serious study of psychology. After a few months, he wired Bertha to tell her they were going to be married during the December holidays. Their wedding took place in New York, and Bertha returned with him to Wisconsin where she enrolled as an art student. Maslow (in Hall, 1968) viewed the first year of their marriage as the "beginning of his life" (p. 37).

Maslow attracted a succession of nurturing and supportive mentors. During his senior year at Wisconsin, he received an extensive background in classical laboratory research while serving as a laboratory assistant to William Sheldon (later known for his attempts to establish a relationship between "somatype," or body build, and personality). Maslow's chief mentor at Wisconsin, however, was Harry Harlow (recognized later for his classical investigations of curiosity and affective motives in rhesus monkeys). As Harlow's first doctoral student, Maslow conducted and published research on the dominance behavior of primates. Receiving all three of his degrees from the University of Wisconsin, Maslow was graduated with the A.B. degree in 1930, the M.A. degree in 1931, and the Ph.D. degree in 1934.

Emergence of a Theory

From Wisconsin, Maslow moved to Columbia University where for eighteen months he worked as a research assistant to Edward Thorndike, director of the psychology division of the Institute of Educational Research at Teachers College. As a Carnegie Fellow at Columbia, Maslow continued his study of dominance, discovering that dominance behavior diminished as intelligence increased in the primate hierarchy. Maslow left Thorndike and Columbia University in 1937 to accept a teaching position at Brooklyn College. He remained a member of the faculty there for fourteen years.

New York in the late 1930s became a gathering place for a large number of influential psychological theorists who migrated to the United States to escape concentration camps in Germany. Maslow (in Hall, 1968; Leonard, 1983) actively sought their company and through his associations with them learned about their interests. Of particular interest were: Max Wertheimer and Kurt Koffka, Gestalt psychologists; Kurt Goldstein, organismic psychologist; Erich Fromm, Karen Horney, and David Levy, psychoanalysts; Alfred Adler, founder of Individual Psychology; and Ruth Benedict and Margaret Mead, anthropologists.

Of his many mentors, Ruth Benedict and Max Wertheimer realized the greatest impact on Maslow's life. In an attempt to learn why these two remarkable people were so special, Maslow wrote privately of them in his journal, recording all the information he could gather about their personal lives—their interests, attitudes, values, and behaviors. In the early 1940s, as his journal entries accumulated, the two descriptions merged into one. "In one wonderful moment" Maslow (1971) realized that he was no longer writing about two different people, but rather about a particular kind of person (pp. 41–42). With this insight, Maslow's concept of self-actualization emerged, and he began an immediate search for others who might qualify for his newly discovered level of psychological health.

Maslow moved to Brandeis University in 1951, where he chaired the psychology department for many years. It was here that he wrote two of his best-known books, *Motivation and Personality* (1954) and *Toward a Psychology of Being* (1962).

In 1961, Maslow's mailing list became the base for the *Journal of Humanistic Psychology,* and in 1962 he helped to organize the Association for Humanistic Psychology. During the summer of that year, Maslow was appointed a visiting fellow to Non-Linear Systems, a high-tech plant in Del Mar, California. There he applied his ideas to management, developing the process now known as Eupsychian (pronounced "You-sigh'-key-an") management.

In 1967, Maslow was elected president of the American Psychological Association. In 1970, he accepted a fellowship of the Laughlin Foundation in Menlo Park, California, to devote full time to writing, an opportunity he had dreamed about for years (Maslow, in Lowry, 1973). Unfortunately, before his dream could be realized, Maslow died of a heart attack. He was sixty-two years old.

Awards and Honors

Maslow's numerous publications (see *The Journals of A. H. Maslow,* vol. 2, pp. 1311–1399, for complete bibliography) must certainly be considered an outstanding achievement. In addition to his writing, Maslow was Andrew Kay Visiting Fellow at La Jolla's Western Behavioral Science Institute, 1961–1962. He was president of the American Psychological Association, 1967–1968. He was named resident fellow at the Laughlin Foundation in Menlo Park, California, 1970. He was the recipient of the American Psychological Foundation Gold Medal Award, 1971; and he was awarded APA's Presidential Citation for Lifetime Contributions, August, 1990.

Resolutions of the Eleven Basic Issues

Maslow, like most of the theorists whose works are presented in this book, did not directly address each of the eleven basic issues. However, his stance on each issue began to acquire shape and meaning as work on the chapter progressed.

Heredity versus Social Determinants

Whether viewed from a biological or a psychological perspective, Maslow (1968b, 1970, 1978) asserts, we are an evolving animal species. While we share none of the total instincts of lower animals, that is, instincts involving all the elements of behavior (nest building in birds, for example), we do inherit instinct remnants or **instinctoid tendencies** (inherited internal prompting or motivational needs).

Although far more subtle than the total or true animal instincts, instinctoid tendencies are rooted in the biological constitution of our species, emerge in the form of deficit needs, and appear in a hierarchy of relative motivational potency and priority (see Figure 10.1). It is these instinctoid needs (along with capacities, talents, anatomical equipment, physiological or temperamental balances, prenatal and natal injuries, and trauma to the neonate) that become the source of an internal prompting, "an inner will to health." The lower the need in the hierarchy, the greater its motivational strength, the earlier it appears in the evolutionary process, and the more directly it is related to survival. Conversely, higher needs are motivationally weaker, may not appear until middle age (if then), and are less directly related to survival.

The higher needs in Maslow's hierarchy are distinctly and uniquely human. Unfortunately, the higher needs of our species require **synergistic** (favorable and facilitating) environmental conditions for their appearance, expression, and gratification. And because they are the weakest of the motivational needs, higher needs are largely unconscious, easily repressed, suppressed, or controlled.

Number and Weight Assigned to Motivational Concepts

Maslow identified five ascending levels of motivational needs for humans, each level weaker and more subtle than the one preceding it. Four of the five levels are basic or deficiency needs (also referred to by Maslow [1968b, 1970, 1978] as deficit or D-needs). The fifth and highest level in Maslow's need hierarchy is the growth need (also referred to as B-need or Being-need). When D-needs are not met, they become pathogenic. B-needs will not emerge until D-needs are sufficiently gratified. The five hierarchical levels of motivational needs listed by Maslow are described as follows.

Physiological Needs   In Maslow's hierarchy of motivational needs, **physiological needs** are defined as the survival needs shared by all animal species (oxygen, drink, food, elimination, sleep, sex, and shelter are examples). Significant deprivation of any one of the physiological needs will dominate all aspects of life and functioning (perceptual, cognitive, emotional, and behavioral).

People who are starving view Utopia as a place where there is always enough to eat. Moreover, they are convinced that a sufficient and continual food supply would solve all their problems and bring them happiness—they would need nothing more. Higher needs, having nothing to do with filling empty stomachs, are waved aside as trivial pursuits. When all energies and capacities are focused on finding food, life is defined in terms of food; there is no involvement in the quest for self-actualization. Intelligence, memory, and habits become only hunger-gratifying tools. Maslow (1970) vividly illustrates the motivational force of the physiological needs when, in contrast to Christian teaching, he asserts: "It is quite true that man lives by bread alone—when there is no bread" (p. 38). However, once hunger is satisfied and there is the assurance that food is and will continue to be available, the next level of needs gradually emerges to become the dominate motivating force.

Safety Needs   Maslow (1970) described the **safety needs** as the inherent need for protection (law, order, security, stability, structure, control, and predictability are examples of the safety needs). Severe deprivation of safety needs results in chronic anxiety that in turn leads to avoidance and compulsive behaviors. Reduction of uncertainty becomes a primary motivation in the lives of safety-deprived individuals. While safety needs motivate humans to avoid injury or an early death, deprivation of these needs can impede or halt positive growth and development. A willingness to exchange personal freedom for security during the emergency of war or a natural catastrophe is but one of many possible examples (Maslow, 1968, pp. 46–47, 49, 54).

Most adults in our society have satisfied their safety needs; however, these needs are clearly evident in very young children, neurotics, and the socially and economically deprived. Insecure children and neurotics typically exhibit fear when encountering the novel. New experiences are avoided through a compulsive narrowing and ordering of their environments. The young child and the neurotic will often adhere to highly structured and compulsively rigid routines when deprived of safety needs; moreover, they will often express their safety needs by searching for a protector, a strong leader they can depend on. In the ordinary adult, the safety needs may be met by a job with seniority rights, tenure, or benefits, various kinds of insurance, a retirement plan, a savings account, or a sound system of investment.

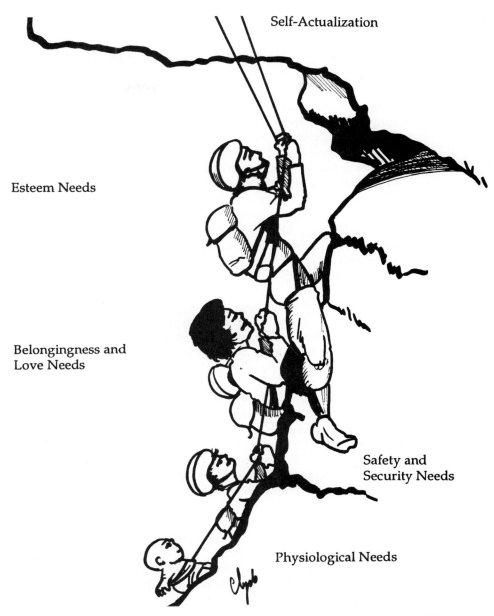

Self-Actualization

Esteem Needs

Belongingness and
Love Needs

Safety and
Security Needs

Physiological Needs

**FIGURE 10-1 For Maslow needs appear in a hierarchical order, each
weaker than the one preceding it**

In contrast, when safety needs are adequately satisfied, people do not find their world, or the people who inhabit it, threatening or dangerous. Unafraid to take risks, they are open to new experiences. The novel and the unexpected are viewed as interesting and exciting, and indeed are actively sought by the confident and secure. Healthy adults, then, are not involved in tension reduction or homeostasis. Rather, they are challenged by the ambiguous, the unstructured, and the unknown.

Belongingness and Love Needs   The third level of needs in Maslow's hierarchy, belongingness and love needs, tends to emerge when physiological and safety needs are relatively well gratified. However, unlike the physiological and safety needs, belongingness and love needs are not commonly satisfied by society. Society, in fact, often imposes restrictions and inhibitions that result in the thwarting of these needs and lead to maladjustment, even psychopathology. Urbanization, the breakdown of the family structure, mobility, and the gap between generations frustrate the human tendency "to herd, to flock, to join, to belong" and create feelings of "alienation and loneliness" (Maslow, 1970, p. 44).

Similar to Erich Fromm's (1941) needs for "rootedness" and relatedness and Martin Buber's (1937/1958) needs for I–Thou affirmation, Maslow's (1954, 1962, 1968a, 1970, 1971) assertion is that humans need to be loved and loving. "No psychological health is possible unless this essential core of the person is fundamentally accepted by others and by himself" (Maslow, 1968a, p. 196). Love, as a deficiency need, is selfish; the person deprived of love is primarily concerned with seeking love from others. When D-love needs are sufficiently gratified, the need and capacity for B-love, a mature love and concern for the well-being and individuality of others, is possible and becomes manifest.

Esteem Needs   Maslow divided the last of the deficiency needs to emerge into two subsidiary types: (1) **esteem needs** that can only be fulfilled by self-respect, when self-evaluations include deserved respect for personal capabilities, competencies, mastery, independence, freedom, and achievement, and (2) esteem needs that can only be fulfilled when the evaluation of others includes recognition, appreciation, standing, status, and praise. Nongratified esteem needs result in feelings of inferiority, helplessness, and the lack of self-regard. Conversely, gratification of esteem needs results in a **self-efficacy** that is based on a realistic self-assessment of personal strength, competence, and significant achievement, rather than on unwarranted status, fame, or adulation. At the public-esteem level, there is the need to "be somebody," but the definition and standards of the somebody one wants to be is extrinsically defined by the crowd. People at the self-esteem level also wish to "be somebody"; however, at this level of development, the somebody they wish to be is self-defined and based on intrinsic values (Schwartz, 1983).

Self-Actualization Needs   If all environment-dependent needs (D-needs) are substantially and consistently gratified, humans gain a fuller knowledge and acceptance of their own intrinsic nature and are motivated primarily by the final and idiosyncratic level of needs (the meta-, growth, or B-needs). Those rare individuals who reach this level experience the desire to know and to understand phenomena that transcend the needs associated with the gratification of their basic needs. At this point, also, self-actualizing needs become stronger, the dominating forces of motivation. Movement at this level, marked by vague feelings of discontent and restlessness, is toward the actualization of unique inherent potentials.

Self-actualization is **idiosyncratic** (varying significantly from one individual to another) and requires a healthful unfolding of all possibilities for growth (Maslow, 1970, pp. 45–46). Feist (1985) writes: "People who have reached the level of self-actualization become fully human, satisfying needs that others merely glimpse or never view at all" (p. 381). This does not, of course, imply that every self-actualizing person will become an Edison or an Einstein. Rather, it means the self-actualizer is fulfilling his or her innate potentials.

Maslow (1954, 1958, 1962, 1963, 1968a, 1971) repeatedly warned, however, that self-actualization is *not* automatic with the fulfillment of the basic needs, for while discovery of the highest potentials is exciting, even exhilarating, it also can be frightening and disabling (see "Psychopathology," this chapter). The highest human potentials carry responsibilities, commitment, and duties. They require the willingness and courage to risk. They also require a healthy, supportive environment with a socialization process that fosters freedom, equality, and trust, and encourages risk-taking behaviors—in brief, an environment that enhances and enriches life. The potentials are there, but the environment must provide the triggering stimulation for their actualization. Self-actualizing needs, the weakest of the instinctoid needs, are thus easily obscured by nonsynergistic environmental influences. A pathogenic culture or environment can overwhelm, stunt, and even destroy self-actualizing tendencies. The biological predispositions of humans require an enriching or at the very least a beneficent culture for their expression and fulfillment.

It is important at this point to remember that Maslow did not offer his theory of motivation as a substitute for a theory of behavior. For Maslow (in Hamachek, 1965), practically all human behavior is both motivated and motivating, but a comprehensive theory of behavior must also acknowledge biological, cultural, and social determinants.

Subjective versus Objective Reality

Maslow's stance on this issue was clearly phenomenological. We perceive events in our environments, and from our perceptions we attempt to create order, structure, meaning, and relationships. Our worlds are private constructs from all we consider important at the moment. In *Psychology of Science*, Maslow (1966) described a hierarchy of knowing ourselves, others, and the world:

> *First comes knowing in the experiential sense; then comes the check on the fallibilities of the senses and of experiential knowledge; then come the abstractions, the theories, i.e., orthodox science (p. 70).*

While Maslow (1966) was convinced that there is no substitute for experience and that "all of life must first be known experientially" (p. 45), he reminded us of the distinction between need-interested or deficiency perception and desireless or Taoistic perception. Deficiency perception is need motivated and thus likely to be distorted—cognitively in error. Taoistic or desireless perception is unintruding, undemanding, non-possessive, thus closer to actuality. He reminded us, too, that experiencing is but the first step. "It must be embedded in knowledge, wisdom, facts, consequences, meanings. It must itself be judged" (Maslow, 1979, vol. 2, p. 855).

Maslow (1970) found that one of the most striking characteristics of the self-actualizing people he studied was that they perceived truth and reality far more efficiently than the general population. In contrast, Maslow (1970) found the perceptions of neurotic persons "not only *relatively* but *absolutely* inefficient," and concluded they were not emotionally sick but rather they were cognitively *wrong* (p. 153, emphasis in original). Because their perceptions are need directed, they perceive reality in terms of their deficiencies. Their feelings and reactions to any situation, then, are based on their perceptions of reality rather than on reality itself.

Early versus Continuous Development

Maslow has not proposed a schedule of specific developmental stages or passages through which humans must progress during their lifetimes; however, his need hierarchy clearly implies a progression of stage-emergent need gratifications "that have a life-history and must be seen developmentally" (Maslow, 1968a, p. 190). While there is no exact timetable, each of the five levels of needs in Maslow's hierarchy emerges only after the level immediately preceding it is at least partially gratified, and gratification largely depends upon **extra-psychic** determinants (such as culture, family, environment, learning). While the culture is a *sine qua non* for the actualization of humanness, human potentialities exist prior to culture. "The culture is sun and food and water; it is not the seed" (Maslow, 1968, p. 161). Only to the extent that culture fosters growth of innate human potentials and capacities is that culture **synergistic** (enhancing to healthy human growth and development).

Infancy Like Rogers (Chapter 9), Maslow (1968, 1971) granted the newborn human the inherent **bodily wisdom** (instinctoid actualizing tendency) that while goaless in early infancy is nevertheless expressed as natural inclinations and propensities. "Very early in life these goaless urges and tendencies become attached to objects ('sentiments') by canalization but also by arbitrary learned associations" (Maslow, 1968a, pp. 190–191). Moreover, not only can the infant differentiate between those experiences that facilitate the actualization of its innate potentials and those that do not, it also trusts fully its inner way of knowing.

Fortunate indeed are those infants whose parents trust in their children's actualizing tendencies and in the natural processes of growth. Viewing the infant as a small bundle of teeming, uncharted possibilities that should be touched, loved, and *permitted to grow,* Maslow (1968a) recommended that parents take a

Taoistic (nonintruding, noncontrolling, receptive, and permissive) stance to childrearing—"not interfere too much, not *make* them grow, or force them into predetermined designs, but rather *let* them grow and *help* them grow" (p. 199, emphasis in original).

Childhood While Maslow recommended that parents take a nonintrusive role and see to it that their children's basic needs are gratified, he (like Adler, Chapter 3) warned against pampering and overindulgence that could be interpreted by children as neglect or lack of love. Reasonable limits must be set to help children avoid the dangers of living, as well as to provide a welcome sense of safety and structure in an otherwise confusing and insensitive world.

Children whose physiological needs have been gratified, and who feel a sense of security and love, can benefit from graded frustrations that test their limits. It is by overcoming frustrations that children learn tolerance and develop the ability to perceive physical reality as essentially indifferent to their wishes. Healthy growth for the child means giving up the techniques used in infancy, in early feelings of weakness and smallness, for adapting to the large, strong, powerful adults, and replacing their early coping techniques with the growth techniques of strength and independence. Growth at this stage involves giving up wishing for the exclusive love of parents, being good because it feels right rather than out of fear, and discovering a personal conscience to replace internalized parents as the sole ethical guide.

Adolescence A lengthy childhood experience gives humans impressive dependency. Adolescents are caught in the dilemma of wanting to remain young and childish *and* simultaneously wanting to mature and become independent. For healthy adolescents, choice in the matter is usually short lived. They are, in fact, growing biologically older, and even the more resistant adolescents learn that society is generally intolerant and unforgiving of those whose behavior does not conform to its dictates.

While intrinsic rewards and pleasures follow the gratification of adolescent growth needs, growth may also be accompanied by pain and fear. With each forward movement, the adolescent risks parting with the familiar and the comfortable. Choosing growth means saying "yes" to a more difficult, demanding, and responsible life. This, of course, requires a degree of will, courage, and strength that adolescents fear they may not have yet developed.

When adolescents deny their inner directions and begin to copy, borrow, and assimilate the lives, wishes, and situations of others, they are denying the essence of themselves and their need to self-actualize. Far more important, however, is the tragic loss of faith in themselves and their visions and, along with this, the loss of trust. "I do not trust what I feel I need and want; therefore, I shall trust what you believe I need and want." In such a statement lies an even more frightening one: "I do not trust what I am and will accept your vision of me."

According to Maslow (1968a), "much disturbance in children and adolescents can be understood as a consequence of the uncertainty of adults about their values" (p. 206). Adolescents soon lose respect for parents who lack a consistent set of values or whose behavior and lifestyle manifest a confusion of values. Worse still, adolescents witnessing their parents' confusion will often simplistically decide that all adults are like their parents and develop a "desacralizing" (nothing is sacred) attitude. Without healthy adult models, they turn to adolescent values (such as those projected in William Golding's *Lord of the Flies*). Adolescent values are growth deficient, hence they stunt any movement toward self-actualization.

Adulthood Convinced that all the needs in his hierarchy of needs were innate, Maslow initially assumed that each need level in the hierarchy would naturally emerge once the level preceding it had been sufficiently gratified. The discovery that many of his subjects (particularly the healthier of his young adult subjects) were not motivated toward self-actualization, even though all the data indicated that their lower needs were gratified, forced a puzzled Maslow to examine further the highest level of human needs. How and why was the need for actualization different from the four preceding need levels? Why did so few of his subjects reach this level of human development? It was in pursuit of the answers to these and similar questions that Maslow uncovered the **metamotivations** (biologically rooted ultimate human values). Maslow's metamotivations are more fully discussed in "Psychological Health and the Good Life" later in this chapter.

While it is true that gratification of the basic needs is necessary for the emergence of the self-actualization process, gratification alone is insufficient. Only those rare individuals who can marshal the will and the courage to embrace the B-values are self-actualizing. Only they encounter the metamotivations. Moreover, Maslow discovered that people seldom if ever become motivated by the meta-needs before attaining full maturity.

Self-actualizing is the long and difficult process of being child, parent, and adult in an unsympathetic world. The process of actualizing involves long years of discipline, training, commitment, and devotion to the ultimate or highest-level needs—the eternal verities, the B-values. Unlike the lower-level D-needs that require coping behaviors, the higher-level needs of self-actualizing call for dedicated growth and urge expression.

The great majority of adults (and nearly all youth), Maslow asserts, are unable to gratify their lower-level needs, for they are still attempting to cope with the love and esteem needs that are so difficult to fulfill in today's culture. Of the few adults who are able to meet all their lower-level deficiency needs, many are unable to risk that final developmental step, to commit themselves fully to the highest human values. Like the Biblical Jonah, they refuse to heed their calling, and run from their destiny (see Figure 10.1, and the Jonah syndrome, "Psychopathology," this chapter).

Determinism versus Freedom of Choice

For Maslow (1971, vol. 1) **freedom** (which he defines as "self-choice and good conditions for self-choice") is an integrated part of the actualizing tendency (p.

430). Natural growth is moving away from external determinants and toward freedom of choice, thinking independently, living authentically, and determining our own values and directions, with the courage to accept the consequences of our choices and actions. When Maslow (1970) speaks of free choice in human beings, he is referring to healthy adults or children "who are not yet twisted or distorted" by introjecting the conditions and disapproval of significant others and the culture.

Freedom, Maslow (1979, vol. 1) asserts, requires "a strength of character" that makes self-choice without anxiety more likely and is formed by practice with graded self-choices, with assimilating freedom and responsibility. Moreover, freedom requires a healthy, enriching, supportive environment that facilitates equality and trust.

Uniqueness versus Universality

Maslow's stance on this issue is clear: We are unique beings. While the actualizing tendency is universal, in the sense that we share many of the same needs, it is also idiosyncratic. The specific forms it takes vary considerably from person to person. No two individuals inherit the same talents, capacities, potentialities, values, and motivations. No two individuals acquire identical levels of knowledge, understanding, tolerance, skills, mastery, and enthusiasm. Our perceptions, emotions, goals, and convictions differ, and no two of us share identical styles of commitment.

Explanation of the Learning Process

As pointed out above, cognitive needs (the need to know and to understand) are tools used for gratifying both basic and growth needs; however, this does not, according to Maslow (1970, pp. 48–51), constitute a definitive answer to the motivational roles of curiosity, learning, philosophizing, and experimenting. Arising from the basic needs, the cognitive needs are true motives. Healthy people are attracted to the mysterious, the unknown, the chaotic, the unorganized, and the unexplained (see "Characteristics of Self-Actualizing People," this chapter). In contrast, deprivation of the cognitive needs may result in such psychopathologies as poor morale, boredom, lack of zest for living, generalized cynicism, suspicion, and depression. Maslow (1970) was certain that the cognitive needs have a striving nature, and "are as much personality needs as the basic needs" (p. 51).

Maslow (1970) was not only puzzled but upset with the traditional extrinsically motivated goals and methods practiced at all levels of the educational system—senseless repetition, arbitrary associations, reward, and pressure to adapt to society's standards. Maslow advocated a radically different conception of learning, of teaching, and of education. "Stated simply such a concept holds that the function of education, the goal of education is self-actualization" (Maslow, 1970, pp. 168–169). He could not understand why "so much of educational psychology concerns itself with means, i.e., grades, credits, diplomas,

FIGURE 10-2   **Like the Biblical Jonah, we often flee our destiny. Maslow refers to this as the Jonah Syndrome**

rather than with ends, i.e., wisdom, understanding, good judgment, good taste?" Maslow, 1970, p. 282). Why, he inquired, were they not asking such questions as:

> *How do people learn to be wise, mature, kind, to have good taste, to be inventive, to have good characters, to be able to fit themselves to new situations, to detect the good, to seek the truth, to know the beautiful and the genuine, i.e., intrinsic rather than extrinsic learning? (Maslow, 1970, 281–282)*

For Maslow, education is learning to grow, and just as important, learning what to grow toward. He also believed that the schools should be involved in the discovery of vocation (Maslow, 1971, p. 181).

Aesthetic Needs   Although he did not include aesthetic needs as a separate need level in the hierarchy of human needs, Maslow (1959, 1962, 1963, 1970) was convinced that **aesthetic needs** (expressed in humans as desires for beauty, order, symmetry, closure, system, and structure) are basic needs, especially so for certain individuals. "They get sick (in special ways) from ugliness, and are cured by beautiful surroundings" (Maslow, 1970, p. 51).

Role Assigned to Self-Concept

According to Maslow (1966), we enter this world with ". . . a model of some kind of real Self, some kind of characteristic which is conceived biologically to some extent" (p. 79). Further, he claimed, our real selves are "constitutional, temperamental, 'instinctoid' " (p. 79), essential, deep, inner cores with "impulse voices" that, if heeded, will impel us forward toward wholeness of self and uniqueness of self, toward full functioning of all innate potentials and capacities. The impulse voices of the real self, Maslow (1971, vol. 1) asserted, are "nice" and "good" (p. 417), a will to health, and should be permitted to emerge naturally.

Unfortunately, much of our energy and striving are in defense against confrontation with the real self. The average person finds the weak impulse voices of the real self frightening. Their softly whispered inner directives, the outcomes of which are unpredictable, often require great risk, commitment, responsibility, and self-discipline. The safest and easiest course is to deny, ignore, or suppress them. The safest and easiest course is also the most costly, for when it is selected too often, we become alienated from our real selves, there is a narrowing of personality, and while the *potentials* of the real self continue to exist, we can lose our actualizing *capacity*.

Conscious versus Unconscious Determinants

For Maslow (1968a), the unconscious may be either unhealthy or healthy. The unconscious we experience depends largely on our everyday choices of fear or courage, safety or growth—in short on whether we live in the D-realm or B-realm.

The unhealthy unconscious presented by Maslow (1968a) shares some similarities with the unconscious described by Freud (Chapter 2); that is, it includes the instinctoid needs, unverbalized repressions, suppressions, the primary processes, the forgotten or neglected. Maslow agreed with Freud that much of the deeper **inner nature** (which he defines as the *real self*) is repressed by individuals living in the D-realm, at the deficiency levels of his motivational hierarchy. When functioning in the inflexible safety-seeking D-realm, conscious selves perceive the unconscious real self as ego-alien, frighteningly impulsive, and in conflict with society's directives and the stronger biological and environmental forces.

Unlike Freud's, Maslow's unconscious also houses the higher growth needs—or metavalues and standards—the roots of courage, creativity, joy, and happiness, the good and the ethical—in brief, the full range of the innate potentials and capacities. Actualizing individuals, especially the more creative, are able to relinquish conscious control of their unconscious and face without fear or anxiety the impulses and imagery that emerge from the primary processes. Moreover, they possess the inner strength to acknowledge the limitations of the conscious self and devote themselves to values beyond their own needs. According to Maslow, persons living in the B-realm somehow manage a *fusion* and *synthesis* of the primary and secondary processes, of the conscious and the unconscious, of the deeper inner self and the conscious self.

There are, then, major differences between Maslow's and Freud's concepts of the unconscious. For Maslow (1968a):

> *This ability of healthier people to dip into the unconscious and preconscious, to use and value their primary processes instead of fearing them, to accept their impulses*

*instead of always controlling them, to be able to regress voluntarily without fear,
turns out to be one of the main conditions of creativity (p. 209).*

It is from the unconscious, Maslow asserted, that healthy individuals derive
much of their extra drive, enthusiasm, energy, and dedication that in turn enable
them to pursue their deepest convictions—the metavalues. Indeed, they look
forward to the unpredictable dialogues between their conscious and their unconscious, between their instinctoid tendency and the claims of life. They enjoy,
rather than fear, their new-found capacity for sensing, wondering, learning, understanding, and aspiring.

Although the emphasis to this point is directed toward the role of the unconscious and Maslow's expressed differences with Freud, Maslow (1971) believed
strongly that coping with environmental forces "may be and characteristically is
fully conscious" (p. 4). He stressed repeatedly the necessity of a reasonably
objective view of the self, the accessibility of the self to consciousness, and self-acceptance. Indeed, conscious self-knowledge is for Maslow an essential ingredient
of the inner strength and courage that characterize the free person.

While creativity comes out of the unconscious, it is the conscious self that
must develop and organize a broad and firm knowledge base and achieve the
skill levels necessary for creative change. Creativity requires mastery of the medium in which creative change occurs, and mastery is the result of conscious,
disciplined effort. Experiencing may be the first step to learning, but it is only a
first step " . . . it must be embedded in knowledge, wisdom, facts, consequences,
meanings. It must itself be judged" (Maslow, 1971, vol.2, p. 855).

Role Assigned to Group Determinants

One of the stronger of the human instinctoid tendencies evolved from the early
survival instinct to herd. Animals that were less swift and less strong than their
predators learned to survive by herding. As humans evolved, they formed family
groups, then clans or tribes, and finally villages, cities, states, and nations. They
learned to identify with and develop allegiance to their groups. The instinctive
need of humans to belong, to be accepted and respected, and to contribute in
some way to the benefit of the group, can be either healthy or unhealthy.

Centrality of Reinforcement

Maslow seldom used the term reinforcement. However, reinforcement (though
short lived) is implied in the fulfillment of innate potentials and in the gratification of both deficiency and growth needs that appear in his need hierarchy. A
sense of reinforcement is momentary, because as soon as one need is adequately
met, it is replaced with a new, higher-level need. Still, for a very brief instant, the
individual experiences the feeling that he or she *is* moving in the right direction,
that there is a meaningful purpose to life and living.

For the healthy individual, a sense of reinforcement does not come from the completion of a particular task, but rather from the *striving* and *moving* toward self-actualizing, with full knowledge that self-actualizing is a means rather than an end, a process rather than a state of accomplishment.

Psychological Health and Psychopathology

Maslow deliberately rejected the medical model that defines health as the absence of symptoms and the adjustment model that measures health in accordance with social norms. Not only do the pervasive psychologies of the normal and the average paint a negative, thus limited, picture of the human condition, Maslow (1971) argued, they offer a concept of normalcy and "averageness" that would be better viewed as "a kind of sickness or crippling or stunting that we share with everybody else, and therefore don't notice" (p. 26). Leonard (1983) succinctly states Maslow's position on the normal human condition: "For Maslow, the self-actualizing person is not a normal person with something added, but a normal person with nothing taken away" (p. 332).

For Maslow (1959, see also 1954, 1962, 1968a, 1971), health is the normal human condition. Further, he proposed a level of optimal health that *transcends* the limited distinctions of the medical and adjustment models, one that "frees the person from the deficiency problems of growth, and from the neurotic (or infantile, or fantasy, or unnecessary, or 'unreal') problems of life" (Maslow, 1959b, p. 24).

Psychological Health and the Good Life

As Maslow studied those rare individuals who were living (or who had lived) to their full potential, he discovered that they were motivated by a different set of values than were the great majority of people still striving to satisfy their deficiency needs. This small sample of uncommonly healthy individuals seemed beyond becoming, at least in the sense of striving for specific goals. Indeed, they appeared to have reached a state of *being*, a higher human nature based on ultimate values. Maslow referred to these values as the Being Values or B-values.

Further study by Maslow revealed that while the B-values functioned in many ways similarly to the lower needs, B-values, in contrast to the D-needs, were ends in themselves rather than a means to an end. Still further study uncovered additional characteristics unique to the B-values. As ends in themselves, B-values are the ultimate satisfiers; they bring with their gratification feelings of perfection, completion, fulfillment, and serenity. The B-values define full humanness—only those persons with the will and courage to embrace the B-values are capable of self-actualization, of entering the realm of *being* rather than *becoming*. B-values give the individual's life meaning and purpose, a reason

Heredity	■	Social Determinants
Subjective Reality	■	Objective Reality
Early Development	■	Continuous Development
Determinism	■	Freedom
Uniqueness	■	Universality
Conscious Determinants	■	Unconscious Determinants

Number and Weight Assigned to Motivational Concepts	Maslow identified five ascending levels of motivational needs: physiological needs (survival needs), safety needs (inherent need for protection), belongingness and love needs (need to be loved and loving), esteem needs (fulfilled by self-respect and fulfilled by others), and self-actualization (actualization of unique inherent potentials).
Explanation of Learning Process	Cognitive needs, the need to know and to understand, have a striving nature. Self-actualization of a person is the function and goal of education. Aesthetic needs (desire for beauty, order, symmetry, etc.) are basic needs.
Role Assigned to Self-Concept	We enter this world with a model of the real self. Our real selves will impel us toward full functioning of all innate potentials and capacities. Denial of the impulse voices of the real self results in loss of our actualizing capacity.
Role Assigned to Group Determinants	One of the stronger human instinctoid tendencies evolved from the survival instinct to herd. As humans evolved, they formed family groups, tribes, and finally nations. Humans learned to identify with and develop allegiance to group memberships.
Centrality of Reinforcement	Reinforcement is implied in the fulfillment of innate potentials and the gratification of deficiency and growth needs. Reinforcement for the healthy individual comes from striving and moving toward self-actualizing.

FIGURE 10-3   Schematic Analysis of Maslow's Stance on Basic Issues

for being. Those who refuse the motivation of the B-values suffer a unique form of existential distress (see "Psychopathology," this chapter).

To distinguish the motivating force of the B-values from the much stronger force of the deficiency needs, Maslow coined the term "metamotivation." It stood to reason, then, that he called the rather novel form of psychological distress arising from the frustration of the B-values "metapathology."

Even though very few humans reach the point of development at which they are capable of metamotivation, Maslow (1968a, 1970) was convinced that this rare form of motivation is inextricably linked to biologically rooted, species-specific values. In short, he believed the B-values are an inchoate part of the essential inner core of human nature and exist at birth in embryonic form, awaiting only the proper conditions to emerge.

As mentioned earlier, when Maslow's journal descriptions of Benedict and Wertheimer merged, he realized that he might have stumbled upon a very rare kind of growth-motivated personality. To further satisfy his curiosity, he began a search for other psychologically healthy individuals, people who, like Benedict and Wertheimer, were actualizing their potentials and living at full capacity. With no intention of publishing his findings and only a vague notion of what he was seeking, Maslow (1970) first looked for optimal healthy personalities from among his friends, acquaintances, and students. Finding few subjects in this group who met his subjective criteria, Maslow extended his study to other living and historical personalities.

As he accumulated and refined his data, Maslow (1954/1970) reported eighteen probable subjects, five partial subjects, and thirty-seven potential or possible subjects (p. 152). Although Maslow never revealed the names of living subjects, the following public and historic figures were included in his study:

Jane Addams	Thomas Jefferson
Ludwig van Beethoven	Fritz Kreisler
George Washington Carver	Abraham Lincoln
Eugene V. Debs	Eleanor Roosevelt
Thomas Eakins	Franklin D. Roosevelt
Albert Einstein	Baruch Spinoza
Sigmund Freud	Henry David Thoreau
Johann Wolfgang von Goethe	Walt Whitman

Using a variety of techniques and the case study approach (interview, free association, and projective techniques with living subjects, and analysis of biographical and autobiographical material with historical subjects), Maslow (1970) compiled from his impressions a composite of characteristics expressed by his subjects that clearly distinguished them from the general population.

Characteristics of Self-Actualizing People

Accurate and Full Perception of Reality With their D-needs gratified and their perceptions based primarily on B-cognition, self-actualizers grasp reality firmly. Their perceptions are not distorted by lower needs or defensive postures; indeed, they perceive an "inner rightness" of themselves and of nature. Anxiety and fear are seldom part of their lives. Because they perceive their world and the people in it accurately, they are excellent judges of character and value. The false and dishonest are easily detected and their true motives uncovered. This unusual ability to judge quality is often extensive, including such areas as art, music, and literature. In brief, because their awareness of reality is both efficient and accurate, their choices and predictions are more often correct and reliable—hence, good, healthy, and desirable.

Greater Acceptance of Self, Others, and the World   Accurate perception leads to greater acceptance and tolerance of reality. For the self-actualizer, reality, simply and impersonally, is. Perfection, whether in self, others, or the world, is neither expected nor demanded; thus, there is no need to deny reality or to insist that it be different. With greater acceptance and tolerance of reality, self-actualizers can accept (without shame, guilt, or sadness) the weaknesses and faults they discover in themselves. Moreover, they are equally accepting (without anger, complaint, or the need to instruct and change) of the weaknesses and faults they find in others and the world. Prejudices and stereotypes are neither useful nor rational for them.

It should be noted that the self-actualizer's stoic acceptance and tolerance of reality is not to be mistaken for resignation or compliance. Acceptance and tolerance are significant traits of the self-actualizer, but they are not to be confused with an immobilizing sense of objectivity or an inability to take a responsible stand and to work towards desired goals. In short, they do not include perceived "discrepancies between what is and what might very well be or ought to be" (Maslow, 1970, p. 157).

Spontaneity, Simplicity, and Naturalness   Because self-actualizers are self-accepting, there is no need to adopt a **persona** (mask or role), to manipulate or deceive, or to strive for an effect. They are good and lusty animals with hearty appetites and the ability to enjoy life without regret or apology. They find it comfortable to be themselves, to be spontaneous and genuine. As authentic beings, they find the artificial and contrived distasteful, whether in themselves or others.

While self-actualizers do not permit convention or law to keep them from doing what they believe is right, just, or necessary, they do not go out of their way to make great issues of trivial matters, rules, or customs. They will generally conform to custom, dress, or the social amenities, for example, when their nonconformity would make others uncomfortable. Nonetheless, they can, when they believe the situation warrants their doing so, be unconventional and unbending, regardless of the consequences of their actions.

Problem Oriented   Self-actualizers are strongly focused on problems or issues beyond themselves, and on being problem centered rather than ego centered. Subjects functioning at a lower level may have a career; self-actualizers have a calling. They are committed to a task, cause, purpose, or mission in life that requires much of their attention and energy. They are dedicated people. Their job or mission in life is one they *must* do, as opposed to one they want to do. It is an assigned duty with responsibility and obligation. Their work is their world for them. They are dedicated and absorbed to the point of passion. For the self-actualizer there are few dichotomies—duty and pleasure are the same, as are also work and play, means and ends. They are absorbed, happy, and fulfilled in their life work.

Quality of Detachment and Need for Solitude Again, with D-needs fulfilled, self-actualizers experience less need for others than the majority of people, and they often limit themselves to a relatively small circle of close personal friends. In contrast to the majority of people, they can be more detached and see things more objectively. Their concentration can be intense, making them oblivious of their surroundings. They not only appreciate solitude and privacy, they often demand it. While their quality of detachment and need for solitude can lead to greater objectivity and independence, these same qualities can also create misunderstandings and problems. Those who are less actualizing are prone to view them as aloof, snobbish, unfriendly, or even hostile (discussed in greater depth later, in "Deep Interpersonal Relations").

Autonomy and Independence of Culture and Environment Related directly to those actualizing characteristics previously described is the relative independence of self-actualizers of their physical and cultural environments. Pushed by meta-needs and B-cognition, self-actualizers can rely on their own potentials and resources for their continued growth and development. They do not become confused by means and ends, problems and methods. Maslow (1970) described the meta-needs and B-cognition as "self-contained" (p. 162). B-motivated self-actualizers, then, are confident, inner-directed, active agents independent of their culture and environment. Their self-confidence gives them an inner peace that those who strive for the approval of others usually lack.

Continued Freshness of Appreciation Maslow (1970) discovered that self-actualizing people "have the wonderful capacity to appreciate again and again, freshly and naïvely, the basic 'goods' of life, however commonplace these experiences may have become to others" (p. 163). They retain a constant childlike sense of pleasure and gratitude for the beauty in life and living. Familiarization does not lessen the miracle of life and beauty. Each sunset is refreshing and renewing. Life never loses its miraculous quality. Some of Maslow's subjects found this beauty in nature, some in children, some in lovers, others in music, art, or literature, but for all, it was always fresh, strengthening, and renewing.

Mystic or Peak Experiences Although Maslow (1964a, 1970) believed all humans possess the potential for peak experiences (at least in their milder forms), he found it convenient in this instance to divide his self-actualizing subjects into two groups—"peakers" and "nonpeakers." **Peakers** were those individuals who were open to occasional, unexpected, mystical moments of transcendence and who welcomed the sensation of the mystical, the intense feelings of awe, wonder, humility, ecstasy, and rapture that accompanied those peak moments in their lives. As a group they tended to be aesthetic. **Nonpeakers**, by contrast, were those individuals who rejected or denied their peak experiences. Threatened by their intense feelings, they sought logical, rational explanations, and unable to find them, feared losing control or going insane. As a group, nonpeakers tended to be practical and efficient.

Although not all self-actualizers report peak experiences, those who did felt them most intensely and believed that their lives were in some way transformed and strengthened by these brief but grand, yet indescribable, mystical moments. Though impossible to communicate fully, their peak experiences could be described as feeling at one with the universe, feeling gratified in every way and deeply appreciative, feeling no fear or anxiety and in control of their lives, feeling disoriented in time and space with little awareness of self or ego, experiencing some great insight or bursts of creativity, and finding the experience desirable and good. Convinced that peak experiences are an "embracing of the B-values," Maslow believes each peak experience has a lasting influence on the person's life. He lists seven possibilities of the peak experience:

1. Eliminating neurotic symptoms;
2. Seeing oneself in a more positive, healthy way;
3. Changing the view formerly held of others and of relationships with them;
4. Changing the view formerly held of the world;
5. Releasing of creativity, spontaneity, and expressiveness;
6. Remembering and attempting to duplicate the experience; and
7. Viewing life and living as more valuable and worthwhile.

Gemeinschaftsgefuhl Self-actualizers, though frequently feeling like aliens themselves, identify with all of humanity. They are world citizens. Their interest and concern extend to all people in all nations and cultures. They experience the feeling of brotherhood (similar to Adler's social interest, see Chapter 3) and the genuine desire to help all members of their species, whether friends or strangers.

Deep Interpersonal Relations Although self-actualizers feel deeply and empathically for all of humanity, and while some are venerated and attract large numbers of admirers and followers, they have no need to be friends (or even friendly) with everyone they meet. Indeed, with their B-love and esteem needs gratified, self-actualizers intentionally limit their friendships to a very few close personal friends, usually other equally healthy individuals with whom they can share and communicate. Interpersonal relationships established between healthy individuals are mutual, intimate, and intense, requiring a great deal of time and energy. Relationships of this nature are easily misunderstood by the less healthy, who may feel excluded.

Democratic Character Structure Maslow discovered that all of his self-actualizing subjects held democratic values; in fact, they seemed unaware of such superficial differences as age, sex, race, nationality, and religion. Rather, they responded to individuals, and because they were without the usual prejudices and could relate to others as equals, they were able to learn from any individual possessing knowledge or skills that interested them.

Discrimination Between Means and Ends   Self-actualizers possess an uncanny ability to discriminate between right and wrong, good and evil, means and ends. Further, because of their ability, they are nearly always aware of the moral and ethical implications of their choices and actions. While they do not lose sight of end-goals and seldom vacillate in a selected course of action, they may discover value in the means itself (reading, exercise, eating, for example). A means to an end can become an end in and of itself.

Philosophical Sense of Humor   While self-actualizers have a well-developed sense of humor and often smile or laugh at themselves, their pretensions, and the general human condition, they find nothing funny in hostile attempts to demean or harm individuals or groups for a laugh. Maslow described the humor expressed by his subjects as philosophical or instructive (i.e., some of the anecdotes of Abraham Lincoln, and while their names do not appear among Maslow's final selection of self-actualizing people, also Will Rogers and Mark Twain). Much of the humor of self-actualizers is spontaneous rather than contrived or planned; moreover, it is intrinsic to the immediate situation. "You simply had to be there to appreciate it."

Creativity   For Maslow (1954, 1959a, 1962), creativity is a universal characteristic of and inseparable from self-actualization. The stamp of creativity is a necessary mark of full humanness; hence all his self-actualizing subjects were creative. Once defined fully and no longer limited to just the arts, creativity is evident in whatever tasks his self-actualizers elected to undertake—indeed, in every aspect of their lives. Self-actualizers are open to their experiences and spontaneous in their feelings. They have the power to imagine beyond the immediate, to envision new ways of living. They view people, things, and events in their world with freshness and appreciation. They are strongly motivated by and have a sharp perception of the B-values—of truth, beauty, and wholeness—values that Maslow believes are the foundation blocks upon which true creativity stands.

Resistance to Enculturation   As mentioned earlier, with D-needs gratified and pulled by B-values, self-actualizers are unhampered by the defenses of ordinary people. Their perceptions of reality are more accurate. Their views of themselves, others, and the world are more detached and objective. They are more inner directed by personal values and standards. In short, they are more autonomous, more world citizens than citizens of any particular culture, state, or nation, and as such, more resistant to the shaping of an enculturation process. While they do not waste valuable time and energy fighting issues of little or no consequence, they do become aroused when their personal values, standards, and rights are threatened, and they will fight for meaningful social change and work to turn their visions into reality.

Psychopathology

When instinctoid needs and tendencies are gratified, humans *naturally* move toward self-actualization and health. An indifferent or hostile environment, however, can thwart or block the natural will to health by denying the gratification of instinctoid needs and tendencies, and in so doing, induce fearful regressive pressures that move humans away from health and toward illness. From this perspective, a neurosis—really all psychopathology—is viewed as a deficiency disease, not unlike avitaminosis.

The lower the level on the need hierarchy at which the deficiency needs are thwarted, repressed, or denied, the more severe the psychopathology—the difference is solely a matter of depth or degree. Moreover, as the pathology becomes increasingly severe, accessibility to benefit from need gratification diminishes. There is, according to Maslow, a point of severity where basic-need gratification is no longer sought by the neurotic, for basic need gratification is replaced with neurotic-need gratification. When a basic need has been "neuroticized," it becomes "uncontrollable, insatiable, ego-alien, rigid, inflexible, compulsive, indiscriminating" (Maslow, 1971, p. 383). In addition, Maslow (1968a) asserted, the neurotic "has usually lost his subjective well-being, his will, and his feeling of self-control, his capacity for pleasure, his self-esteem . . . . He is diminished as a human being" (p. 206).

Neuroses, then, are the losses of innate possibilities—failures, for whatever reasons, to gratify the instinctoid needs necessary to achieve self-actualization; in short, a turning or falling away from the natural movement toward health. Anything less than the full and normal becoming of human nature (self-actualization) is, in a very real sense, abnormal.

There is, according to Maslow (1971), a second path to psychological illness. Unrestrained and irresponsible indulgence in basic-need gratification also can twist the essential human nature and result in abnormal personality development (certain of the personality disorders—narcissistic or antisocial personality disorders, for example). Indulgence implies that needs are gratified by others. It tends to "infantilize" and to prevent development of strengths. Worse still, it is essentially condescending. Only to the self-disciplined and responsible is the advice to "follow your own inner dictates" sound advice. The inner dictates of the neurotic, according to Maslow (1968), are defended against, and their expressions are often distorted in dysfunctional and self-defeating ways.

Psychopathology is not limited to the deficiency needs (physiological, safety, love, and esteem needs). Deprivation of the B-needs (the metavalues) is also pathogenic. Maslow (1968, 1971) coined the term **metapathology** to describe the repression or denial of the metavalues—the typical symptoms of this higher form of pathology are feelings of alienation, apathy, boredom, cynicism, futility, joylessness, uselessness, doubt, hopelessness, and an inability to arrive at a satisfac-

Eleanor Roosevelt

George Washington Carver

Walt Whitman

Ruth Benedict

FIGURE 10-4 Maslow's Self-Actualizing Subjects
All photographs are courtesy of the Bettman Archive

tory system of personal values, hence a reason or purpose for being (see Maslow, 1970, p. 71; 1971, pp. 316–332).

Maslow (1968, 1970, 1971) asserts that humans who have reached the realm of self-actualization by fulfilling all deficiency needs can be overwhelmed with timidity and fear by the self they perceive in their most perfect moments. Their psyche shivers at the image of greatness. He describes those who betray their highest potentials by running from their destiny as suffering from the Jonah complex, for like the Biblical Jonah, in awe before great responsibility, they attempt to escape their fate. Embracing the B-values can instill feelings of unworthiness which, in turn, endanger security needs and lead to metapathology, a state of being without values. When security needs are threatened, risks are avoided, mistakes are feared, and behavior is directed in defense against imagined dangers.

Similar to the Jonah syndrome are the feelings of false humility likely to emerge when the nonactualizing compare themselves with those who are actualizing. When humans who have been taught to view humility as a virtue compare themselves to those who have accomplished greatness, they can be appalled by their own arrogance for even daring to make the comparison. In defense against their grandiosity and sinful pride, they betray their highest potentials by setting their sights lower, thus becoming less than they might be. The search for security is cheaper than the soul. "False humility," Maslow (1971) asserted, "stifles creativity" (p.39). Those who would embrace the metavalues and achieve their highest potentials must first overcome their fear of arrogance. Maslow (1971) believed this is possible only after they manage a "graceful integration between humility and pride," a prerequisite for any highly creative work (p. 39). To accept the challenge of greatness must be a staggering, stunning choice, yet to embrace the B-values, nothing less than greatness will do.

In summary, Maslow believed that neurotic people are those who, in fear of being overwhelmed by their instinctual impulses, mistrust and misinterpret their bodily wisdom, then defend against its direction. The results of yielding to neurotic fear are a wasting of life and a diminishing of humanness. Risk, resolve, strength, and responsibility are requirements of the B-values.

As Maslow attempted to define each of the B-values, he found he could only arrive at a complete definition of a single B-value by employing all the remaining thirteen. He had, then, not fourteen separate values, but rather one grand human value system that included, among others, love of truth, justice, beauty, goodness, and usefulness. This system, Maslow discovered, provides all the criteria necessary for the judgment of quality, *regardless of the subject* (i.e., for a painting to be truly beautiful, it must possess also the qualities of truth, goodness, unity or wholeness, aliveness, uniqueness, perfection, necessity, justice, order, simplicity, richness and totality, effortlessness, playfulness, self-sufficiency, and meaningfulness).

During his last years, Maslow (1968) reflected on transcendental possibilities, beyond Third Force Psychology to a still higher Fourth Psychology. He considered a need beyond self-actualization, the need for self-transcendence.

Heuristic Influences: Research Methods and Techniques

Maslow recognized that his investigative methods were unorthodox, his subjects few, his data questionable, and his work more a collection of observations, thoughts, and impressions than a fully developed theory of personality evolved from a strict, controlled experimentation. However, he made no apology for these shortcomings. Rigorous scientific procedures would have kept him from studying the subjective aspects of the human condition, those areas that were of greatest concern to him, and he consciously chose to proceed rather than give up his study of humans at their full psychological height. He was an explorer, an intellectual pathfinder, willing to submit initial observations that point the directions for future scientists. What mattered to Maslow was that he initiated a disciplined study of psychological health with a strength and insight that summoned attention and encouraged additional study. He willed the validation of his findings to those with the courage to follow—to the bolder and more venturesome of the future researchers.

Convinced that his psychologically healthy subjects had to be studied as integrated, organized, purposive entities, and that much of human behavior is meaningless when the subjective is ignored, Maslow (1966) found the methods of scientific orthodoxy totally inadequate for the questions he wanted answered. Rather than surrender his questions, he worked toward a more innovative, comprehensive, and inclusive philosophy of science.

Maslow's Philosophy of Science

Maslow (1966), a self-described "anticonstructionist," presented his case for a holistic science that is open to all levels of knowledge, *whether or not there are methodological tools available for adequately testing its reliability.* "Knowledge of low reliability is also part of knowledge" (p. 73). In *The Psychology of Science*, Maslow (1966) presented a strong argument that overreliance on methodology frequently leads to the overemphasis on the importance of quantification, the tendency to tailor research to fit familiar methodology, and most important, the avoidance of important and consequential issues. "*Any* philosophy of science which serves primarily an excluding function is a set of blinders, a handicap rather than a help" (Maslow, 1968b, p. 218, emphasis in original).

Maslow (1970) readily admitted to the validity of the charges of the experimentalists and behaviorists that his work is inelegant, imprecise, and crude, but then he asked if these are not the very characteristics expected from first efforts to research a new problem (p. 14). Further, he questioned whether it is realistic, or for that matter, wise to insist that the science of new problems be a mature science. "Knowledge has an embryology, too, it cannot confine itself to its final and adult forms" (p. 73).

Maslow's stance is humanistic. He cares for his subjects. He intentionally does not attempt to design a value-free or value-neutral study. "From nonpersonal truth we can learn nothing about human values" (Maslow, in Lowry, 1973,

p. 620). His work is exploratory, a pilot study at best. His conclusions are in the "realm of prescience." But Maslow dared to concern himself with areas of human functioning that the more scientific theorists avoid. He was one of the first to investigate *optimal* human growth and development. More, Maslow had the courage to publish his findings, in spite of anticipated consequences. Schooled and competent in the methods of classical science, he was painfully aware that he was opening himself and his work to criticism, perhaps inviting censure and ridicule from his colleagues.

Maslow placed some of the responsibility for a rigid philosophy of science at the doorsteps of the editors of professional journals when he charged: "A methodologically satisfactory experiment, whether trivial or not, is rarely criticized ... I do not recall ... any paper that criticized another for being unimportant, trivial or inconsequential" (Maslow, 1966, p. 12; see also, 1970). He urged his students and fellow psychologists to be courageous when considering the areas of research they would pursue, and challenges them to choose "growth science" rather than a pathologized "safety science" (p. 34). The struggle, he believed, is intrapsychic—between fear and courage, defense and growth. For Maslow (1966), science has two goals: "one is toward utter simplicity and condensation, *the other is toward total comprehensiveness and inclusiveness*" (p. 72, emphasis added).

Research Methods and Techniques

Consistent with his philosophy of an expanded philosophy of science (Maslow, 1966), Maslow's research methods were initially intuitive. He relied heavily on observation rather than hypothesis testing and deviated markedly from the orthodox conception of statistics, specifically sampling theory. Sparked by the informal study of his mentors Benedict and Wertheimer, Maslow began his study of optimal human health by first selecting subjects from among his friends and acquaintances who he believed personified his ideal of psychological health by living to their full potential, and later from a group of students at Brandeis University who appeared to be healthy, strong, and creative. When this approach yielded too few subjects, he further extended his search to public and historical figures.

The biographical data gathered from his subjects (and whenever possible from their friends and relatives) were used to form global or holistic impressions. These impressions, in turn, were employed to develop a syndrome of psychological health and to refine the original criteria for self-actualization. Maslow then reviewed all his subjects in light of the refined criteria, retaining some and eliminating and adding others. The entire process was repeated with the second group of subjects. Once again, he refined the criteria for self-actualization and selected a third group of subjects. Maslow continued this process until he was satisfied that he had developed an operational definition of the self-actualizing person.

Maslow divided his subjects into three categories: "fairly sure" cases, which included Jefferson, Lincoln, Spinoza, Einstein, and Eleanor Roosevelt; partial cases, which included five contemporary people whose names he refused to reveal; and lastly, "potential or possible" cases, who seemed to be striving for self-actualization and included such people as Eleanor Franklin, Whitman, G. W. Carver, Auguste Renoir, and Adlai Stevenson.

There are flaws in Maslow's study, the most critical of which is the sampling procedure. Because he selected people whom he personally held in highest regard as models of optimal psychological health, he is charged with permitting his own values to influence his definition of self-actualization. By omitting important variables (e.g., intelligence, special talents, education levels, and economic status), he may have biased his study and thus used an élite sample to generalize about the species. In addition to the methodological problems, Maslow is criticized for a rather loose use of language, particularly such concepts as "metaneeds," "metavalues," and "metapathologies."

Current Assessment

Maslow's prediction that future research would validate many of his theoretical constructs is yet to be fulfilled. Indeed, there is some question whether his theory, which at times borders on the philosophical, has been expressed in a manner that permits scientific confirmation or rejection. Research available at this point does not support his theory to any significant degree, and while this does not necessarily mean that Maslow is wrong, there is reason to believe that should this condition continue, scientific interest in his theory might wane. In an overview of need hierarchy theory, Maddox (1984) reports that while foreign countries (particularly Third World countries) continue to debate and research the applicability of need hierarchy to management and organizations, the theory is not receiving the attention and consideration in this country that it once did. "The fact of the matter is that the majority of the articles available from about 1977 until 1984 come from foreign sources and deal with the applications of the theory in developing countries" (Maddox, 1984, p. 1).

One of the key variables in Maslow's general theory of motivation is that human needs are biological and appear in a hierarchy of prepotency that extends over a considerable, but unspecified, period of time. Thus, with rare exceptions, as a more proponent need is increasingly gratified, needs at the next higher level in the hierarchy will attain proportionately greater influence over an individual's behavior. Much of the support of Maslow's theory is of an indirect or philosophical nature (in contrast to carefully controlled empirical studies). For example, other personality theorists and psychotherapists, as well as some biologists, affirm the influence of an actualizing tendency (Goldstein, 1939, 1947; A. Szent-Gyoergyi, 1974; see also Rogers and Allport, Chapters 9 and 8).

With few exceptions, operational definitions are not provided by the theory, and researchers are faced with the obstacle of measurement. As Maddi (1972) points out while Maslow's language is rich in vivid illustrative references, he "names characteristics more for illustration than to promote a set, dependable scheme whereby one can identify and understand various patterns of living" (p. 320).

More than two decades after Maslow (1943) introduced his concept of a need hierarchy, Shostrom (1974), in close adherence to Maslow's theorizing, devised a self-report questionnaire aimed at measuring the various facets of self-actualizing. Called the Personal Orientation Inventory (POI), the questionnaire consists of 150 paired opposing statements and is scored as two major scales, *inner directedness* and *time competence,* and ten complementary scales: *self-actualizing values, existentiality, feeling reactivity, spontaneity, self-regard, self-acceptance, nature of man, synergy, acceptance of aggression,* and *capacity for intimacy.* The degree of reliability for the scales is reported as adequate (it correlates adequately with variables *believed* to be descriptive of self-actualization), and its claim to construct validity is strengthened by exceptional resistance to faking. In addition to an understanding of the inventory and its rationale, interpretation of the POI entails an understanding of Maslow's theoretical concepts of self-actualization. Most of the research with this instrument is correlational—POI scores are correlated with measures of behavior or personality.

Various POI scales correlate positively with subjects rated by trained psychologists as self-actualizing (Shostrom, 1965). Conversely, the POI scales yield negative correlations in studies of alcoholics (Zaccaria & Wheir, 1967), hospitalized psychiatric patients (Fox, Knapp, & Michael, 1968), and convicted felons (Fischer, 1968).

Few studies in management and organization behavior yield evidence indicating that good measurement techniques have evolved; however, "it is difficult to determine if the situation arises from the weakness of the theoretical base or from poor efforts to think through the constructs and how they might be defined in the real world of work" (Schwartz, 1983; Maddox, 1984).

Questionable confirmation was found for Maslow's need hierarchy in Ganguli and Greha's (1978) study of junior and middle Indian subcontinent managers and their need satisfaction/strength patterns. Managers with greater experience in an organization tend to have stronger and higher-need strength than managers with short tenure. Indeed, there was considerable evidence that security needs were important to those managers who had been with the organization the shortest period of time. This would seem intuitively valid, as entering managers are still experiencing organizational socialization and adjustment. Aram and Piraino (1978), in a forced-choice questionnaire study of 1447 individuals in Chile, report that for this sample, the social needs are the most important of Maslow's needs.

Using Maslow's need questionnaire with 110 Dutch workers, Liebrand (1977) found no support for Maslow's hierarchical arrangement of needs. Goebel and Brown (1981), investigating age differences in motivation related to an implicit developmental sequencing of Maslow's need hierarchy, tested 111 (fifty-eight female and fifty-seven male) individuals between the ages of nine and eighty. In the study, five levels of development from childhood to older adults were demarcated. They found statistically significant age differences in motivation for all but the security needs. The need for love was highest at all levels. Self-esteem need importance peaked at adolescence and declined thereafter. Self-actualization needs declined in adulthood and older adulthood, and safety and security needs came into play once again with aged subjects. This study, then, affords little indication that Maslow's hierarchy is valid in relation to human development or that there is a common sequencing of prepotent need realization.

Overall, the validity of most attempts to test Maslow's need hierarchy is questionable. The majority of these studies are based on self-reports of needs, in spite of Maslow's (1970) repeated warning: "Careful study of the conscious motivational life alone will often leave out much that is as important or even more important than what can be seen in consciousness" (p. 22). In brief, Maslow viewed motivation as largely an unconscious process, while most studies designed to test his need hierarchy are based on self-reports, hence conscious processes. In addition, nearly all available research ignores the cognitive and aesthetic needs by focusing entirely on the five basic needs.

Schwartz (1983) doubts the validity of much of the research claiming to test Maslow's theory. He questions whether many of the researchers understand the theory they are attempting to test, pointing out that many of Maslow's critics overlook or ignore the fact that his theory grew out of and is a part of the psychoanalytic tradition.

Applications to Psychotherapy

Unlike many of the personality theorists whose works are presented in this book, Maslow was not a psychotherapist, and while he was a psychologist and an educator, he did not focus on learning. Nonetheless, his motivational concepts are accepted as practical and applied by specialists in a number of disciplines, including counseling and psychotherapy, management, and education.

While Maslow (1970) did not establish a system of psychotherapy, he views psychotherapy as an "unworked gold mine (p. 241)." Further, he believes that psychotherapy rightfully deserves recognition as "an important department of general psychology" (p. 242).

Therapeutic Goals

Maslow's (1970) "transpersonal" psychotherapeutic stance is eclectic: Psychotherapy is "any means of any kind that help to restore the person to the path of self-actualization *and of developing along the lines that his inner nature dictates*" (p. 270, emphasis added). Clearly implied in Maslow's definition is the idea that psychotherapy is a therapy of the instincts; it is good to the extent that it gratifies the client's basic needs—security, love, belongingness, feelings of worth, self-esteem, and ultimately, self-actualization and the B-values.

The Therapeutic Relationship

Because the basic needs can only be satisfied by other human beings, Maslow described the process of psychotherapy as essentially interpersonal. Perhaps he expressed the therapeutic value of the healthy interpersonal relationship most clearly when he wrote:

> *Let people realize that every time they threaten someone or humiliate or hurt unnecessarily or dominate or reject another human being, they become forces for the creation of psychopathology, even if these be small forces. Let them recognize also that every man who is kind, helpful, decent, psychologically democratic, affectionate, and warm, is a psychotherapeutic force even though a small one (Maslow, 1970, p. 254).*

Like Rogers, Maslow (1970) believed that a healthy interpersonal relationship between the client and therapist is a necessary precondition to therapy proper. Unlike Rogers, however, he did not believe that a healthy interpersonal relationship is always a sufficient psychotherapeutic force. The therapeutic relationship, for Maslow, is not an end in itself, but rather a means to an end.

For Maslow (1970), the therapeutic relationship is not unique; it is "simply a subexample of social or interpersonal relationships" (p. 241). Any healthy interpersonal relationship, whether between client and therapist, child and parent, or student and teacher, can be therapeutic. For those therapists who would apply his motivational concepts to psychotherapy, however, Maslow (1970) warned that while some therapeutic good results from all healthy human relationships, not all healthy people are effective therapists. Psychological health is necessary, but so, too, are intelligence, self-insight, self-understanding, and adequate training in the modern techniques and tools of psychotherapy. He warned also that in the case of severe illness (a chronic and stabilized neurosis or an authoritarian personality that perceives kindness as weakness, for example), it is not unusual for neurotic-need gratifications to replace basic-need gratification. Once this occurs, offering the severely ill client a close interpersonal relationship is useless, for such a relationship is feared, mistrusted, misinterpreted, and ultimately refused.

The Therapeutic Process

Maslow (1970) believed that with the severely ill client, depth analysis in the Freudian tradition—an analysis involving both cognitive and emotive methodology—may be the most effective therapeutic approach for achieving conscious insight, self-understanding, and change. Further, he suggested, the major techniques for such an approach are free association and dream interpretation of the meaning behind everyday behavior. (Perhaps it should be repeated here that Maslow had received training as a psychoanalyst, and on a number of occasions sought the assistance of a psychoanalyst when he needed help with difficult problems, experiences he valued most positively, in spite of the limitations and shortcomings he expressed on numerous occasions.)

Group Therapy

Interested in experiential approaches to the exploration, expansion, and expression of consciousness, Maslow was impressed with the potential of various group therapies and growth centers that emerged in the 1960s. Although Maslow's early knowledge of group therapy was largely that of observer rather than participant, he did attempt to introduce intrinsic learning experiences that were directed to the problems of personal growth, identity, and values in some of his psychology classes and laboratories at Brandeis (Chiang, in Chiang & Maslow, 1960, pp. 225–239; see also Maslow, 1971).

Holistically oriented, Maslow was especially interested in the integration of experiential knowing *and* abstract knowing—an interest, incidently, that few of his contemporaries shared. The more traditionally oriented psychologists, including many at Brandeis University, scoffed at the experiential approach to group therapy, and the leaders of the Gestalt approach to therapy (Fritz Perls, for example) manifested boredom when confronted with words and theoretical concepts. For the majority identifying with the humanistic movement, however, Maslow was accepted as the father of a humanistic revolution, and they did apply his concepts in their work. The leader of Esalen, for example, embraced his ideas concerning the need for intrinsic learning and modeled the institute's program on the ideas Maslow expressed in *Toward a Psychology of Being*. Maslow remained more cautious than many of his followers, and as he did when viewing the potentials of individual therapy, warned of the potential dangers of group therapy, particularly the dangers of unqualified or unethical group leaders.

Extended Applications

Maslow's interest in psychological health and the good life led him to look beyond the individual to work and the work environment, to management in the work place, to education, even to science and religion.

Work and the Work Environment

In his study of self-actualizing people, Maslow (1954/1970, 1965, 1971) discovered that not only is work an important means of meeting the deficiency needs (i.e., food, shelter, security, belongingness, dignity, respect, and appreciation), it is a necessary path to self-actualization. Indeed, Maslow was convinced that along with creativity, dedication to a calling or mission in life—*to one's beloved work*—is a universal characteristic of his self-actualizing subjects (see "Characteristics of Self-Actualizing People"). Further investigation of this phenomenon led Maslow to the discovery that work viewed at the highest level of human health is directly related to the B-values; it transcends basic need gratification and gives both purpose and meaning to life. The self-actualizers in Maslow's study were most happy and fulfilled when they were absorbed in their work. Conversely, those subjects who had all basic needs gratified, but who had not yet discovered their life's work, felt incomplete—unfulfilled. They reported that life lacked something. Maslow (1970, 1971) was convinced that for whatever reason, they had not embraced the B-values; they were not motivated by the metaneeds. Their dissatisfaction and unhappiness were really manifestations of a metapathology (see "Psychopathology").

Management

Eupsychian Management (1965) is Maslow's attempt to apply his theory of motivation to management in business, industrial, and social environments. Maslow (1964b, 1965) believes that management techniques should be based on the acceptance of a higher human nature (which includes the needs for fairness, meaningful work, responsibility, creativity, and the metavalues) rather than on manipulation and exploitation. He is convinced that when the conditions of management and the work environment are conducive (synergistic) to individual growth they are good as well for the aims, values, and productivity of the organization. Maslow's need-hierarchy approach has been a cornerstone of management education for two decades, and appears in nearly every introductory management textbook.

Education

Maslow (1968, 1970, 1971) expresses little faith in traditional education which, he believes, attempts to teach, mold, and shape the predetermined values of society in an authoritarian (interfering) way rather than trusting in the natural processes of human growth and permitting actualization to occur in a Taoistic (noninterfering) way. For Maslow (1971), "education is learning to grow, learning what to grow toward, learning what is good and bad, learning what is desirable and undesirable, learning what to choose and what not to choose" (p. 179).

Uncovering individual idiosyncracy cannot be accomplished, Maslow asserts, within the limits of a set curriculum with required courses, grades, credits, diplomas, and degrees. The need to be free for self-development is a essential part of the instinctoid needs. *Self*-actualization, by definition, is *self*-directed and calls for intrinsic motivation and learning. The goal of education, according to Maslow, is to let the student *be*, to encourage or help in a noninterfering (Taoistic) way what exists in embryo to become real and actual. Through excessive pressures and controls, traditional education, Maslow believes, undermines the natural learning process. It is intrusive rather than receptive, extrinsic rather than intrinsic. "The purpose of education, the purpose of all institutions, is the development of full humanness" (Maslow, in Hall, 1968, p. 57).

Maslow (1971) envisions higher education as an experiential retreat where consciousness can be refreshed and B-values can be awakened and fulfilled. For Maslow, education should be concerned first with the discovery of self, then the discovery of a vocation. Once these goals are accomplished, Maslow asserts, the individual will naturally seek to acquire the specific knowledge and skills necessary for the vocation; moreover, he or she will be intrinsically motivated to do well.

Critique

An articulate and persuasive writer, Maslow expresses a deep personal compassion for his species, with all its wonders and weaknesses. The portrait of humanity that emerges with his theoretical brush contrasts sharply in substance, language, and tone to those painted by Freud and Skinner, a contrast that is welcomed by those dissatisfied with the psychoanalytic and behaviorist approaches to human motivation. While he recognizes the many contributions of the psychoanalysts and behaviorists, Maslow criticizes both groups for their negative, limited, impersonal, and valueless conceptions of the human condition.

Maslow's metamotivational theory generates an optimistic confidence in human potential. And while he acknowledges that his description of the self-actualizing human fits better at present with the broader outlines of philosophy than it does with pure science, he questions the worth of a science so rigid that it excludes all levels of knowledge except those that can be governed by its own distinct rules. An excluding science, he asserts, will never be the productive force it is supposed to be for the psychology of the human. Further, he rejects a science that attempts to divorce itself totally from human values by demanding objectivity, causal analysis, and ethical neutrality. Maslow argues that only the goals and ends of science can justify its methods and techniques. His stance is critical, but it is not a defection. Rather, Maslow seeks to enlarge the jurisdiction of science to include all human realities (see "Maslow's Philosophy of Science").

Smarting from the criticism of unrealistic optimism, a vulnerable Maslow (1979) responds in his journal: "It's funny to be called unrealistically optimistic for reporting that a fraction of one percent of the population I know was pulled out as self-actualizing" (p. 415). He reminds his critics also that the very presence of self-actualizing individuals, regardless of how limited their number, does indicate that a higher human nature is possible. Although Maslow focuses on the higher nature of human potentials, he acknowledges the human capability of aggression and destruction that arises from the frustration of basic human needs and the actualizing tendency. It was not Maslow's purpose to call for optimism—rather his call was for realism in the best sense of the word. For Maslow, the subjective side of human nature is as real as the objective—joy and elation are as real as depression; love is as real as hate; courage is as real as fear.

Maslow's theory has a common-sense appeal. It is consistent with the dictates of common sense, for example, that people who are continuously and dangerously hungry are unconcerned with social and political issues. They are willing, indeed eager, to accept that form of government promising to put the most food on their tables. Maslow's hierarchy of needs lacks specificity in some areas;

however, it does offer a broad theoretical framework that can be used to explain and to organize nearly all human motivation.

There is a fairly high degree of internal consistency in Maslow's theory, even though there are occasions when vague and equivocal language makes parts of his theory ambiguous and impossible to test. For example, Maslow asserts that cognitive needs are a precondition to basic needs, yet does not include them as part of his basic-needs hierarchy. It is also important to note that exceptions to the need hierarchy have been cited (Maddi, 1978).

Maslow's penchant for lists can lead to confusion. Long lists of adjectives frequently obscure the meaning of the nouns they modify, just as lengthy lists of verbs can obscure the action that Maslow attempts to describe. In short, precision suffers when the lists become lengthy or contain contradictions.

A need hierarchy of only five levels does give Maslow's theory the deceptive appearance of simplicity. However, as Schwartz (1983) so aptly points out, the simple is not always simplistic. As Maslow repeatedly explains, humans are frequently and simultaneously driven by several needs from different levels of the need hierarchy, and even self-actualizing individuals are not always conscious of all the motivations behind their behavior. Still, while the need hierarchy is inclusive, it does not offer a clear explanation for those exceptional individuals who achieve a high level of psychological health in spite of a poor history of deficiency-need gratification (Maddi, 1972).

Despite the limitations of Maslow's theory—and there are many (see "Heuristic Influences: Research Methods and Techniques")—his writing is provocative. He has stimulated both the thinking and the investigations of numerous professional groups, including psychologists, counselors, educators, administrators, managers, nurses, and social workers. In addition to awakening an interest in a psychology of health and the farther reaches of human potential, he has forced some professionals to consider the limitations of scientific orthodoxy as a tool for understanding human functioning. Further, he has encouraged other psychologists to focus first on significant questions and only then adopt or if necessary create the techniques for answering them, even when they know their techniques are limited and can lead only to answers that are tentative and incomplete.

Annotated Bibliography

Maslow's definitive book, *Motivation and Personality,* was published in 1954. Shortly before his death in 1970, he completed an extensive revision of this work. In addition to his concepts of the hierarchy of needs and self-actualization, Maslow discusses the application of his work to the theories of science, personality, psychotherapy and personal growth, and general psychology. In his revised edition, Maslow states that it is time to begin thinking about the "transhuman, a psychology and philosophy which transcends the human species itself" (p. xxvii).

Intended as a continuation of the 1954 edition of *Motivation and Personality,* Maslow's *Toward a Psychology of Being* became his most popular book, selling well over 100,000 copies in the original edition. Writing of an intrinsic human nature that is motivated by the highest values and aspirations, Maslow (through a collection of papers and lectures) demonstrates that humans can be loving, noble, and creative; indeed, he asserts, destructiveness and cruelty appear to be "violent reactions *against* frustrations of our intrinsic needs, emotions, and capacities" (p. 3). Admittedly "way out ahead of the data," Maslow presents forty-three major propositions of his Third Force Psychology.

Religions, Values, and Peak-Experiences (1964) is Maslow's warning against the polarization and dichotomizing of the natural sciences and religion, or the body and the spirit. For Maslow, dichotomizing is pathogenic, whether it is religion separating from the facts and knowledge of science, or science separating from the values and ethics of religion. In this book Maslow focuses on peak and plateau experiences, the B-values, and the human need for knowledge and spiritual expression.

Maslow's final work, *The Farther Reaches of Human Nature* (1971), is a collection of articles he had selected for the book. His plans to add new material, to write an elaborate preface and epilogue, and to thoroughly rewrite and update the manuscript were left unrealized when he suffered from a fatal heart attack on June 8, 1970. While the *Farther Reaches of Human Nature* is unfinished and unpolished, at least to the degree that Maslow had intended, it is nonetheless a complete and integrated book. The chapters flow together smoothly and easily, and the reader encounters no difficulty with transitions.

Readers who wish to know more about Maslow's life are referred to F. Goble's *The Third Force: The Psychology of Abraham Maslow;* R. J. Lowry's *A. H. Maslow: An Intellectual Portrait;* C. Wilson's *New Pathways in Psychology: Maslow and the Post-Freudian Revolution;* and B. G. Maslow's *Abraham H. Maslow, A Memorial Volume.* Undoubtedly the best single source for insight into Maslow's thoughts from age fifty are his journals, The Journals of A. H. Maslow (two volumes), edited by R. J. Lowry.

References and Suggested Readings

Aram, J. D. & Piraino, T. G. (1970). The hierarchy of needs theory: An evaluation in Chile. *Revista Interamericana de Psicologia, 12,* pp. 179–188.

Aron, A. (1977, Spring). Maslow's other child. *Journal of Humanistic Psychology, 71*(2), pp. 9–24.

Buber, M. (1937/1958). *I and thou.* New York: Charles Scribner's Sons.

Chiang, H., & Maslow, A. H. (Eds.). (1977). *The healthy personality: Readings* (2nd ed.). New York: D. Van Nostrand.

Feist, J. (1985). *Theories of personality.* New York: Holt, Rinehart & Winston.

Fisher, G. (1968). Performance of psychopathic felons on a measure of self-actualization. *Educational Psychology Measurement, 28,* pp. 561–563.

Fox, J., Knapp, R., & Michael, W. (1968). Assessment of self-actualization of psychiatric patients: Validity of the Personal Orientation Inventory. *Educational Psychology Measurement, 28,* pp. 565–569.

Fromm, E. (1941). *Escape from freedom.* New York: Holt, Rinehart & Winston.

Ganguli, S., & Guha, S. C. (1978). Work experience and managerial need patterns. *Management and Labor Studies, 4,* pp. 13–19.

Goble, F. (1970). *The third force: The psychology of Abraham Maslow.* New York: Pocket Books.

Goebal, B. L., & Brown, D. R. (1981). Age differences in motivation related to Maslow's need hierarchy. *Developmental Psychology, 17,* pp. 809–815.

Goldstein, K. (1939). *The organism.* New York: American Book.

Goldstein, K. (1947). Organismic approach to the problem of motivation. *Transactions of the New York Academy of Sciences, 9,* pp. 218–230.

Guinan, J., & Foulds, M. (1970). Marathon group: Facilitator of personal growth? *Journal of Counseling Psychology, 17,* pp. 145–149.

Hall, M. H. (July, 1968). A conversation with Abraham H. Maslow. *Psychology Today. 2 (2),* pp. 35–37, 54–57.

Hamachek, D. E. (Ed.). (1965). *The self in growth, teaching, and learning.* Englewood Cliffs, N.J.: Prentice–Hall.

Jourard, S. (1974). *Healthy personality: An approach from the viewpoint of humanistic psychology.* New York: Macmillan.

Leonard, G. (December, 1983). Abraham Maslow and the new self. *Esquire,* pp. 326–336.

Liebnrand, W. (1977). Maslow's hierarchical arrangement of fundamental needs. *Tijschrift voor de Psychologie en haar Grensgebieden, 32,* pp. 67–80.

Lowry, R. J. (1973). *A. H. Maslow: An intellectual portrait.* Monterey, Calif.: Brooks/Cole.

Maddi, S. R. (1972). *Personality theories: A comparative analysis* (Rev. ed.). Homewood, Ill.: Dorsey Press.

Maddi, S. R., & Costa, P. T. (1972). *Humanism in personology: Allport, Maslow, and Murry.* Chicago: Aldine–Atherton.

Maddox, E. N. (1984). Need hierarchy theory. Paper presented at the Seminar for Organizational Behavior, Department of Management, Florida State University.

Maslow, A. H. (1943). Dynamics of personality organization, I. *Psychological Review 50 (5),* pp. 514–539.

Maslow, A. H. (1943, November). Dynamics of personality organization, II. *The Psychological Review, 50 (6),* pp. 541–558.

Maslow, A. H. (1945). Experimentalizing the clinical method. *Journal of Clinical Psychology, 1,* pp. 241–243.

Maslow, A. H. (1948). "Higher" and "lower" needs. *The Journal of Psychology, 25,* pp. 433–436.

Maslow, A. H. (1954). *Motivation and personality.* New York: Harper & Row.

Maslow, A. H. & Zimmerman, W. (1956). College teaching ability, scholarly activity and personality. *Journal of Educational Psychology, 47,* pp. 185–189.

Maslow, A. H. (1958). Emotional blocks to creativity. *Journal of Individual Psychology, 14 (1),* pp. 51–56.

Maslow, A. H. (Ed.) (1959a). *New knowledge in human values.* Chicago: Henry Regnery.

Maslow, A. H. (1959b). Critique of self-actualization: 1. Some dangers of being-cognition. *Journal of Individual Psychology, 15 (1),* pp. 24–32.

Maslow, A. H. (1962). *Toward a psychology of being.* Princeton, NJ.: Van Nostrand Reinhold.

Maslow, A. H. (1963). The need to know and the fear of knowing. *The Journal of General Psychology, 68,* pp. 111–125.

Maslow, A. H. (1964a). *Religions, values, and peak experiences.* Columbus, Ohio: Ohio State University Press. Paperback reprint: New York: Viking, 1970.

Maslow, A. H. (1964b). Synergy in the society and in the individual. *Journal of Individual Psychology, 20* (2), pp. 153–164.

Maslow, A. H. (1965). *Eupsychian management.* Homewood, Ill.: Irwin–Dorsey.

Maslow, A. H. (1966). *The psychology of science: A reconnaissance.* New York: Harper & Row.

Maslow, A. H. (1968a). *Toward a psychology of being* (2nd ed.). Princeton, N.J.: D. Van Nostrand.

Maslow, A. H. (July, 1968b). A theory of metamotivation: The biological rooting of the value-life. *Psychology Today, 22,* pp. 38–39, 58–62.

Maslow, A. H. (1970). *Motivation and personality* (3rd ed.). New York: Harper & Row. Excerpts in this chapter are from MOTIVATION AND PERSONALITY, Third Edition by Abraham H. Maslow, revised by Robert Frager et al. Copyright 1954, 1987 by Harper & Row, Publishers, Inc.; copyright © 1970 by Abraham H. Maslow. Reprinted by permission by HarperCollins Publishers Inc.

Maslow, A. H. (1971). *The farther reaches of human nature.* New York: Viking.

Maslow, A. H. (1978). The instinctoid nature of basic needs. In R. J. Corsini (Ed.), *Readings in current personality theory.* Itasca, Ill.: F. E. Peacock.

Maslow, A. H. (1979). *The journals of A. H. Maslow* (2 vols.). R. J. Lowry (Ed.). Monterey, Calif.: Brooks/Cole.

Maslow, B. G. (1972). *Abraham H. Maslow: A memorial volume.* Monterey, Calif.: Brooks/Cole.

Schultz, D. (1977). *Growth psychology: Models of the healthy personality.* New York: D. Van Nostrand.

Schwartz, H. S. (1983). Maslow and the hierarchical enactment of organizational reality. *Human Relations, 36,* pp. 933–956.

Shostrom, E. (1974). *Manual for the Personal Orientation Inventory.* San Diego: Educational and Instructional Testing Service.

Szent-Gyoergyi, A. (1974, Spring). Drive in living matter to perfect itself. *Synthesis,* pp. 12–24.

Wilson, C. (1972). *New pathways in psychology: Maslow and the post-Freudian revolution.* New York: New American Library.

Zaccaria, J. S., & Weir, W. R. (1967). A comparison of alcoholics and selected samples of non-alcoholics in terms of a positive concept of mental health. *Journal of Social Psychology, 71,* pp. 151–157.

Part 4

Existential Theories

The theories of Rollo May and Victor Frankl were selected to represent existential theories. As mentioned earlier (Chapter 1), existential theorists are a most diverse group. Indeed, they object strenuously to being classified as a group, and from their viewpoint, not without justification.

It is more realistic to think of existential personality theorists as sharing a leaning toward existential thought than it is to attempt to classify them into a single general school. The classification employed here, then, is primarily one of convenience.

For both May and Frankl, primary motivation is the will of the individual to discover personal meaning. We are motivated by the dynamic of tensions between what we are (including our potentials) and what we ought to be. Existential guilt results from the recognition of the gap between the two poles. To choose and to accept responsibility for our actions calls for courage to take a stand, to accept that which we sense experientially or discover as meaningful.

Both May and Frankl view us as self-aware, self-conscious, choosing, responsible beings in the world, who must confront the inevitability of nonbeing. Both speak of the need to affirm our identity, courage, creativity, and freedom, and to actualize our possibilities. We alone, they assert, are responsible for discovering our own meaning through the choices we make in the course of daily living. It is only through our choices that we can attain authentic selfhood. We must, in the course of living in the world, acquire the courage to exercise both our will to freedom and our will to meaning.

Chapter 11

May's Existential Theory of Personality

Chapter Overview

Introduction

Biographical Sketch of the Theorist

Resolution of Eleven Basic Issues
    Heredity versus Social Determinants
    Conscious versus Unconscious Determinants
    Subjective versus Objective Reality
    Determinism versus Freedom of Choice
    Early versus Continuous Development
    Role Assigned to Self-Concept
    Uniqueness versus Universality
    Number and Weight Assigned to Motivational Concepts
    Role Assigned to Group Determinants
    Explanation of Learning Process
    Centrality of Reinforcement

Psychological Health and Psychopathology

Heuristic Influences: Research Methods and Techniques

Application to Psychotherapy
Therapeutic Goals
Therapeutic Relationship
Therapeutic Process and Strategies
Course of Therapy

Extended Applications

Critique

Annotated Bibliography

References and Suggested Readings

Introduction

There is no single existential theory of personality development or psychotherapy. Existentialism is a divergent theoretical arena; "it is extremely amorphous, shifting in emphasis from country to country, continent to continent, and even individual theorist to individual theorist" (Maddi, 1980, p. 136).

While some agreement exists among existential theorists (e.g., an interest in those unique qualities that make a human being human and give existence meaning), they have not achieved the unanimity of thought necessary for the establishment of a separate, clearly defined theory of personality or system of psychotherapy. Not only do they sometimes disagree on major theoretical assumptions, they also often disagree on the meanings they assign to identical terms. Hence, rather than a special theory or method, existentialism might better be considered an approach to human personality development and therapeutic practice that attempts to make sense of existence by assigning meaning to it. The existential approach to personality and therapy, then, is more an attitude held, prized, and expressed by personologists, counselors, and therapists who identify with existentialism. Rollo Reese May (1977, 1983), whose works were selected as the primary source for this chapter, supports this perspective.

Moreover, May (1977) contends that any attempt to establish a single theory of existential personality or therapy at this time would be a serious mistake. Indeed, he believes that the nature of the existential attitude makes even the idea of a separate school or theory impossible.

In *Existence* (May, Angel, & Ellenberger, 1958), May traces the philosophic lineage of existentialism to nineteenth-century Europe. He cites Edmund Husserl (the founder of modern phenomenology), and Soren Kierkegaard (the tormented Danish philosopher and theist whose rhetorical treatises criticized the prevalent reductionist view of humankind) as two main precursors of existentialism. Ahead of their time, Husserl's and Kierkegaard's works went largely unnoticed until shortly after World War I, when their concerns were echoed in the writings of such European philosophers as Martin Buber, Fedor Dostoevski, Martin Heidegger, Karl Jaspers, Gabriel Marcel, and Paul Tillich.

Rooted in French resistance to German occupation during World War II, existentialism again moved through Europe, and in the 1950s spread to the United States. Jean-Paul Sartre and Albert Camus were two outstanding existential spokesmen of this period. Both were awarded the Nobel Prize in Literature.

Existentialism became a viable force in art, literature, and religion, and as often happens with popular movements, became attractive to intellectuals and university students as well as various dissident groups. A small group of independent psychoanalysts, dissatisfied with the reductionist Freudian view of humankind, believed that existential analysis added both breadth and depth to the therapeutic concepts and understandings presented by Freud. They worked toward the development of an existential approach to therapy. Two of the more influential persons to follow this path were the Swiss psychiatrists Ludwig Binswanger and Medard Boss.

Among the advocates of an existential approach to psychotherapy in the United States are Rollo May, Abraham Maslow, Carl Rogers, James Bugental, Clarke Moustakas, Adrian Van Kamm, and Irvin Yalom. According to May (May, Angel, & Ellenberger, 1958; May, 1977, 1983), the existential approach to therapy provides a sound, flexible philosophy that lends meaning to and can be integrated with many of the current Humanistic or Third Force theories of counseling and psychotherapy, including, for example, four rather different therapies presented in this book (see Chapters 8, 9, 10, and 11).

Although he rejects much of Freud's theory, May (May, Angel, & Ellenberger, 1958), asserts that many of the Freudian and existential positions are complementary and can be integrated. Both positions ask fundamental questions about human existence, focus on the rational and irrational sides of human nature, are concerned with the ways conflict and anxiety impede human growth and functioning, and concentrate upon understanding human nature. Under the influence of Freud, Adler, Kierkegaard, and Tillich and an intense personal experience and interest in anxiety, May developed a theoretical approach that closely follows existential philosophy. For May (1989), personality is "characterized by *freedom, individuality, social integration,* and *religious tension*" (p. 14, emphasis in original). His view of personality is "dynamic, not static; creative, not vegetative" (May, 1989, p. 34).

Biographical Sketch of the Theorist

Early Years

Rollo May was born April 21, 1909, in the small town of Ada, Ohio. He was the second of six children (three boys and three girls) and the eldest son of Earl and Matie May. As a child May detested the name Rollo, which had been selected for him by his mother. She had named him after Little Rollo, a juvenile hero in a series of nineteenth-century character-building books by the New England churchman Jacob Abbott. Throughout May's childhood, Little Rollo's exploits were presented to May as the model for proper deportment. May's intense dislike for his name remained with him until, as a young adult living in Europe, he learned of a medieval Norman leader, referred to as Rollo the Conqueror; the name Rollo suddenly became acceptable.

While May was very young, his father, a field secretary for the YMCA, moved the family from Ohio to Michigan. Through his father's association with the YMCA, May was subjected to a planned regimen of swimming and character-building. He developed a closer relationship with his father than with his mother, who, he said, did not make him feel acceptable. Looking back on his early years, May (cited in *Current Biography Yearbook 1973*) "pictured himself as a loner in childhood, unaware of being friendly and appealing" (p. 282).

Education

May entered Michigan State College, but his stay there was brief. He and a friend had founded a campus magazine, *The Student,* and convinced that they had evidence, published an editorial charging the state legislature with using the college to conceal graft. Expecting dismissal, May set out for Oberlin College in Ohio. After an hour's conference with the dean, he was admitted without formal application. Majoring in English and minoring in Greek history and literature, May received his B.A. degree in 1930. On the basis of his credentials, in spite of the fact that he had no knowledge of the Greek language, May was offered and accepted a position teaching English at Anatolia College in Salonika, Greece. He held this position for three years, and during two summer vacations he visited Vienna, where he enrolled in seminars conducted by Alfred Adler. To support his stay in Vienna, May worked as secretary for the International School of Art, and in his free time studied painting. His work with Adler marked the beginning of May's interest in psychoanalysis.

May returned to the United States in 1933. He had decided to work toward a graduate degree in psychology at Columbia University in New York, but became discouraged when he discovered that the program was behavioral and did not include study of Freud, Adler, and Jung. May then enrolled in the Union Theological Seminary in New York, which he believed would help him find answers to questions that interested him: questions about anxiety, love, hate, war, and peace.

Feeling responsible for his younger brothers and sisters after his parents' divorce, May withdrew from seminary at the completion of his first year and returned to Michigan. He was employed as a student adviser and counselor at Michigan State College from 1934 to 1936.

In 1936, May returned to New York and the Union Theological Seminary. Completing his studies under Paul Tillich (first his mentor and later his best friend, and the teacher from whom May learned more than from any other), May was graduated cum laude with a B.D. degree in 1938.

May began his ministry in a Congregational parish in Verona, New Jersey. After two years that were filled with disappointments, he enrolled in Columbia University to major in clinical psychology. Again his studies were cut short; this time the crisis came in the form of tuberculosis. Faced with a fifty–fifty chance of surviving his illness, May entered a sanatorium at Saranac Lake in upstate New York, where he remained for eighteen months. Facing the very real possibility of death reinforced his existential leanings. During this period May was especially impressed with Kierkegaard's explanation that anxiety is the result of a threat to one's being. He discovered also that he alone had to decide whether he lived or died. He believed that his conscious will to live was the deciding factor in his recovery.

Shortly before completing his doctorate, May became a member of the faculty of the William Allanson White Institute of Psychiatry, Psychoanalysis, and Psychology, and in 1957 he was appointed an adjunct professor of clinical psychology at New York University. May has also served as visiting professor or lecturer at other universities, including Harvard, Yale, Princeton, and Cornell.

Emergence of the Existential Approach to Therapy

Recognized as a classic and prophetic work today, May's doctoral dissertation, *The Meaning of Anxiety,* was published in 1950. After comparing and synthesizing the existing theories of anxiety, May challenged the popular view that health was life without anxiety and argued that anxiety, at least the free-floating anxiety experienced by most people, is not only normal but *essential* to the human condition. For May (1977), existential anxiety is the phenomenon of increased intelligence and characterizes human risk taking and creativity. An inordinate amount of anxiety can paralyze, but existential anxiety motivates positive change. May contends that in an age of anxiety, self-realization is the result of confronting and coping with the tension that emerges with every new possibility and from the threats to being that all humans encounter.

In *Man's Search for Himself,* May (1967b), concerned with the human dilemma of living in a society marked by traumatic change, decimating values, and vanishing myths, offers his readers the opportunity to encounter their "problems of personal integration" (p. viii). Following an approach reminiscent of Karen Horney's *Self-Analysis* (1942) and the humanistic perspective of Eric Fromm (Chapter 6), May guides us to a clear understanding of the causes of emptiness, loneliness, and boredom predicated by various forms of anxiety. Further, he assures us that we have the capacity to achieve greater self-consciousness, and with it, the qualities of honesty, integrity, responsibility, courage, and love in our relationships with others.

Accomplishments and Awards

In 1955, the New York Society of Clinical Psychology presented May their award for Distinguished Contribution to the Profession and Science of Psychology. *Love and Will* (1969) brought May the Ralph Waldo Emerson Award from Phi Beta Kappa in 1970.

May was named visiting professor at Harvard (1965), Princeton (1967), and Yale (1972). He was appointed to the positions of Dean's Scholar at New York University in 1971 and Regent's Professor at the University of California at Santa Cruz in 1973. May has received a number of honorary degrees, including the D.H.L. from the University of Oklahoma in 1970; the LL.D. from Regis College in 1971; and the L.H.D. from Vincent College, 1972, Michigan State University, 1978, Rockford College, 1977, and Cedar Crest College, 1978.

May is a fellow of Branford College of Yale University, the American Psychological Association, and the National Council on Religion in Higher Education. He is a member of the board of directors of the Manhattan Society for Mental Health and the Foundation of Mental Hygiene, and he is a member and past president of the New York State Psychological Association. At present May is a member of the adjunct faculty of Saybrook Institute Graduate School of Psychology, San Francisco.

Resolution of the Eleven Basic Issues

May's resolutions of the eleven basic issues are unintentional. Indeed, the existential approach to personality theory is subject centered rather than issue centered. Despite this, subject and issue approaches often overlap, and while it was necessary to pursue May's resolutions of the basic issues through numerous sources, he did in fact address (directly or indirectly) most of the basic issues selected for the structure of this text. The issue "Centrality of Reinforcement" had to be inferred by the writer.

Terminology and nomenclature employed by existential writers are often elusive and imprecise, as well as difficult to grasp and apply in the therapeutic situation. May, though a stimulating and careful writer, is no exception. Terms such as "daimonic," "being," "potentiality," and "ontological guilt" are vague and difficult to define. Further, as a psychoanalyst, May refers to the psychoanalytic dynamism of his background but always in terms of its meaning for the existential situation in immediate experience. The result many times is a new meaning for a familiar term, requiring adjustment in both understanding and thinking.

Following a basic issues approach imposes an arbitrary and rigid structure on May's unstructured approach. There is always the danger that May, as well as other existentialists who reject any attempt to systematize their approach, might find this structure objectionable.

Heredity versus Social Determinants

For May (1958, 1977, 1983, 1989), we are dynamic, immediate, experiencing beings existing in a world which we have at least partially created. We and our world are a reciprocal totality, a unity, each dependent on the other for existence and neither understandable except in relation to the other. May (1982) describes this reciprocal relationship most succinctly in an open letter to Carl Rogers: "It takes culture to create self and self to create culture; they are the yin and yang of being human" (p. 12). Being and world are therefore intensely personal. We are viewed as subjects who can never be separated from the object we experience without loss of being. Our world exists as we relate to it and design it. Both our being and our world are *in process* and necessarily centered in coexistence. Isolation from self, others, and the world results in feelings of estrangement and alienation—in short, anxiety (in May, Angel, & Ellenberger, 1958).

As beings in the world, we are a part of the nature of the world. We share our biology—thus, many of our biological needs, including the central need to become—with all living organisms. We inherit the need to actualize fully our being in the world, because it is only by fulfilling our potentials that we can live an authentic life. However, we are more than our biology.

Among all the living organisms in this world, we are distinct. Our innate need to become is never automatic. Even under the most ideal conditions, our actualization is never a gift of nature. Unlike other living organisms that have no choice but to follow a predetermined biological program, we are both blessed and cursed with the unique human capacity of self-consciousness. We have the distinct capacity to be aware of ourselves as beings in the world. We can see ourselves as both subject and object, both as "I am" who is acting in the world and the "am" on whom the world acts. Unlike other living organisms, we are aware of our past and can project ourselves into the future. We must, at least to some extent in our striving, choose and affirm our actualization (see "Determinism versus Freedom of Choice"). **Becoming,** for May, is both our destiny and our task in life.

May (May, Angel, & Ellenberger, 1958) contends that we will fulfill our possibilities in the world *only* to the extent that we consciously choose and act on our goals. There is no alternative to decision making if positive development is to be realized. Moreover, our striving and choices are often painful, since they must be made in the face of doubt, loneliness, and anxiety. Biological and social influences can limit and inhibit but not determine our movement and growth. Becoming, then, is our self-conscious search for and expression of our singular identities and personal meanings, a projection of our *potentia* in action. We cannot deny our existence or the reality of the world into which we are thrown, but we can choose to deny our being and our innate need to become.

For the existentialist, there are three modes of **Dasein** (being in the world). In addition to self in relation to self (the **Eigenwelt**) and self in relation to the physical world (the **Umwelt**), the unique human quality of self-consciousness includes self in relation to others (the **Mitwelt**). We experience the need for contact and communication with other beings, for authentic encounter. We need involvement with our fellow beings. In fact, much of our humanness, as well as our sense of significance and purpose, can only be actualized within the social context of significant others.

Being in relationship with significant others validates our existence, affirms our being, facilitates our becoming, and contributes to our sense of meaning and purpose. Moreover, such an interaction is reciprocal; being in the world together benefits related participants. In contrast, when our social needs are frustrated, we experience a sense of abandonment, loneliness, and loss of our sense of self. Without the courage to risk sharing our world with others or to accept the invitation to enter another's world, our social integration, and with it our development, falters and stops.

In summary, we are bundles of constructive and destructive potentials (the **daimonic** side of human personality), and because we constitute a culture, our culture, like ourselves, is partially good and partially evil. We must "actively confront the issues of evil and good in ourselves, our society, and our world" (May, 1982, p. 19).

Conscious versus Unconscious Determinants

May (1966, 1983) rejects any hypothesis of unconscious as an internal state or entity. "One cannot say *the* unconscious, for it is never a place" (May, 1966, p. 125, emphasis in original). The unconscious, then, is not to be thought of as a psychic repository for impulses, thoughts, and wishes. Things (in the sense of entities) also cannot be unconscious. We can and do, however, repress part of our potential and some of our experience. May (1983) contends that when repression is understood from the perspective of our relationship to our potentials, our concept of unconscious must be increased to include our unrealized or repressed potentials. Hence, May (1983) defines the **unconscious** as *"those potentialities for knowing and experiencing which the individual cannot or will not actualize"* (pp. 17–18, emphasis in original).

For existentialists, **consciousness** is the totality of awareness. We develop a distinct self-consciousness, and through our consciousness, a heightened sense of the nature of our possibilities of relating to the world and the responsibility and guilt that accompany this awareness. Consciousness is the source of human freedom, creativity, and change. The greater our awareness, the greater our **intentionality** (an active reaching out and absorbing activity; which underlies will and decision, making them possible), spontaneity, and creativity. May (1977) writes of rare moments of joy and insight, similar to Maslow's concept of peak experience (see Chapter 10). At these times of heightened awareness, our capacity for creative consciousness of self enables us to transcend the usual limits of awareness. In these rare moments we see truth without distortion and experience fully our unity with the world. By **transcending** (moving beyond the usual limits of consciousness through imagination and symbolization), we not only perceive alternative possibilities but also enlarge our human dimensions and decrease determining influences by creating new possibilities of relating to the world. The more vigorous our expression of our psychological needs, the more the *Umwelt* will include taste and subtlety; the *Mitwelt*, intimacy and love; and the *Eigenwelt*, complexity and individuality (Maddi, 1972).

Conversely, when we experience severe **neurotic anxiety** (inordinately and disproportionately strong anxiety), we restrict our consciousness. We ignore our possibilities and avoid our responsibilities. We exchange spontaneity for conformity. By avoiding decision, we give up our margin of freedom and feel controlled. Biology, history, or present circumstances become our alibis. Rather than self-directed, we are other-directed. If our failure to learn the use of symbolization, imagination, and judgment is great, our behavior will resemble that of animals, at least as much as humans can resemble animals (Maddi, 1972).

We are individuals. We each have our own heredity and unique experiences. Moreover, since we are constantly in the process of becoming, it is impossible to define us at any particular moment. We are different at different times. Because we are individuals, we are alone. We must decide and accept responsibility for our decisions. Our self is like no others, and our mental health rests on our acceptance of our uniqueness. When we attempt to assume the self of another, we err. When we deny our unique being, we experience anxiety and guilt.

Subjective versus Objective Reality

Though not a pure phenomenologist (in the sense that perception is considered the sole determinant of behavior), May (1975, 1983; May, Angel, & Ellenberger, 1958) advocates a phenomenological approach to understanding the world of another being. He is convinced that individual reality is reality *as it is perceived*. We live in personal and subjective worlds that we are constantly reconceptualizing and reshaping. Our worlds, experienced through our individual streams of consciousness, are both the process and the product of our private interpretations, for perception is an interpretive process. By expressing our need for form through our creative processes, we ingest sensory data, sift these data through our personal value systems, and then, with imagination and judgment, postulate bodies, lines, surfaces, cause and effect, motion and inertia, shape and content to evolve structure, relationships, meaning, and value. We are co-creators of our phenomenology.

We can only be known as beings in the world, and that can only occur when we permit another to be in our world with us, to experience our being. In *Existence* (May, Angel, & Ellenberger, 1958), May discusses the difference between "knowing" and "knowing about" another person. When we wish to know another person, we must put aside what we know about that person. For the existentialist, **knowing** is to experience the being of another, to see that person becoming. Knowing requires the empathic personal encounter of the I–Thou relationship. Knowing about a person, on the other hand, lacks encounter; it is an I–It relationship. The person becomes an object of knowing. His or her being is not part of the knowing; his or her personhood is diminished.

Determinism versus Freedom of Choice

May's stance on this issue is clear. For humans, freedom is a life sentence. We are confronted with a myriad of possibilities from the time we are thrown into the world to our inevitable exit from it; and for May (1966): "The healthy person is he who chooses wither the gap" (p. 21). In existentialism, living and choosing are synonymous; hence, freedom, a characteristic that separates us from animals, is one of the ultimate concerns of living and must be faced, courageously and responsibly.

This does not mean that our freedom to choose is arbitrary and unlimited. Neither does it mean that we bear the sole weight of responsibility for our actions. Though we have a hand in our destiny, we are not without constraints. As beings in the world, we are limited by the restrictions of that world, including the limits of body, intelligence, social controls, illness, and death. Nature imposes rigid rules for living in this world, and our continued existence depends on our learning to recognize and accept the ground of our existence. The existential concept of freedom does not mean that we cannot be conditioned. Indeed, much of our behavior is the result of conditioning, although May (1977) reminds us that this need not occur.

May (1966, 1969, 1975, 1983) views **freedom** as our capacity to play a self-conscious role in our development, to be aware of ourselves as the determined ones, "to pause between stimulus and response and, thus, throw our weight, however slight it might be, on the side of one particular response among several possible ones" (1966, p. 175). By intentionally maintaining our impulses in a state of unbalance, we can choose the impulse that best serves our purpose. May (1966) does not view freedom as the opposite of determinism; rather, he sees freedom as our capacity to know that we are the determined ones, and then, to play a self-conscious role in our development. He would have us face the proportion of responsibility that is ours to carry in ordinary human existence.

Heredity and environment may establish conditions for living in the world, but as self-conscious beings we are free to be proactive when developing within these conditions. We must decide what we want in life, become committed to a course of action, and choose from the alternative available to us. We are self-defining beings. We can choose to live either authentically or inauthentically. There is no less freedom in one choice than in the other; however, there are different consequences and their resulting sense of guilt.

For May (1963, 1981, 1991), freedom is cumulative. Although freedom can be gained only through choice and affirmation, each choice adds a greater element of freedom to the next choice. Conversely, denial of freedom, that is, choosing not to choose when confronted with alternatives, reduces our existence.

Early versus Continuous Development

Unlike Rogers (Chapter 9), May (1966) does not assume that development (actualization) is simply maturational. He does, however, recognize the formative power of early childhood experiences and postulates transitional stages of consciousness that lead to widening experiences of growth and autonomy.

Consciousness and its fosterling, self-relatedness, are key concepts in May's existential approach to early development as he views consciousness moving through four stages in healthy development:

- First, the innocence of the infant;
- Second, rebellion—the emergence of self-relatedness and the move toward autonomy, usually fairly well developed by the age of two or three. At this point, the values of love and care take on new meaning; "they are not something *received*, but are reacted to by the child with some degree of awareness. The child may now *accept* the mother's care, *defy* it, *use* it, for various forms of power demands or what not" (May, 1966, p. 74, emphasis in original).
- Third, ordinary consciousness of self;
- Fourth, creative consciousness of self or transcendent consciousness—the capacity to stand outside of self.

May (1966) emphasizes the importance of a supportive setting for the child's early years. Like Adler (Chapter 3), May advocates that parents, or parent surrogates, exercise authentic care and support by encouraging independence, exploration, and self-accomplishment. They must value and model self-reliance. Parents who pamper or indulge their children deprive them of a sense of accomplishment. Again, like Adler, May recommends the establishment of limits and the recognition of natural consequences so that children learn to understand that freedom is not absolute. There are limits and restrictions beyond their control that they must learn to accept.

Much of early development, according to May, is learning to break the binds of dependence on the parents. Because anxiety is present in every growth experience, parental support is necessary as children learn to cope with anxiety, give up their past values, and accept the risk of new and mature challenges.

Role Assigned to Self-Concept

For May (1977, 1983), the concept of self embodies all our capacities. Moreover, he includes freedom, choice, and autonomy as facets of the holistic self. Viewed from this perspective, self-consciousness becomes the highest level of human consciousness because it implies transcendence. Our capacity to be aware of ourselves as both subject and object enables us to **transcend** the immediate situation (to see ourselves as ends rather than means, and "to think in terms of 'the possible,'" May, 1983, p. 145). In transcendence we are no longer stimulus bound or limited to the here and now. We have the capacity to detach ourselves from a situation, view it in its entirety (including ourselves in its midst), and expand the possibilities of behaving and relating to ourselves, others, and the world.

May (1983), aware that the term transcendence can create misunderstanding, reminds us that **self-transcendence,** as he uses it, is a characteristic of any normal human being and is evident in all kinds of human behavior (pp. 144–145). Any normal human being, for example, can transcend the boundaries of the present moment by bringing the distant past (via memory) and the long-term future (via imagination) into present existence. We have the capacity to use our imaginations to rehearse different ways of behaving in a given situation. The inability to transcend a specific self–world relationship is the mark of mental disorder, as exemplified by Kurt Goldstein's (1942) brain-injured patients, soldiers who had portions of their frontal lobes missing lost the capacity for abstract thinking—hence consideration of their possibilities. Obsessed with a fixed world relationship, they suffered an inordinately high level of anxiety if anyone so much as rearranged their closets. Transcendence, as it is interpreted by May, is a natural phenomenon, a normal human capacity that is a characteristic of self-awareness.

Self may also be lost through unconcern and retreat into nonbeing. When being becomes too painful, we take refuge in an **existential false self** (a self disguised and constricted in social roles). **Authentic selfhood,** then, can be attained only through dynamic confrontation with nonbeing.

Uniqueness versus Universality

We all share the common experience of being and the ultimate threat of nonbeing. Nevertheless, we are each unique and irreplaceable. Our heredities are uniquely our own (see "Heredity versus Social Determinants"). We have unique personal histories (see "Subjective versus Objective Reality"). Our self-identities are uniquely our own (see "Role Assigned to Self-Concept"). We have the capacity to generate personal values, preferences, attitudes, and viewpoints, and the more we exercise this capacity responsibly, the more likely these characteristics will be distinct and unusual—in short, unique.

If we are certain of anything, it is that we are exactly like no other person—that in the end, we are individuals and alone. Good mental health rests on acceptance of that knowledge. Any attempt to be someone else is pathogenic. Our vantage points are singular and private, only to be understood as we reveal them to others in genuine encounter. The focus, then, of existential psychotherapy is directed to the individual. We must each resolve the contradictions of our being by asserting our individuality in a manner that causes us to take a stand against those forces in nature and in society that would quell our individual natures. Individuality requires both courage and defiance.

Number and Weight Assigned to Motivational Concepts

While we are pushed by our central need to become and are influenced by past experiences, human motivation, according to May (1969), is neither an emergence of needs nor the result of conditioning. He asserts we are motivated by new possibilities, the goals or ideals of which pull us toward the future. Every act of consciousness is thus a tendency toward some action.

Existential anxiety (normal anxiety) and **existential guilt** (perception of the difference between what one is and what one ought to be) can be stimuli for growth and change. Either signals us that all is not well and that it may be time to initiate the steps necessary for new directions in life. Either also signals us that new directions will take us into the realm of the unknown.

Awareness that we are finite and death is inevitable also motivates. The present becomes crucial when we realize that the time we have to realize our potentialities is limited.

Our unique ability to detach ourselves from the actuality of time and place and to see ourselves as both subject and object as we imaginatively play with the feasibility of some act or occurrence allows us to identify, create, and evolve toward new possibilities. **Wishing** for a new possibility is the first step in the process of willing. A wish is inculcated with meaning and hence different from need or drive. A wish is imbued with direction and time; it introduces intentionality and transports us into the future. A wish motivates, because once a wish materializes it calls for decision, a weighing of future implications and consequences. We initiate through wishing. Through choice, we will and enact.

May (1969) cautions us in *Love and Will* not to mistake *willing* for *will power*. Although both contain commitment and resolve, **willing** is related to our potentialities and hooked to the future, while **will power** is based on "oughts" or "shoulds" dictated by society.

Role Assigned to Group Determinants

The implications of *Mitwelt* are clear. The world in which we exist includes other persons and groups, and we need to reach out from our centeredness and aloneness to fulfill our capacity for social interaction and integration. Through shared participation with our fellow beings, we gain both our sense of identity and our consciousness. During periods of nonaffiliation, we experience deeply the painful feelings of aloneness and alienation. The implication of *Mitwelt* is relationships with significant others, and it has been developed fully by Martin Buber, the renowned philosopher, in his I–Thou philosophy. The essence of the I–Thou relationship is genuine **existential encounter** that offers mutual presence and affirmation to both participants, a replenishment of our sense of significance and worth, and a confirmation of our identity as an individual.

We suffer an **ontological guilt** (guilt related to the nature of our being in the sense of imperfections and limitations) against our fellows (May, Angel, & Ellenberger, 1958). Because it is only possible to see others through our own values and biases, we do them an injustice, and to some extent, fail to understand and meet their needs fully.

Moreover, there is always threat. Not only can identification with another or with a group drain our sense of existence, but also to be unaccepted by or rejected from a group threatens us with isolation and aloneness. The greater our identification, the greater the threat. The group can influence, but May (May, Angel, & Ellenberger, 1958) is quick to remind us that it is we who partly determine the meaning of the group, and thus our relationship with it. The meaning of the group depends, at least in part, on how much of ourselves we put into it (May, Angel, & Ellenberger, 1958).

Explanation of the Learning Process

For the existentialist, **learning** originates in and is an integral part of immediate, vivid, experiential sensing. To know fully the meaning of anything, we must participate fully in it. We perceive, organize, and analyze the sensory data of our worlds (including our bodies), then instill our experience with personal meaning. We recall, imagine, and reconstruct the data of meaningful experience and from this process cognitively create new concepts, ideas, attitudes, knowledge—our world view. We review history and tradition and infer knowledge. We learn our mistakes through failure, and we can use our failures to reevaluate our goals and reformulate our plans. By reorganizing and accepting the reality of our world, we gain a clearer sense of our possibilities in it. We become aware of our inevitable death and develop a vivid sense of life and the urgency to experience what we value while alive.

May (1977) reminds us, too, that as humans we inherit a mind that gives us the cognitive capacity for integrative learning that is significantly different from the learning capacity of animals. We are, for example, able to bring so-called time determinants into the learning process; that is, we have the ability to recall how we and others we have observed acted in the past, and by learning from past actions, influence our present actions. Moreover, through imagery, we can project ourselves into the future, and through fantasy, consider possible alternatives, weigh future against immediate consequences, and choose that action we believe will be most responsible and beneficial.

Normal anxiety, present in all efforts to become, can be our most motivating teacher. We learn well, also, from natural consequences. A significant aspect of self-discovery is an awareness of the realities of both ourselves and the world of which we are an essential part. Only when our learning is meaningful do we gain a sense of self-discovery and an intuitive awareness of our possibilities.

Centrality of Reinforcement

While May (1977, 1983) recognizes the potential power of external reinforcement, particularly on the neurotic, he is much more interested in the rewarding inner sense of joy we experience when we are successful in our attempts to actualize. For May, all experiences that facilitate our becoming are rewarding. Being fully in the world is rewarding and imparts a sense of excitement, a zest for life and living.

We are rewarded when our identities are affirmed in close interpersonal relationships and when we can risk genuine, spontaneous encounter. We are rewarded when we experience the freedom to choose in the face of anxiety. We are rewarded in those moments when we are creative. We are rewarded when we are able to call on our capacities and courage.

Psychological Health and Psychopathology

Healthy Personality and the Good Life

The healthy personality, according to May (1989), is not a static state of being, but rather a dynamic, fluctuating source of energy and power that is a byproduct of an individual's expressed **potentia** (latent energies and capabilities). Healthy existence requires a continual emerging and unfolding. However, unlike the innate actualizing tendency proffered by Rogers (Chapter 9) that naturally evolves in a favorable environment, the actualizing process in May's healthy personality does *not* unfold smoothly or automatically, even under the best of circumstances. Indeed, May asserts, psychological health and the good life must be earned. Healthy individuals must intentionally wish, will, choose, and act to fulfill their being in the world. Moreover, human beings, according to May, are responsible for their own health and pathology.

First, humans must *care* about becoming. If they do not, either because they are unable or because they refuse, or if they simply conform to the demands of others or society, they lose both their being and their potentialities. Humans only reach the higher levels of humanness and health through conscious, intentional, courageous, creative, self-directed will, choice, and action. For May, the act of intending health is primary. Intentionality and freedom exercised extend the individual's capacity for decisive, constructive response to existence in the world. Conversely, denial or avoidance of freedom restricts an individual's responsiveness to existence.

Second, the healthy individual views life as an unfinished process, as an ongoing, ambiguous continuum that is neither totally knowable nor totally understandable. Health is not a state of being; one never fully arrives. There is always a gap between what one is and what one might become.

Third, the healthy individual is aware of, accepts, and trusts the unchangeable aspects of self, others, and the world. Acceptance and trust in this instance are not to be mistaken for passivity, however. The healthy individual remains open to those aspects that he or she can change, and when opportunity presents itself, takes decisive action to bring about the change desired.

Fourth, the healthy individual is relatively self-directed, hence relatively free from the constraints imposed by external expectations. He or she decides on personal goals and values and then pursues them, whether or not the goals and values he or she chooses to hold are shared and approved by others. Moreover, the healthy, self-directed individual accepts full responsibility for the success or failure of his or her decisions and actions.

Fifth, **spontaneity** (for May, an indication that the individual has integrated the deeper levels of personality) is an obvious sign of personality health. Thoughts and actions are not contrived to manipulate or confuse either self or others.

Sixth is **integrity** (speaking and living authentically), another important characteristic of the healthy personality. When integrity is a part of personality, the individual's "whole self" is visible to those who are empathic enough to see it.

Heredity		Social Determinants
Conscious Determinants		Unconscious Determinants
Early Development		Continuous Development
Subjective Reality		Objective Reality
Determinism		Freedom
Uniqueness		Universality

Role Assigned to Group Determinants	Group membership influences our sense of identity and consciousness, but we—through our own values and biases—determine the meaning of the group and our relationship to it.
Explanation of Learning Process	Learning entails reorganization and acceptance of that which is experientially sensed during our participation in life. Both anxiety and natural consequences of behaviors facilitate this learning.
Number and Weight Assigned to Motivational Concepts	We are motivated by new possibilities that pull us in the direction of the future.
Centrality of Reinforcement	Reward is experienced as an inner sense of joy derived from successful attempts to actualize our possibilities in this world. Affirmation of identity, courage, creativity, freedom in the face of anxiety, being fully in the world, and becoming are all experienced as rewarding.
Role Assigned to Self-Concept	The concept of self embodies all our capacities. The ability to be aware of self as both object and subject implies self-consciousness or transcendence, the highest level of human consciousness, and expands our possibilities. Only through dynamic confrontation with the threat of nonbeing is authentic selfhood attained.

FIGURE 11-1   Schematic Analysis of May's Stance on Basic Issues

Seventh, **originality** is manifest in the healthy personality. The individual is free to develop his or her uniqueness and creatively fulfill his or her unique potentialities and possibilities of existence.

Psychopathology

For May (1969, 1977, 1983, 1989), psychological health and psychopathology are different only in degree, not in kind. No one is completely healthy, nor is anyone completely neurotic or psychotic. Neither is psychopathology viewed by May (1989) as an organic illness, though he accepts the idea that the roots of neurosis or psychosis may extend back to early childhood trauma. Rather, he sees neurosis and psychosis as a loss of *Dasein* (being in the world) and the resultant undermining of consciousness, intentionality, and will.

The subjugation of *Eigenwelt* results in the loss of self-awareness and self-relatedness, the abandonment of innate potentials and personal values, submission to the direction of others, and conformity to the roles and rules prescribed by society and expressed in the media. Subjugation of *Mitwelt* results in the loss of relationships with fellow beings which, in turn, is accompanied by inordinately strong feelings of rejection, loneliness, and alienation. Subjugation of *Umwelt* results in loss of relationship to the objective world. Subjective behavior alone, although meaningful to the individual, is often dysfunctional, even bizarre and destructive. In short, with the loss of *Dasein*, consciousness is restricted; experiences are repressed or distorted; imagination is deadened; behavior is rigid, compulsive, and defensive; freedom of choice is denied; responsibility is rejected; opportunities are missed or refused; and innate potentials and possibilities are unrealized.

Heuristic Influences: Research Methods and Techniques

As had Allport, Maslow, and Rogers (Chapters 8, 9, 10) May also presented a case for the need of a new, or at least radically expanded and modified, science of psychology. He argued that psychologists' present fidelity to the methodology of natural science was responsible for limiting not only the phenomena psychologists chose to investigate, but also the kinds of questions they asked about these phenomena. Further, he argued, this same fidelity has resulted in an overconcern about method and means. The unchallenged priority of fitting phenomena to method discourages any attempt in psychology to develop a systematic and disciplined study of human personality. Indeed, May asserted, the restraints imposed by logical empiricism leave no place for the holistic study of humans as existing beings in the world. The characteristics that May believes are uniquely human cannot be made to fit the method of natural science. All too often, fitting a phenomenon to method leads to isolated bits of information that do not integrate with the existentialist's view of humanity; such studies are restricting rather than advancing.

May also questioned the objectivity claimed by psychologists employing the natural science approach in their investigations. He is convinced that however much psychologists extol their objectivity and however much they assert that their research is unaffected by their personal beliefs, values, and prejudices, they, like all humans, share the concerns of their time and are guided by their personal intentions, attitudes, and interpretations. Unlike the natural sciences, the subject of psychology is the human being and the "observer is the observed." The constant presence of the experiencing researcher in his or her own research must be considered and accounted for, for presence is never without influence and it is impossible for humans to be detached observers who view all phenomena objectively.

May proposes a "human science of psychology" in which fidelity to life-world phenomena is granted the privileged position. He proposes also a return to the phenomenal origins of all psychological processes and the priority of structure or total processes over elements, things, objects, or ideas. He is convinced that the pursuit of rigorous experimental models has led us away from our subject matter, the human being as human. Method has become more important than substance, and as a result, the journals of personality psychology are replete with articles describing manipulation of variables with little significance to human personality. Indeed, May concludes that many laboratory studies tend to ignore basic human data, and even to denigrate the persons being studied.

To study humans as existing beings in the world, a human science cannot afford to ignore subjective data, the representations humans have about themselves, others, and the world. There must be room for creative, subjective speculation. Otherwise, the newborn idea is rejected rather than developed. There must also be provision, May insists, for the study of phenomena that are uniquely human (cognition, intentionality, meaning, freedom, will, choice, authenticity, dread, joy, elation, awe, and hope are but a very few of these phenomena).

Applications to Psychotherapy

Therapeutic Goals

Antitheoretical in its approach to counseling and psychotherapy, existentialism focuses on the individual client rather than on any a priori definitions or theory of his or her condition. The specific goals of therapy, then, emerge from the therapeutic process. General goals, when they are discussed, are usually voiced in vague and obscure terms. For example, May (in May, Angel, & Ellenberger, 1958) asserts: "The aim of therapy is that the patient *experiences his existence as real*" (p. 85, emphasis in original). Full awareness of existence includes awareness of possibilities and the ability to act responsibly on the basis of these possibilities. Further, May insists that therapy is concerned with something more fundamental than curing the client's symptoms. Any lasting cures of symptoms must be a byproduct of the client's full sensing and experiencing of his or her existence and the confrontation of guilt and anxiety that leads to a redefinition of the individual's perceptions of self in the world.

Corlis and Rabe (1969) maintain that the therapist's goals are "to stimulate the patient's willingness to work through pain, to offer help without the jeopardy of undercutting the other's own effort, to offer him strength without dependence" (p. 13). Corey (1982) describes the goals of existential therapists as expanding their clients' self-awareness and helping them to become aware of the freedom they possess and the responsibility they have for the direction of their lives (p. 64). Frey and Heslett (1975), in contrast, tell us that "existential counselors agree with the general goals of most other approaches to counseling and psychotherapy, but seek to embellish these general goals with existential points of view" (p. 43).

Therapeutic Relationship

Existential therapy is grounded in the immediate, ongoing, subjective experience of both therapist and client *as they encounter each other in the therapeutic situation.* The therapist emphasizes a full, selfless, and sensitive presence. To meet the client in the dimension of encounter during the therapeutic session, the therapist must be able to put all personal needs aside, center fully on the client, communicate a deep caring for the client's welfare, and express a continued faith in the client's potential. The therapist invites the client to move from isolation into an I–Thou relationship, since the process and content of therapy are discovered only in moments of genuine encounter.

For May (1961): "There is no such thing as truth or reality for a living human being except as he participates in it, is conscious of it, has some relationship to it" (p. 17). The real subject of the therapeutic situation, then, is the existing, becoming person who is attending the therapeutic session. Therapy is two persons existing in a world together, and the world, at least for the length of the therapy session, is the therapist's office. The communication that occurs in therapy is one existence communicating with another (May, Angel, & Ellenberger, 1958).

There is a risk in encountering another being, even in the temporary relationship of the therapeutic situation. In genuine therapeutic encounter *both* therapist and client risk change, and "unless the therapist is open to change the patient will not be either" (May, 1983, p. 22). **Self-transcendence** (rising above one's need for centeredness to reach out to another) is required of the therapist. Concern for the welfare and growth of the client takes priority. Self-disclosure as a person is not only a necessary but also an integral part of therapy. The therapist cannot be authentic and remain detached, passive, or hidden. Methods and techniques must emerge from the experience of the encounter; otherwise, they create distance, block understanding of the client's inner experiences, and obstruct the therapist's presence in the relationship. Any method with the purpose of manipulation or of putting distance between the client and the therapist demeans the end. There is no room in authentic encounter for a means-justifies-the-end concept. The therapist must rely on spontaneity and permit methods and techniques to emerge from the relationship.

Like Rogers (Chapter 9), the existentialists believe that empathy is the door to understanding the inner experiences of the client. Unlike Rogers (Chapter 9), existentialists reserve an expression of positive regard for honesty and authenticity.

Genuine encounter is the primary event in the psychotherapeutic situation. "Encounter is always a potentially creative experience; it normally should ensue in the expanding of consciousness, the enrichment of the self" (May, 1983, p. 22). Moreover, both client and therapist experience the effects of genuine encounter and are enriched by authentic interaction in the therapeutic relationship. It does not matter that the therapeutic relationship is temporary because "the experience of intimacy is permanent," according to Yalom (1980), "it exists in one's inner world as a permanent reference point: a reminder of one's potential for intimacy" (p. 404).

Initial Procedures and Strategies

Initiating Therapy. The initial therapy session differs little from the later sessions. The therapist begins where the client is at the moment and proceeds from there. For the client who does not know what to expect from therapy and who has not learned how to work therapeutically, the initial session can be frightening. During the first session the therapist must communicate to the client that he or she not only understands the client's plight but also is both interested and willing to work with him or her toward a resolution. Client and therapist expectations, then, may require more concentration in the first session than in later sessions, but the therapist's presence is the first priority because, in this as in all sessions, the personal encounter is the process and content of therapy.

Structuring and Client Expectations. Structuring can be a valuable therapeutic method for dealing with irrational or unrealistic client expectations. Clients often enter therapy expecting a quick and painless cure, preferably one that requires little, or better still, no effort on their part. When this is the case, the therapist is obligated to define the limits of therapy and may begin by informing the client that there are no simple answers or magical cures to the inherently difficult facts and possibilities of existence. Instead, therapy involves participation and risk and requires the hard and often painful work of self-reflection, self-discipline, and the will to act.

While it is necessary for the client to accept the limitations of therapy, it is important, too, that structuring communicates the therapist's faith in the client's capabilities. The client's participation and courage in therapy can be facilitated by the therapist's acceptance and belief in his or her capacity to change and grow. Although there is no promise of success, there is the message of and reason for hope.

Course of Therapy

Methods and Techniques. More a therapeutic attitude than a precise theory of psychotherapy, the existential approach to therapy focuses on understanding the existence of a single client rather than on any a priori system of theory or techniques designed for all clients. The tendency of many Western theories to view the client as an object to be manipulated, managed, analyzed, or controlled, and to emphasize methods and techniques over understanding is viewed with concern. May (1983) asserts that existential assumptions may provide the therapist with notions for therapeutic technique, but for the most part, specific techniques must be permitted to emerge from the process of therapy and can only be decided on the basis of what will best reveal the existence of a particular moment in the therapeutic encounter. Emphasis on techniques prevents existential understanding by blocking genuine encounter.

Existential therapists display both flexibility and versatility. Not only is there a wide latitude in their methods from one client to another, but also they may draw on a diversity of techniques from one phase of therapy to another with the same client. Though never merely eclectic, since techniques are determined by the encounter and consistent with the existential attitude, existential therapists do not hesitate to borrow procedures from other therapies, including those as diverse as the psychoanalytic, Gestalt, cognitive, and behavioral therapies.

Rooted in the therapeutic relationship, existential techniques are selected to support, nourish, and enhance the encounter of the client and therapist. Techniques can be validated by the understanding that comes from the encounter, and they can be altered to fit the individual client and the therapeutic moment. An existential requirement for the therapist, deep empathic listening, may be the only predetermined technique in existential therapy.

On the surface, it would appear that a diversity of techniques is intuitively employed. While spontaneity and intuition do play an important role in existential therapy, the therapist does not act on whims. Rather, the therapist eclectically selects techniques from his or her experiential knowledge of the client's existence and draws on his or her clinical experience, skill, and judgment. Clinical skills include a high level of presence and the ability to respond empathically, interpretively, and confrontively in a nonintervening, nonpersuading manner. The methods and techniques of the existential approach to therapy cannot be learned, or for that matter, taught, except through the experience of the personal encounter.

Extended Applications

Other Therapeutic Settings

The primary application of Existential Therapy occurs in individual psychotherapy settings. However, many of the basic existential attitudes and insights have been applied successfully in other therapeutic settings, including couples therapy, group therapy, and organizational and management settings (Rogers and Maslow, Chapters 9 and 10).

Dreams

Following his premise that an individual's Dasein and intentionality are both conscious and unconscious, May looked to his client's dreams as one expression of his or her dominant mode of being in the world and of his or her overall intentions or purpose. Dreams offer a promising way for the therapist to move past the client's conscious, stated experiences or explanations of purposes or intentions and to understand some of the more subtle, complex, and threatening aspects of the client's Dasein and intentionality.

May discovered also that when his clients had arrived at a thoughtful decision in therapy, the implications of that decision were often explored in parallel dreams. The purpose of these dreams was, for May, to permit the client to *experience* rather than to *explain* symbols and myths. The dreams of May's clients not only reinforced the careful decision, but also permitted the client to experience the consequences of acting on that decision.

Critique

May's Existential Theory of Personality and Approach to Psychotherapy shares many of the same strengths and weaknesses attributed to all theories that take a strong phenomenological stance (see Chapters 9, 10, 14, and 15, for example). Those personologists who believe that a theory of personality must acknowledge and explain the private, subjective reality of the individual favor the phenomenological approach. Conversely, those who believe that a scientific approach should be concerned only with observable responses are critical of May's theoretical concepts. Perhaps the major criticism of the phenomenological–existential personality theory is that it is more descriptive than explanatory. Phenomenologists do not often address the conditions that are responsible for the individual's perceptions and interpretations. Offering an hypothesis of an inherent tendency to actualize inborn potentialities as an explanation for behavior is evidence neither for the actual existence of such a tendency nor for the source of the potentialities. Critics point out that reasoning for a sovereign motivating force is simplistic and based on circular reasoning. Further, they point out that rather than explaining personality development, they explain developed adults.

Another criticism of the phenomenological approach is that it relies too heavily on self-reports that are problematic. People are often unwilling or unable to give accurate self-reports. Moreover, they may intentionally distort private information.

May is regarded by many as the chief proponent and practitioner of existential psychology and therapy in the United States, and few would deny that his published works have excited both professionals in the field (particularly those involved in the humanistic or Third Force Movement) and the lay public. His theory has been applied successfully to personal and social crises encountered in such diverse fields as medicine, education, pastoral counseling, family life, and religion. Great numbers of counselors and therapists (regardless of the therapeutic theory to which they profess primary allegiance) have incorporated many existential constructs, attitudes, and approaches into the therapy process they employ. May's existential perspective is evident, also, in contemporary art and literature. In short, May's rich and provocative theory offers an alternative view of what it is to be a human being by centering on an immediate, existing person as he or she attempts to actualize potentialities in terms of self, others, and the world in a transitional age.

May's chosen terminology appears to reflect his own intuitive understanding and connotations rather than to please his readers or other writers. While this practice offers his readers a distinctive vocabulary and style of writing, it also invites such criticisms as: "his language lacks clarity;" "his descriptions are too mythical and remote to be practical;" "his terms are vague and insular;" "his language is imprecise and nearly impossible to test;" "his concepts are abstract and difficult to apply in practice;" "his terminology does not meet the precision and testability standards of a scientific theory of personality."

While May's propensity to refer to philosophy is considered a strength by some, others view this practice as a liability. These critics claim that rather than strengthening his position, his extensive references to philosophy distract rather than persuade the scientific community of his theory's scientific status.

May also has the tendency to make broad, sweeping statements without offering supportive data (e.g., most Americans "feel alienated," "have personality problems," "lack meaning and purpose in their lives"). While broad generalizations draw the attention of the reader, they also take on a sermon-like tone or the appearance of a manifesto, rather than a systematic theory of personality.

May's theory appears to lack a consistent set of constructs. Major theoretical constructs in one book may not appear at all in the next. It is difficult not to question the basic importance of a theoretical construct that is emphasized strongly in one work and is ignored entirely in the next.

Annotated Bibliography

At the age of seventy-eight, May considered his book, *The Meaning of Anxiety* (1950), to be the watershed of his career. At its publication, there were no books on anxiety except for those by Freud and Plato. Unlike either Freud or Plato, May believed that normal or existential anxiety was an essential aspect of daily living, and the therapist's ally. He discussed in depth the difference between normal and abnormal anxiety. For May, a person without normal anxiety becomes "deadened".

In *Love and Will*, May (1969) discussed the necessity of integrating the "daimonic" side of human personality and its potential for either (or both) good and evil. Further, he argued, we must learn to recognize and prize our internal devils, for ignoring them, as millions of Germans did in the 1920s and 1930s, makes us their pawns. In this book, also, May focussed on conscious will and unconscious intent, developed his concept of intentionality, and presented its relation to meaningful action and its place in daily living.

It is in *The Discovery of Being* (1983) that May explored the existential approach to psychotherapy and shared with the reader his views on the therapeutic relationship, methods, and technique. This book is recommended highly to clinical psychologists and counselors.

In *Man's Search for Himself*, May (1967) explored the human qualities of honesty, integrity, responsibility, courage, and love which he believed were necessary to overcome the feelings of anxiety, emptiness, loneliness, and boredom that we experience from living in a society marked by traumatic change, decimating values, and vanishing myths.

May, in *Power and Innocence: A Search for the Sources of Violence* (1972), brought his readers an existential view of the problems created by human impotence, innocence, and violence. Powerlessness, May argued, is every bit as corrupting as power. More important, through his in-depth understanding of the positive, creative aspects of power as a source of self-esteem, he offered possible solutions to such contemporary problems as drug addiction, race riots, police brutality, and youth and campus revolts.

May's (1989) revised edition of *The Art of Counseling* (originally published fifty years earlier) is must reading for counselors and psychotherapists. In addition to looking at the fundamentals of the counseling process, the reader will find May's chapters on the role of empathy in the therapeutic setting and the personality of the counselor of particular interest.

References and Suggested Readings

Corey, G. (1982). *Theory and practice of counseling and psychotherapy* (2nd ed.). Monterey, CA: Brooks/Cole.

Corlis, R. B., & Rabe, P. (1969). *Psychotherapy from the center: A humanistic view of change and growth*. Scranton, PA: International Textbook.

Dempsey, D. (1971, May 28). Love and will and Rollo May. *New York Times Magazine,* pp. 28–29, 87, 91, 93, 96, 98–99, 101.

Frey, D. H., & Heslet, F. E. (1975). *Existential theory for counselors*. Boston: Houghton Mifflin.

Harris, T. G. (1969). The Devil and Rollo May. *Psychology Today, 3,* pp. 13–16.

Horney, K. (1942). *Self-analysis*. New York: Norton.

Maddi, S. R. (1972). *Personality theories: A comparative analysis* (Rev. ed.). Homewood, IL: The Dorsey Press.

Maddi, S. R. (1980). *Personality theories: A comparative analysis* (4th ed.). Homewood, IL: Dorsey Press.

May, R. (1960). Centrality of the problem of anxiety in our day. In M. Stern, A. J. Vidich, & D. M. White (Eds.), *Identity and anxiety.* New York: The Free Press, pp. 120–128.

May, R. (Ed.). (1961). *Existential psychology*. New York: Random House.

May, R. (1963). Freedom and responsibility re-examined. In E. Loyd-Jones & E. M. Westervelt (Eds.), *Behavioral science and guidance proposals and perspectives.* New York: Teachers College, Columbia University, pp. 95–110.

May, R. (1966). *Psychology and the human dilemma.* New York: W. W. Norton.

May, R. (1967a). *The art of counseling.* Nashville, TN: Abington.

May, R. (1967b). *Man's search for himself.* New York: The American Library. (Originally published 1963)

May, R. (1969). *Love and will.* New York: Dell.

May, R. (1972). *Power and innocence.* New York: Dell.

May, R. (1975). *The courage to create.* New York: W. W. Norton.

May, R. (1977). *The meaning of anxiety* (Rev. ed.). New York: W. W. Norton.

May, R. (1981). *Freedom and destiny.* New York: W. W. Norton.

May, R. (1982). The problem of evil: An open letter to Carl Rogers. *Journal of Humanistic Psychology, 22,* pp. 10–21.

May, R. (1983). *The discovery of being.* New York: W. W. Norton.

May, R. (1989). *The art of counseling* (Rev. ed.). New York: Gardner Press.

May, R. (1991). *The cry for myth*. New York: W.W. Norton.

May, R., Angel, E., & Ellenberger, H. (Eds.). (1958). *Existence*. New York: Simon & Shuster.

May, R., Rogers, C., Maslow, A., et al. (1986). *Politics and innocence: A humanistic debate*. Dallas, TX: Saybrook.

Moritz, C. (1973). *Current biography 1973*. New York: H. W. Wilson.

Rabinowitz, F. E., Good, G., & Cozad, L. (1989, April). Rollo May: A man of meaning and myth. *Journal of Counseling and Development, 67*(8), pp. 436–441.

Reeves, C. (1977). *The psychology of Rollo May*. San Francisco: Jossey–Bass.

Stone, S. (1977, May/June). The meaning of health: In the works of Rollo May. *Health Education, 8*(3), pp. 2–4.

Van Kaam, A. (1966). *Existential foundations of psychology*. Pittsburgh: Duquesne University Press.

Yalom, I. D. (1980). *Existential psychotherapy*. New York: Basic Books.

Chapter 12

Frankl's Theory of Logotherapy

Chapter Overview

Introduction

Biographical Sketch

Resolution of Basic Issues
  Determinism versus Freedom of Choice
  Uniqueness versus Universality
  Heredity versus Social Determinants
  Number and Weight Assigned to Motivational Concepts
  Subjective versus Objective Reality
  Conscious versus Unconscious Determinants
  Early versus Continuous Development
  Explanation of Learning Process
  Role Assigned to Self-Concept
  Centrality of Reinforcement
  Role Assigned to Group Determinants

Psychological Health and Psychopathology

Applications to Psychotherapy
  Therapeutic Goals
  Therapeutic Relationship
  Therapeutic Process and Strategies
  Course of Therapy

Extended Applications

Critique

Annotated Bibliography

References and Suggested Readings

Introduction

A Viennese psychiatrist and the founder of **Logotherapy** (a therapeutic approach to recover a meaning for life), Viktor E. Frankl asserts that we are the only creatures in evolution with the innate need to seek meaning (**logos**). In addition to the physical and psychological dimensions, Frankl contends, we have evolved a uniquely human third dimension, a spiritual (**noogenic**) dimension which houses an awareness of potentials, goals, and most importantly, meanings. Our unique human spirit is the core of **mental health** (living meaningfully for the future within the present limitations of reality).

Frankl's Theory of Logotherapy is one of the more optimistic theories presented in this book, for it acknowledges the meaning and values of living. Implicit in Frankl's theory is the German philosopher Nietzsche's assertion: "If we possess our *why* of life we can put up with almost any *how*" (4, maxim 12). Meaning is inherent in the circumstances we encounter in life events; hence, our personal meaning *can* change from moment to moment. In short, according to Frankl, we are continually creating ourselves.

How do we recognize these often unrecognizable meanings? Frankl tells us that we are likely to find personal meaning in those experiences we feel are special and irreplaceable. Our "defiant power of spirit" enables us to take a stand in all situations, to focus on the personal meaning inherent in any event, to face the unavoidable tensions of life, and to confront the differences between what we are and what we might become. The question asked in Logotherapy is not what do you expect of life, but rather, what does life expect of you. Growth, for Frankl, is away from adjustment and toward individual conscience and responsibility. The focus is on the future—on the assignments and meanings to be fulfilled in the future.

Few personality theorists have had their theories tested as severely as did Frankl. A survivor of three years in four Nazi concentration camps, including the dreaded Auschwitz and Dachau, Frankl (1963), prisoner number 119,104, learned firsthand that prisoners who were unable to find meaning in the senseless, dehumanizing suffering inflicted in the death camps, who had neither purpose nor person outside themselves to live for, were most likely to surrender their lives.

For Frankl (1963), meaning, freedom, conscience, love, and responsibility are the intrinsic essences of what it is to be human. The **will to meaning** (an innate and exclusively human motivation to seek meaning and purpose through a cause or mission or for the love of another person or for a religious faith) is always present and always healthy. Hence, we are always capable ("respons-able") of transforming despair and suffering into triumph through responsible and mean-ingful choices in the moment (Frankl, 1967). This **noetic dimension** (a unique, healthy spiritual dimension of our unconscious) *can* assist us in growing beyond ourselves, of transcending ourselves. In short, Frankl asserts, we have the capac-ity to rise above any condition that fate may bestow by choosing our existential attitude toward that condition.

Biographical Sketch of the Theorist

Early Years

Gabriel and Elsa (Lion) Frankl had three children, two sons and a daughter. Viktor E. Frankl was born March 26, 1905, in Vienna, Austria. Gabriel Frankl had been interested in medicine as a young man, but he was too poor to pursue his interest. He worked ten years as a stenographer in the parliament of the Austrian monar-chy. He then became an official in the State Ministry of Social Affairs, where he was particularly concerned with matters of youth welfare. In an interview with Mary Harrington Hall (1968) for *Psychology Today*, Frankl said that he knew his father was proud of him when he decided to enter medical school.

In the same interview, Frankl revealed that at the age of sixteen, he had begun corresponding with Sigmund Freud. In one of his letters to Freud, Frankl enclosed a few pages of manuscript reflecting his thoughts on the origin of mimic affirma-tion and negation—its expression by shrugging or nodding, or whatever. Much to his surprise, Freud responded immediately and asked permission to forward his manuscript for publication. In 1924 (Frankl was then eighteen years old), he received a copy of *The International Journal of Psychoanalysis*, which included his article.

Education

Frankl was educated in Vienna. He was awarded two earned doctorate degrees: the M.D., in 1930, and the Ph.D., in 1949, with a major in philosophy. While a medical student, Frankl became a member of Alfred Adler's (Chapter 3) inner circle. He was eventually excluded from the Adlerian Society in Vienna when his theoretical view began to differ significantly from Adler's. In 1928, Frankl founded the Youth Advisement Centers in Vienna and continued to head them for eight years.

Emergence of the Theory of Logotherapy

From 1936 to 1942, Frankl, then a specialist in neurology and psychiatry, headed the Neurological Department at Rothschild Hospital in Vienna. Frankl and Mathilde Grosser were married December, 1941; she died in a concentration camp in 1945. Frankl had received a visa to leave Vienna for the United States, but decided to stay in Vienna since his position there permitted him to keep his elderly parents with him. Frankl's sister emigrated to Australia and survived the war. His brother, however, was captured by the SS as he and his wife sought shelter in Italy. Neither survived the concentration camps. Later, Frankl, his wife, and his parents were taken to the concentration camps. Only Frankl and his sister survived; he lost his wife, who died in Bergen-Belsen, his parents, his brother, and his sister-in-law.

Frankl entered Auschwitz in 1942 with the manuscript of his book in his pocket, but learned immediately that he could keep nothing. Still, he learned that the basic tenets of Logotherapy were justified by his camp experiences. No experience is completely bound. His three-year confinement convinced him that even under the most horrible circumstances, even when stripped of everything, no one could deprive him of his will to freedom. He alone was capable of choosing his attitude toward his situation, and he alone could find meaning in his suffering.

After his liberation from the concentration camp in 1945, Frankl returned to Vienna. It was, he felt, his "special assignment" to stay and assist with the rebuilding of his city (Hall, 1968). The postwar years were most creative and productive for Frankl, possibly because he was able to retain his belief that to condemn an entire group of people, whether Jews or Nazis, is to dehumanize all members of the group. Not only did he publish fourteen books in a short period, he also completed work toward his second doctoral degree in philosophy. Frankl founded and served as the first president of the Austrian Medical Society of Psychotherapy, and he was awarded the Austrian State Prize for Public Education.

In 1946, Frankl was selected to head the Neurological Policlinic Hospital of Vienna, and the following year he was appointed associate professor of neurology and psychiatry at the University of Nevada in the United States. He was appointed a full professor in 1955. He was a visiting professor at Howard University in the summer of 1961.

Frankl married Eleanor Katharina Schwindt on July 18, 1947. They have one daughter, Gabriele (Mrs. Franz Josef Vesely), who is an experimental psychologist.

Honors and Awards

Frankl received the Austrian State Prize for Public Education in 1956; citations from Religion and Education, 1960, and the Indianapolis Pastoral Center; the founders award from West Virginia Wesleyan College, 1968; the Austrian Cross of Honor for Science and Art, 1969; and the prize for Scientific Achievement from the City of Vienna, 1970. Officials of Austin, Texas, named Frankl an honorary citizen in 1976. That same year he was awarded the Quest Medal from St. Edwards University and a plaque of appreciation from the University of the Philippines and the University of Santa Thomas. Honorary degrees awarded to Frankl include the LL.D. from Loyola University, Chicago, and Edgecliff College, 1970, and the L.H.D. from Rockford College, 1972. In 1977, Frankl was the recipient of the Albert Schweitzer Award and the Cardinal Innitzer Award. He received the

Theodor Billroth Medal, the City of Vienna Ring of Honor, and the World Congress of Logotherapy Award in 1980. In 1983, West Germany awarded him the Cross of Merit with Star. And in 1985, Frankl was the recipient of the Oskar Pfister Award.

Frankl lived to see the success of his published works, not only in Austria, but also in numerous other countries. His German works have been translated into Chinese, Danish, Dutch, English, Italian, Japanese, Polish, Portuguese, Spanish, and Swedish. His lecture tours include Australia, England, Hawaii, India, Japan, Mexico, South America, South Africa, and the United States. The English translations of Frankl's book, *Man's Search for Meaning*, though slow to start, sold a million and a half copies—350,000 copies in the United States alone.

The Viktor Frankl Institute of Logotherapy (P.O. Box 2852, Saratoga, CA 95070) has been established for the purposes of training logotherapists and publishing research. The Institute publishes a journal, *The International Forum for Logotherapy*, which reports current research on logotherapy. Joseph Fabry is the executive director.

Resolution of the Eleven Basic Issues

Research on Frankl's resolutions of the eleven basic issues is limited to the publications (lectures, articles, papers, and books) that have to date been translated into English. Unfortunately, this amounts to but slightly more than half of his published works, and these may be characterized as unsystematic and repetitious. Further, his descriptions of the therapeutic approach of logotherapy are somewhat vague, possibly because he presents his approach to therapy as a supplement to existing psychoanalytic systems rather than as a complete therapy.

Frankl addresses most of the eleven issues selected for presentation in this book. The exceptions are the Centrality of Reinforcement and Role Assigned to Group Determinants. The resolutions for these particular issues are based on the present writer's analysis and interpretations of implications found throughout Frankl's English publications. While the writer is confident that the resolutions presented for the issues Centrality of Reinforcement and Role Assigned to Group Determinants are consistent with Frankl's views, there is always the possibility of error or incomplete treatment.

Determinism versus Freedom of Choice

In the hierarchy of basic issues, freedom, or specifically the **freedom of will,** must be considered the primary concept in Frankl's Theory of Logotherapy. Frankl's construct of freedom of will is not freedom *from* biological, psychological, or sociological conditions. We cannot will the circumstances of our lives or the tasks that arise to confront us. Neither does Frankl's construct of our freedom of will make "willing to will" possible. "Will cannot be demanded, commanded, or ordered" (Frankl, 1969, p. 43). Like ourselves, freedom of will is finite; it is a freedom within the limits set by the conditions of life. We are not responsible for our circumstances, but we are responsible for how we respond to our circumstances. Frankl (1963, 1967, 1969) asserts that we are all capable because of our freedom of will to take a stand, to choose our attitude toward the external forces of environment and the internal forces of instinct. Frankl relies on his patients' freedom of will as an instrument of therapy, even in his most seriously disturbed patients. We are, then, according to Frankl, free from fate, free from a predetermined life. By the very attitudes and values we choose, we are capable of rising above ourselves and finding and fulfilling meaning in our lives, even in the most excruciatingly hopeless and degenerating circumstances, such as those that Frankl himself experienced in the concentration camps.

> *Man cannot avoid decisions. Reality inescapably forces man to decide. Man makes decisions in every moment, even unwittingly and against his will. Through these decisions man decides upon himself. Continually and incessantly he shapes and reshapes himself (Frankl, 1967, p. 34).*

Frankl's construct of freedom to will, then, means that the opportunity of change is ever present. "Man is free to rise above the plane of somatic and psychic determinants of his existence" (Frankl, 1967, p. 3). By choosing our attitudes toward the events that occur in life, we give the events personal meaning, though we are never certain that the meaning we choose is the true meaning (see "Subjective versus Objective Reality," this chapter). Because we are finite beings, there is always the risk of erring.

Uniqueness versus Universality

There is no doubt where Frankl stands on this issue: *We are unique beings.* We lead singular lives, and no singular life is repeatable. With the will to freedom and the will to meaning, we each decide the meaning of every experience, and the meaning we give to each experience in a unique string of experiences can change from moment to moment.

Because we are unique, in terms of both essence and existence, we are irreplaceable. Though we are finite beings, there is a kind of permanence in our uniqueness. We matter in the scheme of things. We are far more than organisms shaped by external reinforcements or driven by instincts. Our awareness and the singularity of our existence require us to respond responsibly to life's questions, to make the best use of any moment, and to rise above both internal and external conditions.

Ultimately, Frankl (1969) asserts, we each decide whether we will permit ourselves to be determined by the conditions of life and living. Only we individually can find meaning in our particular circumstance. Meaning is not transferable; it results only from a personal search. Meaning must be individually discovered and defined through the stands we choose to take toward the tasks we encounter in life.

Heredity versus Social Determinants

Unlike other species, we are not programmed by instincts that tell us what we *must* do. Rather we have evolved as a species to the point where most instinctual directives have become biological *predispositions* or *tendencies*. In brief, it is Frankl's position that though we have instincts, our instincts do not have us. Neither are we guided by a strict set of social traditions as were our ancestors. According to Frankl (1967, 1969, 1973), then, heredity and environment are only materials that we select or reject in constructing our unique personalities.

As already mentioned (see "Determinism versus Freedom of Choice"), freedom means freedom in the face of three things: the instincts, inherited disposition, and environment. We are inherently seekers of meaning. Indeed, we are the first creatures in evolution to consciously seek "logos" (Frankl, in Fabry, Bulka, & Sahakian, 1979, p. 37). "The tension between being and meaning is ineradicable. It [the search for meaning] is inherent in being human and, therefore, indispensable to mental well being" (Frankl, 1967, p. 10).

We are capable of **self-detachment** (the capacity of detaching ourselves not only from a situation—or environmental event—but also from ourselves). "What matters is not the features of our character or the drives and instincts per se, but rather the stand we take toward them" (Frankl, 1969, p. 17). **Transcendence** (a characteristic of human existence and a dimension of the noetic) gives us the capacity to transcend the level of the somatic, the psychic, and the social. We are capable of transcending the environment by choosing our attitude toward it. The events that confront us in life imply no values—only the individual freedom to choose our own attitude toward those events and to endow them with meaning— with either vice or virtue.

Number and Weight Assigned to Motivational Concepts

Although Frankl accepts the motivating force of instinctual tendencies and environmental conditions, the primary motivation, for Frankl (1959, 1963, 1969, 1978), is the will to meaning. It is our will to meaning that "most deeply inspires" us, that is "the most human phenomenon" of all motivations. Moreover, will to meaning involves value choices as they relate to the tasks life sets for each of us.

Homeostasis, tension reduction, the pleasure principle of the psychoanalysts—none can adequately account for all human behavior. Rather, Frankl (1967) asserts, we are motivated by the existential dynamic of the tensions established between what we are and what we ought to be. We alone decide our individual meaning by the stands we take as we confront life tasks. "What matters, therefore, is the specific meaning of a person's life at a given moment" (Frankl, 1963, p. 171).

Although empirical studies of Frankl's theory are sparse, Crumbaugh, Raphael, and Schrader (1970) conducted a study that appears to support Frankl's theoretical construct of a will to meaning. They studied trainees in a religious order (a congregation of Dominican sisters) and found that the subjects' high scores on the Purpose-In-Life Test (PIL) seemed to indicate that a high degree of purpose and meaning in life is both possessed and necessary for success in the order and correlated substantially with ratings of success in training.

There is no general, abstract meaning of life for all; each of us must decide on a specific, concrete vocation, cause, mission, or assignment that demands fulfillment. Moreover, Frankl (1963) asserts, our meaning must be found in the world rather than within ourselves. "Human existence is essentially self-transcendence rather than self-actualizing" (Frankl, 1963, p. 175). Individual meaning may be a cause to serve, a potential to fulfill, a person to love, or God to serve. Meaning requires **self-transcendence**; it is always directed to something or someone other than to self. Self-actualization is a byproduct of meaning rather than meaning itself.

> *Life can be made meaningful in a threefold way: first, by* what we give *to life (in terms of our creative works); second, by* what we take *from the world (in terms of our experiencing values); and third, through* the stand we take *toward a fate we no longer can change (an incurable disease, an inoperable cancer, or the like) (Frankl, 1967, p. 15, emphasis in original).*

True meaning is enduring. We are never separated from true meaning. It lives with us every day. With true meaning we can never become simply numbers or objects.

Subjective versus Objective Reality

For Frankl (1967), reality is intrinsically ambiguous, for we must each choose from a variety of possible interpretations of our perceptions. Our individual realities, then, are subjective segments that we "cognitively cut out" of an objective world (Frankl, 1967, p. 49). Though our interpretations are subjective, this does not detract from the reality of the world. Therefore, while Frankl endows us with an inherited spiritual dimension, he insists that it must be nurtured in our confrontations with an objective world.

Frankl objects to the point of view held by some existentialists, who, he claims, miss a fundamental truth: Only insofar as we are capable of ignoring or forgetting ourselves are we able to recognize anything of the world (Frankl, 1967). While it is true that "finite human cognition cannot become free of subjective moments . . . this does not alter the fact that the more cognition actually becomes mere self-expression and a projection of the knowing subject's own structure, the more it becomes involved in the error" (Frankl, 1967, p. 50). As long as the world is understood as mere subjectivism, the concept of the world is inadequate, little more than self-expression. We are beings in the world, and the world we are in is a world of objective reality with an obligative quality. While the perspective through which we approach reality is subjective, this in no way detracts from the objectiveness of reality itself.

Conscious versus Unconscious Determinants

In addition to the psychological unconscious of the psychoanalytic theories, Frankl (1985) endows the unconscious with the noetic dimension. He asserts that we are not simply egos driven by an id; we have a spiritual dimension in which are housed "the phenomena of conscience, love, and art" (Frankl, 1985, p. 40):

> *In this noetic realm of our unconscious we make our great existential decisions. From here we draw our artistic inspiration, our religious faith, our beliefs, and our intuitions. From this part of our unconscious comes the muffled voice of our conscience telling us our tasks and, by so doing, directing us to the meanings of our lives (Fabry, 1980, p. 27).*

Freud followed us into the depth of our instincts; Frankl (1985), however, took us beyond instincts to the depth of our spirit. While both offer us a depth psychology that is essentially unconscious, Frankl's noetic or spiritual dimension may be conscious as well as unconscious. "In contrast to the fluid border between conscious and unconscious, the border between the spiritual and instinctual cannot be drawn sharply enough" (Frankl, 1985, p. 26).

Frankl agreed with Freud that the dream was the royal road to the unconscious. However, while he used Freud's method of dream interpretation, Frankl's goal was the disclosure of the spiritual unconscious rather than the instincts.

Early versus Continuous Development

Development, like life itself, is a continuous process, ". . . a time Gestalt, and as such becomes something whole only after the life course has been completed" (Frankl, 1969, p. 41). Frankl, therefore, does not accept the Freudian premise of critical stages of psychosexual development. For Frankl (1969), ". . . the Freudian pleasure principle is the guiding principle of the small child, the Adlerian power principle is that of the adolescent, and the will to meaning is the guiding principle of the mature adult" (p. 41). As we mature we learn that we ultimately determine ourselves by deciding whether we submit to the drives and instincts that *push* us, or to the reasons and meanings that *pull* us.

Since there is no indication of a will to meaning, or of a fully developed conscience in the earliest years of life, Frankl (1969) believes the child must be guided by the experiences and values that previous generations have found useful and meaningful. It is only when we are able to develop a conscience and become capable of taking a stand that is independent of traditions that we are ready to find personal meaning in our lives.

As adolescents mature, they become not only more capable of taking a stand independent of conditions, but also capable of opposing the values that were presented by their elders, especially when their elders' values conflict with their own present experiences and are judged as no longer meaningful. For Frankl, mature and healthy individuals are concerned most with some cause or some person in the external world rather than with any inner condition. They are in pursuit of personal life meanings rather than in a search for individual selves.

Explanation of Learning Process

The purpose of education, in Frankl's view, is to nurture and enhance the student's innate capacity to make sound decisions based on conscience. Rather than encouraging youth to accept the value hierarchy they inherit from an older generation, Frankl believes it is the task of educators to invite and encourage their students to refer to and refine their conscience, to find new values, and to discover their personal rank and order of existing values. Teachers cannot give their students meaning, but they can act as role models by setting examples of personal dedication to the cause of science, truth, and research. Frankl stressed repeatedly the importance of not discouraging the enthusiasm of youth for their concern with values and ideals.

Investigating secondary school pupils' concept of the meaning of life, Nieme (1987), at the University of Helsinki, found that pupils think that topics and questions dealing with the purpose and meaning of life should be treated at school. Sixty-one percent held the opinion that these existential questions of meaning and life are not treated enough at school. They asked for warmer and closer human relationships, more communication, more taking into account of individuality, more knowledge that has meaning for their personal lives.

Role Assigned to Self-Concept

With each decision we make, we are forging our own character, our self. We are not only responsible for what we do but for what we are:

> Facts and factors are nothing but the raw material for such self-constructing acts, and a human life is an unbroken chain of such acts. They present the tools, the means, to an end set by man himself (Frankl, 1967, p. 61).

Our search for meaning is also a search for self. When self-concept becomes the intention, however, self-actualization is impossible. The concern must be **self-transcendence**—forgetting self by looking outward to a cause, another person, or "for the sake of God." **Self-actualization** (becoming the true self) is, Frankl (1978) asserts, "the unintended effect of self-transcendence (p. 35). Indeed, if self-actualization is made an end in itself, "it contradicts the self-transcending quality of human existence" (Frankl, 1969, p. 116). For Frankl (1969), self-actualization is "the effect of meaning fulfillment" (p. 116).

Our intrinsic human capacity to take a stand on whatever may confront us includes our capacity to choose our attitudes toward ourselves. By taking a stand toward our own somatic and psychic phenomena, we can, Frankl (1969) asserts, transcend the self. Frankl's concept of conscience presupposes our capacity to transcend a concept of self and judge and evaluate our thoughts and actions in moral terms. Self-transcendence, Frankl (1969) contends, is a necessary condition for self-realization. Self-transcendence opens the **noological dimension** (the distinctly human spiritual dimension) and the capability of putting a distance between ourselves and our biological and psychological predispositions. *Being* is transcended in favor of *ought*—meaning and value. Meaning and value are only available when we transcend self and pursue meaning and value in a cause or mission, another person, or even chaos and suffering. We become our true selves only when we transcend our being-for-self, only when we relate to something or someone other than ourselves.

When we transcend ourselves, we cannot be involved in idealized images of ourselves, and we cannot become involved in a cause or the world. Overconcern with our self-concept is, in reality, an objectification of ourselves. We become trapped in the concept of self; we are inner directed rather than being open to the world and looking for meaning and value outside ourselves; we are choosing against authenticity. The meaning and value in life emerge out of the stands we take in regard to self, others, and the world. **Self-detachment** (the ability to view ourselves objectively) and humor toward self are necessary for an authentic, vibrant, and vital self.

Centrality of Reinforcement

Certainly reinforcement (at least as defined by the behaviorists who coined the term) is not a central issue in Frankl's Theory of Logotherapy. Indeed, the term "reinforcement" does not appear in any of the English translations of his published works. Implied throughout his writings, however, is the belief that the individual who successfully exercises the will to freedom and the will to meaning finds living a rewarding (reinforcing) experience. That is, the individual who senses that he or she is free to choose his or her attitude toward those somatic, psychological, and environmental events encountered in life and finds personal meaning and purpose also senses reinforcement for making moral and ethical choices and finding meaning in existence.

A sense of freedom brings joy, because choosing is creative, and creative activity provides reason for meaning, which, for Frankl, is the central theoretical concept of psychological health. It is personally rewarding to believe we have the capacity to shape ourselves, whether for good or evil, by the stands we take as we confront the events of life. Life for the individual who believes he or she is in control (rather than a victim of instincts or environmental forces) becomes an adventure rather than a trial. A sense of freedom connotes feelings of well-being, of self-esteem, of confidence or self-efficacy—all personally rewarding feelings. Happiness and actualization (certainly rewarding sensations) are the result of making meaningful decisions based on conscience.

Self-transcendence is contagious, hence reinforcing, just as creativity, innovation, and renewal are reinforcing. In fact, any movement toward the discovery of personal meaning is, for the individual, reinforcing, including dedication to a cause or higher value than the self, love for another person, a religious faith, even revealing the dignity of life by suffering and facing death courageously.

Role Assigned to Group Determinants

Logotherapy focuses on the individual, but the idea that no man is an island is a biological as well as a poetic truth. We are inescapably involved with our fellow beings in the search for meaning. We need community to find individual meaning. We need some grasp of the meaning of our relationship to the whole to retain a vivid sense of our individual attitudes and responsibilities.

Frankl makes a clear distinction between community and mass. **Community** represents families, organizations, institutions, even nations that nurture the individual. When the group is also community, it facilitates the kind of change that enriches and strengthens the individual. Relationships in community are mutually fruitful. When group is community, there is an openness to new ideas; renewal and innovation are continuous processes. In contrast, **mass** is defined by Frankl as a group of one mind, settled by habits and fixed attitudes, intolerant of alternative ways of thinking and doing things. The mass imposes a single view and places powerful destructive restraints on the individual. It supports but one view, which can fragment and destroy the individual's will to meaning.

Individual meanings are multiple and varied. Some are discovered early, others late; some are emotional, others entirely intellectual; some merit the label *religious,* others can only be described as *social.* Regardless, each individual meaning implies a relationship between the person and some larger community of ideas or values, a relationship involving obligations and responsibilities as well as rewards.

Psychological Health and Psychopathology

Psychological Health

Perhaps the best approach to understanding Frankl's concept of psychological health is first to understand *what it is not.* It is not **homeostasis** (a lack of psychic tension). Indeed, Frankl asserts, we need a certain degree of tension for mental health, and if spared tension for any length of time, we either seek or create it. The tension between what we have already achieved and what we ought yet to accomplish, or the gap between what we are and what we should become is necessary for will to meaning and freedom of will, both manifestations of psychological and spiritual health. Neither is psychological health a matter of intentionally seeking pleasure or happiness. Rather, pleasure and happiness result as an effect of finding meaning in our lives. Psychological health is not self-actualization or self-fulfillment. Self-actualization is the *effect* of living out the self-transcendence of existence by serving a cause, loving another person, or even suffering. Moreover, psychological health is not utopia. As an ideal, psychological

Determinism				Freedom
Uniqueness				Universality
Heredity				Social Determinants
Subjective Reality				Objective Reality
Conscious Determinants				Unconscious Determinants
Early Development				Continuous Development

Number and Weight Assigned to Motivational Concepts	Primary motivation is the will to meaning. We are motivated by the existential dynamic of tensions between what we are and what we ought to be. Meaning requires self-transcendence that is directed to something or someone other than self. Self-actualization is a byproduct of meaning.
Explanation of Learning Process	Education's purpose is to nurture and enhance the student's innate capacity to make sound decisions based on conscience. Teachers serve as role models. Topics and questions dealing with the purpose and meaning of life should be treated at school.
Role Assigned to Self-Concept	With each decision, we forge our own character. Our search for meaning is a search for self. The concern is self-transcendence—looking outward. Self-detachment and humor towards self are necessary for an authentic self.
Centrality of Reinforcement	The individual who successfully exercises the will to freedom and the will to meaning finds living a rewarding experience. It is personally rewarding to believe we have the capacity to shape ourselves. Self-transcendence, creativity, innovation, and renewal are reinforcing.
Role Assigned to Group Determinants	We are involved with our fellow beings in the search for meaning. There is a distinction between community, which nurtures the individual, and mass, which places restraints on the individual.

FIGURE 12-1   Schematic Analysis of Frankl's Stance on Basic Issues

health is a process never completed, a struggle never finished, an impossible quest. Finally, psychological health is not adjustment, which is usually equated with the average or norm. There are times when meaning can only be preserved by fighting to change social traditions. Meaning may be found by embracing a political struggle, by taking a stand toward death, dread, despair, disappointment, pain, and disease, by transcending the self and finding meaning beyond life's inevitable tragedies.

Meaning is an individual discovery of a worthy life task waiting to be fulfilled. Healthy movement is toward individual responsibility, toward freedom rather than limitations, toward values rather than cultural traditions, toward challenge rather than trauma, toward the future rather than the past.

As social interest is the measure of psychological health for Adler (Chapter 3), the will to meaning is the single criterion of psychological health for Frankl. "Existential analysis, over and above all illumination of *being,* dares to make the advance to an illumination of meaning" (Frankl, 1959, p. 157, emphasis in original). As Maslow's self-actualizing (healthy) individual is dedicated to one of the B-values or meta-values, Frankl's healthy individual is self-transcending and fully aware that there is a meaning waiting to be fulfilled by him or her in the objective world.

Psychopathology

Based on the premise that meaning fulfillment is the most reliable criterion of true humanness and mental well-being, it follows in Frankl's (1978) theory that the lack of meaning and purpose is a manifestation of emotional maladjustment (p. 84). Indeed, Frankl (1969) contends, the existential frustration and anxiety encountered by many in their search for meaning and life purpose constitute the pathology of our age.

In a cross-validation study of the Purpose-In-Life Test, Crumbaugh (1968) concludes that the data support Frankl's theory "that when meaning in life is not found, the result is existential frustration," manifested in normal persons as existential vacuum and in psychiatric patients as noogenic neurosis (p. 74).

Linger's (1977) study of suicide notes also seems to support Frankl's contention that the lack of meaning in life is a most urgent problem and the reason for much of contemporary anxiety. He found that a significant number of suicide notes in his study expressed the writer's wish to die because life no longer held any meaning. He discovered also that the problem of meaninglessness increased as people aged. For example, while fewer than 25 percent of the suicide notes of people under forty years of age listed the feeling of meaninglessness as the reason for their suicides, 57 percent of the men and 75 percent of the women over sixty years of age expressed extreme feelings of meaninglessness as their reasons for taking their own lives.

According to Frankl (1963): "Man lives in three dimensions: the somatic, the mental, and the spiritual" (p. x). It is the spiritual dimension that *Logotherapy*—healing through meaning—is most concerned with. To be disturbed over the lack of meaning and purpose, while a spiritual agony, may have no connection to disease of the psyche; it is not a neurosis in the strict clinical sense. It is, rather, the result of the frustration of the innate will to meaning, referred to at different times by Frankl (1969) as the "existential frustration" or "existential vacuum" (p. 88).

> *The existential vacuum is no neurosis; or, if it is a neurosis at all, it is a sociogenic neurosis, or even an iatrogenic neurosis—that is to say, a neurosis which is caused by the doctor who pretends to cure it (Frankl, 1969, p. 88).*

Applications to Psychotherapy

It was never Frankl's intent for Logotherapy to replace existing psychotherapies. Rather, he contended, Logotherapy complemented and supplemented existing therapeutic systems. By making us aware of our noetic or spiritual dimensions (will to meaning, meaning of suffering, and freedom of will), Frankl hoped to add the final dimension of our wholeness which he believed was overlooked by practically all existing therapeutic approaches. "I believe there is no such thing as psychotherapy unconcerned with values, only one that is blind to values" (Frankl, 1973, p. xi).

Therapeutic Goals

The goals of Logotherapy are to bring to consciousness the unconscious spiritual factors of the patient's personality, to assist the patient to become conscious of having responsibility, to find or to recover meaning in his or her existence. In addition, it is the task of the logotherapist to stimulate the possibilities of concrete meaning in the patient's life experiences or "consciousness through conscience."

Logotherapy does not view self-actualization, self-fulfillment, self-realization, or self-enhancement as legitimate goals of psychotherapy. Such outcomes, Frankl asserts, are the effect of transcending the self and finding meaning in one's life. Indeed, when actively sought, self-actualization is self-defeating. Like happiness, Frankl (1969) argues, self-actualization ensues when individual meaning is discovered.

Therapeutic Relationship

Frankl agrees with the humanists Rogers (Chapter 9) and Maslow (Chapter 10) that acceptance, empathic understanding, concern, and unconditional positive regard for the patient must be communicated by the logotherapist before therapy proper can take place. Logotherapy, therefore, places significant emphasis on the relationship between the patient and the therapist as an important aspect of the psychotherapeutic process—certainly above method and technique. Frankl does not agree with Rogers that this relationship is sufficient, however. Rather, he asserts, there must be a third member of the I–Thou relationship—*meaning.*

Therapeutic Process and Strategies

Logotherapy is often combined with other approaches to therapy and often appears to employ their methods and techniques. However, in addition, there are two techniques, paradoxical intention and de-reflection, that are applicable for rather specific symptoms or neurotic conditions which are existential in nature.

Paradoxical Intention. Frankl first proposed in 1946 and further developed in 1960 a special logotherapeutic technique which he called **paradoxical intention.**

Paradoxical intention directs the patient suffering the symptoms of anxiety, or often **anticipatory anxiety** (the fear of fear), by intentionally trying to create and increase the feared symptom. For example, if the client fears social situations because he or she breaks out in a cold sweat, he or she is instructed that rather than fight the symptom he or should deliberately invite and exaggerate it—to show how much he or she could sweat, to make sweat come from every pore in his or her body, to form puddles of sweat at his or her feet. Many times when the patient deliberately tries to create and exaggerate a feared symptom, he or she is unable to do so.

While certainly not a panacea, paradoxical intention, Frankl asserts, works with a high percentage of patients, even when the problem (e.g., phobic neurosis, obsessive-compulsive neurosis) has existed for years and the patient is convinced, when beginning to employ the technique, that it cannot possibly work. Many patients who deliberately try to panic cannot; indeed, the harder they try, the less likely it is that they can produce the symptoms of their neurosis.

There are cautions which must be observed before using paradoxical intention. It is not to be used with a severely depressed or suicidal patient. It should not be used before a phobic or obsessive-compulsive neurosis has been determined psychogenic or somatogenic. It is important first to perform thyroid function tests. Electroencephalography may also be required for diagnostic clarification.

De-reflection. De-reflection is employed by logotherapists with patients suffering from hyper-intention (e.g., insomnia—the hyper-intention to sleep). Here the patient is instructed to do the opposite of what he or she so very much wants. Patients who become overanxious because they fear they will not be able to fall asleep are instructed to try to stay awake, to keep their eyes open as long as possible. The purpose is to counteract the patients' compulsive tendency to self-observation. In short, they must de-reflect *from* their disturbance *to* the task at hand or to the partner involved. The key is self-commitment—to ignore the symptoms of their neurosis by focusing their attention away from themselves.

Course of Therapy

The initial steps in the process of Logotherapy are first, beginning the establishment of the therapeutic relationship, and second, arriving at a proper diagnosis of the patient's emotional disturbance. A proper diagnosis of a patient involves the whole person. Physical, psychological, and spiritual factors must be assessed to determine which of the three is the primary factor. Primary physical factors point to psychosis. Primary psychological factors indicate a neurosis. And spiritual factors, when primary, alert the therapist to a noogenic "neurosis."

While identification of primary factors is important, it is important also, from the perspective of Logotherapy, to keep in mind that there are no *pure* somatogenic, psychogenic, or noogenic neuroses. There are only instances in which one of the three factors moves to the foreground (becomes primary) and is, therefore, determined the object of therapy. Also, because the logotherapist is interested in treating the whole person, psychotherapeutic treatment may include physical (medical) treatment, psychotherapy, and logotherapy. In brief, logotherapy, which focuses exclusively on meanings and values, is a supplement to other treatment modalities which do not include the spiritual dimension of humans. Logotherapy was created to fill the gap in other systems of psychotherapy. In the therapeutic process psychotherapy and logotherapy cannot be separated, even though they represent different realms.

Logotherapy is not a symptomatic treatment approach, nor is it concerned with the symptom's psychogenesis. Rather, Logotherapy is primarily concerned with the patient's attitudes toward the symptoms. Attitudinal change and the assumption of personal responsibility are the goals. Freedom of choice, or at least some element of it, is assumed, thus, responsibility for response, choices, and actions is assumed as well.

Essentially, Logotherapy, while often combined with other therapeutic approaches and techniques, is generally a discussion of philosophical or spiritual problems, and suggestion, persuasion, teaching, and reasoning are usually part of the therapeutic process. Lucas (in Fabry, Bulka, & Sahakian, 1979), a logotherapist, lists four stages of therapy:

1. Gaining distance from the symptoms,
2. Modification of attitudes,
3. Reduction of symptoms, and
4. Orientation toward meaning (pp. 95–103).

Extended Applications

The central emphasis in Frankl's Theory of Logotherapy (finding meaning and purpose in the moment) is, according to Bulka (in Fabry, Bulka, & Sahakian, 1979), helpful beyond the medical and psychotherapy areas originally prescribed by Frankl. For Bulka (1979), Logotherapy "speaks effectively to many ills of modern society" (p. 331). While Logotherapy is an autonomous psychotherapeutic system, it is also a rehumanizing, indeed transhumanizing, philosophy for many of the current world conditions, with many similarities to the "fourth psychology" proposed by Abraham Maslow (Chapter 10).

Critique

Frankl provides us with a theory of personality that is especially applicable in a stressed society where individuals suffer existential frustration, inner emptiness, and neurosis originating in current conflicts of values or conscience and are searching for meaning in their existence. In a life without meaning, each day is like the days preceding it, and it is experienced with brief or more lasting consciousness of emptiness and a growing sense of isolation and loneliness. In short, Frankl gives legitimacy, indeed, a necessity, to the question: "Does life have meaning?"

Further, Frankl refocuses our attention toward the noetic or spiritual dimension of humanness, not in a religious or secular sense, but rather as the exclusively human core of healthy personality—our will to meaning, our capacity for choice, love, imagination, creativity, self-discovery, and self-transcendence. He has made us aware that it is possible to find meaning even in suffering and death. Of the existential theories presented in this book, Frankl's Logotherapy may be the most optimistic.

Critics accuse Frankl of being more philosophical, moral, and religious than psychological. Logotherapy Therapy, they contend, is concerned with assumptions about the individual's quest for meaning and the spiritual dimension of human personality, hardly serious considerations of scientific study. These same critics also claim that Logotherapy is more a philosophy of therapy than a distinct system of psychotherapy. Frankl's response is that Logotherapy is not intended to replace established psychoanalytic therapies; rather, it is a supplement to other therapies intended primarily to deal with noetic neurosis. He also argues:

> If we define empirical in the widest sense of the word, . . . if we broaden and widen our visual field for man, finally and hopefully we might recognize that empirical means not only sticking to figures, sticking to statistics, sticking to experiments, but transcending them as well (Frankl, in Hall, p. 62).

Students seeking clear therapeutic methods and techniques are often disappointed in Frankl's theory. Therapists essentially teach the value and philosophy of Logotherapy, rather than using techniques. Again, Frankl responds that preoccupation with method, technique, and procedure gains dominance over the whole process of seeking meaning, and is, thus, potentially harmful to the goals of Logotherapy.

Annotated Bibliography

First published in 1946 as *Arztliche Seelsorge,* Frankl's book, *The Doctor and the Soul,* was the first of his books to be translated into English and published in the United States. Random House published the book under the title *The Doctor and the Soul: From Psychotherapy to Logotherapy.* It is this volume that first introduced Frankl's ideas to American psychotherapists and personologists. The book presents the principles of Logotherapy and asserts that the search for meaning in existence is a primary facet of being human. It is here, too, that Frankl insists that psychotherapists must be concerned with the spiritual dimension of human personality if they are to take a holistic approach to psychotherapy, particularly if they are to help patients suffering a new type of neurosis—noogenic neurosis.

Man's Search for Meaning: An Introduction to Logotherapy (1963) is a revised and enlarged edition of an earlier book entitled *From Death-Camp to Existentialism*. The first part of this book is autobiographical—Frankl's personal experiences in three concentration camps that led him to find meaning in senseless horror and suffering and validated his theory of Logotherapy. The second part of this book is a brief but explicit statement of the basic tenets of Logotherapy. As Allport states in the Preface: "It has literary and philosophical merit and provides a compelling introduction to the most significant psychological movement of our day." *Man's Search for Meaning* is highly recommended reading for every student of Logotherapy, whether beginning or experienced.

In *The Unheard Cry for Meaning: Psychotherapy and Humanism,* Frankl (1978) refutes "pseudo-humanism," which he believes is being presented in popular psychology and psychoanalysis. Here Frankl delves into the remarkable noetic (spiritual) qualities that are exclusively human. He also presents case histories in which the two techniques developed within the framework of Logotherapy (paradoxical intention and de-reflection) are demonstrated.

The Unconscious God (1975) resulted from a lecture Frankl prepared for a small group of intellectuals in Vienna shortly after World War II. The lecture was first published in German in 1947. Of his twenty books, Frankl believed that this was the most organized and systemized. *The Unconscious God* includes a supplementary chapter that outlines the new ideas of the 1950s and 1960s on the theory of conscience and an updated bibliography that covers all of logotherapeutic teaching and practice. Students interested in the relationship of religion and psychiatry should find this volume most helpful.

The goals of Fabry's (1980) *The Pursuit of Meaning: Viktor Frankl, Logotherapy, and Life* are "to popularize logotherapy without vulgarizing it, to simplify its theories without oversimplifying them; and to 'Americanize' its practices by focusing on those aspects that speak to readers in the cultural climate of present-day America" (Frankl, in Fabry, 1968, p. x). Frankl believes that he succeeded. For students who want a summary of Logotherapy in a popular language, Fabry's book is recommended reading.

Students seeking assistance and direction in finding meaning in their lives may wish to read Fabry's (1988) *Guideposts to Meaning: Discovering What Really Matters*. The book is available from the Institute of Logotherapy (address listed in "Biographical Sketch," this chapter).

References and Suggested Readings

Ascher, L. M. (Winter 1978/Spring 1979). Paradoxical intention: A review of preliminary research. *The International Forum for Logotherapy, 1*(1), pp. 18–21.

Birnbaum, F. (1961). Frankl's existential psychology from the viewpoint of individual psychology. *Journal of Individual Psychology, 17*(2), pp. 162–166.

Crumbaugh, J. C. (1968). Cross-validation of our Purpose-In-Life Test based on Frankl's concepts. *Journal of Individual Psychology, 24*, pp. 74–81.

Crumbaugh, J. C. (1972). Aging and adjustment: The application of logotherapy and the Purpose-In-Life Test. *The Gerontologist, XII*, pp. 418–420.

Crumbaugh, J. C., & Maholick, L. T. (1964). An experimental study in existentialism: The psychometric approach to Frankl's concept of noogenic neurosis. *Journal of Clinical Psychology, 20*, pp. 200–207.

Crumbaugh, J. C., Raphael, M., & Shrader, R. R. (1970). Frankl's will to meaning in a religious order. *Journal of Clinical Psychology, 26*, pp. 206–207.

Fabry, J. B., Bulka, R. P., & Sahakian, W. S. (1979). *Logotherapy in action*. New York: Jason Aronson.

Fabry, J. B. (1980). *The pursuit of meaning: Viktor Frankl, logotherapy and life* (Rev. ed.). New York: Harper & Row.

Fabry, J. (1988). *Guideposts to meaning: Discovering what really matters*. Saratoga, CA: An Institute of Logotherapy Press Book.

Frankl, V. E. (1958, September 13). The search for meaning. *Saturday Review*, p. 20.

Frankl, V. (1959). The spiritual dimension in existential analysis and logotherapy. *Journal of Individual Psychology, 15*, pp. 157–165.

Frankl, V. E. (1963). *Man's search for meaning*. New York: Washington Square Press. (Originally published 1939)

Frankl, V. E. (1965). *The doctor and the soul: From psychotherapy to logotherapy*. New York: Vantage Books. (Originally published 1955)

Frankl, V. E. (1967). *Psychotherapy and existentialism: Selected papers on logotherapy*. New York: Simon and Schuster.

Frankl, V. E. (1969). Self-transcendence as a human phenomenon. In A. J. Sutich & M. A. Vich, (Eds.). *Readings in humanistic psychology*. New York: The Free Press, pp. 113–133.

Frankl, V. E. (1978). *The unheard cry for meaning: Psychotherapy and humanism*. New York: Simon and Schuster.

Frankl, V. E. (1985). *The unconscious God*. New York: Washington Square Press. (Originally published 1948, Austrian ed.; 1975, English ed.)

Garfield, C. A. (1973, November). A psychometric and clinical investigation of Frankl's concept of existential vacuum and of anomia. *Psychiatry, 36*, pp. 396–408.

Hall, M. H. (1968, February). A conversation with Viktor Frankl of Vienna. *Psychology Today, 1*(9), pp. 56–63.

Linger, E. (1977). *Meaning and void: Inner experience and the incentives in people's lives*. Minneapolis, MN: University of Minnesota Press.

Lieban-Kalmar, V. (1984, January). Logotherapy: A way to help the learning disabled help themselves. *Academic Therapy, 19*(3), pp. 261–268.

Meier, A., & Edwards, H. (1974). Purpose-In-Life Test: Age and sex differences. *Journal of Clinical Psychology, 30*(3), pp. 384–386.

Missinne, L. E., & Wilcox, V. (1981). *Frankl's theory and therapy*. (Report No. CG-016-342). Paper presented at the 27th Annual Conference of the Western Gerontological Society, Seattle, WA., *EDRS*. (ERIC Document Reproduction Service No. RD 223 933)

Muyskens-Gene, P. D. (1981). The relationship between college students' perceptions of meaning in their lives and Viktor Frankl's theory of meaning in life. *Dissertation Abstracts International, 41*, 3582B. (University Microfilms No. 81-04,752)

Niemi, H. (1987). The meaning of life among secondary school pupils: A theoretical framework and some initial results. *Research Bulletin No. 65, 93 pp. ED280804*.

Ruffin, J. E. (1984, September). The anxiety of meaninglessness. *Journal of Counseling and Development, 63*, pp. 40–42.

Yarnell, T. D. (1971). Purpose-In-Life Test: Further correlates. *Journal of Individual Psychology, 27*, pp. 76–79.

Part 5

Radical Behaviorism

Though he objects to being referred to as a theorist, B. F. Skinner may be the best single American representative and defender of radical behaviorism. For Skinner, practically all human behavior is contingent upon the individual's reinforcement history. Indeed, the subject of this book, human personality, is for Skinner nothing more than a repertory of externally reinforced response patterns. Inner motivational constructs are unscientific, according to Skinner, that can be neither observed nor measured. The idea of a self-concept or an unconscious is irrelevant. Freedom is a merely a myth, perpetuated by early irrational reinforcement contingencies. We are *controlled,* and according to Skinner, the sooner we accept that fact the sooner we can begin to shape the behavior we desire by designing the contingency features of our environment.

Skinner's experimental subjects were often pigeons and rats. He encountered no personal problem generalizing his findings to human learning. Indeed, he firmly believed that the laws of learning are universal, and thus, applicable to all animal species, from the very simple to the most complex.

An aspiring writer as a young man, Skinner wrote a fictional account of an utopian community, *Walden Two,* based on his theory of operant conditioning. The views he expressed in this book created quite a stir, not only in psychology but in numerous other disciplines as well. It is still assigned reading in numerous college courses.

Three of Skinner's books are autobiographical. Advocates and critics alike have found them fascinating, for Skinner's theory was also his philosophy of life, and he remained loyal to that philosophy as long as he lived. Indeed, his last public defense of radical behaviorism occurred only a few days before his death.

Chapter 13

Skinner's
Operant
Reinforcement
Theory

Chapter Overview

Introduction

Biographical Sketch of the Theorist

Resolutions of the Eleven Basic Issues
    Heredity versus Social Determinants
    Centrality of Reinforcement
    Explanation of Learning Process
    Determinism versus Freedom to Choose
    Role Assigned to Group Determinants
    Early versus Continuous Development
    Number and Weight Assigned to Motivational Concepts
    Conscious versus Unconscious Determinants
    Role Assigned to Self-Concept
    Subjective versus Objective Reality
    Uniqueness versus Universality

Psychological Health and Psychopathology

Application to Psychotherapy
    Therapeutic Goals
    Therapeutic Relationship

Initial Procedures and Strategies
Course of Psychotherapy

Extended Applications

Critique

Annotated Bibliography

References and Suggested Readings

Introduction

Unlike the results for most of the personality theorists whose works are selected for inclusion in this book, the data for Skinner's Operant Reinforcement Theory did not emerge from personal experiences in the therapeutic setting. Neither were they borrowed from other sciences. Rather, Skinner's work setting was the laboratory, and convinced that the laws of learning apply to all living organisms and that advances in science occur progressively from the simple to the complex, he often used rats and pigeons for his subjects.

Also unlike most of the theorists presented in this text, Skinner was not interested in formulating a theory of human personality. Indeed, for Skinner, **personality** is simply a term or label personologists use to describe a given individual's characteristic behavior patterns that were shaped as a direct function of his or her ongoing conditioning experiences. In contrast, then, to personality theories that emphasize understanding, common and unchanged aspects of human behavior, and differences between species, Skinner's operant principles of learning emphasize prediction and control, behavior change, and universal laws of learning that apply to all species. A dedicated experimental psychologist and ardent radical determinist, Skinner (1953, 1969, 1971, 1974) focused exclusively on carefully controlled observations of the overt, measurable behavior of a single subject. He saw no reason for formal theorizing and objected strongly to introspection as a method for gathering theoretical data. For Skinner (1953, 1971, 1974), when sufficient facts are known, cause and effect become obvious.

Looking for internal motivations (e.g., instincts, needs, drives, and traits) and underlying motives (e.g., unconscious forces, innate striving or actualizing tendencies), Skinner (1953, 1971) asserted, serves only to hold back the scientific approach to the prediction and control of human behavior. Not only are mentalistic and intrapsychic concepts and constructs objectively impossible to observe, hence unverifiable, they also have no direct reference to natural events. Our irrational belief in the existence of inner events and ideas, along with the reinforced illusion of will and freedom, Skinner (1971) argued, hold us back from developing the behavioral technology necessary to promote fully the development of our species and society.

For Skinner (1971), the human struggle for freedom is not due to an inherent free will but rather to the avoidance of aversive environmental stimuli. He warned repeatedly that wise decisions and careful planning are necessary for the survival of both species and culture. He believed also that the broad spectrum of behavioral changes necessary to avoid ultimate disaster are highly unlikely to be realized as long as humans continue to believe that they are not controlled by the contingencies of their external environment.

Although Skinner's contributions to the explanation, prediction, and control of behavior gained him the recognition and respect of experimental psychologists and scientists throughout the world, they also made him a predictable target for harsh criticism. Psychoanalysts and humanists in particular find his revolutionary ideas frightening. Poets, philosophers, and theologians have expressed their outrage. His call for a **technology of behavior** (a systematic scientific program to redesign culture to shape and control human behavior for survival) challenges many of the most sacred ideals and questions any concepts of free will and creativity (Skinner, 1971, 1972, 1974).

The fact that Skinner has detractors does not mean that his ideas leave people unaffected or that they lack impact. Skinner was undoubtedly a major force in the personality arena; "there is a definite image of humanity reflected in the behavioristic outlook" (Rychlak, 1981, p. 433). Skinner provided psychology with a massive amount of experimental data to support his conceptual formulations. He stimulated large numbers of young psychologists to continue and extend his scientific approach to the analysis of behavior. He lived to witness the application of his principles to an incredible array of phenomena, including such areas as pharmacology, educational technology, industrial management, and the therapeutic treatment of psychological problems.

Biographical Sketch of the Theorist

The ease with which biographical material can be located for the personologists whose theories are presented in this book appears directly related to their theoretical stance on personality development. Personologists who see little or no relationship between their early years and later achievements (e.g., Allport, Chapter 8) are much less likely to disclose their early histories. In contrast, those theorists who take a hard determinist stance are inclined to discuss their early childhood, particularly those events and experiences they consider highly influential in their personal development. Skinner, a radical determinist who identified himself as a behaviorist, provided his readers with four volumes of autobiography, and although the entries are not dated, Epstein's (1980) edited book, *Notebooks, B. F. Skinner*, offers insights into Skinner's personality development not found elsewhere. In addition, numerous interviews (e.g., M. H. Hall, 1967) with Skinner have been published over the years, and here, too, are glimpses of Skinner's life as he perceived it at that moment. Pertinent information about Skinner's life is both abundant and readily available. The task here is not finding material but rather deciding what material to exclude.

Whether or not readers identify with Skinner's ideas, they are most certain to find his autobiographical works fascinating. Indeed, this writer strongly recommends these works to readers adamantly opposed to the idea of behavioral control. The exercise of crossing swords with an expert from the opposing camp can be a most beneficial (reinforcing?) learning experience.

Early Years

Born March 20, 1904, Burrhus Frederick Skinner was the firstborn son of William Arthur Skinner and Grace Madge (Burrhus) Skinner. He had one brother, Edward James, two years his junior, who died suddenly of a cerebral aneurism at the age of sixteen. The family lived in Susquehanna, a small Pennsylvania railroad town located close to the border of New York, and until he left for college he lived in the house in which he was born.

Skinner (1976a) remembered his early family life as "warm and stable." He could not recall ever being physically punished by his parents (with the exception of an occasion when his mother washed his mouth with a soapy washcloth for repeating a "bad word"), and he considered his parents' disciplinary methods effective in shaping his early behavior. As a child, Skinner never suffered from doubt regarding what was expected of him. His mother's ideas of right and wrong were both rigid and consistent. He was "taught to fear God, the police, and what other people will think" (Skinner, 1983a, p. 25).

The consequences of breaking the law were instilled in him early when his father, an attorney, took him to the county jail to see firsthand the treatment of those convicted of a crime. Skinner (1976) reported a vivid recollection of his grandmother forcing him to look into the red embers of the coal stove so that he might have some idea of "hell and eternal hell fire." He knew that learning was valued highly because it was both encouraged and reinforced in his family.

Skinner (1976) was taught to appreciate music by his father, "a competent performer on the cornet" (p. 11), and his mother, who "played piano in an orchestra and accompanied singers in recitals" (p. 18). While in high school, Skinner earned money playing saxophone in a jazz band that performed twice each week in the local theater. He was graduated second in a class of seven from Susquehanna High School.

Always mechanically inclined, Skinner spent much of his leisure time as a child constructing, among other things, roller skate scooters, steering mechanisms for wagons and carts, a steam-powered blow gun that could fire potato and carrot plugs over the roofs of neighboring houses, kites, model planes powered by rubber bands, a perpetual motion machine that never quite worked, and a room filled with Rube Goldberg-type contraptions. His interest in mechanical devices remained with him, culminating in the many apparatus for his experiments. The so-called **Skinner Box** (an apparatus Skinner designed to conduct many of his laboratory experiments), the **cumulative recorder** (a device for recording and analyzing data over a period of time that makes changes in rate conspicuous), the **teaching machine** (an early version of today's learning software programs), and the **air-crib** (an enclosed crib that is temperature controlled, soundproof, and germproof) are good examples.

It was in high school that Skinner, attempting to prove to his English teacher that Francis Bacon was the author of Shakespeare's plays, first came under Bacon's influence. Bacon's influence was lasting and is expressed throughout Skinner's thinking and writing.

Education

Determined to become a writer, Skinner entered Hamilton College, a small liberal arts school in New York. He fared well academically, earning a Phi Beta Kappa key, and he contributed to campus literary and humor magazines. However, he never adjusted fully to the social environment of campus life. He joined a fraternity but was not a very active participant. Inept in sports, he avoided most athletic activities.

Along with a number of his fellow students, Skinner considered many of the college curriculum requirements irrelevant, and he objected strenuously to being forced to complete them. During his senior year, his objections became more overt, and he engaged in a number of student activities designed to humiliate certain faculty members believed to be pompous and arrogant in their relations with students. Although threatened with expulsion for such actions, he was ultimately permitted to graduate and received his A.B. degree in 1926, with a major in English literature.

Armed with the determination of youth and an encouraging letter from Robert Frost, who had generously agreed to read three of his short stories, Skinner returned to his family home (they had moved to Scranton, Pennsylvania, just before he entered college). There he set up an attic studio and pursued his career in writing. After a year, with nothing of substance to show for his effort, Skinner decided he would benefit from contact with other writers and moved to Greenwich Village. He read extensively while in the Village but wrote little. Skinner was particularly influenced at this time by Bertrand Russell (1872–1970) and Francis Bacon (1561–1626), and through their writing was introduced to the works of Ivan Pavlov and James Watson. This was his first taste of psychology, for he had not taken courses in this discipline while in college. From Greenwich Village Skinner spent the remainder of the year in Europe, and discovering that he had nothing important to write about, decided to give up writing as a career and continue his formal education, this time in psychology.

Skinner entered Harvard University in 1928, and by leading a Spartan life and reading only in the disciplines of psychology and physiology, he completed all degree requirements in an amazingly short period of time. He received the M.A. degree in 1930 and his Ph.D. the following year. His postdoctoral training for the next five years included work as a National Research Council fellow, and later as a junior fellow in the Harvard Society of Fellows, Harvard's most prestigious award for young scholars. In 1936, Skinner married Yvonne ("Eve") Blue, an

English major at the University of Chicago. They had two daughters, Julia (Mrs. Ernest Vargas) and Deborah (Mrs. Barry Buzon), an artist.

Skinner accepted his first faculty position at the University of Minnesota. In two years he published his first book, *The Behavior of Organisms* (1938), which he considered his most important work. It was here, too, that he began work on a novel, *Walden Two,* a story of a utopian commune governed by operant principles. He had no idea at this time that *Walden Two* would, upon publication, make him something of a cult figure. During the nine years he spent at Minnesota, Skinner was remarkably prolific, establishing himself as one of the country's leading experimental psychologists.

From Minnesota, Skinner moved to the University of Indiana where for a brief period he served as professor and chairperson of the department of psychology. In 1947, he delivered the William James Lectures at Harvard, and the following year he joined Harvard's Department of Psychology as a full professor.

Emergence of Operant Conditioning

With the publication of *The Behavior of Organisms* (1938), Skinner presented his early principles of operant conditioning. *Walden Two* (1948), Skinner's only published novel, was an early application of his theory to a utopian community of a thousand people that drew heavy response and inspired the establishment of several experimental communes, as well as a national conference. *Science and Human Development* (1953) introduced a variety of applications of operant learning principles. In *The Technology of Teaching* (1968), Skinner proposed a revolutionary approach to learning in the school setting. He presented his scientific position in *Contingencies of Reinforcement* (1969) and explained its relevance for a wide variety of social problems. After the publication of *Beyond Freedom and Dignity* (1971), in which he predicted disaster if the world did not soon begin to use its knowledge of behavior, Skinner was criticized harshly for asserting that present illusory concepts of human freedom and dignity block scientific planning for a better world. *About Behaviorism* (1974) is a summary of his views of psychology. His last publication, *Enjoy Old Age: A Program for Self-Management* (Skinner & Vaughan, 1983), concerns the application of operant learning principles to aging.

Accomplishments and Awards

In 1941, Skinner was the recipient of a Guggenheim Fellowship. That same year he wrote the initial draft of *Verbal Behavior* (which was not published until 1957). The Society of Experimental Psychologists awarded Skinner the Warren Medal in 1942. In 1951, an honorary doctor of science degree was conferred on him by his alma mater, Hamilton College. After that time, he received another nineteen honorary degrees, including the Sc.D. from the University of Chicago in 1967; the University of Exeter, England, 1969; McGill University, Montreal, 1970; and Ohio Wesleyan University, 1971. Skinner received the Distinguished Contribution Award from the American Psychological Association in 1958. The highest public award for scientific contribution, the National Medal of Science, was presented to Skinner in 1968; only three behavioral scientists have received this award. In 1971, he was the recipient of the APA Gold Medal and the Joseph P. Kennedy, Jr., Foundation Award.

When asked during an interview how he felt about the numerous awards he had received, Skinner (1983a) responded: "By denying creativity and freedom, I have relinquished all chances of being called a Great Thinker" (p. 32). Skinner's theory grew to influence nearly every aspect of his life. He was often depressed or frightened by the honors conferred on him, and attempted to refuse those that would either take time from his work or unduly reinforce specific aspects of it. Still, looking back on seventy-eight years of life during an interview for *Science Digest* (1983), Skinner remarked to the interviewer:

> But fifty-three years after I went to Harvard to study psychology, I can certainly say this: if, at that time, someone had shown me my present position, I would have settled for that. I would have said, I'll take that as a career (in Rosenthal, 1983, p. 106).

Skinner died August 18, 1990. He was eighty-six years old.

Resolutions of the Eleven Basic Issues

For the most part, Skinner's resolutions of the eleven basic issues are strong and explicit, reflecting a belief in and commitment to elementalism, environmentalism, objectivity, reactivity, determinism, knowability, and controllability. There are, however, a number of issues that are not applicable to Skinner's position since he rejected internal cognitive–perceptual variables as determinants of behavior. For Skinner, **behavior** is the direct result of specifiable, unique conditioning histories.

An understanding of Skinner's theory of personality requires first an understanding of his philosophy of science. As mentioned, Skinner was neither a personologist nor a psychotherapist; rather, he considered himself a *scientific behaviorist*. His work was based on the assumptions that it is necessary to view humans as objectively determined, and that human behavior is subject to the laws of science and should, therefore, be approached in the same way scientists approach any natural phenomenon—through careful causal analysis. Furthermore, Skinner was convinced that the drastic modification of social structure necessary for the survival of humankind will occur only when other scientists adopt his basic assumptions concerning human nature.

Heredity versus Social Determinants

Skinner (1938, 1953, 1969,1986a) did not deny the influence of biological determinants upon human behavior; indeed, he ascribed the propensity for reinforcement to genetics. For Skinner, the process of human evolution shapes innate behaviors in much the same way environment shapes learned behaviors. Inherent sensitivity to reinforcement evolved because of its especially strong survival advantage. Life-maintaining and life-enhancing behaviors are reinforced behaviors selected within the environment for survival. Skinner (1986a) recognized, too, the possibility that some human behaviors may be entirely genetic, thus unaffected by external stimuli.

While Skinner did not claim that human behavior is singly a product of the environment, he did minimize the practical importance of both inner states and biological determinants. Biological variability, like inner states, cannot be directly and objectively observed, measured, manipulated, or controlled; hence, biology does not lend itself well to rigid, functional experimental analysis. Again, for Skinner, what cannot be observed directly is unworthy of scientific study. With his focus guided by his belief in the natural laws of science, Skinner relied almost exclusively on environmental stimuli that can be manipulated—hence, controlled—in the laboratory setting.

For Skinner (1948, 1971, 1974), human behavior is not only the function of existing environmental contingencies but also has an effect on the environment. As people's behavior changes, the contingencies of the environment also are altered. Skinner (1948) therefore emphasized the modification, prediction, and planned control of behavior by developing a behavioral technology to change society and culture. The principles of **operant reinforcement**—that is, reinforcement of a behavior that operates on the environment controlling it and, in turn, being controlled by it—are at the base of Skinner's theory. "We control the world around us, but only because that world has taught us to do so and induces us to do so" (Skinner, 1983a, p. 30).

Since Skinner believed all organisms are subject to the same natural laws, the laws of behavior, once discovered, can be generalized from the simple to the complex—from animal studies to humans, from children to adults. Although Skinner viewed humans as vastly more complex than the lower animals, the differences between humans and animals are a matter of degree rather than kind. Further, following the principle that behavior is lawful and determined, the ultimate purpose of the study of human behavior is not only to be able to predict the behavior but also to control it.

Centrality of Reinforcement

A **reinforcement** (any stimulus that increases the probability of a response) may be either **positive** (a rewarding stimulus) or **negative** (the removal of an aversive stimulus, which is also rewarding). It may be either **primary** (an unconditioned reinforcer such as food, water, attention, or sex) or **secondary** (a conditioned reinforcer such as money or tokens). When reinforcement is withheld or interrupted, or stops for a sufficient period of time, a conditioned behavior diminishes through a process known as **extinction.** Reinforcement, then, is essential for both the acquisition and the maintenance of respondent behavior.

Schedules of Reinforcement Focusing on variables that increase or decrease the probability of a response occurring over time, Skinner (1938, 1953, 1974) discovered that different **schedules of reinforcement** (the contingencies under which reinforcement is delivered) had different effects on respondent learning. **Continuous reinforcement** involves reinforcing the organism each time it emits the desired behavior and is usually employed at the initial stages of most operant conditioning. There are, however, a variety of **intermittent schedules of reinforcement** in Skinner's behavioral technology, falling into two general classifications: reinforcement after a regular or fixed time interval, called **interval reinforcement schedules,** and reinforcement after an irregular or fixed number of responses, called **ratio reinforcement schedules.** These two general classifications provide four basic schedules of reinforcement:

1. **Fixed-ratio schedule** (A schedule in which one application of reinforcement is given only after the subject has emitted a predetermined or fixed number of responses): This schedule generates high operant levels since the more the subject responds, the more reinforcement he or she receives. The fixed-ratio schedule is used effectively in industry, where the employee is paid for the number of pieces produced or the number of operations performed. Sales commissions are based on fixed-ratio schedules. Academic promotions and salary increases based on publication of a specified number of research articles or books over a fixed time period is another example of a fixed-ratio schedule of reinforcement.

2. **Fixed-interval schedule** (A schedule in which reinforcement is given only after an established or fixed period of time without regard to the number of responses): Examples of this schedule are paying for work done by the hour, day, week, or month; giving a child a weekly allowance; and administering midterm and final examinations. Response increases over time with a sharp increase immediately preceding the time for reinforcement. In addition, there is often a low rate of response immediately after the reinforcement.

3. **Variable-ratio schedule** (A schedule in which the number of responses for reinforcement is varied randomly around a specified average value): On a variable-ratio schedule of fifteen, the subject is reinforced for every fifteenth response on the average, but rather than coming at the fixed interval of fifteen, the response receiving reinforcement is randomly selected. This schedule produces a high and constant response rate, and extinction is often slow because the subject does not know when the next reinforcement will be forthcoming. The slot machine serves as a good illustration of this schedule.

4. **Variable-interval schedule** (A schedule in which reinforcements are presented on some stated time interval, but the intervals between reinforcements are irregular and impossible to predict): While reinforcement is solely based on time, the subject must make the appropriate response after the interval is over. For example, when performing on a five-minute schedule, reinforcement may be given after eight minutes, two minutes, six minutes, and four minutes. With this

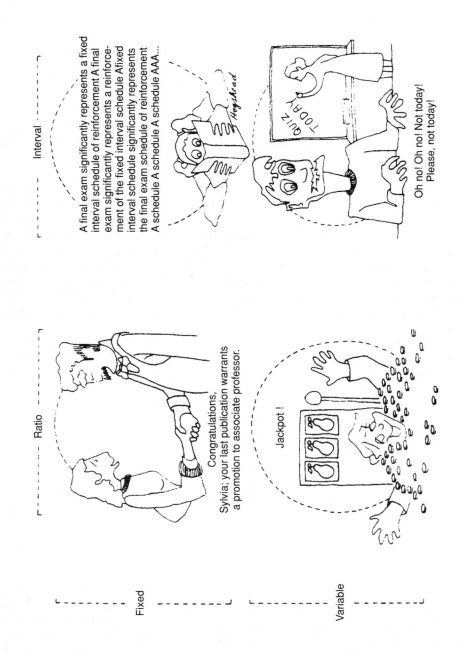

FIGURE 13-1 Skinner's Schedules of Reinforcement

schedule, short time intervals generate a high rate of response, and long time intervals, a low rate. Nevertheless, response rates tend to be steady and are difficult to extinguish. Surprise quizzes, for example, may be effectively employed on a variable-interval schedule to ensure a relatively stable rate of student preparation and study.

Explanation of Learning Process

As the term implies, **respondent behavior** involves a response to or elicited by a specific stimulus in the environment. At its lowest level, a respondent behavior may be a **reflex action** (unlearned, automatic, involuntary responses). The pupil of the eye responds to a bright light by contracting. Food placed on the tongue causes a salivation response. Striking just below the kneecap elicits a forward knee jerk response. No learning or conditioning is involved. Moreover they do nothing to change the environment—the contracting pupil of the eye has no effect on the light that shines into it, nor does the forward knee jerk stop the strike that caused it. Respondent behavior at a higher level is learned or conditioned. A conditioned response involves the substitution of one stimulus for another.

Working with dogs, Pavlov (1927) accidentally discovered that dogs would salivate to neutral stimuli—their keeper's footsteps, for example. In Pavlov's further investigation of this phenomenon, dogs that had salivated when presented with food were presented with the sound of a bell just prior to being fed. After a number of pairings (bell followed by food), the dogs began to salivate at the sound of the bell. The food became a reinforcement. When food no longer followed the sound of the bell, salivation at the sound of the bell decreased in intensity until the conditioned salivation response was extinguished. In short, respondent behavior depends on reinforcement, and when reinforcement is withdrawn the conditioned response is eventually extinguished. Reinforcement is responsible for the continuation of a learned response.

Operant Behavior Skinner believed that operant or emitted behavior is far more significant for human learning than respondent or elicited behavior. The strength and frequency of operant behavior is determined and/or modified by the reinforcement that *follows* it. Unlike respondent behavior, which has no effect on the environment, operant behavior operates on the environment, thus changing it. If the change in the environment is **reinforcing** (provides some reward or eliminates a noxious stimulus) the probability that a person will repeat that behavior is increased. Conversely, should the change in the environment produce no reinforcement, either positive or negative, or should the change produce punishment, the person is less likely to continue to emit the behavior. Perhaps most important, those who provide the reinforcement *control* the person's behavior.

Humans emit a great variety of behavior. Those behaviors emitted and reinforced by the environment grow in strength and form a network or set of patterns. It is these patterns of reinforced behaviors that Skinner refers to when he uses the term **human personality.**

Determinism versus Freedom of Choice

If all human behavior conforms to causal laws, then all behavior is determined by **antecedent factors** (the individual's idiosyncratic reinforcement history). It follows, then, that for Skinner (1969), **free will** and **personal autonomy** are illusions, mere philosophical notions that have been reinforced in the individual's past. As an illusion, freedom holds no place in Skinner's scientific approach to the study of human behavior. Moreover, humans are always subject to **external variables** (their genetic endowment and environmental contingencies).

Skinner's stance on the issue of freedom is not in opposition to freedom, nor is it an adversary of control. Rather, he argues, **control** is a reality; it exists. Further, he warns, control is capricious and will remain so as long as humans continue to hold to the illusion of freedom and do nothing to influence the controlling environmental contingencies.

Through their behavior, humans operate on the environment that controls them. By surrendering their illusory concept of **autonomy** (freedom to choose) and their understanding of the principles of operant conditioning, humans would be in position to develop a behavioral technology that would permit them to plan for and generate controlling environmental contingencies that are favorable to healthy growth and development (Skinner, 1948).

Role Assigned to Group Determinants

Skinner (1953), who believed: "It is always the individual who behaves" (p. 13), rejects common explanations that personify groups as if they were individuals. He dismisses concepts such as the "group mind," "the herd instinct," and "national character" as weak attempts to support an unscientific approach to the study of groups.

Skinner admitted, however, that while it is the individual who acts, it is the group that possesses the stronger effect. We can, as individuals, increase both the probability and the strength of reinforcement by joining a group because the reinforcement contingencies of the group easily outweigh the total consequences that can be generated by its members acting individually. Within a group there is an intensification of effect. Reinforcement for the individual becomes stronger when he or she acts in concert with others.

The larger the group, the more powerful its effect on the individual and the environment. Society, therefore, plays an important role in the establishment of reinforcement consequences essential for the definition, transmission, and maintenance of desired behaviors among its members. Skinner (1953, 1971, 1974) asserted that when behavioral definitions are carefully planned (through functional analysis, for example) and effectively reinforced (through positive reinforcement contingencies), their effect on the individual and the environment are not only immediately beneficial but also contribute to the survival of the species and the culture. Whether a family or a culture, the group is of maximal importance in transmitting rule-governed behavior into its members' personal and unique repertories of responding. It is crucial that the child learn the values first of its particular subgroup and later of its culture to live an effective life as an adult.

Conforming is also a concern in behaviorism. Because some individual responses in a group are positively reinforced while others are ignored or punished, a response conformity is likely established within a group. Skinner believes this conformity may be partially explained by an analysis of imitation. Imitation is likely to be reinforcing. In contrast, membership in several groups, where the behavioral repertoire learned in each does not generalize to the others, often results in several different repertoires—therefore, several different personalities (see "Role of Self-Concept") may emerge. We thus develop separate **selves** (personalities), each appropriate for participation in a particular group. We behave one way in our family group, another in our professional group, and still another way in a group of close friends.

While Skinner did little in the area of group dynamics, he was convinced that group interchange and heightened effect of the group on the environment can be studied most effectively within the framework of natural science. Indeed, he argued, this approach should be used fully before we decide to accept the constructs of social units, forces, and laws that require methods of a different nature (Skinner, 1953).

Early versus Continuous Development

According to Skinner (1953, 1957b, 1969, 1974), environmental contingencies are the major determinants of human personality. Because other humans comprise a large part of the environment, interactions with parents, other family members, teachers, peers, and so on provide most of the reinforcements (and punishments) in the early acquisition of an ever-growing repertoire of behavior. Physical maturation contributes to personality development, but for Skinner, personality is formed and develops as the child acquires a larger repertoire of behavior through exposure to new contingencies of reinforcement.

While Skinner did not subscribe to critical life stages, he recognized that the environmental contingencies affecting children are different at different ages. Behavior reinforced at one age may be ignored or even punished at another. Skinner (1974) reminded his readers: "The child's world 'develops,' too" (p. 67).

For Skinner (1953, 1974), developmental stages do not explain overt behavior. In *About Behaviorism*, Skinner (1974) expressed little regard for the structural concepts of the developmentalists:

> *Compared with the experimental analysis of behavior, developmental psychology stands in the position of evolutionary theory before Darwin. . . . It remained for Darwin to discover the selective action of the environment, as it remains for us to supplement developmentalism in behavioral science with an analysis of the selective action of the environment (p. 68).*

While learning is considered a continuous process, behaviors learned during the early years are especially significant, particularly since the acquisition of new behaviors is often dependent on **unlearning** (extinguishing) old behaviors.

Personality development for classical learning advocates, then, is nothing more than the acquisition of a behavioral repertoire. For Skinner (1968, 1969, 1974), learning and development are synonymous, thus, development, like learning, is dependent on the limitations set by genetic endowment and the existent and potential contingencies of the environment. Physiological development is additionally important because some of the mechanisms necessary for more complex behavioral responses are not present at birth. It remains, nonetheless, the contingencies of reinforcement that play the major role in personality development. In a theory that focuses exclusively on observable behavior and in which all behavior can be traced to external causes, life-stage concepts are not only considered unnecessary to understanding personality development but also confusing, thus wasteful, explanations.

Number and Weight Assigned to Motivational Concepts

Operant responses (approximations of goal behavior) are emitted, reinforced, and strengthened. What appears to be **motivation** is, for Skinner, nothing more than probability of response. Further, he asserted, differing probabilities of response can be accounted for by variables such as degree of deprivation or satiation. From this perspective, hunger and thirst are not inner motives or instinctual drives pressing for action. Rather, they are aversive stimuli brought about by deprivation of food and water. Removal of **aversive stimuli** (noxious stimuli, e.g., deprivations) is reinforcing.

Skinner held the pigeons he worked with to 85 percent of their normal body weight, making food pellets and water reliable reinforcers for shaping desired behavior. Thus, the greater the deprivation, the stronger the aversive stimulus and the more certain the reinforcers—hence, the greater the probability, predictability, and controllability of that behavior.

While Skinner recognized that an inner sovereign motivating force, such as an innate drive toward actualization, or perfection and completion, or individuation, or the instinctual drives of an irrational id, might be construed to explain human motivation and a myriad of other behaviors, he was convinced that all inner theoretical constructs are unscientific, and hence, misleading. Not only do inner motivational constructs contribute nothing to the prediction and control of behavior, acceptance of such constructs stifles any further investigations of the external factors that are the actual cause of practically all human motivation and behavior.

Endowing a star with the inner motivation of providing direction for sailors at sea adds nothing to knowledge of the star's orbit. Knowledge of the star's "behavior" is gained by observing its trajectory over time until the star's movement can be predicted with accuracy. Attributing humans with some invisible inner motivating drive or force adds nothing to the study of their behavior.

Knowledge of human behavior, like a star's movement, Skinner asserted, is best gained through the careful analysis of the behavior observed. Hidden motivations, such as unconscious forces, cognition, instincts, self-concepts, will power, or an actualization tendency, while not denied, fall outside the scope of scientific analysis and are better ignored. Skinner, therefore, limited his data to observed physical events—in the case of human behavior, the behavioral responses and their contingencies.

> *The science I am discussing is the investigation of the relation between behavior and the environment—on the one hand, the environment in which the species evolved and which is responsible for the facts investigated by the ethologists and, on the other hand, the environment in which the individual lives and in response to which at any moment he behaves (Skinner, 1975, p. 48).*

While Skinner (1953) placed internal states outside the domain of scientific analysis, he does not deny their existence. He simply believed that using them to explain an individual's behavioral response is fruitless, since they are not relevant in a causal analysis. Further, to use them to hypothesize a causal role serves only to hold back scientific analysis.

Conscious versus Unconscious Determinants

Skinner flatly rejected either conscious or unconscious entities like those proposed by Freud. Indeed, he rejected all intrapsychic agents. He believed that by turning to the facts on which these inner constructs are based, "it is usually possible to identify the contingencies of reinforcement which account for the intrapsychic activities" (Skinner, 1974, p. 154).

For Skinner, **consciousness** is a social product resulting from a verbal community that arranges contingencies under which we not only see an object or event but also see that we see it. We are a part of a verbal community that insists that we become aware of what we are doing and why we are doing it. Further, the verbal community insists that we talk about it. We are conditioned to observe ourselves; otherwise, we would have no reason to do so. "Our physical world, then, generates both physical action and the physical conditions within the body to which an individual responds when a verbal community arranges the necessary contingencies" (Skinner, 1974, p. 220).

We are conscious in the sense of being under stimulus control. As with all other animals, we feel the pain caused by a painful stimulus. However, we are conscious—aware that we are feeling the feeling of pain—because of verbal contingencies. Different verbal communities reinforce different kinds and degrees of consciousness in their members.

In a sense, all behavior is unconscious until it is observed and analyzed. Moreover, unconscious behavior need not be observed to be effective. We may be unconsciously in pursuit of certain consequences, but our behavior is, nevertheless, best understood with reference to its consequences rather than its conscious or unconscious nature. The causality in behavior does not depend on awareness, so it makes little difference to the behaviorist observing a behavior whether that behavior is conscious or unconscious.

Role Assigned to Self-Concept

For Skinner, what many theorists refer to as **self** or personality is nothing more than a learned repertoire of behaviors, responses acquired through conditioning that are characteristic of a particular individual. Differences in self or personality are nothing more than differences in observed behavior. While complex, each self or personality is constructed, element by element, over a period of time. Skinner's view of self or personality is elemental and in sharp contrast to the holistic views held by such theorists as Rogers or Maslow (Chapters 9 and 10). According to Skinner, **subjectivity** is irrelevant—nothing other than an explanatory fiction.

"The 'role a person plays in life' is a repertoire of behavior, not a 'self' or 'personality.' It is more than a structural concept because it implies an effect" (Epstein, 1980, p. 154). It is clear from this statement that, while Skinner (1953) accepted the phenomenon of self-awareness or self-knowledge, he did not attribute this phenomenon to introspective observation. Rather, our knowledge of emotions, attitudes, values, and internal states consists of the inferences we draw from our direct observations of our overt behaviors and/or from the particular situational context in which these behaviors occur. **Self-awareness** (or self-knowledge), then, is a description of our overt behavior—hence, a function of our reinforcement history. And **self-concept** is neither a construct nor structure of personality but rather a label we employ to describe our observations. Our individual self-concepts will change as we add new behaviors to our repertoire. When, for example, a certain behavior is consistently reinforced, we are likely to emit that behavior and then begin to think of ourselves as persons who are likely to engage in that behavior.

For Skinner, the idea of self-concept is unnecessary in the functional analysis of behavior. As a mentalistic concept—that is, neither observable nor controllable—it is better ignored, or at best, viewed with caution. According to Skinner, self-concept can be misleading and used to account for variability that can be discovered more accurately in the contingencies of reinforcement. As an empiricist, Skinner was unwilling to grant a role to unseen and unseeable hypothetical constructs. He preferred to limit his study to manifest behavior.

Subjective versus Objective Reality

Skinner's stance on this issue was both strong and explicit. He considered **perceiving** to be a behavior, and behavior can be explained solely in terms of objective cause-and-effect relationships. To introduce **subjective experience** (the way we think and feel about incoming stimuli or outgoing responses) is to supplant the external cause of behavior with an explanatory fictional concept. Causality in behavior does not depend on perception. Subjective inner experience is not only irrelevant in Skinner's approach to behavior but also a major source of confusion in contemporary psychology. Once an inner subjective experience is accepted as an explanation for behavior, there is no longer any motivation to look further for the true external causes.

Uniqueness versus Universality

Accused of dehumanizing humans, Skinner (1971) reminded his accusers that "no theory changes what it is a theory about; man remains what he has always been" (p. 206). In *About Behaviorism* (1974), Skinner informed us: "Nothing about the position taken in this book questions the uniqueness of the human species, but the uniqueness is inherent in the sources" (p. 225). We are, in every sense, the locus of these sources, that "point at which many genetic and environmental stimuli come together in joint effect" (Skinner, 1971, p. 168).

Every cell in our bodies is uniquely our own, and we share our personal histories with no other organism. We have each occupied a unique space in this world, making it impossible for anyone else to be subjected to exactly the same reinforcements. Moreover, the gap that exists between each one of us and all others grows with time. With each hour, day, week, and month, we become more uniquely ourselves. Taken a step further, because we act on the environment in our unique ways, we make a difference to the world; we are important.

Psychological Health and Psychopathology

Skinner saw no qualitative difference between healthy and abnormal individuals. Like the term "personality," the terms "healthy" and "abnormal" are only convenient labels, and the laws of learning account for all behavior of all individuals, irrespective of the labels used to describe adaptive and maladaptive behavior.

Healthy Personality and the Good Life

Unlike his theoretical constructs, all of which resulted from carefully designed laboratory studies of lower animals, most of what Skinner (1948) had to say about healthy personality and the good life appears in his utopian novel *Walden Two*. *Walden Two* is Skinner's (1948) fictional application of behavioral analysis to the construction of a workable, effective, and productive pattern of communal government. Here Skinner described a community in which:

> *there is food, clothing, and shelter for all, where everyone chooses his own work and works on the average only 4 hours a day, where music and the arts flourish, where personal relationships develop under the most favorable circumstances, where education prepares every child for the social and intellectual life which lies before him, where—in short—people are truly happy, secure, productive, creative, and forward-looking (Rogers, & Skinner, 1956, p. 1059).*

Heredity		Social Determinants
Uniqueness		Universality
Determinism		Freedom
Early Development		Continuous Development
Subjective Reality		Objective Reality
Conscious Determinants		Unconscious Determinants

Role Assigned to Group Determinants — Group reinforcement contingencies significantly outweigh individual contingencies, and the larger the group, the more powerful its impact on the individual. Different groups reinforce different response repertoires and each group requires conformity of its members. The group is important in transmitting rule-governed behavior.

Explanation of Learning Process — Environmental contingencies determine what we learn and we learn that which satisfies certain contingencies of reinforcement. Learning is cumulative; patterns of responses become increasingly complex as we mature. Effective learning entails the ability to discriminate various stimuli and associate particular responses with particular stimuli.

Number and Weight Assigned to Motivational Concepts — Behavior is contingent on reinforcement histories. Inner motivational constructs are unscientific, contributing nothing to the prediction and control of behavior.

Centrality of Reinforcement — External reinforcement influences both the acquisition and the maintenance of behavior. Reinforcement may be positive or negative, primary or secondary, and different schedules of reinforcement have different effects on respondent learning.

Role Assigned to Self-Concept — Self-concept is an irrelevant hypothetical construct that focuses on introspective observation. Self-awareness and self-knowledge are functions of reinforcement histories. Self and personality are merely learned repertoires of behavior.

FIGURE 13-2   Schematic Analysis of Skinner's Stance on Basic Issues

For Skinner (1988), there is a distinct difference between "feeling well" and "feeling good" about life. To **feel well** is to feel a healthy body free of aches and pains. To **feel good** is to feel a body that has been positively reinforced. "Positive reinforcers please. . . . We say that we are enjoying life or that life is good" (Skinner, 1988, p. 178). **Health and the good life,** Skinner (1988) asserted, are outcomes of scientifically planned environmental contingencies. While humans may fantasize health and the good life by analyzing their feelings, achieving their fantasy is only possible by properly arranging environmental contingencies.

Psychopathology

Note at the outset that the word "psychopathology" is used here only to be consistent with the other chapters in this book. The descriptive adjectives "psychopathological" and "abnormal," in reference to human behavior, are not often found in Skinner's writing. While the definitions of these terms may serve society, they are, according to Skinner, far too general to serve science. Skinner preferred the adjectives inappropriate or maladaptive, even when referring to the bizarre behavior characteristic of some forms of schizophrenia. Indeed, from a behaviorist's perspective, for a therapist to describe a client's overt behavior as "pathological," "abnormal," or "bizarre" is more a declaration of the therapist's lack of knowledge about the client's idiosyncratic learning history than it is a declaration of anything about the client. For Skinner (in Evans, 1968): "A psychotic patient is psychotic because of his behavior. You don't institionalize a person because of his feelings" (p. 42).

All behavior, whether healthy or unhealthy, appropriate or inappropriate, is shaped by environmental contingencies of reinforcement. Hence, all behavior, even the most excessively inappropriate or maladaptive behavior, is *potentially* understandable. Difficulty in understanding another's behavior, or for that matter one's own, arises from the fact that a person's learning history is often unavailable, hence, impossible to know.

Inappropriate behavior is, for Skinner (1972), the result of self-defeating attempts to counteract social control or of unsuccessful attempts at self-control, particularly when either is accompanied by strong emotions or results in severe punishment.

> *An excessive emotional condition, a dangerous mode of escape from anxiety, a troublesome preoccupation with sex, or an excessive enthusiasm for gambling may be nothing more than extreme cases of the effects of environmental conditions (Skinner, 1972, p. 252).*

Skinner (1972) did not deny physiological or genetic causes for maladaptive behaviors; however, he believed that once the principles of learning are understood, most mental disorders are not different from any other behavior. Like other behavior (including "normal" behavior), behavior that is troublesome or dangerous enough to be characterized by society as mental illness may simply be learned, a product of reinforcement contingencies, an idiosyncratic condition of deprivation or satiation, or an emotionally exciting circumstance (Skinner, 1972, p. 252). In such cases, references to inner agencies, conflicts, and unconscious forces *as causal elements* are excluded from a behavioristic explanation.

Because it is troublesome or dangerous, the psychotic's behavior is inappropriate from society's point of view. When behavior is considered inappropriate by society, it meets with negative reinforcement or punishment (behavior under control of aversive stimuli), or the psychotic's rejection of external stimuli in favor of **delusion** (the private creation of his or her own world that may differ significantly from reality). Aversive stimuli are compounded when society labels the maladjusted person as "lazy," "sick," "crazy," "mad," "bad," or "possessed." Once labeled, the maladjusted person is shaped into behaving according to the label. While the secondary gains of "mental illness" become part of this shaping, there is, in addition, the **dependency shaping** of his or her caretakers—the client's passive or willing acceptance of directions and manipulations of those given responsibility for his or her care.

The problem of the behavioral therapist is to identify the maladaptive behaviors in the client's repertoire of behaviors, and through operant techniques, extinguish them. Concurrently, the therapist uses the same operant techniques to shape adaptive behaviors into the client's behavioral repertoire. The psychotic's life history is relatively unimportant except to reveal information about the client's maladaptive behavioral patterns (symptom condition) that is necessary for arranging an effective operant conditioning program. While the client may gain informal insight into his or her problem behavior, from an operant perspective self-understanding is not a requisite for the success of the operant process. Skinner (1953) discussed several of the more common inappropriate behavioral patterns and the environmental contingencies that reinforce them (pp. 363–367).

Applications to Psychotherapy

Armed with an immense literature and impressive body of knowledge based upon scientific inquiry essential to the application of Skinner's operant learning principles, numerous psychologists, counselors, and social workers are employing Skinner's methods of analyzing and techniques of modifying human behavior in diverse settings (i.e., mental health clinics and agencies, psychiatric hospitals, schools and colleges, social agencies, federal and state prisons, psycholinguistics, businesses, and industries).

The operant behaviorists' approach to counseling and psychotherapy is based on clinical applications of Skinner's principles of behavior. While these applications have moved from the laboratory to various clinical, agency, school, and industrial settings, their goals and methods are the same as those established by Skinner in the laboratory: the scientific prediction and control of behavior through contingency management. Behavior modification as a therapy, then, is a compilation of principles and techniques about how to change behavior. It is not a comprehensive therapeutic theory. Further, the principles of learning are value free, giving the therapist no specific directions about what behavior should be modified or who should do it. These principles also do not answer the question of why or when behavioral modification should occur. For those in the field of therapy, these questions center on individual and cultural values, and the answers must come from the therapist and the therapist's professional organizations (e.g., the American Psychological Association or American Association for Counseling and Development, and the state licensing boards).

Therapeutic Goals

For most behavior modification therapists, the client, in a highly interactive process with the therapist, ultimately decides the desired outcomes or goals of therapy. As in most therapies, active client participation is essential. The goals of operant therapy must be explicitly defined in terms of concrete, overt, measurable behaviors, and the process of translating the amorphous feelings of anxiety, depression, helplessness, anger, guilt, fear, and frustration into clearly defined goals for behavioral change can be difficult, especially for those clients who attribute the source of their problems to their feelings.

After an effective relationship has been established, problem assessment and formulation are usually the first steps in therapy proper and involve high degrees of listening and empathy skills on the part of the therapist (see "Therapeutic Relationship"). A thorough understanding of a client's problem, as outlined by Cormier and Cormier (1979), includes the following points:

- Some structuring: An explanation of the purpose of problem formulation;
- Identification and selection of problem concerns: A discussion of general problem situations to obtain a complete picture of the problem, followed by a selection of the concerns that are the most troublesome or difficult, and last, setting priorities and pinpointing the problem that brought the client into therapy;
- Identification of present problem behaviors;
- Identification of antecedent conditions—overt, covert, past, and present—contributing to the problem;
- Identification of consequent contributing conditions: overt, covert, positive, negative, immediate, and delayed;
- Identification of client coping skills;
- Identification of problem intensity: extent, frequency, and duration of problem behaviors.

When both client and therapist thoroughly understand the client's problem, the process of goal selection begins. The importance of establishing clearly defined goals that accurately reflect specific areas of client concern cannot be over-emphasized. Outcome goals not only clarify the client's initial expectations of counseling by delineating what can and cannot be accomplished in counseling, but also specify the direction of therapy. In addition, the goals of therapy establish the techniques, strategies, and evaluation procedures.

Characteristics of behavioral outcome goals are explicitness and attainability. It should be remembered, however, that the client has decision primacy in goal selection. The therapist must decide, on the basis of the client's goals and his or her therapeutic skills, whether or not he or she can help the client attain the goals selected. Major reservations at this point could lead to a reevaluation of the client's goals, referral to another therapist, or termination. Regardless of the decision, the therapist's reasons should be explicit and fully revealed to the client.

As with problem formulation, the goals of therapy must be behaviorally and individually specific and include the conditions under which the desired behavior is to occur, the level or extent of the behavior, an identification and hierarchical arrangement of sub-goals, and client commitment to behavior management efforts.

Therapeutic Relationship

While the behavioristic conceptualization of the therapeutic relationship is different from that of many of the theories presented in this book, it is certainly no less important. The therapeutic relationship is not, for example, the essence of therapy as it is in Rogers's Person-Centered Therapy, nor is it sufficient for therapy. It cannot be used to bring about behavior change or to solve client problems. Indeed, in one of his notes, Skinner (1980) argues that it cannot be used at all since, if genuine, the relationship cannot be turned on or off at will for reinforcement purposes. For Skinner (Epstein, 1980) "it is the contingencies that establish the relation" (p. 262).

Still, most behavior therapists support the importance of the therapist's demonstration of accurate listening, acceptance, understanding, concern, and respect for the client. Cormier and Cormier (1979) suggest that authenticity and spontaneity are potent characteristics of effective therapists. Indeed, they define effective therapeutic relationships from the therapist's viewpoint as "those in which counselors are able to demonstrate their skills without being preoccupied with the skills or themselves" (p. 10). Preoccupation inhibits relating; spontaneity enhances it. Thus, while the relationship between the client and therapist alone cannot be used to solve the client's problems, it is a potential vehicle to foster trust, increase verbal communication, and enhance reinforcement. Overall, then, it is a facilitative factor in producing client change.

It is essential that the therapist spontaneously demonstrates accurate listening, acceptance, empathic understanding, concern, and respect for the client, particularly in the initial stages of therapy during problem assessment and formulation. Accurate participation is encouraged and self-management is emphasized. Moreover, the way the therapist delivers these skills appears to be as important as having them.

Initial Procedures and Strategies

Initiating Therapy. Therapy proper, or the treatment phase of therapy, rests on the foundation built by the client and therapist in the early counseling sessions. During the first phase of therapy, a therapeutic relationship is initiated; the client's presenting problem is functionally assessed and behaviorally formulated; client expectations are explored and clarified; specific behavioral outcomes are defined; and a mutual agreement and commitment to enter the next phase of therapy are confirmed. Client involvement, essential in every phase of operant therapy, is especially crucial in the beginning sessions since the early sessions are where the pattern is set for future sessions.

Structuring and Client Expectations. Experience indicates that initial client expectations can have either a positive or a negative effect on the therapeutic process. While a moderately positive level of client expectation can enhance the probability of therapeutic change, extreme expectations, whether high or low, are often deleterious to the outcome of therapy. Excessively high expectations are usually impossible to realize. Excessively low expectations can be an indication of little or no incentive on the part of the client to participate actively and cooperatively in the therapeutic process.

Structuring (carefully delineating client and therapist roles) is one method of clarifying client expectations and may be employed throughout therapy, as the need arises. By discovering the antecedent stimuli that cause current maladaptive behavior, explaining how that behavior was learned, and describing how relearning occurs in the therapeutic situation, the therapist can often correct the client's unrealistic expectations.

Establishing the goals of therapy is usually effective in clarifying the client's initial expectations of therapy. Clearly defined behavioral goals may help both client and therapist anticipate what can and cannot be accomplished through this particular approach to therapy. Again, because client and therapist commitment is a part of the process of goal alignment, increased client motivation is a natural outcome.

Behaviorally Oriented Interview. Although the interview is not considered an objective method for gathering information required for a functional analysis of the client's behavior, the therapist often relies on the interview when it is impractical or impossible to arrange for direct observation of the client's behavior in the natural environment. A fairly standard procedure is for the therapist to instruct the client on demonstrated methods of self-monitoring and directions for recording specific information about the **ABCs** of behavior control (antecedents, behaviors, and consequences) in a diary or pocket notebook. The client may also be provided a wrist counter or stopwatch to complete a frequency count for baseline assessment of a target behavior.

Self-Management. The ultimate goal of every therapeutic approach is to provide clients with the techniques they need to control their behavior so they can be effective self-managers. Behavior modification is no exception. Although in the end all behavior, including self-controlling behavior, must be accounted for with variables from outside ourselves, we control ourselves, according to Skinner (1953, 1971), precisely as we control the behavior of anyone else—"through the manipulation of variables of which behavior is a function" (pp. 123–124). Interested in the client's right to participate actively in all phases of the therapeutic process, operant reinforcement therapists have developed and demonstrated self-controlling strategies for initiating and maintaining changes in a wide variety of behaviors.

Self-control programs are individually formulated to effect change for clients who are engaging in behaviors that are dysfunctional, self-defeating, or injurious, or who are engaging in a desired behavior too infrequently. Examples of client problems in the first instance are eating to the point of obesity, excessive smoking or drinking, and indiscriminate sexual activity. Self-control strategies, or operant reinforcement programs, are designed to reduce the probability of these behaviors. Examples of client problems in the second instance are inability to speak on one's behalf, failure to exercise adequately, and fear of initiating social contacts. Self-control strategies here are planned to increase the probability of these responses. In therapy, clients may express the desire to work on a program that includes decreasing one response while at the same time increasing another. A self-control program for the obese client may, for example, include decreasing caloric intake by changing eating patterns while simultaneously burning a greater number of calories by increasing exercise.

Behavior therapists using operant reinforcement are not only interested in how schedules of reinforcement determine behavior but also in the role of self-management processes as clients act to alter the variables that affect their behavior. For Skinner (1953, 1971; Epstein, 1980), self-control is an exercise in manipulating the variables that determine one's behavior. Self-controlling manipulations might include such behaviors as physical restraint, physical aids, changing the stimuli that induce unwanted behavior or that make wanted behavior more probable, inducing emotional changes that are likely to assist with desired behavioral outcomes, avoidance of undesirable situations, or rewarding desired behavior while punishing undesired behavior. The self-management techniques are limited only by the number of variables the client and counselor can manipulate successfully.

The obese client discussed earlier may, for example, set a goal to lose two pounds a week for a period of ten weeks. To help himself reach this goal he plans the number of calories he must reduce from his normal diet, a baseline he established from an earlier assessment of his present eating patterns. He decides to remove all unnecessary food from the house and not to purchase food that might be eaten conveniently or impulsively. He places a lock or an aversive sign on the refrigerator door to remind himself that he is not to eat between meals. He serves his meals on smaller plates, eats slowly, chews each bite thoroughly, and places his fork on the plate between bites. He decides, also, to take one five-minute break during each meal. He manipulates antecedent events by avoiding places or situations where snacking usually occurs. When he feels the urge to snack, he walks—this in addition to his regular exercise plan. He charts his weight every three days, rewards himself when he records a loss, and deprives himself of something he particularly enjoys when there is no loss or when he records a gain. As an additional incentive, he gives someone he trusts $200 he has saved for clothes with instructions to return $10 for each pound he loses toward the twenty-pound goal. In those weeks he has not lost two pounds, his friend donates the $20 to a designated charity.

In this example, both the positive reinforcements and aversive consequences are contingent on a specific weight loss. While the client serves as a contingency manager in most instances, the friend functions in this capacity in the last. Contact with others in the program may be helpful to some clients. Success often depends on accurate baseline data and a realistic plan. Charting progress during treatment may also be used to the client's advantage in this plan. The chart becomes an additional reinforcement when he is successful and a punishment when he is not. Complexity of the program depends on the sophistication and involvement of the client.

Token Economy. Based on the principles of reinforcement and extinction, the token economy has been demonstrated as an effective operant approach in group environments. It has been employed successfully in institutional settings such as classrooms, resident care facilities, psychiatric hospitals, and correctional facilities.

In the token economy, tokens or points that can be exchanged for consumer items or privileges are presented to clients for specified desired behaviors. Undesired behaviors go unrewarded or are set up on a cost basis. Initially, target behaviors scheduled for reinforcement focus on order and discipline. For example, single tokens might be awarded to clients who bathe at the designated time, brush their teeth, comb their hair, dress themselves properly, and make their beds. As clients' behaviors improve, reinforcement is increased to a much wider range of socially approved behaviors, and the tokens may be used to purchase a greater variety of goods and privileges. Clients may, for example, use their accumulated tokens to purchase desired consumer goods, acquire greater privacy, attend movies, and participate in field and shopping trips outside the institution.

The initial step in designing a token economy is the identification of clearly specified target behaviors—both those that are desired and to be acquired and those that are undesirable and to be extinguished. Staff involvement at this point is necessary, first to establish baseline behaviors and second to facilitate interest and cooperative participation in the program. Step two focuses on the definition of currency. Although the structure is usually simple, the resources of the institution and the nature of the group being considered usually dictate the form that tangible tokens will take. Items such as poker chips, points on a tally sheet, punched cards or tickets, and gold stars have been used to establish successful token economies.

In the final step, an exchange system is devised. Goods and privileges must be identified and their exchange rate determined. For tokens to maintain their reinforcement and incentive value, their exchange rate and the variety of goods and privileges they may be used to purchase must be increased as clients' behaviors improve.

In addition to improved behavior are the following advantages of implementing a token economy:

1. Once the behaviors have been specified and the program designed, training the staff to participate in a token economy is relatively easy and requires little time and expense.

2. The use of tokens promotes immediacy between the client's response and tangible reinforcement.

3. Tokens serve as positive reinforcements.

4. By manipulating the rate of exchange, clients can be encouraged to work over extended periods of time for single, highly desired reinforcements.

5. By pairing the tokens with verbal reinforcements, the staff enhances the value of intrinsic motivation.

6. A token economy is open to—indeed, facilitates—social reinforcement measures.

7. It is possible to select behaviors that are not normally reinforced by society.

8. By targeting behaviors that contribute to both the short- and the long-term quality of life, it becomes obvious to client and staff members that the program accomplishes more than simply controlling undesirable behavior.

9. The program is designed to ensure that modified behaviors generalize to life requirements outside the institutional setting, making the client's transition to the natural environment easier.

Course of Psychotherapy

Assessment assumes an especially significant and continual role in behavioral modification. The information used by the client and therapist to formulate the target problems for therapeutic focus and by the client for goal selection emerges from a thorough functional analysis of the client's present situation. From this same process the therapist uncovers the information he or she needs to determine the specific methods and techniques of therapy. Finally, the assessment process is used throughout therapy to evaluate the effectiveness of the therapeutic plan. Arguing for the logical relationship of assessment and the objectives of therapy in the initial phase of therapy, Lazarus (1976b) informs us: "Faulty problem identification (inadequate assessment) is probably the greatest impediment to successful therapy" (p. 14).

When a client's behavior has been carefully and directly observed and the specific goals of therapy have been behaviorally defined, therapeutic effectiveness is not difficult to evaluate. The severity of the client's target problems at the time of provisional behavioral analysis can be compared with an analysis of severity at any point in therapy, including termination of treatment.

Extended Applications

During the 1960s and early 1970s, applications of Skinner's laboratory work spread rapidly to numerous human concerns. In addition to psychotherapeutic methodology already discussed, Skinner's operant principles are utilized today in educational, industrial, organizational, managerial, correctional, and military training settings. Instructional software, personalized textbooks, and simulation exercises that are self-paced, immediately reinforcing, and cost effective are readily available to all prepared to state their learning objectives in clear behavioral terms.

Educational institutions from nursery to graduate schools utilize programmed learning in nearly every academic discipline, including the arts. Business and industry, interested in greater efficiency and improved productivity, integrate Skinner's schedules of reinforcement into their incentive programs for both workers and managers. Correctional institutions, both state and federal, employ Skinner's environmental rule and contingencies of reinforcement to engineer a secure, controlled environment with fewer punishments. The armed forces utilize a wide variety of simulated exercises that are not only much less costly but far safer than trial and error experiences (flight training, fighter pilot training, and gunnery are but a few examples). Communities have been patterned after *Walden Two*, Skinner's fictional account of a utopian community of a thousand people.

Critique

Skinner's Theory of Operant Behavior continues to be the theory of choice for many clinical and experimental psychologists. Evidence of their numbers and their research can be found in the active membership of APA's Division for the Experimental Analysis of Behavior and in the journals *Journal of Experimental Analysis of Behavior* and *Journal of Applied Behavior Analysis*. Further evidence for the wide acceptance of Skinner's ideas is the number of psychology and counseling programs in American colleges and universities that teach Skinner's operant behavior principles and research methodology.

There is no question of the high heuristic value of Skinner's theory. Few theories of personality have generated more research, not only in psychology and psychotherapy but in other disciplines as well. Neither is there any question of the wide application of his work (see "Application to Psychotherapy" and "Extended Applications," this chapter). Moreover, Skinner's work cannot be faulted, as are many other theories of personality, for vague terminology. His definitions are both clear and operationally precise. Researchers are able to verify his work without difficulty.

There is also no question that Skinner's position is highly controversial. In addition to the psychoanalytic, humanistic, existential, and cognitive psychologists, Skinner has drawn a great deal of critical fire from practitioners and researchers in a variety of other disciplines, including such areas as psychiatry, philosophy, theology, education, and biology. Some of the more volatile critics are novelists and journalists.

Not only did Skinner present a radically different technology of human behavior, he also called for a complete revision of long-held beliefs about what it is to be human and about what must be done before humans can begin to understand and resolve the pressing issues that threaten their very existence (war and ecology are two examples). For Skinner, autonomy and freedom of choice were illusions. Personality was nothing more than a history of reinforcement.

Skinner did not dispute the possibility of biological and psychological determinants; however, he did question their usefulness and ignore them in his research. Skinner, who was antitheoretical in his approach to the study of personality, argued that until we possess sufficient knowledge of these areas we should not waste time and energy attempting to build theories based on inferred entities (such as an unconscious) or processes (such as cognition). Rather, he asserted, we should limit our research data to overt behavior, that which we can directly observe and measure.

While researchers favor carefully controlled laboratory experiments as a method of studying human behavior, they are aware of the inherent weaknesses of this method. They point out that only very few variables can be controlled in a laboratory experiment (Skinner's experimental variables were usually limited to response and reinforcement) and the multivariable influences of the natural environment affect multiresponse modalities, including the covert response modalities (cognitive and emotive, for example). There were those researchers, too, who questioned Skinners assumption that humans share the behavioral characteristics of infrahuman species (in Skinner's experiments, rats and pigeons). Just as theorists are criticized for not using experimental laboratory research to support their theoretical constructs, so too are those theorists criticized who rely exclusively on experimental laboratory research for the limits of confidence that can be attributed to generalizations drawn from their findings.

Annotated Bibliography

The basic principles of operant reinforcement theory are vividly described in Skinner's utopian novel, *Walden Two*, ". . . but is by no means simply a mechanical dramatization of Skinner's scientific ideas" (Elms, 1981, p. 470). Of all Skinner's books, *Walden Two* is the single work to express subjective accounts or figurative speech in describing the basic elements of personality and social interactions. Elms (1981) argues rather convincingly that the emotional crisis suffered by Burris (one of the two main characters in the book) was very similar to Skinner's own sense of occupational despair and longing for a different life style at the time he wrote the book. Whether or not this was the case, *Walden Two* is not like any of Skinner's publications, either before or since. *Walden Two* is also the one place in Skinner's publications to address directly the healthy personality and the good life.

Beyond Freedom and Dignity (1971) was greeted initially with passionate rejection, a reflection of this nation's emotional investment in the concept of freedom. Later, supporters of Skinner's scientific approach acknowledged parts of the book as plausible, agreeing with Skinner that humans control themselves by controlling the environment.

A Matter of Consequence (1983b) is the concluding volume of Skinner's autobiographical trilogy. The book begins with Skinner's return to Harvard as a faculty member in the department of psychology. *Walden Two* had been published but a few months prior to the book's opening. With his usual honesty and courage, Skinner recounts his disagreements with then current mainstream psychology and offers insight into the intellectual development of an academic career, the influence of which few individuals can match. All who read the first two volumes of Skinner's autobiography will certainly not want to miss the final volume of the trilogy.

Upon Further Reflections (1987) consists of fourteen essays that Skinner published in the eighties. Here, Skinner denounces cognitive psychology for abandoning science to study such areas as introspection, perception, thought, language, and values rather than to continue the scientific analysis of behavior.

Written with Margaret Vaughan, a gerontologist, Skinner's *Enjoy Old Age: A Program for Self-Management* (1983) discusses familiar devices normally associated with old age (e.g., canes, hearing aids, special glasses, etc.), but more importantly, the authors identify forces that work against the elderly and suggest helpful ways of dealing with these forces. It is highly recommended for counselors and psychotherapists who work with elderly clients or clients concerned about aging.

References and Suggested Readings

Bijou, S. W. (1968). What psychology has to offer education—now. In P. B. Dews, (Ed.). (1970), *Festschrift for B. F. Skinner.* New York: Appleton–Century–Crofts.

Carpenter, F. (1974). *The Skinner primer: Behind freedom and dignity.* New York: Free Press.

Chandler, H. N. (1984). Skinner and CAI. *Journal of Learning Disabilities, 17*(7), pp. 441–442.

Cormier, W., & Cormier, L. S. (1979). *Interviewing strategies for helpers: A guide to assessment, treatment, and evaluation.* Monterey, CA: Brooks/Cole.

Dews, P. B. (Ed.). (1970). *Festschrift for B. F. Skinner.* New York: Appleton–Century–Crofts.

Elms, A. C. (1981). Skinner's dark year and Walden Two. *American Psychologist, 36*(5), pp. 470–479.

Epstein, R. (Ed.). (1980). *Notebooks, B. F. Skinner.* Englewood Cliffs, NJ: Prentice–Hall.

Evans, R. I. (1968). *B. F. Skinner: The man and his ideas.* New York: E. P. Dutton.

Greeson, L. E. (1985). Cumulative (personal) record: A case history in self-directed life-long learning. *Lifelong Learning, 9*(1), pp. 21–23.

Hall, M. H. (1967, September). An interview with "Mr. Behaviorist," B. F. Skinner. *Psychology Today.* (Reprint, Ziff–Davis Publishing Company), 7 pp.

Hall, G. (1987). The implications of radical behaviorism: A critique of Skinner's science of behavior and its application. In S. Modgil & C. Modgil, (Eds.). *B. F.Skinner: Consensus and controversy.* New York: Falmer Press, pp. 41–50.

Kinkaid, K. (1973, January). A Walden Two experiment. *Psychology Today, 6*(8), pp. 35–42, 90–93.

Machan, T. R. (1974). *The pseudo-science of B. F. Skinner.* New Rochelle, New York: Arlington House.

Modgil, S., & Modgil, C. (1987). *B. F. Skinner: Consensus and controversy.* New York: Falmer Press.

Pavlov, I. P. (1927). *Conditioned reflexes: An investigation of the physiological activity of the cerebral cortex.* (G. V. Antrip, Trans.). New York: International Universities Press.

Rimm, D. C., & Masters, J. C. (1974). *Behavior therapy: Techniques and empirical findings.* New York: Academic Press.

Rogers–Skinner Debates. (Audio tapes). AACD, 5999 Stevenson Avenue, Alexandria, VA 22304.

Rosenthal, L. (1983, January). Interview: B. F. Skinner, utopia or disaster. *Science Digest,* pp. 14–15, 104, 106.

Rychlak, J. F. (1981). *Introduction to personality and psychotherapy: A theory-construction approach* (2nd ed.). Boston: Houghton Mifflin.

Skinner, B. F. (1938). *The behavior of organisms.* New York: Appleton–Century–Crofts.

Skinner, B. F. (1948). *Walden two.* New York: Macmillan.

Skinner, B. F. (1953). *Science and human behavior.* New York: Macmillan.

Skinner, B. F. (1956). Freedom and the control of men. *American Scholar, 25,* pp. 47–65.

Skinner, B. F. (1957a). *Verbal behavior.* New York: Appleton–Century–Crofts.

Skinner, B. F. with Ferster, C. B. (1957b). *Schedules of reinforcement.* New York: Appleton–Century–Crofts.

Skinner, B. F. (1968). *The technology of teaching.* New York: Appleton–Century–Crofts.

Skinner, B. F. (1969). *Contingencies of reinforcement, a theoretical analysis.* New York: Appleton–Century–Crofts.

Skinner, B. F. (1971). *Beyond freedom and dignity.* New York: Bantam Books.

Skinner, B. F. (1972). *Cumulative Record, a selection of papers* (3rd ed.). New York: Appleton–Century–Crofts.

Skinner, B. F. (1973). Answers for my critics. In H. Wheeler (Ed.), *Beyond the punitive society.* San Francisco: W. H. Freeman, pp. 257–266..

Skinner, B. F. (1974). *About behaviorism.* New York: Alfred A. Knopf.

Skinner, B. F. (1975, January). The steep and thorny way to a science of behavior. *American Psychologist,* pp. 42–49.

Skinner, B. F. (1976a). *Particulars of my life.* New York: McGraw–Hill.

Skinner, B. F. (1976b). The ethics of helping people. *The Humanist, 36*(1), pp. 7–11.

Skinner, B. F. (1979a). *The shaping of a behaviorist.* New York: Alfred A. Knopf.

Skinner, B. F. (1979b). My experiences with the baby tender. *Psychology Today, 12*(10), pp. 28–31, 34, 37–38, 40.

Skinner, B. F. (1979c). Harvard days. *Change, 11*(3), pp. 41–45.

Skinner, B. F. (1983a, September). Origins of a behaviorist. *Psychology Today,* pp. 22–33.

Skinner, B. F. (1983b). *A matter of consequences.* New York: Alfred A. Knopf.

Skinner, B. F. (1986a). What is wrong with daily life in the Western World. *American Psychologist, 41*(5), pp. 568–574.

Skinner, B. F. (1986b). Programmed instruction revisited. *Kappan, 68*(2), pp. 103–110.

Skinner, B. F. (1987). *Upon further reflections.* Englewood Cliffs, NJ: Prentice–Hall.

Skinner, B. F. (1988). The operant side of behavior therapy. *Journal of Behavioral Therapy and Experimental Psychiatry, 10*(3), pp. 171–179. Printed in Great Britain.

Skinner, B. F., & Vaughan, M. E. (1983). *Enjoy old age: A program for self-management.* New York: W. W. Norton.

A Skinner box. (1982, September 17). *Forbes,* p. 184.

Wallace, W. A. (1986). *Theories of counseling and psychotherapy: A basic issues approach.* Boston: Allyn and Bacon.

Wheeler, H. (Ed.). (1973). *Beyond the punitive society.* San Francisco: W. H. Freeman.

Part 6

Rational-Cognitive Theories

George Kelly and Albert Ellis were selected as representative theorists for those theories of personality that can best be described as rational-cognitive theories. They held fast to their belief that cognition plays a significant role in personality development at a time when it was most unpopular to do so. Although many psychologists today refer to themselves as cognitive psychologists, the cognitive movement in psychology is a relatively recent development.

Kelly viewed all humans as amateur scientists; that is, he claimed that we all formulate personal construct systems which in turn predict and control the future events in our lives. In short, he asserted that personal constructs of events direct our behavior, not the events themselves. Like scientists, we test our personal constructs for validity. Imminent threat to our core constructs produces disturbance, and recognition that events fall outside a construct's range of convenience causes feelings of anxiety.

Ellis is also convinced that our cognition mediates between life events and determines our emotions and behavior. When our beliefs about an event are rational, our emotion is appropriate to the event, and our behavior is effective. Conversely, when our beliefs about an event are irrational, our emotions are inordinately strong, and our behavior is ineffective, dysfunctional, or destructive.

Both Kelly and Ellis see us as reactive, thinking beings with the ability to choose from available alternatives. Both hold us responsible for our choices. Both express the belief that we inherit a brain that predisposes us to formulate a personal belief system (Ellis) or personal construct system (Kelly). We exist in the present—the past is only present perceptions or constructs of what has been, and the future is only present anticipations of what might be. Change in personality will occur only with reconstruction of our personal construct or belief systems.

Chapter 14

Kelly's Theory of Personal Constructs

Chapter Overview

Introduction

Biographical Sketch

Resolution of Basic Issues
  Heredity versus Social Determinants
  Subjective versus Objective Reality
  Determinism versus Freedom of Choice
  Conscious versus Unconscious Determinants
  Uniqueness versus Universality
  Early versus Continuous Development
  Explanation of Learning Process
  Role Assigned to Self-Concept
  Number and Weight Assigned to Motivational Concepts
  Centrality of Reinforcement
  Role Assigned to Group Determinants

Psychological Health and Psychopathology

Applications to Psychotherapy
  Therapeutic Goals
  Therapeutic Relationship
  Therapeutic Process and Strategies
  Course of Therapy

Extended Applications

Critique

Annotated Bibliography

References and Suggested Readings

Introduction

George Alexander Kelly's Psychology of Personal Constructs, based on a fundamental postulate and its eleven corollaries (see Figure 14-1), departs radically from conventional personality theories. According to Kelly's (1963) psychology of personality, "there is no *motivation*, no *emotion*, no *cognition*, no *stimulus*, no *response*, no *ego*, no *unconscious*, no *need*, no *reinforcement*, no *drive*" (p. 3, emphases in original). Kelly (1955a, 1963) focuses on anticipation rather than reaction. He emphasizes the creative capacity of an active human intellect to represent the environment rather than merely to respond to it. In short, Kelly (1955a, 1963) views humans as incipient scientists—natural theory builders—who form transient personal constructs through which they view the world of objective events in an effort to predict and control life's circumstances.

Though one of the most systematic and consistent, Kelly's Theory of Personal Constructs is also one of the most novel approaches to human personality. Kelly's theory of personal constructs does not fit neatly into even the most general theoretical classification. Kelly, who resisted all attempts to categorize his theory, would surely find this amusing.

Kelly (in Maher, 1969) reports that Gordon Allport referred to him as an "emotional" theorist; Henry Murray considered him to be an existentialist; in Warsaw he was informed that "personal construct theory was exactly what 'dialectical materialism' stood for;" an orthodox psychoanalyst was convinced that Kelly was really a psychoanalyst; he had been called a Zen Buddhist; he had been classified a learning theorist in a personality text; and a former student invited back for a lecture spent an hour and a half in a seminar corrupting his students with the idea that he was a behaviorist (pp. 216–217). Essentially ahistorical, Kelly was neither concerned for nor interested in the origin of his theoretical constructs—he viewed theorizing as a natural and continual human process in which we all participate.

Writing from the perspective of therapy, Kelly developed a how-to manual for clinical psychologists years before he seriously attempted to formulate a distinctive theory of psychotherapy and personality. In fact, it was not until 1955, with the publication of *Psychology of Personal Constructs* (two vols.), that his work was considered a personality theory. For the next decade, Personal Constructs Theory (PCT) appeared to hold great promise, largely due to graduate students at Ohio State University and various reputable scholars in England.

Since 1965, however, the early promise of Kelly's theory has failed to materialize. Research literature on PCT in this country is sparse. Compared to other theorists presented in this book, Kelly's publications are few. "At death his bibliography listed three papers in major journals, seven contributions to edited

Fundamental Postulate: A person's processes are psychologically channelized by the ways in which he or she anticipates events.

Construction Corollary: A person anticipates events by construing their replications.

Individuality Corollary: Persons differ from each other in their constructions of events.

Organization Corollary: Each person characteristically evolves, for his or her convenience in anticipating events, a construction system embracing ordinal relationships between constructs.

Dichotomy Corollary: A person's construction system is composed of a finite number of dichotomous constructs.

Choice Corollary: A person chooses for himself or herself that alternative in a dichotomized construct through which he or she anticipates the greater possibility for extension and definition of his or her system.

Range Corollary: A construct is convenient for the anticipation of a finite range of events only.

Modulation Corollary: The variation in a person's construction system is limited by the permeability of the constructs within whose ranges of convenience the variants lie.

Fragmentation Corollary: A person may successively employ a variety of construction subsystems which are inferentially incompatible with each other.

Commonality Corollary: To the extent that one person employs a construction of experience which is similar to that employed by another, his or her psychological processes are similar to those of the other person.

Sociality Corollary: To the extent that one person construes the construction processes of another, he or she may play a role in a social process involving the other person.

FIGURE 14-1   The Assumptive Structure of Kelly's Personal Construct Theory: Fundamental Postulate and Its Corollaries

volumes, and a monograph..." (Stringer, 1985, p. 226). The only other publication of Kelly's work is an edited volume by Brendon Maher (1969), a former student and family friend who, with the assistance and encouragement of Kelly's wife, sought to present a selection of Kelly's papers and unpublished addresses that would "properly represent the work of one of the important personality theorists of mid-century" (p. vi).

While Stringer (1985) warns his readers that "the absence of the 'faithful translation' . . . is quite clear in the textbook treatment of personal construct theory," he attributes this absence to the "monumental effort to give structure to a vast array of material ranging right across psychology (personality = psychology)" (pp. 222–223, parentheses in original). Any attempt to add structure to a vast array of material spanning the entire range of psychology, regardless of how general that structure, is certain to be constricting, and readers, personal construct psychologists in particular, "should be attentive to its texts and how they construe" (Stringer, 1985, p. 227). Still, despite the inherent weaknesses of many personality textbooks, Stringer (1985) asserts: "Texts play an important part in personal construct psychology, perhaps an unusually significant part" in keeping Kelly's theory alive (p. 226).

Many of Kelly's students have become leaders in clinical psychology programs throughout the country, but few are presently involved in his theory. Indeed, Kelly's most active proponent today is Donald Bannister (1970, 1977, 1985, Stringer and Bannister 1979), a member of the MPC External Scientific Staff, High Royds Hospital, West Yorkshire, England. Bannister and his colleagues at the University of London established a training and research center that "produced a degree of scientific focus and communicative cohesiveness not found in the more fractionated American community, which lost its social and intellectual leader with Kelly's death" (Neimeyer, 1985, p. 147).

When a theory of personality no longer attracts a group of dedicated, competent followers who discern and test the theory, it inevitably lacks credibility and application. Until the cognitive movement in psychology (Ellis, Chapter 15; Bandura, Chapter 16), such seemed the fate of Kelly's Personal Construct Theory.

Unlike many contemporary personality theories, there are no national institutes that bear Kelly's name, there are no psychology or counseling departments or training programs identified exclusively with his theory, and there are no personologists who specify any particular impact that PCT has had on current thinking regarding personality or psychotherapy. Kelly was not interested in heading a movement or establishing institutes.

Biographical Sketch of the Theorist

The typical biographical sketch is a chronological presentation of events in the subject's life, and this, unfortunately, is no exception. While a review of historical events offers some understanding of the objective experience in Kelly's life, it would, according to Kelly, contribute little insight into the origin of his theory. It is not objective experience that is important for understanding the psychology of personal constructs. It is, rather, Kelly's subjective perceptions and personal constructions of these experiences that influenced his theoretical formulations. Since Kelly left no autobiography or personal journals, his subjective interpretations of life events (his **personal constructs**) are not available.

Early Years

George Alexander Kelly (1905–1967) was born on a small farm in Perth, Kansas, and raised on a homestead in eastern Colorado. He was the only child of devoutly religious parents who had little tolerance for smoking, dancing, drinking, and playing cards. Kelly's father, a Presbyterian minister who, for reasons of health, withdrew from an active ministry to life on a farm, provided his son with a Puritanical work ethic and the traditional values of midwestern America. Kelly's parents believed that life should be lived responsibly, and they would often extend great effort to assist needy and sick individuals and families in their community.

Early Education

Kelly's early formal education was, at best, sporadic. While he attended a one-room elementary school when weather and travel conditions permitted, much of his early education was provided by his parents. Kelly's parents were devoted to their only son; however, realizing that their aspirations for him would unlikely be promoted in the current school situation, they made the difficult decision to send their son, then thirteen years old, to Wichita, Kansas, for his high school education. During the following four years, Kelly attended four different secondary schools.

One might speculate that, from his early farm experience, Kelly developed a practical view of life and living—that which worked was valued. By attending high schools located miles from his parents' home, Kelly had to learn much earlier than most to rely on his own resources. Like Ellis (Chapter 15), Kelly learned to appreciate his early independence, and he, too, learned as an adolescent that it was not the objective events of life that mattered, but rather what he made of those events.

Education

Upon being graduated from high school, Kelly attended Friends University. He transferred to Park College for his final year of undergraduate work, and in 1926 was awarded his B.A. degree in physics and mathematics.

Kelly considered a career in aeronautical engineering and for a short time worked in the field; however, an interest in social problems led him to the University of Kansas, where he majored in educational sociology. Following the completion of his M.A. degree in 1928, his interests shifted, and Kelly turned to education. He began a series of short-term jobs that included teaching speech for the American Bankers' Association, conducting an Americanization class for future citizens, and teaching at a junior college in Sheldon, Iowa. It was here that he met and fell in love with Gladys Thompson, a high school English teacher. They were married in 1931.

Awarded an exchange scholarship in 1929, Kelly spent a year of study under Sir Godfrey Thompson, an eminent statistician and educator at the University of Edinburgh. By receiving permission to complete his examinations at the end of a single year, Kelly earned a Bachelor's degree in education. Although he was not especially interested in the work he undertook with Sir Godfrey Thompson, Kelly did develop an interest in psychology.

Returning to the United States from Scotland in 1930, Kelly applied for the doctoral program in psychology at the State University of Iowa. He was awarded the Ph.D. in psychology a year later.

Emergence of the Theory of Personal Constructs

In the midst of the Great Depression and only recently married, the Kellys experienced difficult times. Kelly accepted a faculty position at Fort Hayes Kansas State College and became involved in the development of the state's psychological services. Kelly was instrumental in establishing a program of traveling psychological clinics which served not only the schools in the state, but also assisted his students by offering them practical field experience comparable to today's psychology internships.

Kelly's early writings focused primarily on the practical problems and issues involved with training and treatment; however, he was at this time beginning to formulate his innovative Theory of Personal Constructs. By 1939, Kelly was using a form of roleplay in his therapeutic approach, as well as a technique of fixed-role therapy (see "Applications for Psychotherapy," this chapter).

In 1943, Kelly was promoted to associate professor. He entered the Navy that same year and was placed in charge of a program for training local civilian pilots. He was later assigned to the Aviation Psychology Branch of the Bureau of Medicine and Surgery of the Navy in Washington, D.C., where he met and worked with other psychologists and members of the medical profession to establish a place for psychology, particularly clinical psychology, within military settings.

In 1945, Kelly accepted an associate professorship in clinical psychology at the University of Maryland. With the return of a large number of emotionally disturbed veterans, there were considerable demands for clinical psychologists. Kelly moved into national prominence when, in 1946, he was appointed professor of psychology and director of clinical psychology at the Ohio State University. Carl Rogers (Chapter 9) had moved to the University of Wisconsin, and Kelly, along with Julian B. Rotter (recognized today as one of the nation's leading social learning theorists), expanded the program in clinical psychology at Ohio State into national prominence. With colleagues and graduate students assisting him to critique and refine his ideas, Kelly completed his major theoretical constructs at Ohio State. In 1955 he published the two-volume work, *Psychology of Personal Constructs*.

After twenty years at Ohio State, Kelly accepted the Riklis Chair of Behavioral Science at Brandeis University in 1965. Kelly viewed this appointment as an opportunity to complete his theoretical work. Unfortunately, he died March 6, 1967, at the age of sixty-two, before he could realize his goal. Two years after his death, B. A. Maher (1969), a former student, edited a collection of Kelly's more important papers, some of which had never been published.

Honors and Recognition

Kelly was elected president of both the Clinical and the Counseling Divisions of the American Psychological Association. He was a founder and Diplomate of the American Board of Examiners in Professional Psychology and served as its president from 1951 through 1953.

Kelly held visiting professorships at several universities in the United States and was in great demand as a lecturer at research congresses and institutions of learning both here and in Europe. While he acquired followers and admirers on both sides of the Atlantic, the British hold the greatest respect for his theory.

Resolution of the Eleven Basic Issues

Kelly addressed nine of the eleven basic issues selected for the structure of this book in his fundamental postulate and the eleven elaborative corollaries. However, he makes no attempt to resolve two of the basic issues (Number and Weight Assigned to Motivational Concepts and Centrality of Reinforcement), except to say that they are part of the assumptive structure of human nature and thus are not issues from the perspective of Personal Construct Theory.

Heredity versus Social Determinants

Upon examining the human species through the perspective of time, Kelly (1955a) concluded that understanding human behavior can be accomplished best by viewing the human as scientist, a rather spontaneous and limited scientist, to be sure, but a scientist nonetheless. Kelly (1955a) was aware that his analogous abstraction (human as scientist) was both a novel and a radical departure from the views of other personality theorists. However, he knew also that the analogy vividly illustrated his particular abstraction of the innate *science-like* aspects of humankind. It expressed the perspective that all of us seek to make predictions about and desire to control our environments. Prediction and control are not limited only to those in the science profession, but rather are shared by all of us.

Even though our endeavors are not as exacting or as organized as are the endeavors of the professional scientist, our views are science-like. He granted that our perceptions of reality are more highly personalized, and our constructions and judgments are less objective. Also, our revisions are seldom open to the scrutiny of others to duplicate. In short, our **personal constructs** (theoretical inventions or hypotheses) are, to a much higher degree, distorted representations of the events on which they are based. Still, Kelly (1955a) asserted, a time perspective confirms that humans have always explored life "by acting out their questions" (p. 18).

In formulating his theory of personal constructs, Kelly amplified his system by developing propositions that follow from and elaborate the fundamental postulate. Kelly formulated eleven of these propositions that he called **corollaries.**

The **fundamental postulate** of Kelly's (1955a) theory of personal constructs, *"A person's processes are psychologically channelized by the ways in which he anticipates events"* (p. 46), indicates Kelly's primary concern for the individual as a psychological process in motion, anticipating and choosing to operate through a structured yet flexible and frequently modified network of pathways as a means to anticipate real events. For Kelly (1955a), life and movement are synonymous. His theory is psychological in focus, and thus, does not explain or account for physiological or sociological systems and their influence upon individuals. Neither is there a need to explain motivation or learning. "Anticipation is both the push and pull of the psychology of personal constructs" (Kelly, 1955a, p. 49). Movement, learning, and anticipation are natural phenomena. We naturally place interpretations (constructs) on our experiences—the events we encounter in life. Because the events that we attempt to predict and control are real psychological processes, we are tied to reality.

Subjective versus Objective Reality

Kelly's stance on this issue is solidly phenomenological. There is no objective reality for the individual; reality exists only in our beliefs, or for Kelly, in our personal constructs. It is not the events of life that determine our behavior, but rather our individual, personal abstractions or representations of the events. Events can be personally evaluated, thus to some degree predicted and controlled. Because we interpret the events of life, we can alter the scheme of things. We are not simply passive respondents to outside influences, hence, we are victims of neither our genetics nor our personal histories. There are always **alternative constructs** (other ways of construing life events).

We "live in anticipation" (Kelly, in Maher, 1969, p. 88). We examine the events in our lives and then draw inferences concerning the meaning of those events. We formulate personal constructs which we use to make predictions. We assess the **predictive efficiency** (validity) of our personal constructs by testing them against the outcome of future events. When there is a practical correspondence between what our personal construct led us to anticipate and what subsequently occurs, we experience a sense of success, and we are encouraged to expand the range of the construct by testing it against related events. If our personal constructs fail the test of prediction, we are likely to conclude, sooner or later, that our construct is useless and consider either revising or abandoning it. Nearly all our behavior, then, can be traced to the characteristics of our system of personal constructs.

Though often labeled a cognitive theorist, Kelly believed this to be an error. Rather, he considered personal constructs to be neither cognitive nor affective (Kelly, 1966, p. 15). He preferred to convey the impression that personal constructs were "too fluid to be pinned down by verbal labels" (p. 15). From his perspective, the personal nature of individual constructs fits comfortably with a phenomenological and holistic stance.

Determinism versus Freedom of Choice

The fifth corollary in Kelly's (1955a) theory is the **choice corollary:** *"A person chooses for himself that alternative in a dichotomized construct through which he anticipates the greater possibility for extension and definition of his system"* (p. 64). According to Kelly (1955a), we may extend our prediction of future events in two ways: we can narrowly define personal constructs, making them more explicit, or we can extend personal constructs, making them more inclusive. The first alternative leads to greater security and certainty about a few things. The second, a more adventurous path, creates temporary uncertainty, but may eventually lead to a broader understanding of and an increase in the predictive range of the our personal construct systems. For Kelly, we are free to choose from among the alternative constructs those that are most useful to predict and control our life events.

Constructive alternativism (the basic assumption that we are all capable of changing or replacing our present interpretations of the events we encounter in life) serves as the foundation upon which all of Kelly's theoretical constructs rest. Clearly implied in this basic assumption is the belief that our behavior is *never* completely determined. There are *always* behavioral alternatives when behavior is viewed not only as what we do, but also as what we might do. Ever present is the freedom to reconstrue our experiences, to view ourselves, others, and the world in any manner that pleases us.

> *Life provides this man with no scientific footholds on reality, suggests to him no narrative plots, offers no rhythmic metaphor to confirm the moving resonance of a human theme. If he chooses to write tragedy, then tragedy it will be; if comedy, then that is what will come of it; and if burlesque, he, the sole reader, must learn to laugh at its misanthropic caricatures of the only person he knows—himself (Kelly, in Maher, 1969, p. 24).*

Conscious versus Unconscious Determinants

Kelly did not find the terms conscious or unconscious particularly useful. As a phenomenologist, he was interested in how we **construe** (view and think about) reality; in short, he was interested in intact cognitive experiences, without concern for their origin. He was convinced, however, that "level of cognitive awareness" was a dimension that ran throughout the construct system. High level cognitive constructs comprised one of the dichotomous poles of Kelly's awareness dimension. **High level constructs** are explicitly symbolized, with readily accessible alternatives and a specific and accurate **range of convenience** (the range of events to which the construct can be applied reliably). At the opposite pole are **constructs of low level awareness.** Low level constructs are implicit, preverbal (i.e., constructs formed prior to language development, those that are incompatible with the current construct system and submerged, or those outside the range of convenience of the present construct system and, hence, out of awareness).

Uniqueness versus Universality

The **individuality corollary:** *"Persons differ from each other in their construction of events"* is Kelly's (1955a) second supporting corollary (p. 55). Our personal constructions are idiosyncratic. We are indeed unique. No two of us interpret our life events in the same way. Not only do we encounter different events, we cannot play identical roles within the same event, regardless of how close we may be or how hard we may try. Two of us forming constructions of the same event will each experience the other as an external figure. We will each experience a different central figure—ourself. Finally, each of us is involved in different aspects of the stream of events. Eyewitness testimony of three individuals who viewed a child struck at an intersection by a car may vary considerably when they are asked to place blame. One may blame the driver for reckless behavior; another the child for darting into the street; and the third, the city council for not approving a traffic light at the intersection when requested to do so six months earlier.

Even though our individual constructions will vary, we can share experiences by construing the experiences of others along with our own; that is, we can share our interpretations of events. This is not inevitable, however, for different cultural identifications or the lack of genuine effort in seeking common ground with others can keep us tied to our different subjective worlds, even though our experiences are similar.

Kelly (1955a) refers to the third supporting corollary: *"Each person characteristically evolves, for his convenience in anticipating events, a construction system embracing ordinal relationships between constructs"* as the **organization corollary** (p. 56). Not only do we each differ in our constructions of events, different constructs can result in incompatible predictions. When this occurs, as it often does, it is necessary for each of us to organize his or her personal constructs in a way that will minimize or transcend the contradictory predictions. Not only are each of our constructions personal, so, too, are each of our **hierarchical arrangements** of the constructs within our personal construct systems. Kelly (1955a) was convinced that "It is this systematic arrangement which characterizes the personality, even more than do the differences between individual constructs" (p. 56).

There can be many levels of ordinal relationships within our personal construct systems. Highest in the hierarchical organization are the **superordinate constructs** (the most comprehensive in the construct hierarchy). A superordinate construct *subsumes* other constructs as one of its elements. The **subordinate constructs** subsumed by a superordinate construct may, in turn, subsume still other constructs. The organizational structure of each of our construct systems, then, "is based on constructs of constructs, concretistically pyramided or abstractically cross-referenced in a system of ordinal relationships" (Kelly, 1955a, p. 61). Our thought is not entirely flexible; rather, it is **channelized,** and follows the network of channels that structure our thinking.

Kelly's organization corollary, then, points to an evolving, personal, idiosyncratic construction system which, while more stable than the individual constructions of which it is comprised, is continually restructuring, thus continually changing shape.

The **dichotomy corollary** reads: *"A person's construction system is composed of a finite number of dichotomous constructs"* (Kelly, 1955a, p. 59). Our personal construct system is comprised of dichotomous (bipolar) constructs (e.g., strong versus weak, security versus adventure, right versus wrong, intelligent versus stupid, etc.); hence, each of us lives with a dichotomous construction system and must place values on the poles of each construct's dichotomies. Not only does a construct tend to force either one or the other of the alternative poles, an assertion about one alternative indicates that the opposite alternative is not characteristic of the favored alternative. For Kelly, it is impossible to see a similarity without simultaneously considering its contrast, a way in which another event is evaluated as different. A construct is always dichotomous. Indeed, it is the dichotomous form of the individual's personal construct system that provides the basis for Kelly's constructive alternativism.

Kelly (1955a) explained the **range corollary** as: "*A construct is convenient for the anticipation of a finite range of events only*" (p. 68). Every construct has its focus and range of convenience; hence, in order to understand the behavior of either self or others, it is necessary to understand not only the construct, but also its focus and range. If, for example, an individual chooses the loyalty pole of a loyal-versus-disloyal construct, prediction of that individual's behavior is only possible when the range of the construct is understood. If the range is broad, the focus of the construct may be on all interpersonal relationships. A narrow range, on the other hand, may limit the construct only to members of the individual's immediate family. A construct is applied only to the events that are considered relevant by the individual holding it; all that is outside the range of the construct is irrelevant. For the individual whose loyalty construct is narrow and tight, one can predict the expectation of complete loyalty from and to immediate family members, regardless of circumstances. Conversely, the same individual would neither expect nor offer loyalty to those outside the immediate family. In summary, to be aware that a person construes some relationships as "loyal" is not helpful for making valid predictions unless one is also aware of the contrasting pole of the construct. It may, for example, be "dangerous," or "untrustworthy," or "unethical," or "weak"—each of which calls for different anticipations.

Kelly's **modulation corollary** accounts for the lawful evolution of the construction system. It reads: "*The variation in a person's construction system is limited by the permeability of the constructs within whose range of convenience the variants lie*" (Kelly, 1955a. p. 77). For Kelly (1955a), modulation refers to change. Personal constructs are more or less **permeable;** that is, they are more or less open to change and alteration. A permeable construct is open to new experience and can be applied to new events not yet construed within the construct in order to make sense out of change. Conversely, a **preemptive construct,** one that is rigid with very limited range of convenience, is impermeable, making change nearly impossible.

In Kelly's (1955a) **fragmentation corollary:** "*A person may successively employ a variety of construction subsystems which are inferentially incompatible with each other*" (p. 83). Our personal construct system is always in a state of flux, so there are times when our construction system tolerates the successive use of inconsistent subsystems. Because of this, predictions of tomorrow's thought and behavior cannot always be inferred from today's. Fragmentation is most likely to be evident when our constructs are impermeable or concrete, or conversely, when they are so loosely defined that we shift rapidly back and forth between constructs.

The **commonality corollary** states: *"To the extent that one person employs a construction of experience which is similar to that employed by another, his psychological processes are similar to those of the other person"* (Kelly, 1955a, p. 90). When two of us share similar constructs, our psychological processes may be similar. It is essential, however, to note that we are not similar because we have experienced similar events or because we manifest similar behavior. Rather, we are similar because our constructs are similar—because we have arrived at a similar meaning when construing events. The emphasis of the commonality corollary is on the process of construing rather than on either experience or behavior.

Early versus Continuous Development

Although Kelly (1955a) insists "Life has to be seen in the perspective of time if it is to make any sense at all" (p. 7), he, like Rogers (Chapter 9), considers personality development a natural and continuous process or movement. **Learning** is an assumed phenomenon, a natural part of the psychological processes of all humans. Unless as developing children we encounter harmful influences that stifle or block our ability to formulate healthy personal constructs for predicting and thus controlling our environment and our future, our movement (changing, evolving, and growing) unfolds naturally and continually. When both the world and we who inhabit it are viewed as always in motion, there is no need to subscribe to a specific hierarchical set of critical developmental stages. Our development, for Kelly (1955a), reflects the evolution of our individual personal construct systems.

Even though Kelly wrote very little of personality development, one would be mistaken to assume that, from the PCT point of view, our early childhood years are unimportant. Kelly (1955a, 1955b) believed that we begin to formulate our personal construct systems very early in life, even before we possess a language to symbolize personal constructs (p. 110; 1955b, p. 668). Unwise or disturbed parents or parent surrogates, through such extreme childrearing practices as overindulgence or pampering, intensive pressure or punishment, and erratic or inconsistent behavior, may weaken or damage our abilities to formulate and elaborate healthy personal construct systems.

The personal constructs formed by overindulged or pampered children are likely to lead to the prediction that their parents will always be there to satisfy their needs and desires. These children evolve dependency constructs that are relatively rigid. The constructs of intensely pressured or punished children may lead to guilt, even subordination of self. When parental behavior is excessively erratic or inconsistent, children may find it difficult or virtually impossible to form constructs that accurately predict their parents' behavior, and the constant invalidation of their constructs results in the painful feelings of anxiety.

Explanation of Learning Process

Kelly's (1955a) **experience corollary** reads: "*A person's construction system varies as he successively construes the replication of events*" (p. 72). Personal construct systems are not permanent. Indeed, they are always in a state of flux. As we test our personal constructs by anticipating future events, those that are not validated must be reconstrued. For Kelly (1955a, 1955b) all personal constructs are tentative—hypotheses that are used to anticipate future events. When our constructs do not meet the **test of validation** (accurate anticipations) they must be discarded or reconstrued. If they are not, the failure rate of future anticipations is likely to increase. It is this process of reconstruction of our personal construct system that forms the basis for learning in Kelly's theory. **Learning,** Kelly insists, like the formulation of constructs, is a continual psychological process. It is not something that happens to us; rather, it is a natural part of being human. **Growth** is the gradual reconstruing of the replication of events over time.

Role Assigned to Self-Concept

Unlike most phenomenologists (e.g., Rogers, Chapter 9), Kelly does not assign a central role to the self-concept. He was, however, interested in the **core roles** we play (the roles we employ to maintain our most significant relationships with others). It is our core roles that are central to our identity or self-concept.

A brief overview of the personality processes that relate to change in the individual's construction system may contribute to a more complete understanding of Kelly's work in general and of self-concept or self-identity in particular. Before beginning this overview, readers should be warned that, while Kelly employs terms common to other theories of personality, he does so from the unique perspective of PCT. Hence, constructs such as "fear," "threat," "guilt," and "anxiety," though related to the way they are used by other theorists, must be construed as Kelly construes them to avoid misunderstanding.

Change in the Personal Construct System   It was pointed out earlier (see "The Fragmentation Corollary," above) that some incompatible constructs in an individual's personal construct system can be tolerated. The individual usually experiences little difficulty when *peripheral constructs* in the system are incompatible. Forced change in *core constructs*—those constructs that govern and maintain an individual's sense of personal identity and integrity—is quite a different matter. Imminent change in the core constructs produces some degree of disturbance, depending, of course, on the extent and nature of that change. Indeed, drastic forced change in an individual's core constructs can be devastating.

Fear is the usual reaction of individuals when they become aware of imminent *incidental change* in their core constructs. Incidental changes in core constructs will not generate irreparable damage to the individual's sense of identity or integrity.

For example, a skater is likely to experience fear if the blades of his or her skates hit an unexpected rough patch of ice and cause thoughts of falling and injury. The risk of falling is incidental to the skater's core constructs because it does not jeopardize either identity or integrity.

The same incident, occurring during the Olympic Games, to a skater who has spent years of practice preparing for this singular event and who has identified crucial aspects of self with faultless skating skill, is likely to be construed as an imminent *comprehensive change* in the skater's core constructs; he or she will react by experiencing *threat*. A fall under these circumstances carries more than the possibility of losing an important contest or risking possible injury; it threatens a loss of dignity and irreparable damage to the skater's reputation as a faultless skater, both of which are essential elements of the skater's core constructs.

Guilt is also a reaction to awareness of change in core constructs, particularly as these changes relate to *core role constructs*. Variance from core role constructs, whether voluntary or not, can result in strong feelings of guilt if the individual invests personal identity in the role structure he or she violates. For example, therapists who construe their therapeutic role structure as empathic, accepting, and caring will experience a strong sense of guilt if they discover that they can only construe their therapeutic role with a certain client as bored, rejecting, and uncaring. It matters not that they were feeling ill or that they are distracted with problems of their own. The reaction of guilt is influenced little by circumstances; it is rather related almost entirely to an awareness that they did not live up to their core role structures.

Anxiety, another common personality term that Kelly (1955a) construes to fit PCT, results from the awareness that perceived important events fall outside the range of convenience of the individual's construct system (p. 495); and in many instances, the individual is unable to construe alternative constructs to explain or anticipate these events. In short, the construction system of the anxious person fails, leading to confusion and an inability to take the necessary corrective steps to resolve the painful dilemma. Events that create an anxiety reaction may be either critical or trivial. So long as they remain outside the range of the individual's personal construct system, they remain unknowable, hence they cannot be confronted, predicted, or controlled. From the PCT perspective, anxiety can be reduced to fear or threat by loosening the construct system sufficiently to increase its range of convenience, hence broadening the perceptual field and adding to the system's capacity to encompass more constructs.

Number and Weight Assigned to Motivational Concepts

Kelly circumvented accepted motivational concepts such as stimulus, needs, and motives by rejecting any assumption of the person as an inert object. We are, according to Kelly (1963/1955), "delivered fresh into the psychological world alive and struggling" (p. 37). Thus, he saw the question of motivation as a "dead issue." The motivation of all humans is the same as the scientist's goal, "ever seeking to predict and control the course of events with which he [or she] is involved" (Kelly 1963/1955, p. 5).

Kelly's (1955a) **construction corollary** states: *"A person anticipates events by construing their replications"* (p.50). It is by formulating a construct that we give substance a shape or event a meaning. Only when we are able to perceive the recurrent themes of constructs are we able to make sense of the events of the world. Meaning is produced by our contrived constructs of likenesses and differences, similarities and contrasts. Replications of both public and private events guide our predictions, hence control, of future events.

Kelly (1955a) labeled constructs "personal," for they reside in us *rather than in the events they were construed to predict and control.* Further, construing is a process, unending and undifferentiated. The world of events begins to make sense only when we find recurrent themes in the experience of the events. Events must be interpreted in terms of beginning and end, similarities and contrasts, before they can be anticipated and controlled. Though it is a mistake to predict that tomorrow will be exactly the same as today, it is possible to predict that there are ways in which tomorrow will replicate today.

Centrality of Reinforcement

There is no place in Kelly's theory for any concept of external reinforcement; indeed, from a PCT perspective, external forces play no role in the shaping of our personalities. It is not the events in our lives that direct our behavior; rather, it is our personal constructs of these events. We are thinking beings who anticipate our own and others' actions by formulating personal construct systems that we then test for validity.

Role Assigned to Group Determinants

The **sociality corollary** in Kelly's (1955a) theory reads: *"To the extent that one person construes the construction processes of another, he may play a role in a social process involving the other person"* (p. 95). While it is not necessary to share identical constructs of another person to understand and communicate constructively with him or her, it is necessary to construe the other person's constructs and understand his or her way of viewing the world. Understanding between two people is more than a similarity or commonality in their thinking; rather, the degree of understanding is the extent to which their personal construct systems subsume each other and permit a constructive role relationship. We only become involved in a role relationship with another when we attempt to infer the other's view or outlook.

Psychological Health and Psychopathology

Healthy Personality and the Good Life

While Kelly (1955a, 1955b) wrote extensively on the subjects of psychopathology and psychotherapy, nowhere in his writing did he address directly the subject of

Heredity				Social Determinants
Subjective Reality				Objective Reality
Determinism				Freedom
Conscious Determinants				Unconscious Determinants
Uniqueness				Universality
Early Development				Continuous Development

Explanation of Learning Process	Personal constructs are in a state of flux. Reconstruction of our personal construct system forms the basis for learning (a continual psychological process). Growth is the reconstruing of the replication of events over time.
Role Assigned to Self-Concept	Core roles are central to our self-concept. Imminent change in the core constructs produce disturbance. Fear, threat, and guilt are reactions to change in core constructs; anxiety is an awareness that events fall outside the range of convenience of the construct system.
Number and Weight Assigned to Motivational Concepts	Motivation of humans is the same as the scientist's goal (predict and control the course of evens). Replications of events guide our predictions and control of future events.
Centrality of Reinforcement	External forces play no role in the shaping of personalities. Personal constructs of events direct our behavior—not the events. As thinking beings, we anticipate actions by formulating personal construct systems that we test for validity.
Role Assigned to Group Determinants	Understanding between two people is the extent to which their personal construct systems subsume each other and permit a constructive role relationship. A role relationship requires an attempt to infer the other's view.

FIGURE 14-2 Schematic Analysis of Kelly's Stance on Basic Issues

personality health or the good life. Neither did he present a list or typology of likely healthy personal constructs. Indeed, the term "health" does not appear in the index of volume one of *The Psychology of Personal Constructs* (1955a), and though it is listed in the index of his second volume (1955b), the pages cited refer to the client's adjustment to ill health, the therapeutic procedures for the clinician's structuring of a client's experiencing of an illness, and the clinician's use of adjunctive services in rehabilitative therapy. This is not unexpected, for as Kelly (1955a) repeatedly warned, PCT ". . . tends to have its focus of convenience in the area of human readjustment to stress" and "should prove most useful to the psychotherapist because we were thinking primarily of the problems of psychotherapy when we formulated it" (p. 12). He warned, too, of the dangers of trying to extend a theory's focus of convenience beyond its boundaries.

Though it may not be advisable to extend the focus of convenience of PCT to include the healthy personality and the good life (particularly in light of Kelly's warnings), it seems appropriate to consider that there are some clear implications in Kelly's theory for building and maintaining a healthy system of personal constructs. What follows, then, is the author's perceptions of these implications.

If, as Kelly (1955a) asserts, humans are best viewed as incipient scientists attempting to predict and control life events by placing alternative constructions on their environment, then the implication is that the more they develop their "science-like" aspects (immediately testing the predictive efficiency of their personal constructs against the reality of their environment, for example) the greater their psychological health. In brief, good science = good health.

Healthy humans, like good scientists, consciously build and continually reconstrue and improve the validity of their individual systems of personal constructs. Moreover, they actively work to enhance and expand both the appropriate focus and range of convenience of their construct systems. The construct systems of healthy people lead to the formulation of testable hypotheses, provoke experiments, suggest predictions of human behavior in a wide range of circumstances, and inspire creative inventions of new approaches to the solution of the problems they encounter.

Healthy humans consciously choose not to be shackled to fixed construct systems. Their constructs are permeable, open to the addition of new elements; hence, they are responsive to new experience and new possibilities. Because healthy humans are not under control of the events in their lives, they have the courage to take risks, to approach life with an active intellect, to pose and answer questions concerning the meaning of their experiences, to try and to test new behaviors, and to revise or abandon constructs that fail the test of predictive efficiency (see Kelly, 1955a, pp. 22–45).

Psychopathology

Kelly (1955b) asserts that PCT is not a theory built upon pathology, but rather a system "designed around the problem of reconstruing life" (p. 830). From this perspective, psychological disorder is defined "as any personal construction which is used repeatedly in spite of consistent invalidation" (Kelly, 1955b, p. 831). For Kelly, then, the disordered person is similar to the rigid or incompetent scientist who refuses to give up a prized, though proven invalid, hypothesis. Personal constructs that are extreme in either direction inevitably result in inaccurate predictions and anticipations. Moreover, they involve high levels of confusion and anxiety that are expressed in either a frenzied search for other ways to construe life's experiences, or in an effort to keep the personal construct system intact, a rigid attachment to the same predictions and anticipations, even though repeatedly proved ineffective. Both paths lead to the breakdown of coping behaviors.

The answer to the problem of "reconstruing life" appears simple: To achieve and maintain optimal psychological health the individual needs only to revise, replace, or abandon invalid personal constructs. In reality, however, *simple* is not always *easy*; indeed, a simple answer can be extremely difficult and require a great deal of courage to translate into action.

An individual's constructions of self, others, and the world are all related and organized into a single construction system. Any threat to this system results in high levels of confusion and anxiety. Invalidation of even a single construct threatens some damage to the system. At the very least, an invalid construct results in loss of the system's efficacy and the individual's capacity to predict and control the course of his or her life. Indeed, the elimination of a superordinate construct could result in the collapse of the individual's world.

Healthy individuals are prepared to face invalidating evidence, to reconstrue their world, and to revise or replace their failing constructs. Disordered persons, however, often lack the courage required to acknowledge invalidating evidence. They are unwilling to endure the painful feelings of anxiety that accompany revision of their personal construct systems. They elect compensation over reconstruction and retain the invalid construct, even the obviously invalid construct, for it is preferable to the hole or gap its loss would leave in the system. As they continue to use a construct that repeatedly fails to work for them, they become maladjusted.

Kelly's Diagnostic Constructs

Kelly (1955b) rejected traditional medical diagnostic categories of psychological maladjustment. He reasoned that their use often predisposed the mental health professional to fit his or her client into a predetermined, stereotypical classification system. This practice focuses attention on the label, often overlooking the client's personal constructs. Further, he argued that a disordered client, once labeled, often accepts and adopts the "official" construct, along with all its related symptoms. To avoid these shortcomings, Kelly (1955b) developed his own set of diagnostic constructs through which psychological disorders might be viewed.

Unlike other diagnostic classification systems, Kelly's diagnostic constructs are also treatment procedures. For example, the person whose construction system is ineffective because his or her personal constructs are too dilated may be helped by learning to perceive life events in a more constricting way.

When a personal construction system fails because there are no superordinate constructs to organize perceptions, the confused and anxious individual will likely attempt to "dilate" (broaden) his or her personal constructs and reorganize them to encompass an ever-widening level of plausibility. When dilation of the individual's constructs is too great, the bizarre is plausible and perceived as reality; the individual may experience hallucinations or delusions. A severe dilation construction disorder, Kelly (1955b) asserts, can lead to what has been traditionally diagnosed as a psychosis and labeled paranoia, mania, depression.

Conversely, the predictions and anticipations of an individual who forms constructs that are too constricted may lead to obsessive-compulsive behaviors— "every prediction, every anticipation must be precise and exact," and the individual develops "a vast array of precise little formulas" to cope with even the minor tasks of everyday life (Kelly, 1955b, p. 489). Following this logic, it is not surprising that Kelly (1955b) views suicide as the "definitive" act of constriction. Depression, according to Kelly, is also the disordered response of individuals who have severely narrowed their perceptual fields. By constricting their personal construct systems, depressed individuals excessively limit their alternatives to act. Major decisions are impossible; indeed, even simple everyday choices, such as getting out of bed in the morning, can be difficult. Unable to formulate alternative constructs, they become overwhelmed by their problems. Suicide, which may be seen by the severely constricted personality as the only solution to insurmountable problems, is always a danger.

Heuristic Influences: Research Methods and Techniques

Considering the increased focus by psychologists on the role of cognition in human personality, the research generated by PCT remains disappointingly sparse. The few empirical studies that have been published in recent years center mostly on the Rep Test (Bannister & Mair, 1968; Bannister, 1985), rather than on Kelly's theory of personal constructs. Kelly himself may be partly responsible for this.

Contrary to many psychologists, Kelly (1955a) did not see either diagnosis or research as a primary objective of the clinical psychologist. Indeed, for Kelly (1955a), "Research, except as it is directed toward the anticipation of the future, is also a minor objective" (p. 186). According to Kelly (1969, in Maher), science is but one system of constructs among many alternatives for the study of nature—particularly human nature—and not always the best system. Indeed, Kelly (1969, in Maher) believed that traditional psychology is "still much too self-consciously scientific" . . . "still much too peripheral to its subject matter," and still much too careful of doing "nothing that a scientist would not do" (p. 226). He was convinced that scientific methodology, if adhered to exclusively, would fetter the personologist, whose main concern should be to get on with the task of understanding human nature. Further, Kelly (1955a, 1955b) repeatedly expressed the view that because it is impossible for the scientist to posit any objective reality apart from his or her own understanding of it, neither the person nor the world is ultimately knowable through a scientific methodology. All forms of nature (human and otherwise) must, Kelly (1969, in Maher) insists, "be regarded as open to an infinite variety of alternative constructions" (p. 116).

In addition, Kelly (1955a) grants the central role of giving meaning to self, other humans, things, and events to the construing individual; thus, in terms of empirical study, advocates of PCT make no attempt to go beyond the data of the individual. The complex and idiosyncratic structure of meaning with which humans confront their world defies most attempts at present scientific methodology. Finally, it should be noted that Kelly (1956) advised his students and readers at the outset that his theoretical statements were "not more than partially perceived personal constructs," with a limited focus of convenience, that would "eventually be overthrown and displaced by something with more truth in it" (p. 33).

Use of the Rep Test in Empirical Studies

Bannister and Fransella (1966) and Bannister and Salmon (1966) have demonstrated the possible usefulness of the Rep Test and Kelly's constructs for understanding thought disorder in schizophrenia. Through use of the Rep Test, they were able to show that the schizophrenic's thought constructs (particularly the interpersonal thought constructs) are less interrelated and more inconsistent than those of the non-schizophrenic. Bannister and Salmon (1966) report that while their schizophrenic subjects did not differ from their control subjects when construing objects, they were far less stable and consistent when construing people. This finding suggests that schizophrenics' thought disorder may be particularly related to interpersonal or role constructs.

In their review of the literature on the relation of couples' constructs and marital satisfaction, G. Neimeyer and Jean Hudson (1985) found evidence for Kelly's (1955a) statement: "Other things being equal, the man confronted with the alternative of marriage will choose marriage if that appears to provide him with an opportunity to enlarge or secure his anticipatory system" (p. 523). Neimeyer and Hudson (1985) offer both empirical and clinical evidence to "support the view that satisfying marital relationships involve a continuous and reciprocal process of personal elaboration" (p. 129). Further implications of personal construct theory for understanding marital relationships are included. Among these are:

1. Like other forms of role relations, marriage represents an elaborative choice (pp. 137–138).
2. Successful marriages have been characterized as mutually elaborative. Partners encourage each other's development by validating and extending their systems of understanding (p. 138).
3. Satisfied spouses are more validating and understanding in their relationships than are dissatisfied spouses (p. 138).

Reporting on a study, the aim of which was to encourage teachers during their year of professional preparation to reveal and explore meaning as they evolved over the academic year, Diamond (1985) worked with seventeen volunteer students who were reading for the Diploma in Education with a core of educational studies in a variety of curriculum studies as offered in a secondary curriculum. The subjects completed repertory grids at the beginning, at mid term, and at the end of the school year. While no claims were made for defining a universal pattern in the prospective teachers' constructural patterns, certain overall trends were revealed, in particular the final separation from pupils. The prospective teachers, aware of their personal processes of construction, were enabled "to experiment with and to change, in self-chosen ways, their own views of teaching." In brief, "by knowing what they are, they can form an idea of what they would like to be, and by knowing that, they can work towards it" (Diamond, 1985, p. 34). Implications for teacher education programs were also discussed.

Applications to Psychotherapy

For Kelly (1955a, 1955b), all present theories of personality are miniature construct systems that, at best, are reasonably true within a limited range of convenience—points at which they are particularly applicable or maximally useful. Further, Kelly asserts, a theory's foci of convenience are likely to be those elements upon which the theory was originally formed (pp. 11–12, 22–23, 137, 185, 196, 562). Following this premise, Kelly (1955a) restricts PCT's range of convenience to human personality, and more specifically, to the problems of interpersonal relationships. Though PCT's range of convenience may be expanded to other areas (institutions, for example), Kelly insists that it should prove most applicable to the psychotherapist, for the problems of psychotherapy were the primary focus of his concerns during the time he formulated his theory.

In his major work, Kelly (1955a, 1955b) wrote extensively and explicitly about the role of the counselor or therapist in the psychotherapeutic process, as well as about specific PCT methods and techniques that he believed were particularly helpful in assisting clients to reconstrue their personal construct systems. Indeed, few personality theorists match Kelly's descriptive detail in the application of his theory.

For the purpose of this book, it is necessary to limit any descriptions of the psychotherapist's role and psychotherapeutic methods and techniques to those devised specifically for or adapted to personal construct therapy, and to keep even those descriptions brief. Readers who are attracted to Kelly's theory of personal constructs and wish to learn more regarding its application to counseling and psychotherapy are encouraged to read Kelly's two-volume work, *The Psychology of Personal Constructs* (1955a, 1955b). Those electing to follow this recommendation should be advised that they, like Patterson (1986), may find Kelly's approach to psychotherapy "formidable." Indeed, Patterson (1986) found Kelly's theory so formidable that he suggests that the tremendous responsibility placed on the counselor or therapist and the "extensive study, training, and experience" required of those who would master personal construct therapy might be the major reasons so few counselors and therapists today elect PCT as their theory of choice (p. 304).

Therapeutic Goals

According to Kelly (1955b), not only must the theoretical and philosophical constructs of PCT be rooted firmly in the professional convictions of PCT counselors and therapists, PCT counselors and therapists must also possess a number of skills and values:

1. They must possess the ability to subsume and utilize the wide variety of personal construct systems that their clients bring with them to therapy; that is, they must be able to construe their clients' personal constructs as their clients construe them.

2. They must possess highly developed observational skills; specifically, they must be alert and sensitive to a wide variety of cues, whether in the self-statements of their clients, biographical data, autobiographical data in the characterization sketch, health records, interviews, documents, reported dreams, tests, presented problems, or the reports of others. Further, Kelly claims, this level of observational skill is possible only when the counselors and psychotherapists themselves have well-elaborated construct systems and a large variety of well-structured experiences.

3. They must possess the ability and the courage to employ propositional constructs.

4. They must possess a clear construction of the psychotherapeutic role for the courage and persistence they will require in the face of threat or guilt.

5. They must possess a high degree of creativity so that they can devise techniques and formulate constructs that will assist their clients in the reconstruction of their personal construct systems.

6. They must be versatile enough to work with clients from all walks of life and to place themselves in their clients' roles.

7. They must possess the verbal skill to express their clients' obscure constructs in words; that is, they must be able to talk their clients' language and to identify key words for elaborating their clients' constructs.

8. They must be aggressive (from a PCT perspective); that is, they must hold an active experimental attitude toward life and toward therapy, aggressively formulating testable hypotheses and actively applying them to see what happens.

Therapeutic Relationship

Kelly strongly recommended that the therapist communicate to the client a "credulous attitude;" that is, that he or she accepts what the client says. The client's statements must be accepted with respect, even if the truth of the statements is in doubt. This is possible first, because the therapist believes personal constructs are real for the person holding them, and they represent real events, and second, because the therapist knows that the reality of the client's constructs are not necessarily the reality of the actual event. It is the construct that must be understood, for the client behaves in terms of the controlling construct rather than the event itself.

Therapeutic Process and Strategies

Self-Characterization Sketch and Fixed-Role Therapy   Derived specifically from the theory of PCT, *Fixed-Role Therapy* is based on observations of the effects of dramatic experience. It begins with a *self-characterization sketch,* which is an invi-

tation by the therapist to the client to write a sketch of him- or herself. The invitation is intentionally structured loosely and stated along these lines:

> *I want you to write a character sketch of Harry Brown [the client's name], just as if he were the principal character in a play. Write it as it might be written by a friend who knows him very intimately and very sympathetically, perhaps better than anyone even really could know him. Be sure to write it in third person. For example, start out by saying, Harry Brown is . . . . (Kelly, 1955a, p. 323).*

The self-characterization sketch presented by the client is, along with other supportive material, used by the therapist, or better still, a group of experienced PCT clinicians and therapists, as the basis for writing the fixed-role sketch.

The fixed-role sketch, carefully designed to set the stage for the resumption of movement in the client's life by shifting the client's present constructions, invites the client to explore the contrasting behaviors of the person in the fixed-role sketch. The role created by the PCT therapist(s) in the fixed-role sketch should remove the client's impermeable constructs, selectively add new conceptual elements that: do not fit neatly into the client's present construct system, consider available opportunities in the client's life for validation, and include a framework for construing others in a manner that aids the client in establishing role relationships. The fixed-role sketch is presented to the client as a "make-believe" experimental effort so that the he or she need feel no threat to his or her core-role or self-constructs and no personal investment in its success or failure. The client is then asked to adopt and experiment with some of the fixed-role behavioral elements for a specified time period (usually from two to twelve weeks) by pretending to be the person presented in the sketch.

Cycles of Construction

The C–P–C Cycle (Circumspection-Preemption-Control)   In PCT, the C–P–C Cycle relates to decision-making in which the client's core-role or self-constructs are involved. The C–P–C Cycle begins with circumspection, a loosening process that enables the client to look at his or her construct elements propositionally or in a multidimensional manner. After looking at numerous alternatives, the client narrows them by deciding which issue or aspect is most relevant or crucial (preemption), and finally, the client makes a choice (control). The client will choose that alternative in a dichotomized construct that he or she anticipates will extend and define his or her construct system (see "Elaborative Choice Corollary" above).

The Creativity Cycle   Creativity, Kelly (1955a, 1955b) asserts, begins with a loosening of constructions, involves exploration and experiment, and terminates with tightened and validated constructions. A loosened construction is one characterized by varying the alignment of its elements. A tightened construction involves the rigid assignment of elements within the construct's contents. The Creativity Cycle, according to Kelly, begins with the person experimenting minimally with each transient variation of elements within a construction, then seizing the more likely alignments, tightening them, and finally subjecting them to a major test of validation.

Dreams For Kelly (1955b), dreams represent the most loosened construction that a client can express in words, and to recount a dream is to engage in loosened constructions which the client has not dealt with (p. 1037). Further, Kelly asserts (1955b), dreams may permit the client to picture him- or herself on the opposite end of one of his or her construct dimensions. As such, dreams may be an indication that the client is preparing to experiment with contrasting behavior or impulsive behavioral experiments. Dreams may represent, also, a client's verbalized or preverbal constructs. When the client reports a preverbal dream, the report is likely to be vague, filled with visual imaging, and void of conversations.

Kelly (1955b) also discusses "mile-post dreams" which he characterizes as vivid, embracing elements from other dreams, marking a transition in the underlying construction system of the client, usually followed by transition in the client's thinking during interviews, and expressing new behaviors which are about to emerge spontaneously (Kelly, 1955b).

From the PCT perspective, "it is not the dream as an entity or as a biographical event that principally concerns us. We are more concerned with the loosened construction which it represents" (Kelly, 1955b, p. 1037). It is a mistake, Kelly believes, for the counselor or therapist to jump immediately into an interpretation of a client's dream. Interpretations should be held until the counselor or therapist wants to assist the client to move toward the tightening of constructions.

Course of Therapy Although strongly cautioned against fixed roles, Personal Construct Therapy usually follows three general phases: role definition or structuring, acceptance or credulous attitude on the part of the therapist, and working through the problem(s) or modification of ineffective constructs or the formulation of new constructs.

A therapeutic relationship is achieved when the therapist subsumes part of the client's construction system. This requires an empathic understanding of the client's view of life events (see "Therapeutic Relationship" above).

Therapy proper is a reconstruction process. Once the client's construct system is analyzed and ineffective constructs are identified, the therapist and client *as a team* work to alter ineffective constructs or to formulate new constructs that will assist the client to anticipate and control life events more effectively (see "Therapeutic Process and Strategies," above). From the PCT perspective, psychotherapy is the utilization of technical assistance (the *Role Construct Test* [REP Test], for example) in the formulation and testing of more viable personal constructs; thus, it is the restructuring of the client's construct system.

Extended Applications

Institutions

Although Kelly (1955a, 1955b) stated repeatedly that his theory's foci of convenience were restricted to psychotherapy, he did not hesitate to point to the implications of PCT for various social institutions, particularly schools, prisons, hospitals, mental health clinics, and welfare agencies. The most important implication is that institutions, like individuals, can best be understood when construed as having construct systems and using these systems to predict and control future events.

Kelly learned early in his career, while providing his traveling psychology clinics to rural schools, that the problems teachers and administrators saw in portions of the student body were better understood when construed as problems of the school than as problems of the students. When a school's view of its students is characterized by the superordinate construct *lazy–industrious,* and the construct is applied preemptively, laziness is the predicted student response to all learning activities, and more, the prediction is validated nearly every time it is tested.

All too often, the constructions that social institutions and agencies formulate of their clients, and hence, their own roles perpetuate the very behaviors that they are directed to eliminate. What is likely to happen in a prison when *prisoner–nonprisoner* becomes a superordinate construct and is applied preemptively? What treatment of clients might be manifest in a welfare agency that applies the superordinate construction *lazy–industrious* preemptively? How will a portion of the student body feel and act if the college or university views them through the superordinate construct *dumb–intelligent*? What happens to the person in the hospital that preemptively holds to the superordinate construct *insured–noninsured*?

Nations

In retrospect, it would appear that PCT's range of convenience might also be extended to nations. Was the Holocaust of Nazi Germany the result of the superordinate construct *Aryan–Jew,* applied preemptively? Was it the superordinate construct *revolutionary–counterrevolutionary,* preemptively applied by Mao Tsetung's Cultural Revolution, that led to the execution or imprisonment and "rehabilitation" of so many people in China? Can one point to the superordinate construction of *owner–slave* to explain the inhumane treatment of blacks during an early period of American history? What superordinate constructions are in play in various nations today? How might these constructions affect world trade agreements, peace treaties, weapon abolishment, diplomatic relationships? What steps might be taken to define and to assist in the abandonment of potentially dangerous superordinate national constructs, or if abandonment is unrealistic, to tighten these constructs by delimiting them?

Critique

Strengths

Many personologists and students of counseling and psychotherapy (Patterson, 1980; Ryckman, 1985; Sechrest, 1977, 1983, among them) believe that the potential of Kelly's theory of personal constructs for understanding human personality is far greater than has been realized. Their belief in the potential of PCT appears to be shared by the great majority of personality textbook authors. The present author's survey of twelve popular textbooks on personality theories published in the last ten years (most in their second and third editions) reveals that 83.3 per cent included Kelly among the major theorists they selected for presentation. Indeed, with the current trend to recognize the influence of cognitive factors in the development and maintenance of human personality, Kelly is increasingly considered one of the major contributors to the field. Belief in a theory's potential, however, erodes swiftly when membership in a theory group and research in the literature decreases. Unless there is a sudden and remarkable resurgence in both interest and action, the future for Kelly's Personal Construct Theory looks rather bleak.

Comprehensive, Integrated, Systematic, Precise   Kelly offers a comprehensive, integrated, and systematic theoretical formulation, that like Rogers's (Chapter 9), is clearly and explicitly stated in propositional form. Moreover, Kelly carefully and completely defines his terminology so that his readers can follow without great difficulty the internal logic with which his fundamental postulate and each of the ten corollaries are developed and elaborated. Considerable detail is necessary, for as Patterson (1980) remarks: "Although the basic postulate and its corollaries are amazingly simple, their elaboration is amazingly complex" (p. 384).

The REP Test   Kelly's Role Construct Repertory Test has been used successfully to identify the important constructs individuals use to construct the significant people in their lives. This test, even more than the theory from which it was developed, has attracted a great deal of attention and generated most of the research studies by PCT advocates.

Weaknesses

All theories of personality have their weaknesses; Kelly's Theory of Personal Constructs is no exception. If PCT is to survive as a visible and influential theory of personality, it must experience an immediate revitalization. Inclusion in personality textbooks, though important, is not enough. Neimeyer (1985) identifies four critical problems that he believes must be resolved if revitalization of construct theory is to take place: "its intellectual isolationism, its crisis of methodology, its relation to the cognitive therapies, and its movement toward professional organization" (p. 167). Because his concerns are echoed by others in the field (see Patterson, 1980; Ryckman, 1985; Sechrest, 1977), they merit attention here.

The Insulated Stance of PCT Purists   Whatever his reasons, Kelly's failure to acknowledge the contributions of his predecessors in the formulation of his theory detracts from the significance of his own work. By working in isolation, Kelly gave the impression that he considered earlier theoretical efforts irrelevant.

Not only did Kelly neglect to recognize allies in existentialism and phenomenology, whose contributions both Patterson (1980) and Maddi (1980) believe might have aided him to greater specification of his theory, he intentionally disregarded biological considerations, unconscious processes, situational influences, and prior experiences as possible determinants of human behavior. Unfortunately, as Neimeyer (1985) points out, later advocates of construct theory, particularly the British purists, continue to adopt Kelly's stance on the issue of isolation.

Kelly introduced his view of *human as scientist* at a time when the field of personality was dominated by views of *human as instinctual* and *human as conditioned*. According to Neimeyer (1985), there were certain advantages in Kelly's dissociation from the dominant views at the time he first presented his theory. Moreover, these advantages, typical of nearly every new group or specialty, were worth the risk of seeming misinformed, or at the very least, uninformed. Kelly's obvious disdain of psychoanalysis and behaviorism drew others with similar feelings to his theory when he was trying to establish a new and radically different theory group. Further, Kelly's strategy of neglecting his "historical roots" facilitated "more cohesive communication ties" and focused "the developing group's efforts on a manageable set of theoretical problems" (Neimeyer, 1985, p. 151). However, though Neimeyer (1985) offers possible justification for Kelly's early acts of omission, he does not accept today's construct theorists' tendency to continue this practice. "What is understandable (perhaps even necessary) for first generation network members can be a serious failing among second or third generation specialists" (Neimeyer, 1985, p. 151, parentheses in the original). Isolation of the construct theory group, in Kelly's own terms, encourages impermeable and constricted elitism, and renders any possibility for a meaningful interface with other theories (particularly the phenomenological, existential, and cognitive theories) highly unlikely.

Methodological Crisis As noted, a common criticism of PCT is the limited research it has generated over the years, especially in recent years. Further, nearly all the research studies in PCT employ some variant of the repertory grid technique, and virtually all focus on an analysis of conceptual structures. Many critics of PCT, as well as some of its strongest advocates (i.e., Sechrest, 1983; & Neimeyer, 1985), find the methodology of PCT research too restrictive and provincial for testing the theoretical constructs of a theory that strives for a model of the person as active, construing, forward looking, and rational. There is still the need for more sophisticated methodology that will help to determine how personal constructs are acquired and developed.

PCT and Other Theories For Kelly (1955a, 1955b), all events, whether internal or external, could only be validated by the individual's perception of correct anticipation. All aspects of personality were explained by Kelly as an extension of an individual's personal construct system, a concept that is a bit too parsimonious and intellectual for many personologists, including many cognitive and social learning theorists.

Other critics of Kelly's theory were concerned over his lack of interest in such personality variables as heredity, development and childrearing, motivation, emotions, and learning. They charged that his cognitive view of personality, though certainly consistent, was too one-sided and simplistic. Still others (Maddi, 1980; Ryckman, 1985; Hall & Lindzey, 1985) pointed to some of the gaps in Kelly's theory, in particular the omission of details on how personal constructs are acquired and developed; the lack of an explanation for differences between individuals in their construct systems; and the fact that his evidence was largely correlational in nature (see "Heuristic Influences" for further discussion of weaknesses in research).

Annotated Bibliography

Kelly, G. A. (1955). *The Psychology of Personal Constructs* (2 vols.). New York: W. W. Norton.

Kelly's presentation of personal construct theory first appeared with the publication of these two volumes. Volume I introduces Kelly's concept of constructive alternativism, the philosophical position on which his theory is based. Chapters 2 and 3 acquaint his readers with the fundamental postulates of PCT, then elaborate this with eleven corollaries and the nature of personal constructs. Kelly next gives his views of the clinical setting, the Role Construct Repertory Test, self-characterization, and fixed role therapy. Volume II presents in detail his views about clinical problems and the PCT strategies for dealing with them. The chapters that follow focus on assessment for therapeutic intervention, psychopathology, and various aspects of psychotherapy.

Bannister, D. (Ed.). (1985). *Issues and Approaches in Personal Construct Theory.* London: Academic Press.

Bannister invited a variety of people whom he considered committed to PCT to write on any theme or topic that concerned them. As might be expected, the book is diverse in topics; nonetheless, each chapter focuses on the central aspects of Kelly's theory or elaborates on those parts of the theory that are more obscure.

Maher, B. (Ed.). (1969). *Clinical Psychology and Personality: The Selected Papers of George Kelly.* New York: John Wiley.

While some of Kelly's papers selected by Maher for publication in this volume appeared earlier in journals, the major portion of his selection consists of works previously unpublished but delivered to academic audiences. For purposes of organization and ease of understanding, Maher's edited volume is divided into three sections: Theory, Psychotherapy, and Specific Problems. In addition, the book contains a brief biography and a complete bibliography of Kelly's published works. The initial paper, "Ontological Acceleration," may be one of Kelly's best for those seeking a greater understanding of his theory. This volume also presents Kelly's stance on science and research methodology.

References and Suggested Readings

Bannister, D. (Ed.). (1970). *Perspectives in personal construct theory.* London: Academic Press.

Bannister, D. (Ed.). (1977). *New perspectives in personal construct theory.* London: Academic Press.

Bannister, D. (Ed.). (1985). *Issues and approaches in personal construct theory.* London: Academic Press.

Bannister, D., & Fransella, F. A. (1966). A grid test of schizophrenic thought disorder. *British Journal of Social and Clinical Psychology, 5*, pp. 95–102.

Bannister, D., & Mair, J. M. (1968). *The evaluation of personal constructs.* New York: Academic Press.

Bannister, D., & Salmon, P. (1966). Schizophrenic thought disorder: Specific or diffuse? *British Journal of Medical Psychology, 39*, pp. 215–219.

Diamond, C. P. T. (1985). Becoming a teacher: An altering eye. In D. Bannister (Ed.), *Issues and approaches in personal construct theory.* Orlando, FL: Academic Press.

Dunnit, G. (1988). *Working with people: Clinical uses of personal construct psychology.* New York & London: Routledge.

Kelly, G. A. (1955a). *The psychology of personal constructs: A theory of personality* (vol. 1). New York: W. W. Norton.

Kelly, G. A. (1955b). *The psychology of personal constructs: A theory of personality* (vol. 2). New York: W. W. Norton.

Kelly, G. A. (1956). Man's constructions of his alternatives. In G. Lindzey (Ed.), *Assessment of human motives.* New York: Rinehart & Winston, pp. 33–61.

Kelly, G. A. (1963/1955). *A theory of personality.* New York: W. W. Norton.

Kelly, G. A. (1966). A brief introduction to personal construct theory. In D. Bannister (Ed.), *Perspectives in personal construct theory.* London: Academic Press.

Kelly, G. A. (1969a). The strategy of psychological research. In B. Maher (Ed.), *Clinical psychology and personality: The selected papers of George Kelly.* New York: John Wiley & Sons, pp. 114–132.

Kelly, G. A. (1969b). Personal construct theory and the psychotherapeutic interview. In B. Maher (Ed.), *Clinical psychology and personality: The selected papers of George Kelly.* New York: John Wiley & Sons, pp. 224–264.

Maddi, S. R. (1980). *Personality theories: A comparative analysis* (4th ed.). Homewood, IL: The Dorsey Press.

Maher, B. (Ed.). (1969). *Clinical psychology and personality: The selected papers of George Kelly.* New York: John Wiley & Sons.

Neimeyer, R. A. (1985). Problems and prospects in personal construct theory. In D. Bannister (Ed.), *Issues and approaches in personal construct theory* (pp. 143–171). London: Academic Press.

Neimeyer, G. J., & Hudson, J. E. (1985). Couples' constructs: Personal systems in marital satisfaction. In D. Bannister (Ed.), *Issues and approaches in personal construct theory.* (pp. 127–141). New York: Academic Press.

Patterson, C. H. (1980). *Theories of counseling and psychotherapy* (3rd ed.). New York: Harper & Row.

Patterson, C. H. (1986). *Theories of counseling and psychotherapy* (4th ed.). New York: Harper & Row.

Ryckman, R. M. (1985). *Theories of personality* (3rd ed.). Monterey, CA: Brooks/Cole.

Sechrest, L. (1977). Personal constructs theory. In R. J. Corsini (Ed.), *Current personality theories* (pp. 203–241). Itasca, IL: F. E. Peacock.

Sechrest, L. (1983). Personal constructs theory. In R. J. Corsini, A. J. Marsella, & Contributors (Eds.), *Personality theories, research, and assessment* (pp. 229–286). Itasca, IL: F. E. Peacock.

Stringer, P. (1985). You decide what your title is to be and [read] write to that title. In D. Bannister (Ed.), *Issues and approaches in personal construct theory* (pp. 210–231). London: Academic Press.

Stringer, P., & Bannister, D. (Eds.). (1979). *Constructs of sociality and individuality*. London: Academic Press.

C h a p t e r *15*

Ellis's Rational-Emotive Theory

Chapter Overview

Introduction

Biographical Sketch of the Theorist

Resolution of the Eleven Basic Issues
  Heredity versus Social Determinants
  Conscious versus Unconscious Determinants
  Role Assigned to Self-Concept
  Determinism versus Freedom of Choice
  Explanation of Learning Process
  Subjective versus Objective Reality
  Early versus Continuous Development
  Uniqueness versus Universality
  Role Assigned to Group Determinants
  Number and Weight Assigned to Motivational Concepts
  Centrality of Reward

Psychological Health and Psychopathology

Heuristic Influence

Application to Psychotherapy
  Therapeutic Goals
  Therapeutic Relationship

Initial Procedures and Strategies
Course of Psychotherapy

Extended Applications

Critique

Annotated Bibliography

References and Suggested Readings

Introduction

For the past thirty years, the theoretical direction of psychotherapy and personality was marked by a gradual but fundamental and profound change that Baars (1986) identifies as the "cognitive shift" or "cognitive revolution." Though seldom credited, Dr. Albert Ellis, the founder and principal advocate of Rational Emotive Therapy (RET), was a major contributor to the early cognitive-behavior therapy movement.

Presenting his first paper on "Rational Psychotherapy" to the American Psychological Association in 1956, Ellis attempted to integrate human cognition, emotion, and behavior. His basic premise, that human cognition mediates and is crucial to both the cause and the alleviation of psychological disturbance, met with immediate and vigorous opposition from all sides. Radical behaviorists viewed humans as passive, conditioned learners and discarded all references to internal states (including cognition) as unscientific. Orthodox psychoanalysts dismissed Ellis's theory as superficial. Existentialists and humanists found the confrontive RET approach to therapy cold and manipulative. In addition, many of the humanists accused Ellis of imposing his personal values and philosophy on his clients.

Ellis established many of the concepts of RET through his personal (see "Biographical Sketch") and clinical experiences, even though he himself claims little originality. Ellis (1975a/1962, 1975b, 1984, Ellis & Grieger, 1977) recognizes that RET borrows liberally from the historical and contemporary traditions of philosophy and psychology, as well as from biology. Ellis (1975b) traces the philosophical origin of RET to various Stoic philosophers, granting special recognition to Epictetus (first century A.D.) and Marcus Aurelius (in full, Marcus Aelius Aurelius Antoninus, 121–80 B.C.). Of the modern psychotherapists, Ellis (1974, 1975b, 1984) credits Alfred Adler (Chapter 3) as the "main precursor of RET." However, Ellis (1974) also notes that Rational-Emotive Therapy represents a distillation and synthesis of ideas from sources as diverse as the phenomenological–existential to the operant conditioning schools of thinking.

While Ellis may claim little originality in his theory, dedicated students of RET readily claim it for him. They "are quick to point to an originality of organization, an infusion of novel ideas, techniques, and materials, and a unique emphasis on the various cognitive, emotive, and behavioristic components of the theory" (Wallace, 1986, p. 193). Further, RET adherents assert, only an original and radical system of psychotherapy would generate so much research, attract so many ardent followers, draw such heavy critical fire from detractors, and leave so few practitioners neutral upon its introduction. Today's counselors and therapists may find RET fairly easy to accept or to reject, but those who choose to ignore either the theory or its founder do so with difficulty.

RET offers a highly structured, comprehensive approach to psychotherapy and to education that focuses on the cognitive and emotional elements of self-defeating behavior. From its inception, RET has presented "a theory of personality change that also implies a theory of personality itself" (Ellis & Whiteley, 1979, p. 15). By stressing human values, RET defines **personality** as consisting largely of beliefs, constructs, or attitudes that are organized into a system or set pattern of thinking (Ellis & Abrahms, 1978). This value-laden system of beliefs, constructs, and attitudes influences human thinking and finds both rational and irrational expression in human perceptions, emotions, and behavior. Experience is mediated by cognition, and as humans think, so they feel and act.

Biographical Sketch of the Theorist

Personologists often enhance and expand their understanding of a particular personality theory by studying the life of the theorist. Even a brief look into the background of Albert Ellis can benefit the student seeking to identify the origin and trace the development of some of the major concepts and hypotheses of RET.

Early Years

Ellis was born in Pittsburgh, Pennsylvania, September 27, 1913; however, from the age of four, he has lived his years in New York City. One of three children (two boys and a girl) in a family marked by a father's absence and a mother's neglect, Ellis discovered early that he had better learn to rely upon his own resources.

Ellis's mother, portrayed by Newhorn (1978, pp. 30–35) as a happy, energetic, and often idiosyncratic individual, who was bothered little by life's trials, and described by Ellis (1972b) as "unequipped to deal with either marriage or child-rearing," was neither consistent nor dependable in her relationships with her children (p. 104). His father, though reported to be intelligent, energetic, and persistent, was also opinionated and volatile (Newhorn, 1978). From the age of twelve, when his parents divorced, Ellis (1972b) seldom saw his father more than once or twice a year, and then only for very brief visits (p. 104). It was at this age also that "Ellis, who had planned to become a Hebrew teacher, questioned much of his early religious teachings; developed an empirical, scientific approach to life; and rejected a devout belief in any authority" (Wallace, 1986, p. 194).

In spite of his parents' shortcomings and "hands-off" child-rearing practices, Ellis (1972b) looked back on his early years as "pretty happy" times. Indeed, he recalled feeling rather good as an adolescent "about being allowed so much autonomy and independence" (Ellis, 1972b, p. 105).

Education

While still in junior high school, Ellis carefully planned his future. His ultimate life goal was to become the Great American Novelist. He was aware that his goal was lofty and that he would have to devote considerable time and energy to writing if he were going to achieve success. He was aware, too, that since others were not likely to support him in his endeavor, he would have to become financially independent before he could totally dedicate his life to writing. Ellis decided that he would first study accounting, then accumulate enough money to retire comfortably by the age of thirty, and finally, without financial concern or the need to publish in order to survive, write *the* novel.

Life's circumstances often dictate revisions of plans formulated in junior high school. Ellis was sixteen when, in 1929, the country was ravaged by the Great Depression. Despite extremely adverse conditions, a determined Ellis managed to complete the requirements of a baccalaureate degree in business administration, and in 1934 he was graduated from City College of New York. While he did not become independently wealthy by the age of thirty, he did find time to write, producing twenty unpublished full-length manuscripts. Realizing that he was "not going to be the Great American Novelist," Ellis (1972b) decided that fiction was not his "forte" and concentrated on nonfiction—"as a vehicle to propound some of my revolutionary views" (p. 109). Ellis may not have achieved the goal he set in junior high school, but he has, indeed, become a writer of some renown.

Ellis entered Columbia University in 1942, and in 1943 was graduated with an M.A. degree in clinical psychology. He began private practice immediately, specializing in marriage and family counseling and sex therapy. Ellis received his Ph.D. degree in 1947, and convinced that psychoanalysis was a deeper and more intensive form of treatment, decided to train as a psychoanalyst. Because the psychoanalytic institutes were considering only those applicants with medical degrees, Ellis waited until he found Richard Hulbeck, a leading analyst from the Karen Horney Institute, who agreed to work with him. Upon completion of analysis in 1949, Ellis began practicing orthodox psychoanalysis under Hulbeck's direction.

Emergence of a Theory

Most current psychotherapies evolved because individual practicing therapists were dissatisfied with the results of the system they employed and sought more effective and efficient techniques for bringing about client change. RET is no exception. As a classical psychoanalyst, Ellis (1975a/1962) discovered that while most of his clients appeared to make great gains in psychoanalytic insights, their perfectionistic, self-condemning, and other-directed behaviors remained unchanged. Insight alone was not sufficient to change ineffective or dysfunctional behavior.

Initially, Ellis turned to neoanalytic theories and more active therapist techniques. Still dissatisfied, he became interested in learning theory and conditioning. With this transition, he became a more effective therapist; however, he discovered that his patients' behaviors were not the exclusive result of social learning and conditioning. Their behavior appeared to result in large part from biosocial predispositions to retain a number of strong, tenacious, irrational ideas, attitudes, and values. Clinical experimentation with various methodologies, increased active-directive therapist involvement, and careful evaluation and incorporation of personal experiences led Ellis away from the traditional therapeutic approaches. He then turned to a self-conceived and innovative system that presented a highly cognitive and active-directive behavioral form of therapeutic intervention and interaction.

In 1954, Ellis began to work diligently toward a rational approach to psychotherapy. Based more on a philosophical than on a psychological model, his new and radical system of psychotherapy was elaborated in a series of articles that culminated in 1962 with the publication of *Reason and Emotion in Psychotherapy*. In 1959, Ellis founded the non-profit Institute for Rational Emotive Therapy in New York City, and he has served as its executive director since 1968.

Honors and Awards

Ellis has become well known for his tireless work in both psychotherapy and writing. In addition to more than 500 papers and articles and numerous instructional tapes and films, Ellis has written or edited more than a book per year for the past forty years. The last count exceeded seventy, but surely more will follow. He has served as associate or consulting editor for ten journals. Ellis is known to work fifteen-hour days and seven-day weeks, but requests for lectures, consultations, seminars, workshops, professional conferences, and personal appearances on radio and television programs are far too many for even Ellis to meet.

Ellis is founder and executive director of two non-profit institutes: the Institute for Rational Living and the Institute for Advanced Study in Rational Psychotherapy, the training and certification headquarters for RET therapists. Branches of these institutes exist currently in ten cities throughout the United States and in Australia, Canada, Guatemala, India, Mexico, and the Netherlands.

In 1971, the American Humanist Association honored Ellis with the Humanist of the Year Award. The Society for the Scientific Study of Sex recognized him for outstanding research in 1972. The APA named Ellis the recipient of their Distinguished Professional Psychologist Award in 1974. In 1976, he accepted the distinguished Sex Educator and Sex Therapist Award of the American Association of Sex Educators, Counselors and Therapists.

Resolution of the Eleven Basic Issues

Ellis was not involved in the selection of the eleven basic issues presented in this book. Neither has he specifically addressed them in any single work. However, Ellis is not one to avoid or ignore any issue, especially a basic issue, and his resolutions are not difficult to extrapolate.

Weighing the significance Ellis assigns to each of the eleven basic issues so they might be presented in hierarchical order was more difficult. The order presented here is a matter of the writer's judgment, and therefore open to question. There is, of course, no assumption that Ellis endorses this hierarchical arrangement.

Heredity versus Social Determinants

Because Ellis believes biological and cultural determinants coexist as a dimension of the complex, unified system that is human personality, he resolves this issue by combining its polar opposites (Chapter 1). We emerge as **biosocial** creatures; that is, we have evolved a brain that biologically gives us the capacity to think both rationally and irrationally, and we socioculturally acquire a predisposition to perceive, think, emote, and behave in specific and set patterns. Unless we consciously alter these patterns, Ellis believes that they persist throughout our lives.

Ellis (1974, 1975a/1962, 1977, 1984) does not endow us with the unconscious, inescapable instincts of the lower animals, as do the psychoanalysts. He does, however, strongly emphasize biological influences in his theory of human personality by identifying a number of **instinctoid tendencies** or **biological predispositions** (animal instincts weakened over the centuries through the process of evolution). Our primary biological predispositions are our propensities toward **rational** (positive, healthful) or **irrational** (negative, pathogenic) belief patterns. We enter this world with tendencies to act and to react in a certain pattern. Moreover, once our belief pattern is established, Ellis asserts, we are inclined to perpetuate that pattern, regardless of the nature of stimuli introduced or the individual growth or stagnation experienced.

Although Ellis is convinced that our idiosyncratic patterns of perceiving, thinking, emoting, and acting are inherited, he recognizes also that we are individually conditioned by the society and culture in which we grow to maturity, by the types and quality of early and ongoing interpersonal relationships we experience, and by the language (signs and symbols) we learn to communicate with ourselves and others. Our socially acquired tendencies are inseparably linked to, influenced by, and reinforced by our hereditary biological predispositions. In short, we are **biosocial** (biological and sociocultural) beings, influenced by a multiplicity of interacting and intersecting biological and sociocultural forces with the potential to influence our personalities.

For Ellis, neither the person nor the environment is a closed system; neither is separable or antithetical. There are complementary and reciprocal interactions between our *inherited* biological predispositions and our socioculturally *acquired* tendencies to think both rationally and irrationally. Conversely, socioculturally acquired tendencies are inseparably linked to, influenced by, and reinforced by innate instinctoid tendencies. This is particularly true of society's absolutes, those beliefs we are conditioned to accept without question—the tyrannical "shoulds, oughts, musts, have tos, and can'ts" that while they may help to perpetuate society, contribute significantly to our irrational belief systems and maladaptive behaviors.

In summary, then, we emerge as biosocial beings. We are biologically and socially predisposed to perceive, think, emote, and behave in specific and set patterns based on belief systems that may or may not function for our best interest. Moreover, our perceptions, thoughts, emotions, and actions are interactional and transactional.

When we perceive an event or object, we think about it; we experience a feeling toward it; and, finally, we act or react in accordance with our feeling. Consider, for example, a young man whose legs are paralyzed as a result of an injury to his spinal cord in an automobile accident being placed in a wheelchair for the first time:

> He sees *the chair being wheeled into the room,* hears *the metallic click of the wheels being locked,* feels *the sensation of being lifted from the bed,* watches *the physical therapist place his feet and legs in the foot rests,* feels *the canvas against his back and the cold chrome under his arms,* grasps *the wheels as the brakes are released,* pushes *and* feels *the sensation of moving forward under his own power for the first time in many months,* decides *that perhaps things are not going to be so bad after all, that he will no longer be so dependent on others, and* experiences *a rush of excitement, anticipation, and hope (Wallace & Maddox, 1981, emphasis in original).*

In brief, the young man perceives, thinks, feels, and acts simultaneously, interactionally, and transactionally.

Conscious versus Unconscious Determinants

Like other mammals, we are conscious, perceptive, experiencing creatures. Unlike other mammals, however, we also are self-conscious and self-perceptive beings. We are not limited to either our biology or our experiences. Our unique self-consciousness makes it possible for us to imagine how our experiences might be different. We can and do anticipate the consequences of our actions.

While some species of mammals have evolved brains that appear capable of thought, we enter this world with brains that not only give us the capacity to think, but to think about our thinking, and further, to think about what we think of our thinking. Sheldon Kopp (1978), in his book *An End to Innocence,* reflects on the unique difference of human thought and the thought of other mammalian species when he writes:

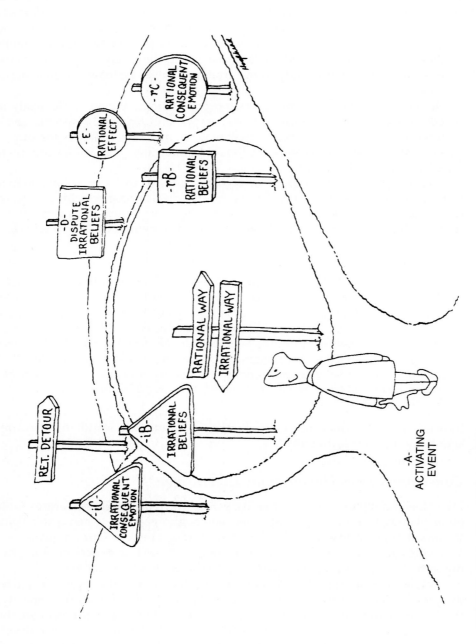

FIGURE 15-1 The ABCs of RET

Other mammals appear able simply to enjoy being momentarily well-fed, warm, and dry. At such times only Homo sapiens are capable of worrying about whether or not the moment will last, of wondering what it is really all about, or of becoming distracted by comparing the moment to some other moment (p. 158, emphasis in original).

The human brain is capable of bipolar tendencies; hence, we as a species can be both rational (self-preserving and pleasure producing) and irrational (self-destroying and misery creating). As individuals, we are predisposed to move more toward one pole than the other. For example, the seriously disturbed individual has a natural predisposition to move toward the irrational pole. With this movement events are perceived in a distorted fashion; cognition is not reality based, emotions are inappropriate and inordinately strong; and behavior is dysfunctional, even bizarre and destructive.

We are verbal animals. Whatever happens to us, whether inner physiological sensations or external events, we think about it, reflect on our thoughts, and talk to ourselves about our reflections. It is our cognitive self-dialogue that largely determines how we feel and act in any given situation because it provides a script for understanding and acting upon perceived experiences. Indeed, this uniquely human inner symbolic interaction gives each of us the ability to create nearly every human emotion and to initiate a large repertoire of physiological responses.

Human Thinking and Self-Talk   Ellis (1962) points out that human thinking often assumes the form of **self-talk** (the inner dialogues that we generate regarding the experiences, encounters, and circumstances that arise in daily life). Our inner dialogues represent the voice of our personal value systems and largely determines ongoing patterns of thought, feeling, and acting or reacting, even though they are not outwardly verbalized.

Because we think continually and automatically about all that transpires in our lives, we may not always be fully, or even partially, aware of our own parallel self-talk; thus, we are often oblivious to our own internal descriptive thinking about our experiences. However, with little effort, we can recall most of our self-talk. Even the most repeated, integrated, or habituated self-talk rests just below the surface of our constant awareness and is subject to recall. Whether aware or not, Ellis asserts, we are predisposed to talk to ourselves about everything that happens to us and around us. Consider again the earlier example of the young man in the wheel chair:

After a few tentative moves forward and backward, he moves out of the room in which he has been confined so long and down the hall toward the Nurses' Station—it is important to him that the nurses see him "on his own." As he nears the service elevator, the doors open, and the luncheon carts are pushed into the corridor. He crashes into the first of these. Some of the trays are knocked to the tiled floor, and the noise seems deafening. Worse, the chair overturns, leaving the young man unhurt, but sprawled on the floor. He tells himself that he was really a stupid fool for even thinking the wheel chair was going to make a difference, that he should have known better than to "get his hopes up," that he would always be a damned invalid, and he ought to accept that fact, that he can't stand having the nurses see him sprawled helplessly on the floor. Now, deeply depressed and angry at himself, he screams at the nurses to take him back to his bed, and to get that "damned wheelchair" out of his room and keep it out (Wallace & Maddox, 1981, emphasis in original).

In every instance, the young man's feelings, first of excitement, anticipation, and hope, and then of anger and depression, were the product of his self-talk. He became excited and felt hope when he told himself and believed that things were not so bad after all, that he could move on his own and would no longer be dependent on others. He felt a sense of anticipation and pride when he told himself that he would wheel past the nurses' station and that they would be pleased to see him progressing so well. He became angry and depressed when he told himself that he was really a stupid fool for even thinking that he would no longer be dependent on others, that he would always be a damned invalid, and that he ought to accept that fact and act like one.

Present Rather Than Past Influences   Ellis (1974, 1975a/1962, 1987, Ellis & Dryden, 1987) asserts that we are not actually disturbed by current or past experiences, but rather by our present attitudes toward and our present interpretations and evaluations of them. Rational attitudes, interpretations, and evaluations perpetuate rational feelings and behaviors. In a very real sense, we are self-determined by the present meaning we choose to give to our experience. Furthermore,

TABLE 15-1   The ABCs of Irrational Thinking and Emotional Disturbance

A. The negative **activating event** (past, present, anticipated, real, or imagined) that is perceived as preventing or blocking the achievement of some basic goal, purpose, or ideal.

B. The personal value or **belief system** that is comprised of both rational or realistic beliefs (rBs) and irrational or unrealistic beliefs (iBs) that people consciously or unconsciously tell themselves when experiencing an activating event.

   rBs—Indisputable, rational beliefs that facilitate the achievement of one's basic goals, desires, purposes, and ideals and lead to appropriate emotions, greater freedom of choice, and more effective behavior.

   iBs—Empirically unvalidated beliefs, often in the form of evaluative, godlike commands and demands (shoulds, oughts, musts, have tos) that interfere with a person's basic goals, desires, purposes, and ideals, thus causing needless discomfort or suffering, such as severe feelings of anxiety, depression, rage, and self-denigration or self-hate.

C. The **consequent emotions** (appropriate and inappropriate) that result as a consequence of "B," and lead to effective or dysfunctional behavior.

D. The rigorous **disputation** of iBs.

E. The new consequent **effect.**

Ellis is convinced that we can learn to recognize and to dispute our irrational beliefs and to accept almost full responsibility for choosing our own thoughts, feelings, and actions.

Return once more to the young male paraplegic, and consider just a few of the cognitive–emotive–behavioral alternatives that are available to him after his mishap:

> *He has been returned to his room, and he is thinking about the accident. He could be telling himself that he is "worthless . . . an invalid . . . half a person . . . without hope," and he might then add: "This isn't fair . . . I can't stand living this way." These thoughts naturally create feelings of inadequacy, alienation, utter hopelessness, extreme anger, and deep depression. And, since emotions often carry implicit behavior-directives, he might be withdrawn, uncommunicative, ready to strike out at any who attempt to help him (Wallace & Maddox, 1981).*

It is relatively easy to understand how this young man is creating misery for himself and all around him by choosing to languish in a quagmire of irrational beliefs, inappropriate and inordinately strong negative feelings, and ineffectual and destructive behaviors. It is just as obvious that little or nothing constructive will occur until he is able to attune to and dispute his irrational self-talk.

This young man could have chosen to view his mishap with the wheelchair more rationally, in which case he might tell himself: "Well, accidents will happen," or "Just my luck to take my first driving lesson during the rush hour," or "It may take me a little longer to operate one of those things than I thought." The young man is dealing with the incident from a rational perspective. He is not condemning himself or rating himself because of the mild misfortune that he encountered on his initial attempt in a wheelchair. Rather, he is telling himself things that put the mishap into accurate perspective, and as a consequence, his feelings are going to be relatively mild. His behavior is not going to lead to an increase in the trauma of his circumstances, and he is not going to alienate himself from those who wish only to help him.

The young man's acceptance of the mishap and acceptance of himself, without radical irrational judgment, prevent him from further limiting his own ability to function as effectively as possible. Indeed, if he limits his self-talk to the statements listed above, he will likely shrug his shoulders, say, "Tough!" and immediately forget the mishap, or he will smile at the humor of "driving his wheelchair in rush hour traffic."

After reading of the young man's wheelchair mishap, it is evident that the biosocial combination of innate and acquired predispositions can lead to difficulty, particularly when the uniquely human ability for self-talk and conviction are added to an already complicated picture. Ellis views us in some degree of precarious balance between the innate tendencies and the environmental forces and influences. On the one hand, we are inclined to act in a certain manner or pattern because of cognitive–emotive–behavioral propensities that are not easily defined or directly observed but that are ingrained in the biological and psychic fiber of the species. On the other hand, we are faced with mountains of true and false beliefs and conditioned expectations that society provides us from the moment of birth via a language that often contributes to irrational thought. However precarious this balance, Ellis holds to the belief that with hard work and long practice, we possess the capacity to weight the balance in favor of rational sensitivity.

Role of the Self-Concept

While Ellis lists self-conceptualizing with the biosocial predispositions that we all share, and while he recognizes that our self-concepts can, at any particular time, exert a significant impact on our feelings of worth and self-esteem, he is firmly convinced that we would do well to get out of the ego-rating business. Indeed, Ellis (1976) contends that humans "do not have to rate themselves, esteem themselves, or have any self-measurement or self-concept whatever" (p. 282).

Ellis (1972a, 1976, Ellis & Abrahms, 1978, Ellis & Harper, 1975, Ellis & Dryden, 1987) defines **self-conceptualizing** as an individual's irrational tendency to use self-ratings, self-judgments, and self-justifications to decide global positive or negative feelings of human worth and intrinsic value. Not only does Ellis (1972a, 1976) doubt the rationality of attempting to rate our worth as humans, he questions both the possibility and the desirability of any global self-rating. To arrive at an accurate self-concept, it would be necessary for us to quantify, add, and average *all* traits, potentials, motives, and behavior, many of which involve abstract values and concepts. Further, Ellis (1976) points out, if the individual self-rater should manage, "through some devious means," to arrive at a global rating of self-worth, he or she would thereby create "a magical heaven (your 'worth,' your 'value,' your 'goodness') and a mystical hell (your 'unworthiness,' your 'valuelessness,' your 'badness')" (p. 283).

When our concept of self depends on performance ratings, anything less than top ratings result in a poor self-concept. A poor self-concept is usually accompanied by anxiety and depression and the tendency to avoid opportunities and tasks that hold any risk of failure. Moreover, because we rate our performances by comparing them with the performances of others, high self-performance ratings can only be justified by rating the performance of others less high or, better still, poor. All others who perform well are a threat to our concept of worth, and we are likely to spend valuable time and energy in an attempt to uncover weaknesses in the performance of others, while simultaneously justifying our own.

Concern and anxiety are the constant companions of those who irrationally equate their performance rating with their self-concept. Each new task, project, or assignment carries the risk of poor performance or failure, thus perpetuating a low self-concept rating and an injured self-esteem which, in turn, lead to still greater anxiety and even greater emotional discomfort and behavioral withdrawal.

Ellis (Ellis & Harper, 1975; Ellis & Abrahms, 1978, Ellis & Dryden, 1987) recommends two separate and distinct approaches to the problems of human worth and the question of the importance of the role assigned to the self-concept.

The first approach, which Ellis defines as the inelegant approach, is offered to those who seem unable to avoid self-rating. During the early development of RET, Ellis referred to the idea of self-concept as a purely tautological and definitional construct. Essentially, this means that we are worthy simply because we exist. In short, there is an intrinsic value in being alive and choosing to remain alive. Realizing this idea had no rational or scientific basis, Ellis later moved toward a second, more elegant and rational approach, to the question of self-concept as an important variable in psychological health: that is, it is more scientifically valid to avoid self-rating entirely.

Throughout his theory, Ellis repeatedly provides his definition of *who* humans are. Humans are fallible, conscious, self-determining, cognitively–emotionally–behaviorally active, biologically and socially influenced and habit-prone beings. As long as we accept ourselves unconditionally and function rationally within this structural arena, we can gain a considerable measure of personal freedom and fulfillment. If, however, we perpetually search for the perfect, hence unattainable self-concept, Ellis believes we are condemning ourselves to a life of ceaseless disappointments and inevitable failures.

Ellis does not discourage our quest for better and more efficient selfhood; he does assert, however, that if the quest is tainted with perfectionism and absolutist expectations or demands, it can and in all probability will produce a great deal of discomfort and disillusionment. **Self-acceptance,** rather than self-concept, is viewed as a necessary prerequisite to stable and positive mental health. Self-acceptance allows us to move ahead with our lives without downgrading or damning ourselves for each setback or disappointment we experience. As we identify and integrate rational self-acceptance into our psychic repertoire, we become healthier and happier beings.

Determinism versus Freedom of Choice

Again, Ellis positions himself near the center of this polarity. He recognizes the existence of causal factors that are beyond our individual wills and efforts to control or to escape. Those behavioral determinants are deeply rooted in our instinctoid tendencies and in our personal-societal-environmental life histories. But just as certainly, Ellis vows that we possess the potential for a wide range of existential freedom and can therefore *choose* to develop rational sensitivity that at least to a limited degree, permits us to transcend our biological and experiential antecedents.

While Ellis (1972, 1979) affords us the freedom to choose rational sensitivity, he cautions us that our freedom is conditional because it does not automatically or implicitly guarantee rational thinking. He reminds us that we are innately inclined to think irrationally and that only our persistent, uncompromising attention to and expression of our freedom to choose rational sensitivity can sustain rational thought, feeling, and behavior.

While we are conditioned by biological and societal influences, Ellis proposes that we condition ourselves via our so-called self-talk network. Ellis believes that within each of us exists a cognitive dialogue that largely affects how we feel and behave in any given experience. From earliest childhood, our self-talk and the incumbent belief or value system upon which it is founded come under the influence of significant others and external groups.

As children, we tend to adopt the values of our parents, our teachers, our friends, and all other people we encounter significantly. As this occurs, our evolving self-talk network takes on characteristics of those individuals and groups with whom we most closely associate regularly. If the values these individuals and groups hold are rational, we learn to express rational self-talk based on realistic values. The opposite is also the case; thus, our self-talk network contains elements of both rational and irrational thought.

Beyond the valuing influence of individuals and groups, our value systems—hence, our self-talk networks—are perpetually molded and shaped by collective societal and societal system's values. We are provided with valuing alternatives from political rhetoric, the counterculture, the educational establishment, the church, the media, government bureaucracy, and other lesser societal forces. There is no guarantee that the conditioned values we encounter are rational and healthy or in our personal best interests.

While this situation is and will likely remain reality, Ellis suggests that we can transcend negative social experiences through development of a keen critical attitude and awareness. Ellis recognizes that the cultivation of rational sensitivity is not easy. However, he believes it to be the most effective way for us to live rationally and to prosper in the present. As we accomplish this, we can express one of the strongest of our natural predispositions—that is, our freedom to choose what we believe and how we behave in our daily lives. Through the confrontation of those ideas that promote irrational thinking and living, we are choosing to consider and eliminate negative valuing influences. We can recreate and maintain a rational value system and a network of self-talk that minimizes personal dysfunction while providing the best ways and means to long-term gratification of our realistic and nongrandiose goals and aspirations.

In the RET ideal, we can and do choose for ourselves what life means to us, how we can and will react to life and to others, and how we use our values, thoughts, emotions, and actions to accept or to alter our circumstances at any given choice juncture in our lives. Ellis believes that our freedom to choose whether we shall be governed by our self-conditioning and the conditioning elements of society or whether we shall choose to become more self-determining, self-aware, self-disciplined, active, and striving determines how alive and fully functioning we are.

Explanation of Learning Process

Ellis readily admits that we are experiencing beings; however, he is quick to demonstrate that we are not limited to our experiences. Our abilities to think, to think about our thinking, and to think about what we think of our thinking permit us to conceptualize our experiences. Essentially, Ellis informs us that we are naturally predisposed to learn and that learning is an important, integral part of our life process and our movement toward more rational living. Thus, for Ellis, learning is central in both the theory and the therapeutic process of RET.

Ellis (1974) accepts many of the main postulates of the learning theorists. He recognizes that sensory data, whether organismic or environmental, can impress and influence each of our minds. However, he insists that our minds, sifting that sensory data through a priori value-laden belief systems, determine the meanings we attribute to our experiences as well as to our emotional and behavioral responses. Were our belief systems comprised only of rational beliefs, our emotional and behavioral responses would nearly always be appropriate and effective. Unfortunately, our belief systems begin to form during those impressionable early years when we are particularly susceptible to the influences of other people, society, and the environment. Because of our dependence and lack of critical awareness, we tend to accept and internalize those values we hear and observe with little discrimination of their rationality. We live in a social world, and it is natural, although sometimes irrational, for us to share the values of that world.

Our belief systems emerge in the form of the declarative and imperative sentences we tell ourselves as we experience ourselves, others, and the world. However, Ellis reminds us that while self-talk crystallizes early and is reinforced constantly in our lives, it is nearly always amenable to change. We are potentially and consciously equipped to transcend these conditioned patterns of valuing and thinking, and with hard work and practice, to move beyond them into a more effective realm of self-facilitation. We can learn to become more rationally sensitive. Ellis's concept of restructuring our self-talk is an exercise in personal self-awareness that allows us to function more effectively and happily.

In conclusion, RET is primarily a teaching process. RET therapists actively and directly teach their clients the logico-empirical method of questioning, challenging, and debating values, attitudes, and beliefs (see "The Process of Therapy"). This process is directed toward cognitive-emotive restructuring and toward greater rational sensitivity and more effective living.

Subjective versus Objective Reality

Ellis has established RET as a rational psychotherapeutic theory and practice. This point alone seems to imply that he believes that a reality exists beyond the phenomenological awareness of the individual. Further, he encourages us to recognize and to come to terms with this reality, particularly in accepting the imperfections of ourselves, others, and the world.

Ellis's firm stance against any supernatural or visionary wheedling, almost any infinite, absolutes, or perfectionism, indicates clearly that he has rooted his theory in the reality of empirical verifications. RET does not allow us the luxury, except in magical, philosophical wanderings, to consider how the world *should* be; rather, we are taught to accept the world as we encounter it in the present. Reality, RET teaches us, is always as it *should* be. The tire with a nail in it *should* be flat. The person who drinks heavily *should* be drunk. The person who overeats *should* gain weight. Demanding that reality *should* be anything other than what it is will not magically make it so.

While it is clear that Ellis identifies with a reality environment, he affords us both the opportunity and the right to make personal statements about the way things are for us. He stresses that our statements, our self-talk, will have an immense effect on our ability to function in the world and with other people.

It is important to note at this point that when we accept the world as it is, we do not automatically relinquish the right to hope, dream, and act in a manner that promotes the collective betterment of that world. In fact, Ellis states that the healthy individual rationally transcends self and moves into an arena character-ized by rational interest in the betterment of the world. We are not victims of cruel fate or ominous foreboding demons, devils, or gods. We are able, when rationally sensitive, to choose for ourselves how externals will affect us, to choose our attitude toward our world.

As we accept our fallibility, without judging this as good or bad, and as we accept the imperfections of reality, regardless of the insanity we may witness, we are placing ourselves on a sounder mental footing. As we approach a position of rational sensitivity and equilibrium, we move closer to an existential stance that puts us largely in control of our attitudes and values and, finally, our actions.

Early versus Continuous Development

The Childhood Years   More than any other species, humans are developmentally immature at birth. Much of the maturation that occurs in human infancy occurs *in utero* in other mammals. By comparison, then, the developmental periods of human infancy, childhood, and adolescence are longer, slower, and more arduous than are similar periods for other mammals. Further, rather than being armed with the determinant instincts of the lower animals, the evolved brain of infants gives them the capacity and propensity for self-awareness. They risk a threat never experienced by the young of other species—an awareness of an over-whelming sense of helplessness and insignificance in a disinterested world. It is during their first years, when human infants are most vulnerable and impression-able, when they are least equipped to discriminate between the real and the unreal or the sensible and the insensible, and when they are most likely to cling to any illusion that offers a reassuring sense of security, that Ellis (1974, 1975a/1962) believes humans begin to develop their personal value systems.

The more intimidated the child by the world, the more the child's personal belief system will be constructed with beliefs to maintain a vision of a world that can be affected and controlled by personal wish, magic, and personification. There is a sense of security in the childhood belief that wishing, wanting, and desiring will make it so. Children gain a sense of being special in the belief that the sun rises specifically to wake them, that stars are there so that they can wish for the things they desire, that the clouds will vanish and the rain stop if they chant a magic verse, or that they can magically be turned into princes or prin-cesses with a kiss.

The irrational beliefs presented in fairy tales and reinforced by family and society are seductive to insecure children. Their irrational beliefs provide them with the temporary illusions of perfection, of being important, of rich rewards for little effort, of magical powers to control others, of a world that is always fair and just. Children are told repeatedly that good is always rewarded, and conversely, bad is always punished. Totally dependent on the significant others in their lives for their very survival, children are quick to believe that these people are always right, that they can do anything, and that they know all there is to know.

It is during their early years, also, that children are indoctrinated to a particular language and gain linguistic control over their behavior. Initially, their behavior is directed by the language of others; later, they learn to use their overt language to direct their own behavior; finally, behavioral control is transferred to internal self-talk (DiGuiseppe, 1982, p. 215). With the value-laden and behaviorally directive symbols of their language they "have the ability to create nearly every human emotion and to initiate a large repertoire of physiological sensations" (Wallace, 1986, p. 197).

While Ellis (1984) recognizes that children's belief systems may be significantly influenced by their culture, their language, their family groups, and the significant others in their lives, he does not hold these forces entirely responsible for irrational beliefs developed during early childhood. Children, Ellis (1984) asserts, bring to their early environments their own powerful innate predispositions to think irrationally as well as rationally.

> *RET holds that a human's environment, particularly childhood parental environment,* reaffirms *but does not* create *strong tendencies to think irrationally and to over or under emote. Parents and culture usually teach children* which *superstitions, taboos, and prejudices to abide by; but they do not originate their basic tendency toward superstition, ritualism, and bigotry (Ellis, 1984, p. 209, emphasis in original).*

In short, Ellis (1979) believes that children bring themselves, their unique "cognitive styles," to early experiences and teachings, "and they largely, though by no means completely, *make themselves* needlessly upset or dysfunctional" (p. 180, emphasis in original). Even if they had the most rational parents and teachers, children would often irrationally escalate their individual and social preferences into absolutistic demands on themselves, others, and the world, because as humans, they are innately vulnerable to irrational thinking and low frustration tolerance.

The Adolescent Years By the time children reach adolescence, many discover that their parents are not perfect, that people they admired and identified with do not always behave admirably, that truth and hard work are not always rewarded, that in a disinterested world everyone must endure misfortune, and that life does not always end happily. In short, exposure to the reality of life and living teaches adolescents that their world, and the people in it, do not fit the belief systems they formulated in childhood.

With the disintegration of their irrational beliefs, adolescents are faced again with many of the crises of their earlier years: the threat of insecurity, ideological confusion, marginal identity, and the painful anxiety that accompanies a myriad of conflicting possibilities and choices. Clinging to the irrational beliefs of their childhood by insisting on a view of the world as it *should be,* adolescents often rebel in a quixotic struggle against the ambiguous and disinterested world that *is.* While society may sanction adolescents' romantically idealized views of the world and their attempts to rebel for a time, the pressure is there to come to terms with reality, and that pressure increases as the adolescent nears adulthood.

For some, the defiant years of adolescent fads and dramatic and heroic postures are short lived. For others, particularly those who willfully cling to an exaggerated sense of self-importance, the inability to accept human imperfections, and the hope of reestablishing their idealized vision of an orderly and comprehensible world, the fight continues into adulthood. The costs of holding to the irrational beliefs of adolescence are ideological confusion, restricted individual freedom, missed opportunities, marginal identity and self-doubt, intolerance, blaming, repeated disappointments, and chronic anxiety.

The Years of Early Adulthood   By the time humans begin their adult years, their evolving self-talk network has inculcated many of the characteristics of those significant individuals and reference groups with whom they most closely associate regularly. Ellis would likely advise young adults to scrutinize carefully all present and future individual and group affiliations, and to select persons and groups that will have the best influence for a rational long-term approach to effective living.

Beyond the valuing influence of individuals and groups, young adults' value systems—hence, their self-talk networks—are perpetually molded and shaped by collective societal and societal systems' values. There is no guarantee that just because they are adults the values they encounter are rational and healthy or in their best interests. Television's impact may serve as a good example. The television set invites humans to tune in to the self-talk network of the masses and to accept currently popular, though often transient, ideals and values. Unless the young adult has developed a keen critical attitude and awareness, it is nearly impossible to grow to maturity without numerous irrational beliefs and priorities. Ideally, adults will begin to develop greater rational discrimination and sensitivity, examine their present belief and value systems, dispute those beliefs that are irrational and lead to inappropriate or inordinately strong feelings and ineffective or dysfunctional behaviors, and replace them with rational beliefs.

There is, then, according to Ellis, a connection between adult dysfunctional behavior and learning experiences as children. However, he strongly affirms our ability to move beyond the influences of the past. In fact, in therapy Ellis would not likely tolerate our lingering in the past or looking for childhood experiences that *cause* us to think, feel, or behave in presently self-defeating ways. He would assert, rather early in the therapeutic process, that nothing we encountered in the past is causing us difficulty. He would inform us that our current manner of thinking is the root of our problem and that anything experienced in the past can be changed in intensity or influence by a change in our present attitude toward it.

Ellis clearly supports the idea of continuous development, since he views rational living as a philosophy and a lifestyle, as well as a psychotherapeutic theory. The more rationally we are able to think, the better we shall feel. Likewise, our behaviors will become less counterproductive and the cycle of rational living will become a part of our ongoing development. Truly, for Ellis, we have the capacity to be rational creators of our effectiveness.

Uniqueness versus Universality

Ellis maintains that we have the resources and the ability to assert and express a unique approach to dealing with the circumstances we create and encounter in life. Our uniqueness is something we largely discover and unfold as we become aware of our potential to choose freely our destinies. Our uniqueness is an integral part of the value systems to which we adhere and live. Our value systems give character to our every thought, feeling, intuition and action. This character sets us apart from any other individual in the world and affords us the opportunity to make completely unique contributions to our happiness and to those individuals and things we value in life. However, it is impossible to say that Ellis ignores the fact that we all share many common biological predispositions and socialization patterns and that these influences play a significant role in how we shall come to know, or even if we shall come to know, our uniqueness.

Surely, the commonality of similar childhood backgrounds, educational experiences, and sociocultural expectations indoctrinates us with a common heritage of thoughts, feelings, and behaviors. We are like our fellow humans because we share so much biological and experiential input with them. Ellis believes that what we do with this input determines whether we come to realization, expression, and functioning at the level we are uniquely capable of attaining. Perhaps it is easiest to express Ellis's conception of this dichotomy by saying that we have the potential to function uniquely within the commonality of humankind.

Again, what we do with what we inherit and experience is important to Ellis because he believes that this activity of self-destiny most explicitly defines us as unique. Finally, Ellis believes that our uniqueness arises also from the degree of development that we may naturally have in a particular or several different activities or abilities. Not everyone is endowed with the same mental and physical prowess, but we all have at our disposal, by choice, the potential to become as fully functioning and well-adjusted as our limitations allow.

Role of Group Determinants

Although primarily a responsible hedonist, Ellis sees us as innately gregarious and relationship prone. He reminds us that from a responsible hedonistic viewpoint, we are usually much happier when we are integrated members of a human community and active participants in an intimate relationship with a few selected members of that community. At the same time, Ellis (Ellis & Harper, 1975) repeatedly cautions us to desire rather than to demand the approval and love of others. It would seem, therefore, that Ellis would likely assert that the importance of group membership is a point that we decide for ourselves and that we had better, for our long-range benefit, use all the rational sensitivity we can muster when we make that decision. We can, as rationally healthy individuals, learn to transcend singular self-interest and become involved in the well-being of others and the development of the community.

As children, we are certainly influenced and shaped by our early group affiliations (see "Early versus Continuous Development"). Our childhood friends, peer groups, and family members beyond the nuclear family provide us with a sense of group membership. As adults, we come under the influence of groups at our place of employment, in our community, and within our social circle that can influence our thinking and behavior. Ellis would likely advise us to choose our group affiliations rationally so that we interact with those groups that have the best influence on us. This implies that we take a rationally critical view of our present affiliations and carefully scrutinize any future affiliations. In the final analysis, we must decide for ourselves what is best for us. This is a power that can work for or against our rational approach to living.

Number and Weight Assigned to Motivational Concepts

Ellis provides a theory of personality that is hedonistic *over the long term*. Motivation is based on the assumption that we naturally prize and pursue pleasure, joy, creativity, and freedom. Indeed, the attainment and enhancement of these pursuits are rewarding. While we find pain, joylessness, creative stagnation, and bondage aversive, we do experience a motivating reward when we manage either to avoid these conditions successfully or to reduce their intensity or duration significantly. Even greater reward is experienced when we confront and overcome the defensive and dysfunctional behaviors we employ to deny or avoid aversive feelings and behaviors. Ellis (1974) asserts that rationally sensitive individuals are motivated to practice responsible hedonism that "emphasizes both the releasing of pleasures in the here-and-now and the long-range goals of future gains through present-day discipline" (p. 13).

Unlike the pleasure–pain dichotomy of the Freudians (Chapter 2), Ellis equates pleasure with effective living and pain with ineffective living. He grants us a wide range of rational and irrational day-to-day cognitive choices. In short, for Ellis (Ellis & Dryden, 1987), we choose our motivational purposes based on our responsible self-interests and short- and long-range benefits. Responsible motivational purposes are reflected also in the goals of RET: 1) survival, 2) achieving satisfaction with living, 3) affiliating with others in a positive way, 4) achieving intimate involvement with a few others, and 5) developing and maintaining a vital commitment to some personally fulfilling endeavor. Again, these are all rewarding and motivating pursuits that may be attained in a wide variety of different approaches. To this end, RET includes many conditioning, counter-conditioning, and self-conditioning techniques to reward and reinforce independent and creative thinking.

RET teaches us to construct our own reinforcement schedules and to use these schedules to enhance the motivating pleasures of effective living. The pleasures of living are facilitated when we are less perfectionistic and absolutist; when we minimize our dire need for love, approval, and success; when we learn to accept rather than to damn ourselves, others, and the world; when we are less procrastinating and more productive; when we become more involved with others; when we risk new and once-frightening behavior; when we rid ourselves of magical thinking, superstitions, and prejudices; or when we become committed to a vital interest or project. In short, when we are rewarded when we minimize the pain and maximize the pleasure of living.

Centrality of Reinforcement

It seems evident, with even a cursory look at the philosophic stance of RET, that Ellis considers reward both an important component of rational, healthful living and an integral part of psychotherapy. As mentioned earlier, RET is based on a theory of personality that when viewed over the long term is frankly hedonistic as well as humanistic. It begins with the premise that we naturally prize and pursue pleasure, joy, creativity, and freedom and that their attainment or enhancement is very rewarding. Conversely, we find pain, joylessness, stagnation, and bondage naturally aversive. Hence, we are rewarded each time we manage to rid ourselves of them, to minimize their intensity or duration, or to confront and overcome the defensive and dysfunctional behaviors we employ to deny or avoid them.

Hedonism, as practiced in RET, is not considered merely the pursuit of pleasure and the avoidance of pain, because this alone is unlikely to reward us with continued enjoyment. The goals of RET, therefore, reflect beliefs and habits congruent with responsible hedonism (Walen, DiGiuseppe, & Wessler, 1980): survival, achieving satisfaction with living, affiliating with others in a positive way, achieving intimate involvement with a few others, and developing or maintaining a vital absorption in some personally fulfilling endeavor. Again, these are all rewarding pursuits and may be attained in a wide variety of ways (see "Course of Psychotherapy," this chapter).

Although RET, particularly in its elegant form, concentrates primarily on **restructuring** our belief or value systems by teaching us to recognize, dispute, and change those ideas and attitudes that lead to inordinately strong emotions and ineffective, maladaptive, or dysfunctional behaviors, our new, more rational beliefs must be subjected to the trial of practice if they are to be meaningful or lasting. To this end, RET includes many conditioning, deconditioning, and self-conditioning techniques to reward and reinforce independent and creative thinking. Further, with RET we are taught to construct our own reinforcement schedules and to use these schedules to enhance our personal styles of living.

In summary, reward, especially self-reward, plays an important part in RET. It is rewarding to be less perfectionistic and absolutistic; to minimize our dire need for love, approval, and success; to accept rather than damn ourselves, others, and the world; to be less procrastinating and more productive; to become

Heredity		Social Determinants
Conscious Determinants		Unconscious Determinants
Early Development		Continuous Development
Subjective Reality		Objective Reality
Determinism		Freedom
Uniqueness		Universality

Role Assigned to Group Determinants	Group affiliation shapes and influences our development. We are naturally gregarious, but we are to desire, not demand, the approval and love of group members. Active participation within a group facilitates greater degrees of personal happiness, but the importance given to group membership rests with our rational sensitivity.
Explanation of Learning Process	We are naturally predisposed to learn, cognitively attributing personal meaning to experiences, as well as emotions and behavior repsonses. Developed early under the rational or irrational influence of others, belief systems emerge as self-talk.
Number and Weight Assigned to Motivational Concepts	Responsible hedonism is the rational approach to life. Long-term self-interest is Ellis's primary concept, and within the parameters of pain avoidance (ineffectual living through irrational thinking) and pleasure (effective living through rational thinking), we choose our motivational purposes.
Centrality of Reinforcement	Reward is experienced with the realization of here-and-now pleasures and the attainment of long-range goals achieved through day-to-day discipline. Effective living is itself rewarding.
Role Assigned to Self-Concept	Self-conceptualizing exerts significant influence on behavior, but when self-conceptualizing includes global self-rating based on behavior, it is irrational. Ellis encourages self-acceptance but discourages self-rating.

FIGURE 15-2   Schematic Analysis of Ellis's Stance on Basic Issues

more involved with others; to risk new and once frightening behaviors; to rid ourselves of the magical thinking of superstition and prejudice; to become committed to a vital interest or project; in short, to minimize the pain and maximize the pleasure of living.

Psychological Health and Psychopathology

Healthy Personality and the Good Life

Consistent with his firm stance against "absolutistic thinking," Ellis (1973) asserts that any certain, invariant criteria for the healthy personality—criteria that would prove valid for all humans at all times and under all conditions—are neither possible nor desirable. He does think, however, that it is both possible and desirable, "on a probalistic, practical basis," to arrive at "some fairly consistent criteria of personality health" (Ellis, 1973, p. 45).

According to Ellis (1972b, 1973, 1974, 1978, 1979, 1987), practically all humans value and regulate their lives by four basic goals or preferences:

1. They prefer life over death.
2. Once they choose life, they prefer pleasure (happiness) over pain (misery).
3. They prefer cooperative and peaceful living in a social group or community over living alone.
4. They prefer to relate reasonably well with most of the people they encounter in their community, and intimately with a selected few members of their social group.

In short, once humans choose to remain alive, it is rational for them to choose also to be happy, social, and loving, since these choices will most likely enhance their chances for personality health and the good life. An important emphasis in RET is that while it is rational for humans to *prefer* love and cooperation of others, particularly significant others, they do not *need*, nor can they rationally *demand* this kind of support (Ellis & Whiteley, 1979).

With the absence of absolutes, Ellis does not prescribe a set of personality traits that guarantees psychological health, happiness, and the good life. He does, however, describe nine personality traits present to varying degrees in rationally sensitive people that enhance the likelihood of taking advantage of the partial freedom and random moments of happiness available in life (Ellis 1966):

Self-Interest. In RET, responsible hedonism is the rational approach to emotional health and the good life. Ellis (1966, Ellis & Whiteley, 1979, Ellis & Dryden, 1987) is convinced that emotionally healthy and relatively happy individuals are first true to themselves and then true to others. Indeed, Ellis (1964, 1972a, 1973, 1975a, 1975b, 1974) views short- and long-range self-interest as the major source of positive, healthy motivation.

In many respects, Ellis's concept of responsible hedonism differs little from the hedonistic stance implied by Rogers's concept of the fully-functioning personality and Maslow's inherent self-actualization tendency (Chapters 9 and 10). For rationally sensitive persons, responsible hedonism is the desire to differentiate between actualizing and nonactualizing experiences and to choose those emotional and behavioral options that facilitate the growth and development of innate potentials. For Ellis (1972b, 1973), personality health and the good life are largely a matter of individual choices.

Whether humans come to realization, expression, and functioning at the level each is uniquely capable of attaining depends on how rationally sensitive and self-disciplined they are when they make their individual choices. "Being healthy and happy is most often achieved by dedicating oneself to loving (rather than to being loved) and/or to working (rather than to needing to achieve)" (Ellis, 1972b, p. 122).

Self-Direction. Emotionally healthy people rely on their own potentials and resources for their continued growth and development. They think of themselves as relatively independent, choice-making, active agents and accept responsibility for the consequences of their choices and actions. While they may *prefer* the cooperation and assistance of others, they do not irrationally elevate their preferences to the status of *needs* or *demands,* nor do they depend on others for their effectiveness and well-being.

Tolerance. Recognizing that all humans are fallible, perfection in self or others is neither expected nor demanded. Indeed, rationally sensitive people grant both themselves and others the right to make mistakes—without blame, anger, shame, or guilt.

Though they accept the human weaknesses and faults they discover in themselves and others, their tolerance is not to be mistaken for resignation, immobilization, or compliance. Mistakes or shortcomings are to be corrected when possible, for life in the long-range scheme of things is more pleasant when lived effectively.

Acceptance of Uncertainty. Emotionally healthy people are very much aware that they live in an uncertain world, a world of probabilities and chance. They are aware, too, that the risk of encountering the uncertainties in their world makes life an adventure and adds challenge and excitement to living. In short, emotionally healthy people enjoy the unpredictability of life. Each moment contains the possibility of surprise and the opportunity to explore the novel. They actively reach out to life, trusting in their own resources, value systems, and decisions.

Flexibility. Rationally sensitive people are intellectually and emotionally flexible. Life and self are continually in flux. They have the courage and resources to be open to new evidence and to revise their view of reality when that evidence calls for revision. In short, they can live comfortably in a disorderly world. Experience is not to be interpreted in absolute terms.

Scientific Thinking. The emotionally healthy are reasonably objective and rational. They are skeptical of dogma and believe empirical validation to be the crucial test of thought and action. They formulate hypotheses about how they would like to see themselves and others behave, then rationally apply the scientific method to their own lives and to their interpersonal relationships.

Commitment. Problem-centered rather than ego-centered, emotionally healthy people are committed to live full and productive lives. More, they are often vigorously and creatively focused on, and structure much of their lives around, some task, problem, cause, or issue beyond themselves. Responsibility and pleasure cease to be a dichotomy, as do work and play and means and ends. They find their work and personal relationships pleasurable and fulfilling. While they may be committed to a few close personal relationships, they do not *need* people. Consequently, their independence and commitment may be viewed by others as cold, unfriendly, or hostile.

While rationally sensitive people refuse to waste their time and energy fighting useless causes, they will work strenuously to turn their visions into reality, to bring about meaningful social change, or to eliminate unnecessary restrictions of their freedom.

Risk-Taking. For those individuals who think rationally, risk is a fact of existence. Emotionally healthy people are open to their experiences and willing to risk the possibility of rejection, defeat, or failure; indeed, risks are accepted as an essential and exciting part of living, if life is to be lived openly and fully. Occasional failure and its accompanying disappointment and pain are viewed as the natural consequences of risk.

Self-Acceptance. A goal of the rationally sensitive is unconditional self-acceptance, just because they are alive and, by mere virtue of being alive, possess some power to enjoy themselves. Acceptance of self and self-worth need not be based on the evaluations of others nor on personal achievements or defeats.

Psychopathology

Rational-Emotive Theory posits that the roots of psychological health *and* psychopathology are based predominately in biology. The same uniquely human cognitive processes that are responsible for the development of a rationally sensitive philosophy of relativism, which is at the heart of psychological health, are responsible also for the absolute values and the grandiose dogmas and demands that are the central features of psychopathology. In short, humans have the innate ability and predisposition to develop either rational and constructive or irrational and dysfunctional motivations and behaviors.

Moreover, Ellis (Ellis & Dryden, 1987, Dryden & Ellis, 1988) asserts that while humans are naturally predisposed to think both rationally and irrationally, they vary in their tendency to favor one mode of thinking over the other. Those individuals with a greater innate tendency toward irrational thinking are more likely to acquire and perpetuate mistaken or distorted perceptions, inappropriate or inordinately strong emotions, and dysfunctional or destructive behaviors.

A study by Charles Newmark, Ruth Ann Frerking, Louise Cook, and Linda Newmark (1973) investigates whether adherence to Ellis's irrational ideas precipitates emotional stress by the use of both normal and psychopathological subjects. Subjects in this study total 338 (193 female and 145 male): 120 psychiatric inpatients, ranging in age from eighteen to sixty-two, whose MMPI profiles were suggestive of neurotic symptomatology; 98 psychiatric inpatients, age range from sixteen to fifty-four, whose MMPI profiles were suggestive of characterologic adjustment patterns, and 120 college sophomores, age range eighteen to twenty-five. A questionnaire designed to evaluate endorsement of Ellis's eleven irrational ideas (each idea presented in a true–false form) was administered to all subjects.

> *The neurotic group was noted to endorse four of the irrational beliefs, a striking contrast to the normal and personality disorder groups, which did not endorse any of these ideas. Additionally, the neurotic group showed a significantly higher endorsement percentage on eight of the irrational beliefs when compared with either normal or characterologic Ss. The latter two groups obtained markedly similar rejection frequencies on all eleven items.*

Charts and statistical information are offered within the article.

Dryden and Ellis (1988) identify two major categories of psychological disturbance in humans: ego disturbance and discomfort disturbance. Self-damning is at the core of ego disturbance and results from the person's absolute demands on self, others, and the universe. The person in discomfort disturbance makes demands on the self, others, and the world also. However, implicit in these demands is the irrational belief that "comfort and comfortable life conditions *must* exist" (Dryden & Ellis, 1988, p. 221, emphasis added).

Heuristic Influences: Research Methods and Techniques

In addition to numerous clinical studies that tend to support the efficacy of RET (DiGiuseppe, Miller, & Trexler, 1979), there is a vast amount of research that appears to bolster many of the theory's clinical and personality hypotheses (Ellis, 1977; Ellis & Whiteley, 1979). While much of the early research generated by RET has its methodological shortcomings, its heuristic value must be rated highly nonetheless. Moreover, outcome research with RET has, with the increased acceptance by psychologists of cognitive factors in personality development, increased in both quality and quantity. Even a cursory review of the literature makes it evident that the amount of research is far too great to be covered adequately in the space allotted to a single chapter heading. Indeed, just listing those studies that appear to confirm the significant role that cognition plays in human emotion, behavior, and personality would require more space than permitted here.

Students who want a more comprehensive view of the research published in support of RET than has been presented here may wish to look at Ellis's (1977a, Ellis & Greiger, 1977, or Ellis & Whiteley, 1979) extensive listing of studies that he asserts confirm thirty-two clinical and personality hypotheses of RET and other modes of cognitive–behavior therapy. Further, because his listing is selective (it ignores those studies that find no evidence for support), students of RET may wish, also, to read the critiques of Ellis's (1977a) review that are provided by professionals in the field, including those of the cognitive–behavior therapists Donald Meichenbaum and Michael J. Mahoney, and the multimodal therapist Arnold A. Lazarus. While these critiques are on the whole positive, they do question certain of the evidence presented by Ellis and the conclusions he drew based on these findings. In addition, the following points are cited:

1. Ellis's review of the literature is intentionally selective.

2. Support for the thirty-two hypotheses does not constitute support for the efficacy of RET.

3. Some of the hypotheses for which research is cited lack specificity and discriminating relationship.

4. While there is clinical evidence for the efficacy of RET, experimental research supporting the efficacy of RET is comparatively sparse.

Many of the criticisms aimed at the research generated by Ellis's theory could just as easily and justifiably be directed at the research of most personality theories today. In fairness to Ellis, students would do well to follow their reading of the critiques cited above with Ellis's (Ellis & Whiteley, 1979) rejoinder (pp. 240–267).

Comparative Studies of RET with Other Therapeutic Approaches

Moleski and Tosi's (1976) study examines the efficacy of RET and systematic desensitization in the treatment of stuttering under the presence and absence of in vivo tasks. Twenty subjects (fifteen male and five female), all patients in the Department of Speech and Hearing, Winnipeg Health Sciences Center, were assigned randomly to one of five groups: (Group 1) RET with in vivo tasks; (Group 2) RET without in vivo tasks; (Group 3) systematic desensitization with in vivo tasks; (Group 4) systematic desensitization without in vivo tasks; and (Group 5) a no-treatment control group. The Moleski and Tosi study demonstrates an overall more efficacious result from the use of RET than from systematic desensitization in reducing stuttering, as well as accompanying anxiety and negative self-attitude. The in vivo technique did not necessarily effect greater results in all measures, but did improve overall performance as compared to groups not using in vivo behavioral assignments. The authors report that the cognitive behavioral approach to stuttering is to be supported over a traditional behavioral approach.

Also representative of the comparative studies is a study by Kenneth Holroyd (1976). Forty-eight test-anxious volunteers were assigned randomly to one of two therapists who provided (1) cognitive therapy, (2) systematic desensitization, (3) a combination of cognitive therapy and systematic desensitization, and (4) a pseudotherapy control procedure. Twelve subjects were also assigned to a waiting-list control group. Holroyd's study assessed test anxiety prior to treatment, at the completion of treatment, and at a follow-up after one month. The group using cognitive–attentional treatment showed significantly greater gains in virtually all measures of test anxiety than any of the other groups.

Noncomparative Studies of RET

Maxwell and Wilkerson (1982) investigated the effects of group RET in promoting rational thinking and self-enhancing emotions among twenty-four college students. The researchers conclude that "the group Rational Therapy program increased emotional stability, serenity, the ability to tolerate frustration, and self-confidence in problem solving and dealing with everyday anxiety regarding achievement" (Maxwell & Wilkerson, 1982, p. 139). Not only did the RET group treatment program provide the subjects with a novel sense of control, but it also gave them repeated practice in exercising RET principles. An interesting implication of this study is the possibility that anxiety may be created not only by the individual's anticipation of stressful situations, but by the absence of a belief that he or she has a choice about the stressful situation's emotional effect.

Thurman (1983) investigated the use of rational-emotive therapy in the treatment of Type A behavior among college students. The findings of Thurman's study indicate that a treatment program on the principles of RET can be used effectively to reduce Type A behavior. "Compared to a no-treatment control group, participants in the therapy group significantly reduced self-reported levels of Type A, speed and impatience, and hard-driving and competitive behaviors, as well as irrational beliefs concerning high self-expectation, anxious overconcern about the future, and perfectionism" (Thurman, 1983, p. 421).

Applications to Psychotherapy

Initially, RET was intended as a relatively short-term one-to-one psychotherapeutic method and applied to the clinical treatment of anxiety, hostility, character disorders, psychotic disorders, depression, addictions, and aging; to problems encountered in interpersonal relationships (love, sex, marriage, and family); to child-rearing and adolescence; to social skills and assertion training; to self-discipline and self-management; and to crisis intervention.

Therapeutic Goals

The essence of RET is "that it is possible to achieve maximum actualization through the use of cognitive control of illogical responses" (Morris & Kanitz, 1975, p. 8). The ultimate goal of the elegant or preferential form of RET is personality change or reorganization through cognitive awareness and philosophic restructuring and the acquisition of a logico-empirical method to maintain that change.

To avoid some of the common misunderstandings or misinterpretations concerning the goals of elegant RET, it is important to note the following:

1. In addition to the elegant, or preferential, form of RET (which makes RET unique among the cognitive therapies) there is the inelegant or general form, the goals of which are specific and indistinguishable from other forms of cognitive therapy.

2. While the two forms of RET therapy have different implications for therapeutic goals, they are not completely distinct and separate. The goals of **inelegant RET** (often expressed as resolving a problem, making a decision, reducing the pain of a symptom, or changing a behavior) may occur through the practice of elegant RET. Conversely, although much less likely, personality change or reorganization can occur through the practice of **elegant RET** (the restructuring of the individual's belief or value system).

3. The RET therapist seldom employs the elegant form of RET exclusively. Ellis and Whiteley (1979) define the RET therapist "as one who *generally* does CEB (cognitive–emotive–behavioral) therapy and who also *specifically* does rational-emotive therapy" (p. 246, emphasis in original). The **elegant** form of RET is preferred because the objective of this form of therapy is not only to help clients eliminate their existing disturbances but also to help them learn a logico-empirical problem-solving process to prevent extreme, sustained, negative emotions and dysfunctional behaviors in the future.

4. While RET therapists will, whenever feasible, actively and directly encourage their clients to recognize and dispute their irrational beliefs so they might gain control of their inordinately strong negative emotional responses, they do not impose any absolutist criteria of rationality. In discussing the term **rational** as it is used in RET, Ellis and Whiteley (1979) tell us that it "refers to people's (a) setting up or choosing for themselves certain values, purposes, goals, or ideals, and then (b) using efficient, flexible, scientific, logico-empirical ways of attempting to achieve such values and goals and to avoid contradicting or self-defeating results" (p. 40).

It is apparent from the resolutions presented earlier (see "Determinism versus Freedom of Choice" and "Uniqueness versus Universality") that RET therapists value highly and accept fully their clients' prerogative to decide their own direction. The RET directive that goal priority rests with the client is possibly best expressed by Walen, DiGuiseppe, and Wessler (1980) when they remind RET therapists that they are not there to stamp out all irrational beliefs in their clients but to help their clients change what they want to change (p. 35).

5. RET supports a philosophy of responsible hedonism: "Go for the pleasures of the moment, but weigh those pleasures against future consequences" (Wessler & Wessler, 1980). RET clients are encouraged to evaluate their decisions, plans, and actions from both a short- and a long-range perspective and to assess the consequences within their value systems. The route to adjustment is enlightened self-interest.

While RET therapists are continually striving to achieve the ultimate goal of elegant or preferential RET, they may approach the ultimate via the accomplishment of the following subsidiary goals:

- To communicate high credibility, professional competence, mutual respect and a genuine interest in and commitment to helping their clients change;
- To communicate unconditional acceptance of their clients;
- To communicate a faith in their clients' abilities to reconstruct their belief systems;
- To help their clients become aware of their natural predisposition to think and to talk to themselves about nearly everything that happens to them, and also to help them realize that this inner dialogue creates most of their feelings and determines how they will act in any particular situation;
- To demonstrate to their clients that they can recall most of their self-talk when they choose to do so;
- To help their clients become aware of how their language contributes to irrational perceptions, thoughts, emotions, and actions;
- To encourage their clients to question and dispute their irrational beliefs, particularly the absolutist beliefs—the "shoulds," "oughts," " musts," "have tos," and "can'ts";
- To teach, actively and directly, their clients a logico-empirical method of questioning, challenging, and disputing values, attitudes and beliefs;
- To convince their clients that they can, with hard and diligent work, weight the balance of their inherent tendency to think both rationally and irrationally in favor of rational thought;
- To demonstrate to their clients that past experiences can only continue to disturb them as long as they actively continue to reinforce and reindoctrinate themselves with the same irrational self-talk that created their disturbance in the first place;
- To encourage their clients to avoid escalating their personal preferences, wants, and desires into the status reserved for needs;
- To help their clients accept the fact that they are only, but totally, human, and as human, fallible;
- To demonstrate to their clients the futility of self-conceptualizing, which results in global positive or negative effect with respect to feelings of self-worth and intrinsic value;
- To acquaint their clients with irrational beliefs commonly held by large segments of the population.

Therapeutic Relationship

Practitioners of RET contend that since people have drastically changed their personalities through a wide variety of direct and vicarious experiences, there probably are no *necessary* and *sufficient* conditions for psychotherapy or for the psychotherapeutic relationship. Therefore, no absolutes guide RET therapists as they attempt to establish a therapeutic relationship with their clients.

Wessler and Wessler (1980) remind therapists, however, that the absence of absolutes does not diminish the importance of establishing a sound working relationship with their clients. The process of therapy is a partnership: two persons working together in pursuit of common goals. There are, then, desirable conditions that seem to facilitate therapeutic collaboration. Walen, DiGiuseppe, and Wessler (1980) believe that the development of a good rapport between client and therapist is an important ingredient for maximizing therapeutic gains. They remind us that the initial approach in RET therapy requires "patience, encouragement, and gentle confrontation" (p. 28). In a paper presented at the First National Conference on Rational Psychotherapy, Young (1981) views relationship building "as a primary consideration in any attempt to practice RET with young people," and presents ten specific expressive techniques that he found particularly helpful in establishing a "trusting, accepting, interpersonal relationship" with the reluctant or frightened adolescent client (pp. 1–3).

Patterson (1980) believes that Ellis communicates a genuine interest in and concern for his clients, and suspects that Ellis's results are more influenced by the relationship he establishes with his clients than Ellis cares to admit (p. 94). The implication of Patterson's position is that the counseling relationship is, in and of itself, therapeutic, a position unacceptable to Ellis and to most RET therapists who view the relationship they establish with their clients as a means to an end, not an end in itself.

As with most therapeutic theories, there are minimal conditions that had best be met if the therapist expects to see a client more than once. Of course, these conditions will vary somewhat from client to client. However, it is important that RET therapists communicate high credibility, professional competence, respect for the client, and a genuine interest in and commitment to helping the client change. Experienced therapists will tailor the emphasis they place on each of these conditions according to their assessment of their clients, as well as to their clients' expectations of therapy.

Because RET therapists believe all humans are fallible, they not only accept fallibility in their clients, but also encourage maximum understanding of and tolerance for human error and frailty. They specifically and vigorously oppose all types of blaming, including self-blame. They fully accept their clients as human beings, regardless of how objectionable or dysfunctional their clients' behavior. In addition to accepting their clients' fallibility, RET therapists communicate a faith in their clients' abilities to reconstruct their belief systems; to perceive, think, and act more rationally and effectively; and to accept the responsibility for their choices. Thus, while seldom communicating warmth or love, RET therapists regularly communicate unconditional acceptance of their clients. The therapeutic relationship of RET does not often produce transference, but should it occur, it is quickly analyzed (via the client's self-talk) and uprooted.

Initial Procedures and Strategies

With the absence of absolutes, no set or prescribed structure is available for the RET therapist to follow when initiating therapy. Although it is possible to learn from experienced therapists, RET therapists not only differ from each other in manner and style but also often vary their therapeutic approach from one client to another or from one session to another with the same client. Each client is unique, and each presents a unique set of conditions or circumstances for the therapist to assess and deal with creatively. Still, RET is an active-directive therapy, and although the client determines the content of the session, the structure, flexibly adjustable to variations in clients, is decided by the therapist.

Initiating Therapy   As with most therapies, the therapeutic relationship of RET is initiated with the first communication between client and therapist. The tone for what is to come is set. First impressions and statements are important. If opening remarks are inane, amounting to little more than the usual social icebreakers, they serve no purpose and, if prolonged, may prove ineffectual or even dysfunctional. The beginning of the session portends the expectations of therapy. The professional, businesslike opening is much more likely to instill client confidence and encourage the client to begin working on the antecedent concerns that have brought him or her to therapy.

Initial rapport building can usually be accomplished fairly quickly with most clients, but others require more time. The referred client, the frightened client, and the adolescent client are often reluctant. They may have little or no confidence in either the therapist or the therapy and may be unable or simply reluctant to talk about themselves. Until their fears and uncertainties have been reduced, any attempt to move into therapy proper is met with resistance.

Client Expectations   RET therapists are seldom interested in an extensive history of their clients, but many want to know whether their clients have ever been in therapy and, if so, the type of therapy they experienced. They may collect this information prior to therapy or during the first session; the purpose is to assess their clients' expectations of and experience with therapy. Congruent expectations of the client and therapist enhance the therapeutic effect. Conversely, incongruent expectations diminish therapeutic efficacy and often lead to the client's decision to leave therapy or to resist it. An accurate assessment of client expectations may help the therapist avoid unnecessary mistakes, as well as wasted time and effort.

Structuring   When the client is experiencing therapy for the first time or when the therapist's assessment of the client's expectations reveals disparity, **structuring** (defining the therapeutic process) may be in order. Intent on identifying and disputing their clients' irrational ideas and beliefs, many RET therapists—the inexperienced in particular—overlook the advantages of structuring when initiating therapy. These therapists tend to move into therapy before their clients are prepared to follow. In addition to an assessment of client expectations to uncover disparities in client and therapist goals, at least some assessment of client readiness for therapy seems advisable. Structuring not only provides a clear definition of RET for the client but also often helps to reduce the client's uncertainties, concerns, and fears about entering therapy, thus facilitating the initiating process and the client's expectation for change.

Structuring, or defining, the therapeutic process of RET typically includes an introduction to the ABC anatomy of emotion, a delineation of therapist and client behaviors and responsibilities, and a specification of and rationale for the goals of therapy. In addition, limits are clearly defined. Therapy schedules and fees are outlined and agreed to. Confidentiality is assured, especially when there is evidence of the vested interest of a third party—for example, the client's parents or a referral agent or agency. Further, many RET therapists use the initiating phase to inform their clients that therapy is not limited to the therapeutic session but that they will often be required to complete difficult assignments between sessions. To emphasize this point, specific readings, designed to define RET further and emphasize the importance of working and thinking about therapy between sessions, may be assigned during the first session. Carefully selected readings, tapes, and films or filmstrips can be used to persuade clients that thoughts are responsible for most emotions. Such supplementary homework assignments may save a great deal of time in future sessions.

RET therapists may judge their attempts at initiating therapy successful when their clients leave convinced that their decision to enter therapy was a good one, that there is a distinct possibility they will receive the help they seek, and that they have a fairly clear idea of what is expected of them and what they can expect from therapy.

Course of Psychotherapy

Because RET is cognitive, emotive–evocative, and behavioral, counselors and psychotherapists who practice it employ a wide variety of therapeutic techniques. Indeed, any therapeutic technique used in accordance with the theory of RET is considered legitimate, regardless of the system from which it was developed. RET counselors and psychotherapists may, for example, employ operant conditioning, self-management, problem-solving, and contract procedures; teach assertiveness and paradoxical intention; make use of biofeedback or instruct their clients in methods of thought stopping and focusing on non-disturbing or peaceful ideas; or give their clients lessons in general semantics and employ confronting humor. It appears, then, that the methods and techniques of RET are limited only by the creativity and ingenuity of the counselor or psychotherapist.

Techniques That Distinguish RET from Other Cognitive Therapies Although RET therapists have adopted the therapeutic techniques of other systems of psychotherapy, they also have developed a number of techniques that are distinctive to RET or that have been adapted to fit the RET format (see Figure 15-1):

Cognitive Disputation of Irrational Beliefs (DIBS). The DIBS technique, which follows the ABC format and which distinguishes RET from other cognitive therapies, is fundamental to RET's elegant solution—the restructuring of the client's belief system. RET therapists use the DIBS to assist their clients to gain and apply three separate but related insights:

1. Point A, the Activating Event in the client's presentation, is not the cause of Point C, the Consequent Emotion often accredited to Point A. Rather, clients feel disturbed and demonstrate inappropriate and self-defeating behaviors because of Point B, their Irrational Beliefs about Point A. That is, they make themselves disturbed, and they alone are responsible for their self-defeating behaviors.

2. Clients are not presently disturbed because of their past conditioning to think irrationally. Rather, they are presently creating their disturbance because they are presently reinforcing their past irrational thinking.

3. Since they are responsible for their past disturbed feeling and continue to reinforce their past irrational thinking, only repeated work and long practice can extinguish their irrational belief patterns of attitudes and values. Realizing that *A* does not cause *C* is not enough. Only the repeated disputing of irrational beliefs and earnest practice of new and actualizing behaviors are likely to bring about positive change in thoughts, feelings, and actions.

The DIBS technique is a process of questioning, usually the Socratic method, employed to teach clients a logico-empirical approach to knowledge and rational sensitivity.

1. What *evidence* do you have for this belief?
2. How do you *know* your belief is true?
3. Why *must* that be so?
4. How would that be so *awful*?
5. How does that belief make you *feel*?
6. Would that really be so *horrible*?

By requesting proof or justification from clients, the Socratic dialogue guides them through sentence-by-sentence disputations of their irrational beliefs. And because neither proof nor justification exists for irrational beliefs, RET clients learn to replace their irrational beliefs with beliefs that are rational. Moreover, by employing the Socratic teaching method, the therapist is teaching a problem-solving method that the client may use to achieve planned changes in the future.

Imaginal and Behavioral Disputation Techniques. Imaginal and/or behavioral techniques are employed after the clients have successfully challenged and disputed their irrational beliefs. The Imaginal Exercise asks clients to return in their imagination to Point A of their presenting problem, then to reveal their feelings at Point C. If, indeed, their feelings have changed as a result of their disputations, they are asked to review their current self-talk to reinforce their newly formed and valid assumptions about life. Conversely, if Point C is the same, there may be irrational beliefs not covered in the cognitive disputation, and the imagery exercise may help bring them to awareness. When this is accomplished, the DIBS technique is repeated.

Rational-Emotive Imagery (REI). Rational–Emotive Imagery is another imagery exercise adapted specifically for RET by Maxie Maultsby (1975), the founder of Rational Behavioral Therapy. Clients are asked to close their eyes and attempt to reexperience one of the inappropriate feelings at Point C. They are then asked what thoughts accompanied their feelings. After revealing their thoughts, they are instructed to shift to a more moderate feeling. Again, they are asked what thoughts they used to achieve the emotive shift. The purpose of REI is to demonstrate to clients that their irrational beliefs create strong negative emotions and that rational beliefs result in moderate, manageable emotions.

RET Homework Assignments. RET homework assignments are designed specifically to urge clients to think about and work on therapy beyond therapy sessions, to encourage clients to challenge and dispute their irrational ideas and beliefs, and to press clients to practice their newly acquired rational sensitivity. Walen, DiGiuseppe, and Wessler (1980) discuss four important characteristics of the RET homework assignment: "Consistency, Specificity, Systematic Follow Through, and Large Steps" (pp. 216–217). Homework assignments in RET may be cognitive, emotive, or behavioral, and they may include one or any combination of the following: reading, listening, viewing, writing, thinking, imagining, conditioning, and acting or behaving. Homework assignments in RET nearly always involve some risk since clients are usually asked to do the very thing they most fear. The client who demands perfection may be asked to select three tasks for the week and intentionally do them poorly. Clients who anticipate rejection from others may be instructed to collect at least three rejections a day for three consecutive days, and to note their self-talk immediately after each attempt. Careful assessment of the risk to the client is made before every homework assignment to be certain that the consequence of the behavior assigned is neither harmful nor damaging. The purpose of the assignment is to challenge the clients' irrational beliefs, not to reinforce them.

Extended Applications

In a very short time, RET was adapted to and found particularly applicable for group therapy. In RET groups, all group members were actively and directly taught to apply the principles of RET to one another. Further, under the supervision of an experienced group leader, group members were encouraged to risk practicing in the group setting new behaviors that fostered the restructuring of their belief systems. RET homework assignments were developed for the same purpose.

Today, RET is taught in schools, colleges, universities, social institutions, political organizations, community and agency centers, and hospitals. Through education and mass media, RET, primarily a psycho-educational process, is taught as a preventive therapy, and has been applied in numerous fields outside the mental health community, including politics, law enforcement, criminality, communication, corporate management and leadership, philosophy, anthropology, education, sports, sex and marriage relations, and parenting.

In addition to being available to professional and lay groups in pamphlets, articles, books, slides, films, audio and video cassettes, RET, since 1983, is available in computer software, and will soon be made available on laser disks. More than twenty standardized tests of irrationality presently exist, and have contributed significantly to psychotherapy outcome research.

Critique

As stated in the introduction to this chapter, Ellis was and continues to be a major force in the "cognitive shift" in psychology, particularly in the areas of counseling and psychotherapy and personality. His early work did much to make others aware that the human brain does more than simply receive, store, and retrieve data. Indeed, for Ellis, the human brain organizes, synthesizes, and transforms raw data (present experience, long- and short-term memory, emotions, and physical sensations) into an idiosyncratic, value-laden belief system that is compulsively expressed in simple declarative and imperative sentences, or "self-talk." Humans are more than their emotions and behavior; they are also cognitive beings. They view reality through the filter of their belief systems; then they talk to themselves about the view. What they think about the view has a greater determining impact on their emotions and behavior than the view itself; that is, they react more to what the stimulus (activating event) prompts them to think than they do to the stimulus.

Like Kelly (Chapter 14), Ellis believes that much of human misery can be traced to illogical and irrational ways people have of construing themselves, others, and the world. Further, he identified twelve of the most commonly held

1. The idea that you must—yes, must—have love or approval from all the people you find significant.

2. The idea that you must prove thoroughly competent, adequate, and achieving, or a saner but still foolish variation: The idea that you at least must have competence or talent in some important area.

3. The idea that when people act obnoxiously and unfairly, you should blame them and damn them, and see them as bad, wicked, or rotten individuals.

4. The idea that you have to view things as awful, terrible, horrible, and catastrophic when you get seriously frustrated, treated unfairly, or rejected.

5. The idea that emotional misery comes from external pressures and that you have little ability to control or change your feelings.

6. The idea that if something seems dangerous or fearsome, you must preoccupy yourself with and make yourself anxious about it.

7. The idea that you can more easily avoid facing many of life difficulties and self-responsibilities than undertake more rewarding forms of self-discipline.

8. The ideas that your past remains all-important and that because something once strongly influenced your life, it has to keep determining your feelings and behavior today.

9. The idea that people and things should turn out better than they do and they you must view it as awful and horrible if you do not find good solutions to life's grim realities.

10. The idea that you can achieve maximum human happiness by inertia or inaction of by passively and uncommittedly "enjoying yourself."

FIGURE 15-3   Ellis's Irrational Ideas

irrational beliefs that result in inappropriate and inordinately strong emotions and in dysfunctional or destructive behavior (see Figure 15-3).

In addition to articulating the role of cognition in human emotion and behavior, Ellis formulated a novel approach to counseling and psychotherapy that employs a large number of cognitive–emotive–behavioral therapeutic techniques that are highly active and directive in assisting RET clients to restructure their belief systems. Unlike that of other phenomenologists, Ellis's approach to counseling and psychotherapy urges RET clients to follow their newly acquired insights with action—specific changes in their behavior. The in vivo homework assignments, for example, are designed by the therapist expressly for this purpose.

RET has attracted a large group of adherents from nearly all schools of therapy and from practically every mental health profession, as well as from such professions as education, social work, business management, law enforcement, and corrections. Not surprisingly, it has also drawn a wide array of critics. Many of the criticisms leveled at George Kelly's Theory of Personal Constructs (Chapter 14) are also directed to RET: (1) Its view of humans is overly rational; (2) it totally disregards unconscious processes; (3) its ahistorical posture results in a lack of interest in human development; (4) it pays little attention to how humans learn; (5) it offers little understanding of human motivation; (6) it does an inadequate job of predicting behavior; (7) it offers little in the way of knowledge of how humans acquire and maintain their belief systems; and (8) it ignores the objective properties of stimuli and situational variables as predictors.

While RET is accepted by many as an effective approach to counseling and psychotherapy, far fewer are ready to include RET as a theory of personality, and those who do question its comprehensiveness. Human cognition, they assert, is a highly complex process, but its complexity is lost in the overly simplified concept of self-talk.

Although the literature of RET research is expanding (see "Heuristic Influences," this chapter), critics point out that inferences about causality are largely drawn from correlation coefficients, rather than from the experimental method. Further, they state that in their present form many of the major hypotheses of RET are ambiguous and untestable. While the clinical evidence for RET is impressive, much of the reported research relies exclusively on self-reports and ignores "noncognitive" processes.

It should be noted that as with the criticisms of all personality theories, some of the criticisms levied at RET are more the reflections of the critics' personal biases and misunderstanding than they are legitimate evaluations of the theory. Many of the weaknesses of Ellis's theory are found also in other phenomenological and cognitive theories.

Annotated Bibliography

Ellis, A. (1975). *Growth Through Reason.* Hollywood, CA: Wilshire Book Company (originally published in 1971 by the Institute for Rational Living).

This book, which contains a series of verbatim therapy transcripts, has been reported as especially helpful for the counselor attempting to enhance his or her skills in RET. It is possible for the reader to follow Ellis and other experienced RET practitioners as they counsel with clients experiencing a variety of problems.

Ellis, A. (1975a). *Reason and emotion in psychotherapy.* Hollywood, CA: Wilshire (originally published 1962 by Lyle Stuart, New York).

This book, written primarily as a textbook, is used widely in counselor education and clinical psychology programs. It is Ellis's first comprehensive presentation of his theory of Rational–Emotive Therapy and is highly recommended for counselor and clinical psychologist candidates.

Ellis, A., & Grieger, R. (Eds.). (1977). *Handbook of rational-emotive therapy.* New York: Springer.

This book is a comprehensive collection of papers on RET. Contributors in addition to Ellis and Grieger include such writers as Arnold Lazarus, Aaron Beck, Michael Mahoney, and Donald Meichenbaum. The major sections of the book are: Theoretical and Conceptual Foundations of RET; Dynamics of Emotional Disturbances; Primary Techniques and Basic Processes; and RET Applied to Children.

Ellis, A., & Harper, R. A. (1975). *A new guide to rational living.* Englewood Cliffs, NJ: Prentice Hall; and Hollywood, CA: Wilshire Books.

Referred to by RET advocates as simply *The New Guide*, this book is a completely revised edition of their classic self-help book, *A Guide to Rational Living* (1961), a book that counselors and psychotherapists have for years most often recommended to their clients. Written in E-Prime (no form of the verb "to be" appears in the book), Ellis and Harper demonstrate how people can themselves challenge and dispute the ten most common irrational ideas they employ to create most of their emotional problems. This book is highly recommended for beginning students in counseling and psychotherapy who are interested in learning more about how the theory of RET works.

Ellis, A., & Dryden, W. (1987). *The practice of rational-emotive therapy.* New York: Springer Publishing Company.

Possibly the best single source for the practice of RET is Ellis and Dryden's (1987) book by that title. Their book offers the most systematic, detailed presentation to date of the most popular clinical modes of RET therapy, including individual, group, couples, family, and marathon therapy. Other books that also do an excellent job of demonstrating the major clinical application of RET are:

Walen, S. R., DeGiuseppe, R., & Wessler, R. I. (1980). *A practitioner's guide to rational-emotive therapy.* New York: Oxford University Press; and

Wessler, R. A., & Wessler, R. L. (1980). *The principles and practice of rational-emotive therapy.* San Francisco: Jossey-Bass.

References and Suggested Readings

Abrahms, E. (1983). Cognition and major mental disorders. In R. Grieger & I. Z. Grieger (Eds.), *Cognition and emotional disturbance.* New York: Human Services Press, pp. 133–145.

Baars, B. J. (1986). *The cognitive revolution in psychology.* New York: The Guilford Press.

Beck, A. T. (1976). *Cognitive therapy and the emotional disorders.* New York: International Universities Press.

DiGiuseppe, R., Miller, N. J., & Trexler, L. D. (1979). A review of rational–emotive psychotherapy outcome studies. In A. Ellis & J. M. Whiteley (Eds.), *Theoretical and empirical foundations of rational–emotive therapy*. Monterey, CA: Brooks/Cole, pp. 218–235.

DiGiuseppe, R. (1982). Problems of children and their parents. In R. Grieger & I. Z. Grieger (Eds.), *Cognition and emotional disturbance*. New York: Human Services Press, pp. 212–225.

Dryden, W. (1989). Albert Ellis: An efficient and passionate life. *Journal of Counseling and Development, 67*(10), pp. 539–546.

Dryden, W., & Ellis, A. (1988). Rational–emotive therapy. In K. S. Dobson (Ed.), *Handbook of cognitive-behavioral therapies*. New York: The Guilford Press, pp. 214–272.

Ellis, A. (1957). *How to live with a neurotic at home and at work* (Rev. ed.). New York: Crown Publishers.

Ellis, A. (1966). The case against religion: A psychotherapist's view. In B. N. Ard, Jr. (Ed.), *Counseling and psychotherapy*. Palo Alto, CA: Science and Behavior Books, pp. 270–282.

Ellis, A. (1972a). *Executive leadership: A rational approach*. Secaucus, NJ: Citadel Press.

Ellis, A. (1972b). Psychotherapy without tears. In A. Burton (Ed.), *Twelve therapists*. San Francisco: Jossey–Bass, pp. 103–126.

Ellis, A. (1973). Can there be a rational concept of healthy personality? *The Counseling Psychologist, 4*:2, pp. 45–47.

Ellis, A. (1974). *Humanistic psychotherapy: The rational-emotive approach*. New York: McGraw–Hill (Originally published 1973 by Julian Press, New York).

Ellis, A. (1975a). *Reason and emotion in psychotherapy*. Hollywood, CA: Wilshire. (Originally published 1962 by Lyle Stuart, New York)

Ellis, A. (1975b). The essence of rational–emotive therapy. In F. N. Ard (Ed.), *Counseling and psychotherapy: Classics on theories and issues* (Rev. ed.). Palo Alto, CA: Science and Behavior Books, pp. 169–189.

Ellis, A. (1976). Rational-emotive therapy. In W. S. Sahakian (Ed.), *Psychotherapy and counseling: Techniques in intervention* (2nd ed.). Chicago: Rand McNally College Publishing Company, pp. 272–285.

Ellis, A. (1977). Rational-emotive therapy: Research data that support the clinical and personality hypotheses of RET and other modes of cognitive-behavior therapy. *Counseling Psychologist, 7*,(1), pp. 2–44.

Ellis, A. (1979). The rational-emotive approach to counseling. In H. M. Burks, Jr., & B. Stefflre (Eds.), *Theories of Counseling* (3rd ed.). New York: McGraw–Hill.

Ellis, A. (1982). Psychoneurosis and anxiety problems. In R. Grieger & I. Z. Grieger (Eds.), *Cognition and emotional disturbance*. New York: Human Services Press, pp. 17–45.

Ellis, A. (1984). Rational–emotive therapy. In R. Corsini (Ed.), *Current psychotherapies* (3rd ed.). Itasca, IL: F. E. Peacock, pp. 196–238.

Ellis, A. (1985). *Overcoming resistance: Rational-emotive therapy with difficult clients*. New York: Springer Publishing Company.

Ellis, A. (1987). The evolution of rational-emotive therapy (RET) and cognitive behavior therapy (CBT). In J. K. Zeig (Ed.), *The evolution of psychotherapy*. New York: Brunner/Mazel, pp. 107–125.

Ellis, A., & Abrahms, E. (1978). *Brief psychotherapy in medical and health practice*. New York: Springer Publishing Company.

Ellis, A., & Dryden, W. (1987). *The practice of rational-emotive therapy (RET)*. New York: Springer Publishing Company.

Ellis, A., & Grieger, R. (1977). *Handbook of rational-emotive therapy*. New York: Springer Publishing Company.

Ellis, A., & Harper, R. A. (1975). *A guide to rational living.* Englewood Cliffs, NJ: Prentice–Hall.

Ellis, A., & Knaus, W. (1977). *Overcoming procrastination.* New York: Institute for Rational Living.

Ellis, A., & Whiteley, Jr. (1979). *Theoretical and empirical foundations of rational-emotive therapy.* Monterey, CA: Brooks/Cole.

Grieger, R., & Grieger, I. (Eds.), (1982). *Cognition and emotional disturbance.* New York: Human Services Press.

Hartig, M., & Kanfer, F. H. (1976). The role of verbal self-instructions in children's resistance to temptation. *Journal of Personality and Social Psychology, 25*(2), pp. 259–267.

Holroyd, D. A. (1976). Cognition and desensitization in the group treatment of test anxiety. *Journal of Consulting and Clinical Psychology, 44*(6), pp. 991–1000.

Keller, F. F., Croake, J. W., & Brooking, J. Y. (1975). Effects of a program in rational thinking on anxieties in older persons. *Journal of Counseling Psychology, 22*(1), pp. 534–57.

Kopp, S. (1978). *An end to innocence.* New York: Macmillan.

Lembo, J. (1974). *Help yourself.* Niles, Il: Charles C. Thomas.

Maultsby, M. C. (1975). *Help yourself to happiness.* New York: Institute for Rational Living.

Maxwell, J. W., & Wilkerson, J. (1982). Anxiety reduction through group instruction in rational therapy. *The Journal of Psychology, 112,* pp. 135–140.

Moleski, R., & Tosi, D. J. Comparative psychotherapy: Rational-emotive therapy versus systematic desensitization in the treatment of stuttering. *Journal of Consulting and Clinical Psychology, 44*(2), pp. 309–311.

Morris, D. T., & Kanitz, H. M. (1975). *Rational-emotive therapy.* Boston: Houghton Mifflin.

Newhorn, P. (January, 1978). Albert Ellis. *Human Behavior, 7,* pp. 30–35.

Newmark, C. S., Frerking, R. A., Cook, L., & Newmark, L. (1973). Endorsement of Ellis' irrational beliefs as a function of psychopathology. *Journal of Clinical Psychology, 29,* pp. 300–302.

Thurman, C. W. (September, 1983). Effects of a rational–emotive treatment program on Type A behavior among college students. *Journal of College Student Personnel, 24*(5), pp. 417–423.

Walen, S. R., DeGiuseppe, R., & Wessler, R. I. (1980). *A practitioner's guide to rational-emotive therapy.* New York: Oxford University Press.

Wallace, W. A. (1986). *Theories of counseling and psychotherapy: A basic issues approach.* Boston: Allyn and Bacon.

Wallace, W. A., & Maddox, E. N. (1981). *Rational-emotive therapy and the rehabilitation counselor.* Unpublished manuscript.

Weinrach, S. G. (November, 1980). Unconventional therapist: Albert Ellis. *Personnel and Guidance Journal,* pp. 152–160.

Wessler, R. A., & Wessler, R. L. (1980). *The principles and practice of rational-emotive therapy.* San Francisco: Jossey–Bass.

Young, H. (1974). *A rational counseling primer.* New York: Institute for Rational Living.

Young, H. (1981). Rational counseling with resistant adolescent clients: Joining forces against a common enemy. *RET Work, 1*(2), pp. 1–4.

Part 7

Social-Cognitive Theory

Albert Bandura was selected to represent this particular theoretical approach to human personality. Initially a social learning theorist, Bandura refers to his mature theory of personality as a social-cognitive theory.

Bandura demonstrated experimentally that much of our learning occurs as the result of modeling another's behavior. Moreover, he demonstrated that learning often occurs in large segments, and though some reinforcement is necessary for retention, learning can and does occur without external reinforcement. In short, Bandura relegates external reinforcement to a facilitative rather than a primary role. Radical behaviorists take issue with Bandura's position, for if accepted, it points to a serious error in their belief that we are solely the products of our external reinforcement history.

Positive incentives (whether formulated cognitively or externally) facilitate development of competencies and interests that are personally satisfying and that promote self-efficacy. Bandura also demonstrated that we develop a personal set of self-standards which we then use to measure our success or failure. If we meet or exceed our standards, an external reinforcement has reinforcement value. Conversely, if we fall below our standards, external reinforcement is ineffective.

Conceptualized in terms of reciprocal determinism, the self acts as a cognitive contributory influence that interacts reciprocally within a system of personal (including cognition), behavioral, and environmental influences.

Anticipatory reinforcement is internal and transcends external reinforcement and control, while at the same time fostering a person's sense of self-esteem and self-regard. Bandura's theoretical stance on the development of human personality, then, is one of reciprocal, or "soft," determinism.

For a relative newcomer to the theoretical arena, Bandura has exerted a tremendous impact on both the experimental and applied fields of psychology. Though some personologists believe he has yet to develop a comprehensive theory of personality, his theory is highly flexible and continues to evolve in light of new research. It seems reasonable to assume that Bandura's theory of personality has not yet reached its full potential. It is equally reasonable to assume that it holds considerable promise of becoming a fully developed personality theory.

Chapter *16*

Bandura's Social-Cognitive Theory

Chapter Overview

Introduction

Biographical Sketch

Resolutions of the Eleven Basic Issues
  Heredity versus Social Determinants
  Explanation of the Learning Process
  Conscious versus Unconscious Determinants
  Early versus Continuous Development
  Role Assigned to Self-Concept
  Determinism versus Freedom of Choice
  Centrality of Reinforcement
  Number and Weight Assigned to Motivational Concepts
  Importance of Group Determinants
  Subjective versus Objective Reality
  Uniqueness versus Universality

Psychological Health and Psychopathology

Heuristic Influence

Applications to Psychotherapy
  Therapeutic Goals
  Therapeutic Relationship

Initial Procedures and Strategies
Course of Psychotherapy

Extended Applications

Critique

Annotated Bibliography

References and Suggested Readings

Introduction

Impressive theoretical and experimental advances in the field of social learning convinced Albert Bandura that the traditional theories of learning were too circumscribed to explain adequately the acquisition, maintenance, and modification of complex human behavior. He was equally persuaded that on both conceptual and social grounds, the predictive efficacy of the psychodynamic theories of personality, with their emphasis on what he believed to be dubious unconscious forces, was poor and their theoretical formulations suspect (Bandura, 1986). Reviewing evidence from carefully controlled experimental research studies that emphasized human rather than animal subjects, Bandura set out to extend and modify many of the accepted learning perspectives. The result of his effort is an interesting, innovative, and optimistic theory of personality development and behavioral change that differs significantly from the classical learning and psychodynamic theories.

Bandura (Bandura & Walters, 1963; Bandura, 1969, 1973, 1977a, 1986) agrees with B. F. Skinner (Chapter 13) that with the exception of the basic reflexes, practically all human behavior (whether manifestly normal or abnormal) is learned. Further—and this is where he and Skinner part company—Bandura (1969, 1977a, 1986) demonstrates that most human behavior is learned in large segments through example, by observing the behavior of others. Indeed, Bandura (1969) suggests that the role of operant conditioning be limited to regulating performance of behavioral sequences once they have been learned through observation. Bandura (1977a) argues that observational learning or **modeling** (vicarious learning—observing the behavior modeled by others) is not only more efficient than operant conditioning but also leads to generalizations beyond the behavior that was observed.

Perhaps Bandura's (1969, 1977a, 1977b) greatest break from traditional learning theory is his focus on human **cognition** (thought, ideation). For Bandura (1977a), "A theory that denies that thoughts can regulate actions does not lend itself readily to the explanation of complex behavior" (p. 10).

Bandura (1977a, 1978a, 1986; Staddon, 1984) is a determinist, but he refers to a **reciprocal determinism.** Personal (*including cognition*), behavioral, and situational factors are continually in a state of triadic reciprocal interaction. The implication of Bandura's reciprocal deterministic stance is that humans not only react to environmental forces or stimuli, but they also select, interpret, organize, predict, anticipate, assign meaning, and transform the environmental stimuli that impinge on them. In short, people play a significant part in the reciprocal interaction that determines who they are and what they do.

With their cognitive processes and capacity to **symbolize** (to use language), humans actively mediate in the direction of their own destinies. If, as Bandura (1977a) asserts, cognition exerts a reciprocal causal influence on behavior, humans enjoy some degree of **freedom** (the number of options available and the right to exercise them) in their actions. Bandura (1977a) expresses it best in the Preface to *Social Learning Theory:* "The extraordinary capacity of humans to use symbols enables them to represent events, to analyze their conscious experience, to communicate with others at any distance in time and space, to plan, to create, to imagine, and to engage in foresightful action" (p. vii).

Based on rigorous experimental studies, Bandura's innovative theory of social-cognitive learning promises to become an exciting force in personality theory, as well as a therapeutic approach. The number of counselors and psychologists receiving training in the theory and applications of Bandura's approach to social-cognitive learning grows steadily. Bandura's concepts have already made a forceful impact in the field of personality development. His theory is being accepted both as a method of research and as a means of changing human behavior.

Biographical Sketch of the Theorist

Early Years

Albert Bandura was born December 4, 1925, to Joseph and Jessie (Berazanski) Bandura. He spent his early and adolescent years on a wheat farm in the remote northern hamlet of Mundare in the province of Alberta, Canada. Mundare is best known for its beautiful rugged terrain and frigidly cold climate.

At that time, Mundare had but one school, only two teachers, and few resources for the twenty elementary and secondary students in attendance. When the responsibility for teaching all subjects for twelve grade levels rests on the efforts of only two teachers, there is little time for individual attention. Bandura learned early that he was expected to rely upon his own academic initiative, a lesson that was to serve him well in later years.

The summer before entering college Bandura took a job working on a road crew filling holes in the Alaskan highway. Many of the men with whom he worked that summer had fled to Alaska to escape "creditors, alimony, and probation officers;" their behavior instilled in Bandura "a keen appreciation for the psychopathology of everyday life" (*American Psychologist,* January, 1981, p. 28).

Education

Bandura was admitted to the University of British Columbia in Vancouver in 1946. Three years later, he received his B.S. degree with the Bolocan Award in psychology. He immediately began graduate work in psychology at the University of Iowa, receiving his M.A. degree in 1951. He was granted the Ph.D. degree the following year. It was at the University of Iowa that Bandura met Virginia B. Varnes, his future wife.

Following a one-year post-doctoral internship at the Guidance Center in Wichita, Kansas, Bandura was appointed to the faculty of Stanford University, a position he held for more than thirty-five years. He was granted a full professorship in 1964, and chaired the Department of Psychology in 1976 and 1977. Bandura was awarded an endowed chair in 1974, the David Starr Jordon Professor of Social Science in Psychology.

Emergence of Social Learning Theory

At Stanford University Bandura found an academic milieu that was close to ideal. In addition to working with distinguished colleagues and gifted students, he was free to pursue his own interests and was often involved in several areas of research concurrently. Always a productive scholar, Bandura has published experimental studies in such areas as the role of observational learning in human behavior (Bandura & Walters, 1963; Bandura, 1971, 1977a, 1977b; Carroll & Bandura, 1982), vicarious reinforcement (1977a, 1977b), aggressive behavior (Bandura & Walters, 1963; Bandura, 1973, 1978b), phobic disorders (Bandura, 1969, 1977a, 1976), human cognition as a mediating agent (Bandura 1977b, 1978a), and psychotherapeutic change (Bandura, 1969, 1977a). Later in his career, his research interests led him to problems in **human agency** (personal control), such as self-referent thought, self-percepts of efficacy (Bandura, 1977a, 1978b, 1980, 1986; Bandura & Cervone, 1983), and self-regulatory mechanisms (Bandura 1977a, 1986). It was from his own and his students' research efforts that social-cognitive theory emerged.

In addition to his teaching and research, Bandura has served on numerous committees, advisory boards, research panels, and federal agencies, and he has been active in the American Psychological Association (APA). He also manages to find time for hiking with his wife and daughters, Mary and Carol, in the Sierras, attending the San Francisco Opera, and enjoying the restaurants in the Bay area.

Accomplishments and Awards

Bandura spent the year 1969 as fellow of the Center for Advanced Study in the Behavioral Sciences at Stanford University. He was a recipient of a Guggenheim Fellowship in 1972. That same year, he received the Distinguished Scientist Award from Division 12 of the APA. In 1973, he accepted the Distinguished Scientific Achievement Award from the California Psychological Association. He was further honored in 1974 by being elected president of the APA. In 1977, he received the James Mckeen Cattell Award. The University of British Columbia recognized his achievements in 1979 by conferring on him an honorary doctor of science degree. In 1980, Bandura received the Distinguished Contribution Award from the International Society for Research on Aggression, was named a fellow of the American Academy of Arts and Science, and was honored by his peers, again, with the Distinguished Scientific Contributions Award, one of the highest awards that can be bestowed on a member of the APA.

Bandura has served as a consultant to government committees and organizations, including the Veterans' Administration. Further, he has served on the editorial boards of approximately twenty professional journals, including a lengthy assignment as series editor of social learning for Prentice–Hall. Bandura has seen his work accepted by increasing numbers of psychologists, therapists, and counselors throughout the United States and Canada, perhaps the greatest recognition granted any theorist.

Resolutions of the Eleven Basic Issues

Like the majority of theorists selected for presentation in this book, Bandura does not specifically address all eleven of the basic issues. The following resolutions represent a combination of Bandura's and the current writer's interpretations of Bandura's response to each issue. Although each resolution was formed only after careful review of Bandura's major works, there is no guarantee that he would grant full endorsement or that he would agree to the writer's hierarchical arrangement.

Most of Bandura's books were included in the search for issue resolution; however, heaviest reliance was placed on *Social Learning Theory (1977a) and Social Foundation of Thought and Action: A Social Cognitive Theory* (1986). It is in these two major works that Bandura presents his readers with the most succinct yet comprehensive views of his unique approach to human learning and personality development.

Heredity versus Social Determinants

Except for our basic reflexes, Bandura (1979a) believes that nearly all behavior is learned and that learning occurs as a result of continuous and reciprocal triadic interaction between personal, behavioral, and environmental determinants. Never do these determinants function independently, and never is any one the sole determinant of our behavior. Rather, they are **reciprocally interlocking** (each influencing the others synergistically).

In this **triadic model,** behavioral factors (B), personal factors (P) including cognition, and environmental factors (E) all operate interactively, as mutual, two-way directional determinants, each reciprocally affecting the other two. As interlocking causal forces, behavior, person, and environment determine each other and together are the cause of all psychosocial functioning.

In this triadic reciprocal determinism the term reciprocal *is defined as mutual action between events, and the term* determinism *signifies the production of effects by events. Because of the multiplicity of interacting determinants, events are associated with effects probabilistically rather than inevitably (Bandura, 1983a, p. 166).*

Reciprocity, in this instance, insists that causes be considered in a two-way direction (see Figure 16-1) and that personal factors include the individual's thought processes.

We contribute to our environmental influences by our thoughts—memories, beliefs, preferences, predictions, anticipations, self-perceptions, and so on—as well as our actions. We partly determine which external events we will observe, how we will perceive these events, what relevance and efficacy the events have for us, and how the information the events convey will be organized and classified for future use. We are, therefore, *partial* creators of both past and present situations in our lives, *but only partial creators.* Numerous other factors (institutional and physical) also contribute to the sequential nature of our life situations.

As beings in the world we cannot be separated from our environment. We influence and in turn are influenced by it. Likewise, we cannot be considered independent of our behavior, because our behavior generates experiences that also influence what we subsequently do and what we become. Further, our present behavior will affect the patterns of our future behavior. Viewed from Bandura's rather optimistic perspective, we individually possess a vast potentiality that can be molded by direct and vicarious experience into a diversity of forms within the boundaries set by our biology.

We are neither unconsciously driven by inner impulses or needs nor helplessly battered by environmental stimuli. Within Bandura's social-cognitive learning approach, covert, symbolic, vicarious, and self-regulatory processes provide an internal deterministic triad of possible behavioral alternatives to given environmental stimuli or circumstances. We have the ability to **encode** (use familiar reductive memory aids or codes) and **symbolize** (use language to describe and elaborate) environmental events and to anticipate, from experience, what particular behaviors will result in specific consequences.

Bandura (1977a) acknowledges that our biology largely defines the limits of what, when, and how adequately we learn. In addition, he recognizes numerous physiological conditions that can motivate us to act. Pain is a good example, as is the aversive stimulation that arises from tissue deficit (i.e., hunger or thirst). Further, Bandura is aware that our heredity can determine physical characteristics that influence the kinds of reinforcements we receive from others in a particular culture, especially the reinforcement we receive from others during the important early years of development and the initial formation of self-efficacy. For example, the attractive child is more likely to receive positive feedback, and the taller of two children is more likely to be perceived as possessing greater athletic skills. For Bandura, however, most of our behavior is learned, and genetic factors are assumed to have a relatively minor role in the overall and ongoing learning process.

While Bandura places greater emphasis on environmental than on biological determinants, he recognizes that our responses, whether affective or physical, are not dependent solely on external stimuli. Our thoughts about environmental events can regulate our responses. We are not simply passive reactors to external influences; there is potential in Bandura's theory for at least some intentional behavior.

In summary, Bandura's stance on this issue is one of reciprocal determinism. Our biology, actions, and environment are potentialities that interact reciprocally, each determining the other.

The strength of each of these three bi-directional deterministic forces varies in different situations and for different activities. There are occasions when environmental factors are the strongest of the three determinants, and other times when personal factors override environmental factors to becomes the predominant influence. There are times, too, when the intrinsic feedback of behavior becomes the central force in the reciprocal system. For the person who has fallen over the side of the boat into swift current, swimming (a motoric response) is the dominant determinant. When taking an important and difficult examination, cognitive factors usually play the major role in reciprocal determinism. The young man entering basic training in the Army may find environmental factors (e.g., the drill instructor) exerting the strongest influence on his behavior. Internal feedback may play the major role in the triadic system for the young person faced with the dilemma of choosing between resignation from a valued position and yielding to a supervisor's request to do something that conflicts with personal standards. Still, in most instances, these three causal processes of psychosocial functioning—

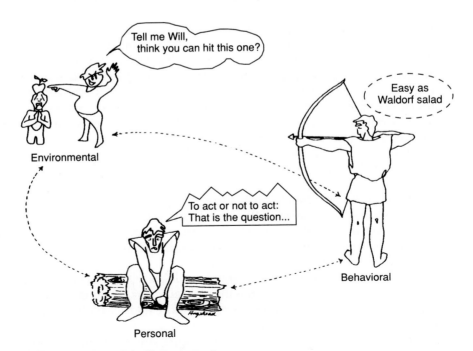

FIGURE 16-1 Triadic Interaction

behavior, environment, and person—are all highly interdependent and interlocking.

Explanation of Learning Process

As its name implies, Bandura's Theory of Social-Cognitive Learning is founded on the phenomenon of learning. Although he does not deny the effect of external reinforcement on learning, by stressing the intervening influence of human cognition Bandura (1969, 1977a) relegates external reinforcement to a facilitative rather than a necessary role in the learning process. He contends that reciprocal deterministic factors other than response consequences often influence what people attend to, and therefore, he assigns external reinforcement to a role compatible with a cognitive orientation and the broad effects of modeling.

Bandura and Walters (1963) and Bandura (1969, 1977a, 1986) demonstrate that we can and do learn novel behavior simply by attending to the performance of others who serve as models. Further, Bandura (1969, 1977a) maintains that much of the learning acquired through modeling is acquired in large segments or in total, without either an overt response to the witnessed behavior or the administration of external reinforcement. In fact, because of our ability to symbolize, modeling is often symbolic rather than behavioral. We can model a behavior by reading or listening to a description of it. We can translate a visual image into symbols that can be stored in memory and recalled far more efficiently than visual images alone.

Once a modeled behavior is symbolized, we can "cognitively" relate anticipated consequences of that behavior to personal standards, values, and goals (see "Self-Regulation"). We can, through the use of symbols, rehearse a wide spectrum of behaviors (e.g., dangerous or feared behaviors) before attempting them or solve complex problems by cognitively testing various alternatives and their anticipated consequences, executing only favored symbolic actions and solutions. A large portion of our learning is not only the result of modeling but also is mediated by cognition.

According to Bandura (1969, 1976, 1977a, 1986) certain interrelated cognitive-perceptual processes must occur for modeling to be effective:

1. *Attention processes:* Exposure to a model is insufficient for learning to occur unless: (a) attention is paid to the model's behavior, (b) the observer's perception is accurate, and (c) the most relevant stimuli are selected for symbolization. Learning is first a perceptual process. Discriminating observation is a requisite condition to the appearance of modeling.

2. *Retention processes:* Observers of modeled behavior must encode and represent symbolically the behavior they observe for learning to occur. Symbolic images are more permanent and easier to store and recall. It helps, for example, if the observers encode the observed behavior episodically and procedurally— mentally talk themselves through the sequential stages of the behavior being modeled.

3. *Motor reproduction processes:* Motor reproduction can occur on two levels: (a) actual practice of the modeled behavior, including feedback regarding accuracy, or (b) internal, or covert, rehearsal of the model's behavioral sequence. For instance, role play helps the individual to rehearse a new skill (e.g, assertiveness) incrementally until it is mastered. Likewise, **imagery** (mental visualization) allows the learner mentally to approximate skill practice and acquisition.

4. *Incentive and motivational processes:* Vicarious or anticipated positive reinforcement, although unnecessary for learning to occur, can increase the likelihood of actual performance of the behavior being observed and learned. In contrast, vicarious or anticipated punishment tends to inhibit actual performance of the behavior being observed and learned.

Bandura and Walters (1963) and Bandura (1977a) point to other factors that may also influence our tendency to perform the modeled behavior we learn. These influences include: (1) our perceptions of the characteristics of the models and their self-attributes, personal standards and valued goals, the complexity of

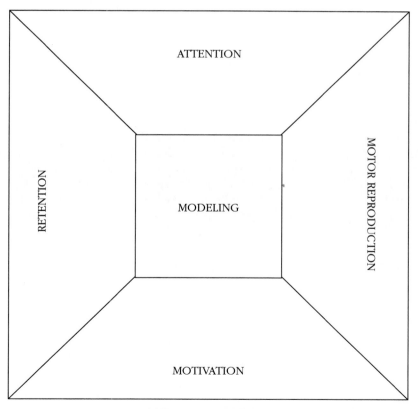

FIGURE 16-2   Four necessary processes for observational learning

the behavior, and (2) the external, vicarious, and anticipated reinforcements the models receive.

We are more likely to repeat a behavior we learn when the model observed is someone similar to ourselves in sex, age, background, and appearance. We are also prone to reproduce the behavior of a model we respect and admire and to whom we attribute prestige or status. We are more likely to be influenced by modeled behavior when we are suffering from low self-esteem or low self-efficacy. We tend to emulate a model's behavior when we observe modeled behaviors that are congruent with our personal behavioral standards and valued goals. And we are more likely to repeat modeled behaviors that have been reinforced, whether that reinforcement is external, vicarious, or anticipated.

According to Bandura (1977b), we function as active **agents** "who transform, classify, and organize modeling stimuli into easily remembered schemes rather than as quiescent cameras or tape recorders that store isomorphic representations of modeled events" (p. 199). We think, aspire, value, plan, and anticipate. We are not, then, mere accumulations of conditioned responses. By recognizing the mediating role of cognition in the acquisition, retention, and expression of behavior, social learning theory increases the dimension of our learning processes to include social behaviors and social reinforcers, as well as the more abstract concepts of language, conversation, personal values and standards of moral reasoning, and the functional influence of precepts of self-efficacy.

The Impact of Chance Encounters on Life Paths Bandura (1982b, 1986) recognizes that chance encounters (unintended meetings with previously unknown persons) may have tremendous impact on the paths we take in life. A personal example of just such an encounter occurred during my first year in teaching. Persuaded by a fellow teacher in a neighboring classroom to join him in a graduate class, I was influenced by my chance encounter with Dwight L. Arnold, a dynamic professor whose enthusiasm for counseling and psychology drew me away from my teaching field and into the counseling profession. More common examples are the numerous married couples who relate the chance encounters that ended in marriage.

The impacts of chance encounters are not always positive. Bandura (1982) writes about Paul "Tex" Watkins, an excellent student who decided to visit an acquaintance while on a tour across the United States. Unknown to him his friend had moved, and living in the cabin at the address his friend had given him was the Manson "family," who recruited Watkins into their way of life.

While predicting the occurrence of chance encounters is impossible, Bandura (1982b, 1986) points out that once they occur, chance encounters are subject to the same reciprocal determinants as all other events. Hence, their probable impact can be assessed.

Conscious versus Unconscious Determinants

Bandura believes behavior is learned and experience must be conscious for learning to occur. He finds neither need nor reason to ascribe any human behavior to elaborate unconscious conflicts, impulses, or motivations that require exposure or alleviation (Bandura & Walters, 1963; Bandura, 1977a). We are not, according to Bandura, driven by mysterious, prohibitive inner forces, nor are we pulled by any innate actualizing tendency. Rather, we are largely conscious, thinking beings. We cognitively select, organize, and transform the stimuli that we encounter. Further, we have the capacity to observe and interpret the effects of our behavior and the behavior of others, to form expectations, and to anticipate behavioral outcomes. We develop personal sets of rules and standards against which we evaluate our actions and gauge the value of both external and self-rewards (Bandura, 1977a, 1982a).

Unlike either the classic psychodynamic or behaviorist approaches, Social-Cognitive Theory (Bandura, 1986) acknowledges self-awareness and other forms of internal regulatory influences on behavior: "Human functioning, in fact, involves interrelated control systems in which behavior is determined by external stimulus events, by internal information-processing systems and regulating codes, and by reinforcing response-feedback processes" (Bandura, 1969, p. 19).

Not only does Bandura (Bandura & Walters, 1963) oppose any concept of an omnipotent (all-influencing) entity in the form of an unconscious mind, he also argues that preoccupation with internal response-producing agents results in neglect of external variables, including variables that have been demonstrated experimentally to exert control over learning and overt social behavior.

Early versus Continuous Development

Bandura (1977a) rejects the idea that early childhood experiences function as permanent determinants that will be expressed in all future behavior. With our capacity to observe, to think, to symbolize, to communicate with self and others, and to set goals and standards of behavior, we often replace early learning with new learning and revised behavior standards. For Bandura (1977a, 1986), thinking in terms of critical life stages is counterproductive in the study of human development. He can find no place in reciprocal determinism for the restraining nature of *stages as concepts.* Critical life stages, Bandura (1963, 1986) asserts, serve only to categorize children into fixed types, and then, unfortunately, to view them in terms of a stereotypical category rather than as individuals with unique thoughts, emotions, and actions. Bandura (1986) prefers to be free of typological stage thinking and to explore potentialities for cognitive development and diversity of cognitive functioning. Further, Bandura (1986) argues: "Stage theories lend themselves to excusing weak instructional programs that are supposed to foster intellectual development" (p. 490). For the stage theorists, Bandura (1986) states: Deficiencies in learning are too often explained away as a lack of readiness.

Although Bandura does not agree with the stage theorists, he does recognize the significance of early childhood.

> *By repeatedly observing that environmental events occur with action but not in its absence, infants learn about contingent relations between actions and effects. Infants who experience success in controlling environmental events become more attentive to*

their own behavior and more competent in learning new efficacious responses than infants for whom the same environmental events occur regardless of how they behave (Bandura, 1986, p. 414).

In a surprisingly short period of time the infant's exercise of control over the social environment begins to play an important role in his or her development of self-efficacy.

It is during our early years, too, that we develop our ability to use symbols, an ability that greatly enhances observational learning, the formation of self-efficacy, and the establishment of internal behavioral and achievement standards, all of which facilitate greater self-control and self-regulation.

According to Bandura (1977a, 1982b, 1986), three factors contribute to human developmental directions: physical maturation, experiences with the social world, and cognitive development. Of these three factors, Bandura considers physical development the least important to social learning, though it is necessary if we are to repeat much of the behavior we observe.

Experience with the environment facilitates social development. First, as children we acquire a repertoire of behaviors. We encounter a social world constituted of models to observe and people (or situations) who apply both positive and negative reinforcements. By experiencing external reinforcement in various situations, we learn which of our behaviors are deemed appropriate and inappropriate within our particular social milieu. We are motivated to behave in ways that are socially approved. Second, we encounter different social environments at different ages, and the changes we experience enhance our development as we move into greater social participation.

During early childhood in particular, we undergo extreme changes in cognitive development. Our attention, memory, and cognitive organization evolve both rapidly and importantly. For Bandura (1977a, 1978a, 1982a, 1986), one especially significant developmental change that occurs during early childhood is our growing capacity to translate observations into symbols. "A great deal of human thought is linguistically based" (Bandura, 1986, p. 498). Cognitive development makes observational learning more flexible, efficient, and lasting. With the ability to use symbols, we can rehearse and store in memory what we observe. Further, as our cognitive ability develops, we gain the ability to recombine symbols and to form hypotheses.

Both physical and social events can be abstracted, formulated, and tested. No longer do we need to see a specific behavior modeled in order to learn it. We can read a description of a behavior and reproduce it. We can listen to an instruction and carry it out. Further, with cognitive development and the use of language, we are predisposed to represent future consequences symbolically and to compare anticipated behavior and consequences with our personal goals and behavioral standards, thus making available the criteria to measure disparities between actual outcomes and the likelihood of desired outcomes.

Families, particularly parents, play major roles in early human development. As children we repeatedly observe and learn most thoroughly the behaviors modeled by family members. We are socialized into the ideologies and lifestyles of our families through constant, complex networks of rewards, sanctions, and punishments. Still, as influential as families are, Bandura (1971a, 1978b, 1986) reminds us that once we develop the capacity for observational learning, *we learn what we see,* and with television especially, what we see as children in our homes, even as very young children, is not always good (see Figure 16-3).

To complicate the process further, the examples adults present to children are often incongruent with the behaviors and ideas they endorse as ideal or optimal. Children must learn to discriminate from differential modeling cues and differential patterns of reinforcement those behaviors they will eventually perform because of the applicability to personal goals and standards.

FIGURE 16-3   Children learn the behavior they see modeled, © David Dimpster/ Offshoot

Self-regulation (self-set standards and goals used to judge success or failure of actions) and control also begin in early childhood (Bandura, 1986, Wood & Bandura, 1989). The greater the child's cognitive abilities, the more active he or she is in accepting and resisting the reinforcements applied and in engaging in self-regulation that mitigates the effects of these reinforcements. Every parent will testify that as children mature, they do not passively receive information and meaning from outside; rather, they actively develop personal encoding strategies, expectations, reinforcement values, and plans of their own. Even relatively small children endeavor to buffer externally imposed reinforcements and to exercise considerable self-control by identifying personal goals and activities and by selecting consequences that reinforce their actions (Bandura 1977a, 1986).

Like Adler (Chapter 3), Bandura (1986) believes that a child's ordinal position in the family can exert differential effects of achievement efficacy and of social efficacy.

> *Comparative efficacy appraisals for siblings close in age will differ significantly from those for siblings spaced farther apart in age. Siblings of the same sex force more competitive ability evaluations than those of the opposite sex. . . . Close age spacing may, therefore, create pressures on younger members to differentiate themselves from older siblings by developing dissimilar personality patterns, interests, and vocational pursuits. The evaluative habits developed in sibling interactions undoubtedly affect the salience and choice of comparative referents in self-ability evaluations in later life (Bandura, 1986, p. 416).*

Role Assigned to Self-Concept

Bandura's (Bandura 1983a, 1984a) model of reciprocal determinism, in which all causal forces are mutually interactive, becomes less confusing with the realization that he places a **self-system** at its center. While functionally similar in many ways to Rogers's (Chapter 9) theoretical construct of self-concept, Bandura (1978a, 1982a, 1986) does not regard the self-system as an autonomous psychic entity with unidirectional control over behavior. Rather, Bandura believes the influences of the self-system are cognitive, contributory influences in a reciprocally interacting system of personal, behavioral, and environmental influences.

The self-system in Bandura's (1978a) theory "refers to cognitive structures that provide reference mechanisms and to a set of subfunctions for the perception, evaluation, and regulation of our behavior" (p. 348). It is the self-system that provides us a sense of identity while giving structure and continuity to our individual personalities over time. The cognitive structures of our self-systems are self-awareness, self-inducements, and self-reinforcement—all of which can influence our thought patterns, actions, and emotional arousal.

Self-Efficacy We form efficacy expectations based on both actual and vicarious experiences. Collectively, our efficacy expectations form a sense of **self-efficacy** that, in turn, exerts significant influence on our choice of and persistence in coping with difficult life tasks (Bandura, 1978a, 1982a, 1982c, 1984a, 1986). The stronger our sense of self-efficacy, the greater our effort and the longer our persistence in coping with difficult and threatening situations; hence, the higher the probability that we will accept risks and deal successfully with frightening or threatening events. Conversely, the weaker our self-efficacy, the less likely we are to exert maximum effort and to persist when tasks are difficult or frightening. See Figure 16-4 for representative empirical studies of self-efficacy.

To account for the different reactions and behaviors of the same individual in different situations, Bandura (1977a, 1986; Bandura & Cervone, 1983) asserts that the strength of a person's sense of self-efficacy varies in different areas. A person with a strong self-efficacy in academic areas, for example, may sense much weaker efficacy in athletic areas or in social situations. Self-efficacy is not a single, global self-image; rather, it varies according to the situation in which the individual finds him- or herself or the problem that presents itself for solution.

Self-Evaluation   Accurate evaluation of self-efficacy has great functional value. In addition to influencing the amount of energy and persistence we will invest in coping with difficult or threatening tasks, our judgments of self-efficacy influence which activities we willingly undertake and which we try to avoid. Those of us who possess a high evaluation of self-efficacy are more likely to view a difficult task as an exciting challenge and approach it with a great deal of self-assurance and anticipation (Bandura, 1986, pp. 390–453; see also Figure 16.4). Those of us possessing low evaluations of self-efficacy, by contrast, are likely to experience

---

Bandura, Cioffi, Taylor, and Brouillard (1988) set out to learn whether perceived self-efficacy in exercising control over cognitive stressors activates endogenous opioid systems. As predicted, self-efficacious nonstressed subjects gave no evidence of opioid activation. Self-inefficacious stressed subjects were able to tolerate increasing amounts of pain stimulation under saline conditions. However, when endogenous opioid mechanisms that control pain were blocked by nalozone the subjects were unable to bear much pain stimulation. This pattern of changes suggests to the researchers that the stress-induced analgesia found under the saline condition was mediated by endogenous opioid mechanisms and counteracted by the opiate antagonist.

In their study, Wood and Bandura (1989) found evidence supporting the idea that the conception of ability with which people approach complex decision making has substantial impact on self-regulating mechanisms that govern performance attainments. When their subjects construed ability as an acquirable skill, their sense of personal efficacy was highly resilient and they continued to act accordingly, even through the challenging preset level of organizational performance eluded them. Conversely, construing their ability as a reflection of innate personal capacity increased the subjects' vulnerability to adverse effects of failure. They also began to doubt their self-efficacy and to lower their organizational aspirations. Further evidence regarding the decision making of subjects in the entity condition indicates that their declining organizational attainments reflect impairment in the use of decisional skills rather than simply a slackening of effort or diminished involvement in organizational activity.

FIGURE 16-4   Representative Empirical Studies of Self-Efficacy

self-doubt and avoidance behavior. Further, Bandura (1982a) asserts: "Those who judge themselves inefficacious in coping with environmental demands dwell on their personal deficiencies and imagine potential difficulties as more formidable than they really are" (p. 123). In contrast, because they are not distracted by imagined difficulties, persons with a strong sense of efficacy are able to focus all of their attention, imagination, and energy upon the solution of a problem; indeed, the difficulties encountered only add to their striving to find a solution.

Self-Regulation Self-evaluation and self-efficacy play central roles in self-regulation and self-control (Wood & Bandura, 1989). Based on our self-evaluations and perceptions of self-efficacy, we subjectively set certain moral and achievement standards for ourselves, which in turn become criteria and incentives for measuring future behavior. Further, we respond to meeting, exceeding, or falling short of our inner standards by rewarding ourselves (e.g., feelings of pride, satisfaction, self-regard) or punishing ourselves (e.g., feelings of shame, guilt, depression).

Whether inner behavioral standards are high or low depends on the reciprocal influences of person and environment; for example, the kind of models we have observed and compared ourselves to (capable, highly skilled models or models praised for relatively simple tasks requiring little preparation and skills); personal perceptions of coping abilities or self-efficacy; and past achievements and failures (Bandura & Cervone, 1986). When our achievements are measured against self-standards and judged equal to or surpassing expectations, we experience positive feelings of self-regard (self-reinforcement). Indeed, even when strong self-efficacy fails to meet inner self-standards, particularly in a task considered important, both effort and determination increase and additional attempts are immediately undertaken to achieve success.

Advocates of Social-Cognitive Therapy have demonstrated that therapeutic outcome and recidivism can best be predicted by considering both the client's perceived self-efficacy and his or her expected outcome beliefs. The combined influence of a client's sense of self-efficacy and outcome beliefs provides the therapist (Bandura prefers *change-agent*) predictive information on the client's likelihood of entering and continuing therapy, the rate of change that can be anticipated during the course of therapy, the client's ultimate success or failure, and where changes are difficult to sustain over a long period (e.g., addictive behaviors calling for abstinence), how the client is likely to respond to a relapse (Bandura, 1986, pp. 390–453).

In addition to affecting behavior, self-efficacy perceptions also affect emotional reactions, particularly in the case of anxiety and stress reactions to novel or anticipated aversive events. When clients believe that they can cope with most problems that arise in life, hence, preventing, eliminating, or minimizing the severity of aversive events, they are less likely to fear the unknown or to anticipate overwhelmingly aversive situations. They also are less likely to experience fear arousal and to employ self-defeating or self-protective avoidance behaviors.

FIGURE 16-5   The Role of Self-Efficacy in Social-Cognitive Therapy

Continued success in meeting self-standards can result in increased self-efficacy and even higher self-standards. Should this occur, achieving an earlier level of performance no longer proves challenging. Conversely, continued failure to meet personal standards of achievement can result in doubt of personal efficacy and the painful feelings of anxiety. This in turn usually leads to avoidance behavior and either resignation or despondency.

According to Bandura (1977a, 1986; Wood & Bandura, 1989), humans prefer self-reinforcements over externally imposed reinforcements. Indeed, external reward for behavior that falls short of a person's inner achievement standards may have no reinforcement value, and hence cannot serve as a reinforcement. Self-reinforcement is stronger than externally imposed reinforcement and maintains behavior more efficiently than external reinforcement. Individuals with a strong sense of self-efficacy and high achievement standards may deny external reinforcement rather than risk self-disapproval and guilt for accepting unmerited reward.

Bandura and Cervone (1986) tested the hypothesis that self-reactive influences exert differential impact on motivation as a function of the level and direction of discrepancy of comparative standard and attainment. Subjects pursued a challenging standard of strenuous activity, then received preselected feedback that their effort fell either markedly, moderately, or minimally short or that it succeeded the standard. They then recorded their perceived self-efficacy, self-evaluation, and self-set goals, and their motivation level was measured. As predicted, perceived self-efficacy contributes to motivation across a wide range of discrepant conditions. Self-evaluation operates as an influential motivator only when attainments fall markedly or moderately short of a comparative standard. Self-set goals contribute to motivation at all discrepancy levels except when attainments are markedly discrepant from the standard. Bandura and Cervone conclude that the relevant self-influence operating in concert at particular discrepancy levels explains a substantial amount of the variance in motivation.

In summary, through self-generated standards, goals, and inducements, anticipated consequences, foresightful actions, self-evaluation, and self-reinforcement, we *do* exercise some self-regulation and self-control over our own behavior. Setting standards and goals promotes skill acquisition, increases a sense of self-efficacy, and adds to interest in the skill or activity being pursued.

Determinism versus Freedom to Choose

Bandura's (1983a, 1984a, 1986) stance on Determinism versus Freedom to Choose also is one of reciprocal determinism. True, we are influenced by the antecedents and consequences of our behavior, but we in turn mediate the influence of these antecedents and consequences through our cognitive processes. Our cognitive processes influence which of the numerous environmental events we attend to, as well as how we perceive and respond to these events.

We can be considered neither causes independent of our behavior and environment nor simple reactors to environmental influences. To the degree that we can influence future conditions by cognitively anticipating the future consequences of our actions, by regulating our present behavior, and by administering self-reinforcing consequences to sustain it, we are *causal contributors* to our life paths (Bandura, 1986).

Our cognitive capacity and ability to work with symbols allow us to create as well as to select our environments. Moreover, the capability of intentional action is rooted in our symbolic activity. We select, organize, and transform the stimuli that impinge on us. We develop values and set behavioral standards and goals to guide our direction and determine our persistence. We develop a sense of personal efficacy that has considerable functional value. Thus, our behavior is at least partially determined by self-produced and self-regulating influences. We can and do, with effective tools of personal agency and social support, give incentive, meaning, and worth to what we do.

Bandura (1974) believes that reflexive conditioning in humans is largely a myth. From a social learning perspective, conditioning is "simply a descriptive term for learning through paired experiences" (p. 859). The assumption that conditioning occurs automatically is in error. Rather, conditioning in humans is cognitively mediated. Our so-called conditioned reactions are, for the most part, self-activated and subject to interpretation or encoding rather than automatically evoked. It is not so much that events occur together in time, according to Bandura (1974), but that we learn to predict them and to rally appropriate anticipatory reactions.

As stated earlier, Bandura (1974, 1977a, 1982a, 1982b) does not view **freedom** as an act of will; he defines freedom as the number of options available to us at any particular time and our right to exercise them. Viewed from this reciprocal perspective, we have the ability to expand our freedom by extending and perfecting our coping competencies and eliminating our dysfunctional self-restraints. The greater the number of our behavioral alternatives, personal skills, and rights as individuals, and the fewer our self-restraints, the greater our freedom. The greater our sense of personal efficacy, the more likely that our behavior is under our anticipatory control.

Centrality of Reinforcement

As indicated in "Explanation of the Learning Process" and "Determinism versus Freedom to Choose," the reinforcement construct in social learning theory incorporates a wider range of influences than do the more traditional theories of learning. Certainly, we are subject to the immediate reinforcement influence of environmental consequences. However, because we possess the unique human capacity of anticipatory thought, environmental consequences are not singular determinants of our behavior nor do they operate automatically and unconsciously. Bandura (1974, 1977a, 1978a, 1982a) argues that our behavior is affected only minimally by external reinforcements of which we are unaware.

According to Bandura (1974, 1982a), we have the ability to shape conditions for our purposes. By cognitively bringing future consequences to bear on our present behavior, we are in position to choose anticipatory or delayed reinforcement over immediate environmental consequences. "The idea that behavior is governed by its consequences fares better," according to Bandura (1978a), "for anticipated than for actual consequences" (p. 356). We further shape our conditions by establishing personal goals and behavioral standards that carry qualitative expectations and conditional reinforcement values. From a social-cognitive perspective, then, reinforcement becomes internal and involves a personal sense of self-esteem and self-regard.

Our actions are often based on foresight, and our most influential reinforcements are often vicarious and self-generated consequences (see "Determinism versus Freedom of Choice"). Environmental consequences exert their greatest influence on our behavior when they are compatible with those consequences under our anticipatory control. As we mature, externally imposed rewards become less important than our sense of self-regard, and immediate gratification becomes less significant than the achievement of our long-range goals or the accomplishment of our self-imposed level of performance. We can, through foresight, proficiency, and self-influence, transcend external reinforcement and control. It should be noted that determinism is not in question because in the view of social-cognitive theory, *all* behavior is caused. Bandura's stance of reciprocal determinism means there is a reciprocal interaction of environmental and personal influences.

Number and Weight Assigned to Motivational Concepts

As Bandura (1977a) points out, there are inherent problems in constructing and testing a theory of motivation "when the existence of that motivation is inferred from the very behavior it supposedly causes" (p. 109). From a social learning perspective, Bandura believes it is preferable to explore how positive incentives, whether external or cognitively formulated, facilitate the development of competencies and interest that serve as enduring sources of personal satisfaction and contribute to a sense of self-efficacy. Following this approach to motivation, **reinforcements** are viewed as *anything* we value under existing circumstances. From this perspective, reinforcements become *incentives* rather than *implanters* of behavior, as proposed by strict behavioral notions (e.g., Skinner). We are motivated to act by reinforcement only when we believe our action and the reinforcement we receive for it are meaningful and useful. We discontinue action and disregard reinforcements that offer no incentive.

Bandura (1963, 1977a) recognizes that aversive stimuli, both internal and external, can motivate action. Examples include the internal aversive stimuli that arise from tissue deficit such as hunger and thirst and external aversive stimuli such as pain. However, he asserts, the major sources of human motivation are those stimuli that arise from cognition and include properties that are both dynamic and structural (Bandura, 1986). We develop anticipatory capacities that enable us to be motivated by expected consequences. "By representing foreseeable outcomes symbolically," Bandura (1977a) claims, "people can convert future consequences into current motivators of behavior" (p. 18).

Much of human behavior is directed toward projected future goals and outcomes. Distant goals require self-motivation, and incremental progress toward these goals via accomplishment of proximal goals. For example, every professor who decides to write a textbook, which may require two or more years of evenings and weekends in the writing, must be self-motivated. No one is there to drive him or her to the computer terminal or the library. Only he or she can set goals or standards that result in the research, organization, drafting, editing, and rewriting necessary to produce a credible text. Proximal goals must be established (e.g., pages per day, specific headings or subheadings, etc.) and self-reinforcements created, for to view the book in its entirety as the only goal would be so distant that it could prove paralyzing.

We have the self-reactive capacity to move from immediate to anticipated consequences once we develop specific standards and goals against which we can measure our performance. We specify conditional requirements for self-efficacy and self-regulation. External reinforcement matters little if we fall below our self-set standards or requirements and is unnecessary if we meet them. Success can be motivating because self-satisfaction is seldom lasting. Once we attain our goal, we raise our sights to even higher levels of performance. The higher our goals, the higher the performance level and the greater the enhancement of our self-efficacy. Cognitive motivation, then, operates through the intervening influence of personal standards and self-evaluation. We judge our performance against others' or against our own past performance. When we can ascribe successful goal attainment to our abilities and efforts, we feel an increased sense of self-efficacy and are motivated to continue and quite often to increase our effort. Conversely, we deny both external and self-reward rather than risk self-censure and the loss of self-efficacy.

Because of the capacity for reciprocal influence, our motivating contingencies are at least partly of our own making. Self-generated incentives are motivating when they are designed to enhance or authenticate personal efficacy. We can, therefore, learn to rely extensively on our goals and approval as motivation for our direction and behavior.

Importance of Group Determinants

As indicated earlier (see "Early versus Continuous Development"), we are indoctrinated into the ideology and lifestyle of our particular family group where, during our most formative years, we observe repeatedly and learn most thoroughly the behavior modeled by family members. Also during this period we begin to form our personal systems of preferences, values, and behavioral standards, as well as our precepts of personal efficacy. Although our opportunities for group affiliation expand significantly as we develop, we appear to have a natural tendency to move toward those groups whose members we perceive share our interests and values. In brief, we give and receive mutual reinforcement to preexisting interests, values, and standards through our group affiliations.

The skills and interests we develop also influence our activities and relationships. The particular social milieus to which we have access are at least partly determined by the potentialities we cultivate and actualize.

In addition to our skills, values, interests, and behavioral standards, the strength of our personal agency will influence our choice of group affiliation. According to Bandura (1982a, 1982b), when we develop competencies, self-precepts of efficacy, and self-regulatory capabilities—that is, strong personal agency—we are more likely to be attracted to groups that offer incentive, meaning, and worth to what we do. Conversely, when healthy social affiliations are lacking, we become vulnerable to coercive or communal groups that offer friendship in exchange for conformity (Bandura, 1982b).

Induction into a group not only brings us into contact with new incentive systems, but also "furnishes a distinct symbolic environment as well" (Bandura, 1982b, p. 752). In addition to feelings of affinity and solidarity, group symbolic systems, whether healthy or unhealthy, help shape group members' ideological perspectives on life and living.

Bandura (1977a, 1982a, 1982b) asserts that the greatest protection we have as individuals rests with groups and organizations whose members have a sense of collective efficacy and can mobilize their efforts and resources to protect individual rights. We are not, according to Bandura (1982a), forced to live our lives as social isolates. We can gain strength in groups. Further, our perceived collective efficacy will influence what we do as a group, the effort we expend as a group, and the length of time we continue to work as a group when the group's efforts fail to produce immediate results. Moreover, he claims, "the higher the perceived efficacy, the greater the propensity to social activism" (Bandura, 1982a, p. 143).

Subjective versus Objective Reality

According to Bandura (1974, 1977a, 1982b), we form perceptions about ourselves and our world by observing and extracting regularities and uniformities of events in our particular environments. By encoding direct and vicarious experiences symbolically, we gain knowledge about priorities and relationships. We anticipate consequences and predict outcomes. We formulate standards and rules and develop incentives and logical verification procedures. We naturally generate perpetuating ideas, attitudes, and habitual patterns of thought. And most important for this issue, we sift all our new experiences of the environment through our current understanding and expectations about ourselves, our behavior, and the world.

Our capacity to symbolize events and our self-valuative and self-regulatory reactions play prominent roles in influencing our perceptions of our world. The concepts we hold at any particular moment exert significant influence on our perceptions of present experiences. Although we are rooted in the reality of the observable and ponderable, we can act on that reality. We have a hand in the creation of what that reality is for us. We have the capacity and we can create the incentive to assert and express ourselves on the world we conceptualize and encounter. We interpret our perceptions and act on our images of reality. In short, we develop a personal integrity that, in turn, influences our perceptions of ourselves, others, and the world.

Uniqueness versus Universality

Bandura has not addressed this issue directly, but his firm stance on reciprocal determinism makes it clear that he views us as unique individuals (Bandura, 1983a, 1984a, 1986). Not only are our experiences, whether actual or vicarious, both numerous and varied, but also we develop highly personal systems of cognitive processes, opening our conceptualizations of every experience to an infinite variety of individual, creative, interpretive shadings. Our realities are subjectively determined images of the world we encounter. Our feelings and actions during and following any experience are uniquely our own. We are, then, neither predictable nor typical. Rather, we are each unparalleled with innate potentials, creative perceptions, and personally constructed attitudes, values, goals, and behavioral strategies.

Psychological Health and Psychopathology

Psychological Health

Although Bandura has not, thus far, directly addressed the subject of "healthy personality and the good life," there are implications for psychological health and effective living in his construct of the self-system and the role it plays in reciprocal determinism, in particular the functions of self-observation, self-evaluation, self-efficacy, and self-regulation. There is some danger, of course, of misinterpreting these implications in ways contrary to what Bandura intends.

From Bandura's social-cognitive perspective, we play a major reciprocal role not only in determining the nature and direction of our lives but also in delineating the specific goals we will pursue and the achievement standards we will use to judge our progress. The question is: "Will the role this self-system plays enhance or harm physical and psychological health?"

Since much of human learning occurs through observation, it is important that what is being observed is also being accurately perceived and objectively evaluated. The implication here, then, seems to be that the healthy person is one whose present perceptions and evaluations of self, others, and the world are realistic and clearly symbolized, both in actuality and potentiality. Moreover, the healthy person is not easily swayed by the opinions of others. Indeed, the healthy person is more likely to trust in and hold onto his or her own perceptions and evaluations.

We humans act in accordance with our precepts of self-efficacy. Implied in this statement is the idea that when we are confident of our abilities to cope with life tasks, we also feel a strong sense of self-esteem and self-worth, and have the

Heredity				Social Determinants
Uniqueness				Universality
Determinism				Freedom
Early Development				Continuous Development
Subjective Reality				Objective Reality
Conscious Determinants				Unconscious Determinants

Role Assigned to Group Determinants	In our formative years, the family group facilitates our formulation of personal preferences, values, standards, and a sense of efficacy. As our social milieu broadens, we tend to move to those groups espousing similar interests and values. Group affiliation promotes mutual reinforcement of preexisting inclinations.
Explanation of Learning Process	Learning occurs via modeling and effective modeling entails attentional, retentional, motor reproduction (actual practice or internal rehearsal), and incentive and motivational processes. External reinforcement is relegated to a facilitative rather than a necessary role in learning.
Number and Weight Assigned to Motivational Concepts	Only those reinforcements experienced as personally meaningful become incentives for behavior. Positive incentives (formulated cognitively) facilitate development of competencies and interests that are personally satisfying and that promote self-efficacy.
Centrality of Reinforcement	Anticipatory reinforcement carries more weight than immediate environmental reinforcement. Anticipatory reinforcement is internal, transcending external reinforcement and control. Further, it fosters a personal sense of self-efficacy.
Role Assigned to Self-Concept	Conceptualized in terms of reciprocal determinism, the self acts as a cognitive contributory influence that interacts reciprocally within a system of personal, behavioral, and environmental influences. An autonomous psychic entity with unidirectional control is disregarded.

FIGURE 16-6   Schematic Analysis of Bandura's Stance on Basic Issues

capacity to give ourselves self-regard. Also implied is that when we experience positive feelings about ourselves, we are also more open to new experiences and change, more likely to view difficult tasks as a challenge, and more willing to risk new behaviors.

With a strong sense of self-efficacy we are also more likely to be influenced by those reinforcements (whether anticipatory or externally imposed) that we deem personally meaningful; indeed, these reinforcements become the strongest incentives for our behavior. The implication: Anticipatory reward carries more weight for the healthy person than immediate environmental reinforcement. Moreover, because anticipatory reinforcement is internal, it fosters an even greater sense of self-esteem and self-regard.

Healthy people value their self-respect above externally imposed material rewards. They rely extensively (though not exclusively) on their own standards and goals as self-approval guides for their personal conduct. Healthy people have greater foresight, more effective proficiency and coping strategies, and a stronger self-influence in the reciprocal, deterministic paradigm.

Because self-regulatory and self-control skills are acquired, they can be taught. Healthy persons have learned to monitor those behaviors they wish to change, to set healthful proximal goals to motivate and guide their efforts over the long term, and to arrange incentives for themselves so that they are more likely to persist in making the healthy behavioral changes they seek.

Psychopathology

Before attempting to present the subject of psychopathology from a social learning perspective, it should be noted that Bandura (1969, 1977a, 1986) does not ascribe to a disease model, nor does he agree with most of the criteria used by the medical model to label certain behaviors psychopathological. Neither does Bandura (1986) accept the psychodynamic model of psychopathology with its powerful internal instinctual controls as the cause of abnormal or deviant behavior.

The designation of behavior as "pathological," Bandura (1969) asserts, involves arbitrary social valuative judgments that are influenced by, among other factors, "the normative standards of persons making the judgments, the social context in which the behavior is exhibited, certain attributes of the behavior, and numerous characteristics of the deviator himself" (p. 3). For Bandura (1967, 1977a, 1986), much of what society labels "pathological" or "symptomatic" is the result of faulty learning, comparatively low self-valuative standards and goals, low self-efficacy, and nonconformist models. In short, most "symptoms" can be traced to an idiosyncratic social-cognitive history.

Although Bandura (1969) emphasizes psychological and cognitive determinants, he is aware that genetic and neurophysiological conditions contribute to behavioral malfunctioning. Even when this is the case, however, Bandura (1969, 1986) believes that biological and psychological factors typically interact in subtle and complex ways to produce maladaptive behavioral patterns. From Bandura's (1986) perspective, then, so-called pathological behaviors are usually dysfunctional behaviors the person has learned in order to cope with self-imposed and environmental demands rather than manifestations of pathology.

Like the traditional behaviorists, Bandura believes all human behavior, including abnormal behavior, is learned. However, when abnormal behavior in humans is viewed through observational paradigms, a much wider range of complex interacting determinants is added to the behavioristic explanation of psychopathology, specifically observational learning, or modeling, and the self-structure influences.

The traditional behaviorist explains phobic behavior as learned behavior that was externally reinforced (see Chapter 13). From the social learning perspective, however, phobic behavior can be mediated through cognitive imagery without external reinforcement. For example, a child observes a parent's mild nervous reaction to a thunderstorm warning on television and then, through self-reinforcement in imagination, the child acquires an extreme fright reaction that is far beyond the mild anxiety manifested in the parent's modeled behavior (Bandura, 1983b). Without ever experiencing external reinforcement, the child has developed an irrational fear of storms and screams at the sound of thunder or the sight of lightning, flees to the safety of a dark closet, and there, crouched in the dark on the floor, shakes and cries until the storm passes. Bandura (1986) believes that through faulty phobic thinking, humans constrain and impoverish their own lives.

The influences of the **self-system**—self-evaluation, self-judgment, self-efficacy, and self-set goals and standards—have each been shown to vastly expand the effect of cognition on motivation (Bandura & Cervone, 1986; Bandura, 1969, 1977a, 1986). Working in concert, these self-influences can lead either to self-motivation and self-reinforcement or to self-punishment and self-devaluation reactions. Depressive reactions, for example, typically arise from extremely high, exacting, personally set self-standards and goals and the resulting devaluing of achievements and the perceived sense of self-inefficacy when the behavior falls short of the expected level of performance. Objective successes, under these conditions, may be viewed as personal failures.

When behavioral standards are extreme and inflexible, the individual demands perfection in every task attempted, whether or not the task is important. Anything less than perfection is perceived a failure. Feelings of inefficacy, worthlessness, and low self-esteem abound. When good is *never* good enough, dysfunctional defensive avoidance behaviors are the norm. Books are never written, or if written, never submitted for publication, because they just are not good enough. Paintings are hidden away in the attic or destroyed so that no one can see that they are not good enough. Music is not performed because the musician fears the performance will not be good enough. With their harsh self-evaluations, perfectionists drive themselves to despondency, inactivity, and depression. Thus, avoidance behaviors are self-defeating and seem only to validate their perceptions of inefficacy.

Chronic anxiety attacks, apathy, resignation, despondency, or depression can soon become a style of life. Moreover, people without a firm sense of personal agency are drawn to others like themselves, delimiting the kinds of behavior they will repeatedly observe, and hence, learn most thoroughly. The result is a mutual reinforcing of perceived inefficacy and depression. Misery not only loves company, it insists on company that is equally miserable.

According to Bandura (1982a): "A comprehensive theory of depression must therefore be concerned not only with the perceived causality of failure but also with the standards by which attainments will be self-judged as successes or failures to begin with" (p. 141). Before change will occur, self-standards and goals must be revised to a realistic level and efficacy expectations must be enhanced to a point where the individual experiences self-regard and feels he or she can cope successfully.

Heuristic Influences: Research Methods and Techniques

The heuristic value of Bandura's theory is unquestionably high. In addition to the steady flow of experimental studies published by Bandura and his students, his theory of social learning has generated both a high degree of interest in and published works from numerous social and experimental psychologists.

The research supporting Bandura's theory is far too extensive to review here, hence this chapter is limited to a few representative studies. The reader who wishes to learn more is referred to Bandura's (1977) book, *Social Learning Theory*, which lists supportive evidence for the critical cognitive role of self-efficacy. Bandura's (1986) more recent book, *Social Foundations of Thought and Action: A Social Cognitive Theory*, cites a broad range of multidisciplinary research that supports such theoretical issues and constructs as freedom and determinism, the role of self-efficacy, sociocultural diffusion of new ideas and social practices, the decision-making process, and cognitive development.

Application to Psychotherapy

Therapeutic Goals

Unlike the therapies of Rogers, Ellis, and May, in Bandura's therapy few accepted social-cognitive goals of therapy apply to all clients. The focus of social-cognitive therapy is instead on the individual client's present behavior or behavioral patterns. Although social-cognitive therapists assist their clients to learn desired or required behaviors and to extinguish maladaptive behaviors that lead to grief, difficulty, or negative consequences, the specific goals of therapy vary from client to client.

Clients in social-cognitive therapy play a major role not only in determining the nature and direction of therapy but also in delineating the specific behavioral changes to be produced. The primary role of the therapist initially is to assist the client to view desired outcomes in terms of specific performance objectives, preferably objectives that are both observable and measurable.

When clients are uncertain about what they want from therapy or when they express goals that are obscure or general rather than specific, social-cognitive therapists may have to assist in a review of the alternative courses of action available to their clients, as well as in an exploration of the probable consequences of following any of them. The goals of social-cognitive therapy are the clients';

however, only when goals are clearly defined in terms of observable, measurable behavior change can the client and therapist arrive at decisions regarding the experiences most likely to produce the outcomes desired. Poorly defined goals leave the client and therapist without any rational, meaningful basis for selecting an appropriate treatment plan and behavioral strategies or for evaluating the effectiveness of therapeutic effort.

Once clients are able to express their problems clearly, social-cognitive learning therapists often assist with the assessment process before devising goals or plans of intervention or action. For example, when and with whom is the problem behavior exhibited? How pervasive and frequent is the behavior? What are the antecedents and consequences of the behavior cited? What were the conditions when the problem behavior originated? Who were the client's role models? How is the behavior maintained? Are there situational factors in the client's living conditions that may be helpful in effecting change? How might these factors be utilized in a program to modify the inappropriate behavioral patterns? Would it be helpful to secure the client's permission to interview other people influential in the client's life who might serve as models of the desired behavior? It may be helpful, also, to specify the conditions under which the desired outcome may be expected to occur.

When behavioral outcomes are complex, they may be divided into a number of sub-goals or steps and sequenced in hierarchical order to ensure optimal progress. Intricate modes of behavior are often best achieved by modeling progressively more complex responses and reinforcing (directly or vicariously) gradual response elaboration.

Therapeutic Relationship

For Bandura (in Bergin & Garfield, 1971), any therapeutic process that focuses on the interview or the relationship as the major method for producing therapeutic change places severe and unnecessary limitations "on the quality, range, and intensity of the experiences that could be created in the therapeutic setting" (p. 653). Convinced that nearly all human behavior is learned and that practically all learning that occurs from direct experience can occur vicariously as the result of observing the behavior of others and its consequences for them, the therapist produces a process of therapy significantly different from the processes of interview and relationship therapies. These differences are evident in the content and focus of therapy, as well as in the agents of treatment.

Skillful interview and relationship techniques may facilitate behavior assessment, goal alignment, and acceptance by the client of the therapist as a model. However, the focus of social-cognitive therapy is on the specific client behaviors requiring modification rather than a series of interviews in which these behaviors, or feelings about these behaviors, are only discussed. Further, rather than confining the therapy session to the office of the therapist, much of the therapeutic process of social-cognitive therapy occurs in the setting in which the client's problem behaviors evolve. While the social-cognitive therapists may serve as models, the agents of therapy are often carefully selected individuals and groups who already have intensive contact with the client or who possess the behavior repertoire necessary to serve as effective models.

Bandura accepts most modes of therapy based on learning principles. However, the emphasis in this chapter is on those specific behavioral enactment methods that are based on modeling principles, methods which have been demonstrated as effective and economical whether for acquiring new patterns of behavior, strengthening or weakening inhibitions of responses that already exist in the client's repertoire, or facilitating the client's perceived self-efficacy.

Initial Procedures and Strategies

Therapy begins with problem definition and assessment. The importance of this initial assessment process in social-cognitive learning cannot be overemphasized because decisions regarding therapeutic approach, strategies, or action plans are based on this definition. Accurate problem definition involves more than identification of the presenting problem. It includes the determination of whether the presenting problem represents all the client's concerns. If the therapeutic process is structured to meet the client's needs, and that is the major purpose of social-cognitive therapy, a thorough problem assessment must be conducted by the client and the therapist to identify all client concerns, including those that for whatever reasons may be withheld or those that are vague and emotion laden. Clarification is necessary to eliminate ambiguity. Clear and accurate specification of problem behaviors is the basis for therapeutic purpose and goal formulation, as well as selection of strategies. Furthermore, conceptualizing the client's problem in terms of specific problem behaviors not only offers both client and therapist a clear and consistent view of the problem but also provides a baseline for future progress assessment.

Clients of social-cognitive therapists are not categorized with any preconceived diagnostic labels like those listed in the *Diagnostic and Statistical Manual of Mental Disorders* (1980), nor are they identified as possessing any generalized or global traits or characteristics like those provided by scores on certain standardized tests. Rather, social-cognitive therapists and their clients work together to define the clients' problems operationally. A clear operational definition not only has the advantage of focusing on specific problem behaviors and the conditions (antecedents and consequences) contributing to them but also avoids the negative global inferences of diagnostic labels and vague traits. Further, operational definitions are much less likely to carry bias into the treatment procedure, thus affecting the way others relate to the client.

Individual and Group Counseling and Psychotherapy

Because the therapeutic process of social-cognitive therapy differs so significantly from those therapies that focus on the interview or on the client-therapist relationship (e.g., Freud's Psychoanalysis, Jung's Psychoanalytic Therapy, Rogers's Person-Centered Therapy), space is allotted here to present some of the major deviations in Bandura's therapeutic approach. For Bandura (in Bergin & Garfield, 1971; see also Bandura 1976, 1977b), any therapeutic process that relies heavily or solely on the interview or the relationship between client and therapist for producing therapeutic change places severe and unnecessary limitations "on the quality, range, and intensity of the experiences that could be created in the therapeutic setting" (p. 653). In social-cognitive therapy, skillful relationship techniques may facilitate behavior assessment, goal alignment, and client acceptance of the therapist as a model. However, unlike Rogers (Chapter 9), who believes the counseling relationship is both necessary and sufficient, Bandura (1969, 1977a, 1986) argues that neither the interview nor the relationship are necessary or sufficient to bring about behavioral change in the client.

Social-cognitive therapists are convinced that all human behavior occurring from direct experience can occur vicariously as a result of observing the behavior of others and its consequences. Thus, rather than focusing on a series of interviews in which the client's behaviors (or feelings about these behaviors) are discussed, the emphasis in social-cognitive therapy is upon those specific behavioral enactment methods that are based on modeling principles. Modeling methods have been demonstrated effective and economical, whether employed in assisting the client to acquire new patterns of behavior, in strengthening or weakening inhibitions of responses that already exist in the client's repertoire, or in enhancing the client's perceived sense of self-efficacy.

The Course of Social Learning Therapy

Modeling is the major technique of social-cognitive therapy. While in certain instances modeling may be the only approach employed by the therapist, in most cases modeling is the dominant component in a more inclusive strategy or action plan designed to demonstrate the client's desired goal behaviors. When part of a larger program, modeling may be supplemented with verbal sets explaining the rationale of strategy, rehearsal sessions in simulated or natural settings, coaching and induction or support aids, client self-directed practice, feedback, homework assignments, and post evaluations or progress assessments.

To assess the effectiveness of therapy, both short- and long-term follow-up inquiries are conducted at selected intervals following termination of therapy. Not only do such follow-up inquiries communicate the therapist's continued interest in the client's welfare, the information gathered through follow-up can be used to determine the extent to which the client is continuing to perform the desired goal behaviors without therapeutic support. Bandura (1969) asserts that success in therapy can only be determined when viewed over the long term.

Models and Modeling While social-cognitive therapists may themselves serve as models to their clients, the agents of therapy are more often carefully selected individuals or groups of individuals who already have established contact with the client or who possess the behavior repertoire and favorable characteristics necessary to serve as effective models. Models in social-cognitive therapy can be live, symbolic, or, in the case of covert modeling, imaginal.

Participant Modeling   According to Bandura (1976), there are four necessary components in participant modeling: explanation of the strategy rationale and instruction, modeling, guided participation, and successful experiences. When the desired client behavior is either complex or fear arousing, it is divided into a series of incremental behavioral responses and arranged in order of difficulty. It is important in participant modeling that the first behavioral outcome demonstrated is one the client can observe without experiencing anxiety, and with the direct support and guidance of the therapist, complete successfully. The object of participant modeling is to promote client competence, and thus, enhance the client's perceptions of self-efficacy (Bandura, Reese, & Adams, 1982).

Selection of an appropriate model is important, also. The therapeutic context often makes the therapist the most likely model candidate. However, greater gains may accrue by using multiple models or, in the case of strong or disabling client avoidance behaviors, **coping models** (persons who have successfully overcome their anxiety or fears by employing the participant model approach in therapy).

In **participant modeling,** the model demonstrates a single behavioral response. The demonstration may be repeated by the same model, or when feasible, by several models—multiple modeling of a goal response lends both variety and credence to the modeled behavior.

Following the demonstration of each modeling sequence in the modeling hierarchy, the client is given the opportunity for guided participation. **Guided participation** includes direct assistance and support of the therapist or the model while the client performs the behavior he or she has just observed. Each practice attempt by the client is accompanied by feedback from the therapist about the client's performance, reinforcement for successful attempts, and when appropriate, suggestions for improving the next practice attempt.

Induction aids are often selected to support and encourage the client during early practice sessions. The therapist or model may elect to assist with or participate directly in the early practice attempts. For example, working with a client who experiences an inordinately strong fear of and avoidance behaviors with snakes, the therapist or model may, at the point when the client is first asked to touch the snake, hold the head and tail of the snake so the client can touch the body. If still hesitant, the client may be provided with a pair of thick gloves.

As therapy progresses, the induction aids are gradually withdrawn. Eventually, the client is expected to perform each behavioral sequence without aids or assistance. In addition, the practice attempts should move from the low-risk situation of the therapeutic setting to the client's natural environment where the risk encountered is often greater. Finally, the client is assigned a series of progressively more difficult homework assignments to be completed between therapy sessions.

Symbolic Modeling Because humans possess the ability to use symbols, models may be presented symbolically—**symbolic modeling** through films, audio or video recordings, photographic slides, imagery scripts, or other written or printed materials. Film or video models are used in therapy much the same way that live models are used, and can become the major component of a more complex strategy or used independently by clients as a self-help or self-directed approach to behavior change. Bibliotherapy is a form of symbolic modeling that has proved particularly effective when model and reader are similar in race, sex, cultural background, and experience or when involved in similar life situations.

Symbolic modeling has been demonstrated as a practical and efficacious modeling approach in therapy. It is highly versatile, and when used repeatedly over time, a cost-effective treatment method (e.g., a film prepared for people afraid of flying may be used as often as there are individuals or groups who wish to overcome their fear).

The particular medium selected for symbolic modeling will depend on the client or group of clients for which it is designed, the specific goal behaviors to be acquired by those who use it, and where and how it is to be used. As with other forms of modeling, the effects of symbolic modeling are likely to be enhanced when the presentation or display is followed with instruction and explanation of the rationale, guided practice opportunities, immediate feedback, and valuative follow-up.

Self as Model When others are viewed as models, there is always the possibility of negative effects (negative model characteristics or model characteristics that remind the observer of earlier nagative conditions) for the observer (Bandura, 1969). Even when the model is carefully selected and possesses many of the favorable model characteristics (prestige and status, same sex and age, and similar cultural and ethnic background), the client may still react negatively. Bandura (1969, 1977a) has discovered that modeling characteristics exert a differential influence on various observers.

For some clients, **self-as-model** can result in closer attention and coding (two necessary requisites for modeling to be effective). Seeing or hearing themselves practice the goal behavior (a third requisite) not only facilitates the modeling process—hence, the likelihood of correct performances—but also offers clients the unique opportunity to learn how they cope with formerly anxiety-provoking and difficult situations. A self-as-model experience can enhance clients' perceived sense of self-efficacy and encourage them to risk attempting new or anxiety-provoking behaviors.

Initially, client-as-model audio or visual tapes that are appropriate for modeling purposes may be difficult to obtain. Therapists may be forced to edit carefully the tapes of the client's early modeling attempts, keeping only those portions in which the client satisfactorily demonstrates appropriate goal behaviors. The edited version of the tape then becomes the model and is played for the client who sees or hears him- or herself practicing the behavior he or she wants to acquire.

To reinforce correct behavior and encourage further rehearsal, the therapist may stop the tape at appropriate intervals to praise a satisfactory performance by the client or to coach the client on ways to improve a particular behavior. To achieve the benefits of repeated modeling, the therapist may ask the client to take the tape home so he or she may view or listen to it, preferably at specified times each day for a set period agreed to by therapist and client.

As with other modeling approaches (participant modeling, for example), the client is encouraged to transfer newly acquired goal behaviors to his or her natural environment. Rather than being confined to the therapist's office, much of the therapeutic process of social learning therapy occurs in the setting in which the client's problem behaviors evolve.

Extended Applications

Bandura's latest major work, *Social Foundations of Thought and Action: A Social Cognitive Theory* (1986), is a synthesis of multidisciplinary research and its application to a wide range of personal and social change in such areas as issues of determinism and freedom, the prevalence and power of learning by observation, the role of perceived self-efficacy in psychosocial functioning, the diffusion of new ideas and social practices, and the process of decision making and judgments. In addition to psychologists and psychotherapists, this work has much to offer to educators, sociologists, communication specialists, ecologists, political scientists, politicians, business and industrial managers, lawyers, and judges.

Bandura (1986) is convinced that social change (whether positive or negative) is achieved most rapidly by applying a dual strategy of the social-cognitive learning approach with an understanding of **social diffusion** (knowledge of how new ideas and social practices spread within a society or from one society to another). He cites research that demonstrates how human judgment, values, and conduct can be altered successfully through television modeling. He discusses in detail numerous examples of extended applications of the social-cognitive approach to learning that when fostered by converging technological changes in television and computers, have influenced personal and social changes in areas as diverse as athletics, ecology, substance abuse, illiteracy, and health practices.

He discusses, also, some of the dangers and negative effects of the social diffusion. In particular, he addresses how this approach can be misused, the issue of determinism and freedom, and the influential role of self-referent thought. "Competent functioning requires both skills and self-beliefs of efficacy to use them effectively" (Bandura, 1986, p. 391). In some cultures there are no incentives for new ideas or change. Indeed, the consequences of advocating change may be punishment from the powerholders and influential vested interest groups. Futility and despondency, as well as anxiety, result when people perceive themselves as unable to influence the events and social conditions that significantly affect their lives. They refuse to take an active part in social change because they seriously doubt that their effort will produce any positive outcome. In such cultures, the people resort to apathy and depression.

Critique

With its focus on social, vicarious, symbolic, and self-regulatory determinants in psychological functioning, Bandura's Theory of Social-Cognitive Learning not only fills some of the theoretical gaps left by other learning theories but also provides a more convincing and optimistic rationale for human personality development and behavior change. Moreover, Bandura's theoretical constructs are supported by an extensive and impressive body of high-quality, innovative, carefully controlled experimental research in a wide variety of topics, including observational learning, cognitive influences, fear acquisition, self-regulation, self-referent processes, and therapist strategies.

Few contemporary psychologists have exerted greater impact on their profession than Bandura. Optimistic expectation for future developments in Social-Cognitive Theory appear to be justified.

No theorist of human personality and psychotherapy is immune to criticism. Personologists have examined the theory of social-cognitive learning and found it wanting in dealing with the structure and organization of personality. This shortcoming, they claim, results in a poorly integrated theory. Although Bandura's social-cognitive theory is broader than most behavioral approaches, it shares the major criticism leveled at behavioral strategies: It does not attempt a comprehensive presentation of personality. Liebert and Spangler (1990) point out that while Bandura's theory "alludes to general principles, it deals with only a few narrow, selected areas of personality functioning [e.g., locus of control, perceived self-efficacy, delay of gratification, and goal setting]" (p. 508).

Bandura's (1986) strong bias against psychoanalysis brings return fire. Psychoanalysts point to the lack of consideration for unconscious influences and conscious and unconscious conflict. Many critics argue that Bandura's contention that improved perceptions of self-efficacy explain successful client change in *all* psychotherapies is too broad a claim for a theory that gives only a narrow account of human personality.

Other critics believe that ignoring genetic and hormonal—indeed, all physiological factors—limits the potential effectiveness of social-cognitive theory. And still others fault Bandura for placing excessive confidence in situational tests to assess personality.

Bandura has been criticized, also, for not setting the boundaries of his theory—defining its predictive and applicative strengths and limits. Some fault social-cognitive theory for not adequately addressing human emotions, such as joy, shyness, elation, jealousy, and prejudice. Others find Bandura's explanation for psychosis far too general to be meaningful. And as mentioned earlier, while there are implications in the theoretical concepts of self-efficacy and self-regulation for the psychological healthy, Bandura has yet to address directly the subject of healthy personality and the good life.

Some therapists find Bandura's social-cognitive theory difficult to adopt or apply to therapy. Others, who believe in the therapeutic value of the counseling relationship, believe that his deemphasis on the relationship between the counselor and client is unacceptable.

Annotated Bibliography

Bandura's (1977) book, *Social Learning Theory,* is highly recommended as an introduction to his work. This small volume offers its readers a concise overview of the conceptual framework of Social Learning Theory and a look at the substantial body of experimental evidence that shaped it. In particular, the reader is made aware of the prominent roles played by vicarious, symbolic, and self-regulatory processes of psychosocial functioning.

When students are familiar with the basic theoretical constructs of social learning, they are prepared to advance to Bandura's more recent efforts to explain human thought, motivation, and behavior. *Social Foundations of Thought and Action: A Social Cognitive Theory* (Bandura, 1986), is an excellent addition to the professional libraries of personologists, counselors, and therapists—indeed, to the library of anyone concerned with the applications of social learning to everyday life. In this book, Bandura examines the influential roles of perceived self-efficacy and the basic issue of freedom and determinism. He analyzes the preponderance and potence of learning through observation and the human judgment and decision-making processes. He addresses sociocultural diffusion of novel ideas and social practices. And he compares his theory of cognitive development with the theory of Piaget (1986).

Chance encounters and life patterns, an issue neglected by most personality theories because their occurrence cannot be predicted, is addressed by Bandura (1982) in the July, 1982, issue of the *American Psychologist.* The thesis of this article is that chance encounters can and often do play prominent roles in shaping human lives. Social learning provides a basis for predicting the impact of chance encounters, and Bandura analyzes the personal factors and milieu properties that govern the branching power of chance encounters on human lives.

References and Suggested Readings

Awards for distinguished scientific contributions: 1980. (January, 1981). *American Psychologist, 36,* pp. 27–42.

Bandura, A. (1969). *Principles of behavior modification.* New York: Holt, Rinehart & Winston.

Bandura, A. (1971). Modeling processes and aggression in children. In S. Cohen (Ed.), *Child development: A study of growth processes.* Itasca, IL: F. E. Peacock, pp. 357–366.

Bandura, A. (1973). *Aggression: A social learning analysis.* Englewood Cliffs, NJ: Prentice–Hall.

Bandura, A. (1974). Behavior theory and the models of man. *American Psychologist, 29,* pp. 859–869.

Bandura, A. (1976). Effecting change through participant modeling. In J.D. Krumboltz & C. E. Thorensen (Eds.), *Counseling methods.* New York: Holt, Rinehart & Winston.

Bandura, A. (1977a). *Social learning theory.* Englewood Cliffs, NJ: Prentice–Hall.

Bandura, A. (1977b). Analysis of modeling processes. In E. M. Hetherington & R. D. Parke (Eds.), *Contemporary readings in child psychology.* New York: McGraw–Hill, pp. 191–207.

Bandura, A. (1977c). Toward a unifying theory of behavioral change. *Psychological Review, 84*(2), pp. 191–215.

Bandura, A. (1978a). The self system in reciprocal determinism. *American Psychologist, 33,* pp. 344–358.

Bandura, A. (1978b). Social learning theory of aggression. *Journal of Communication, 28,* pp. 12–27.

Bandura, A. (1980). Gauging the relationship between self-efficacy judgment and action. *Cognitive Therapy & Research, 4*(2), pp. 263–268.

Bandura, A. (1981). In search of pure unidirectional determinants. *Behavior Therapy, 12*(1), pp. 30–40.

Bandura, A. (1982a). Self-efficacy mechanism in human agency. *American Psychologist, 37*(2), pp. 122–147.

Bandura, A. (1982b). The psychology of chance encounters and life paths. *American Psychologist, 37,* pp. 747–755.

Bandura, A. (1982c). The assessment and predictive generality of self-percepts of efficacy. *Journal of Behavior Therapy & Experimental Psychiatry, 13,* pp. 195–199.

Bandura, A. (1983a). Temporal dynamics and decomposition of reciprocal determinism: A reply to Phillips and Orton. *Psychological Review, 90,* pp. 166–170.

Bandura, A. (1983b). Self-efficacy determinants of anticipated fears and calamities. *Journal of Personality and Social Psychology, 45*(2), pp. 464–469.

Bandura, A. (1984a). Representing personal determinants in causal structures. *Psychological Review, 9*(4), pp. 508–511.

Bandura, A. (1984b). Recycling misconceptions of perceived self-efficacy. *Cognitive Therapy and Research, 8*(3), pp. 231–255.

Bandura, A. (1986). *Social foundations of thought and action: A social cognitive theory.* Englewood Cliffs, NJ: Prentice–Hall.

Bandura, A., & Walters, R. H. (1963). *Social learning and personality development.* New York: Holt, Rinehart & Winston.

Bandura, A., Adams, N. E., & Beyer, J. (1977). Cognitive processes mediating behavioral change. *Journal of Personality and Social Psychology, 35,* pp. 125–139.

Bandura, A., & Schunk, D. H. (1981). Cultivating competence, self-efficacy, and intrinsic interest through proximal self-motivation. *Journal of Personality and Social Psychology, 41*(3), pp. 586–598.

Bandura, A., Reese, L., & Adams, N. E. (1982). Microanalysis of action and fear arousal as a function of differential levels of perceived self-efficacy. *Journal of Personality and Social Psychology, 43,* pp. 3–21.

Bandura, A., Taylor, C. B., & Williams, S. L. (1985). Catecholamine secretion as a function of perceived self-efficacy. *Journal of Counseling and Clinical Psychology, 53*(3), pp. 406–414.

Bandura, A., & Cervone, D. (1983). Self-evaluative and self-efficacy mechanisms governing the motivational effects of goal systems. *Journal of Personality and Social Psychology, 45*(5), pp. 1017–1028.

Bandura, A., & Cervone, D. (1986). Differential engagement of self-reactive influences in cognitive motivation. *Organizational Behavior and Human Decision Processes, 38*(1), pp. 92–113.

Bandura, A., Cioffi, D., Taylor, C. B., & Brouillard, M. E. (1988). Perceived self-efficacy in coping with cognitive stressors and opioid activation. *Journal of Personality and Social Psychology, 55*(3), pp. 479–488.

Bergin, A. E., & Garfield, S. L. (Eds.), (1971). *Handbook of psychotherapy and behavior change: An empirical analysis.* New York: John Wiley & Sons.

Carroll, W. R., & Bandura, A. (1982). The role of visual monitoring in observational learning of action patterns: Making the unobservable observable. *Journal of Motor Behavior, 14,* pp. 153–167.

Liebert, R. M., & Spiegler, M. D. (1990). *Personality: Strategies and issues* (6th ed.). Pacific Grove, CA: Brooks/Cole.

Piaget, J. (1986). *The construction of reality in the child.* (M. Cook, Trans.). New York: Ballantine Books. (Originally published 1954)

Staddon, J. E. (1984). Social learning theory and the dynamics of interaction. *Psychological Review, 91*(4), pp. 502–507.

Wood, R., & Bandura, A. (1989). Impact of conceptions of ability in self-regulatory mechanisms and complex decision making. *Journal of Personality and Social Psychology, 56*(3), pp. 407–415.

Conspectus of the Theories

Chapter Overview

Introduction

A Conspectus of the Eleven Basic Issues
    Heredity versus Social Determinants
    Conscious versus Unconscious Determinants
    Determinism versus Freedom of Choice
    Early versus Continuous Development
    Psychological versus Reality Environments
    Uniqueness versus Universality
    Role Assigned to Self-Concept
    Number and Weight Assigned to Motivational Concepts
    Explanation of the Learning Process
    Role Assigned to Group Determinants
    Centrality of Reinforcement

Psychological Health

Therapeutic Process

Final Commentary

Introduction

A single conceptual structure comprised of eleven basic issues was used in this book to assist you with your examination, understanding, and evaluation of fifteen major theories of personality. In this chapter, that same conceptual structure serves to uncover similarities and differences in ideology and psychological health. Although the focus of this chapter is on the similarities and differences of the fifteen theories, further comparisons, whether of substance or content, are encouraged and facilitated by a separate table of contents that traces each of the eleven basic issues across chapters.

A Conspectus of the Eleven Basic Issues

Heredity versus Social Determinants

Although practically every personality theorist presented in this book recognizes heredity as a determinant force in the development of personality, few grant greater recognition to heredity than Freud. For Freud, human nature is essentially biological. Social and cultural forces are viewed as inevitable sources of conflict. What we become is largely a function of internal dynamics. Jung also asserts that we are driven by inner, unconscious, hereditary forces, in particular by an inherited collective unconscious that contains the history of human evolution in the form of archetypes.

Neoanalytic theorists (i.e., Erikson, Fromm, and Horney) recognize hereditary determinants, but grant an expanded role to ego and to the impact of social and cultural determinants when compared to Freud. Erikson, for example, asserts that social factors actually support the ego by providing us with social roles and identities. Further, most neoanalytic, organismic, and existential theorists assert that through the evolutionary process, most basic animal instincts, along with their fixed, predetermined directives, have become supplanted by or subordinated to innate possibilities, tendencies, or predispositions that need not always be followed and that may, in certain instances, be ignored or transcended, or require conscious development. Social interest, a central characteristic for mental health in Adler's theory, for example, is much weaker than the herding instinct from which it evolved, and hence, must be consciously developed.

Though each theorist recognizes that we are biological beings, Adler, Allport, Rogers, Maslow, May, Frankl, Kelly, and Ellis view us as purposive. While the theories of Horney, Allport, Rogers, and Maslow endow us with an innate actualizing tendency that when followed gives us an inherited bodily wisdom, they recognize, as well, the impact of positive and negative cultural and societal forces on the fulfillment of innate potentials. Fromm, in particular, warned us that sick societies breed sick people.

Allport (1961) was convinced that "... no feature or quality is exclusively heredity, and none is exclusively environmental in origin" (p. 169). Kelly placed little emphasis on the importance of either heredity or environment. Rather, he proposed that we are all scientists in the sense that we develop personal constructs and then set out to test our constructs in the present. Ellis claims that cognition plays a mediating role between life's activating events and our reactions to them. Rogers, Maslow, Frankl, and May grant healthy individuals the capacity to transcend, at least to some degree, both our biology and our environment. May maintains the position that while heredity plays a significant role, human personality cannot be understood when separated from the world in which it exists. While Skinner recognizes heredity as a determinant of behavior, he ignores it in favor of operant reinforcement, which can be observed and measured. Bandura views personality as the result of dynamic, reciprocal interaction between personal, behavioral, and environmental determinants.

It would seem, then, that most of the fifteen theorists presented here would agree that it is naïve to consider only heredity or only environment as the singular determinant of personality. It would also appear at this point that the ideal fusion of this issue would be to study different heredity factors in interaction with different cognitive and different environmental stimuli. A graphic view of the theorists' positions on this issue is illustrated in Figure 17-1.

Conscious versus Unconscious Determinants

Freud, Jung, Kelly, and Skinner take extreme positions on this issue. For Freud, the unconscious is by far the deepest and most significant stratum of the three levels of consciousness. Moreover, he proclaims that our unconscious is comprised of basic psychobiological motives that create most of our major problems.

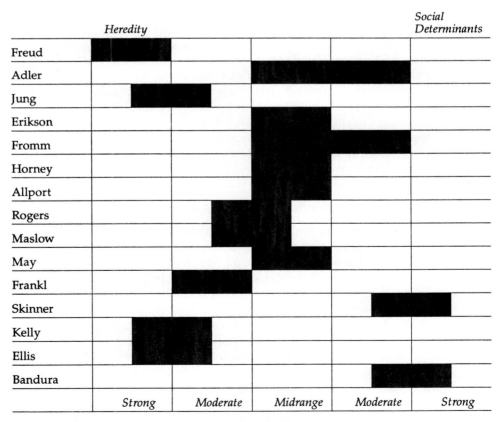

FIGURE 17-1 Heredity versus Social Determinants

Jung's complex theory views a divided unconscious, each division with its own distinct contents and functions. First, there is the personal unconscious and its complexes, and second, a collective unconscious and its archetypes. Skinner, in contrast, finds the unconscious little more than speculation, a presumption impossible to validate scientifically. He therefore sees neither need nor reason to ascribe any human behavior to the unconscious. Kelly provides no construct of an unconscious. Like Allport, Maslow, Rogers, and Ellis, Kelly saw the thinking of healthy adults as primarily conscious and concrete.

Adler, Kelly, Ellis, May, Frankl, Allport, Rogers, and Maslow believe that human behavior is purposive, and collectively they view the unconscious as something we are unable or unwilling to formulate clearly or that we either do not understand or withhold from understanding.

Allport, Rogers, and Maslow refer to an innate bodily wisdom that for the healthy at least, may offer intuitive, hence unconscious, directives. In both instances, this unconscious wisdom is part of the organismic tendency toward being or becoming. May's concept of the unconscious is the repression of potentialities for knowing and experiencing. He, as do many of those theorists who take a teleological stance (Adler, Rogers, Maslow, Kelly, and Ellis), rejects any hypothesis of the unconscious as an internal state or entity.

Nearly all here–now theorists (which includes Rogers, Maslow, May, Frankl, Kelly, and Ellis) work toward awareness of present perception, cognition, emotion, and action. For these theorists, unconscious motivations, while sometimes evident in abnormal behavior, play relatively minor roles in the lives of normal, healthy persons. Indeed, awareness in and of the present is central to the theory of the organismic, existential, and cognitive theorists. Awareness and ownership of present cognition, feelings, and behavior are criteria employed by many of the theorists presented in this chapter to assess therapeutic progress or measure psychological health. A graphic view of the theorists' positions on this issue appears in Figure 17-2.

Determinism versus Freedom to Choose

Freud and Skinner are strict determinists. Neither holds a place in his theory for such concepts as free will, choice, self-determinism, or self-actualization. Freedom is an illusion. Cognition, emotion, and behaviors are but links in a chain of causally related phenomena, determined largely by unconscious instinctual forces (Freud) or antecedent events (Skinner). Thus, while we may appear to ourselves and others as active, choosing beings, our behavior is the result of internal drives (Freud) or external reinforcements (Skinner).

At the other extreme on this issue are the existentialists May and Frankl, who consider us as condemned to freedom and responsibility. Fromm informs us that we have a tendency to escape from freedom. For these theorists, living and choosing are synonymous. Still, the three theorists just mentioned are quick to remind us that their stance on this issue does not mean that our freedom is without limits or restrictions, including the limits of the body, intelligence, social

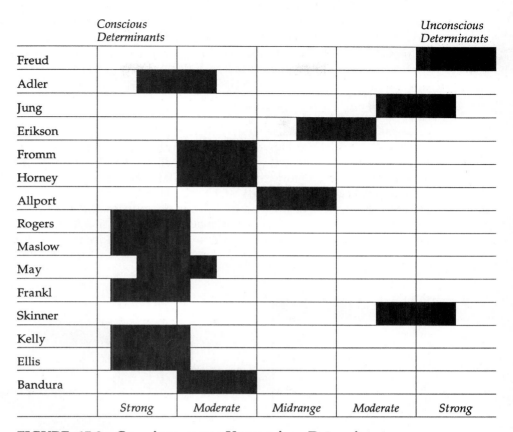

FIGURE 17-2   Conscious versus Unconscious Determinants

controls, illness, and death. Nonetheless, they all consider the surrender of freedom pathogenic.

Rogers and Maslow view us as capable, autonomous, responsible beings, provided we are aware and knowing in the present; in short, as long as we are psychologically healthy and live in the present. Kelly and Ellis maintain that we possess the potential for a wide range of existential freedom. Indeed, they tell us that when our personal constructs (attitudes, beliefs, and values) are rational, we are capable, at least to a limited degree, of transcending our biological and experiential antecedents.

Allport describes freedom as planning–striving–hope, guided by self-image. His principle of functional autonomy is a declaration of freedom. For Erikson, freedom is dependent on the attainment of the virtue of hope.

Bandura's position on this issue is one of reciprocal determinism. While we are definitely influenced by the antecedents and consequences of our behavior, we mediate these influences and consequences through our cognitive processes.

Thus, although we cannot be considered cause independent of our behavior and environment, we also cannot be considered simple reactions to environmental influence. The positions of the fifteen theorists on the issue of determinism versus freedom to choose are represented graphically in Figure 17-3.

Early versus Continuous Development

Practically every theorist acknowledges the importance of the early years on personality formation. However, of the fifteen theorists presented in this book, Freud and Skinner place the greatest emphasis on the continuity of personality development. Their theories clearly imply that events that occur in the present are systematically related to events that took place in the past, because we learned patterns of behavior in the past that determine our present reactions to environmental stimuli. Further, they assert that development is a lawful and consistent process. Jung believed emotional disturbances of children were actually reflec-

	Determinism				*Freedom*
Freud	■				
Adler				■	
Jung			■		
Erikson			■		
Fromm				■	
Horney				■	
Allport					■
Rogers					■
Maslow					■
May				■	
Frankl					■
Skinner	■				
Kelly					■
Ellis				■	
Bandura	■	■			
	Strong	*Moderate*	*Midrange*	*Moderate*	*Strong*

FIGURE 17-3   Determinism versus Freedom of Choice

tions of the emotional disturbances of their parents or parent surrogates. Erikson's developmental stages continue through the entire life cycle.

In contrast, Kelly, Ellis, and to some extent Allport, Rogers, Maslow, May, and Frankl explicitly stress lack of continuity—hence, the lack of predictability and control—in personality development. These theorists emphasize the relative independence of functioning adults from the events of infancy or childhood. Adler, Rogers, Maslow, Kelly, Ellis, May, and Frankl endow us with the existential freedom to choose our attitudes toward any event of the past—thus, the power to transcend the dysfunctional influences of that event in the present. Allport grants healthy adults functional autonomy. In brief, while we are not immune to early childhood experiences, neither are we immutably shaped by them. The majority of these theorists believe that it is possible, in theory at least, to consider both the effects of early experiences and the immediacy of the present in attempts to explain present human behavior (see Figure 17-4).

	Early Development				Continuous Development
Freud	■				
Adler		■			
Jung			■		
Erikson				■	
Fromm		■			
Horney			■		
Allport				■	■
Rogers					■
Maslow					■
May			■		
Frankl					■
Skinner			■		
Kelly				■	■
Ellis				■	■
Bandura			■	■	
	Strong	*Moderate*	*Midrange*	*Moderate*	*Strong*

FIGURE 17-4   Early versus Continuous Development

Subjective versus Objective Reality

The issue of subjective versus objective reality creates a dilemma for all theorists of personality and psychotherapy. How can we possibly know the absolute nature of reality? While all the theorists presented in this book agree that our survival depends on our ability to recognize and adapt to a physical and cultural reality, some, whether in theory or practice, avoid a reality environment as a determinant of behavior. We have only our perceptions of reality to guide us, and our perceptions are limited by imperfect senses and are influenced by individual experiential histories and current expectations.

Rogers tells us that we perceive and attend to what is congruent with our self-concepts. Bandura argues that our current understanding and expectations about ourselves, our behavior, and the world determine our perceptions. May believes our perceptions are influenced by our individual streams of consciousness and personal value systems. Similarly, Ellis insists that we filter our perceptions of reality through our personal belief systems. And Freud and Skinner assert that our past experiences shape our current perceptions. While none of these theorists is a pure phenomenologist, in the sense that perception is the sole determinant of behavior, all are to some degree phenomenological. They vary in the emphasis they give the psychological environment, from Rogers, Maslow, and May, for whom phenomenology is a central concept, to Skinner, who, at least in practice, ignores this issue entirely by concentrating on the principles of operant reinforcement (see Figure 17-5).

Uniqueness versus Universality

A phenomenon recognized by most personality theorists is that while we hold much in common with others of our species, we all sense and experience our uniqueness. Further, just as we are aware that we are duplicates of no other, we are equally certain that we are not the same persons we were in the past. Given this recognized phenomenon of a sensed uniqueness, the issue is not so much a question of uniqueness versus universality as it is a question of emphasis.

Allport, Rogers, Maslow, May, and Frankl grant uniqueness central emphasis in their theories. Ellis proposes unconditional self-acceptance; he views self-rating as irrational and dysfunctional. Skinner explicitly denies the crucial significance of this issue, strongly asserting that what most theorists consider the self is nothing more than a repertoire of acquired behaviors, and as with all acquired behaviors, subject to the principles of learning (see Figure 17-6).

Role of Self-Concept

Self-concept, whether viewed as an association of psychological processes or an accumulation of attitudes and feelings, occupies a conspicuous or central role in many theories of personality and psychotherapy. For May, Rogers, and Maslow, the concept of self emerges from an awareness of being or becoming; in their

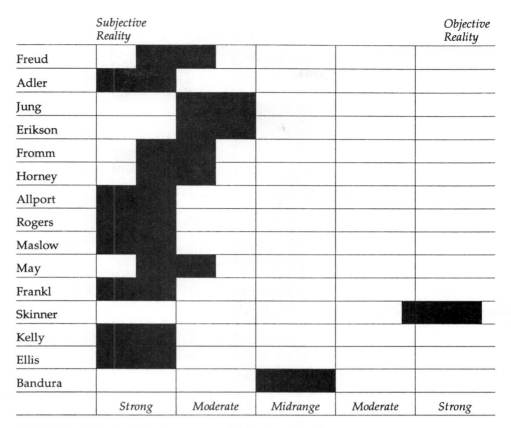

	Subjective Reality				Objective Reality
Freud		██			
Adler	██				
Jung			██		
Erikson			██		
Fromm		██			
Horney		██			
Allport	██				
Rogers	██				
Maslow	██				
May		██			
Frankl	██				
Skinner					██
Kelly	██				
Ellis	██				
Bandura			██		
	Strong	*Moderate*	*Midrange*	*Moderate*	*Strong*

FIGURE 17-5   Subjective versus Objective Reality

theories, self is both process and entity and gives our behavior unity and stability. In Adler's theory, the creative self enables us to rise above the influences of our biology and environment. We creatively use the influences of our biology and environment to construct our unique styles of life. Bandura prefers the term self-efficacy, but as with person-centered theory, a major goal of social-cognitive therapy is strengthening the client's belief in his or her self-efficacy. Horney addresses the influence of the ideal self and the tyrannical shoulds.

While Ellis recognizes the influence of self-concept on our emotions and behavior, he strongly asserts that self-rating (in the sense of rating one's essence or personhood) is irrational. For Ellis, we are, after all, only—but totally—human. Kelly did not assign a special role to self-concept, though he was convinced that any individual who deviated far from his or her core roles experienced guilt. Skinner's conception of learning and behavior focuses almost entirely on reinforcement; thus, with self defined as simply a repertoire of learned behaviors, the self or self-concept plays but a minor role in his theory.

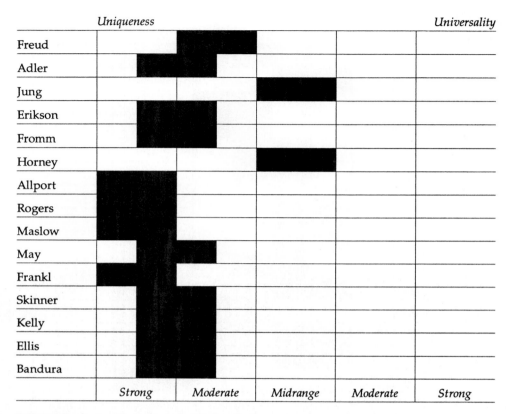

FIGURE 17-6 Uniqueness versus Universality

Number and Weight Assigned to Motivational Concepts

Adler, Jung, Horney, Rogers, and Maslow explain motivation with a single global construct. For Adler, it is a striving toward superiority, perfection, and completion. Both Rogers and Maslow call their motivational concept the actualizing tendency, the need to become fully functioning. There are many similarities between Jung's individuation process and the actualization process described above. Jung refers to his motivational concept as a process rather than a state of being.

For Allport, cognition is a dynamic incentive in motivation; interests, plans, intentions, values, meanings, and wants exert a powerful force of their own and push or pull to action. In addition, Allport's concept of functional autonomy regards adult motives as varied, self-sustaining, contemporary systems, growing out of antecedent systems, but currently functionally independent of them.

While Erikson accepted Freud's concept of libido as a psychic energy force that fuels mental activity, he granted the libido considerably less emphasis and focused more on the innate adaptive force of the ego and the influence of society.

For Kelly, life and motivation are synonymous—we are by nature telic beings, hence inherently motivated to anticipate the future. Bandura also looks to future expectations as forces of motivation.

Skinner, consistent with his experimental approach, ignores any internal, unconscious drives or needs; however, he, too, subscribes to an abbreviated set of motivational concepts based on operant reinforcement principles. Freud's complex theory of psychoanalysis is at the other end of the continuum. Literally thousands of instinctual urges and drives press for fulfillment by creating an intolerable tension in the id.

Explanation of Learning Process

Concern with the learning process in the theories of personality and psychotherapy varies considerably. At one end of the continuum there are the detailed explanations of Bandura and Skinner, and at the opposite end is May, who offers only a general treatment of the learning process.

Allport's stance on this issue is eclectic. While he agrees with many of the findings of the learning theorists, he finds their explanation insufficient when applied to healthy adults, for whom conscious, rational cognition must be considered. For Allport, as for Kelly, humans have a natural disposition to form structures. For both Kelly and Ellis, any change in an individual's personal constructs (Kelly) or belief system (Ellis) exemplifies learning. The value of learning is determined by the validity of the personal constructs or the rationality of the beliefs.

May tells us that learning occurs when crisis is confronted and a new level of consciousness is achieved; anxiety, though painful, is a natural teacher. Adler also focuses on natural and social consequences as instructors of an individual's lifestyle.

Freud, Rogers, and Maslow are satisfied to view learning in terms of global principles that govern all behavior. For Freud, learning occurs through the establishment of cathexes and the defense mechanism of sublimation.

Still, as Hall and Lindzey (1978) point out: "Although there may be some neglect of the learning process, there is an abundance of interest in the products of learning" (p. 684).

Role Assigned to Group Determinants

While none of the theorists presented in this book fails to recognize the importance of the primary group on early development, only Freud views the formative years in the family as critical. Deficiencies that occur during early stages of development are, according to Freud, likely to cause difficulty during adult years; hence, the child's early relationships with members of the family group are critical. Jung informs us that all emotional disturbances of children are reflections of parental failure. Adler also stresses the importance of family relationships on early development. The mother, especially, is responsible for the child's development of social interest, the primary measure of mental health in Adler's theory. In addition, Adler asserts that during this highly significant period of the child's life, unconscious life goals and unique styles of life are developed. Horney's child seeks security. Adler's child senses inferiorities.

Rogers, Maslow, May, and Bandura ascribe responsibility to the primary group for meeting the innate needs of the developing child. For Rogers, a most significant need is the need for positive regard; for May and Erikson, the sense of identity and consciousness; and for Bandura, appropriate modeling is necessary for most early learning and the actualizing of potentials.

For Erikson, a sense of inner solidarity with the ideas and values of some group, a feeling of social support, and validation and meaning to significant others are important determinants of identity and psychological health.

Group membership continues in importance as we move from the formative years into adulthood, and Rogers views the encounter group as an opportunity to provide growth experiences, particularly for those who experience difficulty adjusting to change, clarifying values, overcoming feelings of depersonalization or alienation, establishing interpersonal relationships, or developing self-reliance.

While Skinner is convinced that it is the individual who acts, he is equally certain that the reinforcement of group contingencies easily outweighs the total consequences that can be generated by the group's individual members acting alone. So although Skinner attributes less influence to groups as determinants of behavior, he recognizes that we can enhance the probability and increase the strength of reinforcement by joining a group.

Bandura and Allport have demonstrated that we move toward those groups whose members we perceive to share our interest and values. Further, Bandura asserts that we give and receive mutual reinforcement to preexisting bents through our group affiliations. For Bandura, then, groups partly determine the potentialities we cultivate and actualize.

Centrality of Reinforcement

Theorists vary considerably in the stance they take on this issue. Skinner assigns reinforcement the greatest significance; indeed, principles of operant reinforcement are the basis of his theory. According to Skinner, all learning is attributable to the contingencies of reinforcement.

Both Ellis and Bandura view reward as an important ingredient of learning and an integral part of therapy. Unlike Skinner, however, they grant us the uniquely human capacity for anticipatory thought and give us the capacity to shape conditions for our own purposes.

For Rogers, Maslow, May, and Frankl, external rewards are suspect. These theorists are concerned primarily with internal reward—that inner sense of satisfaction or gratification that comes with all experiences that facilitate the innate actualizing tendency. Erikson defines those experiences that fulfill our identity needs as inherently rewarding. Internal reward is implicit in Freud's concept of the pleasure principle, as well as in the reciprocal relationships in the three major systems of the psyche. Gratification of id's instinctual needs is innately rewarding.

Psychological Health

As stated in the introduction, one of the unique features of this book is the attempt to present the theorists' views of psychological health. As you have already learned, not all personality theorists address this subject directly; indeed, some do not address it at all. Still, in this writer's opinion, whether it was or was not their intent, each theorist offers his or her own unique view of what it is to be psychologically healthy, if only by implication. Further, even a cursory review of the literature reveals that on those few occasions when the theorists selected for presentation in this book addressed the issues of positive personality health and the good life, they did so based on a set of personal values and aspirations which they believed to be consistent with their own theories of personality development. Unfortunately, their views are often laden with more speculation and imagination than fact. This does not, however, lessen the importance of their work. Until we learn more about the nature of psychological health, the study of human personality will be incomplete.

I have learned from my experiences in the classroom that the subject of psychological health is of great interest to students. It provokes the most lively class discussions, for students are eager to learn new ways of fulfilling their possibilities in the world.

When Psychological Health Is Viewed as Utopia

There is a tendency for some theorists to idealize human potential, to present a view of psychological health as Utopia. Theorists who take a utopian stance to the issues of personality health and the good life analyze their imagined *possibilities* of human existence and formulate a universal model of health, rather than the fact of human existence. While arbitrary lists of ideal or utopian human characteristics and behavior are interesting and encourage further thought, discussion, speculation, and research, they do not provide clear direction or methodologies for achieving healthy personality or the good life in the existing world.

The borders separating health and pathology are blurred, and the directions for the person intent on becoming psychologically healthy are unclear. Indeed, by presenting psychological health as ideal, the goals set are unattainable—Utopia is, after all, a nonexistent place, a place to be approached but never reached.

Psychological health as Utopia is a never-ending struggle, a state of being never to be achieved, a possibility always beyond the seeker's grasp. Identified as an elusive possibility, the healthy personality and the good life are never to be fully realized.

While the utopian view of psychological health and the good life may be exciting and the challenge inspiring, it is also both excessive and indulgent. It is the result of a single theorist's reflection and personal bias. To be applied, the ideal view of psychological health must be lived, but it cannot be lived in the Utopia from which it emerged. It assumes knowledge of absolute values in a world with few or no absolutes. Humans live in a world of real objects involved in real events. When health is viewed as Utopia, there is always the possibility of error and change, for psychological health as Utopia creates a world in which there is no variability, contradiction, deception, or suffering, a world as the theorist believes it should be rather than the world that is. Psychological health as Utopia corresponds to the theorist's extension of his or her theory, hence is filled with those biased human characteristics and behaviors that are consistent with that theory. There is always doubt of its applicability in the world that is. Finally, lists of characteristics and behaviors offer no methodology.

While psychological health as Utopia has numerous limitations, extending the application of a personality theory to psychological health is a challenge that cannot be ignored (review the arguments presented by Maslow, Chapter 10). It seems to be the nature of theorists to extend their theoretical constructs and to test their limits (Kelly, Chapter 14). When the ideal is accepted with doubt (rather than faith), we are able to consider the theorists' visualizations as *possibilities* of the psychologically healthy personality. By acknowledging the impossibility of the ideal, we are also able to view it as untested steps or stages on the way to psychological health, rather than as a choice we must make between psychological health and pathology. The most positive views of psychological health hold suggestions that have high heuristic value, suggestions of areas for future research.

When Psychological Health Is Viewed as Normality

As mentioned in Chapter 1, for those personality theorists who work exclusively with human personalities in conflict, not only does abnormal behavior receive primary attention, but also behavior that is in accordance with social norms often becomes the desired goal. When this is the case, there is no further theoretical endeavor to conceptualize ways to transcend the normal in actualization. Personality health strategies and interventions are designed primarily for diagnosis, cure, and prevention of pathology. Individual personality growth, competence, enhancement, and excellence are left to those interested in fostering learning and development.

Psychological Health as Adjustment

For some personality theorists, psychological health is adjustment to the environment; others, however, do not always view adjustment as healthy. Not only do they equate adjustment with the average or norm (see above), they point out that any attempt to fit oneself into the normal distribution curve of certain cultures and societies is pathogenic, or at best a defensive or safe conformity. In short, they maintain that adjusting to a sick society leads to sick personalities.

For the actualization theorists, psychological health requires, at least to some extent, a facilitative environment. Further, they assert that any definition of psychological health must make allowances for imbalances within the individual's personality and between the individual's personality and cultural and societal demands. Refusal to adjust to the demands of a sick society is not only psychologically healthy, but may strengthen the healthy individual's resolve to trust his or her own impulses and intuition, develop higher ideals, and work toward improving the society.

Final Commentary

Though a small sample, the fifteen theories of personality presented in this book are sufficiently representative to demonstrate that theories of personality are diverse. Differences, inconsistencies, and contradictions are evident, both within and across theoretical orientations. It is apparent, also, that there are many similar concepts, though often hidden by the unique terminology of the theorist.

A synthesis of commonalities would seem advisable. However, there are very real obstacles that must be overcome. Patterson (1980) contends that the theorists present the greatest of the obstacles. They are interested in convincing others of the uniqueness and efficacy of their theory. They see little advantage of highlighting similarities with other theories. Considerable significance is attached to the ownership of ideas. Historically, Patterson (1980) informs us, it has been the practice of personality theorists to pit their ideas against all others, indeed, in many instances, to prove all others wrong. They engender a strong faith in their advocates, who are most unlikely to accept the dispassionate observations and critical analysis required for a synthesis of commonalities.

As pointed out earlier, basic issues are value laden. Discussions over their resolutions are often heated. Disagreements will certainly continue. No theory presented here is without its advocates and its critics. Each theory has made significant contributions to our understanding of human personality.

New theories of personality are certain to be formulated, for there is clearly the need to build on the strength of existing theories. There is much we have yet to learn about ourselves, and the basic issues of personality theory (whether those used in this book or others that have yet to emerge) may serve as guides. Movement in this direction is already evident with the growth of social learning and cognitive-behavioral approaches to personality formation and development. Increased attention is being given to genetic determinants. Health psychology and personality theory have much to offer each other in the years ahead.

References and Suggested Readings

Allport, G. W. (1961). *Pattern and growth in personality*. New York: Holt, Rinehart and Winston. (Originally published in 1937)

Bronowski, J. (1955). *Science and human values* (rev. ed.). New York: Harper Torchbooks.

Chiang, H., & Maslow, A. H. (Eds.). (1960). *The healthy personality: Readings* (2nd ed.). New York: D. Van Nostrand.

Hall, C. S., & Lindzey, G. (1978). *Theories of personality* (3rd ed.). New York: John Wiley & Sons.

Harris, S. J. (1972). *The authentic person: Dealing with dilemma*. Niles, IL: Argus Communications.

Jourard, S. M. (1963). *Personal adjustment: An approach through the study of healthy personality* (2nd ed.). New York: Macmillan.

Offer, D., & Sabshin, M. (Eds.). (1984). *Normality and the life cycle*. New York: Basic Books.

Patterson, C. H. (1980). *Theories of counseling and psychotherapy* (3rd ed.). New York: Harper & Row.

Shapiro, D. H., Jr. (1978). *Precision nirvana*. Englewood Cliffs, NJ: Prentice–Hall.

GLOSSARY

Actualizing Tendency *Rogers:* A biological tendency or predisposition within all humans to move toward the actualization and fulfillment of all inherent potentials. *Maslow:* The process of becoming all that one innately is; the movement toward the realization of all inherited possibilities and capacities.

Aggression *Kelly:* One possible response of the individual whose constructs are failing.

Air-Crib *Skinner:* A child's spacious crib that is enclosed in clear safety glass, temperature controlled, soundproof, germproof, and that contains a variety of apparatus that hang from the ceiling to stimulate the child. The Skinners created quite a stir by using the air-crib in raising their second daughter. Skinner now sleeps and works in an air-crib that he designed specifically for himself in his later years.

Anima *Jung:* Unconscious feminine side of man; an archetype in the collective unconscious.

Animus *Jung:* Unconscious masculine side of woman; an archetype in the collective unconscious.

Anxiety *Freud:* A warning of danger to Ego. A strong, pervasive feeling of dread and apprehension without specific cause, accompanied by somatic symptoms, such as palpitations of the heart, tightness of the chest, choking, trembling, faintness, etc. Freud identifies three types of anxiety: objective anxiety—threat in the external world; neurotic anxiety—threat of Id impulses; and moral anxiety—threat of Superego's restrictions or punishment. *Kelly:* Occurs when the events perceived by an individual cannot be construed within his or her construct system.

Archetypal Images *Jung:* Innumerable primordial images activated or invoked by environmental experiences, some of which are more consciously encountered than others. In addition to psychotic symptoms, they can be found in dreams, literature, religious mythologies, art forms, etc.

Archetypes *Jung:* A priori, phylogenetically transmitted predispositions to apperceive a universal emotional core of human experiences, myth, or thought-image fantasy—not a specific idea, image, or belief.

Assessment *Skinner:* Ideally, actual observation of a client's behavior in the natural environment in which it occurs. Behaviorists have developed sophisticated behavioral observation rating instruments and procedures for measuring behavior directly (e.g., frequency, intensity, duration, etc.).

Awareness *Rogers:* Symbolized experiences enter awareness and become part of the individual's phenomenological field.

Behavior *Rogers:* The result of immediate experience as it is perceived and interpreted, and thus only understandable from the internal frame of reference of the behaving individual. *Kelly:* From the PCT perspective, behavior is the person-as-scientist's "way of posing a question." In short, Kelly views human behavior as an experiment in living.

Behavior Modification *Skinner:* Changing behavior through a series of procedures based on reinforcement principles.

Being Cognition Also referred to as B-cognition or B-perception. *Maslow:* Perception and thought at the B-realm (governed by the B-values); the passive, nonjudgmental form of perceiving and thinking that occurs during peak experiences; perception and thought that transcends the lower-level deficiency needs.

Being Motivation Also called B-motivation, metamotivation, and growth-motivation. *Maslow:* Motivation that is beyond deficiency motivation; motivation that arises from embracing the B-values.

Being Values Also known as B-values and meta values. *Maslow:* Eternal or universal values that motivate a few rare individuals to move toward self-actualization.

Biophilic Character Orientation *Fromm:* Love of life.

Castration Anxiety *Freud:* The infant male's fear of the removal of his genital organs in retaliation for his forbidden sexual desires for his mother. The result of the Oedipus complex.

Cathexis *Freud:* The investment of psychic energy in a mental representation or mental image of an object or another person. The greater the amount of energy invested, the stronger the cathexis and the desire for the object.

Causality *Freud:* The conception that events can be explained and understood as the necessary consequence of prior events.

Censor *Freud:* The mental agency responsible for dream distortion and repression.

Circumspection *Kelly:* Applying a series of constructs propositionally.

Collective Unconscious *Jung:* An inherited part of the psyche that houses the archetypes.

Compensation *Adler:* An individual's striving to overcome real or imagined inferiorities.

Complex *Jung:* Clusters of associated feelings, thoughts, and memories with strong emotional content that are housed in the personal unconscious.

Comprehensive Construct *Kelly:* A construct that is applicable to a wide range of life events.

Conditional Regard *Rogers:* Restrictions (usually based on evaluation) attached to one person's regard and worth of another.

Conditioning *Skinner:* Based on linkage between behavior and its consequences.

Congruence *Rogers:* To be all that one truly is; exists when organismic experiences are matched by feelings, awareness, and expression. One of three necessary and sufficient conditions of a therapeutic relationship.

Conscious *Freud:* The part of the psyche that contains all psychic material of which the person is aware at any given moment.

Constriction *Kelly:* A process of narrowing the perceptual field so that anxiety created by incompatibilities with experience is no longer experienced.

Construct *Kelly:* The construct is the core characteristic of human personality. The construct is an idea (abstraction or representation) of a dichotomous nature resulting from idiosyncratic interpretation of experience. All constructs are tentative—to be tested against reality in terms of predictive efficiency—hence, subject to revision or replacement.

Constructive alternatives *Kelly:* A theoretical assumption that humans are always capable of changing or replacing their present interpretations of any event they encounter in life. Because humans are capable of reconstruing their experiences in an infinite variety of ways, human behavior is never completely determined. Constructive alternativism is a basic assumption behind all Kelly's theoretical constructs.

Construe *Kelly:* An individual's process of arriving at an understanding of life experiences through interpretation, deduction, or explanation.

Contextuality *Erikson:* A convincing coherence and order that lifts facts into a context apt to make us realize their nature.

Contingencies *Skinner:* The relationships between behavior and its consequences in a given situation.

Continuous Reinforcement *Skinner:* A schedule of reinforcement in which each desired response is followed by a reinforcement.

Core Construct *Kelly:* A construct that is fundamental to maintenance of self-as-a-person (identity and integrity). Loss of a core construct can damage or destroy the personal construct system. Threat to a core construct will cause a great deal of anxiety.

C–P–C Cycle *Kelly:* Circumspection–preemption–control process for making construction choices.

Creative Self *Adler:* A uniquely human subjective power that gives humans the ability to transform objective facts into personally meaningful events. Not only does this subjective power enable individuals to choose the opinions and attitudes they hold toward their biological and social circumstances, it permits them to search for experiences they believe will fit their life styles. In short, the creative self gives the individual some autonomy over his or her heredity and environment.

Creativity *Maslow:* A universal characteristic of Maslow's self-actualizing people. The ability to generate new or novel approaches to common or unique problems.

Cumulative Record *Skinner:* A method of recording and analyzing behavioral data over a long period of time that makes changes in rate conspicuous.

Dasein   *May:* Being in the world. Self in relation to the self (*Eigenwelt*); self in relation to the physical world (*Umwelt*); and self in relation to others (*Mitwelt*).

Defense   *Rogers:* The behavioral response to threat (perceived or subceived) with the goal to preserve the self-structure.

Defense Mechanisms   *Freud:* Any unconscious defense reaction or strategy employed by the Ego to protect the psyche from anxiety, shame, or guilt that might result from threats from the Id, Superego, or the reality of the external world. Freud identified some of the more common defense mechanisms: repression, regression, projection, compensation, sublimation, reaction formation, and aggression. *Rogers:* Perceptual distortion and denial.

Deficiency Cognition   Also D-cognition. *Maslow:* Need-directed perception; perception based on the judgments of approval or disapproval of others and governed by the deficiency needs.

Deficiency Need   Also referred to as deficiency motivator or D-motive. *Maslow:* Any need governed by the first four levels of Maslow's hierarchy of needs.

Denial   *Freud:* The refusal to accept or, in rare instances, even to perceive a threat outside the realm of the psyche. The irrational idea: "What I don't know can't hurt me."

Desacralization   *Maslow:* A deficiency or defense stance that distorts and diminishes humans, and in so doing, makes life less sacred and less dignified than it is.

Development   *Jung:* A progressively increasing tendency toward differentiation and integration.

Diagnosis   *Skinner:* Identification of environmental antecedents and consequences. Traditional diagnosis focusing on inner processes is considered by behaviorists neither logical, helpful, nor necessary.

Dilation   *Kelly:* The process of broadening the perceptual field so that constructs may be reorganized.

Discriminative Stimuli   *Skinner:* Stimuli present just prior to reinforcement that becomes associated with the response.

Displacement   *Freud:* A defense mechanism. Feelings or actions are unconsciously transferred from a highly threatening object to a substitute object that holds less threat.

Dreams   *Freud:* The royal road to the unconscious. *Jung:* Expressions of natural, creative spontaneity of the psyche; a symbolic process that reveals the inner truth and reality of the individual psyche.

Drive   *Skinner:* Simply a convenient way of referring to the effect of deprivation and satiation and of other operations that alter probability of particular actions to gratify deprivation.

Early Recollections   *Adler:* First memories of early childhood, whether real or imagined, provide important clues to the style of life and basic mistakes. A therapeutic technique to gather information on a client's present style of living.

Ego *Freud:* A structural or topographical concept referring to the organized part of the psyche. The modified part of the Id that has been influenced by the external world. Operates on the Reality Principle and is responsible for the survival of the organism. *Jung:* Located between the unconscious inner world and the external world, ego represents the center of consciousness and mediates and copes with the demands of life and living.

Ego Identity *Erikson:* Accrued experience, an integration of all prior identifications and available, fantasized roles. Also refers to direction and purpose (all we are, want to be, and believe we should become).

Ego Strengths *Erikson:* Sometimes referred to as virtues or qualities: hope, will, competence, etc. A sense of self-efficacy. Never completely achieved.

Elements *Kelly:* Those things and events abstracted or represented by a construct.

Empathy *Rogers:* Accurately perceiving the internal frame of reference of another; relating as if one were the other person without losing the as-if referent in the relationship.

Epigenetic Stages *Erikson:* Life stages that unfold according to an innate plan, span the entire life cycle, and are subject not only to biological forces, but also to a rational and adaptive ego, social processes, and historical factors.

Erotogenic Zone *Freud:* An area of the body capable of producing erotic gratification when stimulated, typically the sexual organs and mucous membranes surrounding bodily openings (i.e., the erotogenic zones of the early developmental stages: oral, anal, phallic).

Eupsychia *Maslow:* The concept of a utopian community that could be created by and for self-actualizing people, a community that permits natural growth to occur.

Eupsychian Management *Maslow:* A healthy form of business, industrial, or societal management that is based on Maslow's hierarchy of needs.

Experience *Rogers:* All visceral and environmental stimuli occurring at any given moment that are potentially available to awareness—experiences may be accurately symbolized and freely admitted to awareness, or may be distorted or denied and prevented from entering awareness.

Exploitive Orientation *Fromm:* The direction of those who expect others to fill their needs. They take what they want through force, stealth, or trickery, whether material possessions, spouse, friend, ideas, or creations. They approach their problems of loneliness by dominating others.

Expressive Movement *Allport:* Motor phenomena (posture, gait, carriage, facial expressions, hand gestures, handwriting, etc.) which are distinctive enough to differentiate one individual from another and which reveal a person's inner motivations and conflicts.

Extinction *Skinner:* Reduction of a learned behavior that is not reinforced.

Extraversion *Jung:* One of two basic ego attitudes toward life (see Introversion); the predominant interest and movement are toward external objects—people, things, and events.

Factuality   *Erikson:* Perceiving a minimum of distortion or denial and a maximum of the validation possible at a given stage of cognitive development and at a given state of technology and science.

Family Constellation   *Adler:* The individual's perceptions and interpretations of the dynamics of his or her family group—the sum total of the relationships and family transactions. The sociopsychological configuration of a family group as perceived by a single member of the family.

Feelings of Inferiority   *Adler:* Perceptions of physical or psychological shortcomings. May be actual or imagined.

Final Fictions   *Adler:* The child's personal, subjective construct of a utopian life goal that the child believes will overcome all obstacles. Formed before language mastery, and hence, never symbolized, this unique final fiction remains largely unconscious and controls the lifestyle, for the child acts as if the final fiction were reality.

Fixation   *Freud:* An inhibition in further libidinal development due to excessive frustration or satisfaction in a critical life stage.

Fixed Interval Schedule   *Skinner:* A schedule of reinforcement in which behavior is reinforced only after a fixed period of time has elapsed, without regard to the number of responses (e.g., pay by the hour, day, week, or month).

Fixed Ratio Schedule   *Skinner:* A schedule of reinforcement in which reinforcement occurs only after the subject has emitted a predetermined or fixed number of responses.

Focus of Convenience   *Kelly:* A construct or construct system works most effectively in predicting certain events. The range of these events is referred to as the focus of convenience.

Free Association   *Freud:* The technique employed in psychoanalysis to bring unconscious material to consciousness. Spontaneously saying everything just as it comes to mind without censoring or editing.

Freedom of Will   *Frankl:* A finite freedom of will within the limits set by the conditions of life.

Fully Functioning Person   *Rogers:* The psychologically healthy person in process of becoming all that he or she potentially is.

Functional Analysis   *Skinner:* Attempt to understand behavior through identification of the environmental conditions that determine its occurrence or nonoccurrence.

Functional Autonomy   *Allport, 1961:* "Any acquired system of motivation in which the tensions involved are not the same kind as the antecedent tensions from which the acquired system developed" (p. 229).

Gemeinschaftsgefuhl, or Social Interest   *Adler:* An innate human potential that when consciously and optimally developed, leads to a sense of community and communal life, involves the individual in the well-being of all humankind, and enables him or her to meet the challenge of life tasks with courage.

Guilt   *Kelly:* From the PCT perspective, guilt occurs when there is a contradiction between the individual's core constructs of self and his or her actual behavior.

Hoarding Orientation *Fromm:* Relates success to accumulating and protecting wealth and power. Anything less than total possession brings a sense of insecurity. Key traits: unimaginative, stingy, stubborn, suspicious, obsessional, and possessive.

Hope *Erikson:* A necessary ego strength for a healthy life. Erikson maintains that life is impossible without hope.

Hostility *Kelly:* An individual's attempt to extort validating evidence for a prediction that is failing.

Id *Freud:* Latin for "it." Used to designate the unorganized part of the psyche. Descendant of the Unconscious. Contains everything inherited or repressed. Operates on the Pleasure Principle.

Idealized Self *Horney:* A glory orientation, masking unconscious self-contempt and characterized by pursuit of a grandiose image of a perfect self and accompanied by the neurotic claim: "I am a superior being and must be treated as such."

Identification *Freud:* The process by which a person extends his or her identity into someone else, borrows identity from someone else, or focuses or confuses identity with someone else.

Idiographic Laws *Allport:* Laws derived from and applicable to the data of a single individual, a single case. A concept to explain that some behavior of a single person would not be applicable to any other individual.

Individuation *Jung:* An autonomous, inborn process of self-actualization rarely, if ever, realized fully; a key developmental concept in Jung's analytic psychology.

Inferiority Complex *Adler:* Exaggerated and intensified pathological feelings of inferiority, including the attitudinal belief that difficulties presented by life problems cannot be overcome through personal, appropriate, cooperative effort.

Instinct *Freud:* An innate motivating force, as numerous as bodily needs. Freud classified all instinct into two major types: Eros, which includes the sexual instincts, and Thanatos, which includes the destructive or aggressive instincts.

Instinctoid Need *Maslow:* An instinct remnant, a biological tendency or predisposition, an innate but weak urge that can be easily overwhelmed by learning or culture.

Introversion *Jung:* One of two basic ego attitudes (see Extraversion); the predominant interest and movement is inward, toward thoughts and feelings.

Irrational Beliefs *Ellis:* Beliefs that are followed by inordinately strong emotions and ineffective, dysfunctional, or destructive behavior. Irrational beliefs block us from achieving long-range goals.

Jonah Complex *Maslow:* Taken from the Biblical story of Jonah. Maslow used this term to describe those individuals who had seemingly gratified all D-needs, yet resisted or denied the growth-needs. A fear of and tendency to run from those potentials viewed in one's most perfect moments.

Libido *Freud:* The psychic energy linked to the sexual instinct, often used as a synonym for sexuality. Freud later expanded the meaning of libido to include both life (Eros) and death (Thanatos) instincts. *Jung:* A synonym for all forms of psychic energy.

Life Goal *Adler:* The unique creation of the individual in response to his or her perceptions of heredity and environment. Constructed by the child before adequate language development, hence never formulated in words (see "Final Fictions," above).

Loose Construct *Kelly:* Leads to predictions that can vary in time and situation or occasion.

Mandala *Jung:* A Sanskrit word translated as "magic circle"; symbol of wholeness, perfection, and unity—the symbol of the self-archetype, thought to aid in integrating the psyche.

Marketing Personality *Fromm:* Those who measure their worth as they measure commodities, by how well they sell themselves on the open market. Genuine interpersonal relationships are impossible.

Mental Health *Frankl:* Living meaningfully for the future within the present limitations of reality.

Metamotives See also B-values. *Maslow:* Motives that are after or beyond striving or desiring; motives that transcend the deficiency needs.

Metapathology *Maslow:* A high-order, existential, psychological disorder resulting from the denial or deprivation of the metavalues (B-values or metaneeds); a lack of zest, meaning, purpose, or will in life.

Modeling *Bandura:* We can and do learn novel behavior simply by attending to the performance of others who serve as models. Learning acquired through modeling is acquired in large segments or in total, without either an overt response to the witnessed behavior or the administration of external reinforcement.

Motivation *Kelly:* Discarded as a redundant, hence, unnecessary, term by Kelly, who viewed all living organisms as naturally and constantly in process—behaving, acting, moving, metabolizing.

Narcissism *Freud:* Love of self; the investment of libido in the self (secondary narcissism). An early stage of development immediately following birth (primary narcissism). If fixation occurs, narcissism may persist into adulthood.

Necrophilic Character Orientation *Fromm:* A particularly malignant orientation toward self, others, and the world. Love of death and decay.

Need for Positive Regard *Rogers:* With self-awareness, the need to be accepted, prized, and loved arises; this need can only be satisfied by others, particularly by those others perceived as significant in one's life.

Negative Reinforcement *Skinner:* The elimination or removal of an aversive stimulus following a response that is reinforcing and increases the probability of that response in the future.

Neglect *Adler:* One of three major parental errors, the failure to give a child the sufficient care and attention it believes it needs. May result in the child's mistaken perception that the world and its inhabitants are uncaring and hostile.

Noogenic *Frankl:* A uniquely human third dimension, a spiritual dimension that houses an awareness of potentials, goals, and most importantly, meanings.

Object of Devotion *Fromm:* The need for direction and purpose.

Oedipus Complex *Freud:* Group of largely unconscious ideas centering around the strong desire to possess the parent of the opposite sex. Ambivalence for the parent of the same sex—jealousy together with love. Considered by Freud to be a universal phenomenon. Usually resolved through identification with parent of the same sex.

Ontological Guilt *May:* Guilt related to the nature of our being in the sense of imperfections and limitations. Always a threat.

Operant Conditioning *Skinner:* Reinforcing approximations of goal behavior. Usually follows a specific schedule of reinforcement.

Organ Inferiority *Adler:* A real or imagined physiological defect that makes the child feel inferior. All depends on the child's perceptions. With successful compensations, pathogenic goals are avoided. One of three major errors responsible for a pathogenic life style.

Organism (Human) *Rogers:* The total person with all his or her physical and psychological functions.

Organismic Valuing Process *Rogers:* The process used by the organism to determine whether an experience will facilitate or thwart the actualizing tendency.

Pampering *Adler:* The most serious of three major parental errors. Pampering (excessive attention, protection, and assistance) contributes to a child's mistaken perception that he or she is to be served by others. Pampering does nothing to develop social interest.

Parapraxis *Freud:* An unconscious slip of the tongue, memory, or pen, or an action that reveals true feelings or beliefs. Freud used parapraxis to demonstrate the existence of the unconscious.

Peak Experience *Maslow:* Brief, intense, mystical, oceanic experience, accompanied by an altered state of consciousness, and characterized by feelings of wholeness, loss of self, euphoria, ecstasy; a transcending, essentially indescribable experience that Maslow felt was triggered by an embracing of the B-values.

Penis Envy *Freud:* The female child's envy of the male child's penis. Considered by Freud to be universal in women. *Horney:* A little girl's envy of the freedom freely given to little boys.

Peripheral Construct *Kelly:* Construct with only limited application. Loss of a peripheral construct may exert little effect on the construct system.

Permeable Construct *Kelly:* A construct is considered permeable when it is open to the application of new events not yet incorporated into the construct system; permeable constructs make change of the construct system possible.

Persona *Jung:* Mask or façade exhibited in public; individuals' perceptions of the roles society expects of them or the roles they want others to perceive. Persona may mask other archetypes, for example, the anima or animus and the shadow. Serious difficulties arise when the persona masks the self.

Personality *Adler:* Manifestation of an individual's life style. Adler used the terms *personality* and *lifestyle* interchangeably. *Fromm:* The total psychic qualities, the individual's inherited temperament or mode of reaction and the individual's character or object of reaction. *Skinner:* A repertoire of behavior—nothing more.

Personal Orientation Dimensions (POD): Shostrom's (1975, 1977) attempt to improve the POI scale by extending and refining the concepts of actualization measured by it.

Personal Orientation Inventory (POI): A self-report questionnaire designed by Shostrom in 1963 to measure self-actualizing tendencies in individual adolescents and adults.

Personal Unconscious *Jung:* That part of the psyche comprised of experiences not admitted to consciousness by ego, either because they failed to make a conscious impression or because they were suppressed or forgotten. Contents of personal unconscious accessible to consciousness.

Pleasure Principle *Freud:* The goal of the Id: to achieve pleasure (gratify instinctual urge) and to avoid pain (tension and anxiety created by nongratification of instinctual urge).

Positive Regard *Rogers:* A positive feeling of self-worth that is not dependent on the attitudes of others—contributes to self-direction, autonomy, and independence.

Positive Reinforcement *Skinner:* Any stimulus that follows a behavior and increases the probability of its reoccurrence.

Pre-conscious *Freud:* That part of the psyche that includes all material that is not repressed and that can be readily moved to the conscious.

Preemption *Kelly:* Construing in terms of one or the other available construct.

Preemptive Construct *Kelly:* When an element belongs exclusively to the realm of one construct; a preemptive construct does not permit its elements to be applied to any other category.

Preverbal Construct *Kelly:* A construct formulated prior to the individual's development of the language skills necessary to symbolize the construct.

Primary Process *Freud:* An hallucinatory wish-fulfillment process of Id. Unable to contact reality for the object of instinctual urges, the Id can only wish (dream, hallucinate, etc.) for gratification.

Primordial Image See "Archetypal Image." *Jung:* Psyche: A term synonymous with personality, a unity that includes all thought, feeling, and behavior, whether conscious or unconscious.

Proactive Functioning *Allport:* Self-initiated behavior, as opposed to reactive functioning or a responsive attitude to external stimuli.

Productive Orientation *Fromm:* An ideal, hence never totally achievable, character type; represents the ultimate in human health and the ideal in human ethics.

Projection   *Freud:* A defense mechanism whereby the individual unconsciously attributes his or her own threatening impulses, wishes, feelings, or beliefs to others, to things, or to the world.

Propriate Functioning   *Allport:* Thoughts, feelings, and actions are subjectively chosen and express the self or proprium.

Proprium   *Allport:* A core concept in Allport's theory. The proprium serves an organizing and integrating function and provides an impetus to psychological growth and development. The functions of proprium are sense of body, self-identity, self-esteem, self-extension, rational coping, self-image, and propriate striving (Allport, 1961, pp. 110-138).

Prototype   *Adler:* The core of the lifestyle, often evident in the individual's earliest recollections.

Psyche   A term synonymous with personality, a unity that includes all thought, feeling, and behavior, whether conscious or unconscious.

Psychic Energy   *Freud:* The force that powers all psychic activity. Freud assumes that the source of psychic energy is similar to physical energy, and like physical energy, is limited.

Psychic Value   *Jung:* A measure of the relative degree of psychic energy (libido) invested in a specific psychic element.

Psychosis   *Jung:* An invasion of the conscious by unconscious content, partially or completely overwhelming ego.

Punishment   *Skinner:* When behavior is followed immediately by an aversive stimulus or by the removal of a positive reinforcer. Skinner holds that threat or punishment is generally inefficient and leads to escape and avoidance.

Purpose of Behavior   *Skinner:* The purpose of a specific behavior is the consequence.

Q-Sort   An inventory technique created by William Stephenson that consists of a series of self-referent statements printed on cards which the subject is asked to sort into separate piles.

Radical Determinism   Everything humans do is the result of specifiable conditions; that is, every human act is considered to be determined by antecedent factors. Once these conditions or factors have been discovered, human behavior can be predicted and, to some extent, controlled.

Range of Convenience   *Kelly:* All constructs, hence all construct systems or theories, have limits beyond which they are less effective or irrelevant; thus the range of convenience refers to the breadth of events for which the individual finds his or her construct system useful for the task of predicting future events.

Rational Beliefs   *Ellis:* Rational beliefs result in appropriate emotions and effective behavior; they lead to achievement of goals over the long term.

Rationalization   *Freud:* A defense mechanism. Unconsciously employing and accepting a plausible but false explanation to justify irrational behavior and reduce feelings of low self-esteem, guilt, or shame. Conceals true motivation.

Reaction Formation *Freud:* A defense mechanism. Unconsciously repressing threatening beliefs, feelings, or urges, and then replacing them with their opposites. Usually exaggerated, thus evident to others.

Reality Principle *Freud:* Ego operates on the Reality Principle. Responsible for the survival of the organism, Ego delays making an object choice for an instinctual urge until it can find a safe and socially acceptable object.

Real Self *Horney:* "That central inner force common to all humans and yet unique in each, which is a deep source of growth" (Horney, 1950, p. 17).

Receptive Orientation: Individuals with dominant receptive orientations fully expect others to fulfill all their wishes and desires: recipients rather than earners or creators, loved rather than loving; passive, opinionless, submissive, unrealistic, cowardly, wishful, gullible, and sentimental. Left on their own they feel quite helpless.

Reciprocal Determinism *Bandura:* Personal (including cognition), behavioral, and situational factors are continually in a state of triadic reciprocal interaction in the determination of who and what we are. All operate interactively, as mutual, two-way directional determinants, each reciprocally affecting the other two. Sometimes referred to as the triadic model; the cause of all psychosocial functioning.

Regression *Freud:* A defense mechanism. Unconsciously reverting to behavior typical of an earlier, safer period of life. Avoids anxiety of present threats.

Reinforcer *Skinner:* Any stimulus that increases the probability of response.

Relatedness *Fromm:* The need to unite with other beings, to genuinely belong.

Repertoire *Skinner:* Acquired behavioral patterns.

Repression *Freud:* The most common defense mechanism. Unconsciously relegating threatening material to the unconscious and using anticathexis to ensure that it remains there.

Resistance *Freud:* A client's attempt to sabotage the purpose of therapy. May take any form that interferes with the free association process or the analyst's interpretations. Transference is a form of resistance, whether positive or negative.

Secondary Process *Freud:* Ego's use of thought and reason in dealing with the external world, the demands of Id, and the restrictions and threats of Superego.

Self *Rogers:* Far broader than the self-concept, the self constitutes the central concept of Rogers's theoretical approach to psychotherapy and personality; indeed, the self is a basic factor in the formation of personality and the determination of behavior. *Jung:* An organizing archetype, hence a precursor of ego and an innate potential for unity and wholeness; sense of a basic, undivided wholeness.

Self-Actualization *Rogers:* A vigorous expression of the actualizing tendency in experiences that are symbolized in the self as the "I" or "me." *Maslow:* The highest level of Maslow's Hierarchy of Needs; to reach this level of human development and motivation, all D-needs must be sufficiently and consistently gratified and the B-values recognized and pursued. *May:* All our capacities, including freedom, choice, and autonomy; our capacity to be aware of ourselves as both subject and object.

Self-Concept *Rogers:* A self's perception of self—a fairly organized and stable conceptual Gestalt that includes all a person refers to as the "I" or "me" and all the "I" or "me" can do—based primarily on experiences with others perceived as important to the self. *Skinner:* A description of one's own behavior; a person's knowledge of functionally integrated system of responses.

Self-Efficacy *Bandura:* Our individual efficacy expectations which exert significant influence on choice of and persistence in coping with difficult life tasks.

Selfhood *Jung:* An ideal toward which humans strive but never completely achieve.

Self-Ideal *Rogers:* That self-concept the person would most like to possess—a perceived goal.

Self-Regard *Rogers:* Occurs when people trust and like themselves; includes feelings of self-worth and self-confidence and contributes to self-direction.

Self-Regulation *Bandura:* Self-set standards and goals used to judge success or failure of our actions

Self-System *Bandura:* Comprised of self-evaluation, self-judgment, self-efficacy, and self-set goals and standards. May lead either to self-motivation and self-reinforcement or to self-punishment and self-devaluation.

Self-Talk *Ellis:* The inner dialogues that we generate regarding the experiences, encounters, and circumstances that arise in daily life. The voice of our personal value systems.

Self-Transcendence *Frankl:* Forgetting self by looking outward to a cause, another person, or "for the sake of God." *May:* Transcending the boundaries of the present moment by bringing the distant past (via memory) and the long-term future (via imagination) into present existence. The inability to transcend a specific self-world relationship is the mark of mental disorder.

Shadow *Jung:* A global analytic term with both personal and transpersonal (archetypal) connotations having to do with dangerously unrecognized repressions and suppressions split off and unrecognized by ego-consciousness. In addition to a denied or projected "otherness," the shadow is considered the archetype of the human's animal nature.

Shaping *Skinner:* See "Operant Conditioning."

Social Interest *Adler:* Primary criterion of mental health. An innate potential in all humans that must be consciously developed. A feeling with the whole of humanity and a striving for a form of community which must be thought of as everlasting.

Stimulus *Skinner:* Any condition that affects behavior.

Subceived *Rogers:* Experiences (stimuli) that are discriminated but not symbolized, hence not accepted into awareness; in short, discrimination without awareness.

Subception *Rogers:* The process of perceiving experiences (stimuli) without awareness (symbolization) of the perception—the detection of an experience before it enters full awareness.

Sublimation *Freud:* A defense mechanism. Unconsciously gratifying threatening instinctual urges in a socially acceptable manner. Similar to displacement, but the object of displacement represents the social ideal of behavior and often requires a great deal of learning and skill development. All Ego development depends on sublimation.

Superordinate Construct *Kelly:* A construct that includes another construct as one of its elements. Core constructs are often superordinate constructs.

Symbols *Jung:* Outward manifestations of the archetypes; universal representations of the innate wisdom of the collective unconscious.

Synchronicity *Jung:* An acausal connecting principle that manifests itself through meaningful coincidences (i.e., paranormal phenomena that do not follow any known principles of nature); attributed to the nature of archetypes rather than to cause and effect.

Synergy *Maslow:* A harmonious integration; a transcending of the D-realm (i.e., Eupsychia was Maslow's concept of a synergistic community where human and social values are integrated and where the usual dichotomies experienced by those living at the D-level are transcended).

Teaching *Skinner:* The arrangement of contingencies of reinforcement under which the students learn. They learn because of consequences of acts. They remember because of reinforcement for recalling what they learn.

Teleology: The conviction that the human personality can be best understood in terms of future goals.

Third Force Psychology *Maslow:* A dynamic, holistic, and humanistic psychology that is offered as an alternative to psychoanalysis and behaviorism; a psychology that stresses the healthy, positive, and creative aspects of human motivation and behavior.

Threat *Rogers:* Subceived experiences that are incongruent with the self-structure are threatening. *Kelly:* In PCT, threat is brought on by an awareness of an imminent major change in the individual's construct system.

Tight Constructs *Kelly:* constructs that lead to unvarying predictions.

Token Economy *Skinner:* A systematic program of behavior modification in which tokens are awarded for identified appropriate behaviors that may then be exchanged for experiences or objects the clients value.

Traits *Skinner:* Ongoing behavioral processes subject to intervention and change. *Allport:* Personal and consistent ways of acting and adjusting to environments—existential units of personality that are relatively stable and congruent structures.

Transcendence *Fromm:* The need to rise above the animal side of our nature, to create. *Frankl:* A characteristic of human existence and a dimension of the noetic; gives us the capacity to transcend the level of the somatic, the psychic, and the social.

Transcendent Function *Jung:* A superordinate process integrating unconscious with conscious, systems with themselves, and systems overall to create a functioning.

Transpersonal Psychology *Maslow:* A concept of a "Fourth Psychology" that reaches beyond all present concepts of identity and self-actualization to ultimate human capacities and potentialities which have no place in psychology today. The *Journal of Transpersonal Psychology* is the voice of this movement.

Tyranny of the Should *Horney, Ellis:* Pathogenic absolutes (should, ought, must, have to).

Unconditional Positive Regard *Rogers:* Positive regard without possessiveness, evaluation, restrictions, or reservations; in short, warm, trusting acceptance of all a person is in the ongoing moment. One of three necessary and sufficient conditions of a therapeutic relationship.

Unconscious *Freud:* That part of the psyche that includes all material not in awareness and not readily available to awareness. For Freud, the unconscious is by far the greatest portion of the psyche. *May:* ". . . Those potentials for knowing and experiencing which the individual cannot or will not actualize" (May, 1983, pp. 17–18).

Undoing *Freud:* A defense mechanism. Unconsciously adopting ritualistic behaviors that symbolically negate earlier actions or attitudes that threaten guilt, shame, or loss of self-esteem. A form of negative magical thinking.

Variable Interval Schedule *Skinner:* A schedule in which reinforcements are presented on some stated time interval, but the intervals between reinforcements are irregular and impossible to predict.

Variable Ratio Schedule *Skinner:* A schedule in which the number of responses for reinforcement is varied randomly around a specified average value (e.g., the slot machine).

Will to Meaning *Frankl:* An innate and exclusively human motivation to seek meaning and purpose through a cause or mission or for the love of another person or for a religious faith.

Wisdom *Erikson:* ". . . Detached concern with life itself in the face of death itself" (Erikson, 1964a, p. 133). Associated with a meaningful old age.

Wish-Fulfillment *Freud:* A primary process and function of the Id. Forming an image of the object that would gratify an instinctual urge or need.

INDEX OF AUTHORS

(Pages in **BOLD** denote author spread)

Abrahms, E., 470

Ackernecht, L. K., 106

Adler, Alfred, 3, 6, 19, 20, 25, 29, 33, 65, 66, **69–107**, 113, 127, 176, 257, 259, 260, 317, 328, 352, 359, 376, 460, 538, 540, 543, 545, 546, 547, 548, 554, 555, 556, 558, 559, 561, 562, 563, 565

Allen, B. P., 144

Allport, G.W., 3, 6, 7, 20, 113, 140, 145, 151, 203, 216, **247–265**, 335, 365, 399, 538, 540, 543, 544, 546, 547, 548, 557, 558, 559, 562, 563

Angel, E., 355, 357, 361, 366, 367

Ansbacher, H. L., 71, 72, 78, 80, 81, 84, 85, 87, 90, 91, 92, 93, 94, 95, 96, 100, 101, 105, 107

Ansbacher, R. R., 71, 72, 78, 80, 81, 84, 85, 87, 90, 91, 92, 93, 94, 96, 100, 101, 105

Aram, J. D., 336

Aristotle, 3

Arnold, Dwight, 510

Baars, B. J., 460

Bacon, Francis, 401

Bandura, A., 6, 20, 50, 432, **499–534**, 539, 540, 541, 545, 548, 560, 564, 565

Bannister, Donald, 432, 447, 456

Beck, A. T., 6

Bentham, Jeremy, 3

Bergin, A. E., 527

Berne, Eric, 71

Binswagner, Ludwig, 33

Blake, William, 133

Bleuler, Eugen, 116

Bottome, P., 72

Bowman, J. T., 106

Boy, A. V., 289

Breuer, Joseph, 31, 32

Brittain, C. Y., 80

Brome, V., 113, 115, 117

Brouillard, M. D., 515

Brown, D. R., 336

Brucke, Ernst, 31

Buber, Martin, 314, 361

Bulka, R. P., 380, 390

Carroll, W. R., 504

Cattell, R. B., 144

Cervone, D., 504, 514, 515, 516, 517, 525

Charcot, Jean, 3, 31

Chiang, H., 206, 258, 260, 285, 339

Ciaccio, Nicholas, 170, 171

Cioffi, D., 515

Compte, Auguste, 3

Cook, L., 484

Corlis, R. B., 366

Cormier, L. S., 418

Cormier, W., 418

Corsini, R. J., 107

Coulson, W. B., 289, 290, 291

Crumbaugh, J. C., 380

Darwin, Charles, 31

de Laszlo, V. S., 127, 128, 132

De Martino, R., 204
Diamond, C. P. T., 448, 449
Dickman, S., 50
DiGuiseppe, R., 475, 479, 484, 487, 489, 493
Dinkmeyer, D. C., 80, 86, 96, 99, 104, 106
Dreikurs, R., 71, 77, 80, 84, 86, 88, 94, 95
Dryden, W., 468, 470, 478, 481, 484
Duckworth, D. H., 145
Dymond, R. F., 279, 289, 290, 291, 292, 293

Eccles, J., 3
Eckhart, Meister, 190
Elkind, D., 190
Ellenberger, H. F., 19, 32, 33, 64, 71, 72, 94, 95, 117, 148, 351, 355, 357, 361, 362, 366, 367
Elliot, Helen, 273
Ellis, Albert, 19, 20, 29, 71, 228, 238, 427, **459–496**, 526, 538, 540, 541, 543, 544, 545, 547, 559, 563, 565
Epectetus, 460
Epstein, R., 399, 418, 420
Erikson, E. H., 6, 29, 113, 133, 145, 157, **159–184**, 259, 541, 546, 548, 555, 557, 558, 559
Erwin, R. B., 117
Evans, R. I., 166, 169, 249, 278, 289, 415
Ewen, R. B., 115
Ewin, R. B., 50
Eysenck, H. J., 145

Fabry, Joseph, 378, 380, 390
Farley, F. H., 80
Farson, R., 303
Farson, Richard, 272
Feist, J., 106, 315
Fischer, G., 336
Fisher, S., 63
Foa, U. G., 92
Ford, D. H., 10
Fordham, F., 113, 133, 139
Fox, J., 336
Frankl, Victor, 6, 19, 71, 259, 260, 264, **347–392**, 538, 540, 543, 544, 548, 558, 559, 561, 565, 567
Fransella, F. A., 457
Freeman, Annis, 192, 193

Freeman, L., 66
Frerking, R. A., 484
Freud, Anna, 162, 256
Freud, Sigmund, 3, 6, 19, 25–26, 28, 32, **34–66**, 70, 113, 173, 181, 183, 189, 190, 191, 259, 321, 341, 376, 538, 539, 540, 542, 544, 546, 548, 553, 554, 556, 557, 558, 559, 560, 561, 562, 563, 564, 566, 567
Frey, D. H., 366
Fromm, Erich, 6, 20, 29, 71, 145, 157, 159, 191, 195, 197, 200, **201–216**, 236, 259, 263, 353, 539, 540, 557, 559, 560, 561, 562, 564, 566
Frost, Robert, 401
Funk, R., 189

Ganguli, S., 336
Garfield, S. L., 527
Gay, Peter, 28, 29, 30, 58
Geliland, B. E., 106
Glasser, William, 71
Glover, E., 113
Goebel, B. L., 336
Goldman, D., 170
Goldstein, Kurt, 310, 335, 360
Goleman, Daniel, 303
Greenberg, R. P., 63
Greha, S. C., 336
Grieger, R., 228, 460, 485
Gurland, Henny, 192

Hall, C. S., 3, 44, 112, 113, 139, 189, 251, 261, 307, 456
Hall, M. H., 340, 376, 377, 399, 547
Hamachek, D. E., 171, 315
Hanewitz, W. B., 144
Hannah, B., 113, 114
Harper, R. A., 470, 478
Hart, J. T., 292
Hausdorff, D., 190, 191, 215
Heppner, P. P., 275, 301
Herginhahn, B. R., 112
Herrill, J. M., 80, 81
Heslett, F. E., 366
Hesse, Herman, 112
Hippocrates, 3
Hobbs, Thomas, 3

Holdstock, T. L., 274, 278, 283, 284
Holmes, T. R., 144, 145
Holroyd, Kenneth, 486
Holt, Robert, 30, 264
Horney, Karen, 6, 66, 71, 157, 160, 192, **220–241**, 353, 462, 545, 546, 559, 564, 567
Hudson, Jean, 448
Hulbeck, Richard, 462
Hunter, F., 144

Ingram, D. H., 241

Jabin, Norma, 229
Jaffe, A., 113, 114, 117
James, R. K., 106
Janet, Pierre, 3, 116
Jones, Ernest, 30, 32
Jourard, S., 20
Jung, Carl, 3, 6, 19, 20, 25–26, 29, **111–155**, 190, 203, 542, 546, 547, 553, 554, 559, 560, 562, 563, 565, 566

Kanitz, H. M., 487
Kelly, George, 6, 19, 228, **427–456**, 495, 496, 538, 539, 540, 541, 543, 547, 550, 553, 554, 555, 556, 557, 558, 559, 560, 561, 562, 563, 566
Kierkegaard, Soren, 3
Kilpatrick, William, 271
Kivnik, Helen, 161
Kline, P., 40
Knapp, L., 9
Knapp, R., 9, 336
Kofka, Kurt, 310
Koller, P. S., 42
Kopp, Sheldon, 465
Krafft-Ebing, Richard Freiherr von, 116

Landis, B., 199
Landsman, T., 20
Lazarus, Arnold, 485
Leary, T., 228
Lee, L. A., 275, 301
Leman, K., 81
Leonard, G., 308, 310, 323
Levy, N., 144
Lewin, K., 6

Liebert, R. M., 40–41, 61, 65, 533
Liebrand, W., 336
Lindzey, G., 3, 112, 113, 189, 251, 261, 456, 547
Linger, E., 387
Locke, John, 3
Lowry, R. J., 333
Lundin, R. W., 106

Machiavelli, Nicholo, 3
Maddi, S. R., 81, 95, 122, 133, 139, 145, 204, 335, 342, 350, 356, 357, 455, 456
Maddox, E. N., 335, 336, 465, 468, 469
Maduro, R. S., 148, 151
Maher, B., 430, 431, 434, 436, 447, 456
Mahoney, Michael J., 485
Mair, J. M., 447
Mannheim, Karl, 18, 19
Marcus Aurelius, 460
Marshall, J. B., 41
Marx, Karl, 189, 191
Maslow, A. H., 6, 20, 29, 113, 140, 141, 145, 146, 150, 151, 190, 203, 206, 216, 224, 252, 258, 259, 260, 264, 285, **306–343**, 365, 388, 390, 482, 540, 541, 543, 544, 546, 548, 550, 553, 554, 555, 556, 557, 559, 560, 561, 563, 566, 567
Masson, J., 66
Mattoon, M. A., 119, 122, 135, 143, 146
Maultsby, Maxie, 493
Maxwell, J. W., 486
May, Rollo, 6, 19, 29, 71, 145, 264, **349–371**, 526, 538, 540, 543, 544, 548, 556, 561
Meichenbaum, Donald, 485
Mellilo, D., 80
Messer, S., 40
Michael, W., 336
Miller, N. J., 484
Moleski, R., 485
Monte, Christopher, 19, 114, 196
Morris, D. T., 487
Mowat, Joan, 162
Mozak, H. H., 71, 77, 84, 94, 106, 107
Mumford, Lewis, 113
Munley, P. H., 170
Munroe, R., 113
Murray, Henry, 162, 430

Neimeyer, G., 290, 448, 454, 455
Newhorn, P., 461
Newmark, C. S., 484
Newmark, L., 484
Niebuhr, Reinhold, 309
Nordby, V. J., 139
Nystul, M., 81

Odajnyk, V. W., 138, 139
Orgler, H., 72

Patterson, C. H., 449, 453, 454, 455, 489
Pavlov, Ivan, 401
Perls, Fritz, 29, 71, 190, 339
Pew, W. L., 80, 86, 96, 99, 104, 106
Pine, G. J., 289
Piraino, T. G., 336
Potkay, C. R., 144
Progoff, I., 137

Quinn, S., 221

Rabe, P., 366
Raft, D., 170, 171
Raimy, V. C., 292
Raphael, M., 380
Rauschenbach, Emma, 116
Reimanis, G., 93
Resnikov, A., 290
Rice, L. N., 292
Rickman, J., 51
Roberts, G. T., 106
Robinson, D. N., 3, 298
Roe, Anne, 18, 19
Roemer, W. W., 228
Rogers, Carl, 6, 19, 71, 113, 140, 141, 145,
    146, 151, 175, 203, 206, 216, 245, 260,
    269–303, 338, 355, 358, 363, 365, 367, 388,
    434, 441, 454, 526, 538, 541, 543, 544, 546,
    548, 553, 554, 555, 556, 557, 558, 560, 561,
    562, 564, 565, 566, 567
Ross, J., 144
Ross, M., 262, 263
Rotter, Julian, 71, 434
Rubins, J. L., 221
Russell, Bertrand, 401
Rychlak, J. F., 399

Ryckman, R. M., 216, 453
Rycroft, C., 52, 65

Sahakian, W. S., 390
Salmon, P., 448
Schachter, S., 80, 81, 95
Schrader, R. R., 380
Schwartz, H. S., 336, 337, 342
Sechrest, L., 453, 454
Seegert, C. R., 41
Sheldon, W. H., 6
Shevrin, H., 50
Shostrom, E. L., 9, 336
Skinner, B. F., 6, 19, 66, 177, 190, 303, 341,
    397–425, 502, 539, 540, 542, 545, 548, 553,
    555, 556, 557, 558, 560, 561, 562, 563, 564,
    565, 566, 567
Smart, D. L., 80
Smith, R. H., 170, 171
Socrates, 3
Soltz, V., 88
Spiegler, M. D., 40–41, 61, 65, 533
Staddon, J. E., 502
Stein, M., 117
Stephenson, W., 145, 293
Stern, P. J., 113
Stevens, Barry, 275
Stice, G. F., 144
Storr, A., 116, 117
Strean, H. S., 66
Stricker, L. J., 144
Stringer, P., 431, 432
Sullivan, Harry Stack, 6, 192
Sulloway, F., 30, 64
Suzuki, D. T., 204
Sweeney, T. J., 80, 84, 99
Szent-Gyoergyi, A., 335

Tauber, E. S., 199
Taylor, C. B., 515
Teichman, M., 92
Tesch, S. A., 170, 171
Thomas Aquinas, Saint, 3
Thomas, Sir Godfrey, 433
Thurman, C. W., 486
Tillich, Paul, 352
Tomlinson, T. M., 292

Tosi, D. J., 485
Travis, C., 66
Trexler, L. D., 484
Tribbich, D., 40

Urban, H. R., 10

Van Kamm, 351
Vaughn, M. E., 402
Vernon, P. E., 262
Vinacke, W. E., 54, 55

Wakin, E., 190
Walen, S. R., 479, 487, 489, 493
Wallace, Douglas, 170, 171, 296, 301
Wallace, W. A., 55, 92, 148, 461, 465, 468, 475
Walters, R. H., 502, 504, 508, 509, 511
Warren, N., 170, 171
Waterman, A. S., 184

Watkins, C. E., 95
Watson, James, 401
Wertheimer, M., 9, 10, 310
Wessler, R. A., 488, 489, 493
Wessler, R. I., 479, 487, 488, 489
Wexler, D. A., 292
Wheelwright, S. B., 148, 151
Wheir, W. R., 336
Whitbourne, S. K., 170, 171
Whiteley, Jr., 461, 481, 484, 485, 487
Wilhelm, Richard, 118
Wilkerson, J., 486
Wood, R., 514, 515, 516, 517
Wylie, Philip, 113

Yalom, Irvin, 351, 367
Young, H., 489

Zaccaria, J. S., 336

SUBJECT INDEX

Abnormal behavior, Bandura, 524, 525
About Behaviorism, Skinner, 402, 409, 413
Abraham H. Maslow, A Memorial Volume,
    Maslow, 343
Accurate Empathetic Understanding,
    Rogers, 295–296
Active imagination, Jung, 148
Actual self
    Horney, 225, 279
    Rogers, 279
Actuality, Erikson 172
Actualizing tendency, 245
    defined, 553
    Maslow, 307
    Rogers, 276, 277
Adaptive behaviors, Allport, 261, 262
Adler, Alfred,19, 25, 29, 69–107
    anomie, 93
    autosuggestion, 102
    basic issues, 74–90, 537–551
    basic mistakes, 96
    biographical sketch, 71–74
    consensual validation, 94–95
    creative power, 106
    creative self, 75, 87
    criminals, 92–94
    critique, 105–107
    early recollections, 100
    emergence of theory, 73–74
    empirical validation, 95–96
    encouragement, 88, 89
    exogenous factor, 96
    family constellation, 78, 79, 83, 84
    feminist movement, 71
    fictional goal, 76
    final fictions, 76–77
    Freud and, 33, 70
    function behaviors, 102
    hidden agendas, 103
    infant mother relationship, 79
    inferiority, 76, 77, 93
    law of social interest, 70
    life goal, 78
    life style, 79
    masculine protest, 76
    mature theory, 26
    neurosis, 91–92
    organ inferiority, 105
    pampering, 93
    pathogenic lifestyle, 92
    perfection, 76
    psychological health, 90–91
    psychopathology, 91–94
    psychotherapy, 96–104
    psychotic, 92
    resistance, 99
    schema of apperception, 84
    schematic analysis, 89
    self fulfilling prophesies, 103
    self-ideal, 88
    social interest, 20, 76, 79, 90–91
    superiority complex, 93
    surprise tactics, 102
    telic experience, 77
    utopia, 76, 78, 86
    validation of theories, 94–96
Aesthetic needs, Maslow, 320
Aggression, Freud, 28
Aggression, Kelly (defined), 553
Aging, Jung, 134–135, 149
Air-crib, Skinner, 401
    defined, 553

Allport, Gordon W., 247–265
  basic issues, 250–259, 537–551
  becoming, 256
  biographical sketch, 249–256
  body language, 262
  critique, 264
  cultural value, 251
  desire to know, 253
  ego drive, 257
  expressive behaviors, 261–262
  functional autonomy, 252, 254, 255,
    264, 265
  Gestalt psychology, 249
  individuality, 253
  mature personality, 20
  motivation construct, 252
  opportunistic functioning, 256
  personal documents, 262
  personality, 251
  prejudice, 248, 257, 262–263
  propriate learning, 255
  propriate striving, 257, 262
  proprium, 253, 254, 260, 261
  psychological health, 258–260
  psychopathology, causes, 260
  relative freedom, 254
  religion, 248, 262, 263
  schematic analysis, 258
Alternative constructs, Kelly, 436
Amplification, Jung, 147
Anal character, Freud, 46
Anal stage, Freud, 44
Analytic theories, 157–158
Analytic theory of Personality, Jung,
    111–155
  personality types, 125–133
  psychotherapy, 145–149
  stages of therapy, 148–149
  structure of personality, 119–125
Anamnesis, Erikson, 181
Anatomy of Human Destructiveness,
    Fromm, 195
Anima, Jung, 117, 119, 124–125, 126
  defined, 553
Animus, Jung, 119, 125, 126
  defined, 553
Anomie, Adler, 93

Anticathexis, Freud, 37, 38
Anticipatory anxiety, Frankl, 389
Anticipatory thought, Bandura, 518,
    523, 524
Anticonstructionist, Maslow, 333
Antisuggestion, Adler, 102–103
Anxiety
  anticipatory, 389
  basic, 222, 225, 234
  castration complex, 45
  characteristics of basic, 229
  existential, 353, 360
  free floating, 353
  Kelly on, 442
  Kierkegaard, 353
  May on, 359, 360, 362
  neurotic, 356
Anxiety, Freud (defined), 553
Archetypal images, Jung, 146
  defined, 553
Archetypes, Jung, 112, 114, 121, 122–123,
    135, 136, 138
  defined, 553
Art of Counseling, The, May, 372
Art of Loving, The, Fromm, 217
Art therapy, 183
Assessment, Skinner (defined), 553
Authentic encounter, May, 367
Authentic selfhood, May, 360
Autonomy, Erikson, 166
Autonomy, Skinner, 408
Autosuggestion, 102
Aversive stimuli, Skinner, 410
Awareness, Rogers (defined), 554

Behavior, Rogers (defined) 554
Bandura, Albert, 501–534
  abnormal behavior, 524
  anticipatory reward, 523–524
  anticipatory thought, 518
  basic issues, 505–522, 537–551
  behavior, 506
  behavioral enactment methods, 529
  biographical sketch, 503–505
  chance encounters, 510, 534
  critique, 533–534
  determinism, 505–506

disease model, 524
factors in development, 512
follow-ups, 529
freedom, 503, 518
group therapy, 528–529
incentives, 519
influence of television, 513
modeling, 502, 508–510, 513, 529–532
observational learning, 509
ordinal position, 514
perfectionists, 525
phobic behavior, 525
psychological health, 522–524
psychotherapy, 526–532
reciprocal determinism, 502, 507, 517
reciprocity, 505, 506
reflexive conditioning, 518
reinforcements, 519
schematic analysis, 523
self-efficacy, 20, 514–515
self-evaluation, 515–516
self-percepts of efficacy, 504
self-referent thought, 504
self-regulation, 514, 516–517
self-system, 514, 525
significance of childhood, 511–512
triadic model, 505
Basic anxiety, Horney, 222, 225, 234
characteristics of, 229
Basic mistakes, Adler, 96
Basic trust, Erikson, 165–166
Basic Writings of C. G. Jung, The, Lazlo, 152
Becoming Partners: Marriage and its Alternatives, Rogers, 275, 300
Becoming, Rollo May, 355, 363
Becoming: Basic Considerations for a Psychology of Personality, Allport, 250, 265
Behavior
abnormal, 524, 525
adaptive, 261, 262
Bandura, 506
dominance, 310
enactment methods, 529
expressive, 261–263
function, 102
inappropriate, 415
operant, 407

phobic, 525
respondent, 407
Skinner, 403
technology of, 399
Behavior modification, Skinner (defined), 554
Behavior of Organisms, Skinner, 402
Being cognition, Maslow (defined), 554
Being motivation, Maslow (defined), 554
Being needs, Maslow, 311–312
Being values, Maslow, 323, 325, 328, 339
defined, 554
Belief patterns, Ellis, 464
Belongingness needs, Maslow, 314
Beyond Freedom and Dignity, Skinner, 402, 424
Beyond the Chains of Illusion, Fromm, 190
Biological predispositions, Ellis, 464
Biophilic
character, 200
characteristics of, 206–207
defined, 554
Bodily wisdom
Maslow, 316
Rogers, 276
Body language, Allport, 262
Borderline personality disorder, 121

C-P-C cycle, Kelly (defined), 555
C. G. Jung Institute, 118
C. G. Jung Letters, I; 1906–1950, Adler, 152
Care, Erikson, 169
Carl Rogers on Encounter Groups, Rogers, 275
Carl Rogers on Personal Power, Rogers, 275
Case Studies in Psychotherapy, Corsini, 107
Castration anxiety, Freud, 45
defined, 554
Castration complex, Horney, 238
Catabolic functions, psychopathology, 260
Cathexis, Freud, 37
defined, 554
Causality, Freud (defined), 554
Censor, Freud (defined), 554
Censorship, Freud, 36
Center for the Studies of the Person, 275
Chance encounters, Bandura, 510, 534
Channelized thought, Kelly, 438

Character orientations, Fromm
  being, 213–214
  biophilic, 197, 199, 200
  concept of, 190
  exploitive, 202
  having, 214
  hoarding, 202
  marketing, 203
  necrophilic, 197, 200, 201
  productive, 203–204
  receptive, 201–202
Character typology, Freud, 61
  anal character, 46
  fixation, 46
  oral character, 46
Character, Fromm, 190
Childhood and Society, Erikson, 161, 184
Circumspection, Kelly (defined), 554
*Client-Centered Therapy: Its Current Practice,
    Implications, and Theory*, Rogers, 274,
    303
Clinical Treatment of the Problem Child, The,
    Rogers, 270, 274
Cognitive Disputation of Irrational Beliefs,
    Ellis, 492
Collective unconscious, Jung, 13, 112, 117,
    119, 120, 122–125, 135
  defined, 554
Commitment, Ellis, 483
Compensation, Adler (defined), 554
Complex, Jung (defined), 554
Comprehensive construct, Kelly (defined),
    554
Conditional regard, Skinner (defined), 555
Conditioning, Skinner (defined), 555
Congruence, Rogers (defined), 555
Conscience
  Erikson, 167
  Frankl, 384
  Freud, 42
Conscious, Freud (defined), 555
Conscious/unconscious, 11
  Adler, 85
  Allport, 254–255
  Bandura, 510–511
  conspectus, 539–540
  comparative chart, 541

Ellis, 465–470
Erikson, 173–174
Frankl, 382
Freud, 49–52
Fromm, 196–197
Horney, 229–230
Jung, 119–125
Kelly, 437
Maslow, 321–322
May, 356
Rogers, 281
Skinner, 411–412
Consensual validation, Adler, 94–95
Conspectus of the theories, 537–551
Constriction, Kelly (defined), 555
Construct, Kelly (defined), 555
Constructive alternatives, Kelly, 437
  defined, 555
Construe, Kelly (defined), 555
Content analysis, 292
Contextuality, Erikson, 172
  defined, 555
Contingencies of Reinforcement, Skinner, 402
Contingencies, Skinner (defined), 555
Continuous reinforcement, Skinner
    (defined), 555
Core construct, Kelly (defined), 555
Core roles, Kelly, 441
Corollary, 435
  choice, 436
  commonality, 440
  construction, 443
  dichotomy, 438–439
  experience, 441
  fragmentation, 439–440
  individual, 437–438
  modulation, 439
  organization, 438
  range, 439
  sociality, 443
Counseling and Psychotherapy, Rogers, 274,
    303
Creative illness, Ellenberger, 19, 33
Creative self, Adler, 87
  defined, 555
Creativity, Maslow,
  conditions for, 322, 329

defined, 555
Criminals, Adler, 92–94
Criminals, Jung, 92–94, 150
Critical Psychology and Personality: Selected Papers of George Kelly, Maher, 456
Cultural value, Allport, 251
Cumulative recorder, Skinner, 400
    defined, 555

Daimonic, May, 356
Dasein, May, 355, 365, 369
    defined, 556
De-reflection, Frankl, 389
Death instinct, Freud, 35
Defense mechanisms, Freud, 37, 40–42
    defined, 556
    test instruments, 41
    turning against self, 42
Defense, Rogers (defined), 556
Deficiency, Maslow, 330
    defined, 556
Deficit needs, Maslow, 311
    defined, 566
Delusion, Skinner, 416
Denial, Freud, 38
    defined, 556
Dependency shaping, Skinner, 416
Desacralization, Maslow (defined), 556
Desire to know, Allport, 253
Despair, Erikson, 170
Determinism, Bandura, 505
Determinism/free choice, 12
    Adler, 86–87
    Allport, 254
    Bandura, 517–518
    conspectus, 540–542
    comparative chart, 542
    Ellis, 471–472
    Erikson, 172–173
    Frankl, 378–379
    Freud, 49
    Fromm, 196
    Horney, 230
    Jung, 136–137
    Kelly, 436–437
    Maslow, 318–319
    May, 357

Rogers, 282
Skinner, 408
Development, Adler, 77–80
    constructing a life goal, 78
    cultivating social interest, 20, 76, 79, 90–91
    developing a style of life, 79
    family constellation, 78, 79, 83, 84
    feelings of inferiority, 76, 77, 93
Development, Jung (defined), 556
Developmental Psychology, Erikson, 184
Diagnosis, Skinner (defined), 556
Diagnostic and Statistical Manual of Mental Disorders, 528
Diagnostic categories, Rogers, 270
Dialectic humanist, 189
Dialectical materialism, Kelly, 430
Dilation, Kelly (defined), 556
Dimensions of a New Identity: The Jefferson Lectures in Humanities, Erikson, 161
Disciplined subjectivity, Erikson, 180
Discomfort disturbance, Ellis, 484
Discovery of Being, The, May, 371
Discriminative stimuli, Skinner (defined), 556
Displacement, Freud, 38, 48
    defined, 556
Doctor and the Soul, The, Frankl, 391
Dream analysis
    Adler, 100–101
    Erikson, 181–182
    Freud, 60, 62–63
    Fromm, 210, 212–213
    Horney, 237
    Maslow, 338
    May, 369–370
    Jung, 147
    Kelly, 452
Dream symbols, Freud, 62–63
Dreams, Freud (defined), 556
Drive, Skinner (defined), 556
Drives, Fromm, 200

Early recollections, Adler, 103–104
    defined, 556
Early/Continuous development, 13–14
    Adler, 77–80

Allport, 256
Bandura, 511–514
conspectus, 542–543
comparative chart, 543
Ellis, 474–477
Erikson, 164–172
Frankl, 382–383
Freud, 43–46
Fromm, 197–199
Horney, 225–226
Jung, 133–135
Kelly, 440–441
May, 358–359
Maslow, 316–318
Rogers, 278
Skinner, 409–410
Education
  as self actualization, 340
Effectiveness, Fromm, 195
Ego and the Id, The, Freud, 34, 66
Ego development, Erikson's theory, 160,
    165–172
  adolescence, 168–169
  confusion, 169
  development of, 165–172
  ego strengths, 165
  identity, 168, 169, 175–176
  integrity, 170
  late adulthood, 170
  latency stage, 167–168
  locomotor-genital stage, 167
  middle adulthood, 169
  muscular-anal stage, 166–167
  oral-sensory stage, 165
  young adulthood, 169
Ego disturbance, Ellis, 484
Ego, Allport, 257, 259
Ego, Erikson (defined), 557
Ego, Freud's theories, 35, 37–38, 47
  censorship, 36
  defined, 557
  ideal, 42
  object choices, 36
  reality principle, 36
  repression, 36, 37, 48
  strength, 56,
Ego, Jung's theories, 120

attitudes, 126–128
  functions, 128–133
Eigenwelt, May, 355, 356, 365
Elementary Textbook of Psychoanalysis, An,
    Brenner, 66
Elements, Kelly (defined), 557
Ellis, Albert, 19, 29, 459–496
  Adler, 460
  adolescents, 475–476
  basic goals, 481
  basic issues, 464–465, 537–551
  belief patterns, 464
  biographical sketch, 461–463
  biosocial creatures, 464
  childhood, 474–475
  comparative studies, 485–486
  critique, 494–495
  discomfort disturbance, 484
  early adulthood, 476–477
  ego disturbance, 484
  fairy tales, 475
  healthy personality traits, 481–483
  instinctoid tendencies, 464
  irrational thinking, 468
  magical thinking, 481
  neurosis, 484
  psychotherapy, 486–493
  rational living, 476
  rational sensitivity, 20
  responsible hedonism, 478, 479–481, 482
  schematic analysis, 480
  self-acceptance, 471
  self-conceptualizing, 470
  self-reward, 480
  self-talk, 467–468, 471, 474, 475
  stoic philosophy, 460
  televisions impact, 476
  value system, 474
Emotional disturbance, Ellis, 468
Empathy
  Fromm, 212
  Horney, 236
  May, 367
  Rogers, 295
Empathy, Rogers (defined), 557
Empirical validation, 95–96
Encounter groups, Rogers, 271, 284, 298–300

Encouragement, Adler, 88, 89, 103–104
Enjoy Old Age: A Program of Self-Management, Skinner, 402, 425
Entropy, 135
Epigenetic stages, Erikson (defined), 557
Erikson, Erik, 29, 157, 159–184
  actuality, 172
  anamnesis, 181
  and children, 160, 181
  Anna Freud, 160, 162
  art therapy, 183
  autonomy, 166
  basic issues, 163–180, 537–551
  basic trust, 165–166
  biographical sketch, 161–163
  care, 169
  child rearing practices, 164
  competence, 173
  conscience, 167
  contextuality, 172
  critique, 183–184
  despair, 170
  disciplined subjectivity, 180
  dream analysis, 181–182
  ego development, 165–172
  ego identity, 160, 175
  ego integrity, 170
  epigenetic schedule, 163
  epigenetic stages, 160
  free association, 181
  generativity, 169
  guilt, 167
  healthy attitudes, 171–172
  Henry Murray, 162
  hope, 166, 173
  humility, 170
  id, 163, 164
  identity, 164, 168, 176
  industry, 167
  inferiority, 167, 168
  initiative, 167
  intimacy, 169
  isolation, 169
  mutuality, 169
  narcissistic "I's", 172
  otherness, 172
  outerness, 172

  play therapy, 160, 181, 182–183
  psychohistories, 182
  psychological health, 177–179
  psychopathology, 179–180
  psychosocial crisis, 164
  psychotherapy, 180–181
  purpose, 165, 167, 168, 173
  reality, 172
  research, 170–172
  role confusion, 169
  schematic analysis, 178
  shame, 166
  stagnation, 169
  wanderschaft, 162
  way of life, 172
  will, 166, 173
  wisdom, 170
Eros, Freud, 29, 34
Erotogenic zone, Freud (defined), 557
Esalen, Maslow, 339
Escape from Freedom, Fromm, 196, 216, 217
Esteem needs, Maslow, 314
Eupsychia, Maslow, 308, 310
  defined, 557
Eupsychian management, Maslow, 340
  defined, 557
Excitation, Fromm, 195
Existence, May, 350
Existential neurosis, Frankl, 387
Existential theories, 285–288, 324, 347
Existential Theory of Personality, May, 350–351
  consciousness, 356
  encounter, 361
  anxiety and false self, 347, 360
  guilt, 360
  healthy personality, 363–364
  psychopathology, 364–365
  psychotherapy, 366–369
  unconsciousness, 356
Exogenous factor, Adler, 96
Experience, Rogers (defined), 557
Experiential freedom, Rogers, 276, 282
Exploitive personality, Fromm, 202
  defined, 557
Expressive behaviors, Allport, 261–262
  defined, 557

External variables, Adler, 408
Extinction, Skinner, 404
  defined, 557
Extroversion, Jung, 120, 126, 127–128
  defined, 557
  feeling type, 130–131
  intuitive type, 132
  sensing type, Jung, 131
Extrovert thinking type, Jung, 129

Factuality, Erikson (defined), 558
Factuality, Fromm, 172
Family constellation, Adler, 78, 79, 83
  defined, 558
  infant mother relationship, 79
  influence of, 84
  ordinal positions, 80–84, 106
  questionnaire, 99–100
Farther Reaches of Human Nature, The,
    Maslow, 343
Feeling function, Jung, 130
Feelings of inferiority, Adler (defined), 558
Feminine psychology, Horney, 238–239, 240
  and sexuality, 222, 239, 240
Feminist movement, 71
Fictional goal, Adler, 76
Field dependency, 42
Final fictions, Adler, 76–77
  defined, 558
Final Lectures, Horney, 241
Firstborn, Adler, 80–81
Fixation, Freud 38, 46
  defined, 558
Fixed interval schedule, Skinner, 405
  defined, 558
Fixed ratio schedule, Skinner, 405, 558
Fixed-role play, Kelly, 434, 450
Flexibility, Ellis, 482
Focus of convenience, Kelly (defined), 558
Forgotten Language, The, Fromm, 217
Fourth Psychology, 332
Frame of orientation, Fromm, 195
Frankl, Victor, 19, 347, 374–392
  Adler, 376
  anticipatory anxiety, 389
  basic issues, 378–385, 537–551
  biographical sketch, 376–378

community, 385
concentration camps, 375, 377, 379
conscience, 384
critique, 390–391
de-reflection, 389
existential frustration, 387
freedom of will, 378
homeostasis, 385
I-Thou-Relationship, 388
life meaning, 381, 383, 387, 388
logotherapy, 376–377, 388–390
neurosis, 387, 389
Nietzsche, 375
noetic dimension, 376, 382
noological dimension, 384
paradoxical intention, 388–389
psychological health, 385–387
psychopathology, 387
schematic analysis, 386
self-transcendence, 381
values, 383, 388
will to meaning, 375, 380
Free association
  Erikson, 181
  defined, 558
  Freud, 32, 50, 59, 60–61
  Fromm, 212
  Horney, 236
  Maslow, 338
Free will, Skinner, 408
Freedom
  Bandura, 503, 518
  existential, 380
  experiential, Rogers, 276, 282
  Freud, 28
  Fromm, 194
  Maslow, 318–319
  May, 358
  of will, Frankl, 378
  relative, Allport, 254
Freedom of will, Frankl, 378
Freedom of will, Freud (defined), 558
Freedom to Learn for the 80's, Rogers, 275,
    283, 303
Freedom to Learn, Rogers, 275
Freedom, Fromm, 194
Freedom, May, 358

Freud, Biologist of the Mind, Sulloway, 67
Freud Reader, The, Gay, 66
Freud, Anna, 160, 162
Freud, Sigmund, 19, 25, 27–67
  aggression, 28
  analytic interpretation, 61–62
  anticathexis, 37, 38
  basic issues, 34–54, 537–551
  biographical sketch, 30–34
  castration anxiety, 45
  cathexis, 37
  censorship, 36
  character typology, 61
  conscience, 42
  conscious, 49, 51–52
  creative illness, 33
  Darwin's influence, 31
  defense mechanisms, 37, 40–42
  denial, 38
  displacement, 38, 48
  dream analysis, 60, 62–63
  ego ideal, 42
  ego strength, 52
  ego, 35, 37–38, 47
  Ernst Brucke, 31
  eros, 29, 34
  field dependency, 42
  fixation, 38, 46
  free association, 32, 50, 59, 60–61
  freedom, 28
  gratification, 48
  hypnosis, 32
  id, 34, 35–36
  impact of theories, 28, 29
  instincts, 34
  interpretation, 61–62
  Jean Charcot, 31
  Joseph Breuer, 31
  libidinal fixation, 56
  libido, 35
  neurosis, 56
  object cathexes, 44
  object, 34
  obsessional rituals, 40
  Oedipus complex, 45, 56, 65
  personality structure, 35
  physical energy, 34

pleasure principle, 36
preconscious, 49, 50–51
projection, 39
psychic energy, 34
psychoanalysis, 47, 58–64
psychological health, 20
psychosexual stages of development, 25, 43–46
psychosis, 56, 57
rationalization, 40
reaction formation, 39, 48
reality principle, 52
regression, 39
religion, 28
reorganization, 59
repression, 36, 37, 47
resistances, 32, 63
rules of psychoanalysis, 47
schema of apperception, 53
schematic analysis, 53
secondary process thinking, 52
sublimation, 28, 37, 38–39
superego, 35, 42–43
thanatos, 29, 34, 220
theory of psychoanalysis, 29, 32–33
transference, 32, 60, 63–64
tripartite model, 34
turning against self, 42
unconscious, 49, 50
undoing, 40
From Death Camp to Existentialism, Frankl, 393
Fromm, Erich, 29, 157, 188–217
  basic issues, 193–206, 537–551
  being orientation, 213
  biographical sketch, 190–193
  character orientations, 299–304
  character, 190
  child development, 197–199
  criticism, 215
  dream analysis, 210, 212–213
  empathy, 212
  free association, 212
  freedom, 194
  having orientation, 214
  human nature, 193
  human needs, 195–196

individuation, 196, 206
Karl Marx's influence, 189
Meister Eckhart, 190
Oedipus complex, 191, 192
parental influence, 197, 209
pathological societies, 196
personality defined, 190
productive personality, 20
psychological health, 206–208
psychopathology, 208–209
psychotherapy, 211–212
research, 210–211
Ryckman on, 216
SANE, 190
schematic analysis, 207
secondary ties, 195
society and personality, 192, 209,
    213–214, 215
study of Nazism, 192
Fully-functioning person, Rogers, 280
    defined, 558
Function behaviors, Adler, 102
Functional analysis, Skinner (defined), 558
Functional autonomy, Allport, 252, 254,
    255, 264, 265
    defined, 558
Fundamental postulate, Kelly, 435

Gandhi's Truth, Erikson, 161, 182
Gemeinschaftsgefuhl, Maslow, 20, 328
    defined, 558
Generativity, Erikson, 169
Genital stage, Freud, 45–46
Gestalt psychology, Allport, 249
Gestalt Therapy, 29
Gestalt, Maslow, 339
Gray-Wheelwright Questionnaire, 144
Group determinants
    Adler, 80–84
    Allport, 256–257
    Bandura, 520–521
    conspectus, 547–548
    Ellis, 478
    Erikson, 177
    Frankl, 385
    Freud, 54
    Fromm, 199

Horney, 231–232
    Jung, 138–139
    Kelly, 443
    Maslow, 322
    May, 361–362
    Rogers, 284
    Skinner, 408–409
Group therapy
    Ellis, 493–494
    encounter groups, 271, 284, 298, 300
    Maslow, 339
Growth needs, Horney, 224
Growth Through Reason, Ellis, 495
*Guideposts to Meaning: Discovering What
    Really Matters*, Fabry, 392
Guilt, 167, 442
    existential, 360, 361
    ontological, 361
Guilt, Kelly (defined), 558

Handbook of Rational-emotive Therapy, Ellis &
    Grieger, 228, 496
Hedonism, Ellis, 478, 479–481, 482
Heredity/social determinants, 12–13
    Adler, 73
    Allport, 251
    Bandura, 505–508
    conspectus, 538, 539
    comparative chart, 539
    Ellis, 464–465
    Erikson, 163–180
    Frankl, 380
    Freud, 34–35
    Fromm, 193–196
    Horney, 224
    Jung, 119
    Kelly, 435–436
    Maslow, 311
    May, 354–356
    Rogers, 276–277
    Skinner, 403–404
Heuristic influences, explained, 21–22
Hidden agendas, Adler, 103
Hoarding personality, Fromm, 202
    defined, 559
Homeostasis, Frankl, 385
Hope, Erikson (defined), 559

Horney's Ten Neurotic Needs, 226–228, 228
Horney, Karen, 157, 219–241
  basic anxiety, 222, 225, 229, 230, 234
  basic issues, 223–235, 537–551
  biographical sketch, 221–223
  critique, 240
  disagreement with Freud, 238
  dream analysis, 237
  Electra, 220
  empathy, 236
  feminine psychology, 238–239
  feminine sexuality, 222, 239, 240
  free association, 236
  growth needs, 224
  ideal self, 225
  inner independence, 235
  learning, 230–231
  moral values, 231, 236
  neurosis, 224
  neurotic needs, 226–228
  neurotic strategies, 229
  penis envy, 220
  phenomenology, 230
  psychological health, 234
  psychopathology, 234
  psychotherapy, 235–238
  real self, 221, 224
  resistance, 235
  responsibility, 231, 235
  schematic analysis, 233
  security needs, 234
  self analysis, 221, 237, 239–240
  self-image, 225
  self-realization, 220
  spontaneity, 235
  thanatos, 220
  transference, 235
  tyrannical "shoulds", 158, 235
  wholeheartedness, 234
Hostility, Kelly (defined), 559
Human agency, Bandura, 504
Human needs, Fromm, 195–196
Human thinking, Ellis
  irrational thinking, 468
  self-talk 467–468, 471, 474
Humanistic social analysis, Fromm, 188–217
  Ryckman's comments on, 216

Humanists, 245
Humility, Erikson, 170
Hypnosis, Feud, 32

I Ching, Wilhelm, 118
I-thou-relationship
  Frankl, 388
  May, 357, 361, 367
Id (defined), 559
  Erikson, 163, 164
  Freud, 34, 35–36
Ideal self, Horney, 225
Idealized self, Horney (defined), 559
Identification, Freud (defined), 559
Identity and the Life Cycle: A Reissue, Erikson, 161
Identity, 164, 168
  confusion of, 169
  motivation, 176
Identity, Fromm, 195
Identity: Youth and Crisis, Erikson, 161
Ideology and Utopia, Mannheim, 18
Idiographic laws, Allport (defined), 559
Idiographic research, 245
  human personality, 253
Imaginary playmate, Jung, 133
Impulse control disorders, Jung, 124
In Search of Common Ground, Erikson, 161
Incentives, Bandura, 519
Individual and Religion, The, Allport, 265
Individual meaning structures, Rogers, 290
Individual Psychology of Alfred Adler, The, Heinz, 107
Individual Psychology, Adler, 70–107
  antisuggestion, 102–103
  basic issues, 74–90, 537–551
  dreams, 100–101
  encouragement, 103–104
  earliest recollections, 100
  family constellation questionnaire, 99–100
  hidden agendas, 103
  interpretation, 101–102
  psychotherapy, 96–104
  spitting in soup, 103
  structuring, 98–99
  surprise tactics, 102
  the question, 98

Individuality, Allport, 253
Individuality, May, 360
Individuation
    Fromm, 196
    Jung, 133, 135, 136, 137, 139, 158
Individuation, Jung (defined), 559
Infant mother relationship, 79
Inferiority complex, Adler, 76, 77, 93
    defined, 559
Inherent potentialities, Rogers, 277
Initiative, Erikson, 167
Innate organismic valuing system, Rogers, 279
Inner independence, Horney, 235
Insight and Responsibility, Erikson, 161
Instinctoid need, Maslow (defined), 559
Instinctoid tendencies
    Ellis, 464
    Maslow, 322, 330,
Instincts
    defined, 559
    Freud, 34, 48
    Jung, 122
Intention, Allport, 252
Intentionality
    May, 356
    Rogers, 289
International Forum for Logotherapy, Fabry, 378
Interpretation
    Adler, 101–102
    Freud, 61–62
    Horney, 236
Interpretation of Dreams, The, Freud, 66, 116
Introjected values, Rogers, 288
Introverts, Jung, 120, 126, 128, 132
    defined, 559
    feeling type, 131
    intuitive type, 133
    sensing type, 132
    thinking type, 130
Inventory of Defense, Freud, 41
Involvement in Old Age, Erikson, 161
Irrational beliefs, Ellis, 468
    defined, 559
Isolation, Erikson, 169

Issues and Approaches in Personal Construct Theory, Bannister, 456

Jonah complex, Maslow 318, 332
    defined, 559
Journal of Abnormal Psychology, 250
Journal of Individual Psychology, 74
Journals of A. H. Maslow, The, Lowry, 343
Jung and Politics: The Political and Social Ideas of C. G. Jung, Odajnyk, 138
Jung's Analytic Psychology, 111–155
Jung, Carl G., 13, 19, 25, 29, 111–155
    active imagination, 147, 148
    aging, 150
    amplification, 147
    anima, 117, 119, 124–125, 126
    animus, 119, 125, 126
    anthropology, 150
    archetypal projections, 146
    archetypes, 26, 112, 114, 121, 122–123, 135, 136, 138
    attitude types, 126–128
    autobiographical works, 19, 113, 118
    basic issues, 118–139, 537–551
    biographical sketch, 113–116
    borderline personality, 121
    break with Freud, 33
    collective unconscious, 13, 112, 117, 119, 120, 122–125, 135, 138
    complexes, 121–122
    consciousness, 120–121
    criminology, 150
    critique, 150–151
    developmental theories, 133–135
    dreams, 147
    entropy, 135
    extroversion, 120, 126, 127–128
    feeling types, 128
    functions of personality, 128–133
    individuation, 20, 26, 133, 135, 136, 137, 139, 145, 158
    instincts, 122
    introversion, 120, 126, 128
    intuition, 128
    learning process, 136–137
    libido, 122, 135
    mandala, 137, 141, 142

mid-life crisis, 113, 134
neurosis, 141–142
persona, 114, 123, 136
personal unconscious, 121–122, 135, 137
personality types, 125–133, 143–145
principle of equivalence, 135
proto-image, 137
psyche, 119, 135
psychosis, 143
psychotherapy, 145–149
religion, 151
Richard Wilhelm's influence, 118
schematic analysis, 140
self-actualization, 146
self concept, 137
shadow, 119, 121, 123, 136, 139
stages of therapy, 148–149
structure of psyche, 120–125
unconditional positive regard, 144
word association, 116, 150
works of, 116
Jung: His Life and His Work, Jaffe, 152
Jung: Man and Myth, Brome, 152
Jungian typology, 125–133, 143–145

Karen Horney Psychoanalytic Institute and
    Center, 223
Karen Horney: Gentle Rebel of Psychoanalysis,
    Rubin, 221
Karen Horney: Her Life and Contribution,
    Eckardt, 221
    Kelly, 456
Kelly, George A., 19, 429–456
    alternative constructs, 436
    anticipation, 436
    anxiety, 442
    basic issues, 435–443, 537–551
    biographical sketch, 432–435
    C-P-C Cycle, 451
    channelized thought, 438
    constructive alternativism, 437
    core roles, 441
    corollaries, 435–440, 441, 443
    creativity cycle, 451
    critique, 453–456
    cycles of construction, 451–452
    diagnostic constructs, 446–447

dialectical materialism, 430
dreams, 452
fixed role play, 434, 450
fundamental postulate, 435–436
guilt, 442
pampering, 440
personal constructs, 432, 435, 437, 441
phenomenology, 436
predictive efficiency, 436
preemptive construct, 439
psychological health, 443–445
psychopathology, 445–446
psychotherapy, 449–454
Rep test, 447, 448–449, 452, 453
research, 447–449
schematic analysis, 444
schizophrenia, 448
Zen Buddhism, 430
Knowing, May, 357

Latency stage, Freud, 45
Latent dream content, Freud, 62
Law of social interest, Adler, 70
Learning process, 15–16
    Adler, 85–86
    Allport, 255–256
    Bandura, 508–510
    conspectus, 547
    Ellis, 472–473
    Erikson, 174–175
    Frankl, 383
    Freud, 48–49
    Fromm, 205
    Horney, 230–231
    Jung, 136–137
    Kelly, 441
    Maslow, 319–320
    May, 362
    Rogers, 282–283
    Skinner, 407
Libidinal fixation, Freud, 56
Libido
    Freud's theory, 35
    Jung's theory, 122, 135
Libido, Freud (defined), 560
Life Cycle Completed, The, Erikson, 161
Life for Our Time, A, Gay, 57,

Life goal, Adler, 78
  defined, 560
Life History and the Historical Movement,
    Erikson, 161
Life, style of, Adler, 79
Logical empiricism, 365
Logos, Frankl, 375, 380
Logotherapy, Frankl, 375, 376–377, 387,
    388–390
  de-reflection, 389
  freedom of will, 378
  paradoxical intention, 379–389
  stages of, 390
Loose construct, Kelly (defined), 560
Love and Will, May, 353–354, 361, 371

Magical thinking, Ellis, 481
Man and the Science of Man, Rogers, 290
Man for Himself, Fromm, 216, 217
Man's Search for Himself, May, 353, 371
*Man's Search for Meaning: An Introduction to
    Logotherapy,* Frankl, 337, 392
Mandala, Jung, 137, 141, 142
  defined, 560
Manifest content, Freud 63
Mannheim, Karl, 18
Marketing personality, Fromm, 203
  defined, 560
Marriage, Rogers, 301
Marshall Personality Measure, 41
Marxian personality theory, 189
Masculine protest, 76
Maslow's philosophy of science, 333–334
Maslow, Abraham, 29, 306–343
  actualizing tendency, 307
  aesthetic needs, 320
  anticonstructionist, 333
  assessment of, 335–337
  basic issues, 311–323, 537–551
  being values, 323, 325, 328, 339
  biographical sketch, 308–311
  bodily wisdom, 316
  child development, 316–318
  creativity, 322, 329
  cultural synergism, 316
  deficiency disease, 330
  deficiency needs, 311, 323

  dominance behavior, 310
  dream interpretation, 338
  Esalen, 339
  Eupsychia, 308, 310
  existential distress, 324
  fourth psychology, 332
  free association, 338
  freedom, 318–319
  Gestalt, 339
  group therapy, 339
  inner nature, 321
  instinctoid tendencies, 311, 322, 330
  Jonah syndrome, 318, 332
  mentors, 309, 310
  metamotivation, 318, 324, 341
  metapathology, 330
  metavalues, 321, 332
  mystic experiences, 327–328
  need hierarchy, 312–315, 336
  neurosis, 330
  parental values, 318
  peak experiences, 327–328
  philosophy of science, 333–334
  psychopathology, 330–332
  psychotherapy, 337–339
  self-actualization, 315, 318, 339
  self-actualizing characteristics, 325–330,
  self-efficacy, 314
  Taoistic influences, 317, 340
  unconscious and Freud, 321–322
  work environment, 339
Maslow: An Intellectual Portrait, Lowry, 343
Masochism, Horney, 238
Matter of Consequence, A, Skinner, 19, 424
Maudsley Personality Inventory, 144
May, Rollo, 19, 29, 347, 349–371
  Adler's seminars, 352
  anxiety, 353, 360, 362
  authentic encounter, 367
  basic issues, 354–366, 537–551
  becoming, 355, 363
  biographical sketch, 351–354
  consciousness, 356
  critique, 370–371
  daimonic, 356
  dasein, 355, 365
  eigenwelt, 355, 356, 365

existentialism, 350–351, 356, 357, 358, 360, 361
  guilt, 360, 361
  individuality, 360
  integrity, 363
  intentionality, 356
  Kierkegaard, 353
  knowing, 357
  mentors, 350–351
  mitwelt, 355, 356, 365
  neurosis, 364
  neurotic anxiety, 356
  originality, 364
  pampering, 359
  personality, 363–364
  phenomenology, 357, 370
  potentia, 363
  psychosis, 365
  psychotherapy, 366–369, 370
  significant others, 355
  spontaneity, 363
  Tillich's influence, 352
  transcendence, 356, 359
  umwelt, 355, 356, 365
  unconsciousness, 356
Meaning
  life, 381, 387, 388
  structures of, 290
  values and, 384
  will to, 375, 380, 387
Meaning of Anxiety, The, May, 353, 371
Memories Dreams and Reflections, Jung, 113, 118
Mental health, Frankl (defined), 560
Metamotivation, Maslow, 307–343, 318, 324, 341
  defined, 560
Metamotives, Maslow (defined), 560
Metapathology, Maslow, 330
  defined, 560
Metavalues, Maslow 321, 332
Mid-life crisis, 113
Middle child, Adler, 82
Mind of Her Own: The Life of Karen Horney, Quinn, 221
Mitwelt, Maslow, 355, 356, 365
Mob violence, Jung, 138

Modeling, Bandura, 508–510, 513, 529
  coping models, 530
  defined, 560
  participant modeling, 530
  self as model, 531–532
  symbolic modeling, 531
Moral values, Horney, 231, 236
Motivation and Personality, Maslow, 310, 342,
Motivation, Allport's construct, 252
Motivation, Kelly (defined), 560
Motivation, need hierarchy, Maslow, 308
Motivational concepts, 17
  Adler, 75–77
  Allport, 251–253
  Bandura, 519–520
  conspectus, 546–547
  Ellis, 478–479
  Erikson, 176
  Frankl, 380–381
  Freud, 48
  Fromm, 199–201
  Horney, 228–229
  Jung, 135–136
  Kelly, 442–443
  Maslow, 311–315
  May, 360–361
  Rogers, 277
  Skinner, 410–411
Multimodal therapy, Ellis, 485
Mutuality, Erikson, 169
Myers-Briggs Type Indicator, 144
Mystic experiences, Maslow 327–328

Narcissism, Freud (defined), 560
Narcissistic "I's", Erikson, 172
Nature of Personality, The: Selected Papers, Allport, 250
Nature of Prejudice, The, Allport, 265
Nazi concentration camps, 375, 377, 379
Nazism, Fromm's study, 192
Necrophilic character, Fromm, 200, 201
  defined, 560
  parents, 197
Need for positive regard, Rogers (defined), 560
Need hierarchy, Maslow, 311–315

criticism of, 336–337
Negative reinforcement, Skinner, 402
    defined, 560
Neglect, Adler (defined), 562
Neoanalytic theories, 157–158
Neopsychoanalytic theories, 157–158, 163
Neurosis
    Adler, 91–92
    Ellis, 484
    Frankl, 387, 389
    Freud, 56
    Horney, 224
    Jung, 141, 143
    Maslow, 330
    May, 364
Neurosis and Human Growth, Horney, 241
Neurotic anxiety, May, 356
Neurotic need gratification, Maslow, 330
Neurotic needs, Horney, 226–228
Neurotic Personality of Our Time, Horney,
    223, 241
Neurotic, Adler, 91–92
New Guide to Rational Living, A, Ellis &
    Harper, 496
*New Pathways in Psychology: Maslow and the
    Post-Freudian Revolution*, Wilson, 343
New Ways in Psychoanalysis, Horney, 23, 241
Noetic dimension, Frankl, 376, 382
Nomothetic research, 245
    human personality, 253
Noogenic, Frankl, 375
    defined, 561
    neurosis, 389, 391
Noological dimension, Frankl, 384
Normality, 20
Notebooks, B. F. Skinner, Epstein, 399

Object cathexis, Freud, 44
Object choice, Freud, 36
Object of devotion, Fromm, 195
    defined, 561
Obsessional rituals, Freud, 40
Oedipus complex
    defined, 561
    Erikson, 157
    Freud, 45, 56, 65
    Fromm's reinterpretation, 191, 192

On Becoming a Person, Rogers, 303
Only child, Adler, 82–84
Ontological guilt, May, 361
    defined, 561
Operant conditioning, Skinner, 402, 410
    defined, 561
Operant Reinforcement, Skinner, 302,
    398–424
Opportunistic functioning, Allport, 256
Oral character, Freud, 46
Oral stage, Freud, 43–44
Ordinal positions
    Adler, 80–84, 106
    Bandura, 514
Organ inferiority, Adler, 105
    defined, 561
Organism (human), Rogers (defined), 561
Organismic theories, 245
Organismic valuing process, Rogers
    (defined), 561
Otherness, Erikson, 172
Our Inner Conflicts, Horney, 241
Outcome goals, Skinner, 417
Outerness, Erikson, 172

Pampering
    Adler, 93
    defined, 561
    Kelly, 440
    May, 359
Paradoxical intention, Frankl, 388–389
Parapraxis, Freud (defined), 561
    parents, 197, 199
Particulars of My Life, Skinner, 19
Pathogenic secrets, Jung, 148
Pathological societies, Fromm, 196, 209
Pattern for Growth in Personality, Allport,
    250, 265
Peak experiences, Maslow, 327–328
    defined, 561
Penis envy
    defined, 561
    Freud, 66
    Horney, 220
Perfection, Adler, 76
Perfectionists, Bandura, 525
Peripheral construct, Kelly (defined), 561

Permeable construct, Kelly (defined), 561
Person-Centered Theory, Rogers, 270–303
    characteristics of, 274
    learning, 283, 284
    psychological health, 285–288
    therapy, 274, 293–298
    research on, 291–293
Person-Centered Therapist, 294
Person in Psychology, The, Allport, 265
*Person to Person: The Problem of Being
    Human,* Rogers, 275
Persona
    defined, 562
    Jung, 114, 123, 136
    Maslow, 326
Personal agency, Bandura, 521
Personal autonomy, Skinner, 408
Personal Constructs Theory, 430–432, 436
    diagnostic constructs, 446–447
    structure and corollaries, 431
Personal constructs, 432, 435, 437
    change in system, 441–442
    hierarchical, 438
Personal documents, Allport, 263
Personal orientation, Shostrom, (defined),
    562
Personal Orientation Inventory, 336
Personal unconscious, Jung, 121–122, 135,
    137
    defined, 562
Personal values, 9
Personality
    Allport, 20, 251
    borderline, 121
    daimonic, 356
    Ellis's healthy traits, 481–483
    Freud's structure of, 35
    Fromm's definition, 190
    fully functioning, 280
    ideographic research on, 253
    Jungian structure, 120
    Jungian typology, 125–133, 143–145
    May's definition, 363–364
    nomothetic research, 253
    Skinner's healthy, 398, 413–414
    society's influence on, 192, 209, 213–214,
        215

Personality and Social Encounter, Allport, 250
Personality defined, Allport, 251
Personality theory
    basic issues, 11–26, 537–551
    history, 3–4
    integrative theory, 7–11
    scientific definition, 4
Personality, Adler (defined), 562
Personality: A Psychological Interpretation,
    Allport, 250, 264
Phallic character, Freud, 46
Phallic stage, Freud, 44–45
Phenomenology 245
    Horney, 230
    Kelly, 436
    May, 357, 370
    Rogers, 277
Phobic behavior, Bandura, 525
Physiological needs, Maslow, 312
Play therapy, Erikson, 160, 181, 182–183
Pleasure principle, Freud, 36
    defined, 562
Pleasure-pain continuum, 17
Polar opposites, 8
Portable Jung, The, Campbell, 152
Positive regard, Rogers (defined), 562
Positive reinforcement, Skinner, 404
    defined, 562
Positive self-regard, Rogers, 278, 280–281
Potentia, May, 363
*Power and Innocence: A Search for the Sources
    of Violence,* May, 372
Practice of Rational-Emotive Therapy, The,
    Ellis & Dryden, 496
*Practitioner's Guide to Rational-Emotive
    therapy,* Walen, DeGuiseppe, &
    Wessler, 496
Preconscious stratum, Freud, 49, 50–51
    defined, 562
Predictive efficiency, Kelly, 436
Preemptive construct, Kelly (defined), 562
Prejudice, Allport, 248, 257, 262–263
Preverbal construct, Kelly (defined), 562
Primal repression, Freud, 37
Primary process, Freud, 36, 44
    defined, 562
Primary reinforcement, Skinner, 404

Primordial image, Jung (defined), 562
Principle of equivalence, Jung, 135
Principles and Practice of Rational-Emotive Therapy, Wessler & Wessler, 496
Proactive functioning, Allport (defined), 562
Process scale in therapy, Rogers, 297–298
Productive functioning, Allport (defined), 562
Productive personality, Fromm, 203
    defined, 562
Projection
    archetypal, Jung, 146
    defined, 563
    Freud, 39, 563
Propriate functional autonomy, Allport, 256
Propriate functioning, Allport (defined), 563
Propriate learning, Allport, 255
Propriate striving, Allport, 257
Proprium, Allport, 253, 254, 260, 261
    defined, 563
Proto-image, Jung, 137
Prototype, Adler (defined), 563
Proximal goals, Bandura, 520
Psyche, Freud (defined), 563
Psyche, Jung, 119
    Jung's structure of, 120–125, 135
Psychic energy, Freud (defined), 563
Psychic value, Jung (defined), 563
Psychoanalysis and Religion, Fromm, 216, 217
Psychoanalysis, Freud, 29, 58–64
    analysis of resistances, 32, 63
    analysis of transference, 32, 60, 63–64
    dream analysis, 60, 62–63
    free association, 32, 50, 59, 60–61
    rules of, 47
Psychoanalysis, Freudian, 60–64
Psychohistories, Erikson's, 182
Psychological health
    Adler's theory, 90–91
    Allport's theory, 259–260
    Bandura's theory, 522–524
    Ellis's theory, 481–483
    Erikson's theory, 177–179
    Frankl's theory, 385–387
    Freud's theory, 54–56
    Fromm's theory, 206–208
    Horney's theory, 234

Jung's theory, 139–141
Kelly's theory, 443–445
Maslow's theory, 323–330
May's theory, 364
Roger's theory, 285–288
Skinner's theory, 413–414
Psychological health, 20–21
    as adjustment, 550–551
    as normality, 550
    as utopia, 549–550
Psychological Types, Jung, 117
Psychology of Dementia Praecox, The, Jung, 116
Psychology of Personal Constructs, The Kelly, 430, 431, 444, 449
Psychology of Science, Maslow, 315, 333
Psychopathology, 29–21
    Adler's theory, 91–94
    Allport's theory, 260
    Bandura's theory, 524–526
    Ellis's theory, 483–484
    Erikson's theory, 179–180
    Frankl's theory, 387
    Freud's theory, 56–57
    Fromm's theory, 208–209
    Horney's theory, 234–235
    Jung's theory, 141–143
    Kelly's theory, 445–446
    Maslow's theory, 330–332
    May's theory, 364–365
    Roger's theory, 288–289
    Skinner's theory, 415–416
Psychopathology, Allport's catabolic functions, 260
Psychosexual stages of development, Freud, 43–46
    anal stage, 44
    genital stage, 45–46
    latency stage, 45
    oral stage, 43–44
    phallic stage, 44–45
Psychosis
    Adler, 92
    defined, 563
    Freud, 56, 57
    Jung, 143
    May, 365

Rogers, 289
Psychosocial crisis, 164
Psychosocial stages of development,
    Erikson, 165–170
    research on, 170–172
Psychotherapy
    Adler, 99–102
    Allport, 261
    Bandura, 526–532
    Ellis, 486–493
    Erikson, 180–181
    Frankl, 388–390
    Freud, 58–65
    Fromm, 211–212
    Horney, 235–238
    Jung, 145–149
    Kelly, 449–454
    Maslow, 339–341
    May, 366–369
    Rogers, 293–298
    Skinner, 416–422
Psychotic, Adler, 92
Punishment, Skinner (defined), 563
Purpose in Life Test, Frankl, 380
Purpose of behavior, Skinner (defined), 563
Purpose, Erikson, 165, 167, 168, 173
Purpose-in-Life-Test, 380
Pursuit of Meaning, The, Fabry, 392
Pursuit of Meaning: Viktor Frankl,
    Logotherapy, and Life, The, Fabry, 392

Q-sort Technique, 144
Q-Sort, Stephenson (defined), 563
Q-technique, 293

Radical Behaviorism, Skinner, 395
Radical determinism, Skinner, 398
    defined, 563
Range of convenience, Kelly (defined), 563
Rational beliefs, Ellis, 477
    defined, 563
Rational living, Ellis, 477
Rational-Emotive therapy, Ellis, 460, 486–493
    activating event, 492
    client expectations, 490
    cognitive disputation of irrational beliefs,
        492
    criticisms, 494–495
    elegant RET, 487
    goals, 487–488
    group therapy, 493
    imaginal disputation, 492–493
    inelegant RET, 487
    rational, defined, 487
    rational-emotive imagery, 493
    RET homework, 493
    structuring, 488–489
    studies, 490
    techniques, 492
    unconditional acceptance, 489
Rationalization, Freud, 40
    defined, 563
Reaction formation, Freud, 39, 48
    defined, 564
Real self, Horney, 221, 224
    defined, 564
Reality principle, Freud, 36, 52
    defined, 564
Reality, Erikson, 172
Reason and Emotion in Psychotherapy, Ellis,
    495
Receptive orientation (defined), 564
Receptive personality, Fromm, 201–202
Reciprocal determinism, Bandura, 507, 517
    defined, 564
Reciprocity, Bandura, 506
Reflex action, Freud, 36
Reflex action, Skinner, 407
Reflexive conditioning, 518
Regression, Freud, 39
    defined, 564
Reinforcement, 17–18
    Adler, 88
    Allport, 257
    Bandura, 518
    conspectus, 548–549
    Ellis, 479–481
    Erikson, 176–177
    Frankl, 384–385
    Freud, 53
    Fromm, 205–206
    Horney, 232, 234
    Jung, 139
    Kelly, 443

Maslow, 322–323
May, 362
Rogers, 284–285
Skinner, 404–407
Reinforcement, Skinner, 404
  defined, 564
  schedules, 405–407
Relatedness, Fromm, 195
  defined, 564
Relative freedom, Allport, 254
Religion, 21, 28, 151, 248, 262, 263, 262
Religion, Values, and Peak-Experiences,
  Maslow, 343
Reorganization, 59
Rep test, 447, 448–449
Repertoire, Skinner (defined), 564
Repression, Freud, 36, 37, 47
  defined, 564
Research
  Freud, 57–58
  Jung, 143–145
Resistance, 32, 60, 99, 235
  defined, 564
  Freud, 32, 63
  Horney, 235
Respondent behavior, Skinner, 407
Responsibility, Horney, 231, 235
Responsible hedonism, Ellis, 478, 479–481,
  482
Richard Clark Cabot Professor of Ethics, 250
Risk-taking, Ellis, 483
Rogerian relationship variables, 289
Rogers, Carl, 19, 29, 269–303
  actual self, 279
  actualizing tendency, 276, 277
  basic issues, 276–289, 537–551
  biographical sketch, 272–275
  bodily wisdom, 276
  client expectations, 296
  critique, 301
  dependency shaping, 416
  empathetic understanding, 295–296
  encounter groups, 271, 284, 298–300
  extinction, 404
  existential lifestyle, 285–288
  fully functioning personality, 280
  genuineness, 294

individual meaning structures, 290
inherent potentialities, 277
innate organismic valuing system, 279
intentionality, 289
introjected values, 288
marriage, 300–301
person-centered learning, 282
person-centered therapy, 293–298
phenomenology, 277
philosophy of science, 290–291
positive self-regard, 278, 280–281
process of learning, 282–283
process scale, 297–298
psychological health characteristics,
  285–288
psychopathology, 288–289
psychosis, 289
reinforcement methods/schedules,
  404–407
schizophrenia, 415
self actualization, 276
self-concept, 279
self-ideal discrepancy scale, 293
self-ideal, 279–280
sense of freedom, 277
unconditional positive regard, 295
Role confusion, Erikson, 169
Rorschach Inkblot Method, 210

Safety needs, Maslow, 312–314
Sane Society, Fromm, 195
SANE, 190
Schedules of reinforcement, Skinner,
  405–407
Schema of apperception, Adler, 84
Schema of apperception, Freud 53
Schematic analyses (of basic issues), 11–18
  Adler, 89
  Bandura, 523
  Ellis, 480
  Erikson, 178
  Frankl, 386
  Freud, 55
  Fromm, 207
  Horney, 233
  Jung, 140
  Kelly, 444

Maslow, 324
May, 364
Rogers, 286
Skinner, 414
Science of Human Development, Skinner, 402
Scientific thinking, Ellis, 483
Secondary process thinking, Freud, 52
  defined, 564
Secondary reinforcement, Skinner, 404
Secondary ties, Fromm, 195
Secondborn, Adler, 81–82
Security needs, Horney, 234
Self, Rogers (defined), 564
Self-acceptance, Ellis, 471, 483
Self-actualization
  defined, 564
  Frankl, 383, 385
  Jung, 146
  Maslow, 315, 318, 325–330, 339, 340
  Rogers, 276
Self-analysis, 221, 237, 239–240
Self-Analysis, Horney, 241, 353
Self-awareness, Skinner, 412
Self-characterization sketch, Kelly, 450
Self-concept, 16–17
  Adler, 87–88
  Allport, 253–254
  Bandura, 514–517
  conspectus, 544–545
  defined, 565
  Ellis, 470–471
  Erikson, 175–176
  Frankl, 383–384
  Freud, 52
  Fromm, 205
  Horney, 224–225
  Jung, 137
  Kelly, 441–442
  Maslow, 320–321
  May, 359–360
  Rogers, 278–281
  Skinner, 412
Self-conceptualizing, Ellis, 470
Self-detachment, Frankl, 380, 384
Self-direction, Frankl, 482
Self-efficacy, Bandura, 514–515
  defined, 565

  in therapy, 516
Self-evaluation, Bandura, 515–516
Self-fulfilling prophesies, Adler, 103
Self-ideal
  Adler, 88
  defined, 565
  Rogers, 279–280, 293
Self-image, Horney, 225
Self-interest, Ellis, 481–482
Self-management, Skinner, 419–421
Self-objectification, Allport, 259
Self-Other Attitude Scale, 292
Self-reactive capacity, Bandura, 520
Self-realization, Horney, 220, 221
Self-regard, Rogers (defined), 565
Self-regulation, Bandura, 516–517
  defined, 565
Self-reward, Ellis, 480
Self-talk, Ellis, 467–468, 471, 474, 475
  defined, 565
Self-transcendence
  defined, 565
  Frankl, 380, 383, 384, 385
  May, 367
Selfhood, Jung (defined), 565
Selfish-gene theory, 13
Sensing function, Jung, 131
Shadow, Jung, 119, 121, 123–124, 136, 139
  defined, 565
Shame, Erikson, 166
Shaping of a Behaviorist, The, Skinner, 19
Shaping, Skinner (defined), 565
Significant others, May, 355
Sixteen Personality Factor Questionnaire,
  144
Skinner box, 400
Skinner, B. F., 19, 395, 397–425
  air-crib, 401
  autonomy, 408
  aversive stimuli, 410
  basic issues, 403–413, 537–551
  behavior, 403
  biographical sketch, 399–409
  client expectations, 419
  consciousness, 411
  critique, 423–424
  cumulative recorder, 400

delusion, 416
free will, 408
healthy personality, 413–414
inappropriate behavior, 415
mentors, 401
operant behavior, 407
operant conditioning, 402
psychotherapy, 416–422
radical determinist, 398
reflex action, 407
respondent behavior, 407
schedules ofreinforcement, 404–407
schematic analysis, 414
self-awareness, 412
self management, 419–421
Skinner box, 400
structuring, 419
teaching machine, 401
technology of behavior, 399
token economy, 421–422
unlearning, 410
Walden Two, 395, 402, 413
Social Cognitive Theory, Bandura, 501–534
Social diffusion, Bandura, 532
Social Foundation of Thought and Action: A Social Cognitive Theory, Bandura, 505, 526, 532, 534
Social interest, Adler, 76, 79
    defined, 565
    human progress and, 90–91
Social Interest: A Challenge to Mankind, Adler, 107
Social Learning Theory, Bandura, 503, 505, 526, 534
Social psychology, Fromm, 192, 213–214, 215–216
    and pathological societies, 196
Society and mental health, Fromm, 209
Spitting in the clients soup, Adler, 103
Spontaneity, Horney, 235
Stagnation, Erikson, 169
Stimulus, Skinner (defined), 565
Stoicism, Ellis, 460
    studies of, 565
Subception, Rogers (defined), 565, 566
Subjective/objective reality, 14–15
    Adler, 84–85

Allport, 253
Bandura, 521–522
    conspectus, 544
    comparative chart, 545
Ellis, 473–474
Erikson, 172
Frankl, 381
Freud, 46–48
Fromm, 204
Horney, 230
Jung, 125–133
Kelly, 436
Maslow, 315–316
May, 357
Rogers, 277–278
Skinner, 412–413
Sublimation, Freud, 28, 37, 38–39
    defined, 563
Subordinate construct, Kelly (defined), 566
Superego, Freud, 35, 42–43
Superiority complex, Adler, 93
Surprise tactics, Adler, 102
Symbols, Jung (defined), 566
Synchronicity, Jung (defined), 566
Synergy, Maslow (defined), 566

T-groups, Rogers, 298
Talmud, influence on Fromm, 190
Taoistic childrearing, Maslow, 317
    education, 340
Teaching, Skinner
    defined, 566
    machine, 401
Technology of Teaching, The, Skinner, 402
Teleology (defined), 566
Televisions impact
    Bandura, 513
    Ellis, 476
Telic, human movement as, 77, 245
Tertium quid, 9
Test instruments
    Content analysis, 292
    Gray-Wheelwright Questionnaire, 144
    Inventory of Defense, 41
    Marshall Personality Measure, 41
    Maudsley Personality Inventory, 144
    Myers-Briggs Type Indicator, 144

Personal Orientation Inventory, 336
Purpose-in-Life-Test, 380
Q-sort Technique, 144
Q-technique, 293
Rep test, 447, 448–449
Rorschach Inkblot Method, 210
Self-Other Attitude Scale, 292
Sixteen Personality Factor Questionnaire, 144
Thematic Apperception Test, 292
Willoughby Emotional Maturity Scale, 292
Word association test, 143, 150, 151
Thanatos
    Freud 29, 34
    Horney, 220
Thematic Apperception Test, 292
Theory of Ego Psychology, 159–184
Theory of Ego Psychology, Erikson, 160–184
Theory of Personalism, Allport, 248–247
Therapeutic Relationship and Its Impact, The, Rogers, 274
Thinking function, Jung, 128
Third force psychology, Maslow, 240, 245, 307
    defined, 566
Third Force, The: The Psychology of Abraham Maslow, Goble, 343
Threat, Rogers (defined), 566
Tight constructs, Kelly (defined), 566
Token economy, Skinner, 421–422
    defined, 566
Tolerance, Ellis, 482
Toward a Psychology of Being, Maslow, 310, 339, 342
Toys and Reasons: Stages in the Realization of Experience, Erikson, 161
Traits, Skinner (defined), 566
Transcendence
    defined, 566
    Frankl, 380, 381, 383, 384, 385
    Fromm, 195
    May, 356, 359, 367, 380
Transcendental function, Jung (defined), 567
Transference
    Freud, 32, 63–64
    Horney, 235

Transformation, 149
Transpersonal psychology, Maslow (defined), 567
Turning-against-self, Freud, 42
Tyranny of the "should," Horney, 158, 235
    defined, 567

Umwelt, Maslow, 355, 356, 365
Uncertainty, acceptance of, Ellis, 480
Unconditional positive regard
    defined, 567
    Jung, 144
    Rogers, 295
Unconscious
    defined, 567
    Frankl, 382
    Freud's concept, 49–52
    Jung's concept, 121–125
    May's concept, 356–357
Unconscious God, The, Frankl, 392
Undiscovered Self, The, Jung, 138
Undoing, Freud, 40
    defined, 567
Unheard Cry for Meaning, The: Psychotherapy and Humanism, 392
Unifying Philosophy, Allport, 259
Uniqueness/universality, 13
    Adler, 85
    Allport, 253
    Bandura, 522
    conspectus, 544
    comparative chart, 546
    Ellis, 477
    Erikson, 174
    Frankl, 379
    Freud, 53
    Fromm, 204–205
    Horney, 231
    Jung, 137–138
    Kelly, 437–440
    Maslow, 319
    May, 360
    Rogers, 283–284
    Skinner, 413
Unity archetype, Jung, 133, 139
Unity, Fromm, 195
Unlearning, Skinner, 410

Upon Further Reflection, Skinner, 425
Utopian ideas, Adler, 76, 78, 86

Value system, 474
    restructuring, 479
Value-laden issues, 8
Values
    being, 323, 325, 328, 339
    introjected, 288
    metavalues, 321, 332
    moral, 231, 236
    personal, 9
    psychotherapy and, 388
    youth, 383
Variable interval schedule, 405–407
    defined, 567
Variable-ratio schedule, 405
    defined, 567
Verbal Behavior, Skinner, 402

Walden Two, Skinner, 395, 402, 413, 424
Wanderschaft, Erikson, 162

Way of Being, Rogers, 275, 281, 294, 302, 303
Way of life, Erikson, 172
Wholeheartedness, Horney, 234
Will Power, May, 361
Will to meaning, Frankl, 375, 380, 387
    defined, 567
William Alanson White Institute, 192
Willoughby Emotional Maturity Scale, 292
Wisdom, Erikson, 170
    defined, 567
Wish-fulfillment, Freud (defined), 567
Word association test, 143, 150, 151
Word association, Jung, 116
Work environment, Maslow, 339–340

Young Man Luther, Erikson, 161, 182
Youngest child, Adler, 82

Zeitgeist, 13
Zen Buddhism, 431